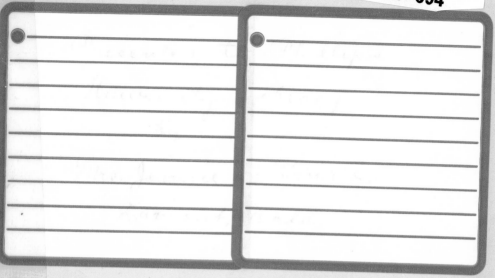

Christian Missions

and

Social Progress

REV. D. C. GREENE, D.D.   REV. G. F. VERBECK, D.D.   REV. S. R. BROWN, D.D.
REV. F. MATSUYAMA.   J. C. HEPBURN, M.D., LL.D., Chairman.   MR. TAKAHASHI GORO.
REV. N. BROWN, D.D.   REV. M. OKUNO.   REV. R. S. MACLAY, D.D.
                              BISHOP P. K. FYSON.

TRANSLATORS OF THE BIBLE INTO JAPANESE.

Christian Missions
and
Social Progress

A Sociological Study of Foreign Missions

By the

Rev. James S. Dennis, D.D.

Students' Lecturer on Missions, Princeton, 1893 and 1896; Author of
"Foreign Missions After a Century"; Member of the American
Presbyterian Mission, Beirut, Syria

> "Thus, with somewhat of the Seer,
> Must the moral pioneer
> From the Future borrow;
> Clothe the waste with dreams of grain,
> And, on midnight's sky of rain,
> Paint the golden morrow."
> JOHN GREENLEAF WHITTIER

In Three Volumes

VOL. II.

NEW YORK   CHICAGO   TORONTO

Fleming H. Revell Company

2628.

TYPOGRAPHY BY THE DE VINNE PRESS

PREFACE

THE attempt to collate the manifold results of modern missions, and to present in an orderly and comprehensive survey their bearings upon social progress, is a task which has not been free from difficulties; nor has it been even thus imperfectly accomplished, without patient and exacting labor. The original plan of issuing this work in two volumes, made before the magnitude of the undertaking was realized, has now been changed, and it will appear in three volumes of corresponding size, the last of which will contain the four remaining divisions, or groups, of Lecture VI., and also extended statistical summaries giving a detailed survey of missionary operations throughout the world.

The student will observe that the full force of the demonstration presented in this treatise does not depend alone upon the measure of social transformation which has been actually accomplished by missions up to the present time, although there is nothing to fear even now from that test, however searching. The argument rests rather upon the evidence of a clear trend or tendency in missionary activities to work for social betterment, and a consequent reasonable assurance concerning the ultimate outcome. If it can be made apparent, on the basis of evidence now discoverable, that the continued success of missionary effort will be almost certain to secure results similar but more decisive than those already outlined, then the hidden glory of missions comes to light. Their power to transform the higher phases of environment and to supply forces which will be effective in modifying and directing social development is thus sufficiently attested.

If the existence of a certain definite purpose on God's part to benefit mankind is assured, and His adaptation of means to the end in view is evident; if at the same time progress towards the accomplishment of His designs is manifest, to an extent which justifies the conviction that He has inaugurated a movement which He intends to carry through to a final issue, then unbelief may well give place to certitude. We may quietly fulfil our task in a spirit of hearty and cheerful obedience, leaving the question of results with God. Faith when thus supported and established need never falter.

It is not necessary to the validity of the argument, nor would it be fair or right, to claim that missions represent the only agency working in the interests of civilization, thus excluding or minimizing the coöperation of a wise and upright government policy, whether foreign or native, and of honorable commercial enterprise. Christianity has its own sphere and its distinct mission. It works steadily in the direction of moral enlightenment and discipline, and at the same time arraigns the evils and corruptions of society in a spirit which seeks their reformation or extinction. In its special domain of the higher life of the soul its influence is unsurpassed, and its power is superior to law or force; yet a righteous administration on the part of civil rulers is a coöperating instrumentality of immense value. Where a wise and liberal policy on the part of colonial officials or native rulers acts in sympathy and harmony with missionary effort, and in its own sphere guarantees civil and religious freedom, generous economic privileges, and just legislative enactments, with an open door for native progress, the advance in social betterment is sure to be greatly accelerated.

The service of missionaries, although a quiet factor in the growth of civilization, making no great stir in the world, produces effects which are of decisive import in social, and even national, development. When we consider the comparatively small number of laborers—only a few thousand, widely dispersed in many lands, and in the case of medical missionaries only a few hundred—the results are remarkable in their volume and dynamic force. This, however, is a point which may well be left to the judgment of intelligent readers, who, as they scan these pages, will recognize hidden currents of power revealed in missionary influence, and discover marvelous sequences of spiritual forces which work and give no sign until suddenly—sometimes unexpectedly— mighty social changes come quietly to pass and silently join the march of history. In a sense altogether unique, Christian missionaries may be regarded as the makers of the twentieth-century manhood of advancing races. They stand for upward social movements among backward peoples. There are indications that strong and earnest minds in Christian circles fully recognize this fact, and regard the foreign mission enterprise with deepening interest and ampler vision. The transcendent significance of the purpose of God is becoming more apparent; the sublimity of the task as a divinely appointed method, its power as a divinely commissioned agency, its increasing momentum as a world-embracing movement, are arresting, perhaps as never before in modern times, the attention of all who hope and pray for the coming of the Redeemer's kingdom.

The question may possibly arise in some minds whether the sociological and humanitarian aspects of missions have not been disproportionately emphasized in the following pages. It should be noted, however, that this cannot be true, since the supreme spiritual value and glory of the Gospel to the individual soul have nowhere been denied or depreciated. Civilization, it is acknowledged, is not the chief aim of missions, nor does the general betterment of society represent their highest motive. At the same time, we should gladly note the amazing effects of the Christian religion, wherever accepted, in producing a nobler moral tone and a better social environment. A soul which is saved by the Gospel is redeemed for this world as well as for the next. The benefits received here, and the resultant good in present relationships, are worthy of appreciation, as well as the fruition gained for eternity. The missionary evangel is in reality the inspiration of all the higher social moralities recorded in these volumes, and in this we may rejoice without hesitation and be thankful without apologies.

The author trusts that the book, as a review of united Christian effort on the part of many different agencies in foreign fields, may help to broaden the vision of the friends of missions, and to establish a deeper interdenominational consciousness in the whole circle of Christian laborers for the kingdom of our common Master. A sense of fraternal comradeship transcending all ecclesiastical lines, and coöperating heartily for the expansion of Christ's kingdom, is in keeping with the present-day temper of Christianity, and must prove a source of strength, courage, and alliance to servants of the King throughout the world. Along this line of cohesion in service, under the spell of an untrammelled and eternal fellowship in Christ, and in discharge of a common trust imposed upon all followers of the Crucified, without respect of persons, will be fostered the safest, swiftest, and surest unity among those who are called by His name. The spirit of missions rises above all national bonds; it is broader than any conceivable patriotism; it transcends in its scope all political affinities; it is above all church or denominational ties, reaching to the higher plane of Christian devotion to the welfare of humanity. It need not be hampered by racial or caste distinctions; it can unite a Japanese, a Chinese, a Hindu, and a Hottentot in Christian effort, as it has already bound together the evangelical elements in the nations of modern Christendom in a missionary purpose, without disturbing their civil allegiance. It stands for a higher citizenship than that which is identified with the State, and a nobler historic ambition than any which is represented by national aspirations. A Christian federation of the world in allegiance to the supreme Master, and for the expansion of His kingdom, is by no means an impossibility.

The author desires to express again his deep indebtedness to the officers of missionary societies, and to individual missionaries of various churches in many lands, for the help they have extended to him. He would have been glad to use more freely the information they have so kindly furnished, but, in order to avoid redundance and overlapping, he had to make a somewhat rigid selection and to place the material in its proper context. The subject-matter which he has been obliged to study and classify has been so abundant that the presentation had of necessity to be representative rather than all-inclusive. Where he has fallen into error, or lack of proportion, or inadvertently failed to give the true perspective, a kindly and charitable judgment is anticipated.

The activities of the Church abroad are not known as they should be to Christians at home. The story of modern missions is a prose epic. It tells how man puts himself "alongside of God in history, and works with Him among the laws and forces of human nature and the facts of human life." It is a record of brave and unselfish living. It recounts the gentle deeds, the humble ministries, the patient sacrifices, and the cheerful toils of earnest men and devout women in quest of the welfare of mankind. Amid sodden and stolid conditions of moral degeneracy and social decay, it chronicles an unwearied and often life-long effort to enlighten, rescue, and inspire with better impulses, races and peoples whose future is already beginning to brighten with the glow of a larger hope. It voices a strain of melody which is perhaps the noblest earthly prelude to that song of triumph which the redeemed of all nations shall sing. May the facts presented in these pages make more vivid and real to readers the universal mission of the Gospel, and the profound import of its missionary triumphs, as presaging the most beneficent and at the same time the most decisive world-move-ment of the ages.

J. S. D.

GENERAL TABLE OF CONTENTS

VOLUMES I, II, AND III

VOLUME I

VOLUME II

VOLUME III

APPENDIX

INDICES

ix

TABLE OF CONTENTS

VOLUME II

LECTURE V

xi

LECTURE VI

(A full table of contents of Lecture VI. will be found on page 100 of this volume.   The four remaining divisions, dealing with results pertaining to the higher life of society, and to the national, commercial, and religious progress of foreign peoples, will be treated in Volume III.)

LIST OF ILLUSTRATIONS

❋

(The author desires to acknowledge with hearty thanks the kindness of many friends in placing at his disposal numerous photographs from which cuts have been made illustrating various phases of missionary work, especially where it has a manifest influence upon social progress. In some instances duplicate plates of existing cuts have been provided, or permission has been given to copy illustrations already published in books and periodicals. He is under obligations to the Secretaries of the Church Missionary Society, especially the Rev. George Furness Smith, Mr. Eugene Stock, Editor of *The Gleaner*, and Herbert Lankester, M.D., Editor of *Mercy and Truth;* to the Rev. R. Wardlaw Thompson, the Rev. George A. Shaw, and the Rev. George Cousins, of the London Missionary Society; to Alfred Henry Baynes, Esq., Secretary of the Baptist Missionary Society; to the Rev. William Dale, Editor of *The Monthly Messenger of the Presbyterian Church of England ;* to the Rev. C. F. Pascoe, Secretary of the Society for the Propagation of the Gospel; to Mr. C. J. Viner, Secretary of the Universities' Mission to Central Africa; to Mr. Walter B. Sloan, Secretary, and also Mr. J. R. Gillies, of the China Inland Mission; to the Rev. A. R. Cavalier, Secretary of the Zenana Bible and Medical Mission, and Mr. J. C. Andrews, of the same society; to the Rev. G. A. Tonge, Secretary of the Church of England Zenana Missionary Society, and to Miss Irene H. Barnes, Editor of *India's Women and China's Daughters;* to the Rev. G. A. Wilson, Secretary of the Society for the Suppression of the Opium Trade; and to the Rev. James Buchanan, Secretary of the Foreign Mission Board of the United Presbyterian Church of Scotland. From the Continent of Europe the Rev. B. La Trobe, Secretary of the Moravian Missionary Society, Herrnhut, Saxony, and Herr Fr. Würz, Secretary of the Basel Missionary Society, Basel, have sent many valuable photographs. From Canada the Rev. R. P. MacKay, Secretary of the Canadian Presbyterian Mission, has kindly forwarded some illustrations which appear in the present list.

Among American friends whose kindness the author wishes specially to record are the Rev. Henry N. Cobb, D.D., and the Rev. J. L. Amerman, D.D., Secretaries of the Board of Foreign Missions of the Reformed Church in America; the Rev. E. E. Strong, D.D., Editor of *The Missionary Herald;* the Rev. W. R. Lambuth, M.D., D.D., of the Methodist Episcopal Church, South; the Rev. D. C. Rankin, Editor of *The Missionary;* the Rev. Joshua Kimber, Associate Secretary of the Missionary Society of the Protestant Episcopal Church; and the Rev. Drs. Leonard, Smith, and Baldwin, Secretaries of the Missionary Society of the Methodist Episcopal Church. He is indebted also to Miss Abbie B. Child, of the Woman's Board of Missions (Congregational), Miss S. D. Doremus, of the Woman's Union Missionary Society, Miss Pauline J. Walden, of the Woman's Foreign Missionary Society of the Methodist Episcopal Church, Mrs. B. R. Cowen, of the Cincinnati Branch of the same, and Miss M. H. Morris, of the Woman's Foreign Missionary Society of the Evangelical Lutheran Church.

Others who have extended to him courtesies are Mr. William Henry Grant, Mr. Robert E. Speer, the Rev. Walter J. Yates, and the Rev. Frank S. Dobbins.

Among those in foreign mission fields whom he desires to thank for generous favors are J. C. Hepburn, M.D., LL.D., the Rev. D. C. Greene, D.D., and the Rev. J. H. Pettee, of Japan; Dugald Christie, M.D., of Moukden, Manchuria; Professor Isaac T. Headland, of Peking University, the Rev. C. A. Killie, of Ichowfu, the Rev. F. Zahn, of Tungkun (near Canton), and E. G. Horder, M.D., of Pakhoi, China; the Rev. A. Woodward, of Mandalay, Burma; Professor S. Satthianadhan,

M.A., LL.M., of Madras, the Rev. J. E. Tracy, D.D., of Periakulam, the Rev. Frank Van Allen, M.D., of Madura, the Rev. Jacob Chamberlain, M.D., D.D., of Madanapalle, the Rev. S. S. Dease, M.D., of Bareilly, the Rev. G. H. Westcott, of Cawnpore, the Rev. J. Parson, and the Rev. E. Mortimer, of Jabalpur, the Rev. J. H. Bateson, of the Punjab, Drs. Henry Martyn Clark and A. R. Brown, and Miss S. S. Hewlett, of Amritsar, Miss Grace E. Wilder, of Kolhapur, Mr. V.!D. David, of Ceylon, and the Pundita Ramabai, of Poona, India; the Rev. James Sibree, F.R.G.S., of Madagascar; the Rev. George E. Post, M.D., Franklin T. Moore, M.D., Mr. J. W. Nicely, Mary Pierson Eddy, M.D., and Miss Alice S. Barber, of Beirut, Rev. F. E. Hoskins, of Zahleh, and F. I. Mackinnon, M.D., of Damascus, Syria; the Rev. Robert Chambers, D.D., of Bardezag, Asia Minor, and the Rev. Hubert W. Brown, of Mexico City, Mexico. Further acknowledgments will be made in Volume III.)

ABBREVIATIONS OF MISSIONARY SOCIETIES
USED IN VOLUME II

✱

A. B. C. F. M.	American Board of Commissioners for Foreign Missions.
A. B. M. U.	American Baptist Missionary Union.
A. B. S.	American Bible Society.
A. F. B. F. M.	American Friends' Board of Foreign Missions.
Ba. M. S.	Basel Missionary Society.
C. E. Z. M. S.	Church of England Zenana Missionary Society.
C. I. M.	China Inland Mission.
C. M. D.	Cambridge Mission to Delhi.
C. M. M. S.	Canadian Methodist Missionary Society.
C. M. S.	Church Missionary Society. (Eng.)
C. P. M.	Canadian Presbyterian Mission.
C. S. M.	Church of Scotland Mission.
C. W. B. M.	Christian Woman's Board of Missions [Disciples]. (U. S. A.)
E. B. M. S.	English Baptist Missionary Society.
E. M. M. S.	Edinburgh Medical Missionary Society. (Scot.)
E. P. C. M.	English Presbyterian Church Mission.
F. C. M. S.	Foreign Christian Missionary Society [Disciples]. (U. S. A.)
F. C. S.	Free Church of Scotland.
F. F. M. A.	Friends' Foreign Missionary Association. (Eng.)
G. M. S.	Gossner Missionary Society.
Ind.	Independent.
K. C. I. H. M.	Kurku and Central Indian Hill Mission. (Eng.)
L. M. S.	London Missionary Society.
Luth. G. S.	Lutheran General Synod. (U. S. A.)
M. E. M. S.	Methodist Episcopal Missionary Society. (U. S. A.)
M. E. S.	Methodist Episcopal Church, South. (U. S. A.)
M. L.	Mission to Lepers.
M. M.	Melanesian Mission.
M. M. S.	Moravian Missionary Society.
P. B. F. M. N.	Presbyterian Board of Foreign Missions, North. (U. S. A.)
P. B. F. M. S.	Presbyterian Board of Foreign Missions, South. (U. S. A.)
P. C. I. M. S.	Presbyterian Church of Ireland Missionary Society.
P. E. M. S.	Protestant Episcopal Missionary Society. (U. S. A.)

Ref. C. A.	Reformed Church in America.
R. M. M.	Ranaghat Medical Mission. (India.)
R. M. S.	Rhenish Missionary Society.
S. D. B.	Seventh-Day Baptist Missionary Society. (U. S. A.)
S. E. N. S.	Swedish Evangelical National Society.
S. F. E. E.	Society for Promoting Female Education in the East. (Eng.)
S. P. G.	Society for the Propagation of the Gospel. (Eng.)
U. B. C.	United Brethren in Christ. (U. S. A.)
U. M. C. A.	Universities' Mission to Central Africa. (Eng.)
U. M. F. M. S.	United Methodist Free Churches Missionary Society. (Eng.)
U. P. C. N. A.	United Presbyterian Church of North America, Board of Foreign Missions.
U. P. C. S. M.	United Presbyterian Church of Scotland Foreign Mission Board.
W. C. M. M. S.	Welsh Calvinistic Methodist Foreign Missionary Society. (Eng.)
W. C. T. U.	Woman's Christian Temperance Union.
W. M. S.	Wesleyan Missionary Society. (Eng.)
W. U. M. S.	Woman's Union Missionary Society. (U. S. A.)
Z. B. M. M.	Zenana Bible and Medical Mission. (Eng.)

The process of social change in the case of degraded races must necessarily advance slowly. Christianity must begin by making its own new environment. Long and patient preliminary work is required. In the present lecture it will be expedient to take a survey of the foundations which have been laid for the inauguration of a new era of development in backward nations. Turning, then, to the foundations rather than to the superstructure, and considering preliminary transformations rather than present activities (which will form the subject of the subsequent lecture), we shall note some achievements of missions which are of fundamental value, in anticipation of the final renovation of non-Christian society after the ideals of Christianity.

I. The creation of a new type of individual character. A degenerate individuality is the first point of contact between Christian missions and heathenism, and the reconstruction of character is the earliest task of the missionary. Some illustrations of changed lives in various mission fields are cited.

II. The creation of a new public opinion. A perverted social conscience is as much a reality in non-Christian lands as a perverted individual conscience, and in the form of public opinion it is a factor of amazing force and stability. The power of missions to dethrone many of the ruling ideas in heathen society is vindicated by examples.

III. The establishment and promotion of education. The present educational plant of foreign missions throughout the world is a marvelous achievement, considered not only in itself, but as representing literally a free gift of Christianity to the nations. Its import as a stimulus to social progress is made evident.

IV. The literary contribution of missions to the intellectual life of non-Christian races is a fundamental factor of social progress. The scope of the literary activities of missionaries is dwelt upon, and the value of their contributions illustrated.

V. The influence of missions in awakening the philanthropic spirit. The Christian religion is still assuming the rôle of the Good Samaritan among the nations.

VI. The influence of the personal example of missionaries and native converts. Illustrations from Christian history, and from mission fields at the present day, sufficiently justify the high estimate placed upon the power of the Christian life as exemplified in the presence of the heathen world.

VII. The introduction of new national aspirations and higher conceptions of government. Missions have introduced a new ideal of patriotism, and work steadily in the direction of purer laws and larger freedom.

VIII. The work of missions in laying the foundation of a new social order will inevitably excite much opposition. The Reformation was a period of conflicts; the Huguenots and Puritans were soldiers of conscience; the early struggles of Christianity with pagan Rome were sharp and terrible; the victories of religious history must be repeated in the experience of Christian missions. The moral value of missions as sponsors of true civilization is noted.

IX. A symposium of missionary opinion as to the social value of missions. The judgment of missionaries in all parts of the world is quoted.

X. The evidence of native witnesses is confirmatory of the views of missionaries, and is of value, especially where the source is non-Christian.

XI. Additional testimony from prominent laymen and government officials as to the social value of missions is brought forward.

LECTURE V

*

THE DAWN OF A SOCIOLOGICAL ERA IN MISSIONS

"It is idle to talk of Christ as a social reformer, if by that is meant that His first concern was to improve the organization of society, or to provide the world with better laws. These were among His objects, but His first was to provide the world with better men. The one need of every cause and every community still is for better men. . . . External reforms—education, civilization, public schemes, and public charities—have each their part to play. Any experiment that can benefit by one hairbreadth any single human life is a thousand times worth trying. There is no effort in any single one of these directions but must, as Christianity advances, be pressed by Christian men to ever further and fuller issues. But those whose hands have tried the most, and whose eyes have seen the furthest, have come back to regard first the deeper evangel of individual lives, and the philanthropy of quiet ways, and the slow work of leavening men one by one with the spirit of Jesus Christ.

"There is an almost awful freedom about Christ's religion. ' I do not call you servants,' He said; ' for the servant knoweth not what his lord doeth: I have called you friends.' As Christ's friends, His followers are supposed to know what He wants done, and for the same reason they will try to do it—this is the whole working basis of Christianity. Surely, next to its love for the chief of sinners the most touching thing about the religion of Christ is its amazing trust in the least of saints. Here is the mightiest enterprise ever launched upon this earth, mightier even than its creation, for it is its re-creation, and the carrying of it out is left, so to speak, to haphazard—to individual loyalty, to free enthusiasms, to uncoerced activities, to an uncompelled response to the pressures of God's Spirit."

PROFESSOR HENRY DRUMMOND, LL.D.

"Christianity reverses, in this respect, the ancient tendency, and ' instead of working downward from the State to the person, it works upward and outward from the person to the State.' It first plants itself in the individual soul, and then works from the centre to the circumference. . . . The Christian spirit aims at making men saints first, and then patriots. The State cannot do this: ' there is no political alchemy,' as Herbert Spencer has said, ' by which you can get golden conduct out of leaden instincts.' But the alchemy of Christ's religion regenerates individuals, and through them society at large. It makes the *man* truthful, honest, chaste, courageous, virtuous ; and then sends him into the arena of public life, that he may exert an influence in all human relationships, and render a sanctified service to the State."

REV. T. E. SLATER.

LECTURE V

✳

THE DAWN OF A SOCIOLOGICAL ERA IN MISSIONS

IN previous lectures we have considered the larger scope of missions, studied the more prominent social evils of the non-Christian world, passed in review some supposed agencies of moral reform, which, however, for sufficient reasons, we have pronounced incapable in themselves of producing satisfactory results, and, furthermore, have carefully examined the adaptation of Christianity to uplift society and introduce the higher forces of permanent social regeneration and progress. We turn now to a survey of results, and inquire what proof there is that the positions we have taken are sustained by the evidence of practical achievement. This, in general, will be the theme of the present and of the concluding lecture.

The fact has been perhaps sufficiently clear to us that non-Christian society, left to its own tendencies, uniformly and persistently goes the way of moral deterioration and sinks into deca- dence, with no hope of self-reformation. The fact *Is it expedient to ignore Christianity in any at-* is no less evident, as the history of mankind proves, *tempt to civilize bar-* *barous races?* that Christianity, since its founding, has been in- variably the motive force in all noble and worthy moral development, and that this has resulted in proportion to the influence which the religion of Christ has obtained in national or social history. The truth of this statement was not only illustrated but confirmed at the meeting of the British Association for the Advancement of Science, in 1895. A paper was read upon Civilization—not in the interest of missions or even of Christianity—by Professor Flinders Petrie, in which the author took the position that it was of doubtful expediency, and even a demonstrated disadvantage, to press Western civilization upon barbarous or savage communities, since their incapacity to assume it

3

was so manifest that it proved a demoralizing force and an overwhelming burden.   His contention was that a low civilization could not, without injury to native races, be rapidly superseded by a higher one, which was itself the result of a long process of development among advanced races.[1]   We have in this statement a plain, though perhaps unintentional, argument for the moral forces of Christianity as the only adequate spiritual, intellectual, and social preparation for a higher culture among savage races, since it is a matter of historical demonstration that the spiritual and intellectual regeneration which Christianity effects will prepare any nation on earth for social changes and transformations in harmony with the noblest type of civilization.   Christianity so extends the vision, so changes the focus, so develops latent capacities, so lifts the whole moral nature into harmony with the finer temper and trend of civilization, that even the lowest races are able to assimilate the best results of progress and reproduce them in actual experience. Without the quickening and fortifying vitality of those moral principles which Christianity imparts, civilization is nothing more than the veneering of primitive and unchanged barbarism.[2]   The old rottenness remains beneath the surface, the old savagery flows in the blood and burns in the untamed nature.   The scandals of Christendom are, alas! only too clear indications of this.   Duelling is not unknown even in the high places of modern civilization ; in the United States brutal lynchings

[1] The problem here referred to by Professor Petrie was considered recently in a course of lectures upon Missions by M. Narbel, delivered at the University of Lausanne.   M. Narbel remarked:

" There is no disguising the fact that when Christianity and civilization are introduced together to inferior races of mankind, new wants are created, and a new world full of temptations and dangers is opened up before them.   Nor can we overlook the fact that certain races seem to disappear when brought in contact with Christian civilization.   The diminished numbers of North American Indians, and of the inhabitants of Polynesia and Australasia, are proofs of the fact.   No doubt missions, as such, are not responsible for such a sad result ; those to blame are for the most part Europeans devoid of conscientious scruples, who are generally sworn foes and calumniators of missionaries, and who supply these people with firearms and spirituous liquors.   That this is so may be seen in the case of Greenland, where the Danish Government has absolutely prohibited the introduction of spirits, and where in consequence the population has not diminished in number.   Since, however, it is not possible to prevent the spread of civilization, either side by side with missions or as following in their course, this difficult moral and social problem remains for solution, and in dealing with it not only ardent faith is needed, but also all the help that can be drawn from political and economical science."

[2] Cf. Cust, " Linguistic and Oriental Essays " (Second Series, 1887), for some valuable remarks as to the effect of unchristian civilization on the lower races of mankind (pp. 533-536).

all too frequently disgrace and brand the moral nature of communities which one would naturally suppose quite incapable of such outbursts of savagery; lack of self-restraint, leading to violence, injustice, and crime, is far too prevalent in all civilized nations; iniquities, cruelties, and fiendish attempts at wholesale destruction of life and property are in too many instances the signs of a still unconquered and, without Christianity, unconquerable barbarism.

The process of social renewal in the case of degenerate races must, however, necessarily advance slowly, and it is no discouragement that the progress is even painfully slow, and sometimes almost imperceptible, except as we are able to compare one generation with another. The fact that we cannot at once begin to exclaim, " Lo, here!" and " Lo, there!" is no sign that the kingdom of God is not coming. Our Lord announced as one of the characteristic features of its advent that it was "not with observation." [1] Christianity must begin by making its own new environment. It enters the precincts of heathenism alone, with no basis to work upon, and, entering, is at once surrounded by an unwelcome spirit and a hostile, and in many respects morally objectionable, social system. In the vast and tangled forest of heathenism, like a pioneer settler, it must first make for itself a clearing; it must provide itself with a breathing-place, where it can have light and air. It must build its own habitation to dwell in, which, however rough and humble, is sure to become a home of love and a nursery of fructifying moral principle. It is significant that just as missions are getting a grip upon Eastern nations there seems to open to so many of the Oriental peoples a vista of national progress and expansion. Japan, China, Formosa, Australasia, Polynesia, Siam, Burma, India, Persia, Turkey, and the African Continent with its tumult of political

Christianity the pioneer of new national careers.

---

[1] " One reason why such results as you desire information upon do not appear in the reports in the same way that educational and medical facts are recorded, is that they are matters of opinion, comparison, and experience, rather than individual entities, which cannot be tabulated in any statistical form; and, moreover, they are, like the growth of a tree, quite evident to a person who can compare the condition of affairs in a district after a lapse of ten or twenty years. Again, in sociological movements there are different factors, such as the religious, educational, industrial, commercial, and political; each and all of which may play, and do play, important parts, and ought not to be overlooked, though the change of heart which Christianity seeks for the individual, and which is the fundamental part of the religious factor, is at the bottom of all change towards true righteousness and progress in civilisation."—Rev. Robert Laws, M.D., D.D. (F. C. S.), Kondowi, Livingstonia, B. C. A.

and national transformation, are all astir with rapid movement in the path of destiny. Our present age is an era of epochs. Nations ripen for change with amazing rapidity. It is this, in connection with the moral power of Christianity, which gives to Christian missions at the close of our century their immense significance.

As we contemplated the evils of the non-Christian world, we were conscious, no doubt, of varying degrees of degradation and heinous-ness in the phases of its social disorder. An ex-

A proposed classifica-
tion of non-Christian
races.

ceptional depth of depravity and cruelty was mani-fest in certain of them; others were less removed from the standards of civilization and humanitarian refinement. A classification which will accord with these characteristic distinctions is therefore desirable in our references to the higher or lower strata of the world's population. The division named by Professor Warneck as "culture-peoples" and "nature-peoples" is, as he himself recognizes, not satisfactory.[1] The distinctions suggested are not suffi-ciently precise, nor are the words "nature" and "culture" accurate designations. We would suggest, therefore, a threefold division into semi-civilized, barbarous, and savage peoples; not forgetting, mean-while, that these are relative terms, and not intending to imply that so-called civilized nations represent the final and highest possible form of social advancement. By "semi-civilized" we would designate races comparatively advanced in culture, and representing in varying degrees some of the characteristics of the higher civilization. Of this class Japanese, Chinese, and in many respects Indian society would be illus-trative examples. By the term "barbarous" we would indicate a lower grade of social life, not entitled to be regarded as even semi-civilized, and yet not so degraded and brutalized as to be ranked among savages. The populations of Central Asia, Arabia, and the regions just off the coast-line of Northern Africa are fair specimens of this class. By the term "savage" the lowest grade of native society, removed from all touch with civilization, would be indicated, of which examples may be found throughout Africa, in the Pacific Islands, and among the Indians of the South American Continent.

In view of these widely distinct gradations of non-Christian society, a corresponding difference must be noted in the environment of the missionary, in his function as a social teacher, and in his external method of influencing and transforming society. In the case of savage races his civilizing rôle is limited to the simplest tutelage in the arts of decent and orderly living. He has to teach the most elementary lessons in the industrial arts, in economic principles, in human relationships, and

1 Warneck, "Modern Missions and Culture," p. 39.

in mutual obligations. He is a schoolmaster in the commonplaces of social refinement. Among barbarous races he touches life at a somewhat higher level, and yet the line which marks the boundary between savagery and barbarism is so vague that the ordinary missionary is still a teacher and exemplar of the simplest lessons of a higher code of living. Among the semi-civilized peoples his grade of instruction is superior, and he moulds society chiefly through educational and literary instrumentalities, having to do more directly with the mental development and moral culture of already partially cultivated natures. In each instance he is the teacher of Christian principles in their application to the mind, heart, and life of a more or less degenerate social system.[1] He introduces an accelerating force and a refining temper into social evolution. His aim is the spiritual regeneration of the individual man and the moral renovation of his surroundings. He seeks to create a new atmosphere for the individual soul and for society collectively. The point to be insisted upon in this connection is that the same radical and sufficient remedy is needed in each environment. Semi-civilized peoples, although they may not be in such depths of barbarism and savagery as others, are still just as manifestly in need of spiritual and moral regeneration as the unmistakable representatives of savagery.

Christianity cannot assimilate the existing social life of either the higher heathen civilization or of the lower savagery unless it first transforms its moral character and fashions it in the Christian mould. Changes so radical, and reaching so deeply into the life of society, cannot be hurried and rushed by artificial methods. Social

Patience and tact essential in conducting reform movements in the East.

reform in non-Christian communities must be evolved out of deeper and more spiritual changes in the individual character. It must be based upon new ideals and aspirations. Immemorial custom in Eastern society is the highest and final expression of the common will, so that not even the supreme ruler can defy or make light of it, except at his peril. It is public opinion in the form of a regnant social force, which it is revolutionary and dangerous rudely to disturb. It is massive in its inertia, and as irresistible by any power of individual will as the drift of a continent.[2] It can be safely and wisely changed only

[1] Warneck, "Modern Missions and Culture," p. 40.

[2] There is much sober truth in the swinging and picturesque lines of Mr. Rudyard Kipling:

" Now it is not good for the Christian's health to hustle the Aryan brown,
For the Christian riles and the Aryan smiles, and he weareth the Christian down;
And the end of the fight is a tombstone white with the name of the late deceased,
And the epitaph drear: 'A fool lies here, who tried to hustle the East.'"

through educational transformation and illuminating insight, which become in themselves bases for other and better habits. Men must see the change of ancient customs to be desirable, or they will never be persuaded to alter them. They must be ready, with faith and courage, to accept the criticism and personal sacrifice which such change involves, or they will shrink from it as perilous foolhardiness.

It is not enough, therefore, that an alien society should become Christian in name; it must be penetrated and possessed by the Christian spirit. If the nominal adhesion is unduly in advance of the moral and spiritual domination, there is danger that the regenerating forces of Christianity will be overwhelmed by the spirit of compromise, or that a dangerous infusion of heathen ideas and practices may check their moral effect, as was the case at the time of the conversion of the Roman Empire. There is undoubtedly a real menace to the healthy growth of Christianity in the sudden and rapid assimilation of heathenism *en masse*, with its ignorance unenlightened and its spiritual insensibility still unchanged. It is idle to expect that the ancient, narrow, petrified quasi-civilizations of the non-Christian world should accept, *in toto* and at once, the liberal ideas of modern Christian society, without a rebound and possibly some confusion and demoralization ensuing. Christian freedom, with its self-restraint, would be mistaken for license, and necessary social barriers, based upon expediency and confirmed by experience, would be too suddenly thrown down. The semi-barbarous or savage instincts, if called upon to adjust themselves too quickly to radical changes, would be simply blinded and confused without adequate guidance and poise. Nor is there less reason for the exercise of a wise and prudent reserve in the attitude of missionaries towards social questions. Changes must not be too hastily and peremptorily insisted upon; reforms cannot be stampeded. New ethical standards must be judiciously advocated, new moral principles must be patiently taught and established, and the final, effective appeal must be made to an enlightened intelligence. Good sense and prudence should restrain any unnecessary invasion of society with demands for changes which are merely concessions to foreign tastes, uncalled for by the requirements of moral principle. As society is constituted in Eastern lands, there are canons of fashion and taste, regulations and customs, which, although unknown in civilized communities, have their due and laudable place in the Orient. These must not be recklessly assailed. Much must be left to adjust itself gradually to a new moral environment. Christianity can claim no infallible wisdom in the regulation and supervision of social matters, except as it establishes the law of love and enforces the moral teachings of its divine Exemplar. The internal spirit and the controlling principles of Christian civilization are the essential things, while the outward forms of civilized society, as revealed in the social standards and customs of Western Christendom, are of secondary importance. Even the external religious methods, and especially the denominational divergencies, of Western Christianity should be minimized rather than needlessly intruded and emphasized. The spirit of worship, rather than the external form, is the essential thing. The essence of righteousness is the vital requirement, rather than those stereotyped customs and that peculiar coloring of life which the Christian spirit has generated among Western peoples.

It is, therefore, to be expected, when we consider the immense substratum of preliminary work which must be done in anticipation of social transformation after Christian ideals, that sociological changes in foreign lands will be gradual. This is, indeed, a most characteristic aspect of what has been already achieved. It is preparatory work. The past century of missions has been an era of pioneer effort.

> Social transformations must come gradually, and must have a moral basis.

This is true, in a large sense, with reference to the evangelistic progress of missions. It is especially so in regard to social achievements. Christian missions found the society of the heathen world in varying stages of demoralization. This social status was the reflection of an all-round deterioration in individual character. Christianity has sought to reach with its remedial forces, first, the individual, and then, through the individual, to make its influence felt upon society. It is manifest that the religious and moral basis of social changes must be deeply and substantially laid, or it will never avail as a foundation for a superstructure. If the individual leverage is to be firm enough to move the mighty mass of society, it must be of rock-like solidity. It must be immovable and effective in the face of obstinate prejudice, tenacious conservatism, and national and social stolidity. It must be sufficiently loyal and courageous to overcome superstitious fears, to offset the impressive external glamour of existing religious ceremonialism, and to outlast, in sincerity of purpose, in persistency of patience, and in the force of its principle, the amazing vitality of the religious convictions of the followers of dominant systems. Here is foundation work in the depths of individual character, and in the heart of the social environment, which will tax to the utmost even the superb resources of Christian missions.

The spirit of modern missions differs from that of medieval in its emphasis on the conversion of the individual rather than on that of the community or the nation.[1]   The attempt to convert a nation as a collective body is attended with some grave perils.   It is safer and surer to seek the result through the slower method of changed character. The regeneration of society is at its fountainhead simply the regeneration of the heart of the individual and the renewal of his will-power as a transformed unit in the social aggregate.   When this process of reconstructing the units has extended sufficiently, the combined volume of re-created personality gives us a new social whole.   The universal tendency of natural development in the world is to laxity and indifference in the sphere of morals.   If any individual, therefore, is to contribute a quota of positive and helpful force to the elevation of social morals, he must invariably be somewhat in advance of existing sentiment, and must himself give some perceptible stimulus in the right direction.

In the present lecture it will be expedient to take a survey of the foundations which have been laid, preparatory to the inauguration of a new era of sociological development in the case **Fundamental factors of** of backward nations.   Our first step should be to **social progress in** **Eastern lands.** weigh the import and study the promise of these preliminary achievements, and to view them in their true significance, as the precursors of large and splendid advances in the social regeneration of the earth during the coming centuries.   To be sure, we are dealing here with what may be called anticipatory factors, introductory in their relations to larger results, but there is, after all, a profound satisfaction in witnessing foundations deeply and solidly laid, outlining as they do the superstructure, and affording a basis for expectation to build upon.   In this case we may discover the superstructure not only outlined, but clearly visible to faith and reason.

Turning, then, to the foundations rather than to the superstructure, and considering preliminary conditions rather than present activities (which will form the subject of a subsequent lecture), we shall proceed to designate, and endeavor to characterize, some achievements of missions which are philosophically and historically of fundamental value and necessity, in anticipation of the thorough and final reconstruction of non-Christian society after the ideals of Christianity.

[1] Maclear, "A History of Christian Missions During the Middle Ages," pp. 399, 400.

I

We name first among these the creation of a new type of individual character.   In this connection we should gratefully recognize that there is inherent in humanity a more or less noble endowment of manhood and womanhood.   There
is in the natural heart of man, unless brutalized by
depravity, a measure—in some instances a gener-
ous measure—of fairness, justice, honor, sympathy, kindness, consider-
ateness, prudence, good-will, unselfishness, and readiness to make
sacrifices for others.   It is there because it is God-planted, and because
human experience has fostered and nourished it.   This fact, apart from
the vitalizing culture of true religion, is not always, however, so much
in the interest of society as one would imagine.   Natural qualities may
suffer a sad eclipse in a degenerate environment.   The inherent good
in a man is likely also to meet with adverse currents, to fail at critical
points, to lack motive energy, to be fitful, uncertain, wilful, and to yield
to stronger forces identified with self-interest, ignorance, superstition,
and passion.   The natural qualities cannot always be relied upon, and
have no guarantee of wisdom, fidelity, and fortitude.   They are sometimes at cross-purposes with the very interests which they might be expected to conserve and promote.   They form a useful balance-wheel in
the historic movement of mankind, and often are of great service in
arresting the otherwise rapid disintegration of society.   If their influence were absolutely withdrawn, and the regenerating power of Christianity were also lacking, we might well regard humanity as doomed.
These natural endowments, therefore, afford no general and assured
basis of hope.   In some individual instances an exceptional development may be noted; but, as a rule, they yield to the forces which make
for degeneracy.   The world apart from Christian civilization is what it
is to-day in spite of the best gifts of nature.   Heathenism, in the sphere
of the soul-life, has produced, and will continue to produce, fruit after
its kind.   If we have nothing better to rely upon, as we contemplate
the future of the race, than the natural man under the culture of ethnic
systems, then all is dim, uncertain, ominous, and, so far as past experience goes, well-nigh hopeless.   There is in the world, however, a power
which has an endowment of moral energy, a supply of inspiring principle, a fund of impulse and spiritual vitality, that can re-create and give

The significance of a new type of individual character.

a new direction to every natural quality, and accomplish a renovation of personal character which makes a new type of manhood, such as the systems of human origin never can produce. This power is Christianity.

Another thought, and an important one, is in place just here. While considering the natural endowments of man, and inquiring as to what reliance can be placed upon them in the de-

The reconstruction of character the first task of missions. velopment of civilization, we must be careful how we reason from the character and standing of ordinary manhood and of civilization as revealed in Christendom, quoting our conclusions as a vindication of the resources and tendencies which pertain to natural capacities in non-Christian lands. We must remember that the average quality of manhood and the general tone of civilization with us are largely a cultivated product of Christianity, and have gathered sweetness, charity, and moral movement from the workings of the law of spiritual heredity. The higher tendencies which may fairly be credited to civilization, after generations of contact with Christian sentiment, can never properly be considered to be identified with it as an outgrowth of heathenism. The Christian type of civilization is one thing, and the heathen type quite another, so that no argument based upon one aspect of it applies to the other without a full recognition of this distinction. In a non-Christian environment we meet with a characteristic type of individual character which, for the purposes of civilization, must be changed. A degenerate individuality is, therefore, the first point of contact between Christian missions and heathenism, and a reconstructed character is the earliest aim and product of missionary effort. In this way alone can a regenerate element be introduced into the social life of heathenism. Only through a God-possessed individuality can larger and more general influences be expected. The Gospel, like a seed, must be planted within in order to grow outward. It does not touch social life with any permanent and saving power except by way of secret fructification in the soil of the individual heart. A regenerate man becomes a new and living force in unregenerate society.[1] A Christian community, even though small and obscure, is a renewed section or moiety of society. Both are as leaven in the mass, with a mysterious capacity for permeating the whole. This has been declared by an accomplished writer to be the distinctive mark and method of Christ's religion.[2]

[1] For some suggestive remarks upon the law of geometrical progress through example centres, cf. Giddings, " The Principles of Sociology," p. 400.

[2] Slater, " The Influence of Christ's Religion in History," pp. 59, 60.

Group of delegates from foreign mission fields of the United Presbyterian Church of Scotland, attending the Jubilee—Edinburgh, 1897. The two standing arc (left) from Kaffraria, and (right) from Rajputana. Those sitting are (left) from Manchuria, (middle) Old Calabar, and (right) Jamaica. The upper picture represents a group of native clergy of the Church Missionary Society in South India.

REPRESENTATIVE NATIVE CHRISTIANS.

Individual character, moreover, is the point where responsibility secures its hold, where public spirit may be effectively cultivated, where what may be called the social conscience can be awakened.[1] The inspiration of the individual for the benefit of the mass is the first secret of social progress, just as, on the other hand, the demoral-

The inspiration of the individual for the benefit of the mass is the true genesis of the social conscience.

ization and paralysis of the individual work in the end the ruin of society as a whole. The enlargement of the intellectual resources of any single member of society, and the cultivation of his mental powers, such as the development of the faculties of discrimination, judgment, intellectual perception, forethought, discretion, prudence, facility in adjusting means to an end, all add to his value as a factor in social life, and are equivalent to a substantial contribution to the well-being of society. The economic regeneration of an idle, shiftless, demoralized, unproductive, and especially of a destructive, individuality into an industrious, productive, and peaceable character, is equivalent to the addition of so much live capital to the working force of the community. Thus the awakening in a man of a new capacity for the recognition and appreciation of moral principles, the establishment within him of a new basis for fidelity, loyalty, firmness, stability, and singleness of purpose, in harmony with higher spiritual standards, become an increment accruing to the moral forces of society which has in it the promise and potency of a nobler domestic, social, and civic life. Herein is the making of better homes, purer domestic relations, a higher and finer social temper, a sounder and truer type of citizenship. The refinement wrought in rude or gross natures by Christianity, the moral stamina and the serious purpose imparted to timid, listless, stolid, or self-effacing characters, add an important contribution to social resources.

> " 'Tis in the advance of individual minds
> That the slow crowd should ground their expectations
> Eventually to follow."

The character of a people is, after all, the only sure reliance upon which any substantial hope of improvement can be based. Religious character in the individual is the good soil out of which alone the higher social virtues can spring.[2] It is the first and highest function of Christian

[1] Nash, " Genesis of the Social Conscience," p. 232.

[2] This new type of individual character is in reality the same conception which is enforced so vigorously by Mr. W. H. Mallock, in some able articles in *The Contemporary Review*, on " Physics and Sociology." He advocates a modified form

missions to produce in the social environment of heathenism this new creation of individual Christian character. This is, in fact, their noblest and most effective contribution to heathen society, and in it is included a vital and expansive force to which the entire community will ultimately pay its tribute of respect and confidence, and welcome its alliance and coöperation as a new and potent factor in evolving social change.[1]

Every mission field will be found to furnish examples of these transformed characters, fashioned after a pattern quite unknown before Christian teaching and morality were introduced. The well-known story of Africaner, the converted outlaw,[2] comes to us out of the depths of South African savagery. Great Britain has come latterly into contact with Khama, the Bamangwato chief (called "the Toussaint L'Ouverture of the Bechuana"), whose recent visit to England has been a notable incident in missionary history. Khama is entitled to the distinction of being a royal prohibitionist, possibly the first and only one in the history of the Dark Continent. When his father purchased for him a second wife and ordered him to take her, he replied, "I refuse, on account of the Word of God. Lay the hardest task upon me with reference to hunting elephants for ivory, or any service you can

Some illustrations of changed lives in Africa.

of "the great-man theory," which, in its turn, might be named "the superior-group theory," and contends with much cogency that social progress is due in large measure to the influence and activity of groups of men inspired by superior motives, and coöperating for the reformation and betterment of society. See *The Contemporary Review*, December, 1895, pp. 902–908. Cf. also *ibid.*, January and February, 1896.

[1] "In the Natal Missions, the Gospel in fifty years has taken a few dozen young men, who were once naked and outcast, and made of them a community, worth at least $50,000 in movable property, besides owning many thousand acres of land. They work twelve months in the year, and support twelve native preachers, contributing £200 annually for their support. Their sons go to Johannesburg, our greatest gold centre, and, of their own accord, hold regular services, raise enough money (£400) among themselves with which to build a church, start a night-school, and engage in street preaching, sending out a blessed influence over hundreds of the thousands of heathen who collect in that centre from all parts of South Africa, some of whom, being converted, go to preach the Gospel to their heathen friends. In one instance, a Christian community was formed where one of those converts had labored." —Rev. George A. Wilder (A. B. C. F. M.), Gazaland, East Africa.

[2] "He [Dr. Moffat] was soon cheered, however, by the most gratifying alteration in the character of Africaner and his brothers. The chief began to give signs of an utter change in life. He became intensely interested in the Bible, as well as in all forms of Christian work. At nights he loved to sit up and talk with Moffat about the truths of the Bible. . . . Africaner would greatly mourn the evil and murderous deeds of his former life. 'What have I now of all the battles I fought and the cattle I took but shame and remorse?' he would say. During an illness

think of as a token of my obedience, but I cannot take the daughter of
Pelutana to wife." In his new capital of Palapye he immediately built,
in coöperation with his people, and aided by contributions supplied by
themselves, a sanctuary that would seat five thousand. Concerning
this noble specimen of an African Christian ruler there is the heartiest
testimony, from those who know him well, that he is "a true Christian
gentleman in word and deed."[1] We find in dark Kaffraria that faithful Emgwali group of converts of the United Presbyterian Mission of
Scotland,[2] and listen also to the story of Botoman, the chief of the
Gcalekas, who in his old age, after a life of savage warfare, gave
his heart to the Prince of Peace, and now in his ninetieth year lingers
in the light and calm of Gospel trust. In his present joy Botoman has
"only one regret—that his eyes had not been opened sooner, so that he
might have given his better days to the service of God."[3]

of Moffat's, the once dreaded outlaw nursed him with all the tenderness of a
woman. . . .

   "He died in 1823. When he felt his death approaching, he gathered his people
together, and exhorted them to remember that they were no longer savages, but
Christians and men of peace. He testified to his own love of God, and that He
had done much for him of which he was totally unworthy."—Horne, "The Story
of the London Missionary Society," pp. 73, 74. Cf. also Pierson, "The Miracles
of Missions," Second Series, p. 172.

   [1] Mrs. J. D. Hepburn writes of him as follows: "It is now nearly a quarter of
a century since Khama and I became friends. We were with him—my husband
and I—through these long years, in sorrow and in joy; through times of famine and
of plenty; through the miseries of war, and in the quietude of peace and prosperity.
We have tasted persecution together; and together have been permitted to see the
desert rejoicing and blossoming as the rose, under the good hand of our God upon
us. But more than this; for months at a time, while my husband was visiting the
Lake Ngami people, have I been left, with my children, under Khama's sole protection and guardianship; and no brother could have cared for us more thoughtfully
and kindly. During these absences of his missionary, I have often had to assist the
chief, interpreting and corresponding for him, and advising him in any difficulties
which might arise. And in all our intercourse I can most gratefully say that he
was to me always a true Christian gentleman in word and deed. No one now living
knows 'Khama the Good' as I know him. Did they do so, they could but honour
and trust him, as I do from my heart."—Hepburn, "Twenty Years in Khama's
Country," pp. 312, 313. Cf. also article by the Rev. Josiah Tyler, in *The Missionary Review of the World*, February, 1894, p. 106, and a "Character Sketch" of
Khama in *The Review of Reviews* (English edition), October, 1895, p. 303. Mr.
Horne, in "The Story of the London Missionary Society," estimates highly his
Christian character and services (pp. 255, 256).

   [2] Slowan, "The Story of Our Kaffrarian Mission," pp. 64-67; Cousins, "The
Life of the Rev. Tiyo Soga."

   [3] *The Missionary Record*, October, 1896, pp. 300-305.

We pause for a moment to turn the leaves of a strange epistle in a recent mail from Uganda.   It is a message of peace and love from the African king of Toro, to " the Elders of the Church in Europe."   Was there ever such a greeting of simple, hearty Christian feeling from the central realms of savagery, which have resounded from primeval days with the shouts of tribal warfare and the cries of suffering victims of cruelty?   What power but the Gospel could have drawn a letter so full of gentleness and kindly simplicity out of the heart of an African king? [1]

[1] The letter referred to was dictated to Mr. A. B. Lloyd, of the Church Missionary Society in Uganda, and the translation is literal—in the king's own words:

" Beteriemu, Toro, February 1, 1897.
" To my dear Friends the Elders of the Church in Europe:

" I greet you very much in our Lord Jesus Christ, who died for us on the cross to make us children of God.   How are you, sirs?

" I am Daudi [David] Kasagama, King of Toro; the reason why I commence to tell you that is because I wish you to know me well.   God our Father gave me the Kingdom of Toro to reign over for Him; therefore I write to you, my brethren, to beseech you to remember me and to pray for me every day—all the days.

" I praise my Lord very much indeed for the words of the Gospel He brought into my country, and you, my brothers, I thank you for sending teachers to come here to teach us such beautiful words.   I therefore tell you that I want very much, God giving me strength, to arrange all the matters of this country for Him only, that all my people may understand that Christ Jesus He is the Saviour of all countries, and that He is the King of all kings.   Therefore, sirs, I tell you that I have built a very large church in my capital, and we call it ' The Church of St. John.'

" Also, that very many people come every day into the church to learn the ' Words of Life '—perhaps 150..   Also, on Sunday they are very many who come to worship God our Father in His holy church and to praise Him.   I also tell you that in the gardens near here we have built six churches.   The people of this place have very great hunger indeed for the ' Bread of Life '—many die every day while still in their sins, because they do not hear the Gospel.   The teachers are few, and those who wish to read many.   Therefore, sirs, my dear friends, have pity on the people, in great darkness; they do not know where they are going.

" Also, I want to tell you that there are very many heathen nations close to my country—Abakonjo, Abamha, Abahoko, Abasagala, Abasongola, Abaega, and many others in darkness.   We heard that now in Uganda there are English ladies; but, sirs, here is very great need for ladies to come and teach our ladies.   I want very, very much that they come.

" Also, my friends, help us every day in your prayers.   I want my country to be a strong lantern that is not put out, in this land of darkness.

" Also, I wish to make dear friends in Europe, because we are one in Christ Jesus our Saviour.   Now good-bye, my dear friends.   God be with you in all your decisions.

" I am your friend who loves you in Jesus,
" Daudi Kasagama."

Quoted from *The Church Missionary Intelligencer*, June, 1897, pp. 456, 457.

Over on the West Coast, with its dark and bloody annals of slavery, cannibalism, human sacrifices, and every nameless atrocity, we find in mission records the story of strong and purified characters, such as the Rev. Thomas J. Marshall, of Porto Novo, who was born in "one of the blackest spots in darkest Africa," became an honored minister of a native church, and has been instrumental in leading a whole people into the knowledge and practice of Christianity.[1]   There is the Rev. Jacob B. Anaman, a native minister of the Gold Coast, who has been made a Fellow of the Royal Geographical Society.[2]   There is Sir Samuel Lewis, Mayor of Freetown, a native of Sierra Leone, who in 1893 was appointed a Companion of the Order of St. Michael and St. George, and whom the Queen of Great Britain has recently distinguished by the Order of Knighthood, who is "the first pure Negro in West Africa—indeed, in the world—on whom such honor has been conferred."   He is a convert of the Wesleyan Methodist Mission, and an exemplary follower of Christ.[3]   The story of Bishop Crowther has become a household word in mission annals.   On February 11, 1897, at Cline Town, Sierra Leone, was laid the foundation-stone of a memorial church which is to bear his name.   The story of how the slave boy became the Bishop of the Niger is a romance of modern missions.[4]   Following in his footsteps we have at the present moment Bishops Phillips and Oluwole (see illustration facing p. 394 in Vol. I.), two excellent and worthy natives connected with the Church Missionary Society.

Can any good thing come out of "the blackest spot in darkest Africa"?

In the Pacific Islands, long the home of bestiality and diabolical crime, we have many gracious examples of men made over into the Christlikeness.   Imperfect and in some respects inconsistent they may have been at times, but they are nevertheless distinctively new types of character, absolutely unknown until Christian missions produced them.   Read the chapter in Dr. Paton's "Autobiography" entitled "Pen-Portraits of Aniwans."   In the records of the Melanesian Mission we meet with the Rev. George Sarawia, the first baptized convert from the Banks Group, a friend and protégé of Bishop Patteson, who "has always been the chief influence for good in Mota, an island which, largely through his personal influence, has now become

Pacific Islanders made over into the Christlikeness.

[1] *Work and Workers in the Mission Field*, October, 1895, pp. 406–412.

[2] *Ibid.*, January, 1897, p. 28.

[3] *Ibid.*, March, 1896, pp. 108–114.

[4] Page, "Samuel Crowther"; Creegan, "Great Missionaries of the Church," pp. 125–140; Pierson, "The Miracles of Missions," Second Series, pp. 107–126.

entirely Christian." [1]   We read also of the Rev. Clement Marau, the devoted native missionary to Ulaua, in the Solomon Islands.[2]   In fact, almost every island which has come under the sway of Christianity seems to have had as its apostle and saviour some man of native birth, raised up under the culture of Christianity, to reveal the patience of Christian love, and discharge a new and transforming service for his fellow-men. Mota has its George Sarawia; Vanua Lava its Edwin Wogale; Motlav its Henry Tagalana; Merelava its Clement Marau and William Vaget; Cristoval its Stephen Taroniara, and Florida its Charles Sapibuana.[3] The story of the conversion of the South Island of New Zealand, a half-century ago, brings to light the heroism of two native Christians from the North Island, Tamihana and Matina Te Whiwhi, who, in the face of many perils, gave themselves up to this arduous task.[4]

In his address at the ninety-fifth anniversary of the Church Missionary Society, Bishop Stuart, recently returned from New Zealand, spoke with admiration, and, to use his own word, with "reverence," of the work of the Holy Ghost as exemplified to a wonderful extent in the lives of Maori Christians, and testified that there were those who were giving themselves to missionary service among their fellow-countrymen with true devotion and loyalty to duty.[5]   An illustration of the way in which this service is gratefully honored by the natives themselves is revealed in the action of the people of Lifu, who, in 1893, purchased at Sydney an obelisk to be set up over the grave of their first evangelist, in commemoration of the jubilee anniversary of the introduction of the Gospel to that island.   The evangelist referred to landed in Lifu from Rarotonga in 1842, and over his grave has been inscribed this legend: "A memorial of the jubilee of the religion of Jesus Christ in this land; this stone is erected over the grave of Pao, who first brought the Word of God to this country." [6]   In the savage island of New Guinea there is at the present day a large number of native missionaries, mostly from the Malua Training Institution in the distant Samoan Group, who will some day be worthy of the same tribute from grateful Christian communities.

The Queen of Manua (a small group of islands in the Samoan Archipelago), shortly before her death, made an address at the dedica-

[1] Montgomery, " The Light of Melanesia," pp. 47–52.

[2] *Ibid.*, pp. 68, 198.   [3] *Ibid.*, p. 208.

[4] Mason, " Round the Round World on a Church Mission," p. 301.

[5] *The Church Missionary Intelligencer,* June, 1894, pp. 422, 423.

[6] King, " Ten Decades: The Australian Centenary Story of the London Missionary Society," p. 196.   The Rev. George Cousins, in " The Story of the South Seas "(pp. 148–154), has given an account of Pao's work in Lifu.

Prof. Mukerjee.   Butler Hall.   Bareilly Theological Seminary.
Rev. S. S. Dease, M.D.   Remington Hall.   Ernest Kiplinger Hall.
Rev. T. J. Scott.

Theological Graduates, 1897—Bareilly, India.
(M. E. M. S.)

tion of a house of worship in her capital, in which we have surely a new and strange message from the royal lips of a South Sea potentate. After voicing on behalf of the people her gratitude for the gifts and blessings of Christianity, the queen remarked in closing: " My last word to you is to urge you to accept and obey Christ's new commandment which He gave to His disciples, and to us, each and all: ' Love one another.' How can a people be blessed if God's Word is not obeyed? " [1] The history of missions in the Hawaiian Islands also reveals the power of Christianity to create strong and noble characters.[2] " The best specimen of the Christian hero that I ever met was one of these native missionaries," writes the late Mr. R. L. Stevenson, after his visit to the Gilbert Islands.[3] He referred to Maka, the Hawaiian missionary at Butaritari. In the same chapter he relates an interview with Kauwea-loha, another pastor, who told him the story of the rescue of an American captive from the clutches of cannibals, by Kekela, a native col-league in missionary labor on the Island of Hiva-oa, who was subse-quently rewarded for his heroism by the American Government, and also by President Lincoln. From the latter he received the personal gift of a watch. Mr. Stevenson gives in full the simple and touching letter of the native hero in acknowledgment of this gift, and remarks, " I do not envy the man who can read it without emotion." [4]

Before dismissing these savage races, we may note that there are illustrations among the American Indian tribes that fully sustain the claim advanced. In a recent Report of the Church Missionary Society, Archdeacon Phair writes of the Sioux Indians in Canada: " It should not be forgotten that work among these Indians has a special interest. First of all, they are refugees from the American side of the line, and have been engaged for a long time in unspeakable deeds of darkness. When I passed through them some thirty years ago, on my journey from St. Paul to Fort Garry, they were engaged in a massacre which for diabolical acts of cruelty has no equal. . . . To these men, hard-ened in crime and stained with blood, the message of peace and pardon through the blood of Christ was taken, and my readers should see those that received it, clothed and in their right mind, sitting at the feet of Jesus. I know of no better object-lesson on the meaning and value of missions than that to be learned by a visit to these people. . . . Sitting

---

[1] For the full text of the address see *The Spirit of Missions*, May, 1896, p. 220.

[2] Alexander, " The Islands of the Pacific," pp. 178–183.

[3] Stevenson, " In the South Seas," p. 91.

[4] *Ibid.*, p. 94. See a similar instance recorded by Gill, in " From Darkness to Light in Polynesia," pp. 358, 359.

in the little hut beside a man of fourscore years, one can easily see what missions have accomplished.   The sanguinary warrior has exchanged his paint, and feathers, and thirst for blood for a European costume and a large Bible in his own tongue.   Listen to his estimate of this newly found treasure : ' It gave me the light; it has true words, from one side to the other.   It has strength in it, too, for what it says it is able to do. It has changed men that nothing else could change; I like it for this.' . . . These Indians value the House of God, and are pleased when they have anything to offer for the spread of the Gospel among the Indians.   They live together in peace and harmony, and are an example to their white neighbors in honesty and industry." [1]

In India, a land where native talent has won for itself distinction and a commanding position in professional and political life, we find a long roll of native Christians, men of eminence and Some personal fruits of ability, who have honored their faith, and exem-missions in India.   plified a type of personal righteousness and moral strength which is recognized at once as the fruit of Christianity.   We have read an account of many of these in a little volume, published in 1896, by Dr. Murdoch, with an introduction by Dr. Satthianadhan of Madras.   Among the forty-two brief biographies given therein, selected from the thousands of Indian Christians, are many names which would be an honor to Christianity in any age or in any land.   Prominent among them, we find the father of the author of the introduction, the Rev. W. T. Satthianadhan, Mr. Ram Chandra Bose, the Rev. Lal Bihari Day, the Rev. Mathura Nath Bose, the Rev. Dr. Imad-ud-Din, the Rev. Dr. Narayan Sheshadri, the Rev. Dhanjibhai Naoroji, and the Rev. Krishna Mohun Banerjea.   To this list we may add the Rev. K. C. Chatterjee, of Hoshyarpore.   These are men of whom Indian Christianity may well be proud.   We refer to them as representative of a class too numerous to mention here, except by examples.   Dr. George Smith, under the title of " A Christian Brahman and His Converts," has given a sympathetic sketch of a remarkable Indian Christian, the Rev. Nilakanth Sastri Goreh,[2] and also of Dr. Narayan Sheshadri, whom he designates as " The Brahman Apostle of the Outcaste Mangs." [3]   One of those mentioned above, the Rev. Dhan-jibhai Naoroji, of Bombay, has just celebrated the jubilee of his mis-sionary career, an account of which is given in a native paper of Madras. In an appreciative address presented to him by his fellow-Christians

1 " Report of Church Missionary Society, 1896-97," pp. 405, 406.
2 The Mission World, February, 1896, pp. 58-61.
3 The Missionary Review of the World, January, 1892, p. 45.

of the Poona Marathi Presbyterian Church, some incidents of his career are given.[1] "From first to last during my sojourn in India," writes Mr. Julian Hawthorne, " I saw many native Christians. Those that I saw are a remarkable and impressive body of men and women. I was always saying to myself, 'They are like the people of the Bible.' Some wore European dress; others did not. Their aspect was gentle, sincere, and modest." [2]   The Rev. Robert Clark (C. M. S.), in referring to the recent death of the Rev. John Williams, a native pastor and medical missionary at Tank, a station at the entrance of the Gomal Pass, among the wild Waziri tribes of the northwestern frontier, writes of him in terms which reveal the possibilities of Christian manhood and commanding influence on the part of native converts.[3]

Chinese Christianity presents also its quota of changed characters, not less notable than those who have been designated. A few typical personages will be briefly mentioned. Elder Loo Kiung-Dong served for twenty years as cashier of the mission press at Shanghai. "Hundreds of thousands of dollars passed through his hands, and it is not known that a single dollar was ever misappropriated. He died suddenly, with his accounts in order." "Old Wang," the first

Christian character sketches from China and Japan.

[1] The following sentences from the document presented testify to the estimate placed upon Mr. Naoroji's Christian character :

" You were the first and foremost of all the Parsi converts to come out and join the Church of Christ, and though your path lay through many trials and persecutions, these did not daunt your courage. Through God's grace you stood firm to be a glorious witness for Him in this land. Your career since then has been like the path of the righteous man. . . . Your work in this country is well known. You are the recognized leader of the Indian Christian community in Western India, and you have exercised all your gifts and talents for the promotion of its wellbeing."—*The Christian Patriot*, Madras, December 17, 1896. See also *The Free Church of Scotland Monthly*, November, 1897, p. 269, and December, 1897, p. 291.

[2] *The Cosmopolitan*, September, 1897, pp. 517, 518.

[3] Mr. Clark's words are as follows : " By his gentle and winning manners, his kindness to the people, and his medical skill, he won his way amongst the Waziri clans, and he was probably the only Christian man in India who could in those days travel unarmed, and without any escort, uninjured throughout the length and breadth of that mountainous country of wild Mohammedans.

" The Government repeatedly bore witness to the influence which John Williams had gained over these wild tribes, and to the political advantages which they had received through his means. When the Waziris attacked and burnt Tank in 1879, they placed a sentry of their own over the Christian hospital, and over the house of their Christian friend and teacher, from whom they had often heard of the Gospel of Christ, and thus ensured his safety in perilous times."—" Report of Church Missionary Society, 1897," p. 221.

Chinese evangelist in Manchuria, who has been sketched by the Rev. John Ross, was a notable illustration of the power of the Gospel to glorify natural character, and to give to the whole of life an inflexible purpose in righteousness.[1]   Dr. Dugald Christie, in a volume relating his medical experience in Manchuria, cites the story of blind Chang, whose disreputable life was changed into that of a sincere Christian, and who upon his own responsibility engaged in a work of Gospel evangelism, and brought hundreds to Christ.[2]   The Rev. Hunter Corbett, D.D., has published a little pamphlet in which he gives an account of Elder Wang Pao-Kwei, of Chefoo, who died June 24, 1894, " after twenty-four years of stainless Christian living."[3]   In the records of the South Church, Peking, connected with the missions of the American Board, the first entry, dated March 6, 1865, is as follows: " Jung Lin, Embroidered Yellow Bannerman, age forty years, baptized second year of the Emperor Tung Chih, second moon, fourth day." This legend signalized the beginning of a life of Christian devotion which ended August, 1895, after thirty years of consistent living, in the midst of many temptations and much violent persecution.   For a quarter of a century he officiated daily, except Saturdays, seldom failing to be in his usual place, in a chapel which was opened in a prominent street of Peking.   He was a quaint and unusual character, but through his eccentricities there shone out the light of a new life, which was spent in truly apostolic service.[4]   In Hinghua lives Hung-Deh-Ging, who since his acceptance of the Gospel, some six years ago, has voluntarily preached Christ to his countrymen, and has been instrumental in opening many centres of Christian work in that vicinity. The Rev. S. L. Baldwin, D.D., in a volume of missionary biographies, has portrayed the earnest life and abounding labors of Sia Sek Ong, the exemplar and advocate of native liberality in the Foochow Mission of the Methodist Episcopal Church.   In concluding the sketch, Dr. Baldwin remarks of him : " His work abides in the hearts and lives of those whom he brought to Christ, and in the influences he set in motion for the awakening of a new life among his people."[5]   Mrs. Bishop writes that Joldan, the Tibetan postmaster in the British office at Leh, "is a Christian of spotless reputation," whose humble spirit and consistent character make him a living epistle in that dark land.[6]

[1] Ross, " Old Wang, the First Chinese Evangelist in Manchuria."
[2] Christie, " Ten Years in Manchuria," pp. 28–30.
[3] The Church at Home and Abroad, March, 1895, p. 212.
[4] The Missionary Herald, April, 1897, p. 137.
[5] " The Picket Line of Missions," pp. 151–182.
[6] Bishop, " Among the Tibetans," p. 101.

Group of Ordained Pastors—Swatow District.

Cambridge Students, Amoy.   Three Amoy Pastors.

Amoy Pastor, Wife and Child.

A PAGE OF CHINESE CHRISTIANS.

(E. P. C. M.)

In Japan the record is similar. God-fearing, devout, and true-hearted Christians testify by their changed lives to that moral renewal which comes with intelligent loyalty to Christ. The story of Ansai Takeichi, who has been called a Christian statesman of Japan, is told in one of our recent magazines.[1] Dr. De Forest's account of a Japanese lieutenant who was engaged in the Formosan campaign, condenses into a few sentences the striking record of what a Japanese Christian can do.[2] A life that comes nearer home to American readers is that of Sanjuro Ishimoto, late professor in the Meiji Gakuin, Tokyo, who died at Princeton, New Jersey, November 2, 1895, where in connection with the College and Theological Seminary he was seeking a higher preparation for future service in his native land.[3] The files of *The Japan Evangelist*, and the current records of Christian biography, yield numerous examples, such as the lamented Dr. Neesima, the late Mr. Sawayama of Osaka, Mr. Ishii of Okayama, Mr. Ibuka of Tokyo, Mr. Takahashi, Mr. Matsuyama, Mr. Tomeoka, and many others, which show that Christianity in Japan, as elsewhere, means a new and ennobled type of manhood.

We must not forget to note in this connection that woman has also an honored place in the roll-call of character throughout mission fields. Such beautiful lives as those of Mrs. Anna Satthianadhan and her daughter-in-law, Krupabai, and Mrs. Tabitha Bauboo, all of Madras,[4] Mrs. Ahok of Foochow,[5] Mrs. Iap of Amoy,[6] and Mrs. Teng of Peking,[7] and many also in the neighboring kingdom of Japan, such as the late Mrs. Ishii of Okayama,[8] Mrs. Kashi Iwamoto [9] and Mrs. Yajima,

---

[1] *The Church at Home and Abroad*, September, 1895, p. 220; quoted from *The Japan Evangelist*, June, 1895, p. 275.

[2] "This one Christian officer prevents his whole regiment from drinking *saké*, forms a temperance society among his soldiers, prohibits prostitution in a Chinese city of 70,000, establishes Christian service in the city, and raises $3500 from Chinese and Japanese with which to erect a monument to the memory of the soldiers who fell in battle, and then resigns to go back to Formosa as a Christian official, with seven other Christians under him."— *The Missionary Herald*, September, 1896, p. 352.

[3] Consult a sketch of Mr. Ishimoto's life, by the late Rev. Dr. James M. McCauley, in *The Japan Evangelist*, April, 1896, pp. 205–209.

[4] Murdoch, "Sketches of Indian Christians," pp. 25–53. Cf. also *The Church Missionary Intelligencer*, September, 1896, pp. 670–677.

[5] Barnes, "Behind the Great Wall," pp. 60–90.

[6] *The Mission Field* (Ref. C. A.), February, 1897, p. 326.

[7] *Woman's Work for Woman*, February, 1895, p. 42.

[8] *The Asylum Record*, December, 1896, p. 5.

[9] *The Japan Evangelist*, April, 1896, pp. 229–237.

both of Tokyo,[1] are sufficient evidence that Christianity will give a pure and saintly charm to the character of womanhood the world over.

Thus out of the humble annals of missions a fresh chapter in biography might be written, which would lose nothing in comparison with the story of victorious lives in other generations.

> " Saints of the early dawn of Christ, Saints of Imperial Rome,
> Saints of the cloistered Middle Age, Saints of the modern home,
> Saints of the soft and sunny East, Saints of the frozen seas,
> Saints of the isles that wave their palms in the far Antipodes."

II

A second achievement of missions, of strategic import and fundamental value, is the creation of a new public opinion.   Changes in public opinion are usually so impalpable in character,

The strategic import of a Christianized public opinion.

and so imperceptible in progress, that it is sometimes difficult to discover them, and almost impossible to realize at once their significance.   Prevailing public sentiment in heathen lands is usually the child of generations, even of centuries, of unchanging habits of thought and modes of living.[2] It is almost invariably rigid, tenacious, uncompromising, and so entrenched in the personal, social, and religious life of the people that it generally eludes and often defies any attempt either to dislodge or change it.   A perverted social conscience is as much a reality in non-Christian lands as a perverted individual conscience, and in the form of public opinion it is a factor of amazing force and stability.   It has back of it the dominant spirit of national or tribal history, and is usually in line with those regnant forces which have always swayed the fallen nature of man.   Christian missions are among the very few influences which can seriously or permanently disturb it.   In fact, the spiritual energies of Christianity represent almost the only power which with any transforming results has ever grappled with it aggressively, under the inspiration of a positive purpose.

Public opinion may be said to exist under varied aspects.   It is found generally in the form of a sodden, stagnant incubus upon the social consciousness, saturated with evil traditions, characterized by an elusive, mirage-like expansiveness, inaccessible in its vastness, yet so

---

1 *The Japan Evangelist,* February, 1896, pp. 170–172.

2 On the genesis and importance of public opinion, cf. Giddings, " The Principles of Sociology," p. 147,

Aged Christians of the Kobe Church, converts from Buddhism. All are widows. They have formed themselves into an association known as the " Rojin Kwai" (Old Ladies' Meeting), for Christian edification and fellowship.

JAPANESE CHRISTIANS WHO HAVE KEPT THE FAITH.

(M. E. S.)

surely and insistently present that when you touch it you seem to come at one and the same time into contact with the whole mass, upon which, however, even the earnest, aggressive Christian reformer is unable apparently to make the slightest impression.   If he seems to impinge upon it at any one point, then the whole immense body appears to rally its weight and influence against him at that very point of contact.   Then there is the proud, alert, defiant, and determined phase of it, which meets one with militant energy and patriotic spirit, and offers a stout and unrelenting resistance to every attempt at modification.   There is the sentimental and rhapsodical phase, the indifferent and contemptuous temper, the selfish, the conservative, the timid, the weak and nerveless species of it.   It brings to its aid and protection, in opposition to all efforts to change it, the feeling of reverence for the past, so strong in Oriental countries, the commanding influence of custom, the force of habit, the love of things as they are, and have been, and shall be.   It is a marvelous thing, this power of public opinion among those who have never been accustomed to independence of thought and life, and have always sat beneath the shadow of pervasive intellectual and moral traditions and persistent social trends which have dominated their lives for centuries.   Moreover, in lands where personal despotism has full scope, the people have been accustomed to take refuge in the stability and protecting conservatism of ruling public opinion as a check upon irresponsible power, and this has added much to its controlling position in their esteem and to its immovable fixedness.   It has done them at times a service similar to that rendered to the American political system by a federal constitution, in giving consistency and continuity to the form of government.

It is hard for us to realize what a hindrance there is to mission progress in this force of public opinion, and what difficulties must be contended with in overcoming it.   Christian missions attack it in detail by influencing individual conviction, which, in its cumulative volume, slowly crystallizes into changed public sentiment.   Here, then, is a sphere of activity and indirect achievement which must be entered and effectively occupied before we can expect any permanent social transformation.   It is manifest that Christian missions, under these circumstances, as a condition of success, must necessarily have a large scope of influence and a wide range of action, and that the accomplishment of any effective service for society in this sphere of transformation will tax fully their best energies and most ample resources.   There is need of a powerful crusade in the interest of social progress in discrediting and overthrow-

Public sentiment a stronghold of heathenism.

ing ruling ideas which can never be dislodged, and hardly even disturbed, by the ordinary factors of social development. Superstitions, traditions, prejudices, fears, customs, moods, fancies, tastes, modes of thought, and hereditary tendencies, backed by invincible habit, dominate and fashion social life to an extraordinary degree in the wide realms of the Orient. The results of social evolution, as they have crystallized in the ruling ideas and practices of society, must, to a certain extent, be undone or dissolved, or at least so modified by a process of Christian involution that a new current will be put in motion. The ideals of men must be changed. We should not forget to note here that this brings a distinct gain to the world in having the devotion, enthusiasm, and sincerity, which are in many instances undoubted characteristics of the religious life of non-Christian races, directed into Christian channels of aspiration, while the practical aim is so rectified as to bring an increment of moral energy into the service of philanthropy and virtuous living. The whole process of social development is thus born again to the possibility of better results; it is charged as by an electric current with a fresh and aggressive spirit.

As human history needed the Incarnation to introduce into its moral current the principle of a new life, and to impart to its worn-out and devitalized powers the new spiritual energy which Christ brought into the world, so the social life of degenerate races needs to be seized from without by a revivifying moral power. Dr. Robertson Nicoll speaks pointedly and truly upon this urgent theme when he writes: " Christianity utterly refuses to be expressed as an earthly evolution. It claims to be a heavenly innovation. Jesus Christ was no product of Jewish heredity and environment. He came into this world from beyond it. He has made a new beginning in human history, because He was a new Person on the stage of time, whose entrance and whose exit were alike mysterious and appropriate to Himself. Christianity declares that the moral order, or disorder, of the world has been altered once for all by a moral impact from without—an impact which Christians believe to have involved, naturally enough, physical correspondences. *God hath visited and redeemed His people.* The Incarnation and the Atonement are our human names for divine acts in which God Himself intervenes to cure the evil and misery of mankind. And henceforth all things are different, since that visitation and redemption." [1] Christianity, then, and Christianity alone, brings the power of recovery to heathen society. The way in which it does this is often at first very indirect and obscure in its workings, but after a time, in the light of assured re-

---

[1] Editorial in *The British Weekly,* July 15, 1897.

sults, the pathway of great and beneficent changes becomes luminous with the glow of Christian influences. The workings of Christian principles and the force of Christian character can be plainly seen.[1]

The introduction of new ideas is the positive side of the creation of a new public opinion, while the destruction of old notions is the negative. The difference is that the former is constructive, while the latter is destructive. The one points to the establishment and confirmation of new sentiments; the other to the discrediting *Some ruling ideas which must be dethroned.* and discarding of old traditions, which are an incubus to be removed in order to give play to new ideals. Let us endeavor to specialize some of these ruling ideas which must be deprived of their controlling

---

[1] " That the new spirit now actively at work in India is the spirit of Christ and of His religion, is clearly shown by a study of the moral and social condition of the native Christian community. This community is now the most progressive body in the country, abundantly proving that Christianity is a vital principle, a motive power, a transforming force, far transcending any force of nature. Each step in its progress has been the natural outcome of the change that the religion of Christ accomplishes in individuals. The native Christian community has risen from a low degree of numerical and social importance to a recognized position of commanding influence and conscious strength. This progress is largely due to the immunity from the social drawbacks under which the Hindu community labours. They have ceased to be restrained by tyrannical social customs and caste prejudices. And it is the Gospel of Christ that has made them free. They are also better educated in youth, better treated in sickness, more promptly aided in times of scarcity, more continuously disciplined throughout life, than any other class in the country. The absence among them of that great social evil, the early marriage system, and the increasing number of intelligent wives and mothers, largely account for their present position. The simplicity of their religious and social life is one of their greatest privileges. Unlike Hindus, whose religious existence is one series of expensive ceremonies from birth to death, they have no burdensome rites to perform, and learn to practise economy in weddings and funerals. Hinduism drains the purse, and exhausts the time and strength, of its votaries. The moment a Hindu becomes a Christian he leaves the land of slavery and breathes the air of liberty. In moral tone and purity, and in many a social improvement, the native Christians take the lead. One has only to compare Christian with Hindu homes to be assured that it is the leaven of Christ's religion that can alone quicken the inert mass of Hindu society. Industry has been developed among them; they are beginning to learn the dignity of labour; and the industrial schools started by missions have proved a great boon to the community, many of whom have taken to honest trades, and are doing remarkably well. The moral, social, and intellectual progress of this community is the natural outcome of the life-giving power of Christianity. Here we have abundant evidence that the Christian faith is the most powerful lever for the uplifting of a people. Self-consciousness and independence are true indications of power; and this community is becoming conscious of its strength."—Rev. T. E. Slater (L. M. S.), Bangalore, South India.

influence in the interests of higher social progress.   Among them may
be named the provincial self-exaltation, usually associated with a withering estimate of the foreigner, prevailing so conspicuously in China,
and of which other nations are able to present no insignificant illustration.   The provincial conceit of Japan pales only in the presence of
that of China.   Japan, however, does not allow national pride to blind
her to the excellencies and advantages of Christian civilization, a large
share of which, with singular wisdom, she is ready to adopt, so far as
there is no conflict with her exclusive predilections.   China has always
stood in the twilight of her own enormous shadow, rejecting everything
that was not indigenous.   Her chauvinism is colossal.   Hatred and
distrust of everything outside of China are ruling ideas of the " Middle
Kingdom."   A Chinese mandarin cannot even enter a foreigner's house
without incurring suspicion and losing a measure of his official and social standing.   The extent to which this contempt of outside nations
will carry the Chinese intellect is revealed in an extract from a placard
attached to the gates of the Examination Hall at Singan, at a time
when thousands of students were gathered for literary examinations.
It is not by any means an exaggerated specimen of its kind.[1]   It is the
testimony of *The Indian Messenger*, a native periodical published in the
interests of Brahmoism, that " there is probably at the present moment
no more conceited race on the face of the earth, and with less cause for
self-glorification, if we take into account only their present achievement
and condition, than the people of India."   A recent correspondent of
the London *Times*, writing from Madagascar, speaks of the " unlimited
conceit " which forms one of the principal traits of the Hova character.
Instances need not be multiplied.   It is one of the functions of
missions to let in the light of comparison and teach the saving grace
of humility.

Many absurd errors in scientific knowledge and practical economy
are prevalent.   Antiquated and childish restrictions upon travel abroad
are still enforced in India.   There is everywhere a reluctance to substitute modern facilities for old and cumbersome methods.   Violent
race prejudices separate non-Christian communities into hostile camps,
hinder that free intermingling of humanity which disarms suspicion, and

---

[1] Its legend runs thus: " These few and insignificant nations that be on the
outskirts of this illustrious land are thorny and wild and all barbarian.   Before the
European countries existed China was sage-educated.   The teaching of Confucius
at last reached unto their barbarity, and reaching them reformed them.   Yet an
Englishman ventures to come out and instruct us!   Why, we are his teachers!
(Signed) Master of the Club of Orthodoxy."—Quoted in *The Baptist Missionary
Magazine*, January, 1895, p. 27.

The six smaller cuts represent Indian devotees and holy men, some of whom are torturing themselves in the hope of meriting reward. The lower central picture represents mission boys learning a useful trade in the industrial workshop of the S. P. G. school, Cawnpore.

INDIAN VERSUS CHRISTIAN IDEALS.

retard that fusion of races which is so characteristic of the progress of Christian civilization. A false and narrow patriotism is apt to exalt and cling to features of national life which a larger and wiser knowledge would reject. Caste exclusiveness rules with despotic sway in Indian society, and in milder form among many other non-Christian peoples. Then there are degrading superstitions, demoralizing fears, misguided convictions, criminal abominations, defective standards of honor and integrity, heartless unconsciousness of responsibility and duty where the interests of others are concerned, heedless cruelty, filthiness of the imagination, and a lax estimate of the enormity of crime. There is a low opinion of the status of women and children, and no proper appreciation of the sacredness of either their persons or their rights. One of the best gifts of missions to heathen society is the educated woman. To instruct a girl was a scandal, until missions established a better sentiment, and now it is a thing to be desired. There are loose views of the marriage relation, and an ever-present readiness to judge leniently, if not condone altogether, the vices which an Oriental loves. In fact, there are few ruling ideas in the non-Christian world that are not a barrier to social progress, and there is no available and really effective instrument for dislodging and dispelling them, other than the Christianity which it is the transcendent aim of Christian missions to teach.[1]

[1] "Nothing can be more certain," writes the Rev. S. H. Kellogg, D. D. (P. B. F. M. N.), of Landaur, India, "than that such movements here and there are directly due to the effect of Christianity as a visible power in provoking to good works."

Dr. Kellogg has kindly forwarded the following items culled from Indian papers: "In a recent number of the Madras journal entitled *Progress* an account is given of the subjects discussed at the Eighth Annual Conference of the Kayastha community of Hindus, known as the ' writer ' caste. They were as follows: (1) curtailment of marriage expenses; (2) prohibition of early (child) marriages; (3) sending youths to England for education; (4) technical education; (5) creation of a national fund for the maintenance of widows and orphans, and education of the children of the poorer members of the Kayastha community; (6) female education; (7) prohibition of members of the community from joining any associations, political or religious, which tend to engender ill feeling between the races.

"The *Gyan Patrika* gives the following items, among others, of the programme of the Hindu Social Conference held at Madras, December 30, 1894: (1) the desirability of regulating the marriage age, that is, not allowing men over fifty to marry girls under fourteen; (2) question of facilitating registration of Social Reform Associations; (3) the advisability of discouraging nautch parties at religious festivals and social gatherings; (4) abolition of imprisonment of women in execution of decrees for restitution of conjugal rights; (5) removal of all social hindrances in the way of the reception of foreign travelled men, and also of men marrying widows; (6) the necessity of a more active coöperation with the Temperance Movement.

There is need everywhere in non-Christian society of a new public opinion as to the value of the individual as a factor in social progress and in national greatness. There must be a new recognition of his rights, an appreciation of the sacredness of his liberty, and of the import and value of his personal relations and character. There must be a new public sentiment as to the value of purity, truthfulness, righteousness, honor, fidelity to public trust, and responsibility for the public weal. There must be a new estimate of the moral obligations implied in public service, of the requirements of loyalty in the sphere of public duty, and a discovery of the status of law, justice, and common honesty in public life. There must be a new judgment as to the standards of integrity, honesty, and trustworthiness in business relations. Deceit, fraud, and unscrupulous misrepresentation, now to such an extent dominant in all the commercial intercourse of heathen society, must be dishonored and discredited. There must be a new appreciation of the nobility of virtue and a deeper perception of the loathsomeness of vice. The old degenerate code must give place to the Christian ideal of the sanctities of the home, the sacredness of family life, and the imperative obligations of sexual purity. There must be a higher recognition of the brotherhood of humanity, and all that it implies in the sphere of mutual helpfulness and philanthropic service. There must be a clearer apprehension of the dignity of law and the superiority of principle over personal favoritism or brute force in the exercise of executive authority or the administration of public trust. There must be new views of the dignity of labor, the shame of idleness as a badge of aristocracy, and the absurdity of regarding fancied nobility of lineage as a plea for sloth. There must be a new estimate of man as man, such as will shatter false standards and sunder the bonds of caste.

Some important lessons to be learned.

There is a whole circle of twisted, gnarled, stunted, grotesque, vitiated, demoralized, and iniquitous aspects of public opinion in foreign lands, which must be slowly changed, purified, sweetened, and brought into harmony with Christian teaching. Here is an achievement, at once fundamental and vital in the interests of social transformation, which Christian missions alone are capable of accomplishing with any touch of mastery, or with any permanent efficiency and thoroughness.

not only as regards spirits, but also as regards opium, bhang, and other drugs; (7) the desirability of promoting interdining and intermarriage between the members of recognized subdivisions of the local caste; (8) the desirability of discouraging the disfigurement of widows, in accordance with the prevailing customs."

The process by which this change is accomplished is difficult to discover or illustrate, but the results are apparent to any thoughtful observer.   Slowly but surely the whole public opinion of China is changing in its estimate of the outside world and its respect for Western science, literature, art, culture, and even religion.   It is no slight achievement to convince a Chinese that any change in his conservative outlook or familiar environment will be an advantage; yet that conviction is now lodged in many minds, and the spirit of progress is beginning to breathe upon the dry bones of China.   This is no doubt due to a variety of causes, but chief among them must be named the influence of Christian missions in stimulating thought, awakening aspiration, and enlarging the outlook of multitudes in the empire.   The Hindu point of view is also changing—quietly, almost imperceptibly, new philosophical principles are dominating Hindu thought.   Christian ideas are being absorbed, appropriated, and even asserted, in some instances with only a faint recognition of their origin.   Reform movements are gathering headway in India; old scandals are losing caste; and things that a generation or so ago were openly admired and practised are now decidedly—in some instances pronouncedly—under a ban.   Some of the most brilliant appeals and thoroughgoing arguments in behalf of reform movements are advanced at the present day by Hindus themselves.   The recent inaugural address of R. G. Bhandarkar, Ph.D., C.I.E., Vice-Chancellor of the Bombay University, in taking the Chair as President of the Poona Social Conference, is a strong, dignified, and outspoken plea for radical and monumental changes in the social system of Hinduism.[1]

> *Public opinion in China and India yielding to Christian influence.*

[1] A few paragraphs from the address will reveal its tenor and spirit:

"About sixty years ago, none among us had any idea of the reform of our society, and a conference such as this was out of the question.   But since that time we have come in closer contact with Western civilization, chiefly through the means of English education; and that has led us to take interest in the concerns of Indian society in general, and consider its good to be our good, and has evoked in us feelings of justice and compassion for the various classes that compose our society. . . . And, first, a good many of the proposals have reference to the condition of the female portion of our society.   Gentlemen, one half of the intellectual, moral, and spiritual resources of our country is being wasted.   If our women were educated as they ought to be, they would be a powerful instrument for advancing the general condition of our country. . . . The other points concerning our daughters and our sisters have reference to the unjust and cruel sufferings to which our present social usages subject them, and which no man in whom the sentiments of justice and compassion are developed can find it in his heart to tolerate even for a moment.   The misery of our widows has been the subject of frequent remark.

Dr. Bhandarkar is a Maratha Brahman, and is spoken of as "a profound scholar, a great antiquarian, and an earnest philanthropist and reformer." He is not alone in his views as to the need of extensive reforms in Indian society, and his advocacy of them is indicative of an eventful and aggressive change in the public opinion of the country, which is growing stronger and more militant every year. What is true of India to a marked degree is true, in a measure, of the entire Orient. There is throughout the East a growing restlessness and discontent with present social conditions, and a new spirit, progressive, alert, and aspiring, is asserting itself, indicative of far-reaching changes which are coming in public sentiment. To what extent these changes will be due to the influence of Christian missions may be open to discussion with some, but it is a noticeable fact that among experienced, competent, and candid observers on the spot there is a readiness to recognize the work of missions as the most pervasive and decisive agency in the introduction of new ideas and in the quickening of new aspirations in Eastern society. The opinion of missionaries in all lands, as we shall see, is practically unanimous in regarding the awakening of non-Christian peoples to a better and nobler social destiny as due to the vitalizing touch of Christianity.

We would not say that it is the paramount duty or the primary service of a missionary to take up the rôle of a social reformer. He must be very wise and guarded in this respect. His first business is with the Gospel as the message of God to man, and with the Bible as a book of religious inspiration and divine instruction, although he may do much by his personal influence and advice to encourage

The Christian missionary should be wise and self-restrained in his attitude towards social reforms.

. . . I will only make a general observation, that that society which allows men to marry any number of times, even up to the age of sixty, while it sternly forbids even girls of seven or eight to have another husband after one is dead, which gives liberty to a man of fifty or sixty to marry a girl of eleven or twelve, which has no word of condemnation for the man who marries another wife within fifteen days after the death of the first, is a society which sets very little value upon the life of a female human being, and places woman on the same level with cattle, and is thus in an unsound condition, disqualifying it for a successful competition with societies having a more healthy constitution. . . . I will next call your attention to those points in the resolution which concern the institution of castes. . . . And, generally, allow me to observe that the rigid system of caste which prevails among us will ever act as a heavy drag in our race towards a brighter future. . . . Then, there are other points in the resolution, the aim of which is to remove positive obstacles to our healthy development. The marriage of boys and girls is of this nature. . . . The prohibition of travel in foreign countries I would put under the same head, since it acts as an obstacle to the free expansion of our energies and capacities."—*The Statesman*, January 7, 1896; quoted also in *The Delhi Mission News*, July, 1896.

needed reforms. The religion which he teaches will eventually purify the minds of men, rectify their views, and reform their ways. He should be especially cautious about interfering with social customs and using the Gospel in the advocacy of a new order of things where there is no imperative call for change. He is a teacher of biblical truth, and an advocate and exemplar of Christian morality. If he is faithful in this sphere, he will in the end do a large and beneficent work throughout the entire realm of social welfare.[1] It may be asked here, Are we not giving too wide and indefinite a scope to Christianity as a transforming and rectifying force in social development? It is a fair question, but we should pause before we answer it to consider whether we have fully realized the penetrating and pervasive power of Christianity in human society, the length and breadth as well as the height and depth of its influence over both the individual and the social man. Can we hope for, or need we desire, anything more directly purifying, ennobling, and thoroughly renovating to human society, in all its complex requirements and its desperate shortcomings, than that it should be wholly Christianized?

III

A third function of missions of fundamental import and touching the deep springs of social progress is the establishment and promotion of education. This is one of the noblest sociological aspects of missionary effort. It illumines, vivifies, and inspires the intellectual nature of man, and brings it into the arena of social struggle equipped *The fundamental character of education as a basis of social progress.* for service. Before the modern era of missionary educational facilities, lamentable ignorance prevailed through all the non-Christian world. Half a century or more ago whole communities, tribes, and even nations were under the incubus of its depressing and paralyzing bondage. Even the deceitful semblance of true knowledge, derived from their

---

[1] "Their customs and habits are so ancient and sacred to them that they will not abandon them simply because they are told to do so. Appeals to their reason or moral sense are fruitless, for in the majority of cases these people are unreasonable, and their moral sense needs first to be developed in order to be made productive of good. Neither has the missionary time to engage in secular matters, nor money enough to supply the demands that would be made upon him. Only he whom the Son of God makes free is free indeed. After Christ has entered the hearts of these people and they are made obedient to the Spirit, they will have faith in the missionary's message and the superiority of his social, moral, and religious ideas."—Rev. J. Heinrichs (A. B. M. U.), Vinukonda, India.

ancient but effete classical culture, was, in the case of the more advanced nations of the Orient, not the possession of the people, but the monopoly of a literary caste. The instruction of the young, except in very rare instances, was neglected. Pitiable ignorance reigned everywhere, and the masses of society were the victims of mental blindness and vacuity to an extent which is almost incredible in our enlightened environment.

It is not necessary here to dwell at any length upon this aspect of our theme. It will be more gratifying to point out what a hopeful change has been brought about. The present educational plant of foreign missions throughout the world is a marvelous achievement, considered not only in itself, but as representing literally a free gift of Christianity to the nations. Its import as a stimulus to social progress is self-evident. It is sufficient to say that mission schools and colleges have awakened everywhere a new passion for education. "The entrance of Thy Word giveth light" is true of the mind as well as of the heart. "It is a common thing in China," writes a missionary, "for illiterate men and women, often far advanced in life, as soon as they embrace Christianity, to want to learn to read."[1] A desire for knowledge, especially for acquaintance with the facts of science, seems to spring up in connection with the quickened life of Christian faith. "How this Christianity does open the eyes of the mind!" was the exclamation of a wondering Chinese, after a talk with a missionary about the elementary facts of science. A new wonderland of mental vision and intellectual attainment has been revealed to the young who are thronging educational institutions in every foreign field. Vast areas of the mental life of the world are thus being reclaimed by culture, and prepared through missionary instrumentalities to be productive of a harvest of social benefits to man.[2] Not only is impulse given to the mental

[1] Rev. William P. Chalfant (P. B. F. M. N.), Ichowfu, China.

[2] The following statistics, which have been gathered with much care, will indicate in a measure the extent and significance of the educational contribution of missions to social progress. These figures are good so far as they go, and, were it possible to secure absolute completeness, it is likely that in some items they might be increased from ten to fifteen per cent., when all returns were obtained and tabulated. There are 112 universities and colleges, including preparatory departments, in foreign mission fields, attended by 28,523 students; there are 546 theological and training schools, with 12,178 students; there are 1087 boarding- and high-schools, with 54,376 pupils; 17,773 day-schools, with 780,448 pupils; 324 industrial schools and departments, with 7390 pupils: making a total of 19,842—in all probability it will be found to be nearly 22,000—institutions and schools, with a total, so far as present returns indicate, of 882,915 pupils. The number is probably not far from a full million.

powers, but their development is guided with a view to usefulness. The training imparted is broad in its scope and thorough in its drill, and is mingled with elevating Christian instruction. The elementary, academic, normal, professional, and industrial departments are pervaded by the moral impress and the Christian tone of the Gospel.[1] The gain is far more notable than is realized by the great majority of the supporters of missions, and in such advanced fields as India and Japan has resulted in the formation of scientific, philosophical, and educational societies, the character and scope of which indicate a generous fruitage of culture, and promise noble contributions to the sum of human learning. The foundations of an intellectual development, in touch with the treasures of modern knowledge, have been laid among receptive peoples whose capabilities will perhaps prove a surprise to the world, and result in widespread advantage to the race.

IV

Next to the educational, we must rank the literary contribution of missions as a basal factor in the social progress of non-Christian peoples. This varies in its character and range, from the primer and text-book of the elementary school to goodly volumes dealing with the highest themes of modern culture. The extent and varied character of the literature given by missionaries to the awakened minds and hearts of multitudes, represent the ripest attainments of modern intellectual life. A chief place, very properly, has been assigned to religious literature, including theological treatises, biblical expositions, and manuals of doctrine and apologetics. The scope of these literary activities, however, goes far beyond this, and covers not only books of a scientific, philosophical, technical, and economic character, but a wide range of works in history, ethics, education, literature, and gives information of practical value, entertaining as well as instructive.

Mission literature as a basis of social development.

The crown and glory of this is the Bible, around which all mission literature is grouped, and to which, at least in the consecrated aims of its authors, it is intended to bear a definite relation. In this service on behalf of a sanctified literature, the great Bible and Tract Societies of America and Britain have borne a noble and conspicuous part. The department of the arts, including æsthetics, has not been overlooked;

[1] Cf. Mott, " Strategic Points in the World's Conquest," chaps. iv.–x., xiii.–xvii.

religious poetry, especially Gospel hymns, has been everywhere introduced. Beautiful and inspiring words have been set to music, partly native and partly borrowed from the sacred harmonies of Christendom, so that the religious services, as well as the homes and hearts of Christians, are cheered and brightened with the delights of sacred song.[1]

Religious journals and periodicals are edited and published by missionaries, and through the stimulus of this example the journalistic enterprise of educated natives has inaugurated an extensive issue of newspaper and periodical literature, which is a growing power in the education of society and the shaping of public opinion. The entire or partial versions of the Bible prepared, chiefly during the present century, by missionaries, or by others for missionary purposes, exceed four hundred. This does not include revised versions; each one represents a distinct language or dialect. The new versions, that is, those still in the manuscript stage and at present in course of preparation, are 20. The publishing-houses and mission presses number, so far as has been ascertained, at least 148. The list of annual publications, as nearly as can be traced, is 6,926,163; the number of pages printed each year is about 250,000,000. There are in addition 34 tract societies on mission fields, printing annually, according to recent reports, 8,613,568 volumes and tracts, representing an estimated number of pages not far from 200,000,000. There are published in connection with the various missions 416 separate issues of periodical literature.

Missionaries have reduced many spoken languages to writing, and made them available for literary uses. A careful estimate reveals the fact that not less than 120 languages have thus been made the medium of literary production through the stimulating agency of missions. They have introduced the art of writing, and provided reading primers, elementary grammars, educational text-books, philological treatises, and various grades of dictionaries, as intellectual tools to peoples who have thus been ushered into a new literary epoch.[2] It is

---

[1] See "The Hymnody of Foreign Missions," by the Rev. James H. Ross, in *The Bibliotheca Sacra*, April, 1894.

[2] Commissioner Sir H. H. Johnston, in a recent report, has referred to the literary services of missionaries in the British Central Africa Protectorate as follows:

"High praise must be given to the missionaries of British Central Africa for the extent and value of their linguistic studies. The Universities' Mission has printed several works dealing with the form of Chinyanja which is spoken on the east coast of Nyassa. In the Church of Scotland Mission the Rev. Alexander Hetherwick has published a handbook of the Yao language, and the Rev. D. C.

COMMITTEE FOR TRANSLATING THE BIBLE INTO HINDUSTANI.

American, European, and Native Members.

Delhi, India, 1898.

safe to say that an era of national literature has been in many instances inaugurated by missions, and in cases where such a literature already existed it has been profoundly stimulated and guided into enlarged and fructifying channels. The morning drum-beat of the British Army is said to accompany the sunrise; but even in more literal harmony with fact, may it not be said that the throb of the mission presses—signal of a transcendent dawn—pulsates round the world with the music of their unceasing activity? In Central Africa, as long ago as 1878, a printing-press was established at Blantyre, in connection with the Church of Scotland Mission. The importance of all this intellectual awakening cannot be exaggerated. The advantage of having the new

Scott has compiled a Mañanja dictionary, which is a veritable mine of information as to native habits and customs. In a way, the Livingstonia Mission stands first as regards the value of its contributions to our knowledge of African languages. Dr. Laws has published at different times vocabularies of the Chinyanja, Chikunda, and Chitonga tongues. Dr. Elmslie has written some really valuable works on the Tumbuka language, and on the dialect of Zulu spoken by the Angoni, besides numerous other contributions to African philology. The late Dr. Henry, of the same mission, has published the best grammar extant of Chinyanja, and the late Mr. Bain commenced a vocabulary of the language spoken at the north end of Lake Nyassa. The Rev. David Jones, of the London Missionary Society, has published vocabularies of the Kimambwe, and has compiled (I do not think it is published other than privately) a most valuable study of the interesting Kiguha language, spoken on the west coast of Lake Tanganyika."—Blue Book, "Africa, No. 6 (1894)," p. 36.

A further statement regarding the literary and other services of missionaries will be found in Sir H. H. Johnston's recent book, "British Central Africa," pp. 205, 206. He there remarks: "Huge is the debt which philologists owe to the labours of British missionaries in Africa! By evangelists of our own nationality nearly two hundred African languages and dialects have been illustrated by grammars, dictionaries, vocabularies, and translations of the Bible. Many of these tongues were on the point of extinction, and have since become extinct, and we owe our knowledge of them solely to the missionaries' intervention. Zoölogy, botany, and anthropology, and most of the other branches of scientific investigation, have been enriched by the researches of missionaries, who have enjoyed unequalled opportunities of collecting in new districts; while commerce and colonisation have been so notoriously guided in their extension by the information derived from patriotic emissaries of Christianity that the negro potentate was scarcely unjust when he complained that 'first came the missionary, then the merchant, then the consul, and then the man-of-war.' For missionary enterprise in the future I see a great sphere of usefulness—work to be done in the service of civilisation which shall rise superior to the mere inculcation of dogma; work which shall have for its object the careful education and kindly guardianship of struggling, backward peoples; work which, in its lasting effects on men's minds, shall be gratefully remembered by the new races of Africa when the sectarian fervour which prompted it shall long have been forgotten."

era of literature established under the noble and helpful influences of missions is incalculable, and of hardly less significance is it to have the modern renaissance in the literary development of already lettered people occur under the auspices of Christian culture.[1]   The old literature is usually antiquated, effete, moribund, and useless for the purposes of modern progress.   It is rather an incubus upon the intellect and the heart, and must be supplanted by a culture which is quickened and fed from later sources of supply.

We should not fail to note, moreover, in this connection, that the awakening of literary desires and the cultivation of intellectual and æsthetic tastes have stimulated a large realm of economic enterprise, which will in time give employment to an army of workers engaged in literary production, and in the publishing, editing, printing, and distributing of books and periodicals, thus ministering to the growing intellectual and artistic wants of an educated community.   This conclusion may safely be reached if foreign mission activities in journalistic and literary fields are to result in a general demand for literature which bears any comparison with the present output within the bounds of Christendom, where millions of money are in circulation and hundreds of thousands of workers are busy supplying the intellectual requirements of the age.

The reflecting onlooker cannot fail to note in this connection the inestimable value of the Bible as a part of national literature.[2]   Who

God's Word the supreme gift of missions to Eastern literature.

can gauge the benefit which follows the introduction of God's thoughts into the intellectual, social, and religious experience of man?   Who can weigh the import of placing such a mandatory and sanctioning phrase as " Thus saith the Lord " in the current of the heart-life of a nation?   Who can measure the moulding power of divine instruction concerning the individual life as well as the mutual relationships of human intercourse?   What terms of gratitude are sufficiently adequate to express the indebtedness of a people to those who bring them this grand heritage of our common humanity—God's light upon human duty and destiny? [3]

It is true that the more enlightened nations of the Orient have sacred books of their own, but, in many instances, these very classics

[1] Cf. Mabie, " Essays on Books and Culture," chap. x., " Liberation through Ideas," pp. 121-131.

[2] Pattison, " History of the English Bible."

[3] Cf. Warren, " The Bible in the World's Education "; Northrup, " The Bible as an Educator."

Telugu Bible Translators. 1879.

Translators of the Bible into the Telugu language, 1879.

Theological Class of the Canadian Presbyterian Mission, Central India. Rev. W. A. Wilson seated
in the centre on the left, and Rev. N. H. Russell on the right.

TRANSLATING AND TEACHING GOD'S WORD IN INDIA.

of their religious faith are responsible for a large part of the default and moral scandal of their social condition.   Professor Fairbairn quotes a distinguished scholar as saying: "If you want to prove the truth, the wisdom, the sober and honest history of the Bible, and the purity of its religion, place it among the sacred books of the East.   In these books there are many grains of gold, but they are hid in mountains of the most extraordinary rubbish, and the astonishing thing is that it is the rubbish that calls forth the enthusiasm and admiration of the peoples that own them.   The sobriety of the Bible, the purity of its spirit, the elevation and devotion of its tone, make it occupy an entirely unique place." [1]

Among more backward and barbarous races little, if any, sacred literature which is worthy of the name exists.   Mythological legends, puerile superstitions, fantastic tales of demons, rhapsodical mutterings, solemn gibberish, or the empty rodomontade of medicine-men and witch-doctors, make up the sum total of their sacred traditions.   To introduce the light, the hope, the truth, the wholesome instruction, the guiding wisdom, the restraining commands, and the glowing assurances of a sanctified Christian literature into the intellectual life of nations so bereft, so demoralized, so enslaved by ignorance, is a service of incalculable import and immense beneficence to mankind.   It is a persuasive summons to all that is best in men; it renews their mental forces; it brings them out of the darkness into the light, out of the shadow into the sunshine; and places them where all their spiritual gifts may ripen, their intellectual powers fructify, and their moral capabilities develop for the higher interests of themselves and their posterity.   This is surely one of the most quickening services of Christian missions for the social as well as the mental and spiritual development of mankind.

V

The cultivation of the philanthropic spirit is another of the notable results of missions.   Under direct missionary auspices a large and impressive exemplification of the benevolent spirit of Christianity has been given.   An impulse in this direction has been imparted not only to the native Christian community, but, in a measure, to non-Christian society wherever missions are conducted.   Benevolence both as a grace and a duty has always been part of the historic outcome of

The influence of missions in laying the foundations of philanthropy.

[1] Fairbairn, " Religion in History and in Modern Life," p. 102.

Christianity.   The Christian religion is still assuming as part of its mission activities the rôle of the Good Samaritan among the nations.[1] A social system without the presence and the active ministry of philanthropy is doomed to selfishness and sterility, since the most powerful and winsome incentive to mutual helpfulness, and so to the development of social virtues, is lacking.

It is true that a theoretical, and after a fashion practical, benevolence is part of other religious systems.   Almsgiving is popular in the East, but it is identified with a meritorious system of religious observance. The giving of alms is inculcated as an act of merit, especially for the benefit of religious devotees, who live in filth and idleness, and are an incubus on society rather than a help to it.   In some instances the benevolent instinct seems to turn from living men and women to exhaust itself either upon animals or on an ancestral humanity dead and gone.   It may safely be said that the systematic, universal, persistent practice of philanthropic and helpful ministry to living humanity in its hour of need, for God's sake and for charity's sake, is characteristic of the religion of Christ in a sense unknown in other systems.[2]   It alone teaches in a clear and emphatic way the sacredness of the living body in its earthly environment, and seeks to brighten and cheer human lives, to assuage pain and deliver the sufferer from its dread mastery, to stay

---

[1] Pierce, " The Dominion of Christ," p. 183.

[2] The following statistics include data which have been verified, and may stand as a fairly approximate—not absolutely complete—representation of the philanthropic agencies of missions.   The total of medical missionaries at present is 680; of this number 470 are men, and 210 women.   There are 45 medical schools and classes, with 382 male and 79 female students—making a total of 461.   There are 21 training-schools for nurses, with 146 pupils.   Neither of these statements includes 240 female medical students now in training as physicians, nurses, and hospital assistants, under the care of the Lady Dufferin Association in India.   There are 348 hospitals and 774 dispensaries.   Exact statements as to the number of patients annually treated have been obtained from 293 hospitals and 661 dispensaries, the total patients recorded in these returns being 2,009,970, representing 5,087,169 treatments.   If we make a proportionate estimate for the 55 hospitals and 113 dispensaries from which reports of the number of patients have not as yet been received, the sum total of those annually treated will be not far from 2,500,000.   If we allow an average of three separate visits or treatments for each patient, the total of annual treatments will be 7,500,000.   There are 97 leper asylums, homes, and settlements, with 5453 inmates, of whom 1987 are Christians.   There are 227 orphan and foundling asylums, with 14,695 inmates.   The statistics of temperance-reform and rescue societies have not been obtained with sufficient exactness to report at present.   The same may be said of children's aid societies, prison-reform movements, and other less prominent charities.   More detailed information will be found in the supplemental volume entitled " Centennial Survey of Foreign Missions."

the ravages of disease, to mitigate the agony of incurable maladies, to care for the weak and helpless, to put a stop to bloodshed and savage torture, and to inspire that fine and humane dread of inflicting pain which is characteristic of Christian feeling. Its programme, in the words of its Master, is "to heal all manner of disease and all manner of sickness." Its aim is to dispel the darkness, to brighten the shadows, to give a home to the homeless, an asylum to the orphan, a refuge to the hard-pressed, deliverance to the enslaved, and an uplift of hope and cheer to the despairing. It seeks to open up the path of honest occupation by placing the tools of industry in savage hands accustomed only to wield weapons of violence. Christianity has a whole round of expedients for the rescue of distressed humanity, the mitigation of its sorrows and sufferings and the saving of lives that otherwise would be doomed.

The philanthropic spirit, with its complement of practice, which these expedients represent, is a signal contribution of missions to non-Christian society. Medical missionary service, hospitals for the suffering, and benevolent institutions of various kinds, have sprung up on every shore where Christian missions have planted the Red Cross flag of humanitarian ministry. Suffering nations are already reaping a harvest of beneficent results, and as yet only the first-fruits have been gathered. Stimulus has here and there been given to philanthropic movements under non-Christian auspices which have brought some benefits where hitherto only neglect had been the rule. In South China, for example, what are known as Sacred Edict Preaching Halls have been established to give instruction in Confucian ethics as an antidote to Gospel preaching. Native benevolent societies have also been formed to meet missionary philanthropy on its own ground.[1] A

---

[1] "It cannot be too emphatically told that this Sacred Edict Preaching Hall movement is due entirely to Christianity. Before missions from the West were established and maintained with ever-growing success, not a Sacred Edict Hall existed. There was no attempt to popularize the teachings of the sages or bring these teachings to the doors of the people. The Sacred Edict itself was read and expounded within the precincts of certain official buildings on the mornings of the 1st and 15th of each month. It was a procedure purely formal. The public, with the possible exception of two or three loiterers, did not attend the readings, nor was any endeavor made to induce the populace to hear the Edict. Christianity has evoked a movement, now widespread, to bring all that is best in Confucian teaching to bear on the life of the people, and in any account of what the Gospel is doing indirectly for their moral and social well-being this fact should have prominence.

"Missionary hospitals have led to the founding of native societies in order that Christianity may be met on its own grounds and conquered with its own weapons. The Chinese Benevolent Society of Canton is a most noteworthy institution, possessing what the natives would regard as a magnificent building of lofty and impos-

striking incident is just at hand which reveals what Christianity can do towards the development of philanthropy among races the most ignorant and degraded, and apparently the least likely to respond to humanizing influences.   Many have no doubt noted the announcement in the English journals that among the contributions received by the Mansion House Indian Famine Fund was the sum of £844 from the people of Fiji.   This is a Christian gift.   " Let the fact be noted," remarks the editor of *Work and Workers in the Mission Field*, " and its significance be taken to heart.   Sixty years ago, at the time of Her Majesty's accession to the throne, the entire Fiji group was inhabited by pagan cannibals.   Its heathen darkness was unbroken by any ray of Christian religion or civilisation." [1]

VI

Another fundamental social force of manifest promise is the personal example of missionaries and native converts, whose daily lives are passed in full view of the non-Christian world.

Personal example as a contribution of missions to non-Christian society.

Native example in the past has been, and is still to an immensely preponderating extent, enlisted in the maintenance of existing customs.   There is no source from which a counter-influence may be expected, unless Christianity, in the person of its missionaries and native converts, steps in with the silent power of personal example.   At first this may seem to

ing proportions, situated in Canton where its central offices could be most conveniently established.   Its operations extend far beyond the bounds of the provincial city and immediate neighborhood.   There are four native doctors in attendance daily at the central building.   These men prescribe for all comers.   Their diagnosis is, of course, from the Western point of view incomplete and often absurd.   There is, however, the fact of an institution known throughout China, with a yearly expenditure amounting to many thousands of dollars, and with branches in different parts of the suburbs and in country districts.   Here again is an indirect result of Christianity manifest in the alleviation of suffering through heathen benevolence brought into play by the opposing force of Christian missions.   Before missions were established in the South of China private benevolence was no doubt exercised by many of the wealthy Chinese.   Some of these may have combined to heal the sick, to help the destitute and famine-stricken, and to bestow coffins as gifts when deserving families among their neighbors were found without the means to bury their dead.   But anything in the nature of a public society organized for the express purpose of systematic and regular benevolence, one may affirm, was an unheard-of project."—Rev. T. W. Pearce (L. M. S.), Hong Kong, China.

1 *Work and Workers in the Mission Field*, May, 1897, p. 177.

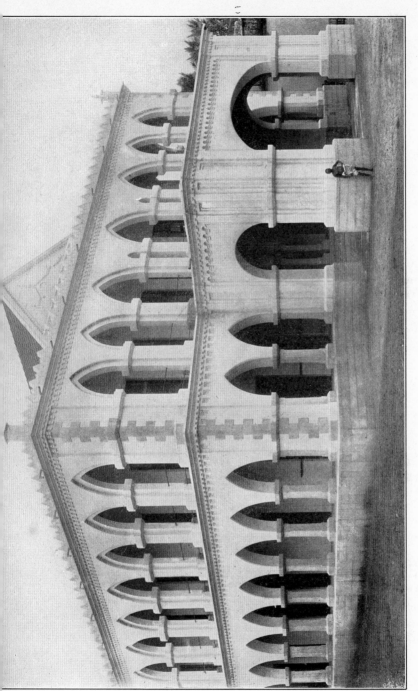

AMERICAN MISSION HOSPITAL, MADURA, SOUTH INDIA.

(A. B. C. F. M.)

A new hospital presented to the American Board by some native Indian princes and philanthropists as a token of their appreciation of the benefits of Medical Missions, and especially of the services of the Rev. Frank Van Allen, M.D., Medical Missionary of the Board at Madura.

be of little value and efficacy as an offset to almost universal tendencies of an opposite character, but the winsome force of a noble and commendable example is often more powerful than the apparently formidable influence against which it contends.[1] Example that is right in itself, and that represents sincerity of conviction, is one of those "little ones which shall chase a thousand." The personal equation is beginning to work in the influence of native Christian communities, and in the contribution here and there of capable leaders in the intellectual, social, and religious life of the Orient. Nor is it too much to expect that Christian missions will give birth in modern times to a St. Chrysostom or a St. Augustine, to a Luther, a Wilberforce, a Howard, and to others of like fame, who have accomplished a noble and transforming work in the realm of human progress.[2] Missions are setting in motion in all lands that stream of consecrated personality which has always characterized Christian history. They are kindling a new enthusiasm for human welfare in nations where, if it ever existed, it has been extinct for centuries. They are opening fountains of individual evangelism where a Gospel yearning for souls has never been known.

The personal character of missionaries themselves is also a factor in the social changes taking place in non-Christian lands which it would

[1] "Just take one phase of His [Christ's] historical action—what He has accomplished through great personalities. Were He dropped out of history, with all the historical personalities He has fashioned, it is hardly possible to conceive what to-day would be. The mightiest civilizing agencies are persons; the mightiest civilizing persons have been Christian men. . . . These were the men who made the century [the sixteenth], but who made the men? In whose name, in whose strength, by obedience to whose will, as they understood and believed it, did they live and act? Did not their inspiration come straight from Christ? Abolish these men, and the sixteenth century loses its significance; abolish Christ, and you abolish the men. Yet what is true of it is true of all the Christian centuries. Subtract the Christian personalities and the ideas that reigned in and lived through them, and you have but the struggle of brutal passions, of men savage through ambition and lust of power; subtract Christ, and you dry up the source of all Christian personalities and ideas, you leave man to go his old blind way, ungladdened by faith in heaven, uncheered by the ideal of a humanity to be made perfect through realizing the mind of its Maker."—Fairbairn, "The City of God," pp. 284-286.

[2] "Our times, which may now and then appear mechanical, commonplace, take deeper significance as we attentively consider the past, especially as we note the far reach of influence in those by whom its movements were chiefly affected. The tremendous force which belongs to any great personality, and the sovereign persistence of its influence among men, become apparent. We gain a profounder sense of the unity of history, as continuous and organic. We see more distinctly the interdependence of centuries on each other, with our indebtedness to many who have labored and struggled before us."—Storrs, "Bernard of Clairvaux," pp. 6, 7. Cf. also Gordon, "The Christ of To-day," pp. 287-292.

be difficult adequately to estimate.[1] How many noble lives marked by a saintly piety, a kindly ministry, a blameless walk and conversation, tireless devotion, heroic fidelity to duty, and unflinching advocacy of the higher spirit and the nobler aims of Christianity, have been passed in the presence of non-Christian society![2] The story of medieval missions is redolent with the charm and sweetness of saintly example and the power of heroic living on the part of men and women who gave themselves to missionary service. St. Columba and his associates were bright illustrations. Of St. Augustine and his missionaries the Venerable Bede writes: "They soon began to make some converts, who were drawn to them by the admiration they felt for the holy innocence of their lives, and the sweetness of the heavenly doctrine which they taught."[3]

Mr. Adams, in his "Saints and Missionaries of the Anglo-Saxon Era" (p. 15), speaking of the first Archbishop of Canterbury, declares that "Bede certainly ascribes the success of Augustine's missionaries to the wonderful impression which their manner of life made on the English." Statements of the same tenor are to be found concerning the personal character and example of the great Continental missionaries

[1] Cf. an article on "French of Lahore," in *The Quarterly Review* (London), January, 1896.

[2] "Missionaries do not need the endorsement of governments or of those who may be termed men of the world. They are quite content to labor with the approval of their own consciences in the sight of God. But it may be well for some who know little of their work to read what *The Japan Mail* says of those who are laboring in the Japanese Empire. This is a purely secular paper, but very ably conducted by men whose theological opinions are by no means in accord with those of the missionaries, yet it says of them: ' They lead the most exemplary lives; devote themselves to deeds of charity; place their educational and medical skill at the free disposal of the people, and exhibit in the midst of sharp suffering and adversity a spirit of patience and benevolence such as ought to enlist universal sympathy and respect. It seems to us that the record is all in their favor. Watching the question closely for many years, we have failed to discover any want of discretion on the part of the missionaries, unless it be an occasional display of unwise confidence in sending unprotected women into the interior.' "—Quoted in *The Missionary Herald*, April, 1896, p. 142.

[3] Adams, "The Saints and Missionaries of the Anglo-Saxon Era," p. 15. Of St. Aidan it is stated in the same volume (p. 105): "St. Aidan's example had a wonderful effect upon the English, and not a few, both men and women, were stirred by it to devote themselves wholly to the service of Christ." Similar statements are made of St. Aldhelm (p. 163), St. Etheldrida (p. 193), St. Hilda (p. 288), St. Cuthbert (p. 328), and of others of the early English missionaries. Cf. also for instructive reading on this point, Maclear, " A History of Christian Missions During the Middle Ages," and Mrs. Rundle Charles, " Early Christian Missions of Ireland, Scotland, and England."

A Corridor of Madura Hospital.   Dr. Frank Van Allen and Native Assistants.   A View from Corridor of Madura Hospital.

GLIMPSES OF THE NEW MADURA HOSPITAL.

(A. B. C. F. M.)

of the medieval period—Columbanus, Willibrord, Boniface, Anskar, Adalbert, Otho, Francis of Assisi, Raymund Lull, and Francis Xavier.[1] Later times in the history of missions reveal the influence of Eliot and Brainerd among the Indians, of Hans Egede in Greenland, of Schwartz in India, and many other saintly characters who served and walked with God before the eyes of degraded and ignorant races.[2] Shall we venture to gauge the power of that object-lesson in brotherhood which, in more recent times, is given in the lives of men like Patteson, Selwyn, Duff, Livingstone, Mackenzie, Calhoun, Thomson, Van Dyck, Gilmour, Nevius, Hill, Verbeck, and Keith-Falconer? "What do modern missions signify?" asks Dr. Fairbairn. "That the most cultivated and high-blooded peoples on earth recognize their kinship and the obligations of their kinship to the most savage and debased. . . . It [the Christian religion] has made civilized man feel that he and the savage are of one blood, that the savage is as dear to God as he is, has as vast capabilities, as boundless a promise of being as his own nature can boast. The religion that has created this sense of kinship and duty is the true mother of man's faith in human fraternity."[3]

The import of example, both on the part of the missionary and the worthy native convert, is not confined to the scope of their individual influence. There is an object-lesson, too, in Christian family life planted in communities as yet very defective in civilization or wholly dominated by savagery. *The Christian family: its power as an object-lesson.* Some have questioned the usefulness, or even the wisdom, of marriage on the part of missionaries. Now, while it is true that there may be some kinds of pioneer work, or special service attended with temporary hardship and peril, in which the celibate missionary has an advantage, yet, as a rule, marriage is a distinct gain as regards both efficiency and scope of influence. Native communities must have their homes, and they need the model presented in the domestic life of the missionary. There is also an aspect of stability, of social dignity and natural accessibility in family life, as well as a refining environment. A Christian home planted in a community which it seeks to mould after its own likeness is an immense gain to non-Christian society.

[1] Maclear, "A History of Christian Missions During the Middle Ages," and "Apostles of Mediæval Europe"; Smith, "Mediæval Missions"; Summers, "The Rise and Spread of Christianity in Europe."

[2] Walsh, "Heroes of the Mission Field," and "Modern Heroes of the Mission Field"; Creegan, "Great Missionaries of the Church"; Haydn, "American Heroes on Mission Fields"; Farrar, "Saintly Workers."

[3] Fairbairn, "Religion in History and in Modern Life," pp. 234, 235.

A word might be said here also as to the status and availability of unmarried women in foreign mission fields.   That there is an open door, a noble opportunity, and a sacred ministry for this class of mission workers is now a matter which need not seriously be argued.   The missionary societies of Great Britain and America have taken the lead in recognizing the possibilities of effective service in the foreign field by unmarried women.   Continental societies have moved more slowly, and in some instances seem to be still open to conviction. At the Bremen Missionary Conference of 1880 the question of sending independent female missionaries was raised, and received with considerable coldness and reserve.[1]   The proposal, however, was earnestly advocated by Dr. Gustav Warneck, but with little success. In the notable report on foreign missions presented at the Lambeth Conference of 1897, there is a distinct recognition, based of course upon experience, of "the value of the work of women" in mission fields.[2]   "Women are needed for missionaries as well as men," writes Sir Harry Johnston concerning British Central Africa.   "On the whole, I think women make better missionaries than men, and are always much more lovable in that aspect.   Let them, therefore, continue to go out to Africa as celibates if they are over thirty-five, but otherwise as married women."[3]   There were 2500 unmarried women connected with all Protestant missionary societies in 1894, and women, married and unmarried, in the foreign fields exceeded the men in number by about a thousand.[4]   At the present time (1899) this number has increased to fully 3500 unmarried, and a total of 8000 married and unmarried women.

The fact that there are social prejudices existing in foreign communities (notably in China) to be overcome, is not a sufficient reason for denying to Christian women their place of privilege and power in mission work.[5]   There are prejudices deep-seated and petrified

The value of woman's service in foreign missions.

[1] Warneck, "Outline of the History of Protestant Missions," p. 213.

[2] "Conference of Bishops of the Anglican Communion, Holden at Lambeth Palace in July, 1897," p. 71.

[3] Johnston, "British Central Africa," pp. 190, 200.

[4] Buckland, "Women in the Mission Field," p. 23.

[5] Just here let us pause for a moment to note how a tactful missionary woman will, day after day, conduct a quiet crusade against those two social monstrosities of China—the crushed and shortened feet, and the elongated finger-nails.

Dr. Mary H. Fulton, of the American Presbyterian Mission at Canton, writes: "I am doing what little I can in my small sphere to show an applied Christianity. In the first place, I try always to be neat in dress.   This invariably calls out complimentary remarks.   They at once compare my pretty and fresh, though cheap, dress with their silken (and generally soiled) robes.   Then they notice my clean,

against almost everything connected with Christianity. Native public opinion is especially out of focus with Christian civilization in its views of woman and her social environment. It regards her in the light of that traditional distrust and detraction which has prevailed for unknown centuries in the East. It is the function of Christianity to teach nobler things concerning womankind, and to enforce its teaching by practice. It may require sacrifice and take time, but the result will be a permanent gain. The portraiture of womanly virtue without the humiliating exactions of the Orient, and the sweet example of womanly service pervaded and inspired by the Christian spirit, dignified and protected by innate purity and refinement, present a social parable which is sadly needed in the Oriental world, and which in many communities has not been given except under the auspices of Christian missions.[1] Then, again, the good which single women can do in the service of their own sex far outweighs in significance and value the injury which may result from the shock to the perfunctory sensibilities of native society in China or elsewhere.[2]

short nails, and contrast them with their long ones,—often fully a finger in length,— which indicate that they are ladies of leisure. They at once want to know *why* I dress so differently from them. It is an easy step to tell them that God, who made us, has put women into the world for *use*, and not merely to live to adorn our bodies, and that there are many poor suffering children and others who need our help. If we have such long nails and bound feet, we cannot go about to help them. They all assent to this, and generally there is an inquiry on the part of some one present if she cannot have her feet unbound. Then you should hear the clamor! A dozen will admonish the one who dared to be so bold as to propose such a thing. ' Had she lost all her modesty that she wanted to go about like a man? ' Now you will laugh, but all my arguments are as nothing compared with showing them a well-fitting, pretty foreign boot or shoe. I have always thought, since feet are such a momentous question in this land, that we should be very careful to make our own as presentable as possible. To see us start off quickly and gracefully and go through the streets so independently often makes them desirous of imitating us, especially when they see women hobbling along painfully, or being carried on the backs of others. The same is true of our homes. I try to make mine attractive in its simplicity. I have a weekly prayer-meeting here just because I want to show my home to these women who have never seen cleanliness and order in their dark, damp, crowded quarters. I give them, after the meeting, tea and sponge-cake, served in pretty cups and plates. Simple as all this is, it lifts them up and out of their sordid surroundings, for the time being, at least, and, I hope, will lead them to make their own houses more homelike. I always urge those coming under my influence to try and be as clean as possible, and I am happy to say that I observe year by year an increasing tendency to the use of foreign soap and handkerchiefs."

[1] Telford, " Women in the Mission Field."

[2] The sphere of missionary women and the value of their services were recently discussed in a very intelligent and sensible paper presented by the **Rev. Fung Chak,**

The presence of missionaries in great emergencies, and in times of calamity and pestilence, has been both an example and a succor to distressed communities.   Recent events in Armenia

[The heroic element in missions, and its social value.

present an impressive illustration of this fact. Both missionaries and their native converts have exhibited a heroism and loyalty which have elicited the respect and admiration of the world.   Amidst the horrible atrocities and sore calamities of the massacres in Armenia, American missionaries have exerted a moral influence, and accomplished a practical service, of the highest value.   They have comforted and cheered native friends during the heartrending terrors of recent years.   Where there has been opportunity for personal intervention, they have checked to some extent the awful cruelties of the Turkish soldiery and their brutal accessories.   They have been the almoners of contributions which the Christians of other lands have sent, and have given trustworthy information to Christendom concerning the extent and unspeakable barbarity of one of the darkest and most inhuman incidents of modern history.   It is no insignificant service to civilization and humanity which is rendered by Christian missionaries scattered throughout the earth on a kind of moral picket duty, when they give authentic and well-

at the Baptist Association of 1896, representing the two Kwang provinces in Southern China.   As the views of a native pastor, the following summary is worth recording:

" Women from the West, as the embodiment of God's love for the world, have crossed the ocean, and, not dreading danger, have come to China to spread the truth, to teach Chinese women.   Let me enumerate some of the benefits which come from women's work here.

" 1. They teach the girls to read.   Most of the Western women who come to China have schools, and employ competent teachers to teach Chinese girls, for the Chinese custom is to make much of boys, but little of girls.

" 2. Foreign women teach our women to know God's doctrine.   Since divine truth is in the Bible, by teaching them to read it for themselves they also teach them propriety, justice, and modesty, and cause them to lead lives of virtue and refinement, to love God, and trust in the Saviour, and be self-restrained and benevolent. . . .

" 3. They benefit the women of China by teaching them the proper way to train their daughters.   It is hard to enumerate the bad customs that prevail.   These are all due to ignorance and want of proper instruction of the women. . . .

" 4. The benefit to national manners.   Although China is great, it is still a land of darkness.   Superstitions and errors fill the land.   But now Chinese female teachers are teaching the Gospel, and opening the way that the women may put away their superstitions and follow the true doctrine. . . .

" Moreover, these Western teachers teach the Chinese the virtue of self-denial in three respects: 1. By their faithfulness in the Lord's service.   Last year the

Smaller Group. Missionaries at Edgehill, Landaur, India.
Larger Group. Mission Workers, Lady Kinnaird Hospital, Lucknow.

CHRISTIAN WOMANHOOD IN MISSION FIELDS.

(Z. B. M. M.)

vouched-for reports of what is going on in lands where irresponsible power has supreme control. It keeps Christian nations in direct, although unofficial, touch with less civilized peoples, and serves also to exert a measure of restraint upon the otherwise unchecked passions of reckless men in places of authority.

There is, on this account, a distinct contribution to the social welfare of non-Christian communities in the object-lesson of missionary and native Christian example. Are not Christian missions, moreover, the only channel through which a gift so precious and potent, so rare and noble, could be conveyed? Let it be noted also that the honors of martyrdom, its sacred inspiration, and the increment of moral power which it gives to the manhood and womanhood of the world, belong in our present century almost exclusively to missions.[1]

The roll-call of missionaries is far too long to allow of any attempt to enumerate more than a few scattered names; yet of all who have ever joined

> " the choir invisible
> Of those immortal dead who live again
> In minds made better by their presence,"

none can be said more truly to realize the beautiful suggestiveness of the poetic conception than sainted missionaries who "live again" in souls purified amidst brooding degradation, renewed amidst moral decay, and beautified amidst the abounding ugliness of heathenism. There are hundreds, even thousands, of these missionary lives

The music of "the choir invisible" in missionary history.

which would furnish ample illustration of this statement, although not a few of those whose examples have proved especially inspiring have lived in comparative obscurity. It is not easy to depict in literary form the secret influences incidental to personality, save as we are able to sketch them in biographical detail, dealing with the life as related to its environment. A few examples must suffice to give us an insight into the subtile and far-reaching effects of individual character.[2]

ladies in our Baptist Mission visited one hundred and sixteen villages. 2. By their earnestness in pressing forward. 3. In accommodating themselves to others. By their sympathy and wisdom, their love and gentleness, their peacefulness and patience, they become acceptable to all. Thus wherever they go they are welcomed; the doctrine is inscribed on their lips, and their manners are admired, and the homes of rich and poor are opened to their teaching; all admire their virtue, in that they uplift the women and pity the girls."— *The Chinese Recorder*, August, 1896, pp. 392–394.

[1] Harris, "A Century of Missionary Martyrs."

[2] In addition to the illustrations given in the following pages, the reader may consult the missionary biographies mentioned in the bibliography at the end of this

The Rev. F. E. Hoskins writes that during a mission tour he was seated with a group of Syrian friends in the little village of Alma, on the southern borders of the Syria Mission field, when the following incident was related. A native Protestant teacher had recently been called to Tyre on business, and as he was passing Alexander's Fountain, not far from the city, he was hailed by a Turkish soldier, who was doing guard duty. The soldier questioned him as to who he was, whence he came, whither he was going, and, finally, what his religion was. Upon his replying that he was a Protestant Christian (*Injeely*), the rough soldier responded promptly: "Were it not for the memory of Mr. Dale, I would smother your religion with curses." Surely here is a lesson concerning the power of a loyal Christian life. "Somewhere and somehow," writes Mr. Hoskins, "that man had been brought into contact with Mr. Dale.[1] The influence of his consecrated life had pierced the rough exterior and softened the heart of the soldier, so that years after Mr. Dale's death he was constrained to dismiss that humble native brother from Alma, not with cursing, but with ' Go in peace.' "

The late Rev. Charles W. Forman, D.D., of the American Presbyterian Mission in Lahore, has left as his legacy to Indian society the influence of fifty years of saintly living. How deeply the power of his personal example entered into the lives of those around him may be gathered from the tributes from native sources which were called forth by his death.[2]

lecture. He will find also much. to confirm the estimate placed upon the value of missionary character and example in the shorter biographical sketches scattered through the current missionary literature of recent years. Cf. also article by Julian Hawthorne, in *The Cosmopolitan*, September, 1897, p. 512.

[1] The Rev. Gerald F. Dale, Jr., went to Syria as a missionary by appointment of the American Presbyterian Board in 1872, and died in Zahleh, Mount Lebanon, October 6, 1886. He was a man of ideal missionary enthusiasm, gifted with power to touch and influence others, and has left an impress which seems to be ineffaceable upon thousands of Syrian hearts.

[2] " *The Tribune* of Lahore, a non-Christian journal, referred to him editorially as follows :

" 'It will be long before Lahoris forget the sweet and benign face of the great American missionary. We doubt whether any other man, European or Indian, has taken as great a part in the making of the Punjab of to-day as has Dr. Forman. A history of his educational work would be almost the educational history of the province. Though he is no longer working in the flesh in our midst, the spirit of his work will beacon us onward. His memory will long be a pillar of light to our people.'

" *The Indian Standard* writes : ' We do not hesitate to say that no man of this century has exerted a larger personal influence on the people of the Punjab.'

" *The Civil and Military Gazette* remarks : ' It is, perhaps, not saying too much

Of the late Miss Eliza Agnew, a missionary of the American Board in Ceylon, the natives were accustomed to say that she was "the mother of a thousand daughters." She lived in Ceylon forty-three years without returning to her native land on furlough. For forty of these years she was the Principal of the Oodooville Girls' Boarding-School, a flourishing educational institution, where during her lifetime she had under her personal care more than a thousand pupils. Six hundred of these graduated after taking the full course, and every one of the six hundred left the school a professing Christian. Many of them engaged in mission work as Bible-women and teachers. It is said of her that through the influence and power of her blameless life "she made the position of an unmarried lady missionary honorable in Ceylon for all future time. The highest praise a native seems able to bestow upon an unmarried lady worker in Ceylon is to say that she was like Miss Agnew."[1]

Another devoted missionary life, wonderful in the power of its personal influence, closed, after forty-two years of service, at Singapore, September 14, 1895. Miss Sophia Cooke entered upon missionary work in the Orient at a time when such service was not recognized or appreciated as it is now. She lived to see, in all the great centres of the East, Christian womanhood consecrated to the Master's business, commanding the respect and admiration of the world. Miss Cooke interested herself in various ways in Christian service for the women and girls of that great cosmopolitan city. Much of it was rescue work among Chinese girls, and many apparently hopeless waifs were saved by her. She was busy also in working for the army and navy, and for several years conducted Bible classes for soldiers at her own home, and was herself the founder of the Sailors' Rest at Singapore. Her influ-

to state that amongst all the foreigners who have lived in Lahore no one has been more widely known or more universally respected and beloved by the people than he [Dr. Forman].'

" *The Punjab Patriot* (non-Christian) thus expresses itself as to Dr. Forman's death : ' The occurrence has spread a gloom all over the Punjab, which is full of his old pupils. In the city of Lahore the people have mourned his loss as that of one of themselves. They feel that they have lost in him a real friend. A prince among missionaries, Dr. Forman will long be remembered in this province, not only as a believer and worker in Christ, but for the noble, unselfish life he led through his long career.'

" Not less than three thousand persons of all classes and creeds followed the hearse, hundreds joining the procession as it passed through the city."—Quoted in *The New York Observer*, April 25, 1895.

[1] For portrait and biographical sketch of Miss Agnew, see *The Christian*, London, May 14, 1896. Cf. also *Life and Light*, September, 1894, p. 409.

ence was a large and important factor, and no one was reached by her efforts without coming in contact with her gracious Christian personality. At her death there was a tribute of respect for her memory from those for whom she had labored which was remarkable in its character. Nothing more representative, it is said, was ever seen in Singapore than her funeral, for this devoted woman was laid to rest with almost regal honors.[1]

The lamented Rev. David Hill, of the Wesleyan Mission, Hankow, who died April 18, 1896, was a man of rare qualities, and his life was one of exceptional heartiness in the Lord's service. To him the Industrial School for the Blind at Hankow is largely indebted for its prosperity and usefulness. The boys in its department of carpentry rendered as a last tribute a touching service by preparing his coffin.[2]

In the missionary annals of the Dark Continent we have lives in which we already see the initial fulfillment of the promise that they "shall shine as the stars for ever and ever." These
New stars in the African firmament. lives have introduced into the spiritual history of Africa a personal influence that will never die, but will continue to gather force and to work with ever-expanding energy as the conversion of the Continent progresses. Such names as Schmidt, Krapf, Vanderkemp, Livingstone, Moffat, Mackenzie, Hannington, Mackay, Goldie, Smythies, Maples, Hill, Walker, Bushnell, Grout, Tyler, Bridgman, Scott, Good, Pilkington, and others— some of whom are still living, as the venerable M. François Coillard, of the French Evangelical Mission—occur to us instantly. One of the native clergy, in an address at a great meeting in London, speaking of Bishop Smythies, remarked: "You call him my Lord, but I call him my Father." Of the late Bishop Maples, of Likoma, in Central Africa, one of his colleagues said: "I never knew one with a greater power of inspiring love. He was able to shake off all European insularities, and to be to Africans a real brother."[3] The late Rev. Hugh Goldie, of the Scotch United Presbyterian Mission in Old Calabar, on the West Coast of Africa, is another striking illustration of what a missionary life means to heathen society. The Rev. William Dickie writes of him: "We cannot pretend to estimate the effect of a life like that of Mr. Goldie upon

---

1 *The Missionary Review of the World*, May, 1896, p. 370.

2 For biographical sketches, see *Work and Workers in the Mission Field*, June, 1896, pp. 232–238, and *The Review of Missions* (Nashville, Tennessee), July, 1897, pp. 1–4.

3 For a biographical sketch of Bishop Maples, see *Central Africa*, December, 1895, p. 185. Cf. also his biography, recently issued.

A Group of Kaiserswerth Deaconesses, Beirut, Syria.

the heathen people among whom he lived. He was one of the gentlest of men, with a quiet enthusiasm for souls. The impression which his exalted piety made upon those around him was very deep. Had he cared to speak of the secret of his life, it would have been in the words of the Psalmist, 'Thy gentleness hath made me great.' "[1]

In connection with work for the soldiers, especially in hospitals, during the late war between China and Japan, we have seen frequent references to the faithful ministries of one who might be called the Florence Nightingale of Japan. Miss Eliza Talcott, a missionary of the American Board, gave herself to service in the hospitals, visiting the sick and wounded soldiers both of China and Japan. Many a suffering soldier has been cheered and solaced by her gentle presence and the kindly ministry of her Christian sympathy. An entirely new and beautiful aspect was given to Christianity in the eyes of Japanese and Chinese by Miss Talcott's influence over multitudes of the wounded whom she visited. Chinese officers of high rank have accorded her a hearty tribute of admiration for her goodness.[2]

In March, 1898, the Rev. Guido F. Verbeck, D.D., died at Tokyo, after a period of nearly thirty-nine years of memorable service in Japan. He went there in 1859, and with true devotion and almost incalculable influence identified himself with the modern development of Japanese civilization and culture. His work for Christianity was monumental, while in his personal influence and varied labors for the public and social welfare of the people, his missionary life was typical in its scope and usefulness. He was one of the translators of the Bible into Japanese, and at times a trusted adviser and guide of the Government in the difficult task of adjusting itself to the changes and responsibilities of this great formative era of the Meiji. Dr. H. N. Cobb, in an appreciative sketch of him, does not overrate his unique position in the following estimate of his services: "When the record of the planting of Christianity and the development of a new civilization in the 'Sunrise Kingdom' is fully and truthfully written, it is probable that no name will be found more indissolubly associated with all that is best and most lasting in it than his."[3]

The Florence Nightingale of Japan.

---

[1] For biographical sketch, see *The Missionary Record*, November, 1895, p. 310.

[2] A sketch of Miss Talcott's experience is given in *Our Sisters in Other Lands*, the quarterly publication of the Woman's Missionary Association of the Presbyterian Church of England, for January, 1896, p. 63.

[3] Sketches of Dr. Verbeck will be found in *The Mission Field*, April, 1898, and in *The Christian Intelligencer*, March 16, 1898.

It is impossible, for lack of space, to give more than here and there an illustration of the import of missionary example.   There has been

Some recent tributes to the personal character of missionaries and the social value of their lives. of late, as there seems to be periodically, rather an unusual outburst of criticism and disparagement in certain sections of the public press concerning the life and influence of missionaries; but over against these criticisms have recently appeared many spontaneous tributes, which present an ever-growing volume of testimony favorable to them, from those who have undoubted facilities of observation, and in whose judgment the world will have confidence.   It may not be out of place to gather a few of the more recent of these tributes into our pages.

The disturbances in Turkey have drawn the attention of the Christian world to the labors of resident American missionaries.   The Hon. James Bryce, M.P., in the new edition of his work on "Transcaucasia and Ararat," has a cordial endorsement of their work.[1]   Sir Philip Currie, the British Ambassador to Turkey, has written: "I feel the most sincere respect and admiration for the courage and devotion shown by the American missionaries in Asia Minor, and it is a consolation for want of success in other directions if I have been able to assist them to continue their labors in the cause of religion and civilisation." [2]   Mr. Edward Wistar, who recently visited the interior of Armenia in the interests of the Red Cross expedition, and there met many of the missionaries, remarks concerning them: "They are very tactful, systematic, and efficient in their signally varied tasks, and as adherents to apprehended duty they stand as examples in courage and fidelity worthy to be known and upheld. . . . Having already written and said elsewhere that the American missionaries in Central Turkey are teachers

---

[1] "I cannot mention the American missionaries without a tribute to the admirable work they have done.   They have been the only good influence that has worked from abroad upon the Turkish Empire.   They have shown great judgment and tact in their relations with the ancient Churches of the land, Orthodox, Gregorian, Jacobite, Nestorian, and Catholic.   They have lived cheerfully in the midst not only of hardships, but latterly of serious dangers also.   They have been the first to bring the light of education and learning into these dark places, and have rightly judged that it was far better to diffuse that light through their schools than to aim at presenting a swollen roll of converts.   From them alone, if we except the British consuls, has it been possible during the last thirty years to obtain trustworthy information regarding what passes in the interior.   Their sympathies have, of course, been with the cause of reform.   But they have most prudently done everything in their power to discourage any political agitation among the subject Christians, foreseeing, as the event has too terribly proved, that any such agitation would be made the pretext for massacre."—Bryce, "Transcaucasia and Ararat," pp. 467, 468.

[2] Quoted in *The Congregationalist*, October 15, 1896.

of the Gospel of peace and of submission to the powers that be, I wish now to state, in controversion of statements recently made to the contrary effect, that they are *not* inciters of revolution or disquiet amongst the Armenians." [1]

Mr. Robert E. Speer, in the report of his visit to the Persia Mission of the Presbyterian Board, in 1896, speaks of the strong impress of the personality of missionaries upon their converts, and especially upon their students. He quotes the late Dr. Shedd as saying: "The reminiscences in which our older graduates indulge illustrate the truth that the main element in educational work is the personal. Inscribed indelibly in their hearts is the personality of Mr. Stoddard, and yet more deeply that of Miss Fiske. The strongest impression is the personal, and that is deepest and best in proportion as Christ lives in us. If this be true, one lesson is that we must have personal contact with the pupils, especially spiritual contact." [2] In another section of the document Mr. Speer speaks in high terms of the personal character and standing of the American missionaries in Persia, quoting the testimony of distinguished foreign residents with whom while there he came in personal contact. [3]

Captain Younghusband, C. I. E., whose opinion cannot be said to be influenced by any blind admiration for the missionary idea, nevertheless speaks in strong terms of the missionaries themselves in his volume entitled "The Heart of a Continent." He closes his chapter on "The Missionary Question in China" with the following affirmation : "That some effect is being produced I can vouch for from personal ex-

---

[1] *The Congregationalist,* November 19, 1896.

[2] Report of Robert E. Speer on his visit to the Persia Mission, pp. 41, 42 (printed for the use of the Board of Foreign Missions of the Presbyterian Church in the United States of America, 1897).

[3] "In Persia the missionaries are held in unqualified respect. . . . General Wagner, an Austrian Protestant, who is drill-master of the Persian Army, and close to the Shah, said to me: ' Say to the Americans, I have seen the missionaries and their work at Urumiah, Salmas, Tabriz, and Teheran, and I know them and their work—it is an angel work!' . . . Sir Mortimer Durand, the British Minister, and one of the most efficient men in the British Eastern service, said with equal earnestness that it was impossible for him to speak too warmly of the missionaries and the good they do. And this opinion of foreigners, expressed by General Wagner and Sir Mortimer Durand, could be duplicated from the lips of many native governors and officials, and verified by many incidents of our stay in Persia. Often even those who oppose the work, like the Amir-i-Nizam, one of the most picturesque, able, and unscrupulous men in Persia, of pro-Russian sympathies, hold the missionaries, to one of whom at least he is under great obligations, in high esteem."— *Ibid.,* pp. 63, 64.

perience. I can testify to the fact that, living quietly and unostentatiously in the interior of China, there are men who, by their lives of
noble self-sacrifice and sterling good, are slowly influencing those about
them—men who have so influenced not only a few but many thousands
of these unenthusiastic Chinese as to cause them to risk life itself for
their religion. And if this good work is going on, if Christians are
willing to give up all they hold most dear in this life to help others forward, then is this not worthy of support?—not the support of force, for
even the missionaries do not desire that, but the support afforded by
the encouragement of their fellow-Christians. The slothful, the ignorant, and the foolhardy may well be criticised, and the missionary cause
will only be advanced if such criticism has the effect of stirring them
to increased and more discreet activity. But the true missionary—the
man who devotes his life to the work of imparting to other races the
religion from which his own has derived so much benefit; who carefully
trains himself for this work; who sympathetically studies the religion,
the character, and the peculiarities of the people he wishes to convert;
and who practically lives a life which those about him can see to be
good—should be admired as the highest type of manhood, and it is he
for whom I should wish to enlist the sympathies of my fellow-countrymen in this grave crisis of the missionary cause." [1]

Mr. T. R. Jernigan, United States Consul-General at Shanghai, in
a recent article on " Missionaries and Missionary Work," writes as follows: " My experience as a United States official in Japan and China
covers a period of six years, and during that time no case has come
before me for advice or settlement, involving directly or indirectly the
interest of the Christian Churches, when it has ever been made to appear that the missionaries were not influenced in their conduct by the
highest principles of right and humanity. There ought to be no patience
with the sentiment that goes out to the great outer world, which is separated by the seas from this ancient empire, depreciating missionaries and
missionary work. It is a sentiment that does not commend those who
indulge in it, and cannot be supported by evidence that would be ad-
missible in any court of justice." [2] " In every instance," wrote the late
Colonel Cockerill, from Seoul, Korea, to *The New York Herald*, " the
Koreans who have come in contact with Christian teachers have been
bettered. At least, they lead cleaner lives in the physical and spiritual
sense. . . . Whatever may be said of missionaries in Japan, I will vouch

---

[1] Quoted in *The Church Missionary Intelligencer*, August, 1896, pp. 635, 636.
[2] See the entire article in *The Chinese Recorder*, February, 1897, pp. 51-54, and
March, 1897, pp. 99-102.

that no servant of the Church is leading a life of comfort here. When I think of well-educated, refined women consigning themselves to this doleful, dirty, bad-smelling, absolutely repulsive country, I am amazed. In Seoul the missionaries have clean, comfortable homes inside the walls, which usually shut out much that is disagreeable; but no compound, however well protected, can cut them off from the misery and wretchedness which everywhere abound." [1]

Sir Charles A. Elliott, late Lieutenant-Governor of Bengal, in an address at the Annual Meeting of the Church Missionary Society, in 1896, spoke as follows: " First, then, as to the testimony I have to give regarding the character and life and work of the missionaries in India. It is more than thirty-nine years ago that my acquaintance with them began. . . . I assert that their usefulness is second to none among the beneficial influences which have followed the introduction of British rule into India, and which, under God's Providence, are penetrating and breaking up the darkness and superstition that are still in the country. No one who is a candid observer, and especially no people who are such keen judges of character as the people of India, can fail to watch with admiration the nobility of spirit, the simplicity of life, and the single-minded devotion to a high aim which the missionaries really display." [2] In *The Cosmopolitan* Mr. Julian Hawthorne gives his impression of the missionaries he met in India during his recent investigations into the ravages of the famine. His report is frankly appreciative, and leaves no doubt upon the minds of his readers that he discovered genuine worth in missionaries and a profound humanitarian value in their work.[3]

It is worthy of note that in the far-off Islands of the Pacific, where the work of missionaries rarely falls under the observation of European travellers, testimony concerning the excellence of their lives and the value of their labors is not wanting, and that in some instances it comes from unlooked-for sources. The late Robert Louis *Words of appreciation from unbiassed observers.* Stevenson has spoken several times emphatically on this subject, and in his volume entitled " In the South Seas," has much to say about missions. The following extracts are typical of the spirit in which he writes. He says: " Those who have a taste for hearing missions, Protestant or Catholic, decried, must seek their pleasure elsewhere than in my pages." [4] In one of his " Vailima Letters " he speaks of the

[1] Quoted in *The Gospel in all Lands*, January, 1896, p. 39.
[2] *The Church Missionary Intelligencer*, June, 1896, p. 443.
[3] *The Cosmopolitan*, September, 1897, pp. 517, 518.
[4] " In the South Seas," p. 89.

Rev. James Chalmers (L. M. S.), of New Guinea, as the "most attractive, simple, brave, and interesting man in the whole Pacific."[1]   Mr. Louis Becke has written also in appreciative terms, in one of his novels of South Sea life, concerning the influence and services of the Rev. Francis E. Lawes, a well-known missionary of the London Missionary Society on the Island of Niué.[2]   Dr. Lamberto Loria, of Florence, an Italian scientist, who has spent seven years in British New Guinea, has written a cordial letter to the London Missionary Society, expressing his high estimate of the services of its missionaries in that island.   He confesses to have gone there with a prejudice against all mission work, but his letter shows conclusively that he has recognized with candor and sincere feeling the beneficent influence of that work as it fell under his observation during his stay.   He acknowledges that his opinion upon the subject has entirely changed.[3]   "It was the missionaries chiefly," writes Mr. Burleigh in his recent volume, "who made Madagascar possible for foreigners to live in with safety.   Within fifty years

[1] "Vailima Letters," vol. i., p. 82.   During his visit to Scotland, in 1895, "the freedom of the royal burgh of Inverary" was presented to Mr. Chalmers in recognition of "his career as a missionary and his eminent services in the cause of civilisation and the spread of the Gospel among the heathen."—*The Missionary Record*, October, 1895, p. 299.

[2] "At Alofi (one of the principal towns in Niué) there also lives the one white missionary,—the Rev. Frank Lawes, of the L. M. S.,—the most loved and respected man in the South Seas.   For nearly thirty years he and his wife have lived and toiled on Savage Island.   I say 'toiled,' for his indeed has been a life of real, hard, unceasing toil, and his personal influence and example alone have reclaimed the Savage Islanders from their former savagery and debasing customs."—Quoted in *The Independent and Nonconformist*, September 23, 1897.

[3] His letter is published in full in *The Chronicle*, February, 1897, pp. 37–40. He thus expresses himself with reference to one of the missionaries of the London Missionary Society: "Before closing, I wish to say a few more words about Mrs. Abel.   From what precedes, you may have a faint conception of her singularly happy influence at Kwato.   It is impossible, however, that you can understand it fully.   Only those who lived at Kwato for months can appreciate her and her work at its real worth.   In a community where women are despised she is beloved, esteemed, respected as Mr. Abel, not to say more.   Her wishes are commands, and even the natives are influenced by her sweet good nature.   Her influence is not confined to Papuans, but extends even to the white population.   I, for my part, have to acknowledge that I am going home a better man than when I left Europe, and I am indebted for this entirely and solely to her influence.   Happy are the persons who possess enough nobleness in their hearts to appreciate her qualities. I cannot finish this paper in a better way than by hoping that the London Missionary Society may have the benefit of the services of Mr. and Mrs. Abel for many years to come, and that they may have health and strength to carry on their great work."

they achieved wonders. Civilisation had followed their steps and was dawning into day. . . . They worked, and verily never had men so great a reward, for their success was abundant." [1]

Captain W. H. Manning, late in command of the British forces in Central Africa, thus writes of his contact with missionary service : " I have not touched on the work of the mission among the natives of the Shiré Highlands, and I feel I can very inadequately express my admiration. First you must see the negro boy in his savage state, and then see the finished article as turned out by the Blantyre Mission, and I think you will say that truly the thing is little short of marvellous—from a wild, unkempt, savage urchin, with a rag for a wardrobe, to a pleasant, self-possessed lad, who dresses in spotless white garments, can read and write English, and conducts himself with quiet decorum. To obtain such results, of course, means days of patient teaching and example, in a climate at times trying in the extreme, but nevertheless carried on unostentatiously to the end. The benefit that the Scotch Mission has conferred on the Shiré Highlands is incalculable." [2] Commissioner Sir Harry H. Johnston has written of missions in the same locality, as follows : " Is it of no account, do you think, is it productive of no good effect in the present state of Africa, that certain of our fellow-countrymen—or women—possessed of at least an elementary education, and impelled by no greed of gain or unworthy motive—should voluntarily locate themselves in the wild parts of this undeveloped quarter of the globe, and, by the very fact that they live in a European manner, in a house of European style, surrounded by European implements, products, and adornments, should open the eyes of the brutish savages to the existence of a higher state of culture, and prepare them for the approach of civilisation? I am sure my readers will agree with me that it is as the preparer of the white man's advent, as the mediator between the barbarian native and the invading race of rulers, colonists, or traders, that the missionary earns his chief right to our consideration and support. He constitutes himself informally the tribune of the weaker race, and though he may sometimes be open to the charges of indiscretion, exaggeration, and partiality in his support of his dusky-skinned clients' claims, yet without doubt he has rendered real services to humanity in drawing extra-colonial attention to many a cruel abuse of power, and by checking the ruthless proceedings of the unscrupulous pioneers of the white

---

[1] Quoted in a review of " Two Campaigns—Madagascar and Ashantee," in *The Spectator*, London, September 19, 1896, p. 374.

[2] *The Church of Scotland Home and Foreign Mission Record*, September, 1896, pp. 281, 282.

invasion." [1]   Another remarkable testimony to the value of missions in Africa is from the pen of a German military officer, Lieutenant von François, in his recently published volume on "The Nama and Damara in German South-West Africa." [2]   A further reference to the work of missionaries in Africa will be found in Dr. R. N. Cust's recent volume, "The Gospel Message," in the form of an address entitled "Missionary Heroes in Africa," delivered at Steinway Hall, London. [3]

We need not confine our quotations, however, to the words of foreign visitors or residents.   There are testimonies also from natives of distinction, who, in some instances, are not them-

Some testimonies to the value of missionary example from native sources.

selves converts to Christianity, but who have eyes to see the truth concerning the character and example of missionaries.   A Japanese scholar, in an article on "The Ethical Life and Conceptions of the Japanese," has referred to the power of missionary example in terms which are well worth quoting. "The missionaries," he writes, "have lived good, honest lives, and been careful not to give occasion for scandal; the native Christians, as a rule, have in their lives been consistent with their profession.   All this has been an object-lesson to the people around them.   Besides, during this epoch of revolutionary change, when the old structures of society were crumbling on all sides, when many young men openly proclaimed that to free themselves from all restraints of morality was a mark of enlightenment, and when, moreover, the idea prevailed that

[1] Johnston, "British Central Africa," p. 205.

[2] "What merchants, artisans, and men of science have done for the opening up and civilising of this country is as nothing in the balance compared with the positive results of missionary work.   And this work means so much the more, because all self-regarding motives, such as always inspire the trader or the discoverer, and are to be found even in the soldier, are absent in the missionary.   It must be an exalted impulse which leads the missionary to give up comfort, opportunities of advancement, honour, and fame, for the sake of realising the idea of bringing humanity into the kingdom of God, into sonship to God, and to instil into the soul of a red or black man the mystery of the love of God.   Self-interest is put aside, and the missionary becomes a Nama or a Herero.   He gives continually from the inner treasure of his spiritual life and knowledge.   In order to be able to do that, however, he must unweariedly play now the artisan, now the farmer, now the architect; he must always *give* presents, teaching, improvements, never *take;* he must not even expect that his self-sacrifice will be understood.   And to do this for years, decades even, that truly requires more than human power; and the average mind of the European adventurer, hardened in self-valuation and self-seeking, cannot understand it.   I used not to be able to understand it; you must have seen it to be able to understand and admire."—Quoted from the *Allgemeine Missions-Zeitschrift*, in *The Chronicle*, August, 1896, p. 191.

[3] Cust, "The Gospel Message," pp. 45-53.

there existed no morality in Europe and America, and that those countries were powerful only because they had superior military equipments—
during this time of transition, I say, it was a very great and noteworthy
thing that there should be these men and women from the Far West
to represent to us the ethical and spiritual side of their civilization.   By
their very presence they reminded us of the importance of morality
and religion in the life of a nation.   In this respect their silent, unconscious influence was beyond all estimation.   I have no doubt that with
the further progress of Christianity in Japan, and the consequent more
perfect adaptation of its teachings to the need of the people, it is
destined to exercise a yet more thoroughgoing influence in the development of our ethical thought." [1]

The lamented death of Mrs. Calvin W. Mateer, of the American Presbyterian Mission, at Tungchow, in February, 1898, after many years of
missionary service, called forth a tribute of love and reverence from the
native community, which was remarkable in its spontaneity and sincerity.   In a tablet prepared in her honor and presented on her sixtieth
birthday, she is described as a "venerable, nourishing mother of heroes." [2]

In a recent number of *The Times of India* was published an extract
from a letter of Tahil Ram Gunja Ram, M. R. A. S., a zemindar of Dera
Ismail Khan, in the Punjab, and a Fellow of the Imperial Institute,
London.   He refers to the beneficial influence of Christian missionaries in terms of appreciation and gratitude. [3]   Still another remarkable
tribute to missionaries is from the pen of a Brahman, Mr. V. Nagam Iyer,

[1] Tokiwo Yokoi, of Tokyo, in *International Journal of Ethics*, January, 1896,
pp. 200, 201.

[2] *Woman's Work for Woman*, June, 1898, p. 143.

[3] " Whatever differences in some theological doctrines and dogmas may exist
between Christianity and the Arya Somaj, the enlightened Hinduism, it would be
the meanest ingratitude if I, in common with my countrymen, did not feel grateful
in the fullest possible way to the Christian missionary societies for the good they
have done to India.   These Christian missionaries have been the pioneers of every
reform, whether it be religious, social, or moral.   Without the aid of the Christian
missionary societies the Indian Government would never have been able to do even
a tenth part of what has been done for India.   It was pious Christian missionaries
like Drs. Duff, Wilson, and Forman, whom the Indians up to this time revere
most respectfully, who first established colleges for the education of Indians.   It
was the pious Christian missionaries who first opened female schools, medical
hospitals, and shelters for the Hindu widows who are so much maltreated by Hindu
society.   Though myself a staunch Arya Somajist by religion, yet I say with double
force that no agency has benefited India so much as the Christian missionary societies."—Quoted in *The Zenana*, April, 1896, p. 90.   The letter was originally published in *The Morning Post*, Allahabad, January 4, 1896.

in his chapter on education, in the census report of Travancore.[1] In *The Baluchistan Gazette*, the proprietor of which is a Parsi, appeared not long ago a striking article upon missionary work, which says: "The mission labor, both in the cause of education as well as physical relief, is eminently superior and more effective than that supplied by Government. The mission work, no matter where or among whom it is done, has a moral element which is both soothing and instructive. The missionaries are the bearers of that Great Truth which cannot fail to enter and enlighten the darkest mind and soften the hardest heart, and it is in this that the success of mission labor lies."[2]

VII

Still another point at which missions impinge with moral power upon both the political and social life of lands where they have been es-

The influence of missions in introducing a basis for higher national ideals.

tablished, is exemplified by the stimulus they give in the direction of new national aspirations and higher ideals of government. The new patriotism of India, in contradistinction to the old, inspired as it is with Christian sentiments and ideals rather than with the degenerate notions and fantastic conceits of Hinduism, is the fruit of missions. A truer conception of the spirit and purpose of legislation and of the supreme function of law is slowly but steadily securing recognition. The first principle of justice—namely, the equality of all men before the law—is beginning to emerge from the obscurity into which it has been consigned by the edict of caste. The era of social tyranny in India has been long and dark, but a new standard is now gradually evolving, and men are beginning to take their place in society on the basis of manhood, as heirs of that liberty which Christianity recognizes as theirs by right of birth in God's likeness. Happily, the evidence accumulates on all sides, attesting the influence of missions in over-

---

[1] "By the unceasing efforts and self-denying earnestness of the learned body of Christian missionaries in the country, the large community of native Christians is rapidly advancing in its moral, intellectual, and material condition. . . . But for these missionaries the humble orders of Hindu society would forever remain unraised. . . . The heroism of raising the low from the slough of degradation and debasement was an aspect of civilization unknown to ancient India. . . . I do not think the Brahmans or even the high-caste non-Brahmans can claim this credit." —Quoted in *The Missionary Herald*, October, 1895, p. 391.

[2] Quoted in *Regions Beyond*, June, 1894, p. 224.

throwing and making odious the long-prevalent reign of social despotism.[1]

The very idea of nationality has come to the educated and enlightened mind of India under the auspices of Christianity.[2]   It is the judgment of Professor Max Müller that "the Indian never knew the feeling of nationality."   He is grasping it now in a large and comprehensive sense, which in time must result in the moulding of a great nation by the fusion of numerous tribes and races on the basis of human brotherhood, as well as in community of interest.   In some instances a revived and progressive life has been given to tribes and peoples as a whole, through the entrance of missions.   The Rev. J. M. Macphail, of the Free Church of Scotland Mission in Bengal, mentions the Santals as "a people owing their social salvation to Christian missions."   He states that they were "entirely uneducated and illiterate forty years ago, and would probably soon have been merged into Hinduism, but under the influence of mission work they have maintained their independence, and have made very rapid strides in civilization."   He mentions also the Khasis, in the hills of Assam, who "fifty years ago were among the wildest of warlike tribes, but are now one of the most prosperous and progressive."   Similar statements are made concerning "the long downtrodden Pariahs in the south, who seem at last to be asserting their manhood, and the Mangs, in the Deccan, who are also being rescued from a position of degradation."   This is valuable testimony, as it shows that

---

[1] The Rev. T. E. Slater, of the London Missionary Society, remarked in a lecture delivered before the Indian National Congress at Madras, in December, 1887: "And so Christ's new idea has brought about a marvellous revolution in social and political relations.   Where it is allowed full play, partiality and class legislation are forever doomed; there will not be one law for the rich and another for the poor, but the interests of the entire community will be the object sought. Wherever Christianity is a living force, social wrongs must be redressed, despotic power and oppressive institutions abolished, and law administered and life protected with even-handed justice."

[2] This is true in a measure of other countries than India.   The educational results of Robert College have done much for Bulgarian national consciousness. Upon this point a missionary writes: "The graduates of Robert College are men of power in Bulgaria, and it has been said that the country owes its national existence to that institution.   A striking proof of the results of the agencies referred to among the Bulgarians can be found by a comparison of that nation with adjacent nations among whom no mission work has been done.   The Bulgarians will be seen to be far superior in intelligence and character.   This may be partly due to differences in racial characteristics, but the fact remains that the history of Bulgaria during the last twenty-five years has been a marked contrast to that of the nations adjoining."—Miss Mary M. Patrick (A. B. C. F. M.), Constantinople, Turkey.

Christianity has a tendency to save and elevate barbarous tribes and peoples as a whole, while mere external civilization, when imposed by superior races, interested more in commerce than in evangelism, has rather the opposite effect.[1]

A striking illustration of the lesson Christianity teaches as to the relation of human government to the divine sovereignty is supplied in the address, before referred to, of the late Queen of Manua, in the Samoan Islands. The occasion was the dedication of a church at the capital town. It is full of hearty ascriptions of praise to God, and dutifully acknowledges His mercies to her people. Continuing, she says: "We think much of our kingdom and government. We know we are respected and take our place among the peoples of the earth; yet our kingdom is as nothing before the kingdom of Christ. That is the one kingdom which shall never pass away, a kingdom of kingdoms. 'Blessed is the people whose God is the Lord' was the message given us by the missionary several days ago, and how true that is we know. It is not outward display that shows the real prosperity of a people, but it is those people who give to Christ their hearts, and live godly lives, who shall be truly blessed, and who shall know true prosperity."[2]

The late Queen of Manua, and her aspirations as a Christian ruler.

The testimony of the Rev. J. E. Newell (L. M. S.), of the Malua Institution, Samoa, as to the happy history of this isolated group is especially significant. He writes as follows: "What Christianity might have done for the whole of Samoa if political unity had been established, may be imagined from the condition of a portion of the islands. The small group of Manua—the most easterly of the Samoan Archipelago—has been able hitherto to maintain its political independence. Fortunately, its people have been for the past fifty years united under one chief; and since the introduction of Christianity their government has been Christian, and they have maintained religious unity. No sectarian divisions have been allowed to take root there. They are a prosperous, healthy, contented people, who have been able

[1] Instances of this are given in Kidd's " Social Evolution," in his chapter on " The Conditions of Human Progress."

[2] *The Chronicle*, September, 1895, p. 231; quoted also in *The Missionary Herald*, December, 1895, p. 513.

The death of this good young Queen of Manua is reported in *The Chronicle* of February, 1896, p. 46. She was a sincere Christian, and had a singularly noble desire to govern as a Christian ruler and promote the higher spiritual welfare of her people. It seemed to her a cause of profound gratitude that Christianity had come to her realm, and she found much happiness in giving every facility to missionary work.

Native Church, Old Style.

Native Church, New Style.
Built by students of the Malua Institution.

Special deputation (1897) of the London Missionary Society. Rev. R. Wardlaw Thompson, Secretary, in the centre on the right, and Mr. W. Crosfield on the left.

A GROUP OF MISSIONARIES IN SAMOA.

(L. M. S.)

to maintain peace and unity without any foreign interference or aid. Their morality is not perfect, and the Gospel of Jesus Christ has much yet to teach them; but they are an essentially Christian people in morals and religion, and the most striking result is that obtained in their social life." Christianity has thus proved not simply an individual and social, but even a national, blessing where it has been received by a people and made the basis of common faith and the rule of communal life.[1]

VIII

From what has been said, is it not obvious that a new significance has been given to missions, as instrumental in laying the foundations of a new social order, touching as they do, both directly and indirectly, the deepest springs of the world's progress? We who speak the English language and cherish in our hearts the inspiration of centuries *The work of missions in laying the foundations of a new social order.* of English culture and progress—do we realize, as English-speaking people, the fontal relationship which the stimulus of early missions bears to our subsequent growth, progress, and world-wide achievement as a race? Columba, Augustine, Aidan, Paulinus, Cuthbert, and others like them, were among the first messengers of Christianity to our ancestors. They entered upon a long and serious conflict; yet how truly they worked for the making of the most superb forces of the modern world we can but faintly realize.[2] In their influence upon non-Christian society modern missions are as yet perhaps quite as much destructive as constructive in their results. All through the Oriental as distinguished from the Occidental world, we see the signs of intellectual and moral awakening. An era of spiritual discovery has come,—a period of religious questionings, of painful heart-searchings, of wistful longings, and desperate wrestlings with an overshadowing and dominant past. As

[1] On the power of Christianity to weld into unity of spirit conflicting races, see article by the Rev. K. S. Macdonald, D.D., in *The Indian Evangelical Review*, July, 1887, pp. 5–27.

[2] Mr. J. R. Green, in his " Short History of the English People," referring to the early missionary era in Northumbria, says: " By its missionaries and by its sword it had won England from heathendom to the Christian Church. It had given her a new poetic literature. Its monasteries were already the seat of whatever intellectual life the country possessed. Above all, it had been the first to gather together into a loose political unity the various tribes of the English people, and by standing at their head for nearly a century to accustom them to a national life, out of which England, as we have it now, was to spring " (pp. 69, 70).

Dean Church has finely said concerning the passing of ancient Roman civilization: "When . . . it went to pieces, rotten within and battered by the storms without, it was a portent and calamity which the human imagination had almost refused to believe possible. It was indeed the foundering of a world."[1]

So we may say with reference to the upheavals produced by Christian missions in contemporary heathenism. An era of struggle is at hand. Christianity, true to its own Master, has come "not to bring peace, but a sword." It works by a process of slow intellectual, spiritual, and social martyrdom. It enters the inner heart-life through dazed sensibilities and torn affections. Its convictions are often revolutionary. Myths, superstitions, ceremonies, dreams, aspirations, and customs—in fact, most of the cherished ideals of the past—are doomed. This is natural, indeed inevitable, as an accompaniment of any serious effort to escape from those retrogressive forces which have held dominion in the past, and have so long retarded the moral development of society. Nothing can be more interesting and touching to a sympathetic student of human progress than the phenomena which accompany the awakening of races just emerging from barbarism to the consciousness of the larger knowledge, the nobler morality, and the higher destiny which Christian civilization offers. It is like God's voice saying after long ages of darkness, "Let there be light." It is the sign of a new creative era in social history, in contradistinction to the long, uneventful periods of primitive savagery.

But enthusiasm must needs be on its guard against the expectation of accomplishing these reforms without meeting with checks, and occasionally seeming to fail. An era of such transformation can hardly be entered upon without a conscientious struggle with dominant religious, social, and political power. The Reformation was a period of conflicts. The early struggles of Christianity with pagan Rome were sharp and terrible. The Huguenots and Puritans were soldiers of conscience. The victories of religious history must be repeated in the experience of Christian missions. We may yet have exiles for conscience' sake from non-Christian lands to found new commonwealths for God and humanity. The one great reigning word in Oriental history, and throughout the realms of savagery, is despotism. All national, religious, and social experience is steeped in it. Even ancient republics were oligarchic in practice, and there is little hope that the spell of this monstrous usurpation will ever be broken, except as the

Conflict the inevitable price of victory.

1 " The Gifts of Civilisation," p. 128.

enlightened conscience, aroused and fortified by religious faith, bids defiance to it, and leads in the conflict for its overthrow. Liberty, and in a large sense true civilization, have been born not of philosophy, or of natural or ethnic religious systems, nor have they come with material progress. They have been the product of a religious faith instructed and inspired by God's Word, and filled with the courage and moral heroism which spiritual contact with Christ can give.

> " Freedom is re-created year by year,
> In hearts wide open on the Godward side,
> In souls calm-cadenced as the whirling sphere,
> In minds that sway the future like a tide.
> No broadest creeds can hold her, and no codes ;
> She chooses men for her august abodes,
> Building them fair and fronting to the dawn."

Let us not be alarmed if Christianity creates problems and stirs up conflicts in foreign society. This is no reason for abandoning missions. The cry that they should be given up if they make trouble in heathen society is about as absurd as to call upon us to give up the Christian religion because it antagonizes the evils of the world and refuses to tolerate sin.

The achievements of missions in laying anew the foundations of a better social order have been accomplished, let it be noted, in spite of the counteracting influence and demoralizing ex- ample of degenerate and reckless foreign traders and adventurers, who stand side by side with the missionary all through the non-Christian world.

The moral value of missions as sponsors of true civilization.

Do we realize the immense service of missions as a defender of the spirit and an apologist for the moral integrity of true civilization as distinguished from false ? If the typical foreign resident, in his usual Oriental environment of unrestrained license, had been the only representative of civilization and the only exemplification of supposed Christianity, the influence of his life would have been to the discredit of Christendom and a distinct check to the moral progress of the world. Commissioner Sir H. H. Johnston, in his recent volume, has characterized in a few burning sentences probably the worst type of the average European trader, pioneer, and adventurer in Central Africa. The description need not be localized; it is applicable throughout the length and breadth of the continent. "They are aggressively ungodly," he writes; "they put no check on their lusts; released from the restraints of civilisation and the terrors of 'what people may say,' they are capable of

almost any degree of wickedness."[1] "There is another benefit derived
from mission work which ought not to be overlooked," writes a resident
missionary in one of the cities of Burma. "It helps to correct the bad
opinion of Europeans usually entertained in this country. English
officials often lead lives here which are so immoral that the heathen
idea of Christian England would be simply hideous, were there not some
counteracting influence to modify it. A majority of the European officials who have been here during the last four years have openly lived
with Burman mistresses, and their drinking capacity is something to
excite wonder."

While this is true of a large class of foreigners, yet there are many
conspicuous and noble exceptions, to whom much credit and honor are
due. It remains a fact, however, that Europeans, to a lamentable extent, have lived unworthy lives in the presence of heathen society, and
that also in the larger sphere of colonial, political, and commercial intercourse a dark page has to be recorded concerning the treatment of
inferior races by the representatives of civilized nations, which has been
characterized by many unfair and shameful features.[2] An elaborate historical sketch of the darker aspects of the dealings of civilized nations

---

[1] Sir H. H. Johnston, "British Central Africa," p. 192.

This dark picture may be brightened by a gleam of sunlight from the letter of
a South African missionary. He writes: "Missionaries in Bechuanaland, lay and
clerical, rejoice in many a woman's benediction, whose sons or other loved ones
have found their way into the recesses of Africa, and whose wild career has, thank
God, in many instances, been checked by unexpected contact with something like
the simplicity and purity of the home life from which they had cut themselves adrift.
The amount of good which missionaries in these far-off lands are often able to do
in this way can scarcely be overestimated. Every one who has thus been able to
regain possession of himself becomes a duplicate of the missionary in the influence
of his life upon black and white among whom he moves."—Rev. Roger Price
(L. M. S.), Kuruman, British Bechuanaland.

[2] "The pith and marrow of all the good in our national life is Christ, and it is
the Anglo-Saxon stock, with its sturdy faith and evangelical tradition, which is the
coloniser and civiliser of the world. Apart from Christianity, has not the West
too often been guilty of the most horrible crimes against the 'childhood of the
world'? From whence have come the man-stealers, the drink-sellers, the murderers
and debauchers of weaker races? What would our boasted civilisation have wrought
by this time, if the strong hand of Christian public opinion and law had not stepped
in to deliver those drawn unto death?"—Dr. H. Martyn Clark (C. M. S.), Amritsar, India.

Dr. A. C. Thompson, in his "Moravian Missions," gives instances of shocking
cruelties on the part of the Spaniards in Central and South America and the West
Indies (pp. 166–169). No American of this generation needs to be reminded of the
wrongs of Cuba as emphasizing the barbarous story of Spanish colonial policy.

with inferior races has been given by Dr. Gustav Warneck, in his "Modern Missions and Culture" (pp. 239–306), where he treats of the relation of culture to missions.[1] Nevertheless, noble progress has been made, and many kindly, humane relations have been established. Christian missions are fast reversing the verdict which might otherwise have been rendered had Christendom touched the non-Christian world only through the channels of unchristian lives and selfish political and commercial aims.

In the meantime, an impressive exemplification of the fact has been afforded that Christianity, the substantial fabric,—wholesome, historic, uncompromising Christianity,—can alone adequately prepare a people for the transition from barbarism to refinement, and guide society as a whole to the hearty adoption of nobler principles and higher standards. Civilization can do much to change the outer aspects of communities and nations, but only the master touch of Christianity can mould the inner purpose and renew the secret springs of righteous living. This is true even in Christendom, for it is Christianity alone which in spirit or in very deed fights certain forms of evil and gives a temper of righteousness to life. It is of the essence of Christianity in its relation to human progress to be aggressive. It was born to fight evil. It was instituted and equipped with a view to its achieving by steady effort and inflexible pressure a great historic result, namely, the perfection of human society. Other agencies which give direction and impetus to social evolution work with more or less of haphazard, or with vague tendencies towards a predetermined end, or with only a drifting, undefined possibility, or at best a probability, that a certain, well-defined result

---

[1] The treatment of aboriginal races by British colonists was made a subject of careful examination by a select committee of the House of Commons at the beginning of the Victorian reign. The report was presented to Parliament in June, 1837, and one of the results of the investigation was the formation of the Aborigines Protection Society, which is still actively engaged in its benevolent service. In that memorable report occurs the following paragraph: "It is not too much to say that the intercourse of Europeans in general, without any exception in favour of the subjects of Great Britain, has been, unless when attended by missionary exertions, a source of many calamities to uncivilised nations. Too often their territory has been usurped, their property seized, their numbers diminished, their character debased, the spread of civilisation impeded. European vices and diseases have been introduced amongst them, and they have been familiarised with the use of our most potent instruments for the subtle or the violent destruction of human life, namely, brandy and gunpowder. It will be only too easy to make out the proof of all these assertions."—*The Aborigines' Friend*, July, 1896, p. 26. Cf. also, for further historical data, "Transactions of the Aborigines Protection Society," 4 vols., 1874–96.

will be reached. Christianity, however, lays down its principles, states its methods, sets forth its programme, announces its aim, and proceeds to work aggressively for its accomplishment. It stands for an intelligent purpose in social evolution; it represents a divine factor in human progress.

IX

Among missionaries of long experience and observation there seems to be but one opinion as to the social results of missions. The power

A symposium of missionary opinion as to the social value of missions.

of Christianity to change the tone and environment of society for the better, its inevitable trend in that direction, and in fact its necessity as a persuasive and invigorating force, if results of permanent value are to be secured, are regarded by them as axiomatic truths based upon experience. The judgment which they pass upon these points is practically unanimous, although the difficulty of tabulating and demonstrating these effects at the present stage of mission progress is fully recognized.[1] This conviction, moreover, seems to be expressed with equal confidence by missionaries who live amidst the higher civilization of the Orient, and by those who labor surrounded by the degradation of savagery.

The missionaries in Japan, as might be expected, express their views with a measure of reserve, as the evidence in the case of that progressive and alert people is not as manifest and in-

The judgment of missionaries from Japan.

dubitable as it is found to be in the case of other more conservative Oriental nations. The Japanese are naturally imitative, and have shown themselves to be responsive to Western thought, and to be receptive, in a remarkable degree, to Western civilization for its own sake. European ideas and methods have been welcomed with a measure of zest; modern culture has been unusually appreciated; and the facilities of material civilization have been adopted to a degree hitherto unknown in the conservative East. This fact leaves it, in the opinion of some, an open

---

[1] A veteran missionary writes to the author upon this point as follows: "One difficulty that at once presents itself is in tabulating results of this kind. These indirect influences of mission work are often so silent and imperceptible that we might as well attempt to put into statistical tables the influence of the rays of the sun in fructifying the earth. These are not only felt by the growing crops which we can measure and weigh, but by every living animal and every tree of the forest. Earth, air, and water—all animate and even inanimate creation—respond to their touch."—Rev. Daniel McGilvary, D.D. (P. B. F. M. N.), Chieng Mai, Laos.

question, or at least one which may at present properly be left open, as to what extent Christianity as such has been directly influential in the production of social changes in Japan.[1]

No one doubts that where there is the will and the ambition, on the part of an intelligent nation, or even among its leaders, to absorb a new and higher civilization, astonishing external changes will be brought about with surprising rapidity; but the old, deep question as to the moral quality and the spiritual power inherent in these outer transformations still remains. Material civilization may be accepted with an appearance of highly beneficial results, but will this impart that moral stamina, those righteous aims, and the essential goodness, which alone can give a firm footing and right direction to social progress? In the case of the Japanese, especially in view of their intense national spirit, we can see that it is not easy for missionaries to speak with decision, however readily personal opinion might sanction it, as to just what

[1] It is fair to say that not all the missionaries in Japan express their views with equal reserve. The following excerpts from letters are of interest, although it should be remembered that those who have been less pronounced in recording a positive opinion may not be on that account less decided in their personal convictions:

"The Red Cross Society, now numbering 100,000, is an indirect fruit of Christianity. Asylums and schools for the blind, and hospitals under government or local patronage, are, I believe, fruits of mission work, though in some cases quite indirect. The Railway Mission, Policemen's Mission, Prison Work, and Scripture Union, though more distinctively mission work, are not reported, so far as I know, by any missionary, tract, or Bible society. The generous treatment of the Chinese by the Japanese in the recent war is probably an indirect fruit of Christian seed-sowing. Certainly the extended and elevated education of women, and indeed the excellent educational system of the empire, though in itself by no means Christian, are the result of contact with the nations sending the missionaries, or with the missionaries themselves."—Rev. A. A. Bennett (A. B. M. U.), Yokohama, Japan.

"I need scarcely add, in reply to your inquiries as to the sociological influence of Christian work in Japan, that great moral reforms in the family, in the community, and in the nation have already resulted. In fact, the ethical side of Christianity has impressed the nation more than its supernatural side, the Sermon on the Mount more than the miracles of our Lord. Concubinage has been disgraced, forced into privacy, and lessened; family life has been ennobled and purified; intemperance and the great 'social evil' fiercely attacked; the liberty and right of the individual emphasized, and an unbending and uncompromising ethical standard set up by which the laws and conduct of the nation and the individual are alike judged. Public opinion is already being greatly influenced by this, so that the Christians exert an influence in the nation out of all proportion to their numbers."—John C. Berry, M.D. (A. B. C. F. M.), formerly at Kyoto, Japan.

"Among the Christians of Japan there is, of course, much improvement in home life, in temperance, truthfulness, brotherly kindness, morality, and in the

place should be assigned to Christian missions as an inspirer of social progress in Japan. Missionaries would naturally prefer, under such conditions, modestly to await the verdict of history as to this aspect of their service, and to avoid any expression of opinion which might be offensive to Japanese sensibilities. Upon the question, however, as to whether the social transformation of Japan can be accomplished with moral safety and ennobling results, apart from the controlling influence of Christianity, there is no room for reserve, and no hesitancy need be found in the full expression of conviction. The words of Dr. W. N. Whitney, of the United States Legation, Tokyo, represent a judgment, expressed with moderation, which reflects the prevalent opinion among the foreign missionaries of Japan.[1]

In China, while there is a frank recognition among the missionaries of the fact that the social results of missions develop slowly amidst an habitual conservatism of exceptional intensity, yet all are agreed that nothing has moved and influenced Chinese society so mightily as Christian missions. "Evidently only the new life which accompanies the Gospel of divine grace," writes the Rev. Jonathan Lees (L. M. S.), of Tientsin, "is a force strong enough to purify, elevate, and save this land; but, necessarily, the process must be a gradual one, which has not advanced very far as yet, and the desired result will come at length rather as the outcome of the permeation of the mind of the nation by Christian thought than by avowed effort on the part of missionaries." "I can give you no statistics on the social lines of mission

Some expressions of opinion from China.

elevation of women, and their influence all around is for good. Outside of the Christian Church in Japan, heathenism, superstition, and idolatry still reign in the hearts of the people, and nothing but the grace of God can cast them out."—Rev. J. C. Hepburn, M.D. (P. B. F. M. N.), Yokohama, Japan.

"Almost all of our philanthropic agencies in the United States are employed. The Young Men's Christian Association, orphanages, hospitals for lepers, schools for the poor, temperance societies, etc., are some of the instrumentalities now used. Public societies, public lectures and meetings, constantly call attention to the evils of society, and discuss remedies. Special efforts for special classes, railway men, jinrikisha-pullers, overworked laborers, etc., are made. For the past five or six years all these varieties of work have been energetically carried on."—Rev. G. W. Knox, D.D. (P. B. F. M. N.), formerly a missionary in Tokyo, Japan.

"We are under a certain restraint in Japan which makes it difficult to claim as the direct results of mission work all that we may think to be fairly its due. There is much on every hand which bespeaks the influence of Christian civilization, and, more or less directly, of the Christian Church itself."—Rev. Theodore M. MacNair (P. B. F. M. N.), Tokyo, Japan.

1 See Vol. I., p. 32, note.

influence," writes the Rev. Dr. M. H. Houston (P. B. F. M. S.), of Hang-chow, "but can only say that it is evident to me that the Gospel, when accepted in its fullness, will extirpate all the social evils which now exist in China, some of which are peculiar to an Oriental country."[1]

From Siam, the late Dr. James B. Thompson (P. B. F. M. N.), of Petchaburee, wrote: "It is my firm conviction—based on what I see about me daily—that Christian missions are ele-vating and refining the people of this land, and bringing to them decided benefits, entirely aside from the evangelical results." "In my mind, it is *The testimony from Siam and Burma.* an axiom," writes the venerable Dr. McGilvary, of Chieng Mai, "that the Gospel is fully applicable and equally essential to cure all the evils that afflict the race as such, in one land as well as another." "In the last seven years," testifies the Rev. W. C. Dodd (P. B. F. M. N.), of Lampoon, "I have seen many evidences of the adaptation of the Gospel to remedy the evils that afflict Laos society. We have a peculiarly fortunate field for the investigation of this point, for we are

[1] Some further expressions of opinion by missionaries in China are as follows:

"The elevation of China socially is utterly hopeless, except as it shall be effected by the power of the Gospel."—Rev. C. W. Mateer, D.D. (P. B. F. M. N.), Tungchow.

"Christianity, I boldly declare, has raised thousands in North Formosa to cleaner habits, purer thoughts, nobler aspirations, and more exalted ideas of earthly existence, while looking forward to eternal life."—Rev. G. L. MacKay, D.D. (C. P. M.), Formosa.

"Christianity is the only hope for China, or for any nation. When this is ac-cepted, it will do for China just what it has done for other countries."—Rev. Hunter Corbett, D.D. (P. B. F. M. N.), Chefoo.

"My only hope for this country [China] is from the progress of Christianity. They will no doubt try to appropriate the advantages of civilisation without Chris-tianity, but they will fail, or should they succeed, only ride to a greater fall."— Rev. Alfred G. Jones (E. B. M. S.), Chefoo.

"The longer I live in China, the less do I believe that civilization, so called, will help this people. Christianity, because it strikes at the root of all these evils, —the heart,—is the only power which really elevates man and improves his social surroundings."—B. C. Atterbury, M.D. (P. B. F. M. N.), Peking.

"Christianity is the only religion that has power to check great vices. Placards all over China exhort against the use of opium, but the vice spreads in spite of them; yet if those who are addicted to this evil indulgence become Christians, there is hope for them. Men who testify that the opium habit was to them 'ten thousand hells' now magnify the grace of God that gave them the victory over it."—Rev. J. G. Fagg (Ref. C. A.), Amoy.

"What is apparent in our new and small field may not be great as to its extent, but it is significant as pertaining to all the life and social condition of those influ-

so shut in from the outer world that we have had hitherto but few of the adjuncts of civilization to follow and supplement our labors."

In Burma, missionaries of the American Baptist Missionary Union give unequivocal testimony upon the point under consideration. The Rev. A. E. Seagrave, of Rangoon, declares that, in his opinion, "the Karens have been made what they are by their acceptance of Christianity; instead of a scattered, degraded, and despised people, they have become the possessors of influence and power." The Rev. W. I. Price, of Henzada, writes: "As to the sociological effects of Christian missions among the Karens of Burma, I unhesitatingly say that they are very marked and most salutary, touching and influencing for good every aspect of society." The Rev. W. F. Thomas, of Insein, asserts: "Of the indirect blessings of missions, to which you refer, nowhere is there more evidence than among the Chins, the Karens, and other hill-tribes of Burma, to whom most of my service for fifteen years has been given. Indeed, so conspicuous are these advantages that they are often over-estimated." The Rev. Alonzo Bunker, D.D., of Toungoo, writes: "The Gospel of Jesus is the sovereign remedy for all the ills of barbarism, and the only force that can lift mankind from a lower to a higher level." This opinion is shared by his colleague, the Rev. H. P. Cochrane, who expresses his conviction that "Christianity is the only power that ever will or ever can cause light to shine into this thick darkness." A missionary of the same society, the Rev. P. H. Moore, of Nowgong, Assam, reinforces this opinion, when he writes: "I feel so sure that Christianity is the only effectual remedy for all these evils of society that the matter seems to me hardly to admit of discussion."

The volume of testimony from India is alike instructive and valuable. Among representative opinions are the following: "Nothing can be more certain," writes the Rev. S. H. Kellogg, D.D. (P. B. F. M. N.), of Landaur, "than that such [reform] movements here and there are directly due to the effect of Christianity as a visible power in provoking to good works." "A volume might be written," observes the Rev. T. E. Slater (L. M. S.), of Bangalore, "on this most

Representative views from India.

enced. An entire change is produced in the individual and in the community, large or small, which yields to the influence of the Gospel as introduced by the missionaries."—Rev. Charles Leaman (P. B. F. M. N.), Nanking.

"Public Christian worship, which is a necessary consequence of our work, and the order observed on such occasions, the large numbers in attendance, the character and ability of native pastors and teachers, and the effect of the whole on the community at large, are all in happy contradistinction to the idolatrous services held throughout the country."—Rev. W. Muirhead, D.D. (L. M. S.), Shanghai.

fruitful subject, but I hope I have said enough to show that here in India we have overwhelming evidence that Christian missions have proved an earthly as well as a heavenly benefit to society. They have greatly relieved the wrongs, burdens, and miseries that afflict humanity, and they are an effective agency for stamping out ancient evils, as well as for creating a higher and healthier public sentiment in the country. The Gospel of Christ is eminently adapted to all this; and apart from it I know of no remedial and regenerating power." "The results are very apparent among the Christians," writes Dr. John Scudder (Ref. C. A.), of Vellore. "They have been elevated in every sense. Many of them were born among the lowest and most degraded, but now take their stand among the best, and are exerting a great moral power in the land." The Rev. James E. Tracy, D.D. (A. B. C. F. M.), of Periakulam, confirms this, when he observes: "In all matters of sociological progress our Christian converts stand confessedly far in advance of the community in general, and whatever testimony this fact may bear to the sociological value of our work is valid evidence." "The Christian community," asserts Dr. Pauline Root (A. B. C. F. M.), formerly of Madura, "takes a firm stand for temperance and social purity, and leads in all good works." Dr. Henry Martyn Clark (C. M. S.), of Amritsar, remarks: "Education, civilisation, the relief of pain, the freeing of the slave, the war against uncleanness, and other manifold forms of evil, social and political, which are rife, are all grand and good works. None of them is, *per se*, the missionary's work, but all, properly used, may be the stepping-stones to success. In pursuing his chief aim it is given him to have the joy of bringing many of these blessings, and of seeing them follow in the train of the Gospel." [1]

---

[1] "I have seen enough of Christian evangelism to fill me with joyful hopes. I never met a missionary in India or Japan who was doubtful about the final result. And I have seen enough of the practical workings of Hinduism, Buddhism, and Islam to crystallize into adamantine firmness my previous conviction of their futility to give the soul peace with God, to remove the weight of guilt and grief, to lay the foundation of a vigorous individual and national morality, and to brighten earth with the light of a blessed immortality. The notion that Asia does not need the Gospel of Christ because of the refined and lofty moral sentiments in the sacred books of the East, or because Oriental speakers trained in Christian schools and shaped by Christian environments are able to make an agreeable impression when expounding their faith on Christian platforms, is born of ignorance. The world needs Christ, and to us more than to any other people belongs the fulfilment of the commission to evangelize the nations."—Rev. John H. Barrows, D.D., in an address after visiting India.

From the Turkish Empire we have a word from the Rev. Dr. J. K. Greene (A. B. C. F. M.), of Constantinople, as follows: "A change has already been accomplished, sufficiently great and salutary to prove that evangelical Christianity, if allowed its legitimate influence, would speedily bring about the regeneration of Turkey." The Rev. Robert Thomson, of the same society, writes, also from Constantinople, in substantially the same strain. Dr. Grace N. Kimball, of the American Board, wrote from Van, in Asiatic Turkey: "Christianity is the only force that can be depended upon to renovate society as well as the individual, yet in order to do this we need not less of the policy of saving souls, but more of the broad activities of applied Christianity." Miss Anna Melton (P. B. F. M. N.), of Mosul, sends from the far eastern recesses of Turkey the following luminous testimony: "Although we have not worked primarily for sociological results, yet we have, in quite an encouraging degree, obtained them. The people can now form organizations and conduct meetings according to rules and regulations, which formerly they could not do. Both sexes take pride in keeping their persons and clothing clean, and try to make their houses more like homes. They look more to the health and welfare of the family, desire earnestly the development of their children, and delight themselves in pure, wholesome, and edifying social amusements, in contrast with the drunken carousals about them. They have more of the spirit of helping one another, and more sympathy for a brother in distress. I distinctly recall a case where a poor villager was robbed of all his money, and his neighbors the same day made up the amount."

What is thought in Turkey and Persia.

The author's associates and colleagues in Syria share with him the view that Christian missions have brought social changes of the highest promise to that land. The Rev. H. H. Jessup, D.D., records his opinion, as follows: "To recount the triumphs of the Gospel in the Ottoman Empire would be to write the history of its moral, intellectual, and social progress for the past seventy-five years."[1] The Rev. W. W. Eddy, D.D., refers to the philanthropic services of missionaries in times of massacre and famine, and to their efforts to secure from Turkish authorities the common rights of non-Moslems, to awaken benevolent enterprise, to care for the dependent, the orphaned, and the enfeebled, to minister to the sick and suffering, to elevate the home, and to protest against intemperance, slavery, and injustice to woman. The Rev.

---

[1] *The Church at Home and Abroad*, November, 1893, p. 363. Cf. also *ibid.*, December, 1894, p. 485.

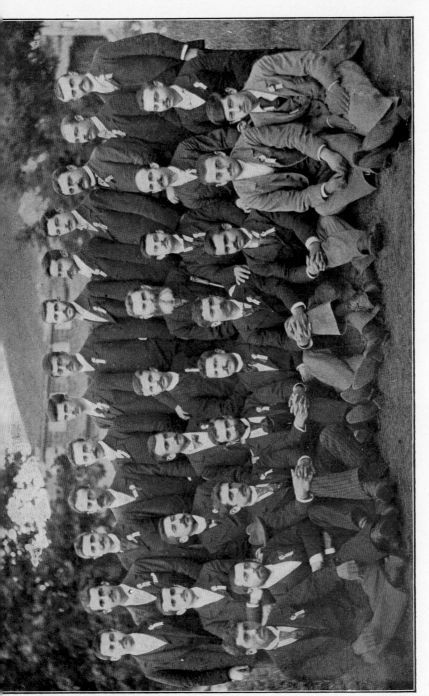

A group of the younger alumni. The Rev. Robert Chambers, D.D., in the second row, fourth from the right.

BITHYNIA HIGH SCHOOL, BARDEZAG, TURKEY-IN-ASIA.

(A. B. C. F. M.)

George E. Post, M.D., who has ministered so skilfully to thousands of suffering Syrians, and for many years has given invaluable instruction to medical students at Beirut, is unhesitating in his judgment that much has been done by Christian missions to ameliorate the social evils of Western Asia. At the end of a long list of specifications he emphasizes the influence of the Gospel in liberating the mind from superstition and the rigors of sectarian animosity. The suspicion, prejudice, and hostility of the various religious elements of society are melting away, and in time will certainly vanish. Similar views, the author knows, are held by President Bliss, Dr. Porter, and Dr. Graham, of the Syrian Protestant College, and by the entire circle of resident missionaries. Dr. Porter writes of the quasi-feudal system and the ecclesiastical despotism which prevailed in Syria until quite late in the present century, but which have now been abolished, or exist only in a very modified form.

In the neighboring Mohammedan realm of Persia, Dr. George W. Holmes (P. B. F. M. N.), of Hamadan, expresses his conviction that "nothing but Christianity can regenerate Persia." Dr. J. P. Cochran (P. B. F. M. N.), of Urumiah, writes: "An educational board is organized by the mission and people, and also a legal board, which is an agent of the people in government affairs. In addition to the services of the missionaries, the sick poor are treated by a number of physicians who have been educated by the mission. There is a Young Men's Christian Association, and also a Christian Endeavor Society. We have started gatherings for the women, where practical questions are considered. Then we have meetings of educated people to discuss questions of the day. An orphanage has been established. We have college alumni and female seminary alumnæ, and at meetings of these bodies, questions are debated and plans formed to help the nation." The Rev. Benjamin Labaree, D.D., for many years a Presbyterian missionary in Urumiah, in a valuable résumé of the social results of missions in Persia, emphasizes the stimulus given by Christianity to higher social aspirations among the people, the philanthropic impulses awakened, the practical influence and service of the missionaries in securing justice and abating outrage when attempts have been made to oppress the subject peoples. "The catalogue of wrongs to Christians redressed," he writes, "of illegal taxes abated, of unjust claims cancelled, of outrages atoned for, through the efforts of missionaries, is a long one." He quotes the perhaps somewhat highly colored language of an English newspaper correspondent as follows: "There is an American colony of Protestants established among the Nestorians.

They lead very heroic and useful lives, and have done more for the improvement of Persian morality and the stoppage of cruelty and persecution than all of the European diplomatic missions put together."

In the West Indies, the Island of Jamaica is an instructive example of what can be wrought by faithful missionary effort, in the interests of civilization among an ignorant and degraded Negro population. Had the Gospel been allowed to enter Cuba, and religious liberty been granted to the people, the state of the island would no doubt have been similar to the conditions now so happily realized in Jamaica. The Rev. James Ballantine (U. P. C. S. M.), of Chapelton, writes: "I can but say that if Jamaica enjoys any measure of the blessings of civilisation, she owes it largely to the Gospel of Christ." "Jamaica is not now a heathen land," affirms the Rev. Adam Thomson (U. P. C. S. M.), of Montego Bay. "It was once so, but at the present time it is in many important respects as much entitled to be called a Christian country as is either Scotland or America. This benign and philanthropic result is mainly traceable to the civilizing and sanctifying influence of Christian missions." Other facts come to hand in a letter of the Rev. W. Y. Turner, M.D., of the same mission. He says: "There are throughout the island various societies having the intellectual and moral welfare of the people in view. These have in almost every case been initiated by the churches, and are connected with them. A system of Penny Savings Banks was introduced by the Government some fourteen years ago, and is worked chiefly in connection with the churches. There were one or two such banks in existence, in association with the churches, before the government system, now universal, was established. There can be no doubt that missions have exerted a great influence upon the lives and habits of the people, and are still doing so. The presence of a missionary has a distinct tendency to repress evil living, as it makes evil-doers more ashamed of sin, and leads to its being shunned. A great improvement has been noticed in this district during the three years we have lived here. There is less quarrelling and fighting, less immorality, and less drunkenness than formerly."

The degraded Negroes of Guiana, Central America, and the West Indies were without one ray of hope until the Moravian missionaries began to labor so heroically for their instruction and elevation. The triumphs and glories of the Moravian missionary epic would alone fill volumes with testimony gathered from the darkest corners of the earth, showing the sanctifying and civilizing power of the Gospel

A word from the West Indies, Mexico, and South America.

among those who may be regarded as preëminently the lost races of the globe.[1]

From the adjacent mainland of Central America, the Rev. E. M. Haymaker (P. B. F. M. N.), of Guatemala City, contributes the following testimony: "That the Gospel is an effective remedy for these social evils in Guatemala is evidenced in the fact that we are bidden God-speed not only by people of Protestant sympathies, but by many Roman Catholics, as well as those representing the liberal body, who so far overcome their antipathy to all religion as to publicly and highly commend Protestantism solely because they recognize its immense and undeniable social value. They realize that it is just what society here needs." From the neighboring Republic of Colombia, the Rev. M. E. Caldwell (P. B. F. M. N.), formerly of Bogota, writes: "Many instances might be given of the power of Christianity to lift up the people of Colombia. It is a power that neither secular education, nor money, nor travel, nor refinement, can give. None of these things has been successful in curing the tendency to impurity or the proneness to untruthfulness, or in building up a stable and virtuous civilization in Colombia. Christianity, and Christianity alone, has been able to make any lasting impression for good."

"Concerning our own people, as a whole," communicates the Rev. J. G. Hall (P. B. F. M. S.), of Mexico, "the evidences are abundant that they are being improved in all their social relations, outsiders themselves being the judges. They live better and dress better, the interior of their houses is more attractive, and they have more material comforts around them; their family relations are happier, and the women and children receive more consideration." The Rev. Hubert W. Brown (P. B. F. M. N.), of Mexico City, writes of his strong conviction that "evangelical missions exert a powerful, pervasive influence upon the thought and life of Mexico." He refers especially to effects produced upon the lib-

[1] Cf. Thompson, "Moravian Missions," Lectures III. and IV.

"Formerly," writes a West Indian planter, in the early days of missions, "we could hardly procure ropes enough on Monday for punishing those slaves who had committed crimes on Sunday, twenty, thirty, and even more being hanged; but, since the Gospel has been preached to them, scarcely two are hanged in a whole year, and these, for the most part, are strange Negroes, who have not been long on the island." More than a hundred years ago, the governor of one of the West Indian islands, in reply to the question as to what security he had against the uprising of the slaves, took the questioner to his window, and, directing his attention to some Moravian mission stations, answered: "This is our security. Negroes who are converted will never rise in rebellion; and their number is so great that the others could never conspire without their knowledge, and they would inform us." (*Ibid.*, pp. 169, 170, 171.)

eral leaders of the State, from the Chief Executive, through governors of States, to the humblest official in many a quiet village or rural district. This influence he designates as "restraining and constraining in character," as "enlightening and beneficial, representing the best thought of foreign Protestant nations, and standing as a monitor or moral norm of right and wrong." He also regards their stimulating and corrective influence over the Roman Catholic Church, especially in arousing the priesthood to a better and worthier life, as already initiating "a moral transformation or counter-reformation." Protestant converts lead "changed lives," and are "a leaven for good in the community where they reside."

Dr. H. M. Lane (P. B. F. M. N.), of São Paulo, Brazil, sums up the net results of the social influence of missions during the past twenty years, as follows: "A marked decrease in the tolerance of open immorality; far less hesitation in classifying the greed and vice of immoral priests, as such; a decline of superstition, and fewer large legacies to the Roman Catholic Church. Women and womanly virtues are more respected; they have been elevated socially to a position unknown in either Spain or Portugal. In a vast circle the Bible is accepted as the only foundation for a code of morals; family life is purer; truthfulness is much more prevalent; African slavery has been abolished without bloodshed. In the new Republic, Protestant Christianity is recognized in many places as a social and political force not to be ignored. In the wake of Protestant missions in Brazil we find the Young Men's Christian Association, with a strong native following, also Christian Endeavor Societies, hospitals, and trained nurses, who are not nuns. Out of our missions have come a periodical literature and a cleaner permanent literature for the young, school-books with a Christian flavor, innocent games, outdoor amusements, ladies' sewing and other societies, co-education, and athletics."

Not less striking is the testimony from those who have had special opportunities for observing the social results of missions among savage races. In fact, the changes that have been wrought among primitive nature-peoples are often more notable than those that may be traced in more civilized communities. From various sections of Africa comes substantially the same verdict as to what is wrought by the touch of Christianity upon native society. "Nothing but the Gospel," declares the late Rev. H. M. Bridgman (A. B. C. F. M.), of Natal, "will ever remedy the evils of society. Nothing else goes to the root of the matter." A missionary of the Universities' Mission at Zanzibar, the Rev.

What is said by missionaries among the savage races of Africa and Madagascar.

G. M. Lawson, says: "Our Christians have usually the greatest repugnance to the objectionable [heathen] practices I have mentioned. If they are ever led to take part in them it is nearly always the result of pressure put upon them by their relations, not because they personally have any taste left for heathenism. No doubt Christianity softens and humanizes all whom it reaches. Christians have a different appearance from heathen, who have generally a hopeless, stolid expression."

"It has been my lot for the past ten years," states the Rev. John W. Stirling (U. P. C. S. M.), of Buchanan, Qumbu, Cape Colony, "to labor in a purely heathen district, among the Kaffirs, yet even that short period has been sufficient to indicate that the Gospel carries in its train the most beneficent of blessings for every department of human life and existence; not only regenerating the moral nature, but affecting the bodily well-being, and radiating brightness all around it. For all existing evils, widespread and dreadful though they be, the Gospel is already proving a panacea." [1]

A well-known missionary of the London Missionary Society in Madagascar, the Rev. James Sibree, asserts: "Wherever so-called civilisation has come into Madagascar without the Gospel, there has been, especially along the coast, degradation and drunkenness, and harm—immense harm—has been done to the people. Some coast tribes, indeed, are rapidly dying out and disappearing, through the vices introduced by wicked white men. There is a very great contrast to all this in the interior provinces, where civilisation came hand in hand with Christianity, and as its fellow helper and worker." [2]

From the dark regions of the Upper Congo, the Rev. George Gren-

[1] The testimony of the late Rev. Hugh Goldie (U. P. C. S. M.), of Creek Town, Old Calabar, is clear and pointed: "Only a small proportion of the people have been won to Christ, but the tribes which our work touches have been greatly benefited by the mission. Though they know not whence the blessing comes, yet wherever the mission has been able to enter, the whole population has been raised from its former state. The atrocities of human sacrifice for the dead, the destruction of infant life, and other deeds of cruelty which filled the land with blood, are abolished. Life is more secure; the dark superstitions which prevented faith in one another are beginning to disappear before trustful social intercourse, and as a consequence the comforts of the present life are more sought after. The 'reign of law' under the British protectorate has entered to do its part, the way having been prepared by the mission."

[2] Mr. Sibree, in a little pamphlet entitled "A Quarter-Century of Change and Progress: Antananarivo and Madagascar Twenty-five Years Ago," has given a glowing account of social, intellectual, and spiritual changes, as well as material advances, among the Malagasy, which may stand as a representative brief of this whole argument for the social results of missions.

fell (E. B. M. S.), of Bolobo, writes : " Those who have not realised the power of Christianity are not slow to say there is no hope for these poor people, but those who have lived longest among them, and have laboured most arduously for their uplifting, say there is hope, but that it is from one source alone.   The only reformation that can possibly regenerate a people so degraded is that which has Christianity for its basis."   " No moral system in the world," adds the Rev. Thomas Adams (A. B. M. U.), of Leopoldville, " can change their condition, except the Gospel, which gives them a new spiritual birth."   In the deep recesses of Central Africa is the smiling missionary oasis of Uganda, of which Mr. Henry M. Stanley writes in the *Atlantic Monthly* for October, 1897 (p. 475).   He speaks of the story of the Uganda missionary enterprise as " an epic poem," and declares that he knows " of few secular enterprises, military or otherwise, deserving of greater praise."   In his opinion, " Uganda is preëminently the Japan of Africa."   " Its unique geographical position, coupled with the remarkable intelligence of the people, will make it as brilliant commercially as it was renowned in pagan days for its martial prowess, and is to-day remarkable for its Christian zeal."   " The number of converts," he states, " has become so formidable that it would task the powers of a hundred white missionaries to organize, develop, and supervise them properly. . . . The results from a moral and Christian point of view exceed those obtained from all the rest of Equatorial Africa " (pp. 476, 481).[1]

[1] In another connection Mr. Stanley writes as follows upon the same theme : " I do not think Americans are fully aware of the marvelous change that has come over Uganda.   Many a time have I been laughed at in the newspapers for my fervid faith in the people of that land.   At first they welcomed the good tidings that Mtesa was entreating the white people to send him missionaries, and applauded the warmth with which the Church Missionary Society responded to the invitation ; but after a while, as the first missionaries sent their doleful impressions home, the zeal for making converts in Uganda cooled down, and people here frequently insisted that it would be better to let the Waganda severely alone.   The Society, however, persisted, though with slight hope of success ; for Mtesa had sensibly deteriorated as he grew older, and when he died, his successor, the present king, being a mere youth and flushed with vanity and lust, emulated Nero.   He ordered the murder of a devoted bishop, hunted the missionaries out of his kingdom, and clubbed, tortured, and burnt the young disciples of Mackay, until it seemed as if there could be no future for Uganda but a quick relapse into heathenism.   Had the Society yielded to the almost universal desire that the missionaries should give up the effort, Uganda would by this time have been one of the darkest regions in Africa.   Faith and perseverance, however, have made it one of the brightest, thereby more than fulfilling my most sanguine hopes.

" There are now 200 churches in the State [later statistics, given in the *Atlantic Monthly*, October, 1897, name 372 as the number], and the number of professing

Group of native church council, Mengo.

Cathedral, Mengo, (side view).

Cathedral, Mengo, (front view).
Will accommodate 4,000 worshippers.

Bishop Tucker's Study, Mengo.
(See page 394, Vol. I.)

CATHEDRAL PICTURES FROM UGANDA.

(C. M. S.)

In a recent report of Sir Claude Macdonald, on the administration of the Niger Coast Protectorate, he refers to missions as follows: "Very much yet remains to be done; religious missions have worked persistently and well, and pointed out to the people the evil of such cruelties and wrong-doings; but there comes a time when their efforts need backing up by the strong arm of the law of civilisation and right." Referring specially to the new training institution of the United Presbyterian Church of Scotland in Old Calabar, he says: "A most important and useful departure has been made by the Presbyterian Missionary Society in starting industrial schools in Old Calabar. These schools are assisted by a yearly grant of £200 from the revenue." [1]

The Islands of the South Seas bring also their quota of testimony. "All my missionary life of thirty-four years," observes the Rev. W. G. Lawes, D. D. (L. M. S.), of Vatorata, New Guinea, "I have been living among so-called barbarous peoples—first on Savage Island, and then here in New Guinea. That Christianity is the only civiliser of such seems to me as unnecessary of proof as that the sea is salt or the fire warm. We find a people debased, ignorant, depraved—in fact, their condition is such that the first chapter of Romans is as true as a photograph. Christianity, if it is anything but a name, must change and reform all this, and benefit the society which accepts and receives it." "When their hearts are touched by the story of the Gospel," writes a missionary from the New Hebrides, "they cast off heathen ornaments, seek clothing, cease from practices once dear to them, and

Strong testimony from the South Seas.

Christians is close on 50,000 [the number is now not far from 65,000]. The islands of Lake Victoria have not been forgotten, for each has its church, with its deacons and elders, who are encouraged in their duties of propagandism by visiting missionaries. Reading and writing have become common acquirements, and the letter now before me from a Waganda chief would indicate the writer as sufficiently advanced to become an excellent clerk. The Gospels are sold by thousands each year; the offertories testify that the religion planted among the Waganda is something more than lip-service. Besides these indications of a rapid advance, the people are turning to with a will to produce food. They are spreading out to make provision for their families, leaving the court which they used to haunt for the sake of its excitement and display. The government steamer, conveyed at an immense cost from the sea to the lake, has just been launched, and the mission vessel is not far from completion. The railway is also advancing steadily into the interior, and is already stimulating the Waganda to put forth greater exertions to make their country worthy of receiving it. The Rev. Mr. Roscoe, who only the other day returned to England after an absence of twelve years, describes the progress as phenomenal."
—*Illustrated Christian World*, December, 1896, p. 10.

[1] *The Missionary Record*, May, 1895, p. 131.

live changed lives." [1] "I am equally certain," writes a missionary of the London Missionary Society in Samoa, "that all allow these [Christian] ideals to be practicable, and that the only power to effect social reform and to prevent disintegration and ruin is the rule of Christ." [2]

Striking and detailed statements are given by a missionary in the Marshall Islands, as follows: "As to results—about one tenth of the population are now church-members. In most of the islands the Church exercises a controlling influence over society. The Christian Sabbath is quite generally observed by all classes. Transgressions of the Seventh Commandment are always regarded as grounds for excommunication, and are no longer gloried in. Licentiousness continues as a besetting sin, and is encouraged by nearly all the foreigners residing in the islands, but it grows more and more disgraceful. Ample clothing is now worn by all. Thieving has mostly disappeared, and lying, though not yet abolished, is growing more and more into disrepute. We never hear of murders committed by a native. Divorces are more infrequent. The people are more wisely industrious, turning their labor to better account, though there is little opportunity to accumulate property. Homes, somewhat like American homes, are no longer unknown, though by no means numerous. The people mostly adhere to their temperate habits, though strongly tempted to use intoxicants introduced by the Germans. There are schools conducted by adherents of the mission on almost all of the islands, and a large proportion of the natives, especially the younger ones, can read and write. Foreigners, whether visitors or traders or shipwrecked mariners, are everywhere treated with hospitality and kindness. Life and property are more secure on all the islands than in any civilized country which I have ever visited or read about. Women are treated with more respect, and marriage is held in greater honor." [3]

On the cheerless coast of Greenland the work of the Danish and Moravian missionaries has created a state of civilization "as Christian as we find in England." [4] Where ferocious cannibals once made the whole coast-line a terror to mariners, there is now safety and hospitality to shipwrecked seamen. Dr. Kane states that "for the last hundred years Greenland has been safer for the wrecked mariner than many parts of our American coast; hospitality is the universal characteristic." [5]

---

[1] The Rev. William Gunn, M.D. (F. C. S.), Futuna, New Hebrides.
[2] The Rev. J. E. Newell, Malua Institution, Samoa.
[3] The Rev. E. M. Pease, M.D. (A. B. C. F. M.), Marshall Islands.
[4] La Trobe, "The Moravian Missions," p. 18.
[5] Thompson, "Moravian Missions," p. 260. The record of their missions in South Africa and Australia presents similar triumphs. (*Ibid.*, pp. 403, 404, 445–451.)

A Native Boy.   Eskimo Christian Women.   A Christian Group.

Candidates for Confirmation.

A Heathen Group.

LESSONS IN PICTURES FROM GREENLAND.

(M. M. S.)

X

The testimony of missionaries to the social benefits of missions can be supplemented by that of thoughtful and observant natives of various lands, and by the opinion of resident merchants and officials, who have in many instances expressed their convictions as to the beneficent results of mission work among native races. "It is freely admitted by intelligent Japanese writers," states Professor John C. Ballagh (P. B. F. M. N.), of Tokyo, "that Christianity is the best regenerator of society." "It is scarcely necessary," writes the Rev. David S. Spencer (M. E. M. S.), of Nagoya, "for a missionary to say that our only hope for the removal of these evils of Japanese society lies in the religion of our Master. This the Japanese—that is, the Christian Japanese—believe, though the belief is not confined to them, for many who make no profession of Christianity boldly say that it is to the religion of Christ they must look for elevation, light, and peace for society."

The evidence of native witnesses in many notable instances confirms the views of missionaries.

Dr. Martin, of Peking, states that "thirty years ago a distinguished native scholar published a paper on the question whether foreign missions or foreign trade had done the most good to China, giving preference to the former. How much have these three decades done to augment that preponderance!" Li Hung Chang, during his recent visit to the United States, in an address to the representatives of the different missionary societies established in China, spoke of the "arduous and much esteemed work" of the missionaries, and referred in terms of cordial comment to the educational and philanthropic services rendered by them, and especially to the help given in fighting the opium curse and in rescuing its victims.[1] Mr. L. T. Ah Sou, a native Christian of Rangoon, Burma (whose opinion is forwarded with a hearty endorsement by Miss Emily H. Payne, of the American Baptist Missionary Union), who himself belongs to the second generation of a native Christian family, writes that while "heathenism does not elevate a man from his ignorance, filth, and superstition, Christianity does that and more. It changes the heart, resulting in a different mode of living and social intercourse. That the Burma of to-day owes much to Christian missions is a fact which cannot be ignored. A native Christian becomes more energetic in seeking his livelihood, more frugal and honest, and cleaner in his person and manner of living."

The Rev. James E. Tracy, D.D. (A. B. C. F. M.), of Periakulam,

[1] See *The Evangelist* (New York), September 3, 1896.

India, in expressing his own strong conviction of the social benefits of Christianity in India, remarks also: "The witness of thousands in high positions among the native officials would sustain me in this view.   It is not long since I saw a statement, credited to the most prominent Brahman in South India, advising the whole Pariah community, which numbers millions, to embrace Christianity as their only hope, since Hinduism had no place for them, and no relief to offer for the evils under which they suffer."   The Rev. W. A. Wilson, of the Canadian Presbyterian Mission, forwards, from Rutlam, India, a communication from an educated Hindu gentleman, of orthodox standing, giving his opinion, even from a Hindu point of view, as to the value of missions in India, which, considering its source, has especial weight.[1]   The Rev. R. M. Paterson, of the Church of Scotland Mission, Gujrat, furnishes also some expressions of native opinion, transcribed from a recent issue of the *Oudh Akhbar*, which are significant in this connection.[2]

The Rev. C. F. Gates, D.D. (A. B. C. F. M.), of Harpoot, Turkey,

[1] Without attempting to quote the entire communication, the following passage may be given as indicating its trend:

"Permit me to say that it is in more than one way that I have been constantly brought into contact with missionaries and native Christians in certain places in Rajputana and Central India,·and have seen their works and heard their preachings for many years.   From what I could gather from this experience of mine, I may say that those who have received the light of Christian teachings have presented quite a different spectacle as regards their habits and social lives.   The foundation of the old bigotries has been utterly shaken in their minds, which has proved in more than one way beneficial to society.   Christianity has always denounced intemperance, immorality, cruelty, self-torture, slavery, neglect of the poor and sick, the subject position of Indian women, caste, superstitious customs, and insanitary conditions, which have come to be looked upon by people at large as so many pernicious evils. . . . In fact, there is a progress with rapid strides towards the amelioration of the conditions of the people."

See also the excerpts from the address of Dr. Bhandarkar, quoted *supra*, p. 31.

[2] The following extracts from this source indicate with sufficient plainness the writer's opinion of missionary instruction as a moral education:

"Recently a Brahman lad, having embraced Christianity in Madras,—which, by the way, is nothing new,—has set our Indian brains going, and, as ' Satan always finds mischief for idle hands to do,' our countrymen have been unusually busy these few days declaring war with the missionaries.   They have evidently forgotten that more than half of our educated brothers, who occupy seats in most of the public and private offices in India, are indebted to Christian missionaries for what little they know.   We all acknowledge that it is absolutely necessary for our children to receive moral training in order that they may be helped to lead a good life in the future, but how this is to be accomplished no one knows.   Beyond what the boy learns in the school, there does not appear to be any other source from which he could be taught morality."

in a private letter to the author, relates an incident which indicates the estimate put by a prominent official upon the social results of Protestantism in a Turkish village. He states that the Governor of Mardin had occasion to make a tour among some of the villages where Protestant mission work had been conducted. As he was about leaving the village of Midyat to return to his home, "the officials and dignitaries of the various communities accompanied him out of the village to escort him a little way on his journey. When the time came for them to take leave of him, he beckoned the pastor of the evangelical community to come forward, and said to him before all the assembly: 'I want you to make the people of this mountain Protestants as fast as possible. I have visited the jails and I do not find Protestants in jail; I have examined the tax lists and I find very few of them in arrears. The Protestant villages are the most peaceful and the best ordered, and the members of that sect are the best citizens, and so I want you to make the people of this mountain Protestants.'" Another missionary in the Turkish Empire, referring to the early reluctance of the Armenian people, clergy and laity, to welcome Protestant missions, contrasts the prevalent sentiment of cordiality at the present time as indicating their appreciation of the benefits which missions have brought them. "To-day," he writes, "the leaders of the Armenian race deeply respect us, and are profoundly grateful for the service we have done. They recognize the fact that it is our work of instruction, in the wide sense of the word, which has awakened in their people a desire for intellectual, social, and spiritual progress, and has given them a clear and impressive idea of what is essential to such progress."

Dr. J. P. Cochran, of the Presbyterian Mission in Urumiah, Persia, has forwarded to the author some opinions expressed to him by prominent natives upon this subject. We have not space to print them, but they indicate an intelligent and sympathetic appreciation of the power of Christianity as a remedy for social evils. "The Persians," writes Dr. George W. Holmes, of the Presbyterian Mission at Hamadan, "recognize their degeneracy, and realize that there is no hope of their redemption except through something outside of themselves. In conversation with a prominent *mujtahad* recently, in Kermanshah, he bewailed the fact that, while all these good teachings, as he put it, were to be found in his own land, it was left for the Christians to practise them, while the Moslems paid no heed to them."

The Rev. J. Pearse (L. M. S.), of Madagascar, has forwarded the translation of a carefully written article by a native, on "The Blessings we receive from the Bible apart from Salvation." His intelligent treatment of the theme furnishes an interesting brief on the whole subject from the native standpoint.[1]

The Rev. George W. Chamberlain, of the Presbyterian Mission in Bahia, Brazil, relates the following incident. In conversing recently with the chief magistrate of a large district, he was interested to hear him remark that one of the most turbulent sections, which had formerly given him a great deal of worry, was now in charge of an inspector who had become a Protestant. The magistrate had recently paid a visit to the old inspector's home, and found him a devout student of the Bible, and soon discovered that through the influence of that book he had gathered the moral force to rule his constituency. The principles which he found in the Scriptures had been applied to the social questions which used to occasion so much trouble, and had secured a peaceable and happy solution. "If I could have in every quarter of this district," remarked the magistrate, "a man like that, my office would be a sinecure; I should have nothing to do."

XI

In addition to the sources from which we have gathered credible testimony as to the actual influence of Christian missions upon heathen

Valuable testimony from laymen and government officials as to the social value of missions.

society, there is still some important evidence which might be collated from the writings of merchants, officials, and other laymen not personally identified with missions, but who nevertheless speak from observation. Sir Bartle Frere, formerly Governor of Bombay, in a lecture on "Christianity suited to all forms of Civilisation," delivered on behalf of the London Christian Evidence Society, in 1872, remarks: "Whatever you may be told to the contrary, the teaching of Christianity among 160,000,000 of civilised, industrious Hindus and Mohammedans in India is *effecting changes moral, social, and political*, which for extent and rapidity of effect are far more extraor-

[1] The paper may be summarized as follows: (1) the influence of the Bible in changing evil customs, several of which, such as divination, divorce, polygamy, idolatry, slave-dealing, and infanticide, are specially referred to; (2) the power of the Bible in banishing immorality; (3) its influence in strengthening and developing character; (4) the inspiration derived from the Bible in calling out and developing every good quality. The writer refers also to the stimulus to education and to general progress in civilization. He enforces his points clearly, and from the standpoint of one who has observed the progress of these social changes.

The First National Christian Endeavor Convention Held in Mexico, Zacatecas, June, 1896.

dinary than anything that you or your fathers have witnessed in modern Europe." [1]

Lord Napier, late Governor of Madras, said: "I have broken the missionary's bread, I have been present at his ministrations, I have witnessed his teaching, I have seen the beauty of his life. The benefits of missionary enterprise are felt in three directions—in converting, civilising, and teaching the Indian people. It is not easy to overrate the value in this vast empire of a class of Englishmen of pious lives and disinterested labors, living and moving in the most forsaken places, walking between the Government and the people, with devotion to both, the friends of right, the adversaries of wrong, impartial spectators of good and evil."

Sir Richard Temple, C.I.E., LL.D., late Governor of Bombay, and Finance Minister of India, in a speech delivered before the Baptist Missionary Society in London, in 1883, pays the following tribute to Indian missionaries: "The names of Carey, and Ward, and Marshman, which you read about, are to me living memories, and not only to me, but to thousands of my fellow-countrymen in the East, and, what is more, to many millions of natives. These are memories of men who were the pioneers of civilisation and of humane refinement, the earliest propagators of Christian literature amongst the heathen. The results, indeed, of their work are to be counted among the peaceful glories of England and a portion of that national heritage which is splendid in the highest sense of the term. . . . As an old Finance Minister of India, I ought to know, if anybody does, when the money's worth is got by any operation; and having myself also administered, from first to last, provinces which comprise nearly half British India, I say that, of all the departments I have ever administered, I never saw one more efficient than the missionary department, and of all the hundreds of officers I had under my command, European officers and gentlemen, I have never seen a better body of men than the Protestant missionaries. Of all the departments I have administered, I have never known one in which a more complete result was obtained than in the department—the grand department—which is represented by the Protestant missions." [2]

Lord Herschell, formerly Lord Chancellor of England, in an ad-

---

[1] Consult for further testimonies, "Laymen's Opinions of the Value of Missions in India," published by the Society for the Propagation of the Gospel, and " Are Foreign Missions Doing any Good? " (London, Elliot Stock, 1894). Cf. also quotations from Sir W. Macgregor, Administrator of British New Guinea, and Sir Charles A. Elliott, late Lieutenant-Governor of Bengal, found upon p. 374 of Vol. I.

[2] Temple, " Oriental Experience," pp. 155, 164, 165.

dress at the meeting of the London Missionary Society in May, 1895, stated with judicial fairness and discrimination his own view of missions: "Can it be doubted," said his lordship, "that owing to the work of this Society tens of thousands of men and women have been led to adopt an altogether different idea of life; that their ideal has been changed, that from being a brutal and degraded one it has become a lofty and noble one? And who can doubt that with the hope set before them, with the faith that inspired them, their lives have not become merely changed, but have been unspeakably happier as well as nobler? How are you going to estimate the value of the happiness conferred on one individual, to say nothing of tens of thousands?" In the English Blue Book containing the Report on the Moral and Material Progress of India for 1871–72, the Secretary of State for India has recorded his estimate of the social benefits of missions in the following language: "The Government of India cannot but acknowledge the great obligation under which it is laid by the benevolent exertions made by missionaries, whose blameless example and self-denying labours are infusing new vigour into the stereotyped life of the great populations placed under English rule, and are preparing them to be in every way better men and better citizens of the great empire in which they dwell."[1] A still earlier testimony concerning the West Coast of Africa is found in the report of a Parliamentary Committee presented in 1842, which attributed the "considerable intellectual, moral, and religious improvement" of the people of Sierra Leone to "the valuable exertions of the Church Missionary Society."[2]

A correspondent from Madagascar, in a communication to *The Times* (London), writes on April 30, 1895, of his impressions of the civilizing results of missions in terms of surprise and admiration. "I was, indeed, amazed," he writes, "to find here so high a degree of civilisation—and it does not appear to be a civilisation that lies merely on the surface. In no part of the world that I have visited can our missionaries show anything approaching to the admirable results apparent in the central highlands of Madagascar, and there is no reason why they should not in time bring the barbarous outer tribes similarly under their beneficial influence. Even those travellers who, coming from South Africa and elsewhere, have formed a poor opinion of missionary work, are compelled to testify to its marvellous success in Madagascar."

Commissioner Sir H. H. Johnston, to quote again from his recent

---

1 Blue Book, No. 172, p. 129. Cf. for further extracts from the same Blue Book, "Are Foreign Missions Doing any Good?" pp. 57, 58.

2 "Report of Church Missionary Society, 1897," p. 68.

volume on British Central Africa, has devoted a chapter to " Missionaries." He speaks of them in the main with great consideration, and
pays repeated tributes to their services, which he regards as of high
value. The few deprecating criticisms he makes are, in cases where
they apply, not undeserved, and his views as to the desirability of
banishing cant, censoriousness, and arrogance from the missionary
vocabulary and demeanor are such as all true-hearted and sensible
missionaries will cordially endorse. " No person," he writes, " who desires to make a truthful statement would deny the great good effected
by missionary enterprise in Central Africa. . . . Any thoughtful,
cultured man, no matter of what religion, who is alive to the interests of humanity in general, must after careful examination of mission
work accord this meed of praise to the results which have followed
the attempts to evangelise Central Africa. . . . Missionary work
in British Central Africa, believe me, has only to tell the plain truth
and nothing but the truth to secure sympathy and support. . . . There
is an undoubted tendency on the part of missionaries to hold and set
forth the opinion that no one ever did any good in Africa but themselves. That they have done more good than armies, navies, conferences, and treaties have yet done, I am prepared to admit; that they
have prepared the way for the direct and just rule of European Powers
and for the extension of sound and honest commerce, I have frequently
asserted; but they are themselves to some extent only a passing phase—
only the John-the-Baptists, the forerunners, of organized churches and
settled social politics. . . . When the history of the great African
States of the future comes to be written, the arrival of the first missionary will with many of these new nations be the first historical event
in their annals. . . . Who can say, with these facts before him,
with the present condition of the natives in South Africa to consider,
with the gradual civilisation of Western Africa, that missionary work
has been a failure or anything but a success in the Dark Continent? " [1]

[1] Johnston, " British Central Africa," pp. 190, 192, 204, 205. Some further
sentences from the same volume should be quoted: " It is they, too, who in many
cases have first taught the natives carpentry, joinery, masonry, tailoring, cobbling,
engineering, bookkeeping, printing, and European cookery; to say nothing of reading, writing, arithmetic, and a smattering of general knowledge. Almost invariably
it has been to missionaries that the natives of Interior Africa have owed their first
acquaintance with the printing-press, the turning-lathe, the mangle, the flat-iron,
the sawmill, and the brick mould. Industrial teaching is coming more and more
into favour, and its immediate results in British Central Africa have been most
encouraging. Instead of importing printers, carpenters, store clerks, cooks, teleg-
raphists, gardeners, natural-history collectors, from England or India, we are grad-

Commander Charles O'Neil, of the United States Navy, has recently written his impressions of American missionaries in Turkey.[1] Professor W. M. Ramsay, in his recent book, entitled "Impressions of Turkey," thus records his conviction concerning the value of missions, based upon observations made during twelve years of personal sojourn and travel in Asia Minor: "I was driven by the force of facts and experience to the opinion that the mission has been the strongest, as well as most beneficent, influence in causing the movement toward civilisation, which has been perceptible in varying degrees among all the peoples of Turkey, but which has been zealously opposed and almost arrested by the present Sultan, with the support of the six European Powers."

The Hon. Charles Denby, formerly United States Minister to China, in one of his official despatches expresses in the most cordial terms his sense of the value of missionary efforts in that empire.[2] Mr. Valentine Chirol, a special correspondent of *The Times* (London), in his published volume, entitled "The Far Eastern Question," in the chapter on mis-

ually becoming able to obtain them amongst the natives of the country, who are trained in the missionaries' schools, and who, having been given simple, wholesome local education, have not had their heads turned, and are not above their station in life" (p. 205).

[1] "My experience with the American missionaries in the Ottoman Empire was most favorable to them, and whenever the occasion presents itself I do not hesitate to commend them and their work. I can always be relied on and referred to as a warm friend and ally of our countrymen and women who are laboring in the cause of Christianity and education in Turkey; they have done and are doing noble work, the far-reaching influence and value of which cannot be overestimated."—Quoted in *The Church at Home and Abroad*, August, 1897, p. 123.

[2] "As far as my knowledge extends, I can and do say that the missionaries in China are self-sacrificing; that their lives are pure; that they are devoted to their work; that their influence is beneficial to the natives; that the arts and sciences and civilization are greatly spread by their efforts; that many useful Western books are translated by them into Chinese; that they are the leaders in all charitable work, giving largely themselves, and personally disbursing the funds with which they are entrusted; that they do make converts, and such converts are mentally benefited by conversion. . . . Missionaries are the pioneers of trade and commerce. Civilization, learning, and instruction, breed new wants which commerce supplies. Look at the electric telegraph, now in every province in China but one. Look at the steamships which ply along the coast from Hong Kong to Newchwang, and on the Yangtse up to Ichang. Look at the cities which have sprung up, like Shanghai, Tientsin, Hankow—handsome foreign cities, object-lessons to the Chinese. Look at the railroad now being built from the Yellow Sea to the Amur, of which about two hundred miles are completed. Will any one say that the fifteen hundred Protestant missionaries in China, and perhaps more of Catholics, have not contributed to these results?"—Quoted in *The Missionary Herald*, August, 1895, p. 316.

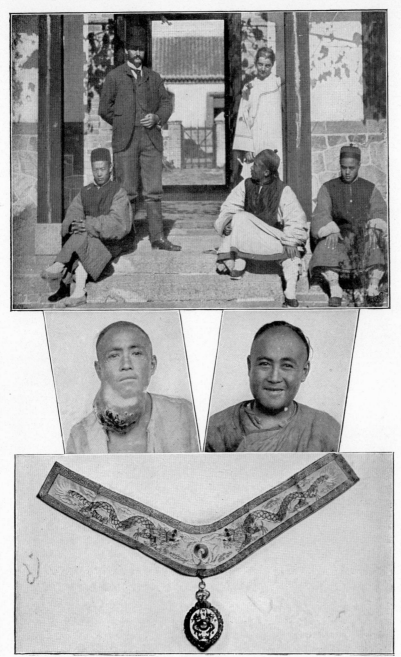

Dr. A. W. Douthwaite, a lady nurse, and students, on veranda of hospital, at Chefoo.

A successful operation—the patient before and after.

Insignia of the "Order of the Double Dragon," conferred on Dr. Douthwaite by the Emperor.

A REPRESENTATIVE MISSIONARY PHYSICIAN IN CHINA.

(C. I. M.)

sionary outrages in China, refers to missionaries and their work with uniform courtesy and appreciation.[1]

" In comparing India at the beginning of the century with the India of to-day," writes the Hon. John W. Foster, " a great improvement is to be noted in the moral and social conditions.   The prohibition of human sacrifice and of torture in the religious rites, of the burning of widows, of the killing of female children, and the efforts at reform in the practice of child marriage, are all direct results of the exposure and condemnation by the missionaries.   The establishment of schools and colleges, which was inaugurated by the missions, has created a widespread zeal for education hitherto unknown in the land.   The awakened interest of the Brahmans in the purification of their religion, and the efforts of reformers to establish a Hindu worship more in accord with the enlightened spirit of the age, are the direct outgrowth of the preaching of the Gospel of Christ.   If not a single conversion to Christianity could be recorded in the past century, these reforms and blessings alone would be an abundant reward for all the labors of the missionaries, and the money contributed by the churches for their support." [2]

It would seem that the spontaneous testimonies to the social influence of missionary example and the favorable comments upon the benefits to society of missionary effort, quoted in the present lecture, should be sufficient, for a time at least, to vindicate missions from aspersions.   We have little expectation, however, that this will be so, since it is not likely that the unfriendly critics of missions will read them, and, moreover, if it has been possible in the past for some to fail so completely to discover the good that has resulted from missions, it is probable that others in their turn will express the same hasty and misleading opinions concerning them.   In the judgment of some of

[1] " Two points alone need be borne in mind.   First of all, foreign missionaries, whatever we may think of them, are just as much entitled to protection in the lawful pursuit of their calling, under the treaties to which China has subscribed, as the foreign merchant or the foreign official.   Secondly, even if, judged by a mundane standard, the material results have not been proportionate to the amount of blood and treasure expended, missionary work in China is not only a proselytising but also a humanising agency, and every missionary establishment is a centre from which civilising influences radiate over the whole area of its operations. . . . Missionary work is practically the only agency through which the influence of Western civilisation can at present reach the masses " (pp. 79, 80).

[2] From an address by the Hon. John W. Foster, given at the Union Missionary Meeting of the Presbyterian Churches of New York City, at Carnegie Hall, November 15, 1895.

our readers such an array of *testimonia* may seem unnecessary and perhaps unbecoming, but in view of the strange susceptibility of many minds to every wind of reckless comment upon missionaries and their work, from whatever source it blows, a reassuring word from witnesses whose opinion inspires confidence seems occasionally to be in place.

In concluding this survey of the fundamental transformations wrought by missions in non-Christian society preparatory to coming changes in the higher life of the nations, we must return with emphasis to that consummate and crowning feature of their influence—their capacity to produce Christianized manhood. This individual product is the essential and ultimate basis of an ideal social status. We need not insist that this ideal can never be attained apart from Christianity; it is enough to show that it never has been attained, and the irresistible inference is that it never will be. Christendom is a convincing testimony that Christianity at least works in the right direction, while the non-Christian world sufficiently indicates that everything else works in the wrong direction. We may leave it an open question how far Christendom has advanced towards perfection. It is a closed question that, where Christianity has not wrought for the social welfare of man, the tendency has been towards deterioration. Christian missions in the light of history are the social hope of the world. We see as yet but the breaking of the dawn, but the time will come when the soft glow of the morning shall brighten and expand into the full light of day, and there will be God's peace and God's righteousness in all the new earth.

LITERATURE AND AUTHORITIES FOR LECTURE V

The student should consult also the bibliographies of Lectures I. and IV., in Volume I. Many books of value are omitted in the following list, especially in the biographical section, because already included there.

Biographies of missionaries and native Christians are specially noted here, as a luminous source of evidence confirmatory of the positions taken in the preceding lecture. Older biographical issues will be found in the bibliography at the end of Volume I. of the "Report of the Centenary Conference, London, 1888," and in the Appendix to Volume I. of "The Encyclopedia of Missions."

N. Y. = New York.	C. = Chicago.	B. = Boston.
P. = Philadelphia.	L. = London.	E. = Edinburgh.
	n. d. = no date.	

I. RECENT STUDIES IN MISSION HISTORY

ALLEN, W. O. B., and McCLURE, EDMUND, *Two Hundred Years: The History of the Society for Promoting Christian Knowledge, 1698-1898.* L., S. P. C. K.; N. Y., E. & J. B. Young & Co., 1898.

BARNES, IRENE H., *Behind the Pardah: The Story of C. E. Z. M. S. Work in India.* L., Marshall Bros., 1897.

BARROWS, Rev. J. H., *The Christian Conquest of Asia.* N. Y., Charles Scribner's Sons, 1899.

BARRY, Rev. A., *The Ecclesiastical Expansion of England in the Growth of the Anglican Communion.* L. and N. Y., The Macmillan Co., 1895.

BEACH, Rev. HARLAN P., *Dawn on the Hills of T'ang; or, Missions in China.* N. Y., Student Volunteer Movement, 1898.

BRAIN, BELLE M., *The Transformation of Hawaii.* N. Y. and C., Fleming H. Revell Co., 1899.

CALDECOTT, Professor A., *The Church in the West Indies.* L., S. P. C. K.; N. Y., E. & J. B. Young & Co., 1898.

CAVALIER, Rev. A. R., *In Northern India: A Story of Mission Work in Zenanas, Hospitals, Schools, and Villages.* L., S. W. Partridge & Co., 1899.

Classified Digest of the Records of the Society for the Propagation of the Gospel in Foreign Parts, 1701-1892. L., Office of S. P. G., 1895.

COILLARD, Rev. FRANÇOIS, *On the Threshold of Central Africa: A Record of Twenty Years' Pioneering among the Barotsi of the Upper Zambesi.* (Translated from the French by his niece, Catherine W. Mackintosh.) L., Hodder & Stoughton, 1897.

ELMSLIE, Dr. W. A., *Among the Wild Ngoni.* E., Oliphant, Anderson & Ferrier, 1899; N. Y., Fleming H. Revell Co.

GALE, Rev. J. S., *Korean Sketches.* N. Y. and C., Fleming H. Revell Co., 1898.

GALLOWAY, Bishop C. B., *Modern Missions: Their Evidential Value.* Nashville, Tenn., Publishing House of the M. E. Church, South, 1897.

GIFFORD, Rev. D. L., *Every-day Life in Korea.* N. Y. and C., Fleming H. Revell Co., 1898.

GRAHAM, Rev. J. A., *The Missionary Expansion of the Reformed Church.* L., A. & C. Black, 1898; N. Y., published by Fleming H. Revell Co., under title of *Missionary Expansion since the Reformation.*

GUINNESS, M. GERALDINE, *The Story of the China Inland Mission.* 2 vols. L., Morgan & Scott, 1894.

GUINNESS, LUCY E., *Across India at the Dawn of the Twentieth Century.* L., The Religious Tract Society; N. Y. and C., Fleming H. Revell Co., 1899.

HODDER, EDWIN, *Conquests of the Cross.* 3 vols. L., Cassell & Co., 1891.

HOLE, Rev. CHARLES, *History of the Church Missionary Society to A.D. 1814.* L., Church Missionary Society, 1896.

HOPKINS, Dr. S. ARMSTRONG-, *Within the Purdah.* N. Y., Eaton & Mains, 1898.

JOHNSTON, Rev. JAMES, *China and Formosa.* L., Hazell, Watson & Viney; N. Y. and C., Fleming H. Revell Co., 1897.

LANG, Rev. JOHN MARSHALL, *The Expansion of the Christian Life.* E. & L., William Blackwood & Sons, 1897.

LEONARD, Rev. D. L., *A Hundred Years of Missions; or, The Story of Progress since Carey's Beginning.* N. Y. and L., Funk & Wagnalls Co., 1895.

LOVETT, RICHARD, *The History of the London Missionary Society, 1795–1895.* 2 vols. L., H. Frowde, 1899.

MACKENZIE, Prof. W. DOUGLAS, *Christianity and the Progress of Man.* N. Y. and C., Fleming H. Revell Co., 1897.

M'LAREN, Mrs. DUNCAN, *The Story of Our Manchuria Mission.* E., Offices of United Presb. Church, 1896.

Make Jesus King. Report of S. V. M. U. Conference in Liverpool, 1896. (Order of Mr. L. B. Butcher, S. V. M. U. Office, 93 Aldersgate Street, London, E. C.)

MARTIN, Rev. CHALMERS, *Apostolic and Modern Missions.* N. Y. and C., Fleming H. Revell Co., 1898.

MORSHEAD, A. E. M. ANDERSON-, *The History of the Universities' Mission to Central Africa, 1859–1896.* L., Office of the Universities' Mission, 1897.

MUIRHEAD, Rev. W., and PARKER, Rev. A. P., *Ninety Years of Missionary Work in China.* Shanghai, Presbyterian Mission Press, 1897.

NOBLE, FREDERIC PERRY, *The Redemption of Africa: A Story of Civilization.* 2 vols. N. Y. and C., Fleming H. Revell Co., 1899.

ORR, Rev. JAMES, *Neglected Factors in the Study of the Early Progress of Christianity.* L., Hodder & Stoughton; N. Y., A. C. Armstrong & Son, 1899.

REID, Rev. J. M., *Missions and Missionary Society of the Methodist Episcopal Church.* 3 vols. (Revised and extended by the Rev. J. T. Gracey, D.D.) N. Y., Eaton & Mains, 1896.

RITTER, Rev. H., *A History of Protestant Missions in Japan.* Tokyo, The Methodist Publishing House, 1898.

SPEER, ROBERT E., *Missions and Politics in Asia.* N. Y. and C., Fleming H. Revell Co., 1898.

STEWART, Rev. ROBERT, *Life and Work in India.* P., Pearl Publishing Co., 1896.

STOCK, EUGENE, *One Hundred Years: Being the Short History of the Church Missionary Society.* L., Office of the Church Missionary Society, 1898.

STOCK, EUGENE, *The History of the Church Missionary Society: Its Environment, its Men, and its Work.* 3 vols. L., Office of the Church Missionary Society, 1899.

STONE, Rev. R. H., *In Afric's Forest and Jungle.* N. Y. and C., Fleming H. Revell Co., 1899.

STORROW, Rev. E., *Our Indian Sisters.* L., The Religious Tract Society, 1898; N. Y., published by Fleming H. Revell Co., under the title, *Our Sisters in India.*

STOTT, GRACE, *Twenty-six Years of Missionary Work in China.* L., Hodder & Stoughton; N. Y., American Tract Society, 1897.

Student Missionary Appeal (The). Official Report of the Third International Convention (Cleveland, 1898) of the Student Volunteer Movement for Foreign Missions. (Address F. P. Turner, Bancroft Building, 3 West 29th Street, New York.) 1899.

TAYLOR, Bishop WILLIAM, *The Flaming Torch in Darkest Africa.* (Order from Rev. Ross Taylor, 150 Fifth Avenue, New York.) 1899.

THORNTON, D. M., *Africa Waiting; or, The Problem of Africa's Evangelization.* L. and N. Y., S. V. M. U., 1898.

VAN DYKE, Rev. HENRY, *The First Christmas Tree.* N. Y., Charles Scribner's Sons, 1897.

WARNECK, Dr. GUSTAV, *Abriss einer Geschichte der Protestantischen Missionen, von der Reformation bis auf die Gegenwart.* Berlin, Martin Warneck, 1898.

WARNECK, Dr. GUSTAV, *Evangelische Missionslehre.* Ite Abt., 1892. IIte Abt., 1894. IIIte Abt., 1897. Gotha, Perthes.

WATSON, Rev. ANDREW, *The American Mission in Egypt, 1854 to 1896.* Pittsburgh, United Presbyterian Board of Publication, 1898.

WOLF, Rev. L. B., *After Fifty Years; or, An Historical Sketch of the Guntur Mission of the Evangelical Lutheran Church of the General Synod in the United States of America.* P., Lutheran Publication Society, 1897.

II. BIOGRAPHIES OF MISSIONARIES AND NATIVE CHRISTIANS

(A selected list, mostly of recent issues.)

BARBER, Rev. W. T. A., *David Hill, Missionary and Saint.* L., Charles H. Kelly, 1898.

BATTERSBY, CHARLES F. HARFORD-, *Pilkington of Uganda.* L., Marshall Brothers, 1898.

BENHAM, MARIAN S., *Henry Callaway, M.D., D.D., First Bishop for Kaffraria.* L. and N. Y., The Macmillan Co., 1896.

BERRY, Rev. D. M., *The Sister Martyrs of Kucheng: Memoir and Letters of Eleanor and Elizabeth Saunders.* L., James Nisbet & Co.; N. Y. and C., Fleming H. Revell Co., 1897.

BIRKS, Rev. HERBERT, *The Life and Correspondence of Thomas Valpy French, Scholar and Missionary, First Bishop of Lahore, 1825-1891.* 2 vols. L., John Murray, 1895.

BOVET, FELIX, *Count Zinzendorf: A Pioneer of Social Christianity.* (Translated and condensed by the Rev. T. A. Seed.) L., Charles H. Kelly, 1896.

BROCK, WILLIAM, *A Young Congo Missionary: Memorials of Sidney Roberts Webb, M.D.* L., H. R. Allenson, 1896.

BRUCE, Mrs. WYNDHAM KNIGHT-, *Khama, the African Chief.* L., Kegan Paul, Trench, Trübner & Co., 1893.

BRYSON, MARY F., *Fred. C. Roberts of Tientsin; or, For Christ and China.* L., H. R. Allenson, 1895.

BRYSON, MARY F., *Life of John Kenneth Mackenzie, Medical Missionary to China.* L., Hodder & Stoughton; N. Y. and C., Fleming H. Revell Co., 1895.

BUCKLAND, Rev. A. R., *John Horden, Missionary Bishop: A Life on the Shores of Hudson Bay.* L., Sunday-school Union, 1895; N. Y., Thomas Whittaker, 1896.

BUCKLAND, Rev. A. R., *Women in the Mission Field, Pioneers and Martyrs.* N. Y., Thomas Whittaker, 1895.

CAREY, WILLIAM, and Others, *Serampore Letters: Being the Unpublished Correspondence of William Carey and Others with John Williams, 1800–1816.* New edition, edited by Leighton and Mornay Williams. N. Y. and C., Fleming H. Revell Co., 1898.

COUSINS, Rev. H. T., *Tiyo Soga, the Model Kafir Missionary.* L., S. W. Partridge & Co., 1897.

COX, Rev. W. S., *Early Promoted: A Memoir.* (Compiled by His Father.) L., Sampson Low, Marston & Co., 1897.

CRAIGHEAD, J. G., *The Story of Marcus Whitman: Early Protestant Missions in the Northwest.* P., Presbyterian Board of Publication, 1895.

CREEGAN, Rev. CHARLES C., and GOODNOW, Mrs. JOSEPHINE A. B., *Great Missionaries of the Church.* N. Y. and B., Thomas Y. Crowell & Co., 1895.

DENNIS, Mrs. JAMES S., *Sketch of the Life of Rev. Simeon Howard Calhoun.* N. Y., American Tract Society, 1898.

DONCASTER, E. P., *Faithful unto Death: A Story of the Missionary Life in Madagascar of William and Lucy S. Johnson.* L., Headley Bros., 1897.

FAULKNER, ROSE E., *Joseph Sidney Hill, First Bishop in Equatorial Africa.* L., H. R. Allenson, 1895.

GILMOUR, JAMES, *of Mongolia: His Diaries, Letters, and Reports.* (Edited by Richard Lovett, M.A.) N. Y. and C., Fleming H. Revell Co., 1892.

GOODWIN, HARVEY, *Charles Frederick Mackenzie.* L., Bell & Son, 1864.

GRACEY, Mrs. J. T., *Eminent Missionary Women.* N. Y., Eaton & Mains, 1898.

GREEN, Dr. SAMUEL FISK, *Life and Letters of.* (Compiled by Ebenezer Cutler, D.D.) Printed for family friends, 1891.

HALL, ROSETTA SHERWOOD, *The Life of the Rev. William James Hall, M.D.* N. Y., Eaton & Mains, 1897.

HARRIS, S. F., *A Century of Missionary Martyrs.* L., James Nisbet & Co., 1897.

HAYDN, Rev. H. C., *American Heroes on Mission Fields.* First series. N. Y., The American Tract Society, 1890.

HEANLEY, Rev. R. M., *A Memoir of Bishop Edward Steere.* L., Bell & Son, 1888.

HUGHES, THOMAS, *David Livingstone.* L. and N. Y., The Macmillan Co., 1889. Reprinted 1898.

HUGHES, Rev. THOMAS P., *Heroic Lives in Foreign Fields.* N. Y., E. R. Herrick & Co., 1899.

Hü YONG MI, *The Way of Faith Illus-*

trated: Autobiography of Hü Yong Mi, of the China Mission Conference. Cincinnati, Curts & Jennings, 1896; N. Y., Eaton & Mains, 1899.

IWAMOTO, Mrs. KASHI, the First Graduate of Ferris Seminary, Japan; with a Collection of Her English Writings. (Address R. Brinkerhoff, 25 East Twenty - second Street, New York City.) 1896.

JESSUP, Rev. H. H., The Setting of the Crescent and the Rising of the Cross; or, Kamil Abdul Messiah : A Syrian Convert from Islam to Christianity. P., The Westminster Press, 1898.

JEWETT, FRANCES GULICK, LutherHalsey Gulick, Missionary in Hawaii, Micronesia, Japan, and China. B., Congregational Sunday - school and Publishing Society, 1895; L., Elliot Stock, 1897.

JOHNSON, Rev. C. R., Bryan Roe : Soldier of the Cross, Missionary in West Central Africa. L., C. H. Kelly, 1896.

KEELING, ANNA E., What He Did for Convicts and Cannibals : A Biography of the Rev. Samuel Leigh, the First Wesleyan Missionary to New South Wales and New Zealand. L., Charles H. Kelly, 1896.

LAMBERT, CHARLES WILLIAM, The Missionary Martyr of Thibaw: Brief Record of Life and Missionary Labours in Upper Burmah. L., S. W. Partridge & Co., 1896.

LAPSLEY, SAMUEL NORVELL, Missionary to the Congo Valley. By His Father. Richmond, Va., Whittet & Shepperson, 1893.

LAURIE, Rev. THOMAS, Woman and the Gospel in Persia: Memoirs of Miss Fidelia Fiske. N. Y. and C., Fleming H. Revell Co., 1892.

LEWIS, ARTHUR, George Maxwell Gordon : The Pilgrim Missionary of the Punjab. L., Seelye & Co., 1890.

LLOYD, Rev. EDWIN, Three Great African Chiefs, Khámá, Sebelé, and Bathoeng. L., T. Fisher Unwin, 1895.

McDOWELL, W. F., PIERSON, Rev. A. T., BINGHAM, JENNIE M., and Others, The Picket Line of Missions : Sketches of the Advance Guard. N.Y., Eaton & Mains, 1897.

McMASTER, Rev. A. A., The Life and Letters of the Rev. Arthur Fraser Sim, First Missionary at Kota-Kota. L., Office of the Universities' Mission to Central Africa, 1896.

MAPLES, ELLEN, The Life of Chauncy Maples, D.D., Bishop of Likoma, British Central Africa. L. and N. Y., Longmans, Green & Co., 1897.

MARAU, Rev. CLEMENT, Story of a Melanesian Deacon. (Translated by R. H. Codrington.) L., S. P. C. K., 1894.

MARRAT, Rev. JABEZ, Missionary Veterans in South Africa. L., Charles H. Kelly, 1894.

MARSHALL, ELSIE, For His Sake : A Record of a Life Consecrated to God and Devoted to China. L., The Religious Tract Society, 1896; N.Y., Revell Co.

MARWICK, Rev. WILLIAM, William and Louisa Anderson : A Record of Their Life and Work in Jamaica and in Old Calabar. E., Andrew Elliot, 1897.

MOFFAT, JOHN S., The Lives of Robert and Mary Moffat. New edition. N. Y., A. C. Armstrong & Son, 1888.

MYERS, Rev. J. B., Thomas J. Comber, Missionary Pioneer to the Congo. L., S. W. Partridge & Co., 1888.

NARUSE, JINZO, A Modern Paul in Japan : Life of Rev. Paul Sawayama. (Introduction by the Rev. Alexander McKenzie, D.D.) B., Congregational Sunday-school and Publishing Society, 1893.

NEETHING, W. J., Missionary to Africa, Made Exceeding Glad: A Brief Memoir. L., James Nisbet & Co., 1897.

NEVIUS, HELEN S. C., Forty Years in Shantung : The Life of John Livingston Nevius. N. Y. and C., Fleming H. Revell Co., 1895.

NIXON, OLIVER W., How Marcus Whitman Saved Oregon. C., Star Publishing Co., 1895.

PAGE, JESSE, Captain Allen Gardiner, Sailor and Saint. L., S. W. Partridge & Co., 1897.

PARSONS, ELLEN C., A Life for Africa : Rev. Adolphus Clemens Good, Ph.D., American Missionary in Equatorial West Africa. N. Y. and C., Fleming H. Revell Co., 1897; E., Oliphant, Anderson & Ferrier, 1898.

PATON, Rev. JOHN G., Autobiography for Years 1886-1897. N. Y. and C., Fleming H. Revell Co., 1898.

PATON, MAGGIE WHITECROSS, Letters and Sketches from the New Hebrides. N. Y., A. C. Armstrong & Son, 1895.

PHILLIPS, Mrs. J. L., Dr. J. L. Phillips, Missionary to the Children of India. L., Sunday-school Union, 1898.

PIERPOINT, Rev. R. D., In Uganda for Christ: The Life Story of John Samuel Callis, B.A. L., Hodder & Stoughton, 1898.

PIERSON, Rev. ARTHUR T., Seven

Years in Sierra Leone : The Story of the Missionary Work of William A. B. Johnson. N. Y. and C., Fleming H. Revell Co.; L., James Nisbet & Co., 1897.

PITMAN, Mrs. E. R., *Missionary Heroines in Eastern Lands.* L., S. W. Partridge & Co., 1895.

RANKINE, W. HENRY, *A Hero of the Dark Continent : Memoir of the Rev. William Affleck Scott, Church of Scotland Missionary at Blantyre, British Central Africa.* E., William Blackwood & Sons, 1896.

RANNEY, RUTH W., *Lives and Missionary Labors of the Rev. and Mrs. Cephas Bennett.* B., N. Y., and C., Silver, Burdett & Co., 1892.

ROBSON, WILLIAM, *Griffith John, Founder of the Hankow Mission, Central China.* L., S. W. Partridge & Co., 1888; N. Y. and C., Fleming H. Revell Co., n. d.

ROSS, Rev. JOHN, *Old Wang : The First Chinese Evangelist in Manchuria.* L., The Religious Tract Society, 1889.

ROWE, Rev. G. STRINGER, *James Calvert of Fiji.* L., C. H. Kelly, 1893.

RUTHERFORD, Rev. JOHN, *Missionary Pioneers in India.* E., A. Elliot, 1896.

SABATIER, P., *The Life of St. Francis of Assisi.* (Translated by Louise Seymour Houghton.) L., Hodder & Stoughton, 1896.

SCHAUFFLER, Rev. W. G., *Autobiography of.* (Edited by His Son.) A. D. F. Randolph & Co., 1888.

SCHOFIELD, A. T., *Memorials of R. Harold A. Schofield, M.A., M.B. (late of the China Inland Mission).* New edition. L., Hodder & Stoughton, 1898.

SHARROCK, Rev. J. A., *Bishop Caldwell : A Memoir.* Madras, S. P. C. K., 1896.

SINKER, Rev. ROBERT, *Memorials of the Hon. Ion Keith-Falconer, M.A., Missionary to the Mohammedans of Southern Arabia.* L., George Bell & Sons, 1890.

Sketches of Indian Christians. (Collected from various sources ; with an Introduction by Mr. S. Satthianadhan.) Madras, Christian Literature Society, 1896.

SMITH, GEORGE, *Bishop Heber, Second Bishop of Calcutta, 1783-1826.* L., John Murray, 1895. (Biographies of Martyn, Carey, and Duff, by Dr. George Smith, will be found entered on p. 69 of Vol. I.)

SMITH, GEORGE, *Life of Dr. John Wilson.* L., John Murray, 1878.

SMITH, Mrs. JOHN JAMES, *William Knibb, Missionary in Jamaica.* L., Alexander & Shepheard, 1896. (Biographies of Knibb written by Hinton, 1847, and by Sargent, 1849.)

STEVENS, Rev. GEORGE B., *The Life, Letters, and Journals of the Rev. and Hon. Peter Parker, M.D., Missionary Physician and Diplomatist.* B., Congregational Sunday-school and Publishing Society, 1896.

STEVENS, Rev. SUMNER W., *A Half-Century in Burma : Memoir of Edward Abiel Stevens, D.D.* P., American Baptist Publication Society, 1897.

STOCK, SARAH G., *Missionary Heroes of Africa.* L., Office of the London Missionary Society, 1897.

TAYLOR, CHARLES E., *The Story of Yates the Missionary.* Nashville, Tenn., Sunday-school Board of the Southern Baptist Convention, 1898.

TAYLOR, Bishop WILLIAM, *The Story of My Life.* N. Y., Eaton & Mains, 1896; L., Hodder & Stoughton, 1897.

TRESTRAIL, Mrs., *Elizabeth Sale, the Zenana Missionary.* L., The Baptist Tract and Book Society, 1898.

TUCKER, Rev. H. W., *Life of Bishop George Augustus Selwyn.* 2 vols. L., Wells Gardner, Darton & Co., 1886.

TURNER, H. F., *His Witnesses.* (A Record of Some of the Martyrs of the Fuhkien Mission.) L., Simpkin, Marshall, Hamilton, Kent & Co., 1895.

UCHIMURA, KANZO, *Diary of a Japanese Convert.* N. Y. and C., Fleming H. Revell Co., 1895.

WALSH, Rt. Rev. W. P., *Heroes of the Mission Field.* Fourth edition. N. Y., Thomas Whittaker, 1898.

WALSH, Rt. Rev. W. P., *Modern Heroes of the Mission Field.* Fourth edition. N. Y., Thomas Whittaker, 1898.

WARD, GERTRUDE, *The Life of Charles Alan Smythies, Bishop of the Universities' Mission to Central Africa.* (Edited by the Rev. E. F. Russell.) L., Office of the Universities' Mission to Central Africa, 1898.

WATSON, MARY E., *Robert and Louisa Stewart* (of Kucheng). L., Marshall Brothers, 1895.

WILLIAMS, F. WELLS, *The Life and Letters of S. Wells Williams.* N. Y., G. P. Putnam's Sons, 1888.

YONGE, C. M., *Life and Letters of Bishop John Coleridge Patteson.* New edition. 2 vols. L. and N. Y., The Macmillan Co., 1898.

SYNOPSIS OF LECTURE VI

The first three only of these classified groups appear in this volume.

I.—RESULTS MANIFEST IN THE INDIVIDUAL CHARACTER. (1) Temperance Reform; (2) Deliverance from the Opium Habit; (3) Restraint upon Gambling; (4) Establishing Higher Standards of Personal Purity; (5) Discrediting Self-Inflicted Torture or Mutilation; (6) Arresting Pessimistic and Suicidal Tendencies; (7) Cultivating Habits of Industry and Frugality; (8) Substituting Christian Humility and Proper Self-Respect for Barbaric Pride and Foolish Conceit; (9) Cultivation of the Personal Virtues.

II.—RESULTS AFFECTING FAMILY LIFE. (1) The Elevation of Woman; (2) Restraining Polygamy and Concubinage; (3) Checking Adultery and Divorce; (4) Seeking the Abolishment of Child Marriage; (5) Alleviating the Social Miseries of Widowhood; (6) Mitigating the Enforced Seclusion of Woman; (7) Improving the Condition of Domestic Life and Family Training; (8) Rendering Aid and Protection to Children; (9) Diminishing Infanticide.

III.—RESULTS OF A HUMANE AND PHILÂNTHROPIC TENDENCY. (1) Hastening the Suppression of the Slave-Trade and Labor-Traffic; (2) Aiding in the Overthrow of Slavery; (3) Abolishing Cannibalism and Inhuman Sports; (4) Arresting Human Sacrifices; (5) Banishing Cruel Ordeals; (6) Initiating the Crusade against Foot-Binding; (7) Promoting Prison Reforms and Mitigating Brutal Punishments; (8) Securing Humane Ministration to the Poor and Dependent; (9) Organizing Famine Relief; (10) Introducing Modern Medical Science; (11) Conducting Medical Dispensaries, Infirmaries, and Hospitals; (12) Founding Leper Asylums and Colonies; (13) Establishing Orphan Asylums; (14) Promoting Cleanliness and Sanitation; (15) Mitigating the Brutalities of War; (16) Instilling a Peaceable and Law-Abiding Spirit.

IV. RESULTS TENDING TO DEVELOP THE HIGHER LIFE OF SOCIETY. (1) The Introduction of Educational Facilities; (2) The Development of Industrial Training; (3) Modern Methods of University Extension; (4) Christian Associations for Young Men and Young Women; (5) The Production of Wholesome and Instructive Literature; (6) The Quickening of General Intelligence; (7) The Abolishment of Objectionable Social Customs; (8) The Disintegration of Caste.

V. RESULTS TOUCHING NATIONAL LIFE AND CHARACTER. (1) Cultivating the Spirit of Freedom and True Patriotism; (2) Promoting the Reconstruction of Laws; (3) Aiding in the Renovation of Administrative Methods; (4) Elevating the Standard of Government Service; (5) Furthering Proper International Relations; (6) Contributing to the Intellectual and Scientific Progress of the World.

VI. RESULTS AFFECTING THE COMMERCIAL AND INDUSTRIAL STATUS. (1) Commending New Standards of Commercial Integrity; (2) Promoting Better Methods of Transacting Business; (3) Seeking to Introduce a Better System of Finance; (4) Developing Trade and Commerce with the Outer World; (5) Introducing Material Civilization and Modern Facilities.

VII. RESULTS DUE TO REFORMED STANDARDS OF RELIGIOUS FAITH AND PRACTICE. (1) The Advantages of a more Spiritual Conception of Religion; (2) The Influence of the Decline of Idolatry; (3) The Gain to Society from the Overthrow of Superstition; (4) The Social Effects of Associating Morality with Religion; (5) The Benefits of Exemplary Religious Leadership; (6) The Social Results of Religious Liberty; (7) The Social Uplift of Sabbath Observance.

LECTURE VI

*

THE CONTRIBUTION OF CHRISTIAN MIS-
SIONS TO SOCIAL PROGRESS

"The course of humanity has been an onward course. Individual men have gone back, individual nations have gone back, but humanity itself has never receded. And wheresoever Christianity has breathed, it has accelerated the movement of humanity. It has quickened the pulses of life, it has stimulated the incentives to thought, it has tuned the passions into peace, it has warmed the heart into brotherhood, it has fanned the imagination into genius, it has freshened the soul into purity. The progress of Christian Europe has been the progress of mind over matter. It has been the progress of intellect over force, of political right over arbitrary power, of human liberty over the chains of slavery, of moral law over social corruption, of order over anarchy, of enlightenment over ignorance, of life over death. As we survey that spectacle of the past, we are impressed that the study of history is the strongest evidence for God. We hear no argument from design, but we feel the breath of the designer. We see the universal life moulding the individual lives, the one will dominating the many wills, the infinite wisdom utilizing the finite folly, the changeless truth permeating the restless error, the boundless beneficence bringing blessing out of all.

"In the culture of the past Thou [Christ] art the only modern. None felt with Thee the sympathy for man as man. They felt for man as Greek, as Jew, as Roman; but not as man—not as hopeless, friendless, landless. Thou hast descended below all accidents—below race, and clime, and kindred. Thou hast gone down beneath all qualities—beneath beauty, and virtue, and fame. Thou hast broken the barriers of caste; Thou hast reached the last motive for charity—the right of hunger to bread. O Son of Man, Thou hast been before us. Thou hast outrun our philanthropy; Thou hast anticipated our benevolence; Thou hast forestalled our charity. Thou hast modelled our infirmaries; Thou hast planned our orphanages; Thou hast sketched our asylums; Thou hast devised our houses of refuge; Thou hast projected our homes of reform. Thou hast vindicated the claims of the returned convict; Thou hast asserted the sacredness of infant life; Thou hast given a hand to the climbing steps of woman. Thou hast outstripped both Peter and John in the race to the ancient sepulchres of humanity; at the end of all our progress we have met Thee."   REV. GEORGE MATHESON, D.D.

"If we have considered some of the temptations of the first Christians, if we know a little of the terrible environment of evil by which they were encircled, we must not, as we too often do, forget how they conquered the world. It was not by any despairing withdrawal from city and market; not by any proud isolation in selfish security; not by any impatient violence; but by the winning influence of gracious faith, they mastered the family, the school, the empire. They were a living Gospel, a message of God's good-will to those with whom they toiled and suffered. Pure among the self-indulgent, loving among the factious, tender among the ruthless, meek among the vainglorious, firm in faith amidst the shaking of nations, joyous in hope amidst the sorrows of a corrupt society, they revealed to men their true destiny, and showed that it could be attained."

BISHOP BROOKE FOSS WESTCOTT, D.D.

LECTURE VI

*

THE CONTRIBUTION OF CHRISTIAN MISSIONS TO SOCIAL PROGRESS

OUR survey of the function and efficiency of missions as instrumental in preparing the way for social changes, by introducing new forces, giving needed stimulus, and providing the unique equipment required, must now be supplemented by a more detailed review of present activities of a sociological import in many fields. Having studied the scope and fundamental conditions of social progress as affected by missions, let us now seek to enter the very workshop, inspect the tools, observe the machinery in motion, understand its processes, and see with our own eyes the results it produces. The subject is so multiform, our tour of inspection so extensive, and the variety of detail so bewildering, that a concise treatment of this theme is not possible except in a somewhat superficial and panoramic fashion. We must therefore beg the reader's indulgence if at times an unsatisfactory brevity or inadequacy of treatment seems to mark references to institutions and movements of great importance and noble practical usefulness.

There is little in this modest survey after the manner of those "drum and trumpet histories" referred to by Mr. Green in the introduction to his "History of the English People," yet there are voices here—quiet and unobtrusive it may be —which awaken nobler passions than those which are associated with military triumphs. There may appear to be a certain element of confusion in the clashing and commingling of so many currents of social influence, yet this is not untrue to the real facts of the case. Civilization grows complex as it advances, and, like the branches of a tree, ramifies and subdivides itself into many intricacies. If we picture to ourselves the living and varied

The historic value of missionary transformations.

103

streams of Christian influence which take their rise in mission fountains and push their way into bold contact and seemingly hopeless conflict with the mighty currents of heathen thought and life, we recognize the shifting, fitful, and somewhat confused phases of social results which must follow. Apparently the insignificant volume of those forces which represent the transforming and sweetening power of nobler ideals is absorbed and lost in the great rush and impetus of the dominant trend, but there is a persistency and a richness of spiritual essence in the springs of influence which God originates which will in the end purify and possess any higher life into which they may flow. There is at the present time no resultant of Christian civilization in the world which has not been thus clarified by long and patient struggle on the part of nobler elements introduced for that very purpose.

Let us note at the outset that we are not dealing in this connection primarily with the spiritual or evangelistic outcome of missions. We are endeavoring rather to ascertain and emphasize their more indirect results in the sphere of social reformation and progress. For the sake of convenience, as in our study of "The Social Evils of the Non-Christian World," the varied aspects of the subject may be classified into groups or clusters, and first among these we shall notice that in which personal character is chiefly affected.

I.—RESULTS MANIFEST IN THE INDIVIDUAL CHARACTER

In the ultimate analysis of society—to repeat a statement which has often been emphasized in these pages—the personal character is the stronghold of social virtue as well as of social vice. Whatever missions may do for communities and races must be done first in the individual members. We turn, therefore, with interest to scrutinize the results of mission work in transforming single lives into nobler and finer associate lives.

1. TEMPERANCE REFORM.—That intemperance is a curse to society is a truism in morals.[1] It destroys the character, the economic worth, and the practical usefulness of its victim, and turns him rather into a centre of demoralizing influences. He becomes, in fact, a dangerous

[1] A little volume by the Rev. A. E. Garvie, B.A., B.D., on "The Ethics of Temperance," is of special value in the study of this subject.

element, an incubus, and in the end an outcast from society.[1] It cannot be ignored in this connection that the introduction of intoxicants into non-Christian lands (especially Africa) is a crime for which the greed and depravity of unworthy representatives of civilization are largely responsible. It must be a relief to Christian sensibilities that missions the world over are contending earnestly against this giant curse.[2]

Great honor is here due to the world-wide efforts of the Woman's Christian Temperance Union, which has sent to the foreign fields a succession of accomplished missionary advocates of temperance to quicken devotion to principles and promote helpful adjustment of forces. Organized societies in Christian lands having in

A world-wide movement on behalf of temperance.

view the protection of native races from the ravages of strong drink have also accomplished a valuable service. The latter agencies are at present represented by a United Committee for the Prevention of the Demoralization of the Native Races by the Liquor Traffic—a Committee composed of representatives of twenty-one societies of a missionary, philanthropic, or temperance character. The story of the great polyglot petition of the World's Woman's Christian Temperance Union is well known,[3] and it was the testimony of the late Miss Frances E. Willard, the originator of the idea, that the organization of which she was the President had been greatly aided by missionaries in all parts of the world, whose sympathy and practical coöperation had been of the highest value. Her own words of testimony are notable: "It is needless to say that but for the intelligent and consecutive work of foreign missionaries, the World's W. C. T. U., now a living, organic force, would be merely a plan on paper." [4] The Aborigines Protection Society of England is giving careful attention to the drink traffic in Africa, as appears from its latest reports. Its keen sense of responsibility, and full recognition of the enormous dangers of the situation, appear in its memorials to the British Government, its public meetings, special literature, and practical efforts to stay the surging ravages of the

---

[1] Cf. "The Civilisation of Our Day," James Samuelson, editor, for an essay on "The Drink Question and Temperance Efforts," pp. 222–228.

[2] Cf. "The Drink Traffic and Foreign Missions," by the Rev. Frank S. Dobbins, in "Temperance in all Nations," vol. ii., p. 319.

[3] *Regions Beyond*, June, 1895, p. 260. Cf. article on "Woman's Work for Temperance," by Mrs. George Kerry (E. B. M. S.), in *The Indian Evangelical Review*, April, 1896, p. 445.

[4] *The Heathen Woman's Friend*, November, 1894, p. 129.

evil. The time limit of the general act of the Brussels Conference, fixed at six years from January, 1892, has now expired, and it will be the urgent aim of this and other organizations interested in the subject to secure some more effective action dealing with the liquor problem in Africa.[1]

In foreign fields, with hardly an exception, Christian missions have organized bands and societies for the advancement of temperance work and the restoration of the fallen, and are endeavoring through every channel of influence to restrict the manufacture and sale of intoxicants and to prevent their use by native converts. The cause of temperance has its place on the programme of missionary conferences. It is advocated in the papers and periodicals issued for circulation among natives, and has an honored prominence in mission literature.

An examination more in detail of the status in different mission fields may well turn our attention first to Africa. A noble personality, singularly wise and heroic, arises at once to greet us out of

Khama, and his brave crusade against strong drink. the deep shadows of what is fast becoming a rum-cursed continent. It is Khama, the native South African chief and Christian convert, who has exercised his authority in prohibiting the drink traffic within his domains.[2] He has recently (1895), with two other African chiefs, paid a visit to England, the purpose of which was to secure the maintenance of existing political relations with the British Government, and also to request its good offices in protecting his country from the threatened invasion of liquor. In this he seems happily to have succeeded, at least for the time being, having received the express commendation of the Queen in approval of his sturdy hostility to the entrance of intoxicants among his people, and being assured of the support of Her Majesty's Government in the endeavor to maintain his remarkable position on this question.[3] A despatch to the British

---

[1] *The Aborigines' Friend: Journal of the Aborigines Protection Society*, July, 1896, p. 36; May, 1897, p. 137.

[2] Cf. references to Khama on pages 14 and 15 of this volume.

[3] A character sketch, entitled "Khama: A Romance of Missions," will be found in *The Review of Reviews* (English edition) for October, 1895, which contains much of striking interest concerning the character and history of this notable African. Cf. also *The Chronicle* of the London Missionary Society, November, 1895, p. 285. In the latter periodical we find an account of a reception given to Khama at a Centenary Meeting of the London Missionary Society, and a report of the brief address he made upon the occasion, in which occur the following pointed sentences: "I have a request to make of the English Christians: to pray that we may be helped in the great and difficult task in which we are engaged. We are black, and when we come among white we seem to go astray; therefore I rejoice because of the help. I

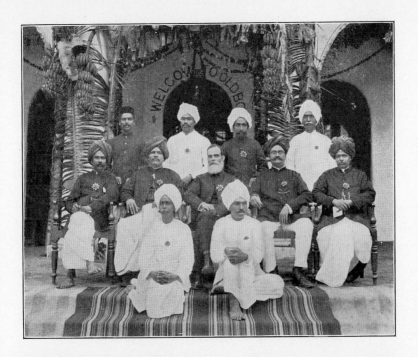

Photo by Russell & Sons, London.

High Caste Indian Christians.
(C. M. S.)

Khama and his attendant chiefs while on a visit to England in 1895. Rev. W. C. Willoughby
(L. M. S.), of Palapye, South Africa, standing on the right; Khama seated next to him.

NOTABLE GROUPS OF AFRICAN AND INDIAN CHRISTIANS.

authorities, previously written by this wise-hearted chief, is a unique State paper, and indicates the high-water mark of Christian statecraft where full play has been given to the moral power of missions. These are Khama's words: "It were better for me that I should lose my country than that it should be flooded with drink. Lobengula never gives me a sleepless night, but to fight against drink is to fight against demons, not against men. I dread the white man's drink more than all the *assegais* of the Matabele, which kill men's bodies, and it is quickly over; but drink puts devils into men and destroys both bodies and souls forever. Its wounds never heal. I pray your Honor never to ask me to open even a little door to drink."[1] It would be well for Christendom apparently if some of our foreign mission converts could have a hand in the legislation against the drink traffic which is so sadly needed outside of Africa. The heroic struggle of Khama still goes on, but as European demands grow exacting he finds his opposition more difficult to maintain. Will those who profess to represent civilization at last strike down the hero who is struggling to save his people from the power of a desolating scourge?[2]

rejoice especially because the Christian Church in England is making war against strong drink; therefore I say we have a common enemy whose name is Strong Drink. Let us fight him together. I personally have been engaged for years battling with this enemy, because I saw how it would destroy my people and my government. . . . In our country we have things that trouble us very much, and we do not know whether we shall live nicely in that country; but we look to God, for He knows all the circumstances. He knows how to conquer all things. May He conquer all evil things, so that we may go forward in all good things. I give thanks to Jesus for the way in which the Christian Churches have received us, and for what you do for us."

[1] Letter from Khama to Sir Sydney Sheppard, March 7, 1888, quoted in *The African News*, December, 1893, p. 12, and in *The Review of Reviews* (English edition), October, 1895, p. 303.

[2] The latest aspect of this strange warfare is a letter from Khama addressed to the United Committee on the Liquor Traffic, received by them early in 1897, which has been made the basis of an inquiry in the House of Commons as to whether any action would be allowed which might be in contravention of the pledges given to Khama by Her Majesty's Government. The point at issue was whether the Government would license refreshment-rooms on the railway passing through Khama's territory, thus making them public places for the sale of intoxicants. Khama's letter is as follows:

" To the Assembly of Those Who Help Nations of Strangers in Resisting Liquors:

"I have seen your letter and rejoiced. I rejoiced exceedingly as when I saw you in England, you who are big men; I am thankful because you stand in the word which you spoke to us in England. And concerning liquor, I am still

In passing we may contrast the principles which govern Khama
with those that have controlled the neighboring Boer Government in
the Transvaal, where the licensing of the drink traffic and the freedom
with which a native can obtain intoxicants have produced a shocking
prevalence of drunkenness.   It is reported that twenty-five per cent.
of the total number of native employees in the mining industry are
rendered unfit for work every day by liquor; and in an independent report, dated June 20, 1893, from the Manager of the Salis-
bury Mine, it is stated that "nearly half the natives were drunk or
incapacitated from the effects of the big drunk on Saturday."   For the
same reason a high percentage of fatal accidents is recorded, and it is
asserted that "the amount spent yearly on drink by natives on the Rand
cannot be estimated at less than a million and a half pounds, and it
more probably amounts to two millions."[1]   We leave it to the judgment of the reader as to whether the policy of Khama would not only
be the more Christian but also the more civilized attitude on the part
of the Government.

In other sections of South Africa a strenuous warfare is waged under
missionary leadership to check this terrible evil.   The Committee on
Temperance of the Synod of the Free Church
Mission in South Africa presented, in 1896, a telling report based upon detailed inquiry, showing
the almost unanimous attitude of opposition on
the part of native congregations to the traffic in intoxicants, and the
prevalence of total abstinence to a remarkable extent among all church-

Vigorous policy of the
native churches.

trying, but I do not think I can succeed.   Here in our country there are Europeans
who like liquor exceedingly, and they are not people who like to save a nation, but
to seek that a nation may be destroyed by liquor; and they are not people who like
to be persuaded in the matter of liquor; but you who are people of importance in
England, I know that you like to save people so that they may live in the land.   And
I cause you to know that we have seen the path of the train in our land.   And
concerning the path of the train, I rejoice exceedingly.   But I say concerning the
path of the train there is something in it which I do not like among you; it is the
little houses which will be in the path to sell liquor in them.   I do not like them,
for my people will buy liquor in them.   And I say help me in this matter, for it is
a thing which will kill the nation.   And I cause you to know, because you are
people who do not like nations to be destroyed in the land.   Now I end [my words].
I say be greeted, my honoured friends.   To see your ink is like seeing you in
England.   " Your friend,
                                                                             " KHAMA."

The Missionary Record, March, 1897, p. 97.

[1] Cf. article on " The Drink Question in the Transvaal," in *The Saturday Review*, March 20, 1897, p. 285.

members.[1]   In some churches this requirement is made a condition of membership.   In an account of temperance efforts among the Zulus it is stated that through the length and breadth of the mission of the American Board total abstinence is a fundamental rule of admission to church-membership.[2]   Work on behalf of temperance is successfully conducted in the Natal Mission of the American Board,[3] and in the Kaffraria Mission of the United Presbyterian Church of Scotland.[4] Concerning the policy of the missions around Lake Nyassa similar statements regarding the temperance movement might be given.   "At all the stations," writes the Rev. Donald Fraser, of the Livingstonia Mission of the Free Church of Scotland, "the Christians have of their own accord met and pronounced against the drinking of beer.   They see that drunkenness has been followed by murder, uncleanness, and foolish talking, and that the whole country is being devastated, in order to raise the beer crop, so they have agreed together and said, 'We will neither make beer nor drink it.'"   As foreign intoxicants have not yet penetrated to the interior sections of the Continent, where access is difficult, the question of temperance has not assumed the importance in the Church Missionary Society's work in Uganda which we may expect it will later when the completion of the railway shall make that region accessible to traders.[5]   It is interesting

---

[1] *The Christian Express* (Lovedale), October 1, 1896, p. 147.

[2] *Life and Light for Woman*, June, 1894, p. 265.

[3] " A temperance society in our mission has done great good.   It is called ' The Blue Ribbon Movement.'   It began about fifteen years ago.   A great many have become abstainers who are not members of any church, but it is expected that members of our mission churches should take this pledge.   It reads like this : ' I promise to give up all native beer, and also to abstain from all other intoxicating drinks.   I ask God to help me to keep this pledge.' "—Miss Gertrude Hance (A. B. C. F. M.), Esidumbini, Natal, South Africa.

[4] " A new feature of our work is to be found in the Band of Hope.   This temperance movement originated among the women.   On February 25th the leading women of the church from various out-stations, to the number of about forty, met here [Mbonda] for the purpose of forming the Band.   This branch of our work is directly under the superintendence of Mrs. Soga.   At the initial meeting thirty-one names were affixed to the roll.   Branches have since been started at most of the out-stations, and much good has resulted in the way of strengthening and purifying the characters and lives of many of the church-members and others.   At present there are about one hundred and fifty names on the roll."—" Report of the United Presbyterian Church of Scotland Foreign Mission Board, 1897," p. 38.

[5] The views of Bishop Tucker are worthy of note just here as revealing the personal attitude of this leader of missions in East Central Africa towards the question of temperance.   He says : " I have been a teetotaller for twenty years.   So far from regretting it, I would commence it sooner if I had the chance again.   I find

to note, however, that already temperance societies are being formed among the Christian natives, with a view to the restriction among them of the use of indigenous intoxicants.[1] Mr. R. H. Leakey, of Koki, in Uganda, reports that "about ninety per cent. of the adults are more or less addicted to drinking, but happily nearly all the Christians are total abstainers." [2]

The whole West Coast of the Continent, in practical defiance of the Brussels Act of 1890–91, has been cursed by the desolations of the rum traffic. This Act professed to regulate the supply

The social aspects of the rum traffic in Africa.

of spirituous liquors to natives in different parts of Africa, but it has proved to be so inoperative that its efficiency has been of little value, especially along the coast-line and in sections of the Congo Valley. The interior regions, either on account of difficulty of access or government prohibition (as in the Niger territories and part of the Congo State),[3] are little touched by the scourge. We note this paragraph in a recent number of *The Christian:* "Mr. Chamberlain has given the matter of the liquor traffic on the coast of Africa great consideration, and finds that eighty per cent. of the total revenue of the Niger Coast Protectorate, and sixty per cent. of the revenue of the Gold Coast and Lagos, are derived from the liquor trade."[4] There is reason to hope that the British Foreign Office will make the effort to secure an international agreement with a view to the limitation of the traffic. Sir George T. Goldie, K.C.M.G., President of the Royal Niger Company, has recently said that he has "long been convinced that the whole African movement will end in failure, unless European spirits are practically excluded." He characterizes the rum traffic as "by far the most im-

that in Africa not only is a teetotaller better fitted to cope with the climate, but he is better fitted for the great physical exercise which he has to undergo. I have marched some ten thousand miles in Africa, and have never felt the want of anything like a stimulant. Indeed, I feel sure that if I had not been a teetotaller it would have been impossible to undergo the fatigue involved in some of the marching." The Bishop is said to have walked about a thousand miles in a recent pastoral visit.

1 *The Church Missionary Intelligencer,* July, 1893, p. 506.
2 " Report of Church Missionary Society, 1897," p. 136.
3 " The Statesman's Year-Book, 1897," p. 195.
4 *The Christian,* June 17, 1897. This statement concerning the Niger Coast Protectorate should not be understood as referring to the Royal Niger Company's Territories, where the importation of liquor is prohibited above the seventh degree of north latitude—thanks, we believe, largely to the personal influence of Sir George T. Goldie. " Report of Church Missionary Society, 1897," p. 64.

Native Teachers.

Theological Class of the
Adams Training School.

Girls' School Building.

Graduating Class, 1897.

Pupils in Girls' School, Adams.

IN TRAINING FOR CHRISTIAN LIFE IN SOUTH AFRICA.

(A. B. C. F. M.)

portant African topic of the day." [1] It is interesting to note in this connection that throughout all the missions of the West Coast of Africa there is a vigilant and vigorous temperance movement to arrest the ravages of this dread enemy of the African. In the Congo Valley, the missions of the American Baptist Missionary Union have instituted severe prohibitive measures upon the subject of intemperance, requiring total abstinence of all church-members. "We fought for temperance," says the Rev. Henry Richards, in a recent report of his station, Banza Manteka, "and now we have a strictly temperance church." [2] If we pass to Egypt and the northern coast of the Continent, we find missions to be the same saving power, and almost the only thoroughgoing and consistent influence in favor of abstinence. [3] It may be said, in fact, that Christian missions in Africa are fighting the battle of temperance with zeal, and that they represent a most important phase of organized effort in that direction.

In the neighboring Island of Madagascar we discover the Malagasy Christian Woman's Temperance Society, with its fine record of courageous and devoted service on behalf of sobriety. The French commander had hardly established himself as the military master of the island when, to his surprise, he was visited by a deputation of native Christian women, not in a spirit of fear with a timid plea for mercy and forbearance, but as representing the Madagascar Branch of the World's Woman's Christian Temperance Union, to thank him for his stringent regulations concerning the sale of intoxicants. [4] "As regards temperance," writes the Rev. James Sibree

Courageous friends of temperance in Madagascar.

[1] *The Missionary Record,* August, 1895, p. 228. Cf. article by Major F. W. Lugard, on "The Liquor Traffic in Africa," in *The Nineteenth Century,* November, 1897.

[2] *The Baptist Missionary Magazine,* July, 1894, p. 353.

[3] "Another evil of widespread power among the native Christian sects, when our mission began, was intemperance. Although it was a rare thing to see a drunken man on the streets, yet drunkenness and debauchery were prevalent among the Copts. I am very happy to say that there has been a wonderful improvement in this regard, and I am not afraid to assert that this amendment is entirely due to the influence of mission work in the schools and churches, and to the dissemination of Christian literature, and also in no small degree to the personal efforts of missionaries with the people in their homes. I am sorry, however, to have to say that the habit of drinking has rather increased than otherwise among the Mohammedan inhabitants, because while they naturally avoid contact with the missionaries, they are brought into close relationship with the foreign drinking populations in connection with business and government work."—Rev. Andrew Watson, D.D. (U. P. C. N. A.), Cairo, Egypt.

[4] *The Missionary Review of the World,* June, 1896, p. 430.

(L. M. S.), of Antananarivo, "a large number of people have now taken the pledge, and there is a body of women workers who are earnest and zealous in holding meetings for the cause." Where is there, by the way, a temperance society which for its size can present a more inspiring and creditable report than one just received from the busy headquarters of the Malagasy Christian Woman's Temperance Society? [1]

In the South Sea Islands "the fight against intemperance has been resolutely waged by our missionaries." [2] This legend might stand for all mission work in the South Seas, from the time

A resolute fight in the South Seas.

of John Williams, when European traders began their nefarious introduction of intoxicants. There is no darker stain on the history of commerce than the persistent efforts of traders to purchase the native products with ardent spirits. In this they were only too successful, and the disease of drunkenness swept over the islands. Nearly everywhere the work was thrown back, and "but for these little handfuls of true and faithful Christians the whole race might have gone back into savagery." [3] From that time (1836) onward to the present, temperance strict and uncompromising has been the watchword of missions in the Pacific Islands. In Apia, Samoa, which is popularly known among the sailors of the South Seas as the "Hell of the Pacific," the London Missionary Society has opened a coffee-house and free reading-room especially for foreign sailors, and reports that there are flourishing Gospel Temperance and Christian Endeavor Societies in connection with the Apia church. [4] We read that in the Gilbert Islands, where the American Board is at work, one of the group, Butaritari, has a Christian king, and that in his realm "strict temperance laws are en-

1 Here is a brief summary of its annual report: " (1) Some of the members have diligently visited people in their homes and conversed with them about the evils of drinking, and every two months the work accomplished is reported to the committee. In this way 311 persons have been induced to sign the pledge. (2) Some members visited the owners of houses where rum was sold, and with the exception of two, who said, 'I will think about it,' all so visited promised to discontinue the sale of drink in their houses. (3) In the month of May the Society held services in the churches in town, and obtained 87 pledges. (4) Some members undertook to hold meetings in the country places. This work was very heartily taken up, and everywhere the workers were well received. The pledges taken at these meetings were 1690. (5) Others offered to go to distant places, and the results have been very remarkable. During the year, 12,055 pledges were taken."
— The Missionary Record, March, 1896, p. 92.

2 Horne, "The Story of the London Missionary Society," p. 229.

3 Ibid., p. 51.   4 The Chronicle, May, 1897, p. 112.

forced among the natives, but the white foreigners keep an open saloon in defiance of law." No wonder that the writer of the above sentence asks, "Who are the pagans?" The king appealed to the English, who have assumed a protectorate over the islands, to help him in executing his law against the foreign transgressors.[1] In the Caroline Islands a notable temperance status among the natives had been established before the Spanish occupation in 1887. Of Pingelap it was said that liquor was "banished from the island." The Rev. E. T. Doane wrote concerning Ponape before the coming of the Spaniards, that the making of intoxicating drinks and the traffic in the same had ceased.[2]

In the New Zealand House of Representatives a young Maori chief, who represents his race, has been pushing for legislation that will protect his fellow-countrymen. He pleads for the following striking clause to be added to the Licensing Act of the colony: "That no intoxicating liquor be sold or given to any man of the native race, and that no license be renewed or fresh license be granted within a mile of Maori-land."[3] A petition, in regard to which it is stated that it was signed by thirty of the chiefs and over sixty other representative natives, was recently addressed to the Maori Parliament, which in response forwarded an official appeal to the New Zealand Government, urging the addition of the foregoing clause.[4] At the Centenary of the London Missionary Society (1895) the Rev. James Chalmers, one of its missionaries in New Guinea, made an earnest plea for the entire suppression of the liquor traffic among native races, and reported from his own field that Sir William Macgregor, the excellent Governor of New Guinea, was strictly enforcing his prohibitive law against the selling or giving of strong drink to the natives.

Protection of native races in New Zealand, New Guinea, and Formosa.

On our way to Japan we touch at the Island of Formosa for a word of information from Dr. MacKay, of the Canadian Presbyterian Mission. "On the east coast of Formosa," he says, "I have planted a dozen churches amongst drunken aborigines. The change in the villages since has been amazing. The heathen Chinese around have a common saying that 'the aborigines are now men and women.'"

[1] *The Missionary Herald*, June, 1893, p. 232.
[2] See article by the Rev. E. E. Strong, D.D., on "Spain and the Caroline Islands," in *The American Monthly Review of Reviews*, June, 1898, pp. 706-709.
[3] *Abkari*, October, 1895, p. 108.
[4] *The Sentinel*, July, 1897, p. 86.

The Rev. W. Gauld, also of the Canadian Presbyterian Mission, reports that there is great improvement in the native Christian community with reference to temperance.   Among the non-Christian population of the island, both Chinese and aborigines, except where mission influence has gained the upper hand, there is unhappily an increasing tendency to drunkenness, especially in the ports where foreign liquors are offered for sale.

In Japan there is a vigorous temperance movement, which is not by any means confined to Christian circles.   The history of Christianity in the empire, however, shows that it has taken a pronounced and leading part in advocacy of this reform, and, in the opinion of those who have long resided there, it is the source and promoter of temperance ideas among all classes.   The Rev. Albert Arnold Bennett (A. B. M. U.), of Yokohama, wrote, in 1895, that there were four principal Christian temperance societies in Japan, the Yokohama, Tokyo, Hokkaido, and Teikoku, with an average membership of about 2500 each, and also about eighty others, in which the membership averaged 75 each, making a total of about 16,000 members.   In *The Japan Evangelist* for September, 1897, we find mention of six Christian temperance organizations.   As this data is some two years later than the report given by Mr. Bennett, progress is evident.   Steps have just been taken to form a union of temperance societies by the appointment of a Central Committee, with Dr. Soper, of the Methodist Episcopal Mission, as President.[1]   A further organization into a National Alliance, including all the temperance societies of the empire, is about to be consummated.   There is also a Buddhist temperance society, which is said to number about 30,000 members, half of whom bind themselves to total abstinence, and the remainder take the same pledge either for a limited time, or with special reference to certain Buddhist ceremonies during which drink habits are prevalent.   These larger societies issue periodicals of their own.[2]   The zealous apostle of temperance in the Hokkaido, or "Northland" of Japan, is Mr. Kazutaka Ito, the first

[1] See article on "More Advanced Steps in the Line of Temperance Reform," in *The Japan Evangelist*, September, 1897, pp. 358–361. Cf. also article by the Rev. Julius Soper in *The Independent*, December 16, 1897, p. 17.

[2] "Much has been said and written by the Christians in Japan against the use of liquor, and there are some of the churches that make total abstinence a requisite for admission.   There are thousands of temperance people now in the country, and the weight of Christian teaching and example is doing much to check the great evil. On one of the islands of Japan the sale and use of intoxicating drinks are entirely forbidden.   See *The Japan Evangelist* for December, 1894, p. 64, article by Dr.

convert to Christianity in Sapporo.[1] The pioneer temperance society in that northern island was organized by Christian converts, and Mr. Ito was elected its president. Among the Ainu, who are specially given to drink,[2] it has now a branch, and the movement has spread throughout the Hokkaido, being represented by many auxiliaries.

Christian laborers in the employ of the Japanese railways are organizing Industrial Temperance Societies. Interesting accounts are given in some of the Japanese periodicals of earnest and sustained efforts on the part of many prominent native Christians to establish and foster temperance organizations. Besides the work Japanese Christians the leading spirits in temperance reform. of Mr. Ito, previously referred to, zealous service is rendered by Mrs. Yajima, Vice-President of the Central Committee, who was active in the formation of the first *Kyofukwai*, or temperance union, in Japan, and was its first president,[3] by Mr. Miyama, who is called "the John B. Gough of Japan,"[4] and by Mr. Taro Ando, of Tokyo, who has recently established a monthly temperance journal, and is himself active in this special reform. We read also of the organization by Miss Elizabeth Russell, of the Methodist Mission, of a Y. W. C. T. U. in the boarding-school for girls at Nagasaki. This Union numbers at the present time one hundred and eighty members, and there are still others at Kobe, and in the Bancho Girls' School at Tokyo.[5] Here is a significant incident reported by the Rev. Albert Arnold Bennett, writing from Yokohama. In speaking of a number of recent baptisms, he says: "One of the five baptized last Sunday had been away four years studying the manufacture of wines and other liquors, and expected to do quite a business in that line. We feared his faith would not hold out when he was told he must give up such trade if he became a Christian, but he did stop, and is now seeking a business that will not work ruin."[6]

It is of interest to note in this connection an historical fact reported

---

Soper, entitled 'Japanese Religious Workers.' "—Rev. Henry Loomis (A. B. S.), Yokohama, Japan.

"As to sobriety—drinking largely prevails in Japan, but Christianity enforces temperance in the churches, by the organization of temperance societies, and the requirement of temperance on the part of teachers and scholars in schools."—Rev. R. L. Halsey (A. B. M. U.), Shimonoseki, Japan.

[1] *The Japan Evangelist*, December, 1894, pp. 64–69.
[2] Batchelor, "The Ainu of Japan," pp. 30, 31.
[3] *The Japan Evangelist*, February, 1896, pp. 170–172.
[4] *Ibid.*, June, 1897, p. 282.   [5] *Ibid.*, June, 1897, pp. 282, 283.
[6] *The Baptist Missionary Magazine*, January, 1892, p. 24.

by the Rev. D. S. Spencer, of Nagoya: "At the time of concluding commercial treaties with the Tokugawa Government, the American representative, Mr. Townsend Harris, earnestly advised the Japanese Government to restrict the importation of opium to fifteen pounds per boat, and to put thirty per cent. duty on imported liquor. Japan has profited by following this advice, since the result has been largely to keep out opium and greatly to reduce the quantity of imported liquors. Still the amount received through Yokohama in 1893 was 3500 *koku* (one *koku* equals forty gallons), 5500 *koku* in 1894, and 14,000 *koku* in 1895." This statement indicates a rapid increase in the importation of liquors.

In China the opium evil overshadows the temptation to strong drink. The Chinese as a nation may be regarded as temperate, although not generally total abstainers. In the treaty ports, however, and where foreign intoxicants are introduced, their use is largely on the increase. In many sections of China drunkenness is classed by the missionaries with opium-smoking, and warfare is waged upon both together. "We have temperance societies here," reports the Rev. Charles Hartwell (A. B. C. F. M.), of Foochow, "some of them with three pledges, against opium, tobacco, and alcoholic drinks." The best-known temperance pledge now in use in China is against both wine and opium.[1] There is a National Woman's Christian Temperance Union in China, of which Mrs. J. M. Farnham, an American Presbyterian missionary of Shanghai, is President, and in many of the churches temperance societies have been formed,[2] while in a number of the schools temperance text-books are in use.[3]

In the great realm of India all mission efforts on behalf of this reform are much facilitated and aided by the work of the Anglo-

Chinese Christians no friends of opium or of strong drink.

[1] The following is the form of the pledge: "I . . . voluntarily promise as long as I live not to use wine as a beverage, not to use opium, and to exhort others not to use them; further, that I will not traffic in them. Trusting in the Lord for help, I will forever keep the pledge, and hereby voluntarily sign my name and testimony. . . ."

[2] " Our people have formed a temperance society, and not a few have signed the pledge never to taste any kind of intoxicating drink, and to discourage its use at feasts and at all times."—Rev. Hunter Corbett, D.D. (P. B. F. M. N.), Chefoo, China.

[3] " In many boarding-schools 'temperance text-books' are now used, with special effort to show the ill effects of the use of strong drink, opium, and other vices, on the organs of the body."—Rev. J. C. Garritt (P. B. F. M. N.), Hangchow, China.

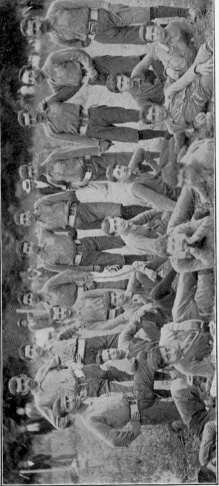

First Temperance Society in Bithynia High School, Bardezag.　　　Football Players, Bithynia High School.

TEMPERANCE AND ATHLETICS IN ASIA MINOR.

(A. B. C. F. M.)

Indian Temperance Association, a society formed in 1889 for the promotion of temperance in India. It has wrought well, with the hearty coöperation of many distinguished natives of India, among whom may be mentioned Mr. Bepin Chandra Pal, Mr. P. L. Nagpurkar, and others, including the late Mahant Kesho Ram Roy,[1] who A growing temperance sentiment in India. served the cause of temperance in India with great eloquence and devotion. According to a recent report (1897) of this Association, it has 260 Indian temperance societies affiliated with it, and over 200,000 pledged abstainers. In 1894 it reported the formation of 53 new societies, in 1896 of 22, and in 1897 of nearly 30. Its indefatigable Secretary, Mr. W. S. Caine, M.P., visited India in the winter of 1896–97, and awakened new interest in the cause. There are also about 90 lodges of the Independent Order of Good Templars, others of the Order of the Rechabites, and a flourishing Army Temperance Association, independently organized, with a present average membership of 23,711, which is thirty-five per cent. of the entire British Army in India.[2] The Rev. Thomas Evans, of Mussoorie, formerly a Baptist missionary, has done yeoman's service in this cause throughout the length and breadth of India, chiefly in connection with the Anglo-Indian Temperance Association.

The Excise Department of the British Government in India involves many complex and difficult problems. Its regulations are defended by some,[3] but sharply denounced by almost all temperance reformers. It is not possible to discuss here the questions involved. It

[1] " Some five years ago, a remarkable movement took place in Benares. In connexion with our association we had a temperance meeting in the town hall, at which, besides my colleague and myself, the Rev. Thomas Evans, a Baptist missionary, and Mr. W. S. Caine, M.P., were the speakers. Among the audience was a Brahman, Mahant Kesho Ram Roy by name, who had been taught in a mission school. He was so impressed by what he heard that, of his own accord, he set about trying to reform some of the castes most addicted to drinking. He got the head men of these several castes together, and persuaded them to make rules against intemperance among their fellow-castemen. All this he carried on for weeks without our help or knowledge. Since then, with our sympathy and advice and occasional help, he has carried on the work—writing books and tracts on temperance, and lecturing in neighboring towns. As the outcome of his efforts, there are now between forty and fifty thousand members of temperance societies in the Benares Division, and the sale of spirits has fallen off to a very considerable extent."—Rev. D. Hutton (L. M. S.), Mirzapur, North India.

[2] *Abkari*, July, 1897, p. 74.

[3] Dr. R. N. Cust, who was formerly a British official in India, and has had much to do with excise regulations, declares them to be conceived in practical wisdom, and with a view to the welfare of the country. While thus defending the government system, he does not deny the immense evils of intemperance in India, and fixes

is sufficient to note that the excise revenue of India has more than doubled in twenty years. In 1874–75 it was £2,633,000; in 1894–95 it was £5,528,000.[1] When we take into consid-

Excise problems of the Indian Government.

eration the fact that total abstinence is the general rule with the great mass of the Indian population, and that the consumption of liquor is confined to about fifty millions, an added significance is given to this lamentable increase of the drink traffic. The various systems of Indian excise are fully explained in a little pamphlet entitled "A Brief Sketch of Our Indian Excise Administration," which is published at the Mafasilite Press, Mussoorie, India. Whether what is known as "farming"—that is, selling the exclusive right of the liquor traffic to some contractor in a designated area—or what is called "the central distillery system" —that is, the establishment of great government distilleries to the exclusion of all private manufacture—or what is named as "the out-still system"—that is, the renting of the distilling right to those who will pay for it—is adopted, the result seems to be one and the same—a constant increment to the business. Of these different methods "the central distillery system" appears to be the least objectionable. Still another expedient in vogue, chiefly in the Bombay Presidency, is known as "the minimum guarantee system." The contractor who, under this arrangement, obtains his privileges through public competition, engages to manufacture a certain amount annually, and if he is not able to dispose of it, to pay the Government the duty on the full amount. The curious result in this case is that while the contractor engages to supply a so-called "minimum" number of gallons, yet invariably the man whose bid promises the highest number as his pledged output is the one who obtains the contract.[2]

Temperance reform in India, therefore, whatever may be true of its inception, is not at present exclusively a phase of Christian missions, as many non-Christian natives of distinction, and multitudes of others

the blame upon merchants who trade in foreign intoxicants by importing vast quantities into the country. "Notes on Missionary Subjects," Part II., essay on "The Liquor Traffic in British India," pp. 121–164. *Per contra*, see a trenchant letter from the Rev. Thomas Evans, on "The Indian Government and the Drink Question," *Abkari*, October, 1895, p. 104.

[1] "Report of the Anglo-Indian Temperance Association for 1896–97." See *Abkari*, July, 1897, p. 75.

[2] Cf. "A Brief Sketch of Our Indian Excise Administration," by A Loyal Briton and a Friend to the People of India, published at the Mafasilite Press, Mussoorie, N. W. P., India. See also an article on "Excise in Bengal," by Bepin Chandra Pal, of Calcutta, in *Abkari*, July, 1897, p. 84.

less distinguished among the people, are its friends and supporters. It may be truly said, however, that mission agents at the beginning, and even now, are in the forefront of Indian temperance effort.   At the last Decennial Con- Christian missions in the forefront of Indian temperance effort. ference in Bombay, a public temperance meeting was held, in which the subject was discussed with enthusiasm and vigor.   The Rev. Arthur Parker (L. M. S.) asserted that in some instances entire Indian castes had pledged themselves to total abstinence as a formal rule, and further reported: "We reckon now sixty thousand persons in the lower castes of Benares pledged to either partial or total abstinence." [1]   This social movement is not by any means confined to the lower orders, as the Anglo-Indian Association in a late report mentions thirty-eight Kayastha temperance societies and clubs in affiliation with itself.   The various somajes have had an active and influential part in Indian temperance agitation, and lend their powerful aid to the Anglo-Indian Temperance Association. The great Indian reformers, with hardly an exception, have been advocates of this movement.   It is stated, upon the authority of a prominent member, that "in the Brahmo Somaj there is not a single person who is guilty of intemperance." [2]   The Rev. R. A. Hume (A. B. C. F. M.) was the founder of the Bombay Temperance Union, which in connection with various other organizations has become part of what is known as the Bombay Temperance Council, inaugurated in December, 1896. [3]

"Mission work," writes the Rev. James M. Macphail (F. C. S.), of Chakai, Bengal, "has had a remarkable effect in creating a conscience on this matter, even among those of the Santals who have not yet embraced Christianity.   As a rule, when they become Christians they give up voluntarily and entirely the use of intoxicants."   A Canadian Baptist missionary, the Rev. John Craig, of Akidu, states: "In this mission we are all total abstainers, and expect our converts to follow our example.   We have reason to believe that very many of them do so.   Many missionaries are helping in the prohibition movement. I am trying to stir up the Sudras and others to petition for the closing of liquor-shops in the various villages.   Nearly every one admits that they bring only loss."   "At Ongole," writes Mrs. Ellen M. Kelly (A. B. M. U.), "we have a Christian Temperance League, to which both men and women are admitted as members.   In our Christian com-

---

[1] "Report of the Bombay Conference, 1892–93," p. 756.
[2] *Abkari*, October, 1894, pp. 151, 152.
[3] *Ibid.*, January, 1897, p. 7.

munity here total abstinence is insisted upon." The Arcot Mission of the Reformed Church of America is stated by the Rev. Dr. Chamberlain, its veteran missionary, to be "in itself a total abstinence society. No missionary joins it, no native assistant enters its employ, without thereby taking the pledge. No members are received to the Church without pledging total abstinence." In connection with the summary of results at the recent jubilee celebration of the Gossner Mission among the Kols, it was reported that although drunkenness had not entirely disappeared, yet among the Christians eighty-five per cent. avoided all use of spirits.[1] In many of the higher educational institutions temperance societies are formed, as, for example, in St. John's College (C. M. S.), Agra, where it is said that "more than two hundred of the students are members of the Students' Temperance Association."[2]

In Assam the missionaries of the American Baptist Missionary Union have waged a most successful campaign against intoxicants. In all their churches, and in many of the villages where Christians reside, total abstinence is the rule.[3] In some of the large tea-estates special temperance work has been established.[4] "Christianity is the only way of salvation for this country in respect to intoxicants, since the heathen are becoming more and more addicted to their use." Thus writes the Rev. Robert Evans, of Mawphlang, and he adds: "But there are some thousands of Christians in our churches who refrain from liquor altogether, and their children are brought up

Christians almost to a man total abstainers in Assam and Burma.

---

[1] *The Mission World*, February, 1896, p. 79.

[2] " Report of Church Missionary Society, 1897," p. 205.

[3] *The Baptist Missionary Magazine*, September, 1892, p. 404; Bailey, "A Glimpse at the Indian Mission Field," p. 69.

[4] "'I began work in a tea-estate a few years ago. The manager, an Englishman, was not at all favorably inclined towards mission work. But hear his testimony. He said: 'Before, the people were awful drunkards, and Sunday, when work stopped on the tea-garden, was a day of drunkenness and rioting; but since a good number have become Christians on the estate, all is quiet on Sundays, and the Christians are sober and total abstainers.' In one large Kol village, called Bebejia, all the inhabitants, Christians and heathen, have become total abstainers from intoxicants, and fine heavily all transgressors. This is perhaps the only abstaining village in India. The majority of its inhabitants have become Christians. All our converts promise to be total abstainers before we baptize them. They are a well-to-do, prosperous people, whereas before becoming Christians they spent a great deal of money for liquors and opium."—Rev. C. E. Petrick (A. B. M. U.), Sibsagor, Assam.

without knowing the taste of it." The same is true of Burma, where missionaries of the American Baptist Missionary Union also labor. "The thirty thousand communicants," writes the Rev. W. I. Price, of Henzada, "are almost that number of total abstainers from the use of intoxicating liquors. No sin or misdemeanor is more promptly dealt with by the Karen churches than the use of intoxicants as a beverage." Another missionary of the same society, the Rev. W. F. Thomas, of Insein, in speaking of the attitude of the churches to temperance, affirms that "total abstinence from all that intoxicates forms a plank in the membership of every church connected with our Mission, among the Burmese as well as among the hill tribes, who were universally addicted in their heathen days to the use of drink. So resolute are the churches in enforcing their restrictive principles that there is not the call for the W. C. T. U. in this country that there is elsewhere." Total abstinence is declared by the Rev. D. A. W. Smith, D.D., a colleague of Mr. Thomas at Insein, to be "the first benefit of a public character which the Gospel has brought to the Karens." In the neighboring kingdom of Siam, up in the deep recesses of the Laos country, a missionary of the American Presbyterian Board, the Rev. W. C. Dodd, reports that the "Lao church is a body of teetotalers. Wherever Christianity has been accepted and practised by the people it has reformed the victims of strong drink. I think, too, that a public sentiment against intemperance is being aroused in the regions contiguous to our mission stations." "The Church in Siam," writes Miss Mary L. Cort, formerly of the Presbyterian Mission, "is itself a great temperance society."

If we turn now to Western Asia, we find that missions in the Turkish Empire have created a strong sentiment in favor of abstinence, and have put under a decided social ban in many communities the habit, all but universal years ago, of offering wine and arrack to callers. The custom has disappeared almost entirely from Protestant families, and also from many not included in the Protestant community.[1] "It is an interesting fact," writes the Rev. J. L. Barton, D.D., for many years a missionary in Asiatic Turkey, "that when the Gospel was received by the people they read therein the necessity of temperance; the churches began to advocate it, although it was opposed to the customs of the country, and in many places the total abstinence pledge was demanded from those who wished to become members of

A strong temperance sentiment in mission churches throughout Turkey and Persia.

[1] Dr. George C. Raynolds (A. B. C. F. M.), Van, Turkey.

the Church." [1]   In Persia, as elsewhere, the obligation of temperance has come with the prevalence of Christian teaching.   An incident connected with the revival of 1893 in Urumiah, related by the Rev. F. G. Coan, clearly illustrates this fact.   The Gospel had wrought powerfully in a Persian village not far from Urumiah, and as the grape crop that year had been unusually prolific, the native houses were full of wine, which, as the people knew, would find a ready sale elsewhere. So strangely powerful was the temperance sentiment created in the village by the work of the Holy Spirit that they with one mind determined upon the destruction of their wine crop rather than that its sale should foster intemperance.   It was surely a marvelous spectacle for Persia when immediately after a church service the entire community poured its wine into the gutter as a tribute to the newly awakened conviction concerning the Christian obligation to promote temperance. [2]

From Western Asia, if we journey across the seas, to the English and Scotch Missions in the West Indies, we find substantially the same record as to the influence of missions in promoting temperance. The Rev. James Cochrane (U. P. C. S. M.), of Jamaica, reports that "temperance associations of one kind or another are common all over

[1] " The fifty thousand Protestants of Asia Minor have been largely saved from the evils of intemperance—evils which have pressed sorely upon the non-Protestant population, especially upon the Greeks of the Orthodox Church.   Moreover, the example of the Protestants in this respect has had a salutary effect upon other communities, and but for the unhappy influence of certain European residents settled, or located temporarily, in Turkey, the example of the native Protestants would have been still more impressive."—Rev. J. K. Greene, D.D. (A. B. C. F. M.), Constantinople, Turkey.

The following interesting item is given by one of the medical missionaries of the American Board in Aintab: " The work among the intemperate here in Aintab is unique.   Four years ago a daughter of one of the native pastors, trained in the missionary school, and afterwards a teacher in the Girls' Seminary, went to London to take a course in midwifery.   On returning, her attention was called to the great increase in intemperance, and after holding a series of meetings especially for the women, she decided to open a temperance crusade.   She invited a general attendance at a meeting appointed for a certain time, and in that meeting, she, an unmarried woman, addressed the men.   The audiences increased, not only Christians going, but Gregorians as well, and she soon had a band of a hundred men who had signed the pledge.   There was much commotion.   The Gregorian priests forbade their flock to attend the meetings, but her quiet persistency has overcome all resistance.   Singing has been an important factor in attracting new-comers, and lectures are given frequently, both by the college professors and the physicians. The work is steadily growing, and we hope for much.   This credit surely belongs to Christian missions, as Miss Krikerian owes all her training to our missionaries."—Dr. Caroline F. Hamilton (A. B. C. F. M.), Aintab, Turkey.

[2] *Woman's Work for Woman*, October, 1893, p. 272.

Students in Teachers' Training College, Fairfield, Jamaica.

Students in Training College, St. Thomas, West Indies.

Pupils in Girls' School, Bluefields, Nicaragua.

DISCIPLES OF CHRISTIAN FAITH AND TEMPERATE LIVING IN THE WEST INDIES.
(M. M. S.)

the island, and their membership is creditably and gratifyingly large."
The Rev. J. Morton, D.D., of the Canadian Presbyterian Church
Mission in Trinidad, says: "We have temperance
societies, but they are almost a part of the church   Moral fruitage of
work and life." A total abstinence association is   missions in the West
mentioned as one of the features of the English   Indies.
Baptist Mission in Jamaica.[1] From the little Island of Ruatan, in the
Caribbean Sea, thirty miles off the coast of Honduras, where the
English Wesleyan Methodists are established, a missionary writes that
he has started two Gospel Temperance Societies, and that "they are
going with a real swing, a large number of candidates for initiation
being constantly before them. In fact, drunkenness has so decreased
that the chief official is reported to have said: 'We used to sell two
thousand bottles of liquor a month in the Bay Islands; now we sell
only six hundred.' "[2]

In Central America, under the auspices of the Rev. E. M. Haymaker, a Presbyterian missionary at Guatemala City, "a temperance
and general improvement society for laboring
classes has been organized." Entertaining and   Organized efforts in
profitable methods of interesting the people have   Central America and
been devised, with a view to protecting them upon   Mexico.
holidays and feast-days from the inevitable temptation to intemperance.[3]
The first temperance society in Mexico was organized in the City of
Guanajuato, in 1878, by the Rev. S. P. Craver, of the Methodist
Episcopal Mission at Puebla. He also published a series of articles on
temperance in the leading daily paper of the City of Mexico. There
have since been numerous societies formed by the missionaries, and
a few by others connected with mission work. The Rev. Hubert
W. Brown (P. B. F. M. N.), of Mexico City, writes of the high
percentage of alcohol in some of the distilled liquors used in Mexico, and their great intoxicating properties, especially what is known
as *agua ardiente, tequila*, and *mexcal*. He states that a decided growth
in temperance sentiment is apparent, even since he took up his residence in Mexico thirteen years ago. The recent visit of Mrs. Helen
H. Stoddard, of the W. C. T. U., resulted in the establishment of
many branches of the White Ribbon Army, and her lectures in all the
principal cities of the central table-land have given a stimulus to the

---

[1] " Handbook of Jamaica, 1894," p. 353.
[2] *Work and Workers in the Mission Field*, April, 1896, p. 165.
[3] *The Church at Home and Abroad*, March, 1895, p. 222.

cause.[1]   Mr. Brown adds: "Many men, women, and children have signed the total abstinence pledge. Mrs. Stoddard was well received, not alone by the missionary societies, but also in the government schools, in which she was allowed to speak, and the Mexican press commented favorably upon the movement."

In South America, where intemperance is so prevalent, missionary efforts have been put forth to remedy the evil. At the South American Annual Conference of the Methodist Episcopal Church, held in March, 1895, the Rev. Thomas B. Wood, D.D., of the Peru district, stated in his report that a "special society to agitate and educate for temperance reform was founded in 1894. It has gathered a choice circle of young people. Our native church is squarely in the front rank of this reform. No members are admitted to full communion who are not intelligent and avowed adherents of teetotalism." [2] It is reported also, by a missionary of the same Church in the province of Buenos Ayres, that the "temperance cause is doing uncommonly well." A fine organization is spoken of as associated with the Methodist Episcopal Church in the city of Buenos Ayres.[3] In Chile, in connection with the same denomination, "an important temperance movement has been established, in which the President of the Republic takes an interest and contributes to its support." [4] A similar crusade is also conducted by the American Presbyterian missionaries of both the Northern and Southern Boards in their various South American missions.

Societies "to agitate and educate" concerning temperance in South America.

Do we need any further evidence that throughout the length and breadth of the non-Christian world evangelical missionaries are the friends and advocates of temperance, and that the Christian Church, wherever established, if true to its principles, is bound to give timely and effective help in this strenuous battle with the baneful scourge of intemperance? It is possible that some may be inclined to question the wisdom of making a total abstinence pledge a condition of church-membership; but the effects of intoxicants among many of these native races are so swift and deadly that there is no hope of safety, unless on the basis of moral principle, enforced by conscience, they can be induced to let strong drink forever alone.

[1] Cf. " Report of Missionary Society of the Methodist Episcopal Church, 1897," p. 275.
[2] *The Gospel in all Lands*, August, 1895, p. 404.
[3] *Ibid.*, p. 427.   [4] *Ibid.*, January, 1894, p. 27.

2. DELIVERANCE FROM THE OPIUM HABIT.—Our attention is now turned almost exclusively to China and India, and we find that Christianity, as represented in missions, is instinctively at war with this blighting evil, and is everywhere extending a helping hand to its victims. There is, so far as the writer has discovered, entire unanimity of sentiment among missionaries as to the perils, sorrows, and swift ruin which attend the habitual use of the drug. In China the consensus of opinion is absolute, and the entire missionary body is in an attitude of unqualified abhorrence and alarm in view of the prevalence of the vice, and of hearty antagonism to its extension.

The testimony which missionaries have given as to the calamitous evils which attend the indulgence has been of service to the anti-opium cause, and the influence they have had in moulding public sentiment by stating unitedly and individually the true facts of the case is a valuable accession to the resources of the anti-opium crusade. Their memorials, addresses, contributions to the press, and published reports of facts gathered from careful study on the ground, have yielded a fund of timely information to Christendom. This is no slight service, in view of the official position of the British Government on the subject.[1] At the Annual Meeting of the Society for the Suppression of the Opium Trade, held in London, May 27, 1897, Mr. Benjamin Broomhall presented some startling figures with reference to the Victorian record of the opium traffic. During the Queen's reign the exportation of opium from India has amounted to over 263,000 tons, and the revenue derived therefrom equals £253,-

The opium traffic—a neglected factor in the problem of the Far East.

---

[1] Abundant data concerning opium may be found in the Report of the Royal Commission, issued in 1895, in a series of seven Blue Books. Cf. also the bibliographical references in Vol. I., p. 350, and the section on the opium evil, pp. 80–84. The publications of the British societies for the suppression of the opium trade, especially *The Friend of China, The Sentinel, Abkari,* and *National Righteousness,* are of value. Articles bearing upon the subject will also be found in *The North American Review,* September, 1896, p. 381; *The Missionary Review of the World,* April, 1896, p. 265; *The Church Missionary Intelligencer,* February, 1894, p. 85; *Work and Workers in the Mission Field,* August, 1894, p. 350; *ibid.,* October, 1894, p. 435; *The Chinese Recorder,* January, 1896, p. 21; *The Saturday Review* (London), September 12, 1896, p. 288; *Abkari,* October, 1895, p. 89; *ibid.,* October, 1896, p. 112; and a valuable series of papers published at different times in *The Friend of China,* by the Rev. F. Storrs Turner, complete data concerning which will be found in the number for July, 1897, p. 93. The government view of the matter is found in the Report of the Royal Commission, referred to above, and has been presented also by Dr. R. N. Cust in "Notes on Missionary Subjects," Part II., pp. 93–119.

975,382—an appalling statement, surely.[1] At the same meeting, the Rev. J. Macgowan, of Amoy, who has been for thirty-eight years a missionary of the London Missionary Society in China, gave a graphic account of a visit which he once made to an opium palace in Shanghai. He described most of those who resort thither as young men, and the estimate of the number present at the time of his visit was about one thousand.[2]

In connection with the recent Royal Commission, the testimony of missionaries and their formal memorials on the subject were of permanent value, especially the notable one signed by British Protestant missionaries in China of twenty-five years' standing.[3] Indian missionaries, with but few exceptions, have united in the declaration: " We are unalterably opposed to the participation by the Government in the demoralising traffic in opium, and we record our conviction that it is a sin against God and a wrong to humanity." The Anti-Opium Committee of Urgency in Great Britain is responsible for the following statement: " Every missionary society and every native Christian church in China, Protestant and Roman Catholic, European and American, excludes from the membership of the Christian Church all opium-smokers and -eaters, and all persons who grow, manufacture, or sell opium." Many quotations from individual missionaries whose opinions are of exceptional value, in view of their character and standing, and because of the lifelong observation which their testimony

The settled conviction of the missionary body.

---

[1] " Mr. Benjamin Broomhall, in seconding the resolution, was sure all present would rejoice in the many schemes which had been propounded in honour of the good and long reign of Her Majesty the Queen, and he wished it were possible, amongst other great deeds this year, to abolish the trade in opium. According to a calculation made for him by Mr. Maurice Gregory, during the sixty years of that reign the quantity of opium exported from India to demoralise, corrupt, and destroy our fellow-men in China and the Straits Settlements amounted to 263,404 tons, or half a ton for every hour of the day and night of the whole of that period. They could not wonder that the missionaries on the spot who knew the result of the opium traffic should be loud in their expressions of indignation against any Government which encouraged that which spreads desolation, moral and social, amongst the millions of China. The revenue derived from the traffic by the Government of India during the past sixty years was £253,975,382, or more than one third—four tenths, to be more precise—of the amount of the present National Debt."—*The Friend of China*, July, 1897, pp. 81, 82. Cf. also *ibid.*, October, 1897, p. 98.

[2] *The Friend of China*, July, 1897, p. 83.

[3] Printed in full in *The Chronicle*, of the London Missionary Society, July, 1894, p. 153; *The Friend of China*, August, 1894, p. 19; and *The Missionary Herald*, August, 1894, p. 323.

Opium Smokers in China.

Anti-opium Society, Ningpo.
(U. M. F. M. S.)

Opium Smokers in Persia.

THE OPIUM QUESTION—ARGUMENTS OF THE CAMERA.

represents, might be given. Such men as the late Dr. William Lockhart, Dr. Colin S. Valentine, Dr. James L. Maxwell, Dr. A. Lyall, the Rev. Griffith John, D.D., Archdeacons Arthur E. Moule and John R. Wolfe, the Rev. Arnold Foster, the Rev. Jonathan Lees, the Rev. William Muirhead, D.D., Dr. Duncan Main, Dr. S. R. Hodge, Dr. Robert Swallow, Dr. J. A. Otte, Dr. W. A. P. Martin, and others, might be called not unwillingly to the witness-stand.[1]

The attitude of Christian society in China is uncompromising—in fact, every native church in the empire may be called an anti-opium guild. Formal utterances on the part of mission conferences and ecclesiastical synods indicate clearly the inflexible stand which has been taken.[2] "The Church in China," writes the Rev. Joseph S. Adams (A. B. M. U.), of Hankow, "wages war against opium. No person is ever admitted to the communion who buys, sells, uses, or

The uncompromising attitude of Christian society in China.

---

[1] Dr. Duncan Main's views may be quoted as representing the judgment of a physician: " My opinion about the evil effects of opium-smoking is unaltered. No one in his sober senses can say anything in its favour, unless he talks nonsense. We never come across an opium-smoker or a non-opium-smoker who has anything to say in defense of the habit, and if it were such an innocent affair as some advocates of it try to make us believe, surely we who live among the people from year to year would find it out. I think far too little is made of this most important fact. . . . To me it seems an utter impossibility for any one who lives among the Chinese, speaks their language, knows their lives, and mixes with them from day to day, to do anything else but condemn the base, cruel, and demoralising habit. It affects the Chinaman's person, principles, and purse, damages his constitution, degrades his conduct, and depletes his cash, and in many cases leads to ruin and destruction of body and soul. God grant that every help may be given to those who are fighting against the evil and trying to cure and save the victims of the habit!"—" Annual Report of the Church Missionary Society, 1893–94," pp. 203, 204.

A full statement of the verdict of Dr. J. A. Otte will be found in the " Annual Report of the Board of Foreign Missions of the Reformed Church in America for 1894," pp. 16, 17.

The views of Archdeacon Moule, of Shanghai, and of the Rev. Arnold Foster, of Hankow, were expressed at a " Meeting of Protest " held January 12, 1898, in London. Their forcible addresses will be found in *The Sentinel*, February, 1898, pp. 19–21, and in *National Righteousness*, March, 1898. Mr. Foster's admirable speech is published as a separate pamphlet by the Women's Anti-Opium Urgency Committee, 312 Camden Road, London.

[2] The Presbyterian Synod of Amoy at its session in Shanghai in 1893 adopted elaborate resolutions, the tenor of which was strongly anti-opium. They are recorded in the " Annual Report of the Presbyterian Board of Foreign Missions for 1894," p. 67. The Synod of Amoy of the Reformed Church in America also dealt with the subject in the same spirit, at its meeting in March, 1897. See report in *The Christian Intelligencer*, May 19, 1897.

allows to be used in his house, or cultivates in his fields, any opium. The Church has established native anti-opium societies, having a pledge, a mutual watch cure, a supply of medicines for eradicating the craving, and a plan for extending a helping hand to others.   Books and leaflets exhorting smokers and warning non-users are extensively circulated.   Many thousands of opium fiends are yearly discharged from mission hospitals as cured, but those who remain permanently free from the craving number under ten per cent.   There is a strong public opinion against the drug, which is supported and strengthened by missionary example and teaching."   "The vice of opium-smoking," writes Dr. S. P. Barchet, of the same society, "a trap into which all classes of Chinese have fallen, is the curse of China.   Anti-opium societies have been formed in several native churches, but practically all our churches are pronounced in their opposition, for no one who smokes opium would be admitted as a member."

The protest of the Church is supplemented by the establishment, under missionary auspices, in many parts of the empire, of associations for the suppression of the vice.   The Anti-Opium League in China is an organization which was instituted "to devise and pursue whatever methods the grace of God might enable us to use toward the delivery of China from opium."   The first President is the Rev. H. C. Du Bose, D.D., and its Secretary the Rev. J. N. Hayes, of Shanghai.[1]   "Anti-opium societies," writes the Rev. J. C. Garritt, of Hangchow, "are multiplying rapidly."   A flourishing one is established at Ningpo.[2]   Perhaps, however, the most effective service which is

Philanthropic efforts to save victims of the habit.

---

1 *The Chinese Recorder,* June, 1896, p. 308; February, 1897, p. 92; March, 1897, p. 145; November, 1897, p. 554; *The Sentinel,* August, 1896, p. 98.

2 "I may claim for the Christian Church in China that an uncompromising attitude toward opium has led to painstaking and thorough investigation with a view to convincing gainsayers.   Among the leaflets published last year is a statement concerning the questions addressed to smokers, so that by recording and translating answers signed in the presence of trustworthy witnesses we might contribute to knowledge on the subject.   This testimony to the baleful influence of opium is collected at first hand, and from the smokers themselves, which is surely a distinct advantage.   Out of many papers filled in and signed there was not a smoker who did not wish to be delivered from the bondage of his habit.   If opium is to be restricted or prevented from sapping the strength of China, this result will be brought about in large part by the testimony of the Christian Church.   There is one important fact to be noted in this connection.   Where the smoker is reclaimed and breaks off the habit, it is almost always through his contact with Christianity. It would seem to need the Gospel of the grace of God to accomplish what is required.   All lesser motives to reform are inadequate.   Seldom indeed does a man

rendered by missionaries is in connection with hospitals and opium refuges where special provision is made for treating the victims of the habit with Christian kindness and scientific skill.[1] It is the practice of almost every mission hospital in China to provide special treatment for those who are under its power. Such able and experienced medical missionaries as Drs. Otte of Amoy, Cousland of Swatow, Main of Hangchow, and his predecessor, Dr. James Galt, the late Dr. John Kenneth Mackenzie of Tientsin, Dr. Atwood of Fenchofu, Dr. Machle of Lien Chow, Drs. Pritchard and Atterbury of Peking, Dr. Christie of Moukden, Dr. Davenport of Wuchang, Dr. Douthwaite of Chefoo, and many others, are constantly treating the besotted and helpless victims of the drug.[2] Unhappily, the desperate hold which opium has upon its habitual slaves renders these efforts in many instances futile. It is stated upon the best authority that not more than from five to ten per cent. of those treated are permanently cured, and that in almost every instance of a successful case Christianity is the secret of the cure.[3] His Excellency Li Hung Chang, during a

---

outside a Christian church give up opium when once the craving has been formed. The task before the Church is, on the one hand, to utter her voice against this evil, and, on the other hand, to reclaim and restore its victims."—Rev. T. W. Pearce (L. M. S.), Hong Kong, China.

"Missions have especially benefited the social life of the Chinese by the unceasing and combined warfare against the opium traffic. The Protestant churches, as a whole, give no countenance to opium-smoking, opium-raising, or opium-selling. The benefits bestowed are not merely in curing the Chinese of opium-smoking, but in saving hundreds of people in every city, especially among the women, from the effects of opium-poison, taken to commit suicide."—Rev. Gilbert Reid (Ind.), Peking, China.

[1] Cf. article by Dr. H. T. Whitney, on "The Value and Methods of Opium Refuges," in "Records of Shanghai Conference, 1890," pp. 306–314. See also *The Baptist Missionary Magazine*, July, 1897, pp. 368, 375; *The Missionary*, August, 1897, p. 366; and *Medical Missions at Home and Abroad*, October, 1897, p. 6; *The Review of Missions* (Nashville, Tenn.), July, 1898, pp. 18–28.

[2] "Dr. Mackenzie writes: ' You will see how the work among opium-smokers has been increased. For the first ten months only eight persons agreed to enter the hospital. During the past year [1876] the numbers have increased to two hundred and thirty-five; and during the last month and a half, three hundred and twenty have entered the wards for treatment.' At a subsequent date he writes: ' In one year seven hundred persons were treated for opium habits in the Hankow hospital.' " —Creegan, " Great Missionaries of the Church," p. 150.

In the hospital at Chefoo under the care of Dr. Douthwaite (C. I. M.), two hundred and fourteen opium-smokers were admitted for treatment in one season. See "The Opium Habit," by A. W. Douthwaite, M.D., printed at the *Mercury* office, Shanghai, 1891.

[3] "The only permanent and reliable cure for the opium habit is the hearty

visit to the United States, in 1896, in an interview with the representatives of various missionary societies, referred to the use of opium as one of the great curses of the Chinese people, and expressed in very appreciative terms his gratification with the efforts made by American missionaries to mitigate this evil.[1]

In the Island of Formosa, since it has passed under Japanese rule, measures have been taken to restrict the importation and use of opium.

Japanese policy in
Formosa. Public sentiment in Japan is firm upon this subject, and influential meetings to support the Government in maintaining such a policy in Formosa as prevails in the Japanese Empire have been held in Tokyo. Many difficulties have arisen, and the plan finally adopted is one of limited restriction, which, it is to be hoped, will result ultimately in complete prohibition of the use of the drug, as soon as this can be accomplished with safety. The system now in use is substantially the same as that in operation in Burma, with some additional restraints. It seems desirable that more effective measures should be taken, or at least such as will eventually extirpate the evil rather than perpetuate it under a system of patronage in which there is opportunity for evading ineffective restraints.[2] The attitude of missions in Formosa is indicated by the statement of Dr. MacKay that "throughout our field hundreds have been relieved and thousands kept from the deadly opium habit by the preaching of Jesus Christ, and Him crucified."

adoption of Christianity. Cures abound among natives, but perhaps ninety-five per cent. lapse."—Rev. Donald MacGillivray (C. P. M.), Chu-Wang, China.

" Opium-smokers have been rescued, and their families saved from ruin, when the victims were cured in the early stages of their evil life."—Rev. Frederick Galpin (U. M. F. M. S.), Ningpo, China.

" Unless an opium-smoker is soundly converted, I have very little hope of permanent benefit."—Rev. Hunter Corbett, D.D.(P. B. F. M. N.), Chefoo, China.

" Mr. Li, an opium-smoker for twenty years, renounced the opium habit, and received the Gospel while in the hospital [Hiau Kan]; the period of his probation is nearly over; he has stood firm, and is expecting to be baptized in a few days. Physically and morally he is a new man."—" Report of the London Missionary Society, 1897," p. 51.

1 His words were as follows: " Before I bring my reply to a conclusion, I have only two things to mention. The first, the opium-smoking, being a great curse to the Chinese population, your societies have tried their best, not only as anti-opium societies, but to afford the best means to stop the craving for the opium; and also you receive none as your converts who are opium-smokers."—Reported in *The New York Tribune*, September 2, 1896.

2 The new regulations are printed in full in *The Friend of China*, April, 1897, p. 42.

An opium refuge, Taiyuenfu—victims of the habit under curative treatment. Rev. G. B. Farthing, Superintendent, seated on the right.

THE LIGHT OF HOPE IN SOME SAD FACES.

(E. B. M. S.)

In India the question of opium has two important aspects. One of these relates to the government policy in establishing its own monopoly of production and sale, and especially of exportation to China and elsewhere. The other pertains to its use under licensed facilities in India itself. The opium policy maintained there by the Government is a public question which weighs heavily upon the consciences of a large portion of the British people. Ceaseless and strenuous agitation having in view the withdrawal of the Government from its patronage of the opium traffic, and the entire repudiation of its dismal responsibility for the extensive manufacture and large exportation of the drug, has been going on for many years. The report of the recent Parliamentary Commission was a disappointment in anti-opium circles, but the subject-matter brought to public notice in the printed documents of the Commission is of permanent value, and, in the estimation of a candid reader, may be interpreted quite as much in the interest of the anti-opium agitation as against it. Its report will not carry conviction to those who have any sufficient realization of the moral principles at stake in the whole question. It was perhaps to be expected that a Parliamentary Commission to examine a source of revenue in British India would not fail to take the most lenient view of the moral stringency involved in the problem, and justify to the limit of possibility the attitude of the Government in deference to what, from an official point of view, would seem to be a financial, political, and economic advantage.[1]

A complex problem in India.

There are indications, however, that the Government of India is inclined to a somewhat reactionary policy in favor of restriction, and that to a hitherto unwonted extent it is ready to respond to any reasonable appeal to close opium dens and prohibit as far as possible the extension of the perilous habit among the people. It has, at the request of the Anglo-Indian Temperance Association, promptly suppressed the opium dens of Lucknow, an action quite in harmony with its own declared purpose to do away with the practice of opium-smoking in government licensed shops. Mr. W. S. Caine, M.P., reports a gratifying willingness on the part of the Indian officials to take vigorous repressive measures.[2] It would seem as if the

Is the British Government recognizing the social peril of the opium habit?

---

[1] A valuable abstract of opium statistics for the ten years ending 1895 will be found in *The Friend of China*, April, 1897, p. 60. Cf. also, for a trenchant statement on the subject, *The Illustrated Missionary News*, July, 1898, pp. 100, 101.

[2] *Abkari*, July, 1897, p. 75.

success of prohibition in Burma, combined with an awakened sense of responsibility in view of the growing evil, had quickened the readiness of the authorities to act.   Moreover, the failure, in large measure, of the opium crop for eight successive years [1] has diminished the quantity which the Government has been able to obtain, and this, of course, has involved a forced diminution of income.   Providence appears to be demonstrating in a happy degree the possibility of the survival of the British Government in India without the opium revenue, a fact which there seems to have been extreme reluctance to concede on the part of the friends of the traffic.   The whole question is one of crucial importance to the social welfare of coming generations.   The growth of the habit where there is no effective restraint seems to be inevitable, and, if India is to escape the social desolations that opium has wrought in China, much will depend upon the spirit and activity of the Indian authorities in dealing with the problem.

The sentiment of Christian missions in India is overwhelmingly opposed to opium, although there seems to be on the part of some resident missionaries a spirit of mild tolerance towards the Government, and a disposition to question the presence of any very serious danger to the people of India from the opium habit.

A strong anti-opium sentiment among Indian missionaries.

Even in such instances a distinction is often made between their personal wishes and views, and the attitude which is justified towards the Indian Government.   It is not unlikely that all missionaries, with Dr. Sommerville of Jodhpore, "would rejoice to see the absolute and complete suppression of the opium trade with China, and an entire withdrawal of Government from all share in this trade, and in the production of the drug," while at the same time, with him, some may hesitate to participate in the severe condemnation of the Government which many seem to think is justified.[2]   There is no doubt, however,

---

[1] *The Sentinel,* May, 1896, p. 65; May, 1897, p. 58; *Abkari,* July, 1897, p. 95.

[2] " With regard to the opium and hemp habits, although as a medical man I have been brought into large and frequent contact with the question, and have seen some of the disastrous results which follow the use of these drugs, my experience in Rajputana, where opium is grown to some extent and a much greater amount used, does not justify me in adopting the strong language and extreme statements affected by those who have lately been agitating for the suppression of these drugs as articles of popular use and commerce.   Personally I would rejoice to see the absolute and complete suppression of the opium trade with China, and an entire withdrawal of Government from all share in this trade, and in the production of the drug.   The individual responsibility of Government officers and the distribution of accountability is quite another aspect of the matter, and missionary influence has

that missionary sentiment in India is, with but few exceptions, in an attitude of intense antipathy to any possible extension of the habit among the people, and that the influence of the Christian Church there, as elsewhere, will be in strenuous opposition to any participation on the part of Christians in this degrading and ruinous business.

From Siam there is gratifying testimony to the power of Christian missions in reforming the victims of opium.[1] It is said that "the first government document ever printed in Siam was the King's Proclamation contrabanding opium, issued April 27, 1839, from the mission press of the A. B. C. F. M."[2] The battle is easier among the Siamese because of the opposition of the Government to the traffic.

Persia seems to be in peril from the opium habit. The cultivation of the drug is increasing, and its use is becoming more extensive. Opium dens are found in considerable numbers in the prominent cities of Persia. It is estimated by the Rev. Lewis F. Esselstyn that nearly four million pounds are consumed annually, representing a valuation of over nine million dollars.[3] The annual exportation already exceeds two million dollars in value. Mr. Robert E. Speer, in a recent communication from Persia, asserts that "the opium habit has spread like wild-fire, and medical missionaries who see the inside of Persian life declare that it is as common there as in China." Islam, he declares, is not contending at all against its increase. The Christian churches throughout Persia regard opium in the same category with strong drink, and, so far as their influence extends, are equally unwavering in their opposition to the habit.

Bulletins from Persia, South Africa, Australia, and the South Seas.

From South Africa there are very recent and ominous reports of a growing opium habit among native communities. Paragraphs on the subject in prominent papers give some of the facts.[4] The late Mr. R. L.

---

too often been used to denounce unjustly both men and measures because these were not carefully or properly considered."—Dr. James Sommerville (U.P.C.S.M.), Jodhpore, India.

[1] "Wherever Christianity has been fully accepted by the Lao people, it has reformed the victims of the opium habit. So far as I know, there is only one church-member whose absolute reform in this regard is open to question. And I have personally known many trophies of the grace of God from among the ranks of the opium-users, most of them being reformed without the aid of any medication."—Rev. W. C. Dodd (P. B. F. M. N.), Lampoon, Laos.

[2] *Woman's Work for Woman,* July, 1897, p. 187.

[3] Vol. I., p. 84, note.

[4] "Liquor of the most fiery and poisonous description, specially distilled for native consumption, has long constituted a serious obstacle in the way of those who

Stevenson has called our attention to the existence of an opium traffic dating back many years, practically under the patronage of the French Government, in the Marquesas Islands—a fact concerning which the world knows virtually nothing.[1]

It is pleasant to note that in some of the Australian colonies there is vigorous government action prohibiting the use of opium except for medical purposes, although, unhappily, the law applies only to aboriginals.[2]

3. RESTRAINT UPON GAMBLING.—The ethics of gambling have been thoughtfully and wisely treated in a little volume by Professor W. Douglas Mackenzie.[3] It is an antichristian as well as anti-social vice, and has been rightly called by Lord Beaconsfield "a vast engine of national demoralisation." Its prevalence will quickly work the ruin of the individual, personally and socially, and bring a permanent collapse to all economic prosperity. It has properly been pronounced in its moral aspects a "veiled felony." The public conscience has vigorous spasms of severity and condemna-

The social dangers of gambling.

desire to civilize the Kaffir, and is wrecking the dusky races of Africa, morally as well as physically. Not content with this, the Europeans have now initiated the black man to the charms of opium, the nefarious traffic of which is carried on openly in the Transvaal, where white people keep dens in which Kaffir men and women pay sixpence a smoke. The hideous effects of the opium on the semi-savage Kaffirs who work at the mines are already showing themselves in a very marked degree, and the mine managers are unanimous in declaring that the curse is many times greater than that of alcohol."—*The New York Tribune*, October 11, 1897.

"*The Daily Chronicle* calls attention to the fact, reported from Johannesburg, that in that city ' many Chinamen do a thriving business by supplying Kaffirs with the deadly drug prepared for smoking.' Chinamen, however, are not the only or even the chief sinners in this respect. The nefarious traffic is carried on more or less openly by large numbers of Europeans, who keep dens where Kaffirs and coloured women pay sixpence for each smoke. The sanitary police are said to be quite aware of the abuse, and it is further alleged that a well-known firm supplies Chinamen with the drug."—Quoted in *The Friend of China*, October, 1897, p. 99.

[1] Stevenson, " In the South Seas," pp. 73–75 (Scribner's ed., 1896).

[2] *The Sentinel*, March, 1896, p. 33.

[3] Mackenzie, "The Ethics of Gambling." Cf. also *The Century*, February, 1892, article by C. C. Buel, on " The Degradation of a State, or the Charitable Career of the Louisiana Lottery "; *Harper's Magazine*, February, 1895, article by John Bigelow, on " What is Gambling?"; *The Economic Review*, April, 1897, article by Rev. Arthur Barnett, M.A., entitled " Why are Betting and Gambling Wrong?" The Congregational Sunday-School and Publishing Society of Boston issues a little pamphlet entitled " Gambling, or Getting Something for Nothing."

tion in dealing with it, and sternly prohibits all licensed facilities for its indulgence. The best of laws exist in almost all civilized communities, but are not always enforced as they should be. The recent formation of the National Anti-Gambling League in England, the new restrictions in the Australian colonies, and the vigorous municipal action in many prominent cities of Christendom, all indicate the commendable attitude of civilization towards the vice. The difficulties attending the prohibition of lotteries show the powerful resources of the gambling fraternity, but the persistent warfare which is waged against this evil business reveals the determination of Christian civilization to destroy it.

A singular and most regrettable exception to this general condemnation of gambling, is the readiness of some of the Roman Catholic authorities in South America to establish lotteries for the benefit of their Church and its charitable institutions. The President of the United States of Brazil has had occasion, while refusing to sanction the efforts of the Romish Church to secure lottery privileges, to administer to it a severe rebuke in his State paper declining the request. After showing that such schemes are unconstitutional in Brazil, he concludes with the following paragraph: "Let it be further added that, as the principle of gaming involved in lotteries is an evil condemned by the laws both of morality and of political economy, disturbing labor, ruining the poorer classes, and turning away from productive employment a large mass of capital, it is the duty of those in authority, acting for the best interests of the nation, to restrain, or even, if possible, to extinguish this evil, and not to encourage it, or to incite to its development by the concession of lotteries with a capital so enormous that they are made most seductive and thus most pernicious."[1] Years ago the only opposition to gambling was from Christian

Lottery scandals in South America.

[1] *The Echo of Mission Work in Brazil*, March 30, 1896, p. 5. This Protestant missionary paper of Brazil, published under the auspices of the American Church Missionary Society of the Protestant Episcopal Church in the United States of America, in commenting upon the above document, remarks as follows:

" 1. Here is the official organization of the principal Roman Catholic Church in Rio de Janeiro asking for a lottery concession in order to sustain its institutions.

" 2. Here is the President of the Republic, in vigorous and intelligent language, propounding the principle of religious tolerance, and condemning lotteries as prejudicial to the moral interests of the people.

"The corruption of the representatives of religion saddens us. But the high Christian spirit that breathes in the President's message reveals the noble aspirations and the reform purpose that are now stirring young Brazil."

missionaries. "Theirs was the only voice," writes Dr. H. M. Lane, of São Paulo, Brazil, "raised against lotteries and open resorts of gambling. To-day in some of the States lotteries are prohibited, on account of their evil tendency. The city authorities of São Paulo have recently forbidden the game of *pelota*, and closed the shops of the book-makers."

In spite of general opposition to public gambling in civilized communities, private gambling seems inconsistently to be condoned and tolerated as a necessary feature of individual liberty, although many true and wise words have been uttered by the leaders of thought, denouncing unhesitatingly its deteriorating effects, and branding it as it deserves.[1]

Christian missions have enlisted all their forces against this perilous vice, which has an almost unchecked indulgence throughout vast sections of heathen society. The non-Christian

The passion for gambling in heathen society.

world is fully susceptible to the fascinations of the habit as a method of gaining something for nothing. The gambling spirit, moreover, is in harmony with heathen ways of thinking concerning the supernatural. It is simply one aspect of the universal passion for appealing to unseen agencies, which we find so prevalent in necromancy, divination, witchcraft, and a thousand superstitions that govern even the common life of the people. The turn of luck is a part of the daily expectation of those who know little of an intelligent use of the faculties combined with trust in a divine Providence.

The Japanese Government more than any other seems of late to

---

1 " There is one way of wasting time, of all the vilest, because it wastes not time only, but the interest and energy of great minds. Of all the ungentlemanly habits into which you can fall, the vilest is betting, or interesting yourselves in the issues of betting. It unites every condition of folly and vice ; you concentrate your interest upon a matter of chance instead of upon a subject of true knowledge, and you back opinions which you had no ground of forming, simply because they are your own. All the insolence of egotism is in this, and so far as the love of excitement is complicated with the hope of winning money, you turn yourselves into the basest sort of tradesmen—those who live by speculation."—John Ruskin.

" Now all this is bad, bad, nothing but bad. Of all habits, gambling is the one I hate most and have avoided most. Of all habits, it grows most on eager minds. Success and loss alike make it grow. Of all habits, however much civilised men may give way to it, it is one of the most intrinsically *savage*. Historically, it has been the fierce excitement of the lowest brutes in human form for ages past. Morally, it is unchivalrous and unchristian."—Charles Kingsley, in Letter to his Son.

be making an honest effort to suppress this evil. The number of arrests reported for gambling in Japan, in 1894, was 36,560, of which 51 were for engaging in lotteries. Its legal prohibition in China is generally inoperative. In fact, some of the leading Chinese officials are inveterate gamblers, and lotteries on an enormous scale are frequently established under the highest patronage.[1] It is clearly understood, however, in all mission circles that when a man becomes a Christian he breaks at once and forever with this habit. Church discipline is severe in the case of any one who yields to the temptation. It is interesting to note the frequent references in missionary reports and magazines to the conversion of gamblers and their immediate discontinuance of the habit. In one instance of a lapse on the part of a Christian native at Ningpo it is stated that the repentance was so genuine and the self-condemnation so sincere that the man deliberately chopped off his finger as a method of reminding himself never to do so again.[2] A missionary was once lamenting the little spiritual progress made in a Christian village community in China, when one of the prominent members replied: "Sir, you don't know. Formerly, before we knew the truth, gambling was common; now it has been utterly abolished. Then we had feuds and lawsuits every month; now harmony prevails." It is customary for Christian converts who have been rescued from the vice to give it up *in toto* and enter upon a determined warfare against it.[3]

Native Christians do not gamble.

[1] " As an instance of the practices of China's highest officials, irrespective of the moral precepts to be found in their proclamations, it is interesting to note that the famous Weising lottery has just been farmed by the Government to three of the most prominent men in the empire. These are Li Hau Chang, brother of Li Hung Chang, and ex-Viceroy of Canton; Shao Yu-lien, ex-Governor of Formosa; and Liu Hsueh-hsun, a *chin shih*, or metropolitan graduate, of considerable notoriety in Canton. To obtain the sole right of controlling this lottery these officials pay to the Imperial Government a sum of Tls. 1,600,000, and a further sum of Tls. 1,400,000 is required for working expenses. Estimating their profits from the business at a low figure, over 2,000,000 taels will thus be drawn from the people by means of this officially organized gambling concern."— *The Mail* (London), June 21, 1897.

[2] " Report of the Church Missionary Society, 1897," p. 351.

[3] Horne, " The Story of the London Missionary Society," p. 329; Gordon, " An American Missionary in Japan," pp. 142–144.

" Two men recently came under my observation who previous to conversion had been noted gamblers. When they became believers in the Word of God they forsook their former wicked practices, and are now living honest and honorable lives."
—Rev. A. M. Cunningham (P. B. F. M. N.), Peking, China.

In an account of his conversion to Christianity by Mr. Taro Ando, now prominent in temperance work in Japan, and late Japanese Consul-General to Hawaii, he reports that gambling was very prevalent among the Japanese in Hawaii, until missionary work was established among them, when a great and cheering change took place.[1] In the midst of a Christian service in the Congo Valley, a native in the audience called out to the preacher: "I shall gamble no more. I believe in God's *palaver*, and accept it from this day." "This man had gambled from boyhood," writes a missionary, "gambled day and night."[2] The incident is typical of the power of the Gospel to awaken a sluggish and hardened conscience, and call a halt in the indulgence of a lifelong vice. In a copy of *The Spectator* (London), for January 4, 1896, is found a significant communication from the local Secretary in Madagascar, of the Friends' Foreign Mission Association, in reply to a statement which had been quoted from a correspondent of one of the London papers, asserting that gambling was practised by the Queen and her courtiers. The letter may speak for itself.[3] In a series of papers by veteran missionaries, published in *The Church Missionary*

Illustrations of changed lives.

---

[1] "A Methodist Episcopal missionary, the Rev. K. Miyama, came from San Francisco to engage in work among the Japanese laborers [in Hawaii]. As the result of Mr. Miyama's work, as well as his earnest preaching, laboring specially for the improvement of their morals, gamblers began to throw away their dice, drunkards to dash to pieces their cups, and the disorderly to show signs of genuine repentance. For the time being the troubles of the consulate greatly diminished. The result of all this was that I, who had been such a hater of Jesus (while shrinking from the very thought), began seriously to reflect and inquire whether, after all, the Christian religion was not the efficacious source of this moral reform, and whether it was not a religion well suited to the needs of the ignorant masses." See article by Mr. Taro Ando in *The Gospel in all Lands*, August, 1894, p. 363.

[2] The Rev. W. H. Sheppard, in *The Missionary*, October, 1895, p. 465.

[3] "TO THE EDITOR OF THE 'SPECTATOR.'

"SIR: During the twenty-four years of my residence in Antananarivo, I have been a regular reader of the *Spectator*. I have always been struck with your fairness in being willing to insert communications in correction of any statements made in your paper that are thought to be incorrect. May I therefore ask your usual courtesy with regard to a paragraph in the *Spectator* of August 13th, which has just arrived here? In that number, quoting from the Antananarivo correspondent of the *Times*, the assertion is made that the ' Queen and courtiers take to gambling of the most reckless description.' I am able to give this the most positive contradiction. For many years now there has been no gambling in the presence of the Queen, and it has been strictly forbidden in the Royal Palace. I am perfectly sure that you will do justice to the Christian lady who is still Queen of Madagascar, by inserting this letter.   "HENRY E. CLARK."

Gleaner, is one by the Venerable Archdeacon Phair, describing the past and present status in the Diocese of Rupertsland. His backward glance covers a period of thirty years, since he began his missionary work in that part of the world. He speaks of the "overwhelming argument in the interests of Christian missions" which might be derived simply from the passing of ancient evils and loathsome customs, and the entrance of a sweeter and lovelier life into society. "Gambling, conjuring, dancing, and all sorts of heathenism, have given way before the mighty power of the Gospel."[1] The facts just recorded are surely sufficient to indicate that if Christian missions were allowed to decide the question, gambling would cease wherever they could prevent it.

4. ESTABLISHING HIGHER STANDARDS OF PERSONAL PURITY.— That Christianity is at war with heathen vice and has an urgent message of reproof and prohibition concerning every form of immorality is a fact which has been made plain by all history and experience, and which every reader of the Word of God knows to be true. All that is needful in this connection is to bring forward some illustrative evidence to show that missions have actually introduced new standards of manhood and womanhood, and planted in the individual and social life of once shameless communities a new reverence for the sweet and saintly austerities of the Christian law of purity. In general, it may be said that every evangelical church in mission fields is a society for the promotion of clean living. This battle with immorality is perhaps the most intense phase of conflict with social evil which is known in mission churches. The inflexible principles of Christianity are advocated and insisted upon as a condition for church-membership, and prompt discipline is the rule wherever it is called for by lapses on the part of professing Christians. White Cross, White Ribbon, and Purity Societies are to be found under mission auspices in China, India, Burma, Africa, and elsewhere. In this good work the World's Woman's Christian Temperance Union bears an honored part. Its representatives have visited every continent as missionaries of personal righteousness. The notable services rendered by Dr. Kate Bushnell and Mrs. Elizabeth W. Andrew are well known throughout the Christian world, especially their exposure of the irregularities and scandals connected with the Indian cantonment system, in defiance of legal

Mission churches promote clean living.

1 *The Church Missionary Gleaner*, May, 1894, p. 67..

regulations.[1] In many mission fields special literature on the subject is already in circulation, prepared with a view to local conditions and requirements. Christianity has aroused discussion, stimulated agitation, set in motion aggressive plans, and organized definite practical efforts for the suppression of moral evils and the accentuation of personal righteousness. This is all very different from the *laissez-faire* policy which has hitherto prevailed.

In Japan the agitation originated almost exclusively in Christian circles, but it has commended itself to many of the best citizens of the empire, and has led to movements with the same end in view on the part of those who were not known as professed converts. The Christian press has written boldly and loyally on this theme, and concerted effort has been made to secure government action with a view to the withdrawal of its patronage of vice, and the abolition of the system of license. Several local assemblies in different parts of the empire have been appealed to by Christian reformers, and in some instances resolutions for the abolishment of licenses have been carried. The native Christians of Kyoto, as long ago as 1890, prepared a petition known as "The Kyoto Memorial for the Abolition of Licensed Prostitution in Japan," and forwarded the same to the Chairmen of both Houses of the Imperial Diet. This printed memorial was circulated largely in Japan, and received numerous signatures. It is a thoroughgoing document, dealing with the subject in wise and moderate language, yet presenting facts and arguments with singular clearness, brevity, and force.[2] The appeal, while received with consideration, produced no practical result so far as official action of the Imperial Diet was concerned. In some local assemblies there has been more success, but the lack of pronounced public sentiment in favor of the movement stands in the way of progress. It is evident, however, that there has been a change in the attitude of the Christian public of Japan towards this evil—a change which has extended quite beyond the bounds of these evangelical communities. "Young men who are Christians," writes a missionary, "are noted and praised for their pure

A reform movement among Christians in Japan.

---

1 See "Report of the Committee Appointed by the Secretary of State for India to Inquire into the Rules, Regulations, and Practice in the Indian Cantonments and Elsewhere in India, with Regard to Prostitution" (Blue Book of the British Government, 1893).

2 "The Kyoto Memorial for the Abolition of Licensed Prostitution in Japan, Addressed to Members of Both Houses of the Imperial Diet through Their Presidents" (Kyoto, December, 1890).

Rev. K. Ibuka, President.

Faculty and Graduating Class, Meiji Gakuin, Tokyo.

CHRISTIAN EDUCATION IN JAPAN.

(P. B. F. M. N. and Ref. C. A.)

lives." The leaders in the movement for the abolition of licensed sin are, as a rule, followers of Christ, but not in every case, as there are others—in most instances those who have been impressed by the higher standard of living taught by Christians and exhibited in their lives—who have been prominent in the advocacy of a decided change in the policy of the Government towards this desolating social evil. Societies under native control have been organized in different places for rescuing the depraved, and conducting an aggressive warfare against vice.[1]

A little pamphlet entitled "The Problem of Social Purity in Japan" was issued by missionary ladies of the American Board in that country during the year 1895, containing an address to Count Ito, in the name of the World's Woman's Christian Temperance Union, by the ladies of that Board residing there. It urges action by the Government on behalf of morality and the protection of Japanese girls, stating facts and statistics which clearly indicate the urgent need of official intervention.[2] It contains the interesting statement that the Japanese Christian young men of California, by the aid of their Consul, have been instrumental in entirely stopping the traffic in Japanese girls at San Francisco. The closing words of the appeal reflect the spirit of Christian missionaries throughout the world upon this delicate and burning problem: "We pray your Excellency," they write, "to interfere that this beautiful land of Japan be not made the harlot house of the nations, and that the womanhood of Japan may be a glory instead of a byword and jest to the impure, and a sorrow and

A Christian appeal to Japanese authorities.

---

1 "There died this spring [1895], in Okayama, a young man, Mr. Hama, who has rendered efficient educational and evangelistic service in both Okayama and Tottori prefectures, and who more than any other person was influential in arousing and keeping alive in that region public sentiment on the social purity question. Mr. Noyes reports from Maebashi: ' Socially the important event has been the abolition of licensed prostitution in the province, the act going into effect January, 1894, as the result of fourteen years of agitation. Though the churches as such took no part in the movement, the result is largely due to the efforts of individual Christians, and particularly to the Young Men's Association, who deserve all the praise they have received. Though the act is in force, great efforts are being made to go back to the old system, and a vote of reconsideration recently taken in the prefectural assembly showed a majority of only one in favor of abolition. The vote was forty to thirty-nine. It is plain that unless the Christians bestir themselves the foothold which they have gained will soon be lost.'"—Pettee, "A Chapter of Mission History in Modern Japan," p. 176.

2 "The Problem of Social Purity in Japan," printed by the Yokohama Seishi Bunsha, 1895. Cf. also *Life and Light for Woman*, August, 1895, p. 350.

loathing to the pure of all lands." Our missionaries are thus leading the way, and the better class of natives catch the spirit of reform.[1]

In a thoughtful article by Mr. Tokiwo Yokoi, of Tokyo, Japan, on "The Ethical Life and Conceptions of Japanese," we find the following statement: "But taking the body of for-

Testimony of thought- eign missionaries as a whole, and the native
ful Japanese writers. churches as they are, there is one particular in which they have succeeded in impressing on the mind of the Japanese people a very important ethical truth. I refer to the principle of monogamy and personal purity. I do not mean to say that the Japanese people have been, as a rule, polygamous, or that womanhood among them, especially in the better classes, had not a very high ideal of faithfulness and chastity. But monogamy as the only true principle of social order, and purity as obligatory upon men as upon women, were never clearly understood. If to-day our best ethical opinion has practically endorsed these truths, we must give a large measure of credit to the foreign missionaries who have been living among us for nearly forty years."[2] In Tokyo it is reported that there are now over one hundred Christian writers, of whom the major-ity have formed themselves into an association, meeting quarterly with a view to the discussion of important questions and the public advo-

---

1 " A favorable sign of the times is the manifest anxiety the better class of men and women have with regard to the low moral standard of the people. They realize the danger which threatens the ruin of this fair land through strong drink, licen-tiousness, and idleness. One of the newspapers of Sendai came out with a couple of articles exposing, in a most decided manner, the immorality of the city, and took a stand that few of our newspapers in America are brave enough to take. A Tokyo paper has declared itself an enemy to the *Tenrikyo* faith, on account of its immoral practices, exposing the wickedness of its ceremonies, and pledges itself to fight the society until it is destroyed."—Miss Lavinia M. Mead (A. B. M. U.), in *The Baptist Missionary Review* (Madras), September, 1896, p. 323.

" An event of interest in the national life is the series of papers on morals, written by Fukuzawa Jukichi, whom we may call the most prominent educator in the empire. These papers were written in response to a request by the Education Department of the Government for treatises on the subject from which might be selected material for the preparation of a course of ethics for the public schools. Mr. Fukuzawa's essays, while not giving the source, are clearly drawn from Chris-tianity. They are acknowledged by the native press to be by far the best that have been offered. Monogamy and other Christian practices are advocated in these essays. The family life as we see it only under Christianity is portrayed in glowing colors."—Rev. E. H. Jones (A. B. M. U.), Sendai, Japan, in *The Baptist Missionary Magazine*, January, 1897, p. 15.

2 *International Journal of Ethics*, January, 1896, p. 200. Cf. also *The Church at Home and Abroad*, April, 1896, pp. 354, 355.

cacy of such views as they are able to agree upon. "This association has already declared itself as opposed to licensed prostitution in Formosa."[1] The President of the *Kodo Kwai*, an organization for fostering morality among the people, is the Hon. Shigeki Nishimura. In a lecture delivered not long ago in Sendai, although not himself a professing Christian, he declared that the remedy for national perils was in "emphasizing the supreme importance of morality." "There are indications," says a Japanese periodical, "that Mr. Nishimura's thinking has been influenced by Christianity. It is sincerely to be hoped that he will in time see that the best and most stable basis for ethical culture is the Gospel of Jesus Christ."[2]

A Japanese Christian woman, Mrs. Yajima, the President of the National Woman's Christian Temperance Union, has presented to the Japanese Diet for seven consecutive years a peti-

A patient crusade for higher standards of morality in Japanese society.

tion in the interests of purity, asking "that men and women receive the same punishment for social crimes." It was rejected every year, until 1897, when it was accepted and passed by the House of Lords. "Every church bell in Japan," to quote a prominent journal, "ought to have rung, and every Christian should have hastened to send this faithful mother heart a letter of appreciation and sympathy."[3] The influence of Christianity in the direction of higher standards of morality is not merely indicated by incidents like the above, but is freely acknowledged by men of prominence, as well as by the secular press.[4]

India is a land where the tendencies to impurity are strong, and where much that is flagrant and debasing has been prominent in social and religious life for centuries. Christian missions

Changed sentiments in India on the subject of moral purity.

have introduced new standards of self-control, and have created a public sentiment which was quite unknown in the past.[5] It is no uncommon

---

1 *The Japan Evangelist*, February, 1896, p. 195.

2 *Ibid.*, November, 1896, pp. 63, 64.   3 *Ibid.*, April, 1897, p. 221.

4 "One of the large native daily newspapers in Northern Japan says: 'Our forty millions to-day have a higher standard of morality than we have ever known. There is not a boy or girl throughout the empire who has not heard of the one-man, one-woman doctrine. Our ideas of loyalty and obedience are higher than ever. And when we inquire the cause of this great moral advance, we can find it in nothing else than the religion of Jesus.'"—Quoted in *The Spirit of Missions*, January, 1895, p. 8.

5 "I am constantly receiving testimony from native friends who are not Christians of the value of our teaching and influence on private and public morality, and my own observation goes to confirm this testimony. Within the circle of my own

thing at the present time in India to find the essence of social and moral reform advocated with eloquence and urged with high and sincere purpose by eminent natives, who in some instances are Christians, and in others are not. Such bright and able journals as *The Indian Spectator* and the *Subodha Patrika*, of Bombay, *The Indian Social Reformer* and *The Christian Patriot*, of Madras, and *The Indian Messenger*, of Calcutta, serve as the media for expressing the views of these reformers. The annual meetings of the Indian National Social Conference, and frequent gatherings of various local associations in many sections of India, give much attention by means of discussions, lectures, resolutions, and practical efforts on the part of their members, to social problems, and it is especially noticeable that among these the cause of moral purity is coming to the front.[1]

experience many men do not now flaunt their immorality as they were wont to do, and, strange as it may seem, are rather abashed in the presence of Christian life and opinion. Such a thing was absolutely unknown until the advent of Gospel teaching, and these changes in public sentiment, even though they are limited and partial, are a welcome sign of the influence of missionary effort, direct and indirect."—Dr. James Sommerville (U. P. C. S. M.), Jodhpore, Rajputana, India.

Another missionary, referring to the transformations in public opinion, remarks: " Gradually Christian teaching and example are awakening public feeling against all licentiousness. Years ago the Hindu New Year, or *Holi*, was the occasion for a general indulgence in vice and obscenity. No woman was to be seen on the streets. The most filthy and disgusting songs were sung in public, and vile abuse was bandied from one to another. Now very little of all this is to be seen or heard in or about towns and cities. The respectable classes have risen against it, and common sentiment taboos the old objectionable custom. The public conscience has been touched, and higher and better conceptions of moral purity are commending themselves to the people."—Rev. D. Hutton (L. M. S.), Mirzapur, India.

" The lessons and examples of Christian morality are gradually changing the old idea of indulgence and slowly creating a conscience and a will for self-control, while it is Christian men who are leavening the country with a spirit of shame concerning the dancing-women."—Rev. L. L. Uhl, Ph.D. (Luth. G. S.), Guntur, India.

[1] In *The Indian Social Reformer* for April 12, 1896, is the report of a lecture delivered by Mr. N. K. Ramasamayya, B.A., B.L., at a public meeting of the Madras Hindu Social Reform Association, upon " Morality in India, Past and Present." It is full of quickening thought, and pervaded by a sentiment of deep admiration, and even reverence, for pure morals. His words of instruction and exhortation to his fellow-countrymen are eloquent and uncompromising. Referring to the well-known scandal of the nautch, he remarks : "The institution of dancing- or nautch-women, shamefully called *devadasis*, attached to our temples is a standing monument of our moral degradation. In this connection I cannot but allude to the rites of *Vamacharis*, which are most infamous. Yet they are celebrated in the sacred name of religion." In a more hopeful strain he speaks of the present outlook for reform, as follows: " The moral tone of the people is now greatly elevated. The introduction of Western education has gone a great way in promoting good morals

A reform which is just now very prominently before Indian society is known as the anti-nautch movement, which originated some years ago at Madras among Hindus themselves.[1] The agitation is vigorous, and, under the patronage not merely of Christians but of Hindus, forms a part of almost every public discussion upon social questions. Influential natives of Madras have recently petitioned British officials to withhold their patronage of this institution.[2] The subjoined resolution on the subject, taken from the records of the Ninth Indian Social Conference, held at Poona in December, 1895, will serve to indicate the spirit with which this agitation is conducted. It was resolved by Mr. Raman Bhai, of Ahmedabad, and carried unanimously, as follows: "The Conference records its satisfaction that the anti-nautch movement has found such general support in all parts of India, and it recommends the various Social Reform Associations in the country to persevere in their adoption of this self-denying ordinance, and to supplement it by pledging their members to adhere to the cardinal principle of observing on all occasions, as a religious duty, purity of thought,

The growing agitation against the nautch scandals.

in India. Morality is the foundation of all other reforms. It is a necessary and important factor of religion, of sociology, and of politics. It is the groundwork on which the whole fabric of reform should be built. If it is weak, the superstructure, however grand and imposing, even if reared with all possible care, will inevitably come to the ground. In our times the merit of any religion is tested by its morality."

Many extracts similar to the above, representing the awakened and militant reform sentiment of enlightened Hindu society, could be culled from Indian papers. That all this is an indirect result of Christianity is not difficult to believe.

[1] "Its aim is to discountenance the presence and performance of dancing-girls at public functions and private entertainments. These women—of whom there are some twelve thousand in the Madras Presidency alone, according to the recent census—represent an old class of courtesans, designed for service in the temples, and resembling the *hiero-douloi* of the ancient temple of Venus at Corinth. Their presence, with their music, songs, and dancing, has been hitherto considered indispensable at Hindu weddings and on other social occasions."—"Report of Work among the Educated Classes in Connection with the London Mission, Bangalore, for the Year 1893," p. 14.

[2] The following significant paragraph is taken from the Madras journal entitled *Progress*, for February, 1896: "When it was known that Lord Elgin would visit Madras, the wealthy citizen who distinguishes himself by entertaining Viceroys was urged by social reformers not to have nautch-girls, but he gave no heed to the appeal. At the entertainment, when the Viceroy and the Governor were sitting side by side, a nautch-girl suddenly came forward, and began her performance. The Viceroy and Governor then spoke to each other; their feelings were communicated to their host, who was standing near a pillar, with the result that the performance was stopped. This account is on the authority of an eye-witness. It is hoped that hereafter nautch-girls will be omitted from the programmes of such entertainments."

speech, and action, so as to purge our society generally of the evils of low and immoral surroundings." [1]   Another hopeful feature of this conflict is the formation of Purity Societies in different parts of India, the spirit and purpose of which are in accord with such organizations as the White Cross Army, the White Ribbon Society, and others of various names.   While calling attention more especially to the organized work and public movements on behalf of social righteousness, we should not forget the mighty influence of Christian missions in kindling new moral aspirations in the individual heart.   This aspect of the subject may be less conspicuous and not so easily discoverable, but its effectiveness is incalculable.

The renewed discussion on the regulation and consequent legalization of vice, as embodied in what are known as the Contagious Disease Acts, is once more prominently before the British public, especially in connection with the moral status in India.   That it is a difficult question is not to be denied, and it is evident also that there is a difference of opinion upon the subject among those who sincerely desire public morality and are truly seeking the social welfare. The standpoint from which the matter is viewed is all-important. It may be regarded as preëminently a moral question, to be decided in the light of biblical standards, or it may be looked upon from the heights of *laissez-faire* officialism, and be judged in the light of social expediency, with little solicitude for the higher principles involved. That the moral aspects of the question are deserving of first consideration must surely be maintained.   In the end, if these are honored and conserved, the best interests of all concerned will be promoted. It is claimed upon a basis of sufficient evidence that the policy of compromise and so-called "regulation," as represented in the Contagious Disease Acts, fails altogether as a moral restraint, and is worthless as a practical expedient.[2]   The spectacle of a civilized government thus facilitating immorality by system and supervision is at once startling and deplorable.   Surely there is a better way—one which will aim both to save the tempted and rescue the victim.[3]

Is there a Christian basis for " regulated vice"?

---

[1] *Progress*, February, 1896, p. 89.   Cf. also *India*, March, 1896, p. 91.   Further information will be found in a letter from the Rev. John S. Chandler (A. B. C. F. M.), published in *The Independent*, August 17, 1893, pp. 16, 17.

[2] *The Sentinel*, March, 1896, p. 31.

[3] Several periodicals, both in England and America, are issued in support of the cause of social purity and national righteousness.   Prominent among them is *The Sentinel*, published by Dyer Brothers, Rose Street Corner, Paternoster Square,

We cannot dwell longer upon this subject. A careful scrutiny of almost every mission field will discover signs of Christian influence in the direction of a higher morality. Much might be said of the encouraging advance under the auspices of missions in Jamaica and throughout the West Indies. A missionary writes from the Levant:

The White Cross a universal symbol of mission teaching and influence.

" The morals of the people have been greatly improved, and it may fairly be claimed that the constant insistence by missionaries and native Protestant preachers upon a pure morality has not been without salutary effect upon the non-Mohammedan communities of Turkey." [1] From China, Siam, Burma, and the islands of the Pacific, similar testimony would be forthcoming. " In Madagascar," writes the Rev. James Sibree (L. M. S.), "immorality is certainly greatly diminished, and a purer family life established." A paper written by a native Christian of that island, on " The Blessings Received from the Bible apart from Salvation," contains the following sentences: " The Bible has affected the former immoral habits of the people. Many are now living a changed life. Our former ways of living were shameful in the extreme; nevertheless they were rejoiced in. That state of things has undergone a complete change." Even in Africa a moral tone has been established in Christian communities which is in striking contrast to all heathen conceptions. In the " Report of the United Presbyterian Church of Scotland for 1897," under the head of Kaffraria, is the following significant statement from the pen of the Rev. Alexander Welsh, concerning progress at Emgwali: " The White Cross Society has about fifty members now. We hope it will continue to grow and do good work. Purity meetings have been held at various places in the district." Surely there can be no reasonable question as to the indubitable trend of mission influence throughout the world in the direction of establishing higher standards of personal purity and introducing the blessed leaven of social righteousness amid the demor-

London, where books and tracts dealing with the problem of social purity may be obtained. In America the official organ of the Woman's Christian Temperance Union, known as *The Union Signal*, holds a corresponding position, and the efforts of that powerful organization, having various branches throughout Christendom and also in many foreign mission fields, are turned with increasing energy to the subject of social purity. International conferences at stated intervals, and an international organization for the abolition of State regulated vice are among the instruments at work to develop public sentiment and deepen the reverence for a purer code of morals. *The Philanthropist*, the organ of the American Purity Alliance, is devoted to the same cause.

[1] The Rev. J. K. Greene, D.D. (A. B. C. F. M.), Constantinople, Turkey.

alizing laxity of heathenism.   To the honor of Christian missions it
may be said that not one sign of compromise or unhallowed license
characterizes their attitude towards this circle of loathsome vices.
The highest and noblest standards of purity are always advocated
by missionaries, and to a remarkable extent are reflected in the personal life of native converts.

5. DISCREDITING SELF-INFLICTED TORTURE OR MUTILATION. — The
extreme expedients of heathen asceticism are due to the delusive hope
of merit-making, or are the consequences of the
false conception that maceration of the flesh is the
destruction of sin.   Superstitious fear or the
frenzy of religious fanaticism also accounts for
some of these self-inflicted tortures and mutilations.   The Gospel is
the true remedy for such strange and pitiful follies, because it teaches
the way of peace in Christ.   It restores the desperate and despairing
victim of religious delusion to "his right mind."   Many who are now
thus "sitting and clothed" were for weary years struggling for hope
and comfort by means of supposed meritorious sufferings, often self-
inflicted, and sometimes prolonged and severe.   In times of sorrow and
fear the heathen are accustomed to give way to inconsolable grief,
accompanied usually by frenzied self-laceration.   The Gospel imparts calmness and faith, and a trustful spirit of submission to the
Heavenly Father's will.   The contrast observable at Christian funerals
conducted with decorum, and free from the wild scenes and cruel excesses so characteristic of heathenism under similar circumstances,
is striking in its exhibition of the power of Christianity to calm
and sustain the soul in its hours of need.   The British Government
has put a stop to some of the worst of these tortures in India, but the
spirit which prompts them cannot be banished by legal enactments,
and there are besides many less notorious kinds of painful austerities
not within the range of civil law, which only the enlightening wisdom
and grace of the Gospel can discredit.   Wonderful illumination of the
mind and speedy change of habit concerning these fanatical cruelties
follow the entrance of missions into savage life.   "We find," writes
the Rev. H. McKay (C. P. M.), of Round Lake, Canada, "that the
cruelties of self-torture are put away by Christian Indians."[1]   No one

The Gospel a message of sanity and peace to deluded minds.

---

[1] "Our native preachers, to the number of sixty or more, denounce self-torture;
Christians condemn it; and now even the magistrates are issuing proclamations
against it.   From year to year, of late, cruel rites have been forbidden; for example,

who understands at all the tone and temper of Christian faith can doubt that just here it has healing and saving power.

6. ARRESTING PESSIMISTIC AND SUICIDAL TENDENCIES.—The frequency of suicide in civilized countries has been the occasion for much recent comment in the public press. In an article on " Suicide and the Environment," in *The Popu-* The antisocial trend of *lar Science Monthly* (June, 1897), Mr. Robert N. pessimism. Reeves states upon good authority that since 1860 it has increased in the New England States to the extent of thirty-five per cent., and gives it as his opinion that " this percentage, with but slight variations, will probably apply to all other States of the Union where there is great industrial and commercial activity." Information derived from the Bureau of Vital Statistics in Washington indicates that while the rate of increase in population from 1850 to 1890 registers 1.70+, the increase in suicides in the same period registers 7.00+. The number reported in 1850 was 491, and 3932 in 1890, or, upon another basis of computation, the proportion in 1850 was 2.11+ to every 100,000 persons, and in 1890 it was 6.00+.[1] Still later statistics give the number of suicides in 1896 to be, so far as ascertained, 6520, being an increase of 761 over the record for 1895. Psychologists, philanthropists, and moralists have studied the subject with care, but apparently they can do little to remedy this disastrous increase in the tendency to self-destruction. Where the natural love of life is not sufficient, nothing seems to act as an effective deterrent, except the fear of God and the conscientious restraints of religion. Mere civilization, if it is godless, is of little avail in checking it. Among all the social forces which act as an antidote to suicidal propensities there seems to be no doubt that the most helpful preventive influence is a pure and well-ordered family life.[2] The Bible teaches that self-destruc-

last year (1894) the Tamsui magistrate forbade sorcerers to afflict their persons, as was the custom. Formerly many devotees died as the result of self-torture with fire, knife, club, etc. Now there is a very great improvement. As far as Christianity is accepted, the efficacy of self-torture is disbelieved, and others besides Christians are beginning to doubt it."—Rev. W. Gauld, M.A. (C. P. M.), Tamsui, Formosa.

[1] Article by James H. Taylor, D.D., in *The Independent*, April 30, 1896.

[2] In the article by Mr. Robert N. Reeves, already referred to, statistics are given which fully confirm this statement. " It has been found," he asserts, " that in a million of husbands without children there were 470 suicides, and in the same number with children there were but 205. Of a million wives without children

tion is a sin, and in the light of domestic and social obligations it becomes also a crime, yet one which it is impossible to regulate by any provision of the criminal code.

If amidst all the optimistic aspects of society in Christendom the dark and awful refuge of suicide is so popular, it can hardly surprise us that in an environment of heathenism this tragic expedient should be far more frequently adopted. The atmosphere of the non-Christian world is strongly pessimistic. The teachings of its philosophy and religion regarding the future life encourage the expectation that a further opportunity, or at least some change which is more desirable than the present lot, is to be found in another state of existence, while that sacredness which Christianity gives to life is absent. Dr. Faber, a learned scholar in Confucianism, regards its doctrines and practices concerning woman as the cause of the tendency among Chinese women to commit suicide.[1] The Rev. Arthur H. Smith speaks of suicide among the wives and daughters in China as very common, —even epidemic at times,—and gives as a reason the unhappy status of woman, especially in her marital life. He describes the way in which young girls band themselves together to seek self-destruction rather than consent to marriage, and remarks that "the death-roll of suicides is the most convincing proof of the woes endured by Chinese women."[2]

Suicide a popular remedy for the ills of heathenism.

That Hindu philosophy is pessimistic is not difficult of proof. Its doctrine of the Supreme Being—a virtual nonentity, without attributes of personality or force of will—gives no cheer and courage to faith. Its ascetic view of existence, its dismal doctrine of metempsychosis, and its hopeless legalism, all cast the sombre shadows of pessimism far and wide. The universe is gloomy, life is hard and sad, and the future is darkened by cheerless mysteries. If we follow

The pessimistic outlook of the Hindu and the Buddhist.

157 committed suicide, as against 45 with children; widowers without children, 1004; with children, 526; widows without children, 238; with children, but 104. These figures are eloquent pleaders in favor of family ties as conservators of life."

[1] "The Memorial Arches erected to persons who have committed suicide, especially to widows, are throwing a sad light on the morality of a community where such *crimes* are necessitated. Confucianism is responsible for it by the low place it allows to women, by the wrong feeling of honor it awakens in men and women, and by the meagre religious consolation it can provide for the afflicted. Death is sought as the only escape from unbearable misery."—Article on "Confucianism," by the Rev. Ernst Faber, Dr. Theol., in "The China Mission Hand-Book" (1896), pp. 5, 6.

[2] Smith, "The Natural History of the Chinese Boy and of the Chinese Girl: A Study in Sociology," pp. 19, 26.

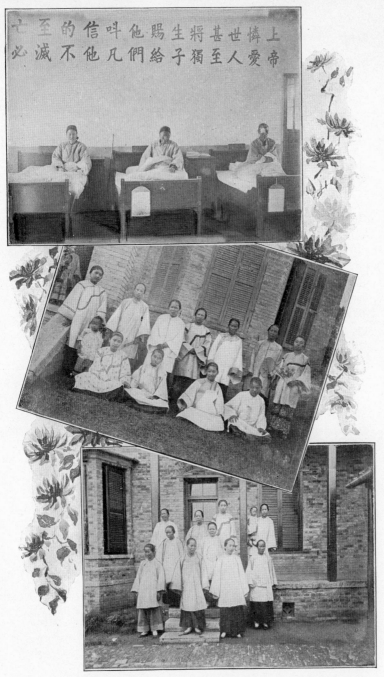

上帝愛世人甚至將他獨生子賜給他們叫一切信他的凡不信他的人必至滅亡

Patients in Nanking Hospital.   Inscription on the wall, John 3 : 16.

Pupils in the Woman's School, Nanking.

Pupils in Bible Training School, Nanking.

CHRISTIAN OPTIMISM IN CHINESE FACES.

(M. E. M. S.)

the trail of heathenism, nature-worship, and demonology, into the recesses of the non-Christian world, we find our pathway deeply shadowed by the same depressing hopelessness.

It can hardly be questioned by any candid mind that the Gospel, when accepted, brings a flood of precious light and a supply of comfort and hope into these dreary and saddened realms of pessimism. What the world needs everywhere is the sanity, courage, and cheer of Christian optimism. Hope is the antidote to despair, and a restraint upon the hideous suggestions of suicide, and this support is just what the Gospel provides wherever it is received. In an article on "Japan's Debt to Christianity," by the Rev. James I. Seder, of Tokyo, he writes: "Christianity is substituting optimism for the former pessimism. The old religious ideal was 'to leave the world of suffering' and enter Nirvana, or be absorbed into the universe and practical nothingness; the new ideal is to stay in the world and help to reform it." [1] In a printed report from a China Inland missionary in the Province of Hupeh occurs the following significant statement: "About one hundred lives of would-be suicides have been saved."[2] Almost every missionary physician in China is frequently called upon to give professional aid in the case of some one who has attempted suicide by opium, and in many instances the ministrations not only to the body but to the mind persuade the victim to refrain from such attempts in the future.

In an account of the Mission of the United Presbyterian Church of Scotland in Old Calabar, it is stated that as far back as 1878 an agreement between the British Consul and the leading men of the country contained an article forbidding suicide. Consul Hopkins acknowledged that "such an agreement would have been impossible but for the long-continued residence and teaching of missionaries." [3] Christian converts the world over rarely commit suicide, unless mentally unbalanced. They live in comparative happiness and comfort, with a glow of spiritual peace and hope brightening their earthly lot, with cheerful views of their present existence, and a clear

Suicidal tendencies disappear among native Christians.

---

[1] *The Missionary Review of the World*, September, 1895, p. 656.

[2] *China's Millions*, October, 1892, p. 133.

[3] Dickie, "Story of the Mission in Old Calabar," p. 78. The article referred to reads as follows: "Any persons taking the esere-bean wilfully, either for the purpose of committing suicide, or for the purpose of attempting to prove their innocence of any crime of which they may have been accused, shall be considered guilty of attempting murder, and shall be fined as heavily as their circumstances will permit, and shall be banished from the country."

assurance of immortality in Christ. The Gospel ministry of hope is an unspeakable blessing to multitudes, who without it would remain the victims of pessimism.

7. CULTIVATING HABITS OF INDUSTRY AND FRUGALITY.—In the case of some Asiatic peoples, as, for example, the Japanese and Chinese, frugality and industry are to a marked degree natural traits of character. The *samurai* among the Japanese and the *literati* among the Chinese must be counted as exceptions, but as a rule the masses do not need to be taught either the dignity and usefulness of labor, or the rewards of frugality. Economic conditions, to be sure, may have compelled them thus to recognize the necessity of labor, and it is not unlikely that the notions which regulate the attitude of the higher classes in both countries to all industrial occupation would have a far more extensive following were it possible for the people as a whole to avoid the necessity of toil. It is, after all, the Christian conception of work which is contesting sharply the theoretical platform of the two-sworded and long-nailed gentry in these lands, and has already made considerable inroads upon the stability and hitherto undisputed dignity of their position.

The influence of Christianity in infusing a conscience into the spirit of common labor, in stimulating and brightening daily toil, and in imparting a sacredness to the ordinary duties of life, is a worthy part of its blessed record upon earth.[1] The early Christian missionaries of Europe were the pioneers of industry as well as of religion. It was they who introduced the ideal of peaceful and industrious toil in settled homes as an offset to the wild life of adventure and brigandage which was the ambition of early barbarism. "The ensign and emblazonry of the entire history of the monks during those early ages," Montalembert declares to be "Cruce et Aratro."[2] Christianity has ennobled toil and to a large extent delivered it from the contempt which according to the notions of the heathen seemed to

Christian missions advocate and stimulate honest industry.

---

[1] Eph. iv. 28; 1 Thess. iv. 11, 12; 2 Thess. iii. 10–12.

[2] Storrs, "The Divine Origin of Christianity," pp. 308, 618. The following quotation from Montalembert is given by Dr. Storrs on page 618: "It seems to me that we should all contemplate with emotion, if it still existed, that monk's plough [Theodulph's], doubly sacred, by religion and by labor, by history and by virtue. For myself, I feel that I should kiss it as willingly as the sword of Charlemagne or the pen of Bossuet."—Montalembert, "Monks of the West" (London ed., 1861), vol. ii., pp. 376–379.

be attached to it.[1]   It has steadily sought to be "the moral regenerator of labor wherever it is, and its moral founder wherever it is not."[2]

A glance at missions in the South Seas and the African Continent will yield telling illustrations of this.   War, feasting, hilarity, and idleness were magic words with the average native of the Southern Isles early in the present century.   The transfiguration of work in Africa and the South Seas. The first lesson of the missionary was an inspiration to better things.[3]   Many of these islands are now under European, especially British, protection, while commercial as well as agricultural industries are rapidly assuming importance.   If we ask why these islanders are such apt pupils in the school of Western civilization, the true answer will be, because they have been through a long preparatory training at the hands of the missionaries, who first subdued, reclaimed, and instructed their savage natures so that they were ready for the advent of Western methods and restraints.   The industrial results of missions in the South Pacific may take rank as one

---

1 Uhlhorn, "The Conflict of Christianity with Heathenism," pp. 105, 106.

2 Warneck, "Modern Missions and Culture," p. 81.

3 "It was in 1818 that Mr. Williams and Mr. Threlkeld settled at Raiatea [Society Islands], under the famous chief Tamatoa.   The inhabitants welcomed them with every demonstration of delight, and provided a great feast, which included five hogs for Mr. Williams, five hogs for Mrs. Williams, and five hogs for the baby! With characteristic energy and practical common sense, Mr. Williams devoted himself to stimulating the people to all kinds of good works.   He became ' guide, philosopher, and friend' to them all.   Apparently there was nothing he could not make, from a house to a constitution; and even the notorious indolence of the Raiateans gave way under his energetic leadership.   The main settlement of natives lay in an exposed position, which resulted in their huts and crops being frequently destroyed by storms.   Largely at Mr. Williams's instigation, there was an ' exodus' of the entire settlement.   A new town was formed in a more healthy and sheltered position.   Good houses were built, wells were sunk, a beautiful place of worship erected, gardens planned and planted, until the whole place was a monument to Mr. Williams's genius and industry. . . . Every year the fruits of the new religion began to appear.   The people grew in industry and morality."—Horne, "The Story of the London Missionary Society," p. 44.

" The innate indolence of the natives has given place to industrial pursuits, and in several instances to the acquisition of industrial arts.   Many of them have become useful mechanics.   The men are now able to build and furnish with their own hands comfortable dwellings, and they are also frequently engaged for the same purpose by the white settlers.   The women make decent clothing for their families, and all are well clad.   In the eastern islands the natives can build small, well-constructed sailing vessels, on good models, and are able to man and navigate them themselves.   They carry on trading operations with distant islands, and occasionally sail to South American and other ports."—"The Pacific in 1795 and Now," by the Rev. S. Ella, in *The Chronicle*, September, 1894, p. 212.

of the most unique social and economic transformations that the world has ever witnessed.[1]   In the "Report of the London Missionary Society for 1891" is the following paragraph, referring to the people of the Hervey Islands, which had then passed under British protection: "With growing intelligence and the increase of their wants there has been a development of thrift and industry.   They are building one-hundred-ton vessels, and are extensively engaged in planting coffee and cotton."   The effect of such institutions as those at Malua and on Norfolk Island is to alter the whole current and trend of native ideals.[2]

A great change is apparent in the New Hebrides.   A correspondent of a newspaper of Auckland testifies that "the Rarotongans are the most advanced of all the South Sea Islanders in European industrial civilization.   They have become efficient artisans and mechanics; they build houses after the colonial type, also wagons and boats; they work extensive plantations and cotton-ginning machines; they are good seamen, valued for their docility, industry, and contented disposition.   They cultivate largely oranges and limes; of the former they export millions; from the limes they express the juice and ship it in small barrels, some two thousand gallons yearly being sent away from the island.   They also export cotton, coffee, bananas, arrowroot,

The industrial civilization of the New Hebrides.

---

1 *The Chronicle*, August, 1894, p. 180; September, 1894, p. 212.

2 "In 1844, Rev. Charles Hardie, with Rev. G. Turner—who in the previous year had been obliged to flee for his life from the Island of Tanna in the New Hebrides—established a self-supporting boarding-school for higher education at Malua, on the Island of Upolu.   They purchased three hundred acres of land covered with wild jungle and bordering on a lagoon, erected buildings, and enrolled one hundred students, in classes of twenty-five, for a four years' course of study.   With the aid of the students the land was cleared of brush and planted with ' ten thousand bread-fruit and cocoanut trees, thousands of bananas, and yams, taro, maize, manioc, and sugar-cane, and a road was made in circuit around the tract, and shaded by the cocoanut palm.'   Besides cultivating the soil and catching fish from the lagoon the students learned useful mechanical arts.   The produce of the land and the fish of the lagoons supplied all their wants.   In this school pupils were received from the New Hebrides, New Caledonia, and Savage Island, as well as from the Samoa Islands. Its graduates have become the teachers of the common schools, the pastors of churches, and foreign missionaries; and here over two thousand teachers and native ministers have been trained.   In the year 1891 ninety-five graduates were acting as ordained pastors in the Samoa and other groups of islands.   The Malua Institution has been rated as foremost in importance of the missionary agencies in Samoa."— Alexander, "The Islands of the Pacific," pp. 284, 285.

Similar statements might be made concerning the Norfolk Island Training Institution.   See Montgomery, "The Light of Melanesia," p. 15.

and copra. Thus they thrive, and are contented and happy, because free and unoppressed, and at liberty to enjoy the fruits of their labors." [1] Would this remarkable statement be possible were it not for the toils and sacrifices of missionary labor for so many years in that primitive environment of loathsome savagery? "Jehovah's Arrowroot" is the watchword of a recent and flourishing industry in these islands, by means of which the natives pay for the printing of the Gospels at Melbourne for their own use. "Better work than fighting" is the new rallying-cry.[2] In the great island of New Guinea the pioneers of orderly living, the reclaimers of swamps, the builders of decent dwellings and neat chapels, and the first patrons of the modern arts of life, have been the agents of the London Missionary Society.[3] The orange and coffee trees and the cotton-plant were introduced in some of the South Sea Islands by the early missionaries.

The African has learned the very alphabet of industry and frugality from Christian missions. Such institutions as that of the Free Church of Scotland at Lovedale, South Africa, not only guide young men and women into paths of spiritual light, but transform the life that now is into a happy and useful career by teaching some industrial art which makes them of value to the world, and gives them the privileges and joys of self-supporting service.[4] No one in the home churches can realize, and the missionaries themselves hardly appreciate, the immense social changes in the direction of orderly and useful living

Africans made valuable to the world by mission training.

[1] Quoted in Alexander, "The Islands of the Pacific," p. 273.

[2] Paton, "Letters and Sketches from the New Hebrides," p. 298; *The Free Church of Scotland Monthly*, January, 1895, p. 15.

[3] Horne, "The Story of the London Missionary Society," p. 410.

[4] Dr. James Stewart, who is at the head of this noble enterprise, thus refers to the department of industrial instruction and its scope: "Among a people in barbarism, or emerging from it, there is almost entire ignorance of the arts of civilised life and a certain indolence, which is often a serious barrier to the acceptance of the Gospel. There is also the danger of unsatisfactory results, if all that goes on under the name of education is confined to a knowledge of books and attendance at school classes. Knowledge merely puffeth up, but manual labour taught with charity certainly edifieth the individual—in the original sense of that word—as well as the African social state. The following trades are taught—Carpentering, Wagon-making, Blacksmithing, Printing, Bookbinding, and even Telegraphing; the latter only to a few. In addition, all who are not indentured to these trades engage in some kind of manual work about the place for a certain number of hours daily, in the gardens or fields, or on the roads, and in keeping the extensive grounds in order. A large farm is also cultivated to supply food, and this affords work in the sowing, hoeing, and reaping seasons, as well as at other times during the year."—"Lovedale, South Africa," p. 5.

which have been inaugurated in hundreds of African communities. "The kraal-going missionary has made the kirk-going people," is the quaint epigram which describes the result of the United Presbyterian Missions in Kaffraria. This is not, however, the whole truth, since that same missionary has turned the warrior into the modern plowman, and put tools of precision into idle hands. Industrial missions and also industrial features in the curriculum of missionary training are no longer an experiment in many African fields. Plows, which, in the dramatic language of a native admirer, are said to "do the work of ten wives," have broken furrows of civilization in African society. Self-supporting industry has brought a new consciousness of self-respect. The "eight-and-twenty plows seen by one visitor to Lutuli," an out-station of the Scotch United Presbyterian Church, in the wilds of Kaffraria, are not to be passed over as too insignificant a fact to be noted.[1] It throws a bright light over the earthly lot of many whose lives were, not long ago, all out of focus with any true usefulness in the world.

Mr. Slowan, in his little volume on the Kaffrarian Mission writes, referring to the missionary: "He it is who has taught the Kaffir —not only by precept, but by the far more effec-

The heathen *versus* the Christian hut — an object-lesson in mission economics.

tive means of example—to value irrigation and the use of tools; to feel the need for decent clothes; to wield the pen and the spade instead of the *assegai;* while in his hands the mission station has become an object-lesson of industry, progress, and beauty, which the dullest intelligence can apprehend. Of two huts in the same kraal you may tell, before

---

[1] Slowan, "The Story of Our Kaffrarian Mission," p. 73.

The late Rev. H. M. Bridgman (A. B. C. F. M.), of Umzumbe, Natal, has communicated the following interesting facts concerning the natives of that vicinity: "They see that among enlightened people it is no disgrace, even for a man, to work. All this change has of course necessitated the purchase of thousands and tens of thousands of 'Hillside Plows.' They now see that in this way they get larger crops. I should say that the plows are American, also the thousands of small axes. These plows cost from sixteen to twenty dollars each. We may say that this material advance is largely the result of the teaching of missionaries, for they first taught the natives to yoke and break in their oxen, and to plow."

The Rev. G. A. Godduhn (P. B. F. M. N.), Gaboon, West Africa, writes as follows: "In our mission we have never had industrial schools, but have imported different kinds of tools, and taught the natives to use them, and showed them, above all, that labor was honorable. When I came to Batanga we could hardly get men to work for us, and the few who came were often sneered at and ridiculed, because 'they sold their skin for money,' that is, they worked for wages. During the last few years more men were available than we could employ."

you cross the threshold, in which the heathen lives and in which the Christian." [1] Mr. Joseph Thomson, the African explorer, reports in *The Geographical Journal* that the Blantyre church (see illustration in Vol. I., p. 459), built under the direction of a missionary of the Church of Scotland, but by the hands of native workmen, is "the most wonderful sight I have seen in Africa." [2] Hard by Nyassaland has been planted the Zambesi Industrial Mission, in the Shiré Highlands. The French Protestant Mission in Basutoland has seven hundred young men in its normal and industrial schools, and counts as one of its triumphs the converting of the native "from the condition of a loafing savage to that of a laborer."

The Livingstonia Mission of the Free Church of Scotland has made possible an industrial outlook to thousands of Tonga laborers who were only a few years ago dwelling in hopeless poverty and fear, on account of their cruel neighbors, the Angoni. Even the latter have been turned from their trails of blood and plunder to the paths of honest toil. [3] Bishop Tucker, in an account of a visit to Taveta, situated in a section of British territory west of Mombasa, at some little distance from the coast, gives a sketch of an industrial as

Paths of honest toil over ancient trails of blood and plunder.

1 Slowan, "The Story of Our Kaffrarian Mission," p. 97.

2 In Mr. J. S. Keltie's recent volume, he refers to this structure as follows: "A church has quite recently been erected in the heart of what is still savage Africa; a creditable and even handsome church it is, with many graceful points of architecture. It stands in the Blantyre Highlands, consecrated by the name of Livingstone, near the banks of the Shiré River, to the south of Lake Nyassa. It is a region that for centuries has been devastated by slave-raiders and native wars, a district which, when Livingstone passed through it in his sad last wanderings, was in a deplorable condition. For some years, however, that region has been in the hands of Scotch missionaries and Scotch traders. Thousands of acres are under coffee plantations, and thousands more have been taken up by English planters to be brought under cultivation. The natives, who a few years ago lived in the wildest savagery, come hundreds of miles voluntarily to beg for work in these plantations. Many of them have been trained to various trades. This church, then, designed by a Scotch missionary, was built entirely by the natives with free labour. He and his colleagues taught the natives to make bricks, burn lime, and hew timber. Here there is not the least suspicion of compulsion, and the result is wonderful."—Keltie, "The Partition of Africa," pp. 453, 454.

3 "Dr. Laws tells us that on his journey up the Zambesi and Shiré to the lake he saw traces of the Livingstonia Mission from the sea-coast at Chinde to Lake Nyassa. Most of the porterage on the rivers is done by Tonga boatmen, lads from the mission schools being captains of the boats and canoes, or employed in other stations of more or less trust and usefulness. The African Lakes Company employs no fewer than 1400 Tonga, while among the other settlers and planters on the Shiré

well as spiritual transformation wrought by resident missionaries, which
has in it the making of a new race in those African forests.[1] In the
first report on trade and labor in the Uganda Protectorate, by Mr.
Berkeley, issued by the Foreign Office of Great Britain early in 1897,
the progress of the Waganda in developing a spirit of industry is commended, and efforts are reported in the direction of teaching new
employments and introducing improved methods in the place of old
ones.   It does not appear in the account to what extent this progress
is due to missionaries, but the fact that they have been such an important element in the opening of Uganda certainly will justify crediting
a measure of it to mission work.   A glance into the life and services of
Alexander Mackay will fully support this inference.   He speaks of his
own hard toil, sometimes for the purpose of earning his food, and while
occasionally lamenting that he could not give more strength to the
religious instruction of the people, he adds in one of his letters the
following significant sentence: "But somehow or other I get a good
deal of that [spiritual missionary work] done also, and in a place like

Highlands other 4000 are employed. They have not all come from the Bandawè
schools, nor are they all even professing Christians; but it is the mission which
has made their honest labour possible. When our missionaries first went to Lake
Nyassa, these Tonga were starved fugitives, fearfully inhabiting rocky islets on the
lake shore, afraid to grow food or keep cattle lest they should bring the dreaded
Angoni down upon them. He reports also in the Shiré Highlands many Angoni
labourers. These men, who once disdained all labour but that which was involved
in killing their fellow-men or wild beasts, are now earning an honest livelihood."—
The Free Church of Scotland Monthly, January, 1895, p. 14.

In a private letter to the author, from Kondowi, Livingstonia, Dr. Laws, who
is at present connected with the Free Church of Scotland Missions in British
Central Africa, writes as follows: "I am at a new place here, which we hope to
occupy as a training institution for native teachers and pastors, and also as a technical school for handicrafts. A bit of work on which I have been engaged was laying
out and making a road to the plain below. I had a gang of men with me, and the
majority of these belonged to the Angoni tribe. The last time several of these
had been in this neighborhood was on a war foray, and now they were helping in
making a road for the use of the people they had formerly hunted as partridges on
the mountains. Fourteen years ago these Angoni refused to carry a load—'they
were warriors, not slaves!'—work was beneath them. War forays are rare among
them now, and even those who are opposed to the Gospel have to acknowledge the
Word of God as a power in the land, the censure of which it is not wise of them by
their conduct openly to incur."

[1] "The name given to it is Mahoo, i.e., Happy Land; and to very many young
men and boys it is proving a veritable happy land. I find that there are now some
forty-six boys under Christian instruction at Mahoo; these all live upon the station,
and maintain themselves entirely by their own labour. A certain proportion of

this, where the people are above doing any labor, my example in the workshop may not be lost." A writer in *The Church Missionary Intelligencer*, in commenting upon this passage, remarks: "Overwork is not one of the curses of uncivilised races, and no Factory Acts or Eight Hours Bills are needed to protect them from it. If they are to be elevated to the dignity of true Christian life in this world, they must be taught industry as well as the other virtues, and the actual practice of the missionaries is the best, and often the only, means of inculcating it." [1]

The stations of the Universities' Mission to Central Africa are scenes of industry, neatness, and good order. If we at home could only behold the smiling faces and cheerful demeanor of the happy natives who live in them, it would add an ineffaceable charm to mission work. The Rev. J. S. Wimbush (U. M. C. A.) writes that the object of that missionary society is to teach the African "that time and strength and brains are God's gifts, and are given to be used. It insists upon the duty of work, and then it steps in and shows him new ways of using these gifts. It teaches him to build with stone instead of with reeds and mud; it acquaints him with carpenters' tools, and instructs him how to use them. Having taught him to read and write, it introduces printing-presses, and teaches him to print books and magazines in his own language. It sends out steamships, and shows him how to manage a steam engine. The Universities' Mission has in the last two years supplied Sir H. H. Johnston, Commissioner for British Nyassaland, and his assistants, with native printers, carpenters, cooks, and a telegraph clerk, and Baron von Eltz, the German Governor, with cooks and a carpenter. The same Mission has two steamships on the Lake, the smaller of which is in entire charge of a native engineer, and the larger (sixty-five feet long) is worked by native engineers under the direction of a European. All these have been taught by the Mission."

The Gospel of smiling faces and cheerful hearts.

time each day is allotted to general education in school, which each boy attends. Four days a week, cultivation, and building, and manual labour of some kind or other for the general good, are undertaken regularly. Each boy, moreover, has allotted to him a small garden, or *shamba*, some forty yards by twenty. The produce of this piece of land is his own property, and he is allowed one day in the week for cultivating it. Thus the work of the station is carried on, and the whole made self-supporting."—Letter of Bishop Tucker, in *The Church Missionary Intelligencer*, June, 1895, p. 452.

[1] *The Church Missionary Intelligencer*, September, 1894, p. 672.

Industry, let it be noted in this connection, is not the natural bent of an African's desire. His ideal is summed up in idleness, questionable amusement, and war. It becomes, there- **The industrial triumphs** fore, no common victory to turn him into an eco- **of missions in Africa.** nomic producer, and make him an honest toiler among his fellows. This is being done, however, through missionary influence, both direct and indirect, in many sections of the Continent.[1] Industrial features are, in fact, a part of almost all mission work in Africa. The establishment of such plants as are found, under the direction of the Mission of the Lutheran General Synod of America, at Muhlenberg, Liberia, on the West Coast, the Zambesi Industrial Mission on the East Coast, and the missions started by Bishop Taylor in the southwestern sections of the Continent, promises a practical betterment of the African, which in its import is second only to his growth in godliness.[2] The Lutheran

[1] The Rev. J. P. Farler (U. M. C. A.) writes of a visit to a native Christian community, an offshoot of the Mbweni station, where a number of converts had founded a new village, built their own church, and opened an industrial centre on their own account. This is the strange legend of Kichelwe, as reported by Mr. Farler: "Guided by one of the school-boys, I took a long walk through the plantations and visited many of the houses of the people. I found that natives from the interior had joined them, and also Mohammedan Swahili from the coast, attracted by the peace, order, and prosperity of this settlement, all submitting to Christian instruction. They told me that they cultivated fruit and vegetables, and sold them to the Germans at Dar-es-Salaam, and also raised fowls, getting good prices for them and their eggs. They assured me that they were happy and prosperous. The Mohammedans respect them, and the Germans are favourably disposed towards them. Now this is a purely native mission, self-supporting, and without any English supervision. A priest visits them once a month to celebrate the Holy Eucharist for them. This is something very different from the 'travellers' tales' about native converts begging rice and food from the whites. These people are self-supporting and self-respecting, desiring nothing from the mission but spiritual assistance. Managing their own affairs, orderly and self-disciplined, in their native deacon they have a minister of a very high character, and are guided by him. Perfect order is maintained, while there is absolute freedom. I don't know of anything that has pleased me more than this self-contained group of native Christians, drawing outsiders into their community by their own inherent qualities, living their own Christian lives and asking no assistance from any one."—*Central Africa*, October, 1895, p. 154.

[2] The Rev. George Grenfell (E. B. M. S.) writes from Bolobo, on the Upper Congo, that "missions, by means of the technical training they are furnishing, and by reason of the habits of industry they are inculcating, are also contributing in no small measure to the future development of the people. It is as important for the missionary's chief purpose as it is for the country that habits of industry should be formed. It cannot be conceived that Christianity should really influence the heart of the uncivilised negro and leave him content in the midst of his old circumstances

Industrial pupils of the English Baptist Mission, Bolobo, Upper Congo. (Engineers, Printers, Carpenters, Brickmakers and Bricklayers.)

CONVERTS TO THE GOSPEL OF INDUSTRY IN AFRICA.

(E. B. M. S.)

Mission Board above referred to has established an industrial farm on the West Coast of Africa, where various trades and occupations are taught to the pupils. In all, ten thousand acres are under cultivation, owned in small holdings by about three thousand natives, every one with his own share in the prosperity of the entire plant. Each family lives in its own home under Christian influence, and the members of the community support church organizations with their own earnings.[1] Along the Congo new industries have been introduced by the Baptist missionaries.

India, with all its poverty, is in certain features of its social life a land of foolish extravagance and ruinous waste. Conformity to expensive customs, especially those incidental to marriages and funerals,[2] and general improvidence, is largely responsible for the enormous debts which rest like an incubus upon so many. Agitation upon the subject of marriage expenses, with a view to their reduction, is now part of the programme of social reform. Conferences and conventions pass resolutions condemning the needless prodigality and costly exactions incidental to these occasions, and urging efforts at curtailment.[3] A former Governor of Madras said upon this point: "He who could persuade his countrymen to give up their, to us, astounding expenditure on marriages would do more for South India than any government could do in a decade." The British Govern-

Lessons in domestic economy for extravagant India.

—his old unclean and immoral surroundings. Those who have had experience of mission work in Africa recognise how difficult it is for church-members to maintain consistent lives unless the old idleness is exchanged for industrious pursuits."

1 "Report of Third Conference of Officers of Foreign Mission Boards and Societies in the United States and Canada," held in New York, February, 1895.

2 "I was invited to the obsequies of a man of some position in the city here a few years ago, my card of invitation bearing the serial number 7000, an indication of the huge crowds sometimes collected on the occasion of a marriage or the celebration of the death ceremonies in a rich or influential man's family. Many families, afraid to incur the social stigma which would result from the non-observance of these ceremonies, have had their whole savings swallowed up by the expenses incurred; others have been plunged into debt from which they never recovered; and many more have been absolutely ruined."—Dr. James Sommerville (U. P. C. S. M.), Jodhpore, Rajputana, India.

3 The resolution on this subject passed at the National Social Conference of 1896, at Calcutta, was as follows: "That the Conference notes with pleasure the efforts made by caste associations and conferences in the North Provinces and the Punjab to curtail needless expenditure on marriage and other rites, and it trusts that the leaders in every caste will frame regulations on their behalf, and enforce them strictly on all occasions."—*The Indian Social Reformer*, January 17, 1897, p. 155.

ment can do little in its official capacity to regulate the matter, yet we read in a recent Indian paper that Sir Dennis Fitzpatrick, "an astute and experienced administrator," is endeavoring to inaugurate in the Punjab "a social movement for the reduction of the expenses of the Hindu marriage." The paper commends the effort, and refers in deprecatory terms to the way in which "the earnings and savings of a whole lifetime are frittered away on an outlay which, however unreasonable, the Hindu must make, and after daughters are disposed of he is left almost penniless." [1] The Government does not propose to legislate, but only to extend moral support to such an undertaking on the part of the people. The Bengal Governor, it is stated, has taken steps to follow the precedent established in the Punjab.

In other respects, especially by the establishment of savings-banks, the British Government is seeking to encourage providence and fru-

Provident funds and thrifty ways among Indian Christians.

gality among the people of India. No more efficient efforts are made, however, in this direction than those which have been inaugurated under missionary and native Christian auspices. Such organizations as the Madras Native Christian Provident Fund, the Madras Native Christian Benefit Fund, and its branches, the Bengal Christian Family Pension Fund, the Palamcotta Native Christian Benefit Fund, and others, are gaining headway, and introducing a wise economic policy into Christian communities. In some cases individual missionaries, as, for example, Dr. Mowat (F. C. S.), of Jalna, are endeavoring to remedy the fatal drift of Hindus into the vortex of debt by establishing provident funds worked on the coöperative system.[2] In connection with the Basel Missions in India and Africa what is called a Missionary Commercial and Industrial Society has been formed, and is doing a useful service. In India a proposal to form "Agricultural Colonies" is also under consideration.[3] *The Christian Patriot*, a prominent native paper of Madras, has been discussing the establishment of what it calls Mission Banks, for the purpose of encouraging thrift among native Christians. A lengthy editorial in the issue of May 7, 1896, is based upon information that such a bank has actually been established by the Rev. Bernard Lucas, of Bellary, and is successful.[4] An undertaking of this kind, however well meant, involves some grave considerations. These, no doubt, will be carefully weighed by missionaries before assuming permanently

---

[1] *Progress*, March, 1896, p. 108.   [2] *The Missionary Record*, May, 1895, p. 145.
[3] *The Chronicle*, May, 1895, p. 136.   [4] See article on " Mission Banks,"
by Mr. Lucas, in *The Harvest Field* (Mysore), May, 1896, pp. 161-172.

responsibilities which in the long run can be delegated perhaps more wisely to secular agencies under Christian lay management.

At the meeting of the Indian Christian Association at Cawnpore, in December, 1896, a significant feature was an industrial exhibition representing native Christian handiwork from all parts of India. Widely scattered Christian communities from the chief centres of work were participants. Prizes were given, and the excellence and skill which were manifest commanded much admiration. The Bishop of Lucknow, who presided over the exhibition, gave a powerful opening address on "The Dignity of Labor."[1] Among the incidents which excited much interest was the success of the American Mission in teaching shorthand and the use of the typewriter to Hindu young men. 'The Government," it is stated, "and also private firms, were ready to employ all the pupils that the mission school could turn out, and many of them had secured lucrative appointments." In all, forty-seven prizes and certificates were awarded. One of the items of missionary news from India, in a recent number of *The Free Church of Scotland Monthly*, is an account, by the Rev. A. Andrew, of the Chingleput district, of a "Christian Harvest Home." The celebration was not merely a harvest home in the ordinary sense of the term, but it was turned to good use as a time of religious instruction. The addresses conveyed to the hearers lessons of spiritual husbandry, while offerings to the Lord from the products of their toil were made with much delight and enthusiasm. The narrator remarks finally that the occasion "proved conclusively that the Christians in the new settlements had learned habits of thrift and independence." Such harvest festivals are becoming more frequent throughout the Christian communities in South India.[2]

Industrial exhibitions and harvest festivals under mission auspices in India.

---

[1] The Bishop's address is summarized as follows by the Rev. William Fenwick Walpole, in a communication published in *The Independent*, May 21, 1896: " He reminded his hearers that Christianity had emancipated them from the trammels of caste. The Brahman could not engage in any trade he wished. He could not touch leather, or embark in paper manufacture and many other occupations. The law for the Christian was, ' *Whatsoever* thy hand findeth to do, do it with thy might.' The whole range of industry was thrown open to the man who walked in the new light. Indian traditions tabooed work. Christianity blessed and ennobled it to the followers of the Son of the carpenter. They should be as ready to drive a plow as to drive a quill, to make a desk as to sit at one, to dig a potato as to eat it. He exhorted them by integrity and thoroughness, to force their way to the top, and to so conduct themselves as to command the respect of their employers as well as win recognition in the market, where there was always room for the best articles."

[2] *The Free Church of Scotland Monthly*, August, 1897, p. 185.

Mr. Wellesley C. Bailey, in a published account of his visit, early in 1887, to Ebenezer, the chief station of the Indian Home Mission to the Santals, situated in the northern part of Bengal, speaks of its industrial work with enthusiasm. After referring to his tour of inspection to work-shops, brick and lime kilns, gardens, printing-press, and book-bindery, he informs us that the boys and girls are taught to work in a way which is useful, and as they will have to do, in their own villages.[1] The Christians of Ebenezer and vicinity, number all told about ten thousand, and, in addition, a colony of about seven hundred communicants, have emigrated to Assam, where they have established themselves as a Christian community.[2] A missionary lady in India, more than fifty years ago, taught the manufacture of what is known as Nagercoil Lace, which has grown to be an extensive industry in the hands of native Christian women.   It has gained medals at the London, Madras, and Paris exhibitions.   The profits of this lace trade are devoted to the promotion of female education, and several schools are thereby maintained.   The industrial plants of the Society for the Propagation of the Gospel, at Nazareth, and of the Wesleyan Mission, at Karur, both in South India, are especially notable for their extent and usefulness.   A Hindu village priest, as reported by the Rev. Dr. Chamberlain, once remarked to him: " Sir, what is it that makes your Veda have such an influence over the lives of those who embrace it? " And, referring to the people of his village who had become Christians within a year, he remarked: " Formerly they were lazy, and sometimes drank, lied, and cheated, as those around them do, but see what a change it has made in them—now they are sober, industrious, well-behaved, and thrifty.   Why, there is not such a village in all this region."[3]

Prize medals for mission industries.

In Burma and Siam the economic influences of Christianity are also working for the betterment of social conditions.   The Karens are almost entirely agriculturists, and a missionary writes concerning them: " The best-cultivated fields in this district belong to Christian Karens, and they are showing a commendable degree of carefulness in the use of property.   Among the cultivators of the soil they are least under the power of the money-lender."[4]   The meas-

No better fields in Burma than those of the Christian Karens.

1 Bailey, " A Glimpse at the Indian Mission Field," p. 68.
2 *Ibid.*, p. 68.
3 " Report of the Bombay Conference, 1892," vol. i., p. 47.
4 The Rev. W. I. Price (A. B. M. U.), Henzada, Burma.

ure of self-support and cheerful independence in the religious life of the Sgau-Karens is phenomenal. In 1880, they had raised $135,000 in endowments for educational work, and were supporting pastors, village schools, and some native missionaries of their own. As long ago as 1875 and 1877 they sent one thousand rupees to famine sufferers in Toungoo and among the Telugus.[1] A single statement concerning the Laos population of Upper Siam will certify to the influence of missions in encouraging thrifty ways, especially among the Christian converts. The Rev. W. C. Dodd (P. B. F. M. N.) writes as follows: "We can clearly discover the evidences of growing thrift. In the stations of our mission, the natives, heathen as well as Christian, are building better houses and fences, wearing nicer clothes, and using better implements to do finer work. When the late Governor of Lampoon was accused by some of his advisers of being too pro-foreign in his policy, he replied: 'Yes, I am in favor of the coming of the foreigners [the missionaries]. You all know what kind of fences and houses used to be in Chieng Mai; see the difference to-day. What has made it? The coming of the foreigners. Let them come to Lampoon; soon you will see the difference here too.' He gave the ground for a mission compound because he was keen enough to see the sociological benefits that would result."

In the West Indies and in sections of South America a spirit of thrift and a readiness to work have been greatly stimulated by the efforts of missionaries. The African Negro in Jamaica has been made

---

[1] The following statement concerning their subsequent progress is worth quoting: " Since 1880, under Mr. Nichols, they have continued to advance. They have endowed their high school, ' the best in all Burma,' with about $50,000; they have about 425 students of both sexes, a fine printing-office, and an extensive sawmill and machine-shop. Both board and tuition are free to those who can pass the examination. They have enlarged their great Memorial Hall, and built and endowed a hospital. The discipline of the churches is strict; their pastors are well and thoroughly trained; their benevolence is maintained on a system which reaches every member; and in their dress, furniture, domestic life, and social condition, they compare favorably with the country churches in the United States."—Bliss, " Encyclopædia of Missions," vol. i., p. 48.

In a special report on " Self-Support in Mission Fields," presented by the Rev. Henry F. Colby, D.D., at the Annual Meeting of the American Baptist Missionary Union, in 1895, striking facts are recorded regarding the remarkable spirit of liberality among the Burmans in contributing to the support of their Christian institutions. If any one doubts the stimulus which Christianity has given in some instances to the economic development of the people among whom it has been introduced, let him read this carefully prepared and elaborate report on the subject, which will be found in *The Baptist Missionary Magazine*, July, 1895, pp. 199–204.

a better man from an industrial and social as well as a religious stand-point by the training of Christian teachers.[1]   At the southernmost extremity of the South American Continent, in the wild realms of

Tributes from neglected lands and races to the material advantages of missions.

what has been called the "Land of Fire," are the missions of the South American Missionary Society, under the care of the Bishop of Falk-land.   Through the influence of its Christian efforts social changes have been brought about which have been the wonder of scientists and others who have chanced to visit those distant and inhospitable regions.   In an article by Mr. Robert Young, F.R.S.G.S., published in *The Mission World* for April, 1896, are statements which show conclusively that Christian enterprise has carried into the dark-ness of that hideous savagery a hope and stimulus for the life that now is, which have produced a happy transformation in the whole material outlook of the population.   Special reference is made to the mission established at Ushuaia, Tierra del Fuego, which has become "a well-conducted Christian village, with cottages instead of wigwams, a church, a school-house, and an orphanage."   The people, under the instruction of Mr. Bridges, a missionary of thirty years' residence, are spoken of as "developing habits of industry in planting and fencing gardens, felling trees, sawing them into planks, building cottages, and making roads.   Cattle and goats have been introduced.   An orphanage has been erected, of which all the planking and fittings were prepared on the spot."   A letter from Mr. Lawrence, who was stationed at Ushuaia in 1894, as a missionary of the South American Missionary Society, states that "there are daily demands upon us which require attention, especially where the industry of the natives depends so much upon the active exertions of the missionaries.   The people of Tierra del Fuego need teachers who can interest themselves in everything that pertains to their temporal welfare as well as spiritual benefit, and in every-day life, whatever their occupation may be, can lead them on, by example, to make the best use of time."[2]   Mr. Bridges, in 1886, obtained from the Argentine Government an extensive grant of land along the shores of Beagle Channel, about thirty miles to the east of Ushuaia, with the view of working it as an industrial farm, which we understand has proved successful.

From these fragmentary and scattered references to this interesting aspect of the results of missions we must now turn to other themes.

[1] Robson, "The Story of Our Jamaica Mission," chap. ix., entitled "The Jamaica of To-day: its People and Social Progress."
[2] *The South American Missionary Magazine*, November, 1894, p. 165.

Enough has been said to indicate that could the facts all be gathered, it would be found that missionary pioneers have planted seeds of industry and frugality in thousands of communities, which in the future will bear fruit in a rich and beneficent material progress.

8. SUBSTITUTING CHRISTIAN HUMILITY AND PROPER SELF-RESPECT FOR BARBARIC PRIDE AND FOOLISH CONCEIT.—Some attention has been given to this subject in the previous lecture (p. 28), where the importance of creating a new public opinion was discussed. Certain it is that humility and meekness are Christian rather than heathen qualities, and that the enlightening influences of missions tend to fix the true basis of self-respect as well as dissipate the false standards of ignorance and conceit. As a rule, the Asiatic imagination is under the spell of utterly meretricious ideals of greatness, while the savage conception of what is worthy of admiration is not only hideous but evil. The very things which make men monstrous, and hinder all higher progress, are regarded with pride by barbaric society. Heathen conceit is apt to vaunt itself in that which in reality is either foolish or shameful. Christianity is a message of sanity to the mind; it clarifies the mental vision; it brings men into touch with really great and good ideals, and delivers them from the power of the false, degenerate, and demoralizing notions of their traditional environment. It suggests a humble heart as of more value than a big head.

Transformation of old Asiatic ideals.

Chinese pride, usually so stolid and complacent, is feeling the effect of some serious shocks in these latter days. The outer bastions and towering battlements are beginning to lose their monumental stability, although so far it is merely the military power and the worldly éclat of the empire that seem to be in question. The assumption of intellectual superiority and moral sufficiency is hardly touched as yet, except among Christians or others who have been specially enlightened by contact with Western culture. The most progressive statesman of China—Li Hung Chang—offered a prize, in the spring of 1894, for an essay on " Reform in Religion," a strange sign of the times in Chinese contemporary history.[1] China, when she apprehends the truth that there is any need of reform in her religion, will have advanced leagues onward towards her higher destiny. Hardly a man can be found outside the Christian communities who will confess this, and true courage

[1] Cf. " China's Appalling Need of Reform," by the Rev. T. Richard, in *The Chinese Recorder*, November, 1894, pp. 515-521.

and fidelity are required to teach the Chinese this unwelcome truth. That Christian converts do see it, and that they have the moral nerve to acknowledge it, is a mark of special grace and enlightenment.[1]

In Japanese periodicals are to be found with increasing frequency articles written by educated natives who frankly recognize that even Japan has much to learn intellectually and religiously from Christian sources. Missions can hardly do a more useful service to an alert and progressive people like the Japanese than to awaken a consciousness of moral and religious need, and guide them to the heavenly wisdom which is in Christ. It is only thus that genuine and worthy self-respect can be nourished in place of flighty conceit. Reasonable self-esteem rather than empty vanity is the secret of individual stability as well as of national strength.

In India lessons of humility are hard to teach, and far more diffi-cult to learn. Conceit is the very atmosphere of Hinduism; pride is the very essence of the Moslem spirit. The Hindu glories in the fact that he is a philosopher, and that in his caste exclusiveness he is "not as other men"; the Moslem prides himself upon the dignity of his title and the merit of his practice. Only the Christian enters the kingdom of his Master as a little child. It may be said in general that everywhere Christianity teaches that "except ye become as little children, ye shall not enter the kingdom of heaven." No more helpful lesson than this could be taught to the proud-hearted heathen world. "I am like a child, knowing little and wanting to learn," were the words of an Indian chief among the Kitkatlas, who had become a captive of the cross.[2] Humility is one of the chief graces of Christian experience, and while it is in no sense a blow at proper self-respect, yet it surely banishes once for all the clamorous boastfulness of heathen pride. It destroys also that unteachable assurance which is such a barrier to the entrance of enlightening and progressive ideals.

Some invaluable lessons for those who are "not as other men."

9. CULTIVATION OF THE PERSONAL VIRTUES.—That Christianity teaches and demands of its followers sincerity, honesty, truthfulness, and other personal virtues inculcated in the Moral Law of God, and also develops in the character such graces as charity, meekness, and

---

1 "Christianity weakens that overweening pride and self-satisfaction which offer an effectual barrier to all progress."—Rev. Donald MacGillivray (C. P. M.), Chu-Wang, China.

2 *The Church Missionary Gleaner*, February, 1892.

forbearance, is a simple truism which needs no demonstration. All that is called for, then, in this connection, is some credible evidence that Christian missions are introducing and establishing among native converts these graces of personal character, and habits of correct living, to an extent which justifies the assertion that they are nurseries of practical godliness.

Personal character and straight living the touch-stones of mission success.

It does not invalidate the force of this demonstration if it proves to be, so far as our discovery of it is concerned, less perfect and convincing than we could wish. We must remember that Christianity allows an almost startling freedom to the play of inclination and will, and that character even under the culture of Christian influences is in a true sense a growth rather than a ready-made product. It is surely beyond question that the tendencies of Christianity, when it is once received and appropriated by the spiritual nature, are to quicken and nourish the personal virtues which the Word of God both commends and commands. It must not be forgotten, however, that in so doing, especially in mission fields, the Gospel code must contend with a combination of dominant heredity, adverse environment, and overmastering temptation, which adds immensely to the difficulty of moral renovation, and gives a peculiar intensity to the struggle for a renewed spiritual nature. It requires more Christianity to the square inch of personal character—if the expression is allowable—to produce a given amount of moral stamina where a thoroughly demoralized heathen nature is to be made over, than where a naturally high-toned and responsive individuality is to be brought into deeper accord with a moral code already perhaps instinctively revered, and in large measure observed.

In Japan a new standard of truthfulness is identified with Christian character, and this is true also as regards honest dealing. Whatever may be claimed as to the superior natural qualities of the Japanese, it is frankly acknowledged that their Christian living is on a much higher moral plane.

A new value to truthfulness and honesty in Japan.

"The influence of Christianity," writes the Rev. Henry Stout, D.D. (Ref. C. A.), of Nagasaki, "upon those who have accepted it, in such matters as kindness and common honesty, is recognized and admitted by all who know anything about the facts, the incorrigible haters of Christians excepted." In a comprehensive article on "Japan's Debt to Christianity," by the Rev. James I. Seder, of Tokyo, this is clearly specified. He says: "Lying is considered in a different light than it formerly was. Christianity is setting forth the high ideal of perfect truthfulness and is pressing its claims. As an instance of far-reaching influence upon the whole national life, which shows that veracity and truth are being sought, it may be mentioned that some of the best scholars of the empire are engaged in sifting the national history and mythology in order to ascertain the facts. Truth is coming to be valued and desired; and although it still meets with great opposition, it will win its way here as elsewhere. Another instance from the humbler walks of commercial life may also be noted. Said a Buddhist orange-merchant to the writer recently, while praising his oranges: 'I don't lie; I am a Christian.' Although, at the very moment he spoke, his foot slipped from the path of truth, as the idols and shrines in and about the house testified, yet the restraining ideal was present." [1]   A striking and pathetic incident from an entirely different source reveals the estimate which Japanese military officials entertain of the truthfulness of Christians as such, even though found in a distant island and among enemies. The story of the Christian martyrs of Formosa at the time of the Japanese invasion is full of touching significance as well as tragic sadness. They were trusted by the Japanese because they were Christians and would not deceive them; they were martyred by the "Black Flags" because they would not play false to the invaders.[2]

That the Chinese have felt this subtile power of the Gospel to beget in the heart a love for truthfulness and a respect for honesty is equally capable of proof. "It has been done in hundreds

The Christian is worthy of being trusted in China.

and thousands of cases," writes the late Rev. J. A. Leyenberger (P. B. F. M. N.), of Wei Hien, and adds, "I have seen with my own eyes the marvelous change." The Rev. P. W. Pitcher (Ref. C. A.), of Amoy, relates the following incident: "A certain heathen village proposed

---

[1] *The Missionary Review of the World,* September, 1895, p. 656.

[2] The Rev. Thomas Barclay, a missionary of the Presbyterian Church of England in Formosa, has recently visited Moatau, the scene of the massacre of native Christians by the "Black Flags," just before the Japanese occupation of Taiwanfu. The following curious explanation of why these Christians were executed is given in *The Monthly Messenger:* "The hatred aroused by the Japanese advance, and (singularly enough) the good opinion of Christian character entertained and manifested by the Japanese generals, were responsible for the attack on the Christians of Moatau, and for the executions of those at Kagi, further to the north, by the Black Flag leaders. The Japanese, marching through an unknown and difficult country,—intersected by precipitous ravines,—were in the habit, when they came to a village or town, of enquiring if any Christians were in the place. If so, they seized them and compelled them to act as guides, because, as they said, *Christians could be trusted not to deceive.* For the same reason the Pescadores preacher was taken on shore by the Japanese force which held these islands, when it landed to coöperate with the army marching south of Taiwanfu. The Black Flags were thus

to raise a sum of money for a special object. When it came to the question, who should hold the funds when collected, it was unanimously agreed to place the cash in the hands of a church-member, because, as they all said, 'he is an honest man.' A splendid recognition!"[1] In the "Annual Report (1894) of the Shensi Mission of the English Baptists," it is related that at one of their stations a heathen man was asked whether he saw any good points about the Christians. "Yes," he replied, "there are three things I am bound to admire: (1) There is no need to watch our crops around their village. (2) They neither sow, sell, nor swallow opium. (3) They cause little trouble in paying their taxes."[2] Here is rare and downright honesty accredited to Chinese Christians towards their neighbors and, what is more remarkable, towards their Government. There is much unanimity in the testimony of missionaries as to the sincerity of native Christians and their steadfastness in times of trial and persecution. The cruelties to which they are exposed, and the fearful weight of hatred, contempt, and ignominy which is rolled upon them, would crush the spirits of any but sincere and loyal believers.[3]

In a formal and elaborate "Statement of the Nature, Work, and Aims of Protestant Missions in China, Laid before the Tsung-li Yamen November 14, 1895," with a view to its being presented to the Emperor as an exposition of the real intent and significance of missionary enterprise, the supreme aim of Christianity as the promoter of virtuous living is insisted upon with much detail. Among its many paragraphs bearing upon this point is the following: "Christians are taught to speak the truth, to deal justly, to love mercy, to be orderly, chaste, peaceable; to avoid fraud, theft, adultery, and all evil; to seek after and practise all good. The object of the religion they profess is to make them good men and women, and to prepare them in this life

---

able to accuse the Christians, with a show of truth, of assisting the foreign invaders, though this assistance was rendered only under compulsion. There is comfort in the sorrow, in the two facts: that there were no Christian defections, and that Christian character stands high in Japanese opinion. It strengthens the hope that the missions will be befriended by the new Government."—*The Monthly Messenger*, April, 1896, p. 82.

[1] "Christianity is the only power that can cure lying, and it has been done in many individual cases. The heathen have noticed this transformation, and will trust the Christians where they will not trust each other, even though they despise these very Christians for their religion."—The late Mrs. C. W. Mateer (P. B. F. M. N.), Tungchow, China.

[2] *The Chinese Recorder*, March, 1895, p. 126.

[3] *The Church at Home and Abroad*, January, 1896, p. 40.

for a better life to come."[1] That this is the real message of Christianity to China as a programme of social righteousness who can doubt? And that many sinful natures and disorderly lives are transformed seems equally sure. On the southwestern borders of China, in the interior recesses of Northern Siam, are the Laos people, among whom the American Presbyterians are conducting a flourishing and fruitful mission. Concerning them Dr. J. W. McKean writes that "it is freely and voluntarily acknowledged by both princes and common people that the Laos Christian is honest, or, as they put it, is 'honorable.'"

Let us turn now to India, and we find amid its varied and teeming population that there are new moral currents in motion, not only in

A new moral outlook in India.

Christian but even in non-Christian circles, which are tending towards righteousness. Standards are being set up which, although not strictly observed, are frankly recognized. The Rev. Francis Ashcroft, of Ajmere, a United Presbyterian missionary from Scotland, in a thoughtful article on "The Preparation for the Gospel in India," dwells at some length on the influence of Christianity upon the moral outlook of educated young men, and emphasizes the change which is apparent not only in their point of view but in their personal attitude towards Christian conceptions of God, of duty, and of practical morality. "Uprightness, purity, truthfulness, honor, almost the whole ethics of Christianity, with the exceptions [of some aspects of religious ceremonialism] already noted, have been accepted by the young party as universally binding. Alas, that in their own individual experience they should have so little weight! Still, it is something to have the ideals of the Christian presented as those of the Hindu, and vice and sin condemned by both."[2] Of the natives who have been brought under Christian teaching and example a missionary writes: "They are more polite and refined in their manners, more truthful in their conversation and statements, and exhibit in dealing with others a greater regard for uprightness and honorable conduct. There is a higher moral tone among them. This is so generally recognized that persons thus influenced are expected to exhibit a superior standard of moral and social life."[3] "The pronounced and positive attitude of Christianity," writes another missionary, "regarding lying and bribery has its effect far and wide on both converts and pagans who come in

[1] *The Chinese Recorder*, February, 1896, pp. 68, 69.
[2] *The Missionary Record*, August, 1894, p. 223.
[3] The Rev. D. Hutton (L. M. S.), Mirzapur, India.

contact with it; that effect, however, is slow, and results are not seen in a short time." [1]

The indirect effects of Christian teachings as they ramify in unsuspected directions are sometimes more striking in the evidence they give of Christianity's power to propagate moral ideals than is the testimony which comes to light in connection with direct conversion. In a district where the individual fruits of evangelism seem to be meagre, incidents are reported which reveal the hidden influence of Christian morality among those who are apparently untouched by its evangelistic appeals. In the case of a group of men called upon to bear witness in a court of justice regarding their landlord, it is naturally to be expected that their testimony would be in his favor, since he has the power to help or to harm them. "To his utter astonishment, their statements tell against him, for they have heard the Word of God, and their lips refuse to utter the suggested lie, although they know that this refusal will bring upon them wrath and persecution." Still another fact is reported concerning "a little company of shopkeepers who have banded themselves together, not to keep up their prices, nor to increase their gains, *but to carry on their trade without lying.*" [2]

In Mohammedan lands, especially in the Turkish Empire, not alone among Moslems but also among nominal Christians, duplicity and dishonesty are only too common. One of the most brilliant moral qualities that can pertain to a man in Western Asia, giving him a distinction as rare as it is wonderful, is to be known as truthful and honest. The badge of simple truthfulness is, by general consent, the " Victoria Cross " of morals in the Orient. This characteristic is recognized as belonging in a very unusual degree to Protestants. "It is a common saying," writes a missionary, "that our converts are more truthful than any other class of people. This truthfulness has its effect upon others outside, and, almost unconsciously, a higher standard of honesty is established." [3] The Rev. Robert Thomson (A. B. C. F. M.), of Constantinople, writes in the same strain of "the confidence reposed in Protestants," and the Rev. J. W. Baird, of Monastir, declares that they are "trusted more than others." "It has been recognized," writes Dr. Caroline F. Hamilton, of Aintab, that "treachery is unknown among our Christians." In a land where this failing is so prevalent it is a spiritual triumph for Christianity to awaken

The "Victoria Cross" of morals in the Orient.

---

[1] The Rev. L. L. Uhl, Ph.D. (Luth. G. S.), Guntur, India.
[2] *The Church Missionary Gleaner*, July, 1895, p. 99.
[3] The Rev. John A. Ainslie (P. B. F. M. N.), Mosul, Turkey.

in the hearts of its followers a sense of honor and a respect for obligation.

In the case of savage races, as in Africa and the South Sea Islands, where human nature has lost its moral fibre, it is not to be expected that the personal virtues can be cultivated easily and rapidly where the very elements of character must not simply be renovated but recreated; yet there is much which is beautiful and striking in the power of the Gospel to give a new and hopeful bias to the most degraded natures. If men who during centuries of moral stagnation have never hesitated for an instant to be untruthful and dishonest, can be brought even to a stage of revolt and struggle with such temptations, a great change will have been produced. That every native who professes Christianity becomes at once and forever free from moral lapses would be an absurd and improbable contention, but that the Gospel exerts a wonderful and helpful influence in the right direction is indubitable, and it is no less certain that nothing else can produce this renewed character. The Rev. H. D. Goodenough (A. B. C. F. M.), of Johannesburg, reports that as the result of investigations made by himself among the prisoners in the jails at Stanger, Maritzburg, and Durban, it was found that out of a total of 47 in Stanger only 1 could read and write, and out of a total of 168 in Maritzburg only 10 were able to read and write, while at Durban out of a total of 287 only 32 could read and write. It does not appear that any of those who were educated to this extent were Christians, but the figures are significant as indicating that the great majority had never been in touch with mission influences. A further investigation at Maritzburg, made by the Rev. John Bruce, a missionary of the Free Church of Scotland, revealed the fact that, during a period of six months, out of three or four hundred pupils in his school not one had been arrested for any misdemeanor.[1] The Rev. George A. Wilder (A. B. C. F. M.), Gazaland, East Africa, writes: "In 1892 the Portuguese Governor at Lorenzo Marques applied to the Swiss Mission for men to send as carriers with their Boundary Commission, because, as he said, 'these are the only natives we can trust not to run away.'"

The testimony of missionaries in regard to the moral renewal of the personal character of Christians in the South Seas is cumulative, and cannot be questioned by any candid mind. The Rev. William Wyatt Gill may be regarded as a representative witness. He writes

Marginal note: Savage heredity will yield to Christian grace.

---

[1] *The Christian*, July 2, 1896, " Letter from South Africa."

Teachers of the Girls' Central School, Antananarivo, (Miss Briggs in front row, Miss Craven in middle, and Miss Sibree on the left in last row.)

Antananarivo College, (requisitioned by the French authorities.)

Group of Tutors and College Students. (Rev. James Sibree on the right, Rev. A. W. Wilson on the left.)

THE FRUITS OF CHRISTIAN INSTRUCTION IN MADAGASCAR. (L. M. S.)

concerning the results of mission work in the Pacific Islands: "The abolition of human sacrifices, war, cannibalism, polygamy, idolatry, and a crushing despotism, is due to Christianity. The thief has become honest, the immoral pure in life, the cruel-hearted kind." [1]

Another aspect of this subject is the influence of Christianity in cultivating the physical virtues of cleanliness and neatness. It is universally acknowledged that converts almost invariably mend their ways by banishing uncleanness both from their persons and their surroundings. There is hardly a mission field where the Christians cannot at once be distinguished from the heathen by the attractiveness and wholesomeness of their personal appearance. Christian homes are pervaded by an atmosphere of refinement and a simple charm of orderly neatness which are unmistakable to any one who is at all familiar with the ordinary domestic habits of the natives. Dr. H. M. Lane (P. B. F. M. N.), of São Paulo, Brazil, relates an incident illustrating this truth: "A rich planter, travelling along a country road one Sunday, heard singing in a mud hut, a little way from the road. He went in, and found about twenty persons, men, women, and children, singing Protestant hymns and having their regular Sunday worship. They were poor people, but on inquiry he learned that they were prospering on their little farms, and were happy; also, he noticed how clean and orderly they were. All along the rest of the road he found only squalid poverty, many intemperate and vicious people, as he had been accustomed to meet in that class of society. He said to the missionary whom he met a few days after, that if Protestantism bred virtue, industry, and cleanliness, such as he had seen in that little group, he hoped it might overrun the whole land." [2] That cleanliness is next to godliness in the programme of the Gospel seems to a remarkable extent to be capable of visible demonstration. "A few weeks ago," writes the Rev. A. M. Cunningham, of Peking, "a certain woman, noted for her filthiness and indecency, began attending the sessions of a class for Bible study. Almost immediately an improvement was noticed in her personal cleanliness and general appearance." Of the Chinese who arrive in San Francisco, stolid, dirty, and repulsive, the Rev.

Outward neatness a sign of inward cleanliness.

---

1 Gill, " Life in the Southern Isles," p. 16.

2 " A gentleman who lived just in front of the meeting-place of one of our congregations once told me that he had been watching the people for several years as they came and went to and from their services, and that he had been particularly impressed by the great improvement in their personal appearance."—Rev. J. G. Hall (P. B. F. M. S.), Ciudad Victoria, Mexico.

I. M. Condit (P. B. F. M. N.) writes that a happy change comes over those who can be reached by the Gospel. " It is interesting to see the dirt gradually disappearing from face and hands," and neatness both in clothing and persons becoming habitual with those who were in these matters apparently incorrigible.[1] There seems to be a happy magic in Christianity to cleanse both within and without.

II.—RESULTS AFFECTING FAMILY LIFE

The reconstruction of the family, next to the regeneration of individual character, is the most precious contribution of missions to heathen society, and we may add that it is one of the most helpful human influences which can be consecrated to the service of social elevation. In the effort to hallow and purify family life we stir the secret yearnings of fatherhood and motherhood ; we enter the precincts of the home, and take childhood by the hand ; we restore to its place of power and winsomeness in the domestic circle the ministry of womanhood ; and at the same time we strike at some of the most despicable evils and desolating wrongs of our fallen world. Nothing in the history of human society, except the teaching and example of Jesus Christ, has wrought with such energy and wisdom in introducing saving power into social development as a sanctified home life. If parental training can be made loving, faithful, conscientious, and helpful, if womanhood can be redeemed and crowned, if childhood can be guided in tenderness and wisdom, if the home can be made a place where virtue dwells, and moral goodness is nourished and becomes strong and brave for the conflicts of life, we can conceive of no more effective combination of invigorating influences for the rehabilitation of fallen society than will therein be given.

Christian homes essential to the renovation of heathen society.

Let us now inquire what Christian missions have accomplished in transforming and purifying the conditions of family life and mitigating the evils which appear in its special environment. What have they done for the elevation of woman, the central figure in the home, to deliver her from the humiliation and suffering incidental to those great historic curses of Oriental society, polygamy, concubinage, adulterous laxity, and easy divorce? What have they wrought for the

The magnificent rôle of missions in purifying and protecting the family.

---

[1] " Christianity makes the converts more cleanly than they were formerly, but aside from this there is no very general change in respect to food and dress. Of

abolishment of child marriage and the alleviation of the social miseries of widowhood? What have they effected—not, let it be noted, with indiscreet precipitancy, but with wise caution and sobriety—to secure the release of woman from the condition of enforced seclusion and minimum privilege which traditional custom in the Orient has imposed upon her? What influence have they exerted to better the practical aspects of domestic life, to improve family training, and to render aid and protection to helpless children, so often the victims of cruelty or infanticide where no organized societies are instituted specially to guard their welfare? Questions like these open a broad field of most interesting results, which it would be delightful thoroughly to explore. The scope of the inquiry is so large that it is expedient to treat it in detail under separate heads.

1. THE ELEVATION OF WOMAN.—A brief account of the actual condition of woman in non-Christian society has already been given.[1] The subject which concerns us here is what missions have done towards rescuing her from this unhappy lot. We shall not dwell upon the theme in its historical amplitude. Some fine passages in the writings of Dr. Storrs may be consulted by those who desire to obtain an inspiring view of what Christianity accomplished for woman in the old Roman world and in medieval times.[2] Christendom, so far as it has been penetrated and moulded by the spirit of Christ, is ready also with its contribution of decisive testimony; and who can doubt that womanhood is blessed and revered in Christian lands as it is nowhere else in the world?

Turning now to mission fields, we find abundant evidence to sustain our contention that Christianity is the good angel of woman's life, and the creator of a new and happier environment for her social development. Emphasis may be laid at once upon the ennobling and refining influence of the Christian religion in the heart of woman, and its manifest elevation of her personality and life. This result cannot be questioned by any one who has had an opportunity to observe in Eastern lands the transformations in her character, ways of living, and even her personal appearance, wherever she has come under the power of

The elevation and education of woman a notable aspect of mission progress.

course the Christians are more truthful than the heathen, and more faithful in all the relations of life."—Rev. Charles Hartwell (A. B. C. F. M.), Foochow, China.

[1] Vol. I., pp. 103–113.

[2] Storrs, "The Divine Origin of Christianity," pp. 146–153. Cf. also Warneck, "Modern Missions and Culture," pp. 173, 174.

the Gospel of Christ.   Christianity, moreover, refines and purifies man's estimate of woman, and insures to her a measure of respect and fealty of which she can by no means be assured under any other religious cult.

The whole movement for female education in non-Christian lands has sprung up in connection with Christian missions. How true this is may be illustrated by the fact that in India, among all nationalities and sects, out of a total of 2,756,135 pupils under instruction in all educational institutions, only 162,248 are girls, that is, about one seventeenth of the entire number. In the Christian community of India, however, out of a total of 95,650 pupils in schools, 35,064 are girls, or over one third of the whole. These figures represent but a small proportion of the aggregate of Indian women, so small indeed is it that we may accept as true the editorial statement of *The Indian Social Reformer* that "in the year 1897 six out of every thousand women in India are not illiterate." [1] The exact number, according to the Indian census of 1891, was 127,726,768 illiterate females out of a total of 128,467,925 whose condition was ascertained, leaving—and the number includes all those under instruction in schools—a remnant of 741,-157 who can either read and write, or are likely to do so soon. The result, as will be seen, is that ninety-five per cent. of the women of India (i.e., of those represented in the returns) are illiterate; and if we consider those who are twenty-five years of age, or over, the percentage rises to ninety-nine and a half per cent. of illiterates, which indicates that female education is almost confined to the present generation. [2]

[1] Cf. article on "Sixty Years of Social Progress" in issue of June 20, 1897, p. 332.

[2] See article on "The Indian Census and Female Education," by the Rev. W. Stevenson, in *The Missions of the World*, October, 1894, pp. 328-331. Substantially the same statements are made by Professor Gokhale, in a paper on "Female Education in India," read at the Education Congress of the Victorian Era Exhibition, held in London, July, 1897. After a very careful review of the present status in India, he emphasizes the fact that the advance up to the present time has been almost entirely confined, so far as girls are concerned, to the department of primary education, a fact which is illustrated in the Bombay Presidency, where out of more than "nine hundred schools for girls there are only sixty for secondary education, and even these are, for the most part, European, Eurasian, or Parsi schools." He gives in the course of his paper the following statistics, the significance of which cannot be misunderstood: "Even the progress in primary education, which appears so striking, marks, after all, only the commencement of the great work that in reality lies before us. The following figures will make my meaning clear. In the Madras Presidency, according to the last census, out of a total female population of 20,000,-000 only 250,000 can read and write or are under instruction, which gives a ratio of 1 in 80. In the Bombay Presidency the figures are 100,000 out of a total female

In addition to the foregoing figures, there are 12,028,210 females in India concerning whom no educational returns are made—the total female population, including that of the Native States, being 140,469,-134. Just what proportion of this large number not included in the statistics should be counted as among illiterates does not appear, but it seems probable that the great majority should be so ranked. The statement seems to be justified, therefore, that, if all the facts were tabulated, the number of illiterate women in India would represent a large fraction over ninety-nine per cent.[1] A further insight into the import of these facts may be obtained by studying the distribution of illiteracy given by Mr. Baines, the Census Commissioner, which shows that of girls from five to fifteen years of age only ninety-three in ten thousand are under instruction—less than one in every hundred. Between the ages mentioned is the period which in all countries should include the maximum proportion of those who are under instruction. In India this is less than ten in a thousand. The manifest inference, since all girls there are likely to be married before fifteen years of age, is that, only one out of every hundred marriages at the present time is with a girl who has received an education and will carry into her home any glimmer of knowledge. Another point of view reveals the equally dismal fact that during the current year, out of every fifteen educated men who marry in India fourteen of them must take illiterate wives, and thus inevitably darken their homes at the outset with the shadow of ignorance.[2]

Dr. Bhandarkar, who is said to be the "foremost Sanscrit scholar in Western India at the present day," asserts that in ancient times Indian women were allowed the privileges of education, and that many of them were distinguished by their knowledge of Vedic literature. In fact, the position of woman, as indicated in the earliest sacred writings of the Hindus, was far superior to her present status.[3] That her social

population of about 13,000,000, thus giving a ratio of 1 in 130. In Bengal, out of 37,000,000 females, only 150,000 can read and write or are under instruction, which means a ratio of 1 in 250. In the Punjab the figures are 35,000 out of a total of 11,500,000—a ratio of 1 in 330. In the North-West Provinces we have 50,000 females who can read and write or are under instruction, out of a total of 23,000,-000, which gives a ratio of 1 in 460. The Central Provinces have a female population of 6,500,000, and of these only 12,000, i.e., 1 in 540, are attending schools or can read and write. Comments on these figures are really superfluous."—*The Indian Magazine and Review*, August, 1897, p. 407.

[1] The statistics upon which these estimates are based are found in the Census Report, and in "The Statesman's Year-Book for 1898," pp. 122, 127.

[2] *The Missions of the World*, October, 1894, p. 331.

[3] Consult address of Professor Gokhale, in *The Indian Magazine and Review*, August, 1897, p. 401. See also *ibid.*, April, 1897, pp. 202–204.

condition has deteriorated with the centuries, and is now practically hopeless in an environment of Hinduism, can hardly be disputed.[1]   It is equally clear, on the other hand, that the educated woman, who is fast winning her way to a place of dignity and power not only in India but in all non-Christian lands, is a distinctive product as well as a characteristic trophy of missions.

Much has been done in India for the social advancement of woman, although there is seemingly little in the previous statements to justify

the assertion.   British rule, however, facilitates effort on her behalf, and there are striking results to be noted, full of high promise.   Sir William W. Hunter, in an address at the annual meeting of the National Indian Association, in 1895, emphasized "the great services which have been rendered by the missionary bodies towards female education in India."   In the course of his remarks he said: "You will find that almost all the educated women of India who have made their mark in our day are native Christians, or were educated under missionary influence."[2]   At the same gathering, Sir Charles H. Crosthwaite, a former Lieutenant-Governor of the North-West Provinces, gave substantially the same testimony, when he stated: "We have a medical school in Agra, where we train girls to be assistants in hospitals for women. When we first started the class we secured a few girls, Hindu and Mohammedan, who had been educated; but very soon the supply was exhausted, and I found that there was hardly any one fit to receive medical education except those native Christian girls who came from mission schools."[3]   The same statement was made with much emphasis by Professor Gokhale, in his address at the Education Congress.   Referring to the Bombay Presidency, he said: "The credit of making the first organized effort to educate Indian girls belongs to the American missionary society which opened, in 1824, the first native girls' school in Bombay. . . . Last year there were nine hundred schools for girls, with an attendance of over eighty thousand pupils."   In regard to the Madras Presidency, he remarked: "The first attempt at providing schools for native girls was made in 1841 by the missionaries of the

Valuable results of female education in India.

---

[1] "No man eats with a woman, not even with his own wife; nor does he accept food that has already been partaken of by a woman.   The wife brings the meal to her lord; he eats what he wants, and leaves the rest for her.   At first this created an embarrassment at the celebration of the Communion, as the men said they could not touch the cup and eat the bread after it had been passed round among the women; but the missionaries refused to yield, and the difficulty has practically disappeared from among us."—Rev. James M. Macphail (F. C. S), Chakai, Santalia, Bengal.

[2] *The Indian Magazine and Review,* June, 1895, p. 295.

[3] *Ibid.,* June, 1895, p. 289.

Miss Kimmins and her co-workers.
Smaller Group.

Girls' High School, Bombay.
Larger Group.

EDUCATIONAL WORK AT BOMBAY, INDIA.
(Z. B. M. M.)

Scottish Church. . . . Last year there were in the Madras Presidency over one thousand schools, attended by nearly one hundred and ten thousand girls."[1] Similar testimony could be given for all parts of India. Miss Cooke at Calcutta was the pioneer in 1822.

The famous despatch on education, issued in 1854 by the British Government, largely through the influence of Dr. Duff, found the work of instruction under missionary auspices already inaugurated throughout the country.[2] It is difficult for us to realize the import of this educational movement on behalf of women. Indian men look upon it as a radical upturning of their whole social environment, and one to which it is almost impossible for them to adjust themselves. It appears to them to be as ominous as the revolutionary theories of anarchists. It seems like an unsettling of society, involving the possible overthrow of religion itself. In the light of this fact, however, we can discover the significance of the change which is so rapidly taking place in the whole outlook of female education in India. We cannot fail, moreover, to recognize its importance as an element in social progress, since no matter how rapid and splendid may be the advancement which is identified with the education of men, if the women are still in ignorance, no permanent improvement can take place. The hope of any substantial advantage is reduced to a minimum "if a man when he marries finds himself belonging to one century and wedded to a century far back."[3] "Social reform," writes Dr. Downie, of Nellore, "can never advance until the zenana is broken up and women are educated."

In what has been called the "Social Movement" in India prominence has been given to all that concerns the elevation of woman. Indian conferences and associations are discussing the subject in all its aspects, with a liberality of sentiment and an intelligent appreciation of its important bearings upon the higher life of society which mark an immense advance in native opinion. At the meeting of the Indian National Social Conference—not a missionary or even

The elevation of woman a prominent subject of discussion in the new "Social Movement" in India.

---

[1] *The Indian Magazine and Review*, August, 1897, pp. 404, 405.

[2] A writer in a recent issue of *The Hindu*, a prominent non-Christian paper, indicates that candid native opinion does not hesitate to give due credit to the missionary as a pioneer of education in India. He says: "It is now becoming the fashion among our educated people to cry down the labors of Christian missionaries, and even to vilify them. But an ounce of solid work is worth a pound of windy oratory. Judged by this principle the Christian missionary must be esteemed to be one of the greatest benefactors of our country. While the educated Indian has not yet got beyond the talking stage in the matter of female instruction, the Christian missionary has honeycombed the country with girls' schools."

[3] *The Indian Magazine and Review*, June, 1895, p. 297.

distinctively Christian organization—held in Calcutta, December, 1896, a strong resolution was passed emphasizing the desirability of female education.[1] In the address of Professor Gokhale, before mentioned, the theme is treated at length with ability and enthusiasm, as the following sentences will indicate: "A wide diffusion of female education in all its branches is a factor of the highest value to the true well-being of every nation. In India it assumes additional importance by reason of the bondage of caste and custom which tries to keep us tied down to certain fixed ways of life and modes of thought, and which so often cripples all efforts at the most elementary reforms. . . . It is obvious that, under the circumstances, a wide diffusion of education, with all its solvent influences, among the women of India, is the only means of emancipating their minds from this degrading thraldom to ideas inherited through a long past, and that such emancipation will not only restore our women to the honoured position which they at one time occupied in India, but will also facilitate, more than anything else, our assimilation of those elements of Western civilisation without which all thoughts of India's regeneration are mere idle dreams, and all attempts at it foredoomed to failure. The solution appears simple enough, and yet no problem in India is surrounded with greater difficulties or requires a more delicate and patient handling."[2]

Addresses in a similar strain are now to be heard at all the numerous gatherings of native Indians in the interest of social reform. To mention only some of the more recent examples, the late Mr. Manomohun Ghose, in a paper on "The Progress in Bengal During the Last Thirty Years," speaks of the marvelous change in Hindu opinion with reference to the education of women, and of the great advance made towards the emancipation of Indian women from the bondage of igno-

---

[1] The resolution is as follows: "That in the opinion of the Conference the permanent progress of our society is not possible without a further spread of female education, and that the best way is (1) to proceed on national lines by employing in female schools female teachers of good character and descended from respectable Hindu families; (2) to establish training-schools to secure a sufficient number of qualified female teachers; (3) to open home classes for grown-up ladies who cannot attend regular schools, with extra female teachers to visit and help at stated intervals such ladies as read at their homes; (4) to employ a Pandita versed in Sanscrit to read passages from the Puranas and impart religious and moral instruction to ladies; (5) to take steps to publish text-books suited to the requirements of female schools; and (6) to impart instruction in needlework, hygiene, culinary art, domestic economy, and the training of children, in secondary schools."— *The Indian Evangelical Review*, January, 1897, p. 384.

[2] *The Indian Magazine and Review*, August, 1897, p. 399.

rance.[1] Mr. K. G. V. Aiyer, B.A., of the Madras Christian College, in a lecture before the Hindu Social Reform Union of Bangalore, May 31, 1896, uses the following language in describing the purpose of social reform efforts in behalf of female education. He says: "The movement aims at the elevation of woman to the same level in society as man, so that she may prove to be his honorable companion and efficient helpmate in life. . . . I believe that all of us here understand full well that by keeping our women in darkness and ignorance we do not help the next generation to become superior to us in those qualities which are necessary in the struggle for existence."[2] Mr. N. G. Chandavarkar, in a forcible and learned address before the Madras Hindu Social Reform Association, devotes a considerable portion to the urgent need of better educational facilities for women.[3] These addresses are but specimens, and reveal how alert the educated mind of India is upon this special phase of the social reform programme.

A strong representation of the native press is helping on this agitation by an enlightened and vigorous advocacy of the necessity of female education as essential to the higher civilization of India. A few extracts from the columns of *The Hindu*, a leading non-Christian journal, will indicate the strenuous and unequivocal character of the views entertained on this subject: "The community of native Christians has not only secured a conspicuous place in the field of higher education, but in the instruction of their women, and in availing themselves of the existing means for practical advancement, they are far ahead of the Brahmans. The native Christians are a very poor community, and it does great credit to them that they so largely take to industrial training. The progress of education among the girls of the native Christian families, and the absence of caste restrictions among them, will eventually give them an advantage for which no amount of intellectual precocity can compensate the Brahmans. We recently approved of the statement of a Bombay writer that the social eminence which the Parsis so deservedly enjoy at the present moment is due to these two causes, namely, that their women are well educated, and they are bound by no restrictions of caste."[4] In another issue of the same paper is the following: "If we were wise in our generation we would

The native press a spirited advocate of a higher life for women.

---

[1] See *The Indian Social Reformer*, February 22, 1896, p. 190.

[2] See *Ibid.*, June 7, 1896, p. 309.

[3] See the entire address published as a Supplement to *The Indian Social Reformer*, November 29, 1896.

[4] Quoted in *The Baptist Missionary Magazine*, May, 1894, p. 126.

strain every nerve to sustain and accelerate this advance by realizing the influence of woman in national and social progress, and by taking all necessary steps to promote female education. The old ideal of obedience is an outworn conception; it is necessary to grant her freedom, so that she may move with the times and become the companion, guide, and helpmate of man."[1]   *The Indian Spectator* remarks: "We look to the young men of India to battle with this evil arising from the ignorance of woman, by insisting on the education of their wives and sisters."[2]   These paragraphs sufficiently reveal the spirit and courage with which the progressive wing of the native press is contending that higher privileges and a larger life shall be the lot of Indian women.

Now the point which may fairly be insisted upon in connection with these evidences of a momentous change in the public sentiment of India upon the subject of the elevation of woman

Missions a decisive factor in awakening these new aspirations.

is that these new aspirations on her behalf have resulted from the missionary movement for her education. The best thought of the country is throbbing, perhaps unconsciously to itself, with the quickening power of this stimulus. It is at the present time advocating, defending, and aggressively supporting a missionary idea which it has adopted as its own. No one who is not familiar with the past trend of Indian opinion can realize the radical import of this change, and the almost insurmountable difficulties which confront it.[3]

[1] Quoted in *Progress* (Madras), January, 1896, p. 79.

[2] Quoted in *The Indian Social Reformer*, July 12, 1896, p. 350.
The Rev. W. A. Wilson (C. P. M.), Rutlam, relates a significant incident. He says: "An instance was lately brought to my notice of a young man, a student at college, who resisted the efforts of his friends to bring about his marriage in his boyhood, and refused to marry until he had taken his degree. Having at last chosen a young girl, he took steps to have her educated before marrying her."

[3] "When missionaries first attempted to commence work amongst the girls, it was with the greatest difficulty that they could induce parents to allow them to learn. Before this time, girls who were intended for a life of prostitution had received some instruction in order that they might prove more attractive to their visitors; hence education in women was associated with immorality. In order to overcome their prejudice, parents had to be paid to allow their daughters to attend school. Then the conservatism of the older members of the family most strongly opposed it, on the ground that the gods would be angry and show their displeasure by removing the husbands of girls who had been taught. Were the history of the progress of female education in India written, it would contain many stories of schools almost deprived of scholars owing to one of them becoming a widow, and the old women pointing to her case as a certain instance of the displeasure of the gods falling upon her and her family for departing from their time-honoured customs. But gradually this prejudice was destroyed by the quiet and persistent efforts of the

Turning now to another phase of the indirect influence of missions on behalf of Indian women, we note the rapid increase of organizations specially devoted to their welfare. Young Women's Christian Associations are established at Calcutta, Bombay, and Madras, with many smaller auxiliaries in various places. This effort was inaugurated under the auspices of the World's Young Women's Christian Association. There is at Bombay a Missionary Settlement for University Women, founded by Christian students of educational institutions for women in Great Britain. There are also native societies, such as "The Association of the Daughters of India," supported by the Christian women of North India with a view to a helpful religious and intellectual ministry to their less favored sisters. "The Union for West India," with a membership of over one hundred, is composed of Christian women, native and foreign. Hindu Ladies' Social Clubs are found in Bombay, Calcutta, and Baranagar. At Madras a lectureship for Indian ladies has been established, through the good offices of Mrs. Isabel Brander.[1] Home classes for native women are conducted in different centres. It is impossible to make more than a fragmentary reference to these various efforts, but enough has been said to show that Indian society is awakening to a more unfettered life, and that unprecedented proposals on behalf of larger liberty and higher advantages for women are meeting with favor in all directions.

The growth of societies in India for the advancement and culture of womanhood.

If we inquire now what response has been made on the part of Indian girls to the new educational opportunities given them, an inspiring chapter is unfolded. In some instances the graduates of mission schools have passed university examinations, and a few among them have carried off the honors. The first native lady to take the degree of M.A. in Bengal was Miss C. M. Bose, a Christian convert, who has since become the principal of Bethune College, Calcutta, the only government college for native women in India, and from which candidates are now sent up for university examinations. Miss Cornelia Sorabji, a member of a native Christian family of distinction at Poona, achieved a brilliant success at the Deccan College, Poona, and the Bombay University. She subsequently pursued a course of legal educa-

The quick response of Indian girls to these new opportunities.

ladies of various missionary societies, until nowadays in a very great number of the houses of the middle and upper classes are to be found those who have been regularly sent to school and are able to read and write fairly well."—Wilkins, "Modern Hinduism," pp. 373, 374.

[1] *The Indian Magazine and Review*, September, 1896, p. 479.

tion in England, was graduated at Oxford with honor, and was admitted to practise as a barrister, being the first woman of India to attain that position. She has recently delivered lectures at Wilson College, Bombay, on "The Legal Status of Women in India," and at the Gujarat College of Ahmedabad, on "English Literature and Language." Miss Alice Sorabji, her sister, has lately passed most creditably the B.Sc. examination at the Bombay University, being the first Indian lady to take that degree. Miss Lilavati Singh, educated at the Lucknow College, was one of the first to obtain the B.A. degree from Calcutta University. Miss Toru Dutt, of Calcutta, was the first woman in India whose poetry attracted the attention of European critics, and although she died in Aug., 1877, at the early age of twenty, she had won for herself a place of honor not only by her Christian character but on account of her intellectual gifts.[1] We read also of three Brahman girls from the Maharani's Girls' High School at Mysore, who have just passed the matriculation examination at the Madras University. This is probably the first instance of high-caste Hindu girls appearing for public examination at a modern university.[2]

Another Christian woman of exceptional gifts and fragrant memory was the late Mrs. S. Satthianadhan, of Madras, known as Krupabai, the first Indian woman to attain eminence as a novel-

The life-story of Krupabai.

ist. She was born in 1862, a daughter of one of the earliest Brahman converts to Christianity in the Bombay Presidency, and was educated in a zenana mission school. Subsequently, as the first Indian woman to enter a medical school, she became a student at the Madras Medical College, which was the first in India to open its doors to women. This courageous example has now been followed by many of her countrywomen who have chosen a medical career. It is difficult for us to realize what it cost this brave young girl to face the prejudices of Indian society and begin a course of medical study. She left her home in Bombay, and proceeded resolutely to Madras, intent upon the accomplishment of her purpose, whatever hindrances might beset her. She was kindly received into the family of the Rev. W. T. Satthianadhan, and began her studies at the college. In "Saguna," one of her novels, she has described her reception when she first entered the lecture-hall. Her appearance was the signal for enthusiastic welcome on the part of the assembled students, who rose to their feet and cheered her for her courage and independence in venturing to join their ranks. Her unas-

[1] Chapman, "Sketches of Some Distinguished Indian Women," pp. 91–112.
[2] The Indian Social Reformer, March 7, 1897, p. 206.

Prof. S. Satthianadhan, M.A., LL.M.,
of the Presidency College, Madras.

The late Mrs. S. Satthianadhan,
(Krupabai.)

Satthianadhan Memorial Hall, Madras.
(In Memory of Mrs. W. T. Satthianadhan.)

Tinnevelly College, (C. M. S.)

CHRISTIAN EDUCATION THE HOPE OF INDIA.

suming and gentle demeanor, as well as remarkable scholarship, won for her the respect and admiration of both teachers and students.[1]

Mrs. Satthianadhan, although the first Indian woman to enter upon the study of medicine, was not the first to take the medical degree.[2] She was obliged to give up her chosen profession, as the strain of its duties proved too severe for her physical strength. She was married, in 1883, to Professor S. Satthianadhan, B.A., LL.M., of Madras, an educated gentleman who had taken his degree from Cambridge University, and was occupying at that time a position in the Indian Government service. He is now a professor in the Presidency College, Madras, and the President of the Young Men's Christian Association of that city. His wife was well known as an authoress, and has been eminently useful in the sphere of philanthropic ministry. Her novels, "Saguna" and "Kamala," and also her "Miscellaneous Writings," have been published both in Madras and London. She was an ardent advocate of the noblest Christian ideals for Indian women. Her death occurred in 1894, and, as a fitting memorial of her life, a scholarship for women in the Madras Medical College has been instituted, and also a medal in the Madras University to be awarded to the Indian girl who passes the best matriculation examination in English. Both these tributes to her memory were gifts from her friends.

Others might be mentioned, as the Pundita Ramabai, whose work

[1] Murdoch, "Sketches of Indian Christians," p. 48.

[2] M. de Menant, in the *Nouvelle Revue*, gives a very instructive account of Anandibai Joshee, the first Hindu lady on whom was conferred a medical degree. "The daughter of a rich native landowner, this lady pioneer was born thirty years ago [1865] at Poona, and, like most of her countrywomen, was married at the age of nine years, becoming a mother four years later. Through lack of proper medical attendance her child died, and it was then that the young girl made up her mind to devote her life to bringing adequate medical aid to her cloistered countrywomen. Fortunately, her husband, an intelligent and kind-hearted man, was given a government appointment in Calcutta, and, once there, he allowed his wife the extreme liberty of behaving like a European woman. In 1882, in spite of the great opposition of her family and of her husband's friends, she made up her mind to go and study medicine in the United States. Before leaving India, she held a great public meeting, which was attended by both Europeans and natives, and explained her reasons for wishing to undertake what she was about to do. At the Woman's Medical College in Pennsylvania she passed [1886] eighth out of forty-two students. It is sad to add that, after all these trials, the valiant girl fell seriously ill, and was ordered back to India, where she died at the age of twenty-one, having conquered by her courageous action even the most narrow-minded members of her caste."—*Progress*, June, 1895, p. 143. Cf. for a biographical sketch of Dr. Joshee, Chapman, "Sketches of Some Distinguished Indian Women," pp. 48–69.

at Poona for widows and famine-sufferers is so well known, and Mrs. Hensman, of Madras, sister of Professor S. Satthianadhan; but these typical examples, representing what Christianity can do for Indian women, are sufficient to indicate the bright and useful career which it opens up to them.[1]

Training and normal schools are preparing hundreds of young women to enter the profession of teaching and to render valuable service in promoting female education, a sphere of mission work which is so soon to overtax the resources of foreign agencies. The Victoria School at Lahore, not itself under missionary auspices, has been for several years under the direction of unmarried Christian ladies of Indian birth, and is a prophecy of what is to come in woman's work for woman in India. In nine years the attendance at this school and its branches has risen from two hundred and fifty to seven hundred and fifty. "Everywhere," says *The Church Missionary Intelligencer,* "the same

The growing distinction of the Christian women of India.

---

[1] *The Indian Christian Messenger,* a prominent journal, publishes, with very natural enthusiasm, the following paragraph concerning the achievements of Indian Christian women: "We may with pardonable pride point to the noble essay of the girls of our own community, evincing capability to a degree that marks them as destined to play an important part in advancing our country. Who was the first Indian lady that graduated in arts? Miss Chundra M. Bose, a Christian. Who was the first Indian lady that graduated in medicine? Miss Mary Mitter (now Mrs. Nundy), a Christian. Who was the first Indian lady that graduated in law? Miss Cornelia Sorabji, a Christian. Who was the first Indian lady that encompassed the wide, wide world, both old and new, in search of knowledge and means for the amelioration of the condition of millions of Indian widows? Pundita Ramabai, a Christian. Who are as yet the only Indian ladies whose writings have earned the approbation of European critics? Miss Toru Dutt and Mrs. S. Satthianadhan, Christian ladies. Who have rendered signal help towards making an accomplished fact that eminently Christian movement for which millions of Indian females bless the honored name of Lady Dufferin? The Indian Christian girls. Confining ourselves to our own North-West Provinces and Oudh, we may well continue: Who was the lady that first graduated as M.A.? Miss S. Chuckerbutty, a Christian. Who was the lady that attained a position hitherto unsurpassed by any lady candidate amongst M.A. candidates of the Allahabad University? Miss Lilavati Rapheal Singh, a Christian. Who was the first lady in Bengal that graduated in two subjects with the degree of M.A.? Mrs. Nirmala Shome, a Christian."—Quoted in *The Christian Patriot,* April 16, 1896.

It may be further said, in the same strain, that out of twenty-three native female graduates in Bengal thirteen are Protestant Christians, and the only Indian lady who edits an English weekly newspaper in Calcutta is the daughter of an illustrious native Christian of Bengal. The *Somaprakas* of Calcutta, a non-Christian journal, exclaims at the conclusion of an editorial upon the above theme: "Lo, what a marvellous progress these Christians have made! Verily, their Lord is with them."

tale is heard of honour paid to Christian ladies by their non-Christian fellow-countrymen; for this school is only one of many like institutions under management which is exclusively non-Christian, not to say in some instances antichristian, where the dignity and true womanliness of Christian ladies inevitably asserts itself too strongly to be ignored or forced into the shade."[1] This, let it be noted, is in that very land where a generation or so ago, when the first girls' school was talked of in Calcutta, an astounded native remarked: "These missionaries will soon begin to educate our cows, since they think it possible to educate girls."[2]

The elevating influence of missions on behalf of the women of China is as unmistakable as any evidence of the fact which can be found in India. Chinese women are acknowledged to be capable and possessed of natural dignity of char-   A higher destiny for acter, but in the blighting environment in which   Chinese women. they have lived for centuries their endowments have withered and their life has stagnated. Christianity, when its full opportunity comes, will make a noble and saintly type of womanhood in China, which will be an honor to the kingdom of God, and an untold power in the social development of Asia. Hitherto, these Chinese women have, as a rule, been so schooled in humiliation, and so constantly taught the lesson of their inferiority, that hope has died; but the woman's heart still lives, and the touch of Christ will awaken it to its higher destiny.[3]

1 *The Church Missionary Intelligencer*, August, 1897, pp. 604, 605.

2 " In point of higher education the native Christian community stands second only to the Brahman, and in female education no other class of the native population of India has made such rapid progress. In this community are to be found women who have with great credit carried off the highest academical distinctions at the disposal of the Indian universities, and among them are to be found cultured and accomplished ladies who will be valued as acquisitions in any good and polished society. It is chiefly from the ranks of native Christians that the Government has to get female doctors and agents for the education of the women of India. In the year 1895–96, out of a total of 309 females undergoing training in normal schools in the Madras Presidency, 240 were native Christians."—Satthianadhan, " Sketches of Indian Christians," Introduction, p. ix.

3 " The theory of heathenism is that man is everything and woman nothing. She has no recognized civil rights as compared with man, but, in the first place, is under the jurisdiction of her parents, and afterwards of her husband. The former can dispose of her as they please, either to a life of immorality or to a man of their own choice as a husband. In either case she has no voice in the matter. The latter can divorce or sell her if he chooses, and unless she has powerful relatives who may oppose, she cannot resist his will. Public sentiment and law declare that she must

Dr. Martin relates how he once saw in a Chinese temple, upon a festal occasion, some two or three thousand women reciting prayers to Buddha. He inquired, "Why are all the worshippers women, and what are they praying for?" The response was: "They are praying that they may be born into the world as men, so inferior are they taught to consider their present condition." That they have elements of personal and social value is recognized by Dr. Martin, when he further remarks: "Morally, however, they are China's better half—modest, graceful, and attractive. Intellectually, they are not stupid, but ignorant, left to grow up in a kind of twilight, without the benefit of schools. What they are capable of may be inferred from the fact that, in spite of disadvantages, many of them are found on the roll of honor as poets, historians, and rulers. Some of the brightest minds I ever met in China were those of girls in our mission schools."[1] The Rev. Arthur H. Smith, D.D., confirms this opinion in the following statement: "The women are seen to be able to learn, often faster than the men. This compels respect in a land where learning is so valued." It is a promising fact that schools for girls and classes for women are becoming popular in China, and are winning recognition with less distrust and friction than in some other countries.

Woman's work for woman in China, on the part of native Bible-women and teachers, presents very cheering and encouraging aspects. Dr. MacKay, of Formosa, in a chapter upon "Native Workers for Native Women," gives us the following information: "Some of the most zealous and successful workers, who were one with the little band of students in our early struggles, and who bravely, and almost single-handed, stemmed the tide of bitter persecution, were women, of whom fragrant memories are still cherished by the church there." The whole chapter is a vivid portrayal of woman's life in

be under the power of man. The sages, statesmen, and great thinkers of bygone ages have never said anything in her defence, and generation after generation has but transmitted the idea that her position is inferior to that of man."—Rev. J. Macgowan (L. M. S.), Amoy, China.

"With very rare exceptions, women are never educated. Of heathen women possibly one in two or three thousand can read. One of the stock arguments against the education of girls, and in favor of foot-binding, is that these measures are necessary to make them docile. If they were educated and had natural feet, they would gad about and do nothing, or become independent and ungovernable. The masses of the women are kept busy with cooking, spinning, weaving, and sewing. Those who are rich spend their time in embroidery, gossip, and gambling. The Christians are more generally teaching their wives to read, and educating their daughters."—The late Mrs. C. W. Mateer (P. B. F. M. N.), Tungchow, China.

[1] Martin, "A Cycle of Cathay," pp. 82, 83.

Formosa, and of the service which has been rendered by devoted Bible-women.[1]

There seems to be an incongruity between the theoretical ideal regarding woman which is found in the literature and philosophy of China, and the every-day practice which has prevailed for centuries in Chinese society. There are famous books of instruction about woman, and especially addressed to her, such as " The Four Books for Girls " and " The Classics for Women," as well as " The Records of Illustrious Women in Ancient Times "; but these literary monitors seem to wield only a feeble influence in real life either over the minds of men or in moulding the lives of women. The Rev. James Ware, in a little volume recently published, entitled, " A Peep into a Chinaman's Library," quotes the verdict of Dr. Faber, of Shanghai, concerning these biographies of famous Chinese women. Dr. Faber's views of the character and tone of the subject-matter therein contained are given in a brief summary.[2] It is clear that a Chinese woman can entertain but little hope that her lot will be changed through the teachings of the Classics.

[1] MacKay, " From Far Formosa," chap. xxxii. Cf. also a sketch of woman's life in China, in an article by Mrs. George S. Hays, in *The Missionary Review of the World*, February, 1897, pp. 102, 103.

[2] Dr. Faber's researches into this extensive field of Chinese literature have led him to record the following results : " (1) The imperial harem has always been a source of moral pestilence to China. (2) This harem is imitated, according to means, by every mandarin and wealthy person throughout the empire. As long as these harems are tolerated, it will be found impossible to reform Chinese social life and bring it to a condition approaching health. (3) Polygamy shows its worst influence on female nature; it excites a number of base passions which have caused unspeakable misery in China, and continue to do so. (4) The general neglect of female education causes a corresponding disastrous influence of courtesans. (5) Most of the ' Famous Women ' belong to ancient times and to the highest ranks in Chinese society. (6) Female virtue is in modern China almost exclusively of a passive nature, too often consisting in nothing but a stupid imitation of ancient example. (7) None of the stories point to spiritual comforts, nor to the hope of a better world. Though there are accounts of females said to have reached the state of immortality, it will be difficult to discover a Chinese woman striving after the same success. (8) We find, on the whole, very few Chinese women famous for noble qualities, the greater number being objectionable from the standpoint of Christian morality. (9) We find infanticide mentioned, by which not only the child but motherly affection is murdered. Though Buddhism warns against destruction of human life, the crime has increased in the course of time, and is not yet recognized as murder punishable by law. Thousands of female babies are destroyed every year. (10) Suicide is encouraged, as a woman belongs to her affianced and has no business to live on after his death. (11) The stories of supernatural females show perfect agreement with modern emancipation theories in Western lands. (12) Vice is made as famous as virtue in these stories. Chastity seems only insisted on in

Now let Christianity try what it can do to help her and to bring in an era of happier life and nobler destiny.

That an age of Christianized womanhood has begun in China may fairly be claimed, although as yet the relative proportion of Christian women in that vast population is exceedingly small. This fact, however, only adds to the impression one derives of the value of that infinitesimal leaven as it works in the hearts and homes of Chinese women. Education is advancing, and schools for girls are multiplying, many of normal standards and high curriculum having already been founded. Classes for adult women are popular, and training-schools for Bible-women, such as the one Miss Adele Fielde conducted for many years at Swatow, give special promise of usefulness. Christian homes have been established, and higher standards of respect and consideration towards woman have secured recognition to a remarkable extent in such an unimpressible community.

An era of Christianized womanhood has begun in China.

Still more noticeable is the fact that Chinese women are entering the medical profession, and are already acquitting themselves with credit. A class for women is conducted at the Canton Hospital, under Drs. Niles and Fulton, and there are other classes in connection with several of the larger hospitals of the empire. The first student of medicine among the women of China who received a foreign diploma and returned to her native land to practise her profession was Dr. You Mé Kying (written in English "You May King"). She was the daughter of a native pastor, and was born in 1864. After the death of her father and mother, which occurred in her infancy, she was taken into the family of Dr. D. B. McCartee, then a missionary of the American Presbyterian Board at Ningpo. She received a careful education, mostly under the personal direction of Mrs. McCartee, and afterwards came with Dr. McCartee's family to America, where she eventually entered the Woman's Medical College of the New York Infirmary for Women and Children, and was graduated at the head of her class in 1885. In 1887 she was sent out by the Board of Foreign Missions of the Reformed Church in America as a medical missionary to Amoy, where she served in that special sphere for a year.[1] Subse-

Medical honors for Chinese women.

regard to women engaged or married, not as of any moral value in itself. (13) Chinese women cannot have a purifying influence upon Chinese social life under the present circumstances."—Ware, " A Peep into a Chinaman's Library," pp. 42–45.

[1] "Annual Report of the Board of Foreign Missions of the Reformed Church in America, 1887," p. 13. For a sketch of Dr. Kying, see *The Medical Missionary*

Dr. Mary Stone (left), and Dr. Ida Kahn (right).
(See pages 193, 361.)

Dr. Hu King Eng.
(See page 193.)

Educational Possibilities for Chinese Women.
(M. E. M. S.)

quently Dr. McCartee and his family removed to Japan, and this led her to enter the service of the American Methodist (Southern) Board, as a missionary physician at Kobe, where she remained for five years. Her marriage afterwards to Mr. E. de Silva brought her again to America, where she now (1898) resides in San Francisco, California.

Another—apparently the second—Chinese woman to enter the profession with a Western diploma was Dr. Hü King Eng, who finished her preparatory course at the Ohio Wesleyan University, and, after completing her studies at that institution, entered the Woman's Medical College at Philadelphia in 1888, though illness deferred her graduation until 1894. She returned to China in 1895, as a missionary of the Woman's Foreign Missionary Society of the Methodist Episcopal Church. She is a granddaughter of one of the earliest native Christians in China, and was herself baptized in her native land. Her father was a converted mandarin, his two sons entering the ministry of the Methodist Mission, and this daughter (born in 1866) adopting the profession of medicine. Upon her return to China she was greeted with an ovation by mandarins and coolies, all ranks of society paying honor to her gifts, and recognizing with respect the remarkable character of her achievements. She is now known as the " Miracle Lady." One instance is related of a Chinese wheeling his blind old mother in a wheelbarrow a thousand miles to consult her. It is worthy of note that Dr. Hü King Eng and Miss Marguerite Wong,[1] both of whom were educated at mission schools, were appointed by the Chinese Government as delegates to a Woman's Congress planned to be held in London in 1899. The former has lately been asked to accept the position of physician in the household of Li Hung Chang. The medical profession is now increasingly popular among Chinese women. The graduation, with special honor, of Drs. Meigii Shie (Mary Stone) and Ida Kahn from the medical department of the University of Michigan in 1896 is an interesting incident in two respects—they left a record in both character and scholarship which is not often surpassed, and are among the Christian pioneers in the ministry of healing to their countrywomen.[2] They returned to China in September, 1896.

Record, August, 1887, pp. 81, 82. Cf. also a statement by the Rev. Robert Aikman, D.D., in *The Church at Home and Abroad*, April, 1898, p. 288.

[1] Since her appointment Miss Wong has been married to Dr. Lim Boo Keng. She gives an interesting account of her meeting with Li Hung Chang, in *Woman's Missionary Friend*, December, 1896, p. 173.

[2] " President Angell, of the University of Michigan, so widely known in China since his diplomatic service there in 1878-79, ' by the authority of the Honorable Board of Regents,' conferred the degrees upon seven hundred and forty-five stu-

In the various medical classes for women in China there are also many bright and capable students who are preparing for a life of special usefulness.

Letters received from missionaries in China contain frequent references to the changed status of womanhood, due to missions, which is already noticeable, and is growing more and more pronounced. "It is common," writes the Rev. W. P. Chalfant (P. B. F. M. N.), of Ichowfu, "to hear outsiders comment admiringly on the improvement in our Christian women.   Native ideas upon the subject of the rights and capabilities of women are steadily changing."   The Rev. J. Macgowan (L. M. S.), of Amoy, speaks of the "new sentiment that permeates every Christian household.   The result is seen in the gradual elevation of woman, and the different position she holds from that which obtained when I first arrived in China.   Certain rights are secured to her that heathen women dare not claim.   Parents may not marry their daughter to a heathen, unless it is impossible to get a Christian, nor to any man of known bad character.   They may not dispose of her to be a concubine or second wife, neither can they compel her to be betrothed to one to whom she herself, for moral reasons, has an antipathy.   If they do not regard the welfare of their girls in these matters, the Church steps in and utters its voice in their behalf.   Again, a man may not ill-treat his wife, or, except for one offence, divorce her, or take another wife, unless he is prepared to come under the discipline of the Church.   Hitherto woman has had no champion to stand by in her defence.   Now she has, and one that is prepared to right every wrong in her social life." [1]

Benefits which Christianity is bringing to the women of China.

dents.   They marched to the platform and received their diplomas at his hands, but to none was there accorded such a universal outburst of applause from students and visitors as to these two little Chinese women. . . . The demonstration was also participated in by the medical faculty, the only time any of the staff joined the students."— *Woman's Missionary Friend*, August, 1896, p. 42.

[1] "At the present time," writes the Rev. T. W. Pearce (L. M. S.), of Hong Kong, "each Christian home is an object-lesson, and the influence of Christianity in purifying and elevating domestic life is acknowledged by many non-Christians. The women of the churches take their part in Christian effort and usefulness. Attached to our own church is a Dorcas Society composed of Chinese women, to the number of twenty or more, who spend one morning of each week in sewing garments as a contribution to the benevolent work of the church."

"The position of the women," writes the Rev. W. Gauld (C. P. M.), of Tamsui, Formosa, "in Christian households is so decidedly improved that many heathen parents try to obtain Christian husbands for their daughters.   Twenty years ago it was with very great difficulty that a Christian man, even a preacher, could find a

The Japanese, perhaps more than any other Oriental people, have responded with quick and intelligent appreciation to Western ideas concerning a higher type of womanhood. The women of Japan are naturally gifted with more refinement and graciousness than can be found among most Asiatic peoples, and there is reason to expect that when the finer elements of Christian womanliness are added, a character of rare beauty and excellence will result, which will prove a blessing to Japanese society, and add a winsome dignity to the influence of Christianity in Eastern Asia.[1]

A new type of womanhood in Japan.

Japanese statesmanship has shown itself alert on the subject of female education. To what extent this is due to Christian missions need not be stated with any attempt at definite assertion, but it is evident that one of the features of reactionary policy in Japan has been to check the movement for the higher training and social ad-

wife, but now alliance with such men is sought after, because of their reputation for love and kindness towards their wives."

[1] An actual occurrence reported in a Japanese periodical, under the heading "The Confessions of a Converted Husband," throws a flash-light illumination upon the gentleness and patient sweetness, as well as the Christian faith, of which Japanese womanhood is capable. The account, in the words of the husband, runs as follows: "I awoke one night—it was toward midnight—to hear a voice praying in the garden. It was the familiar voice of my wife. 'O Heavenly Father, is my husband utterly unworthy to be received into Thy grace? I had believed that it was sufficient for all. Am I faulty in my deeds? Do I lack zeal in prayer? I can no longer visit Thy house of prayer. I can no longer read Thy Word. I can no longer sing Thy praise. I have not resented, but bowed to these inordinate commands, simply because I trusted to Thy timely interference. . . . Thy handmaiden is unwilling to make any human being the confidant of her sorrows, for how can she lay open the inhumanity of him to whom she has vowed to be faithful even unto death? Thou alone knowest the bitterness of her grief. O Lord, omniscient and almighty, hear Thou the humble prayer of Thy handmaiden. May it please Thee to lead my beloved husband into repentance. May his heart be opened to accept Thy everlasting Word. Lord, grant my petition, or let me die. If there be aught amiss in my heart or in my daily life by which my husband is kept back from Thy salvation, let me share his fate with him. Thy ordinance united us as man and wife, to be together in joy and in sorrow, and I would be faithful unto death.' Her broken voice came from a heart heaving with emotion. Impressed as I already was with her gentle obedience, with her devoted faithfulness, my thoughts in listening to this prayer can better be imagined than described. Her hot tears burned into my inmost soul. The sacred flame within her consumed all that was obstinate within me. I rushed out to where she was, and knelt down beside her. We both wept, praising God. The moon's serene rays shone down upon us both, as if in token of the heavenly good-will. Ah, yes, it was indeed thus that I became a Christian."— *The Japan Evangelist*, December, 1895, p. 106.

vancement of woman. In recent years public utterances of eminent Japanese officials have revealed a high appreciation of the importance of this aspect of national development. The Marquis Saionji, Minister of Education in 1895, delivered an address at his official residence to all the principals of the normal and middle schools, called especially to meet him, which contained some memorable utterances, although it should not escape our notice that among the nationalistic and anti-foreign leaders of Japan it was received with bitter comment and much opposition. The following quotation from his remarks indicates his attitude. He said: " If a nation wishes to produce good and strong citizens, it needs the cultured influence of woman. This is the reason why foreign nations take great interest in the education of woman. A woman, like a man, needs to develop her faculties and character. Therefore, to us as a nation the education of our women is of the greatest importance."[1] The words of Count Okuma, in an address on the same subject, before the normal school in his native town of Saga, are indicative of a wise and intelligent judgment concerning this entirely new aspect of public policy in Japan. He said: " A nation consists of men and women. Men and women should therefore both be educated. But heretofore the education of women has been very much discouraged. Now, therefore, this project must be greatly encouraged to make up for past shortcomings. Every strong nation has its female education highly developed. In other words, where this has been emphasized, national strength has attained to foundations of firmness and soundness."[2]

The new thought of Japan has been greatly quickened upon this theme. All its aspects are being discussed, both publicly and privately, with interest and enthusiasm. The old conservative element is obliged to defend itself against the lively and vigorous advocacy of the leaders of enlightened progress. The equality of men and women in their personal status and rights is a live question in present-day Japan. The dual standard of morals is being questioned on every side, and " a

The social prospects of woman a live question in present-day Japan.

----

[1] *The Japan Evangelist*, August, 1896, p. 357.

There was held in Kyoto, in 1895, a convention on the subject of government education, attended by over three thousand teachers. Many earnest addresses were made upon the subject of the education of woman. Among others was that of Mr. S. Tsuji, formerly Vice-Minister of Education, who insisted that such instruction must be encouraged. Mr. S. Kiba, the head official in the Department of Technical Education, spoke in the same strain. Mr. S. Akitsuki, principal of the Higher Normal School for Girls, also declared with no uncertain sound his opinion in favor of female education. (*Ibid.*, p. 357.)   [2] *Ibid.*, p. 358.

St. Agnes' School, Kyoto, Japan.

(P. E. M. S.)

JAPANESE GIRLHOOD UNDER MISSION CULTURE.

white life for two" is becoming a watchword in Japanese reform circles. The proposal that the Imperial University at Tokyo should open its gates to women who may be able to pass its examinations has been supported from Japanese sources. The desire that woman should take a more active part in promoting the higher welfare of society and in conducting philanthropic work is freely urged by the Japanese themselves.[1] When the Emperor promulgated the Constitution, in 1889, his wife rode by his side in an open carriage. It is doubtful if in the annals of Japan womanhood ever appeared so prominently in the making of national history.[2] The present Emperor by his respect and courtesy to the Empress has set an example which is calculated to exert a marked influence in elevating the marriage relation and conserving the honor of the home.[3]

The public press of Japan, both Christian and non-Christian, is discussing the subject of the social position of woman in all its aspects, not without some narrowness and ire on the part of nationalistic journals, but, on the whole, with excellent spirit and acute discrimination. Woman is contributing her share to the controversy, and with no mean ability giving an impetus to her side of the question. Such articles as those by Mrs. Gin Ogino, on "The Past and the Future of Japanese Woman Physicians," indicate this.[4] *The Japan Evangelist* has a well-conducted department devoted exclusively to the interests of woman, the subject-matter of which is mostly supplied by Japanese writers. A few of the topics treated therein will show the scope and directness of the advocacy of these higher ideals. Among them, as we glance through the files, we find the following: "Japanese Women in Religion," "The Future of Japanese Women," "Social and Civil Rights of Japanese Women," "Women and Charities," "The Present Condition of Woman's Education in Japan," "The Responsibility of Japanese Women in Leading and Civilizing Asia," "Christian Influence in the

---

[1] Cf. article entitled "Japanese Thoughts on Woman's Education," by Mrs. W. E. Hoy, in *The Japan Evangelist*, April, 1897, pp. 213-217.

[2] Bacon, "Japanese Girls and Women," p. 115.

[3] While this remark is true, the Occidental reader will still be obliged to adjust his sensibilities to an Oriental environment when he learns that "the Emperor added another concubine to his harem during the celebration of the twenty-fifth anniversary of his marriage to the Empress." The present Crown Prince is in fact the son of a concubine. A military officer of the Japanese Government expressed to a missionary the hope "that when the Prince came to the throne he would set a better example."

[4] The original articles appeared in the *Jogaku Zasshi*, but were translated for *The Japan Evangelist* of February and April, 1894.

Home," "New Fields for Japanese Women." Themes like these are surely the signs of nobler aspirations for Oriental womanhood.[1]

The question may well be asked here, Can this change of sentiment and this new trend of thought concerning the elevation of woman be traced in any degree to mission influence? With-
The new trend of thought is largely due to mission influence. out attempting to pronounce too hasty and unqualified a judgment upon this point, we leave our readers, with the facts in view, to form their own opinion. It seems certain that female education, at least, has been an outgrowth of missions. The new respect for woman is to a marked extent identified with Christianity. The higher standards of courtesy and consideration are in large measure traceable to the same source. The better and nobler home life of Japan is certainly Christian. The dishonor to womanhood in the system of concubinage has been revealed and emphasized through biblical teaching. Is it likely that these changes would have taken place in Japanese society, and these subjects of discussion have assumed such prominence, had Christian missions never entered the empire?[2]

---

[1] *The Japan Evangelist*, December, 1895, February, June, and August, 1896, May and June, 1897.

Some statements which are made in one of the articles mentioned may be quoted. In speaking of Christian influence in the home, the following testimony to the honor of womanhood is recorded: "Since the year when war between Japan and China was declared, it has been a hard time for military men both on land and sea. They have endured much for nearly three years. During this period, many wives stained the fair names of their heroic husbands by their shameless conduct, and it is frequently reported that they used the precious savings sent to them by their thoughtful and trusting husbands for most abominable purposes. The Christian wives of Christian soldiers, however, presented quite a different picture, and made the light of their faith shine brightly. Of none of them did we hear any such bad report. On the contrary, appreciating their husbands' severe sacrifices, they kept their homes pure, and performed their duties towards their parents-in-law, as well as attended to the education of their children. So faithfully and wisely were these duties discharged that their husbands, on their return, found their homes happy and in good condition. The difference in their situation, as compared with that of their comrades, filled their hearts with joy and gratitude. Is this not good evidence of the power of Christian influence upon the very foundation of society—the home?"—*The Japan Evangelist*, June, 1896, p. 288.

[2] "The elevation of woman has brought about a change in sentiment, and in practice too, concerning concubinage. The evil has been recognized, and it is no longer considered respectable. Where it is practised it is inclined to hide itself."—Rev. Henry Stout, D.D. (Ref. C. A.), Nagasaki.

"The material and social benefits that have come to Japan during the past twenty-five years—directly and indirectly the results of Christian teaching—are

The history of the establishment and rapid growth of female education in Japan is inseparably linked with missionary effort. The Rev. Henry Stout, D.D., of Nagasaki, writes to the author: "The very idea of education for women must be traced to missions. Speaking from personal experience, the first suggestions of this kind were received with stolid indifference. . . . Women are now regarded not only as capable of education, but as worthy of receiving it. This, I believe, must be set down chiefly to the credit of missions. But it would be unfair to claim all as due to this agency, except perhaps indirectly; for many who have been personally uninfluenced by Christianity have come to see the good to be derived from the considerate treatment of women, have fallen in with the views, and by their own conduct helped forward the movement." It is now (1898) only twenty-seven years since the first mission school for girls was opened in the empire. At present there are about eighty in successful operation, besides those conducted under other than mission auspices. The subject is now so much to the front that annual conferences on the Christian education of woman are regularly held. The more important of these schools are devoted to normal training, and graduate teachers who have no difficulty in finding employment.

many. The greatest of all is the higher estimate that has been put upon woman, and the new ideas in respect to home life, as shown in the educational institutions that have been established by the Government, or by individual enterprise, for the elevation of woman. When I came to Japan twenty-one years ago, *there was not a girls' school in the empire outside of missionary circles.* The provisions which have been made here for woman's education within the past eighteen or twenty years are one of the marvels of the age. There are to-day in Japan hundreds, yea, thousands, of pure women who are moral, and intelligent factors in society, who would not have been such but for the introduction of Christianity."—Rev. Julius Soper (M. E. M. S.), Hakodate.

" Christianity will also do away with the forcible marriage of girls against their will, and to men they have never seen till the evening of the marriage ceremony. One of our believers was told by her parents and brothers that she must marry, and so they presented for her sanction several men, some four or five in a month, and when she refused to be wedded to any one of them, she was taken to the home of a man she had never seen, and married to him. Our Christians said, ' Barbarous,' and we echo the opinion."—Rev. S. W. Hamblen (A. B. M. U.), Sendai, Japan.

" Twenty years ago it was an unheard-of thing for a man to be seen walking with his wife, but now they can be observed not only walking and talking together, but riding in the same jinrikisha. The system of concubinage, which has wrought such evils in family life, is opposed by a growing public sentiment which has been fanned by the direct efforts of Christian people, and others influenced by Christian principle."—Professor John C. Ballagh (P. B. F. M. N.), Tokyo.

One of the finest institutions of the kind in Japan is the College (*Jo Gakuin*) of the American Board Mission at Kobe, which, in 1895, celebrated its twentieth anniversary. At that time it was reported that over 690 pupils had been admitted since its foundation, of whom 132 had been graduated. Of this number 32 were engaged in educational work.[1] Other institutions whose success and usefulness have been conspicuous are the *Joshi Gakuin*, of the Presbyterian Mission (U. S. A.), at Tokyo, the Ferris Seminary, Yokohama, the Jonathan Sturges Seminary, Nagasaki (both of the Reformed Church of America), the Methodist schools at Nagasaki and Hakodate, the Naniwa Girls' School of the American Presbyterian Mission, and the Bishop Poole Memorial Girls' School of the Church Missionary Society, both at Osaka, and St. Agnes' School of the American Protestant Episcopal Church at Kyoto. The total graduating from these and similar schools at the present time may be estimated at about seventy per year. "There are now," writes the Rev. Henry Loomis, of Yokohama, "hundreds of Japanese homes where the daughters have been taught the modern branches, and, what is best of all, they are animated by Christian principles and live devoted lives. In strength of character and singleness of purpose some of these Christian women are the peers of the men, and examples to all Japanese society." There are also, besides strictly literary institutions, others for the education of nurses, as the Kyoto Training-School in connection with the Doshisha, and those for Scripture instruction, where Bible-women are trained, as the Bible School at Kobe. Private classes of this character are conducted at many points. These facts are full of promise when we consider that the missionary purpose is beginning to lay hold upon the Christian conscience of Japan, and that native missionaries, both men and women, are being sent to Formosa.[2]

The phenomenal development of female education in Japan.

---

[1] *The Japan Evangelist*, February, 1896, p. 173.

[2] In an article written by a native Christian lady, entitled "New Fields for Japanese Women," occurs the following paragraph, which reveals a truly Christian instinct concerning missionary obligation: "Japan as a nation has been given the noble privilege of being the first to receive and interpret the civilization of the West. Standing at Asia's gateway, the task assigned her seems to be to open her mind to Western ideas, to assimilate them, and then to give them to her sister nations in a more or less modified form. The Christian religion, like many other gifts from the Occident, must first be studied and reduced to its purest fundamental elements by minds other than European before it can be comprehended by the Asiatic mind. Christianity often comes in forms too highly colored with Western modes of thought for our ready appreciation. It stands to reason, therefore, that we are better able

Ferris Seminary, Yokohama.
(Ref. C. A.)

Graduating Class, 1892.

NEW IDEALS FOR JAPANESE WOMANHOOD.

A glance at what missions have done for woman in Korea opens to us a fresh and almost romantic chapter of beginnings. We are dealing with first things in this story of brightening hopes for Korean womanhood. In *The Korean Reposi-* *tory* for January, 1896, we have a sketch of "Woman's Work in Korea." It opens with the statement that those who have recently arrived can "scarcely realize the difference between the Korea of to-day and the country to which we came more than *ten years ago.*" The first girls' school was established by the Methodist Mission in 1886. Many difficulties and embarrassments had to be overcome in securing pupils, but the last report states that there are now forty-seven in attendance. In the *Heathen Woman's Friend* for September, 1895, is an article by Mrs. M. F. Scranton, of Seoul, entitled "A Social Advance." The incident to which she refers under the above title is that at a public function in honor of the independence of Korea, consisting of a banquet and garden-party at the palace, to which all foreigners and many Koreans of rank were invited, a decided innovation in the customs of the country was inaugurated. This was the presence of the wives of the cabinet ministers, who were to receive with them and take part in the ceremonies of the occasion. One of these officials, whose wife had been educated in the Methodist Mission School, acknowledged to Mrs. Scranton that this was the first time that he had ever publicly introduced her. This fact is, perhaps, an insignificant bit of history, but, as Mrs. Scranton writes, "to us who are here, and who know about the secluded and narrow lives of Korean women, it seems a most important and suggestive event." "We are moving forward," is the comment of the editor of *The Korean Repository*, in reporting a mass-meeting of Christians on the King's birthday, 1897, at which one of the speakers, the editor of *The Independent*, the only English newspaper published in Korea, "made a splendid plea for woman, and the necessity of honoring her." The editor of the *Repository* continues as follows: "It was the first public utterance on this subject we remember hearing."[1]

to approach our Korean and Chinese sisters, as well as those in Formosa, than are our Western sisters. We will have to seek them in their own homes, as we have been sought in ours, and give them our truest and best—in short, give to them, in our turn, what has been so freely given to us. We must remember that we have many things in common—our literature, our social customs, etc., which ought certainly to be a bond between us to prepare the way for mutual understanding."—*The Japan Evangelist*, February, 1896, p. 169.

[1] *The Korean Repository*, September, 1897, p. 358.

A romantic chapter of brightening prospects for Korean women.

If we turn now to note what missions in Mohammedan lands have accomplished for the elevation of woman, we find interesting facts to record.   A carefully prepared article by the late

The beginning of a better day for woman in Moslem lands.

Rev. Thomas Laurie, D.D., on "The Beginnings of the Education of Woman in Syria,"[1] presents a detailed review of the early history of female education in that land, recounting its difficulties, now hardly credible, and also showing its fruits in the lives of a group of remarkable women, who, during the past fifty years, have been an honor to Christianity in Syria.   A memorial column has been erected in front of the mission church at Beirut, in commemoration of the first day-school for girls in Syria, which was opened, in 1835, by Mrs. Sarah Huntington Smith, the wife of Dr. Eli Smith.   On the 18th of April, 1894, at the unveiling of this column, nine hundred native children assembled to celebrate and adorn the occasion.   In 1835 there was this one little day-school for girls, conducted by missionaries of the American Board; at the present time there are thirty-six boarding and day schools for them in Beirut alone, under Protestant, Roman Catholic, Greek, and even Moslem direction.   Protestant schools for girls scattered throughout Syria and Palestine have not less than nine thousand pupils, and if we should count those of all sects and creeds there would be several thousands more.

The first girls' boarding-school in Syria was founded by Dr. and Mrs. De Forest, in 1847.   Since then female education has grown to be almost a specialty in Syrian mission work.   Such admirable institutions as the girls' seminaries of the American Presbyterian Mission at Beirut, Sidon, and Tripoli, and that of the Irish Presbyterians at Damascus, the British Syrian Institution at Beirut, and other schools at Hasbeiya and Zahleh, under the same direction, St. George's School and Orphanage, under the charge of Miss Jessie Taylor, and the Orphanage of the Prussian Deaconesses at Beirut, the training institutions at Shimlan and Shweir, Miss Proctor's school at Shweifat, and that of the Reformed Presbyterian Mission at Latakia, give tangible evidence of the efficiency and extent of female instruction at the present time in Syria. The advances in all parts of the Levant have been hardly less marked. "Female education," writes the Rev. Andrew Watson, D.D., of the United Presbyterian Mission in Cairo, "which was almost unknown in Egypt at the time our work was begun, is now making rapid progress, and almost entirely under mission auspices."   The appreciation of the education of girls which exists at present both in the Turkish Empire

[1] *The Missionary Review of the World*, December, 1895, pp. 891–899.

and Persia is most remarkable in a land of Mohammedan traditions, although the actual advance is as yet far more marked among Oriental Christians than among Mohammedans. The statement of the Rev. W. L. Whipple, for many years the agent of the American Bible Society at Tabriz, that when Dr. Perkins, of the American Board, first went to Persia, in 1834, " there were only two women in the whole Nestorian nation who could read," is sufficiently indicative of the state of things at that time. Happily, at present he can add that "now it may almost be said that it is difficult to find a young woman who cannot read."

From Aintab, Turkey, Dr. Caroline F. Hamilton (A. B. C. F. M.) sends a similar report.[1] " It is a somewhat extreme statement," writes the Rev. Dr. George F. Herrick (A. B. C. F. M.), of Constantinople, "but a true one, nevertheless, that our colleges and high schools for girls have had a wider and deeper social influence than that which they have exerted as purely educational institutions." The higher schools for the training of girls in the Turkish Empire are an honor to modern missions. The American College for Girls at Scutari, Constantinople, the Euphrates College at Harpoot,[2] the Aintab Girls' Seminary, and the Central Turkey College for Girls at Marash, with a score or more of boarding and high schools in other places, form a monumental tribute to the value placed upon the education of woman. In Persia we have only to mention such institutions as the Faith Hubbard School at Hamadan, the Iran Bethel at Teheran, the Fiske Seminary at Urumiah, and the Girls' School at Tabriz, to indicate how thoroughly to the front is this important department of mission enterprise in that dark Mohammedan land.

No one can fully understand the value of the Christian education of girls as a social benefit in Moslem lands without tracing the indirect results which follow and affect in so many ways the status of woman and the customs which pre-   Decisive changes in
vail concerning her. In important respects the   public sentiment and social customs.
traditional policy regarding marriage is almost
revolutionized. Early marriages become impracticable, unless a girl's intellectual training is to be neglected. When she is once educated, her

1 " When our missionaries came to Aintab in 1849 and 1850," writes Dr. Hamilton, " they found two women who could read, among all the Gregorians in the city. Since that day the advance has been marvelous. At present to educate their daughters has become well-nigh fashionable, and, though we regret to say that sometimes it is with the desire to render them more marketable, yet the women reap the benefit, and are certainly better fitted to train their children. The educated mothers are always anxious to send their daughters to the Seminary, and so the lump is being leavened."

2 See illustrations, Vol. I., pp. 275, 277, 287, 293.

superiority of intelligence and dignity and worth of character lead to a degree of respect for her preferences which have never been thought of before.[1]   The whole tone of public sentiment, and especially the standards of Christian consideration and kindness, are slowly but surely elevating the atmosphere of home life.   Parental aspirations and desires pertain to the girls as well as the boys.   " Under the old régime," writes the Rev. Edward Riggs (A. B. C. F. M.), of Marsovan, " the domestic and social condition of woman in the home was most deplorable.   The influence of missions in breaking down evil customs, and introducing Christian liberty into the inner sanctum of the family, is one of the most marked results of the Gospel.   The graduates of our girls' schools, who are now numbered by the hundreds throughout the land, have become teachers, wives, and mothers.   It has been found impossible to place them in the common category of dumb household drudges.   Ordinarily the bride was ridiculously limited in her sphere of activity.   For a long time after marriage she could not under any circumstances speak above a whisper, nor even that without permission of her mother-in-law, whose absolute and abject slave she was expected to be.   Of other tyrannies and absurdities I need not speak.   With the example of a few truly Christian families before her, and the instructions of her school course deep in her heart, and especially if equally united to a young preacher or teacher similarly trained, they soon set a new fashion of married life.   Mutual respect, help, and forbearance take the place of self-assertion and arbitrariness. The example has had its influence far beyond the immediate circle to which it first applied, and a higher view of the marriage relation seems to have spread quite widely."[2]   The advance from the crude and re-

[1] " Education prevents early marriage, and many of our girls teach a few years before being married.   In one small city in our field, I am told there is not an unmarried girl over twenty years of age.   Here in Aintab there are several spinsters, and they show the happiness and usefulness possible in single life— something deemed impossible a few years ago.   Then it was a shame, but now these women are honored, and all are busy workers."—Dr. Caroline F. Hamilton (A. B. C. F. M.), Aintab.

" It is certain that in Syria there is a growing sentiment against the very early marriage of girls.   This is partly due to the idea that they are to be educated—a thing incompatible with early marriages.   Education is a direct agency or fruit of missions."—Rev. Professor George E. Post, M.D., Beirut.

" Girls are no longer married at so early an age; they are now consulted as to whom they will marry, and are often lovingly sought and won, as every true-hearted woman ought to be."—Rev. J. K. Greene, D.D. (A. B. C. F. M.), Constantinople.

[2] " The home has become immeasurably more lovely, and a much happier place for husbands and fathers, and to such the attractions of the coffee-shop and the

pressive customs of former days to this era when educated girls are in positions of dignity and responsibility as school-teachers, members of philanthropic societies, Bible-women, or mothers of Christian families, over which they preside with true refinement, gentleness, and loving fidelity, is indeed inspiring.

In certain sections of the Continent of Africa and the once savage islands of the Pacific, there is a change in the social position of woman which in its magnitude and significance is incomparable. Christian ladies from England have lately (1895) entered interior Africa, and are in heart touch with the women of Uganda. "In the old days," writes a missionary, "woman was but a beast of burden. How wonderful to see her now in many communities beginning to take her rightful place by man's side! It will be a gradual work, the elevation of woman, but we do see it already proceeding. The arrival of the five ladies who accompanied Bishop Tucker last autumn will no doubt greatly accelerate it."[1] In the field of the Universities' Mission also are many ladies who have braved the hardships of an African life. Miss Caroline Thackeray, of Mbweni, in an interesting communication, has given brief biographical sketches of the character and work of a number of native girls who have become mission helpers. It is a loving and cordial tribute to the worth of these young converts who have been lifted out of the depths of heathenism to become teachers and exemplars of the religion of Christ.[2] Had we space to trace the results

Some gold of pure womanhood from mines of African heathenism.

liquor-shop have largely lost their charm. In short, with the elevation of woman, and the heightened sanctity and love of home, has come an improved state of morality generally, and also the abolition of many hurtful customs in society."—Rev. J. K. Greene, D.D. (A. B. C. F. M.), Constantinople.

"The social status of woman has greatly changed. There are many houses, particularly among the Protestants, where the men and women sit down at table together—a thing entirely unheard of when we came here. Often the household purse is in the wife's hands, and she is trusted to make all ordinary purchases, while, under the old system, stealing from the husband by the wife was a most common occurrence."—Rev. George C. Raynolds, M.D. (A. B. C. F. M.), Van.

"Probably a change in the relative position of woman among all races in this land would have occurred in the present generation, even if American missionaries had never come to the country. But whatever of high and healthy tone marks the change actually taking place is traceable directly to the influences thrown into the current by these missionaries. High moral aims, truthfulness, purity of heart and imagination, service—these are the jewels which we teach them to seek and prize for their daughters. It is missionary work alone which has been fruitful of such social results."—Rev. George F. Herrick, D.D. (A. B. C. F. M.), Constantinople.

[1] Pilkington, "The Gospel in Uganda," p. 26.
[2] *Central Africa*, December, 1896, pp. 203-208.

in South Africa, it would be pleasant reading for every Christian heart. The missionary magazines of the societies laboring there contain many articles bearing upon this theme.[1]   In some sections of the West Coast native legislation has been instituted for the protection of woman and the elevation of her status in society.   An illustration of this appears in a letter from Mrs. R. H. De Heer, of Benito, West Africa.   The incident is well worth recording as something new in the State records of an African chieftain.[2]   Native women of refined and gentle spirits and devoted lives, who are serving Christ and doing good among their countrywomen, are found in these old haunts of savagery.   No happier example of this can be mentioned than Mrs. Crowther, the wife of Archdeacon Crowther, concerning whose work Bishop Tugwell has written in terms of high commendation.[3]

[1] Cf. files of *The Chronicle, Work and Workers in the Mission Field, The Missionary Record, The Free Church of Scotland Monthly, The Church of Scotland Home and Foreign Mission Record, The Christian Express* of Lovedale, and *The African Pioneer.*

[2] " A few days ago, our Kombe king came down from his headquarters at Bata to hold the semiannual meeting of parliament, and, after very animated discussions, three or four new laws were promulgated, all bearing upon the improvement of the condition of women.   Some of the Christian representatives were in favor of having payment of dowry, which means purchase of wives to be held as slaves, entirely abolished.   Others felt that the mass of the people were not yet prepared for the innovation, and the attempt to enforce such a law might only lead to rebellion.   So it was decided that the amount of dowry should be somewhat decreased, and that no more infants should be betrothed to grown men.   They are to be left free until they have attained an age when they are supposed to be capable of making choice for themselves.

" Then, heretofore, it has been a law, as binding as that of the Medes and Persians, that in case a man dies his wife must be inherited, like his other property, and compelled to marry such member of the deceased husband's family as shall be decided upon in council by the male relatives, irrespective of any choice on her part. If the woman should have sufficient spirit to rebel, she would be ostracized at once, and looked upon as a suspicious character.   This custom has been a sore stumbling-block to church-members, who have come under discipline again and again for marrying polygamists by whom they were inherited; and in other cases where they refused, they were subjected to real persecution.

" The new law provides that in such cases women shall be left free to make their own election, whether to remain in the family of the deceased husband, seek some other agreeable alliance, or remain even as they are.   Of course, if one leaves the family, the dowry paid will have to be returned, or a portion of it, according to the length of her service with her former owners.   Narrow as this liberty may seem, it means much in comparison with former bondage, and will, we hope, open the way for perfect freedom.   *Our present king is a Christian,* a member of our church, and so far as his light goes he will be in favor of reform."— *Woman's Work for Woman,* January, 1897, pp. 8, 9.

[3] *The Illustrated Missionary News,* November, 1897, p. 186.

Party of C. M. S. Missionaries about to leave England for Uganda, in 1895.
(The first lady missionaries to enter that field.)

MISSIONARIES FOR UGANDA.

(C. M. S.)

In the Islands of the Pacific we have the same charming and inspiring story of rescued womanhood introduced into a happier and nobler life, and given a more worthy place of use- A happier and nobler fulness in society. The extreme and brutal de- life for rescued woman- basement which was once the lot of woman among hood in the islands of those savage islanders makes the change seem the sea. to come slowly, but it becomes all the more conspicuous on that account. In order to be appreciated, careful note must be made of traditional conditions of savagery and humiliation. Even quite recently Dr. Montgomery, the Bishop of Tasmania, in writing of a visit in 1892 to the Santa Cruz group, speaks of a sad fact which he observed in those islands, namely, their ill treatment of the women. "Nowhere else in Melanesia," he writes, "did I notice the degradation of the women as in this spot. They were never seen with the men, but kept to themselves entirely, and if any of them passed a man they were compelled to turn their backs or throw a covering over their faces. Here also the women did all the hard work in the yam-gardens, and carried the loads, while the men attended to the weaving at the looms. The women looked broken down and degraded, while the men were noted for their magnificent bearing and fine physique." He testifies, however, to the influence of mission schools in securing a different treatment of the women, and speaks especially of the example of Christians in showing them consideration and kindness.[1]   "Nothing is so revolutionary as Christianity," writes the Rev. W. W. Gill. "Women, utterly downtrodden in heathenism, are to-day quite able to hold their own in Christian Polynesia, and doubtless the same change will take place in New Guinea as the Gospel wins its way."[2]

In those islands where the London Missionary Society, the English and Australian Wesleyans, and the American Board have established their missions, the progress in female education is a cheering aspect of the results observed. Such institutions as the Girls' Central School (L. M. S.) at Papauta, Upolu, the Girls' Boarding School (A. B. C. F. M.) at Kusaie, in the Caroline Islands, and the facilities for female education in the Hawaiian group, all indicate that this department of mission work has not been neglected. Special attention in the case of Hawaii should be directed to the faithful labors of missionaries like Miss Maria C. Ogden (1827-74), of whom it is recorded that a thousand native girls and young women had come under her personal influence. Did she dream then that she was training the mothers of future citizens of

[1] Montgomery, "The Light of Melanesia," pp. 127, 128.
[2] Gill, "From Darkness to Light in Polynesia," p. 382.

the United States, and would eventually bequeath an endowment of Christian heredity as a free gift to her native land ? In an article by the Rev. A. S. Twombly, D.D., on native Christian women in the Hawaiian Islands, a striking tribute to the early power of missions is given, and even since the days of heathen reaction the permanent fruits of Christianity are clearly manifest.[1] From the New Hebrides a missionary correspondent writes: "The women are now better treated, and, war having ceased with the presence of the Gospel, the men are engaged in agriculture, fishing, and peaceful occupations, so that the women have less hard manual labor. Polygamy and immorality are difficult to eradicate, but the former is banished among Christians, while immorality is greatly lessened."[2]

In the West Indies missionary effort has brought about hopeful reformation in the status of woman. Training-schools have been founded by the Moravians and the American Friends, while the Christian churches established there, themselves the fruits of colonial and foreign missions, and some of them with large constituencies, are giving careful attention to the educational department of their home missionary efforts. Village schools for girls are conducted in many places under the direction of both home and foreign mission agencies.[3] In the sphere of social morals the one fact that legal marriage was virtually unknown among the Negroes of Jamaica when missions entered the island, and that now forty per cent. of the births among them are legitimate, is itself clear evidence that Christian instruction is checking the evils of immorality. In Mexico and Central and South America the introduction of educational facilities for girls is largely due to Protes-

Efforts for female education in the West Indies, Mexico, and South America.

[1] "New schools for girls are springing up, notably the large boarding-school established last year by the Bishop fund. If the race, as such, is doomed to extinction within the next fifty years, as some affirm, if the half-whites are to take the places of the natives, and if it be true that there has been a downward tendency during the last generation in morality and religion, all friends of missions may well congratulate themselves that Christianity has not been a failure, so far as it has been allowed to assert itself against evil foreign influences in the absence of missionary supervision. It still remains a potent power for good, holding back the native woman from superstition and heathen practices, and setting a standard for conscience. Many a Christian Hawaiian woman would stand foremost among American church-members for consistency of conduct and firmness in resisting peculiar tendencies and temptations. Some remarkable examples of true and saintly lives have come to my knowledge."—*Life and Light for Woman,* June, 1895, p. 260.

[2] Rev. William Gunn, M.D. (F. C. S.), Futuna, New Hebrides.

[3] Caldecott, "The Church of the West Indies" (an excellent manual, written in a fine spirit of catholicity).

tant missions.[1] This is especially true among the lower races. In many States of South America and in Mexico fine institutions have been established. If the power which Protestant missions have had in stimulating the whole system of government education in Mexico were fully known, much honor would be accorded to them as a leading influence in favor of female education.

2. RESTRAINING POLYGAMY AND CONCUBINAGE.—The insistence of missions upon the monogamous precepts of the New Testament is a service in the interest of domestic happiness and harmony which is of priceless import to non- Grappling with darling Christian society. It has been the policy of the sins of the Orient. great Oriental religions either boldly to sanction or quietly to condone polygamy, concubinage, and divorce at will. These are darling sins of the Eastern world, and in the social code of savages they are commonplace incidents. Christianity teaches another law, and teaches it without any qualifications. "And they twain shall be one flesh" expresses our Lord's view upon the subject.

While this is true, yet it must be admitted that the inquiry as to the proper attitude of Christian missions towards polygamy is not free from embarrassments. The problem is one with which missionaries have struggled, and upon which they show a divided front; although none of them would be willing to tolerate polygamy as a Christian institution, or to allow professing Christians to marry more than one wife. There is also unanimity among them in the opinion that no polygamist should ever be allowed to *take office* of any grade in the Christian Church, that no further marriage should be contracted by a polygamist who has been once baptized, and that in the case of the death of one of his wives he should not be at liberty to marry another in her place. The parting of the ways among them begins with the question of the admission of polygamous converts to the Church. Some would admit to the sacraments of baptism and the Lord's Supper; others only to baptism; while there are still others who would deny them either ordinance,

[1] " The women in a certain sense are not degraded, and yet in another they are, as they have not their rightful place. Until the entrance of the missionaries into the country, it had not been considered necessary or desirable to educate the daughters. Consequently there are numbers of middle-aged women of ample means and good social standing who can scarcely read or write. Now it is regarded as quite important to give the daughters the same advantages that the sons enjoy."—Miss Charlotte Kemper (P. B. F. M. S.), Lavras, Brazil.

and place the applicant in the attitude of a perpetual catechumen—that is, one accepted simply for religious instruction. In certain missions the term "catechumen" includes also those who are teachers. Again, among those who would admit the polygamist to the Church there is a further division of opinion. Some would require the putting away of all but the wife first married ; others would allow a choice of the one to be retained. In either case it is taken for granted that the support and guardianship of the husband will be extended to the wives thus put away and to their children. There are still those who would require the putting away of all but one wife only so far as full marital rights are concerned, while insisting upon the protection, support, and kind treatment of the others whose relationship is thus modified. The whole problem has been much discussed in missionary literature, and has been recently quite prominently before the Church.[1]

While it is recognized that there are sometimes grave and seemingly cruel results involved in the exaction of a monogamous family life as an imperative demand of the Church of Christ, yet

Can Christian missions compromise with polygamy? it seems to the author to be the burden of Scripture, and the only sound policy in missions, never to put in jeopardy the honor of the Christian Church, or the dignity and purity of the marriage law of the New Testament, for the sake of receiving polygamous families to the communion and fellowship of the visible Church. It is not enough to prohibit a polygamist from holding office; he should not be formally admitted to membership. The perplexities of an English bishop concerning this difficult problem are discoverable in the writings of the late Bishop Maples, a pioneer missionary in Central Africa. His wise and firm adherence to the rule of not baptizing polygamists is worthy of

[1] Cf. Cust, " Notes on Missionary Subjects," Part II., essay on " Polygamy in Christian Churches "; also substantially the same article in his volume entitled " The Gospel Message," pp. 263–291. (A bibliography of literature on the subject accompanies these articles.) Cf. also *The Missionary Review of the World*, February, March, April, and May, 1897, articles by the Rev. D. L. Gifford, on " Polygamous Applicants : What Missionaries Think Should Be Done with Them "; Laurie, " Missions and Science " (The Ely Volume), p. 482; " Report of the Mission Conference, London, 1888," vol. ii., pp. 51–81 ; " Report of the Missionary Conference of the Anglican Communion, 1894 " (George A. Spottiswoode, Editor), pp. 281–303; *The Presbyterian and Reformed Review*, April, 1896, article by the Rev. S. H. Kellogg, D.D., on " The Baptism of Polygamists in Non-Christian Lands "; *The Presbyterian Messenger*, June 20, 1895, article by Professor B. B. Warfield, on the exegetical interpretation of I Tim. iii. 2, 12, under the title " The Husband of One Wife "; *The Monthly Messenger of the Presbyterian Church of England*, October, 1897, p. 270.

Girls at work, St. Matthew's Industrial School, Keiskamma Hoek, S. Africa.　　Boarding Pupils, St. Matthew's School.

THE TRAINING OF WOMANHOOD IN AFRICA.

(S. P. G.)

note.[1] It appears to a plain student of the Bible almost beyond dispute that the Church of Christ cannot recognize a man while still a polygamist as a member of Christ's body.[2] Such a step would create a perilous state of uncertainty as to the inviolability of the moral precepts of Christianity, and open the door to a plausible advocacy of the suspension of Christian standards wherever expediency seemed to justify it.

The supposed authorization for the admission of polygamists to the Church is based upon an inference drawn from the instruction of Paul to Timothy (1 Tim. iii. 2, 12) that "a bishop then must be blameless, the husband of one wife." This is interpreted as implying beyond reasonable doubt that there were men of good and regular standing in the Church of that day who possessed more than one wife. Can this exegesis, built upon inference or implication, be sustained in this case? Surely not, if it is opposed to the plain teachings of Scripture elsewhere, and still less is it allowable if another explanation of the intent of the command is possible which would be in harmony with Scripture and the historic environment of the passage. This harmony with the biblical context and the contemporary facts is maintained if we understand the directions of Paul as meaning simply that a bishop must have a clean record in regard to the temporary alliances so common in that age. He must not have married several women in succession, divorcing them one after another, as was the custom with many. He must be known as "the husband of one wife," to whom he has been faithful, and with whom his relations are holy and honorable. No man, even though he was at the time a convert in the Church and was virtuous and true in his conduct, was to be a bishop if he had a trail of divorces in his previous history and was surrounded by women who were once his wives. In the light of this interpretation the propriety of the requirement becomes at once manifest as a preventive of scandal, and as necessary to the "blameless" moral standing of one who bears office in the Christian Church. It is as applicable to church life to-day as it was in Paul's time. We are sure that this problem in our mission fields, if

---

[1] "Life of Bishop Maples," pp. 71, 75, 265, 303. Cf. also Bryce, "Impressions of South Africa," p. 389.

[2] This rule need not be applied necessarily to the wife of a polygamist, since she is not always in that category, and should not be held responsible for the sins of her husband. The late Bishop Crowther wrote: "We treat a woman who is a wife of a polygamist as innocent, as she has no wish that her husband should have more wives than one, and it is a subject over which she has no control. She is treated in the Church, therefore, as a wife having only one husband. We do not propose a separation if she determines to be faithful to her unbelieving husband."

dealt with in a wise, cautious, and sympathetic spirit, can be so solved as to minimize the hardship, and yet preserve the principle at stake.

The author's experience as a missionary has taught him to appreciate the difficulties of this class of problems, and to sympathize with the desire to spare a new convert the stress and strain of all needless suffering. It has also made it plain to him that it is possible to allow an undue or too decisive weight to the fact that personal sacrifice and trial to the convert are often implied in the upholding of Christian ideals. If in some instances hardships which missionaries might well shrink from exacting are involved in maintaining biblical standards intact, on the other hand it should not be forgotten that the good name of the Church must be preserved and right principles maintained, or great and manifold evils will inevitably follow. Christian missions have not only to sustain the law of Christ in this matter, but they must act in view of the indubitable fact that monogamy is an essential condition of well-ordered society. As Bishop Westcott has remarked: " Marriage is the divine pattern and crown of human communities, the original sacrament of completed manhood." It is one of the primal institutions of human history, established, as we believe, with its monogamous limitation, by the Creator Himself. In the words of Dr. Cust, it is "at once the gratification of a legitimate and holy wish, the machinery of a holy life, and the divinely ordained method of perpetuating a holy people." Polygamy is utterly and hopelessly at variance with these ideas. Upon this aspect of the subject, however, there surely can be no difference of opinion among Christian missionaries.

What seems to be the true attitude of missions towards this question may be described as a combination of official rigor with informal personal kindliness and leniency towards those who are *The true modus vivendi between the Church and polygamous converts.* involved in the entanglements of polygamy. The Christian Church should withhold official recognition of a polygamist as an accepted member of its communion. It should not even baptize him. If, however, he is inclined to religious fellowship with God's people, he should be treated with social respect and kindly sympathy, and admitted to the privileges of instruction and worship. While the door into regular membership ought not to be opened, the hand and heart of the Church should reach to the outer court of social and religious friendliness, and there minister in the spirit of Christ to all such. The problem is one which man cannot eliminate. God only can solve it in His providence and His grace. The Church in her sphere and the polygamist in his must wait with patience for a solution such as sovereign wisdom and power alone can secure. In cases where a polygamist voluntarily has put away all but one wife, and is living in accordance with Christian law, there seems to be no clear reason why baptism and communion should be denied him, if he is otherwise worthy of admission to the Church.

This statement, however, may be qualified in several particulars. The separation should not be compulsory, in defiance of the legitimate rights and wishes of his wives, ignoring obligations he has assumed, and depriving his wives and children of their legal status. In organized society, such as we find in India, where the British Government recognizes the legality of more than one wife, this rule is applicable, far more so than among less civilized tribes, where marriage customs are governed by tradition and usage rather than by legal regulations. If the separation can be accomplished only as an arbitrary and coercive act, then the parties should bide their time outside the visible Church. Once more, this severance should not imply a refusal to extend support, protection, and kindly treatment to wives and children from whom the candidate has separated. If these conditions are complied with, no hardship or privation of an unchristian kind is involved in the transaction. Honorable obligations are not repudiated, and no wrong is done in the name of religion. A polygamist would expect to support his wives if he continued to live in heathenism, and it is no harsh requirement for him to do it as a matter of justice and honor if he embraces Christianity. As regards the choice of one wife with whom he shall maintain lawful relations, it is not absolutely essential that it should be in all cases the first one to whom he was married. This rule may be elastic, and may vary in different circumstances and countries. The first marriage may have been a forced one at a premature age, and so be destitute of the real essence of Christian marriage, which involves a free, intelligent, and responsible choice.

It is evident then, that a man who would become a Christian and enter the Church is bound by the law of the Bible and by the unvarying custom of Christian living to break with polygamy. He must disentangle himself, and begin *A break with polygamy* life over again on a new basis, in the light of Bible *imperative.* teachings, and in accord with Scripture standards. The introduction of polygamous households into the Church would require startling and dangerous concessions, and establish a demoralizing precedent. It is of the first importance that evangelical churches in mission lands should begin rightly in this matter; otherwise they will become involved in a painful and needless struggle with subtle questions of casuistry which they will be unable to solve. That they are incapable of dealing with it aright, in the light of their own wisdom and in the atmosphere of their traditional environment, is only too evident. The formation of a polygamous party in mission churches would involve the grave possibility, if not probability, of eventually so changing the standards of Christian living that the Church itself would become a polygamous institution.[1] An illustration of this tendency is reported from West Africa.[2] Firm and true counsel in their formative period is what the churches need. A temporizing and non-committal evasion of the issue would end in a distinct loss of moral prestige and spiritual influence. The words of Professor Warneck upon this subject are to be commended : " Although theoretically something may be said for a degree of tolerance of polygamy in a period of transition, on the ground of apostolic example, yet practically this forbearance has been of no use, but at the commencement of missions the axe was laid at the root of polygamy as a practice absolutely irreconcilable with the Gospel. That has naturally had many harsh and disadvantageous consequences, especially as the acceptance of Christianity by a chieftain has been now and again prevented ; but it has had the great advantage that the path has been cleared, and the heathen regard the establishment of monogamy as the manifest and necessary consequence of the acceptance of Christianity." [3]

In India, China, Japan, Africa, and all Moslem countries, this question confronts Christian missions on the threshold. The law of one wife, with the further demand of absolute fidelity to marriage vows, is a hard saying to the disciples of heathen culture. It either repels them by its rigorous standards, or it forces them into a dilemma which is especially difficult in the moral and social atmosphere of non-Christian traditions. Sometimes all that missions can accomplish for

[1] " If polygamists are admitted into the Church, the system will not soon be abolished ; the act will give the Mohammedans reason to triumph, and declare that their religion is better than Christianity, which would seem to be changeable in its teachings and doctrine. The heathen will affirm that the life of polygamy as practised by their forefathers was suitable to them, and needs no change. The heathen young men would take advantage of this, and wait till they had married many wives, and then apply to be received into the Church ; if their fathers could be received as such, why should not they? The infidels, who are numerous about this coast, and live ungodly lives, would say to the heathen population, Did not we tell you that the new religion is not consistent in its teachings? Hence we would not practise it. You see we are right in our belief and practice after all."—Extract from the late Bishop Crowther's " Papers on African Missions."

[2] Cust, " Notes on Missionary Subjects," essay on " Polygamy in Christian Churches," p. 11.

[3] Warneck, " Missions and Culture," p. 180.

a generation or more is to let the light of biblical teaching and influence shine, and introduce the example of monogamous family life. There is a quiet power in this, and when communities of Christian families begin to appear, intelligent natives commence to wrestle with a new sociological problem, often with a penetration and insight which are far in advance of their readiness to conform in practice to what in theory is a matter of clear conviction.

Let us plunge at once into the most hopeless environment of unrestrained license, and see if Christian missions have yet modified to any extent the native customs of African society.

"When I first visited Uganda," says the Rev. R. P. Ashe, "it was a shame to a man not to have a great following, and a large number of women who were cultivators of the soil, and therefore a sign of wealth; now in Uganda it is a shame for a man to have more than one wife."[1] The story of how good Bishop Mackenzie founded a Christian community in Central Africa upon the hitherto unheard-of basis of monogamy is told by the Rev. Henry Rowley, in his volume on Central Africa.[2] Dr. W. A. Elmslie, in a letter from British Central Africa, reports the breaking up of polygamous connections among those of the Angoni who have come under mission instruction. The movement called forth much persecution, but the monogamous principle has triumphed, the natives themselves adopting it.[3] The Rev. A. G. MacAlpine, of Bandawè, in the Livingstonia Mission, writes of the renunciation of polygamy and slavery by the Christian community of that place, with the happy result that the practice was unanimously condemned and repudiated by the native church itself.[4] The Rev. F. Coillard, of the French Evangel-

African communities are taught a new lesson in social morals.

---

[1] *The Church Missionary Intelligencer*, April, 1894, p. 282.

[2] Rowley, "Twenty Years in Central Africa," pp. 66–68.

[3] *The Free Church of Scotland Monthly*, December, 1896, p. 294.

[4] Mr. MacAlpine's statement is as follows: "On Thursday, April 2, 1896, we had a meeting for the discussion of the relation of the Church to three questions which come up again and again in our work—Polygamy, Beer, and Slavery. . . . We sat for five hours, and adjourned, to meet again in the afternoon. All the members present wrote their answers to the following questions : (1) Do you believe these practices to be right or wrong? (2) What is your action in the matter? and (3) What about candidates for church-membership? The third question, on the subject of slavery, was divided into two parts—Have you any slaves? and, What do you intend doing with them? On these points the Church maintained the Christian attitude, and declared emphatically its opposition to all three; that, for itself, it had abandoned them utterly, and that none should be admitted to church-membership whose practice was not in keeping with the Church's declaration on these subjects."
—Quoted in *The Christian Express*, December, 1896, p. 183.

ical Mission on the Upper Zambesi, reports that the native conscience has awakened in the matter of polygamy. Khama, the Christian king, has never consented to become the possessor of more than one wife, although his royal position and the invariable custom of his country would make him an unrestricted polygamist.[1] It is the testimony of the Hon. A. Wilmot that in Khama's territory Christianity has had the effect of putting an end to polygamy.[2] Among the Bechuanas it has been the curse of their social system. A recent communication from the Rev. Alfred S. Sharp, of Mafeking, says that "the system is doomed. It is peculiarly interesting to observe how the spread of Christianity offers an insurmountable barrier to its progress, and threatens its very existence. . . . Moreover, there is a growing distrust of the system; the light of the Gospel has shown that it is incompatible with the higher life after which the people are struggling, and, indeed, this very struggle is in itself a war against the practice, and as it increases polygamy must vanish."[3] In Pondoland the prime minister of one of the prominent chiefs proved his faith by his works when he renounced heathenism, since he paid off his debts, made restitution for all money purloined, and gave up his seven wives, retaining only the one to whom he was first married.[4]

We can but feebly comprehend the hard and exhausting contest of pioneer missionaries in the dark recesses of African savagery with such a dominant social evil as unrestricted polygamy.[5] We find in the papers of the late Bishop Crowther, kindly furnished to the author by his son,

---

[1] Hepburn, "Twenty Years in Khama's Country," p. 140.
[2] Wilmot, "The Expansion of South Africa," Introductory Note, p. xxiv.
[3] *Work and Workers in the Mission Field*, February, 1893, p. 62.
[4] *Ibid.*, October, 1894, p. 409.
[5] The late Dr. Good writes of the Bule, an interior tribe of the Gaboon Mission, on the West Coast: "Polygamy is terribly prevalent, and in all this region it is the substitute for slavery. The sole idea in marriage is ownership, and the condition of woman is that of a slave. It is the ambition of every Bule man to marry at least twenty or thirty women; the number of his wives determines his rank. Some chiefs have sixty or eighty. If a man has many wives he need not work, for they will keep his stomach full, and he can sit in the village palaver-house and smoke in blissful idleness all his days. This is the Bule's idea of perfect happiness."—*Woman's Work for Woman*, June, 1893, p. 162.

Another missionary from the Congo Valley writes: "Polygamy makes it so easy for our young people to go wrong. A chief will have many wives whom he will hire out. In the eyes of the natives there is no sin in thus taking a wife, if the man pays; *the sin is in not paying.* We are having a hard fight against these customs. The marriage question is daily being brought up to us."—*The Baptist Missionary Magazine*, July, 1894, p. 357.

Archdeacon Crowther, of the Church Missionary Society Mission in the Niger Delta, some information concerning the early mission policy favored by the bishop. "We do not tolerate polygamy in this our mission," he writes, "whether the person be influential or not, or whether he be rich or poor. With the influential and rich person the renouncing of wives and retaining only one is a test of his sincerity and a mark of that self-denial for Christ's sake which is required of those who are to be new creatures. Merely the forsaking of the worship of idols can hardly be called the test of fleshly lusts and appetites." [1] In the Island of Madagascar "polygamy has nearly disappeared, and divorce can only be obtained after a proper trial before the judges." [2] This statement is confirmed by the Rev. James Sibree (L. M. S.), who writes from Antananarivo: "Divorce and polygamy are becoming more and more rare."

[1] Other testimonies from the West Coast Missions are at hand.

"The greatest social change which has been effected here is the gradual elevation of the people from a state of lowest barbarism to what might be called Christian family life. The majority of our converts have homes of their own, and although the ideal of domestic life perhaps has not been fully realised, there is a change in this respect that no one can fail to see."—Rev. Robert M. Beedie (U. P. C. S. M.), Duke Town, Old Calabar, West Africa.

"The polygamy of the Ondos is of the lowest character. It is associated with polyandry, and is promoted by the custom of parents in forming marriage contracts for their daughters from their infancy, and there are instances in which they are made before their birth, in case the child should be a female. As soon as the contract is made, the parents begin to receive dowry periodically, in the shape of services, money, or food, from the betrothed husband, until the girl becomes marriageable. It is not easy to break through such engagements afterwards. I need not say that the wife is regarded at law as the husband's property. The result is that the older, well-to-do, and great men monopolize all the available women in the country; their younger male relatives are then permitted to have them as concubines. The children born to the concubines during the husband's lifetime are legally his, the natural father regarding them as brothers or sisters, and treating them as such. I need not state that the degradation of women, the low state of morals, and the insecurity of inheritance are the results of this wretched system. The eyes of the people are being opened to the harm done to society by it, but twenty years is too short a time to produce a change, which must come in proportion as Christian families are formed."—The Rt. Rev. Charles Phillips, D.D. (C. M. S.), Lagos, West Africa.

[2] Cousins, "Madagascar of To-day," pp. 136, 137.

"Polygamy was the rule of life among the Malagasy, and created envy, jealousy, and much domestic trouble and family misery. It is now the exception, as there is a strong popular feeling against it, and it is forbidden by law, under a penalty of what would be equal in America to the sum of five hundred dollars."—Rev. J. Pearse (L. M. S.), Fianarantsoa, Madagascar.

A look into the mission records of the South Seas reveals the same strong trend towards the suppression of the evil under consideration.

Those island barbarians, who were notorious polyg-
A social revolution in amists, have experienced a social revolution
the South Seas. which only the moral forces of Christianity could produce. The Rev. J. E. Newell (L. M. S.), of the Malua Institution, Samoa, after enumerating the heathen vices that once prevailed, asks: "What has Christianity done with this condition of life and thought? It at once abolished polygamy and concubinage, and set its ban on all the indecent associations of the event of marriage. It is remarkable how much has been accomplished in this direction by Christian teaching and example, not only in Samoa, but in groups like the Society Islands, where the imaginations of the heart were utterly corrupt and vile." In describing the present status in the Island of Futuna, of the New Hebrides group, the Rev. Dr. William Gunn reports that "Christian marriage is now recognized as the law of the island."[1] In an account of the introduction of Christianity into Mangaia, in the Hervey group, a description is given of how the chiefs, early in the Christian history of the island, "heartily acquiesced in the proposition to abolish polygamy. The powerful chief Parima, who had six wives, set the example by putting away five." The narrator, the Rev. W. W. Gill, adds: "By divorce these women were not condemned to want, as to each was given a plot of land with fruit-bearing trees on it, sufficient for her own subsistence and that of her children."[2]

Bishop Montgomery, in a sketch of Christian progress in Florida, one of the Solomon Islands, quotes a paragraph from one of the missionaries, telling of the way in which Bishop Selwyn in his day dealt with the question of polygamy, which is interesting not only because it shows the tendency of mission influence, but also states a fact which can be shown to be true, at least in some sections of the world, namely, that the abolition of polygamy does not necessarily involve physical cruelty and hardship.[3] Dr. Paton makes similar statements concerning the

[1] *The Free Church of Scotland Monthly*, August, 1897, p. 186.

[2] Gill, "From Darkness to Light in Polynesia," p. 335. See also Horne, "The Story of the London Missionary Society," p. 215.

[3] "Bishop Selwyn makes it a *sine qua non* that a polygamist shall put away all but one wife before he receives baptism. That this is the right course in Melanesia I cannot for a moment doubt, though the case of the woman put away is in some respects a hard one. . . . But she need not be homeless or friendless, or compelled to lead such a life as many of those who take the opposite view of this question assume to be inevitable. There are respectable people who will give her a home for the sake of her work, and with such she can live. Many of these women become

comparative freedom from actual misery and want, which are supposed to be usually associated with the extinction of polygamy in heathen countries. He writes that in the New Hebrides "the heathen practices were apparently more destructive to women than to men, so that in one island, with a population of only two hundred, I found that there were thirty adult men over and above the number of women. As a rule, for the men that have two or more wives the same number of men have no wives, and can get none, and polygamy is therefore the prolific cause of hatreds and murders innumerable." The result has been that wives released from polygamous ties have easily found a better marriage awaiting them, in accordance with the Christian rule. "We had one chief," reports Dr. Paton, "who gave up eleven wives on being baptized. They were, without a single exception, happily settled in other homes."[1] In another connection Mrs. Paton writes: "Polygamy on Aniwa is now a thing of the past."[2] The story of the terrible immorality in the Hawaiian Islands in the days of idolatry and unrestrained heathenism has often been told. The influence of Christianity was an immense moral gain, although it has been qualified to a sad extent by the entrance of a godless element through which the vices rather than the benefits of civilization have been introduced.[3]

Christians, and in the spiritual consolation and freedom from superstitious fear which they then enjoy find greater happiness than they ever had as heathen; and though in their new life there may be somewhat of the hardness which Christianity accepts, yet they would not return to the old conditions, so contrary to the faith in which they now find peace. . . . There remains the significant fact that in these particular islands a strong feeling exists in the minds of the native converts themselves against allowing a polygamist to receive baptism; and I feel sure that if an exception were once made, no matter how hard the case might appear at the time, it would set up a precedent most difficult to deal with in the time to come."—Montgomery, "The Light of Melanesia," p. 219.

[1] "Autobiography of John G. Paton," Part II., p. 267.

In deprecating the criticisms of some who denounce the abolition of polygamy as an unjust and arbitrary proceeding, Dr. Paton writes: "Those will be the most ready to condemn us who have never been on the spot, and who cannot see all the facts as they lie under the eyes of the missionary. How could we ever have led natives to see the difference between admitting a man to the Church who had two wives, and not permitting a member of the Church to take two wives after his admission? Their moral sense is blunted enough without our knocking their heads against a conundrum in ethics! In our church-membership we have to draw the line as sharply as God's law will allow betwixt what is heathen and what is Christian, instead of minimising the difference."—*Ibid.*, pp. 266, 267.

[2] Paton, "Letters and Sketches from the New Hebrides," p. 334.

[3] Alexander, "The Islands of the Pacific," pp. 172–177. Cf. for statements concerning other sections of the Pacific Islands, Cousins, "The Story of the South Seas," p. 154.

Among the Indian races of North and South America polygamy prevailed extensively,[1] with no attempt to question its desirability, and

Higher domestic life among the Indians of America.

still less to challenge its propriety, until Christian missions entered and brought a lesson of higher and happier living.   An illustration of this is given by the Venerable Archdeacon Phair, in his description of a visit recently made by him to Scanterbury station, some forty miles to the northeast of Winnipeg, in the Diocese of Rupert's Land, Canada.   He contrasts the present state of the Indians with his recollection of their horrid barbarism thirty years ago, when he first went among them.   "If the efforts of the Society," he writes, "had accomplished no more in this country than simply transforming this wilderness of heathenism into the happy, prosperous Christian community that it is now, I am convinced the Society would be more than amply repaid.   There is not a conjurer, not a polygamist, not a medicine-man in the whole place."[2]

If we touch the old civilizations of the Orient, we find that either polygamy is firmly established, as in China and, under certain conditions, in India, or that concubinage provides an ample com-

The Korean version of the marital code.

pensation for the legal observance of monogamy, as in Japan and Korea.   The Korean, as Mrs. Bishop states, "is legally a strict monogamist," yet the rather dubious credit to which the Korean husband is entitled on this account is clearly indicated by what the same author says a little further on, where she quotes the remark of a Korean gentleman in summarizing

---

[1] " There is no marriage ceremony among the Navajoes, save bargain and sale. A young man wishing a woman for a wife ascertains who is her father, goes and states the cause of his visit, and offers from one to fifteen horses for the daughter. The consent of the father is absolute, and the one so purchased assents, or is taken away by force.   All the marriageable women in a family can be taken by the same individual ; that is, he can purchase wives so long as his property holds out.   Marital separations are by mutual consent, when both are at liberty to go in search of other companions.   A man or a woman from one village can marry a man or a woman from another.   The men have from one to six wives, sometimes more."—Rev. Daniel Dorchester, D.D., in *The Gospel in all Lands*, July, 1894, p. 302.

" Polygamy exists, but it is limited by the necessity of having to pay a certain amount of property to the father-in-law by way of purchase.   The first wife is always the chief one, but each has to present to her husband a dish of her own cooking every day, besides a poncho [an outer garment] of her own making every year, so that an Indian's house contains as many fireplaces and native looms as he has wives."— "The Araucanian Indians: Their Country, Habits, and Customs," in *The South American Missionary Magazine*, September, 1894, p. 136.

[2] *The Church Missionary Gleaner*, May, 1894, p. 67.

the status of the marriage relationship: "We marry our wives," he quietly informed Mrs. Bishop, "but we love our concubines."[1] Mrs. Underwood refers to the same fact when speaking of the many serious problems of missions in Korea. She remarks: "Another monster difficulty is the plural-wife question. It is indeed a 'rock of offence.' Men are naturally unwilling to give up their families, women to give up their breadwinners and protectors, especially as it is almost invariably the legal first wife who is unloved and neglected, and the concubine who is the companion and choice of the husband's mind and heart. In our sympathy for individual cases it is very hard to look beyond the present. The easy and pleasant thing to do is our temptation, and yet thinking of the future of the Church and the future of poor women even outside the Church it seems to some of us that our only clear, though hard, duty is to take a firm stand against polygamy. At present, however, our mission is almost evenly divided on this question."[2]

The Japanese custom of regarding concubines as entitled to a place in the family is described by Miss Bacon.[3] Among mission converts in both Korea and Japan the biblical rule of strict monogamy is observed. The signs of a wholesale break with the old ways are more and more manifest in Japan,[4] and the progress of Christianity will insure this. A few generations of Japanese Christian example and influence will relegate concubinage to its proper place as one of the scandals of a past social *régime*. The honor placed upon the marriage ceremony by Christians, who to an increasing extent are regarding it as a religious service, adds to the sacredness of the marital bond.

An impending break with the old ways in Japan.

---

1 Bishop, "Korea and Her Neighbors," p. 343.

2 *Woman's Work in the Far East*, November, 1896, p. 92.

3 Bacon, "Japanese Girls and Women," pp. 111–114.

4 "But what has Christianity done in this respect? It is safe to say that there are in practice not one tenth the number of violations of moral rectitude in this direction in Japan to-day as compared with thirty years ago. To have a *mekaki* [concubine] now is a disgrace to a man. The better class of the people are pronounced in their opinions against this sin. Native ministers have preached against it, statesmen have denounced it, missionaries have shown its sinfulness, the Bible has enforced the principles of the Sermon on the Mount, until there is scarce a hamlet throughout the length and breadth of the land where the Christian idea of one woman for one man has not been heard. Thus homes are brighter, women are honored, motherhood is made more sacred, and society is blessed and far more peaceful. The determination of the leading men of the nation to keep step with the progress of the times will furnish the means by which to uproot both concubinage, which has well-nigh disappeared, and the Yoshiwara."—Rev. David S. Spencer (M. E. M. S.), Nagoya, Japan.

Japanese statesmen and educated men are turning their attention to the subject, and a reform of the marriage laws in accordance with the code of Christian civilization cannot be far distant. In *The International Journal of Ethics* for January, 1896, Mr. Yokoi credits missionary influence in Japan with "impressing on the mind of the Japanese people a very important ethical truth—the principle of monogamy and personal purity—purity as obligatory upon men and women."[1]

In China polygamy is the source of many social evils, and it is now acknowledged by enlightened Chinese themselves that if true civilization is to enter, the Christian law of monogamy must be observed. Dr. Faber, in writing of "China in the Light of History," deprecates the mischief caused by the example of the Emperor. He attributes to polygamy a large influence in producing and perpetuating the corruption of the mandarins, since the expenses of polygamous households tempt the officials to practise their methods of extortion.[2] In the "Statement of the Nature, Work, and Aims of Protestant Missions in China," prepared for presentation to the Emperor, it is declared that "Christians marry but one wife," and a brief exposition of the distinctively biblical features of the marriage relation is given.[3] The example of the happy home life of converts is already a power in the land. That progress is necessarily slow can be readily explained, but as Christianity obtains sway over the conscience, and the ideals of a higher civilization win the respect of that conservative people, we shall find the Christian code more and more widely recognized and observed.

In India the question previously referred to, of the admission of polygamous converts to the Church, is one of peculiar difficulty, owing to the fact that British law in that country recognizes polygamy and gives a legal status to more than one wife. Missionaries have held very different views upon the subject. The Presbyterian Synod of India, in 1894, adopted a Memorial to the General Assembly in the United States (Northern Presbyterian), presenting a request that the ultimate decision in all such cases be left to the Synod, and that its missionaries be allowed to act independently in the matter, some

---

[1] *The International Journal of Ethics*, January, 1896, p. 200. Cf. also article by the Rev. J. H. De Forest, D.D., on "The Japan of 1896—Religiously," in *The Independent*, January 14, 1897.

[2] *The Chinese Recorder*, January, 1897, pp. 28, 29.

[3] *Ibid.*, February, 1896, p. 69.

test votes of that body having revealed the fact that a considerable majority would be in favor of the admission of polygamists to the Church. The General Assembly, after carefully considering the matter, expressed its inability, without violating the Constitution of the Church, to thus delegate its powers.[1] Several missionary bodies in India, as, for example, the North India Conference of the American Methodists, are opposed to such admission, and many distinguished individual missionaries are on record as of the opinion that the baptism of polygamous converts is open to serious objection.[2]

Despite the difficulties of refusing to accept a polygamist, the arguments against such acceptance seem to be conclusive. On the other hand, it is equally clear that no proper effort should be spared to mitigate the hardship and trial which are involved in severing such connections. Is a decisive verdict possible? It does not seem necessary to insist upon any radical change in the marital relationship, except in one essential particular, every other obligation receiving due consideration, and the legal position of the wife before the law of the land being in no way disturbed. If, however, such a specialized separation is impracticable or unacceptable, it seems far wiser to defer baptism indefinitely, knowing as we do that salvation is not dependent upon church ordinances, and that only the temporal and visible status is affected, the larger citizenship in the kingdom of heaven being a matter of personal faith in Christ and spiritual contact with Him. Just at the present time, when Indian social reformers themselves are denouncing polygamy and Kulinism, and passing strong resolutions of condemnation in public assemblies, it would be a strange and mystifying anomaly for the Church of Christ to make room for Indian polygamists.[3]

[1] "Minutes of the General Assembly of the Presbyterian Church in the United States of America, 1896," pp. 149, 150. No vote declarative of the judgment of the Assembly on the policy of admitting polygamists was taken.

[2] "Report of the Missionary Conference of the Anglican Communion, 1894," p. 294. The Lambeth Conference of 1888 also recorded a vote against the admission of polygamists. See also a "Reply to the Memorial of the Synod of India to the General Assembly," by the Rev. J. J. Lucas, of Saharanpur.

[3] Some aspects of polygamy in certain sections of India, Burma, and Assam are so offensive to human decency and so rankly odorous with animalism that it would be extremely compromising for the Christian Church to recognize the system as such even in cases where every objection is at a minimum.

"Polygamy and polyandry exist in some parts of Assam, although they are not formally recognized as among the legal customs of the country. Men have their acknowledged wives whom they partly support, but they have also concubines wherever they go. In one part of my district it is almost the rule that married

This discussion of the propriety of admitting polygamous converts to the Church should not be allowed to obscure the fact that missions in India have everywhere set themselves strongly in opposition to polygamy itself, and that it is altogether prohibited within the Christian communion. Among the converted Kols, where the Gossner Mission has recently celebrated its Jubilee, it has wholly ceased, whereas it was a national vice previous to the entrance of Christianity.[1] The Arcot Mission of the Reformed Church in America is on record as follows: "Polygamy has not existed, and will not be allowed to exist, in any of our churches."[2] So far as any formal sanction of the system is concerned, this is in fact the attitude of the entire Christian Church.

In all Moslem lands polygamy and concubinage, as a feature of slavery, are recognized, and have a religious authorization in the Islamic code. It is simply impossible for Christianity to countenance these practices, and for a Mohammedan polygamist to be admitted to Gospel ordinances would be an indelible offense against the dignity and honor of the Christian Church. So far as the author is aware, this is the unanimous opinion of missionaries laboring among Mohammedan populations. The gross views of Moslems upon this subject are utterly irreconcilable with Christian standards.[3] In Babism, a reaction from Persian Mohammedanism, one of the reforms proposed was that polygamy should be discountenanced. It is above

The Moslem code of polygamy is anti-christian.

women invite other men when their own husbands are away. And although the husband would be more or less angry with his wife if he found her quartering any other man, yet he would not consider either his wife or the man to have committed a sin unto death, as he is himself guilty of transgressing in similar fashion. In another part of this district, when a man marries the daughter he marries the mother also at the same time. That is always understood. Both are his wives in the same way."—Rev. Robert Evans (W. C. M. M. S.), Mawphlang, Shillong, Assam.

"*The Civil and Military Gazette*, October 3, 1890, has the following notice: 'A Kulin Brahman over eighty years of age, residing in the far North, lately cast his aged eyes on six sisters, whose ages ranged from *three to twenty-two years!* He made the sporting offer to marry the lot for Rs. 300. The father of the maidens accepted this proposal and paid down the money, but the bridegroom designate beat a hasty retreat with the coin. The father sued him for the money, and obtained a decree, but soon died, and the relatives came to terms with the aged lover, agreeing to pay him Rs. 600 on the fulfilment of the contract.' This case would have passed unnoticed as a matter not worth mentioning had it not entered the law-court. And how many cases there are like this we little know."—Rev. R. M. Paterson, B.D. (C. S. M.), Gujrat, Punjab, India.

1 *The Mission World*, February, 1896, p. 79.
2 Laurie, "Missions and Science" (The Ely Volume), p. 483.
3 Wilson, "Persian Life and Customs," pp. 262–267.

MAIN BUILDING OF WOMEN'S HOSPITAL

Hospital for Women and Children, Nellore, India.
(A. B. M. U.)

Woman's Hospital, Guntur, India.
(Luth. G. S.)

HOSPITALS FOR WOMEN IN INDIA.

all things important that the record of Christian missions wherever they come in contact with Mohammedans should be consistent and unequivocal in maintaining the law of Christ, as any compromise with Islam upon this matter would beyond all peradventure be dangerous and scandalous. Mission policy everywhere has been decisive and firm on this point, and the Christian estimate of marriage is slowly gaining not only respectful recognition, but even a measure of ascendancy, in Moslem circles.[1]

3. CHECKING ADULTERY AND DIVORCE.—Adultery on the part of woman is generally and indeed strenuously condemned in the higher circles of heathen society, and is frequently punished with frightful severity. There is a degree of laxity, however, in some quarters which makes it seem at times as if all standards of virtue and honor were in a state of collapse.[2] The characteristic leniency of pagan morals concerning the same sin on the part of the man is still

Echoes in present-day heathenism of the old pagan code concerning adultery and divorce.

---

[1] " Of course the first thing that meets one in the social realm as a result of missions in the East is the changed condition of women. This is patent to all, but I have recently had the matter more especially called to mind by reading anew Muir's Life of Mohammed, in connection with the Annals of At-Tabari, relating to the same period. Mohammed changed the comparatively free and honorable state of women among the Arabs to one of seclusion and humiliation, a course rendered necessary by his sanction in precept and practice of polygamy, and the almost unrestrained liberty of concubinage and divorce. The degradation of womanhood followed, and one can see plainly how the introduction of Gospel teaching has tended strongly to modify this state of things here in the East."—Rev. Professor Harvey Porter, Ph.D., Syrian Protestant College, Beirut, Syria.

" Polygamy is almost impossible where girls [Moslems] have been taught in our schools. An educated girl can usually control that. The intellectual culture of Moslem women will in time do away with the institution, by making its monstrosity apparent."—Rev. Professor George E. Post, M.D., Beirut, Syria.

[2] " Chinese wives can be sold or leased for a term of years. One of our early inquirers near Ningpo could not be received into church fellowship because while still a heathen he had leased his wife for a term of ten years. When he saw how wrong he had been in doing so, he endeavored to redeem her, but the party in possession refused to release her until the ten years should have expired. Before the time was up, the second husband died, and his family or clan, refusing to allow the woman to return to her original husband, leased her to a third party. Such abominable practices will surely die out as Christianity spreads, and our churches are already a distinct benefit to society in this respect, as none of them will tolerate such customs."
—S. P. Barchet, M.D. (A. B. M. U.), Kinhwa, China.

" As to the degradation of women, volumes might be written. Among officials,

found in the code of social manners throughout the Oriental world. Among savage tribes similar ideas prevail, but in the practice of lower races there is far less restraint than is found in the higher civilization of the Orient. Christianity, from its earliest entrance into heathen society, has contended for a nobler standard, and that conflict in mission fields is still at close quarters and with no attempt to compromise. In the beginning of Christian history some of the early Church Fathers fell into the error of condemning second marriages as not consistent with the inviolability of the one marriage tie.[1] A wiser view upon this matter eventually prevailed, with no relaxing, however, of the abhorrence and inflexible condemnation of the sin of adultery on the part of both the husband and wife. The peculiar sacredness which attaches to the conjugal union is an integral part of Christian teaching in every mission field, while sins against the Seventh Commandment are made a matter of discipline in all the churches, perhaps more frequently in African communities than in others.[2] In some instances legislation for the regulation of divorce has been promoted. The Rev. F. M. Price (A. B. C. F. M.), of the Micronesian Mission, writes of a visit to Butaritari, one of the Gilbert Islands, and thus refers to the king: "This king is really

who often have numbers of concubines, a very common and polite present from one to another is a favorite concubine! Among the common people, who are not able to keep concubines, a wife is often loaned to another man. Wives who cannot bear children are not averse to their husbands getting a secondary wife, or borrowing the wife of some one else. These things are known to be wrong, and are not actually practised under the open heaven, but they are matters of well-known fact."—Rev. J. C. Garritt (P. B. F. M. N.), Hangchow, China.

1 Schmidt, "The Social Results of Early Christianity," p. 198.

2 That the lives of converts in different mission fields are controlled to a remarkable extent by Christian principles of morality, and that church discipline is maintained when necessary, is apparent from the following representative testimonies:

"Husbands and wives are faithful to each other. Many of them train their children in the fear of the Lord, and these children go into the marriage state without bringing dishonor upon themselves, their parents, or the Church of Christ."—Rev. Robert Evans (W. C. M. M. S.), Mawphlang, Shillong, Assam.

"A check has been given to the loose, immoral life which polluted the whole community, and marriage unions according to divine law are being formed."—The late Rev. Hugh Goldie (U. P. C. S. M.), Creek Town, Old Calabar, Africa.

"In the train of the Gospel came also admission to the decencies and dignities of marriage. A low morale is still the sad social characteristic of Jamaica, but, whereas in the old slavery times the nuptial compact was almost unknown, there are now over three thousand marriages solemnized and registered yearly in the island."—Rev. James Ballantine (U. P. C. S. M.), Chapelton, Jamaica.

"Marriage has become the basis of the family, and that, too, through the influence of Christianity, or public opinion, among many who are not yet Christians."—Rev. J. Morton, D.D. (C. P. M.), Trinidad.

a remarkable man for a Gilbert Islander. He is a devoted and consistent Christian, and is doing what he can to give his people just and humane laws and to elevate them to a higher plane of life. . . . He is now framing a law against divorce. He has put away all his concubines and is living with one wife, and trying to encourage the establishment of Christian homes."[1] A similar influence is reported from Madagascar: "Divorce, for any and every reason, and often for no reason at all, used to be an every-day occurrence. Against such unrighteousness there is now strong popular feeling, and it has become much less common than in the past. To put away a wife is now unlawful in Madagascar, and a valid decree can only be obtained by appeal to the State."[2]

That this matter of divorce is one of great difficulty and embarrassment can hardly be questioned by one who is at all familiar with its prevalence even within the precincts of our best civilization. The scandals of divorce legislation and practice in our own country fully justify such an organization as "The National League for the Protection of the Family" (formerly known as "The National Divorce Reform League"), from whose reports facts which are calculated to startle and sober every Christian patriot may be gathered.[3] The pagan system of conjugal ethics has always stultified itself not only in its failure to insist upon a single code of morals for both parties, but in its provision for easy divorce at the will of the husband. The marriage tie is worthless if it can be annulled by the man whenever he is so inclined. Divorce becomes simply the routine form for making adultery respectable. The average Oriental of to-day regards, not unnaturally, the infidelity of his wife with horror and indignation, but, at the same time, he either insists that his own life is not to be scrutinized, or, as is the case in the majority of instances, he sins openly without shame or regret.[4] He grants to his wife no liberty of separation on this account, while he claims the absolute right on his own part to divorce at pleasure, with unrestricted freedom to contract new alliances.

[1] *The Missionary Herald*, November, 1894, p. 488.

[2] Rev. J. Pearse (L. M. S.), Fianarantsoa, Madagascar.

[3] The Report for 1895 shows that divorces in the United States have increased more than twice as fast as the population. In 1867 there were 9937, in 1886 there were 25,535, in 1894 there were over 40,000.

[4] In Persia an iniquitous system of temporary marriages is cloaked under legal forms. A missionary writes: "The system of contract marriages, through which women are passed along from one temporary husband to another, carries with it the degradation of all parties involved."—George W. Holmes, M.D. (P. B. F. M. N.), Hamadan, Persia.

These degrading lapses in theory and conduct are condemned by the Christian view of marriage, which prevails everywhere in mission churches and is insisted upon as an essential part of the social code of Christianity. Wherever biblical standards have been established, chastity is made an inflexible law of Christian living, conjugal infidelity is not tolerated within the Church of Christ, and the right of frivolous and unjust divorce is denied. The immediate effect of this is to elevate the status of woman, secure to her just rights, deliver her from iniquitous discriminations, release her from practical slavery, and prevent gross wrongs. Christian teachings alone are effective in liberating her from fetters which a proud and licentious paganism forged long centuries ago. It is noticeable that the new atmosphere introduced by missions is also lessening the actual practice of divorce where theoretically the right would be claimed.[1] The fact that marriage is in so many instances a matter of bargain and sale by parents or brothers, usually without any reference to the choice of the individuals, insures many disappointments, and is one of the secrets of loveless homes and wanton alliances.[2] The Christian theory and practice of a union of hearts, based upon voluntary choice, is an immense help in securing happy marriages and safeguarding the domestic relations.

Scriptural views of marriage an essential part of the social code of Christianity.

[1] "In places where the influence of missions is felt, there is a lessening of divorce. The education of girls tends very strongly in this direction."—Rev. Professor George E. Post, M.D., Beirut, Syria.

[2] "Marriage customs include the sale of the bride, who takes a dowry of furniture with her to her husband's house. The arrangements are made without the knowledge of the young people, and they are married while still strangers to each other."—Rev. F. P. Gilman (P. B. F. M. N.), Hainan, China.

"A woman is regarded as her husband's property. A man speaks of his wife in the Telugu as ' my chattel.' It is the custom to pay a sum to the father and mother of the bride as purchase-money, and consequently he regards his wife as bought and paid for. It is hardly necessary to say that in arranging a marriage no one would dream of consulting the girl about the matter or asking her consent."—Rev. W. Howard Campbell (L. M. S.), Cuddapah, South India.

"The husband pays for his wife, and she is held as the property of his family, should he die. Should the [deceased] husband have a brother who is pleased with the sister-in-law, he may take her *nolens volens* for wife or concubine. As a rule, the women have one or two children before they marry."—Rev. W. H. Roberts (A. B. M. U.), Bhamo, Burma.

"Women are married, really bartered for a few sheep or cows, soon after entering their ' teens,' and each one becomes the exclusive property of her husband. At his death she is inherited by the male next of kin, who uses her as a second wife. The teaching of the Christian doctrine has done much to alleviate woman's suffering in this station, but even here the dictum that man and woman are equal in God's sight is

Wedding Group of Kaffrarian Christians.

Native Christian Teacher.

Sewing School, Shiloh, Kaffraria.

MORAL TRANSFORMATIONS IN SOUTH AFRICA.

(M. M. S.)

There are those who deprecate any effort on the part of missionaries to change for the better the native customs of betrothal and marriage. In their opinion, what has been should continue to be, and is good enough for all practical purposes. The influence of missionaries has been exerted, however, with persistency and resolute purpose chiefly in two directions: first, in protesting, where this is possible, as in some sections of Africa, against the coöperation of a Christian government in enforcing methods and requirements which are in themselves unjust and objectionable; second, by cultivating in the natives higher conceptions of what is incumbent in well-ordered society, and encouraging them in the reform of this particular evil. The Rev. Brownlee J. Ross (F. C. S.), of Cunningham, Transkei, Cape Colony, writes that while every wealthy native, in order to prove his social standing, had from four to fifteen wives, each wife had at the same time her lover, and this involved no social or moral stigma. The British Government has been countenancing the system, but " Christianity has now almost broken it down." In South Africa it is the so-called "missionary clamor" which has secured a desirable government policy towards the commercial features of a marriage bargain, and has prevented in many instances the coöperation of the authorities in enforcing the wishes of parents where they involved the enslavement and unhappiness of daughters.[1]

being accepted very slowly."—Rev. R. M. Ormerod (U. M. F. M. S.), Golbanti, East Africa.

" In the engagement of a young girl to be married she has, almost invariably, no voice or choice in the matter. The man may be young or old, rich or poor, and his character is not taken into consideration. During the process of betrothment the girl is not permitted to see and converse with her future husband; she must shun his company, as a sign of bashfulness, until the time of their marriage."—Extract from the late Bishop Crowther's Papers on African Missions.

[1] " Another great evil is the sale of girls for wives, which results in practical slavery. The missionaries have insisted that the Government should not be a party to sanction and enforce such sales. I am thankful to say that lately marriageable girls have learned in many instances to defy the law, and to run away to the missionaries for protection, if their parents try to force them to marry any one whom they dislike. I should add, that we put no restraint on these girls to keep them if they wish to go home when, usually within twenty-four hours, their parents come for them. We allow the parents to talk with them to their hearts' content, but we never permit the daughters to be seized and dragged away. The storm is severe while it lasts, but when the parents see that the girl is allowed to go if she wishes, and that she is not willing, then they quiet down, and leave, requesting us to take good care of her. I may say here that it is a disciplinable offense for church members to sell their sisters or daughters."—The late Rev. H. M. Bridgman (A. B. C. F. M.), Umzumbe, Natal.

" Polygamy is another evil. It is made much worse by the custom of paying

4. SEEKING THE ABOLISHMENT OF CHILD MARRIAGE.—A desire for early offspring, in order to insure the observance of the ceremonial rites which among Hindus a dead parent is supposed to require, the universal wish to secure an early alliance for daughters, the pruriency of childhood in the East, and the tendency everywhere to regard marriage only in its sensuous aspects, sufficiently explain the unnatural custom of child marriage.[1] Non-Christian civilization has not been inclined to object to it, and has done little to mitigate its evils. Among the populations of India (see Vol. I., p. 119) it has prevailed to a deplorable extent, and has occupied until quite recently an almost impregnable position in their domestic life. The counter-movement is wholly Christian in its origin, although wherever higher ideals of marriage have been introduced and a non-Christian public sentiment against the custom has been aroused, valuable coöperation on the part of certain Indian reformers who are not believers in Christianity deserves recognition. Christian missions, however, have been the source of the effort to reform, which has been especially stimulated by medical missionaries, who have dwelt particularly upon the physiological and social objections to the practice. "The raising of the marriage age," writes Dr. Pauline Root, "was first agitated by missionary physicians."

The attitude of non-Christian civilizations towards child marriage.

The Missionary Conference of 1877, at Calcutta, addressed a petition to the Governor of Bengal, requesting the appointment of a com-

dowry. In marrying a wife, a man must pay her father as many cattle as may be agreed on. This among the Kaffirs is not wholly evil in its primary intention. The cattle are the support of the wife, should she be put away, or have to leave her husband, owing to cruelty. Usually, however, *uku-lobola*, or the custom of exacting dowry, is grossly abused, owing to human cupidity. A father sells his daughters, with utter disregard for their wishes and affections, in many cases to old and wealthy polygamists; and still more revolting is the use of brute force by an unnatural and inhuman father, should a daughter resist his wishes. It has been found difficult to put a stop to a modified form of this custom within the Christian community, as a father expects dowry for his daughters."—The late Mr. Andrew Smith, M.A., King William's Town, South Africa. Cf. also Bryce, "Impressions of South Africa," p. 391.

[1] "In regard to women, the general feeling is that they are the necessary machines for producing children (Manu ix. 96); and without children there could be no due performance of the funeral rites essential to the peace of a man's soul after death. This is secured by early marriages. If the law required the consent of boys and girls before the marriage ceremony, they might decline to give it. Hence girls are betrothed at three or four years of age, and go through the ceremony of marriage at seven to boys of whom they know nothing, and if these boy husbands die they remain virgin-widows all their lives."—Monier-Williams, "Brahmanism and Hinduism," p. 387.

mission to obtain information concerning the character and extent of the evil.[1] Bishop Thoburn is right in his statement regarding the abolition of child marriage, that "while the missionaries already have the coöperation of many enlightened Hindus, yet when the great consummation is reached, they will be justly entitled to a large, if not the largest, share of the credit due for so great an achievement."[2] One of the most complete and powerful indictments of the custom is from the pen of Mrs. N. M. Mansell, M.D., of the American Methodist Episcopal Mission, now residing at Mussoorie. Her medical knowledge and experience give special force to her statements upon the physical evils incidental to early marriage.[3] Enlightened natives who have taken an early and active part in this crusade are worthy of all honor. The majority of them are either Christians or strongly under the influence of Christian truth. Among the first to render notable service was Keshub Chunder Sen,[4] and later Mr. B. M. Malabari, whose able advocacy in the interest of this and other great reforms adds lustre to his name.[5] Many other distinguished natives might be mentioned as giving valuable support to these efforts.

Special notice should be taken of a very successful movement in Rajputana, which originated through the agency of the late Colonel Walter, C. S. I., then British Agent in that important native State. This excellent Christian officer, recognizing the vast evils which attend the custom of early marriage, proposed in 1887 that a representative committee should consider the question. The suggestion resulted in the formation of a society called, in his honor, the "Walterkrit Rajput Hitkarni Sabha," which may be translated the "Walter-founded Rajput-loving Association." The aim of this organization is to limit marriage and funeral expenses, and to determine the earliest age at which marriage may take place. The members bind themselves by a set of rules limiting the expenditure on both marriages and funerals, and fixing the minimum age for the marriage of boys at eighteen and of girls at fourteen. In view of the difficulties which attend so radical a reform in India, the success of the effort has been remarkable. The results from year to year have grown steadily better, and the in-

Helpful efforts on the part of a British official.

---

[1] Warneck, " Missions and Culture," p. 183.
[2] Thoburn, " India and Malaysia," p. 186.
[3] The document was published in *The Indian Social Reformer*, September 1, 1890, and appears again in the issue of February 13, 1898.
[4] Monier-Williams, " Brahmanism and Hinduism," p. 507.
[5] Karkaria, " India: Forty Years of Progress and Reform," pp. 114–130.

fringements of the rule have constantly decreased. The most recent report at hand—that of 1896—states that out of 5458 marriages among Rajputs the rules of the Association were broken only in about six per cent. of the whole number. In no less than 3021 cases the bridegroom was over twenty years of age, and in 820 cases the bride was over sixteen.[1] The organization is now well established, and its membership is representative throughout Rajputana. The Native States of Baroda and Cambay have followed this example and instituted a similar reform movement.

In the Christian communities of India this harmful custom has been almost entirely abolished. "Child marriage is unknown among our Christian people," writes the Rev. W. Howard Campbell (L. M. S.), of South India. The influence of education works steadily against it, and instances are on record of actual revolt on the part of educated girls. Dr. Rukhmabai, a young woman of high caste, not long ago successfully resisted through the English courts an attempt to force her to consent to an unwelcome marriage, the contract for which was made during her infancy. She afterwards pursued a medical course in England, passing all examinations with credit, and then received the appointment as house-surgeon at the Cama Hospital, Bombay.[2] Legislation upon this subject by the Indian Government is embodied in what is known as the Native Marriage Act, of 1872, which prohibits forced marriages under the age of fourteen for women and eighteen for men, and requires the written consent of parents or guardians when either party is under twenty-one.[3] The old provision of the Penal Code fixed the limit at ten years in the case of a girl as the age before which it was criminal to consummate a marriage. Subsequent legislation, which went into effect in 1891, raised the age to twelve years, and it is to be hoped that a still further provision will place the minimum limit at the age of fourteen, as is already the case in Rajputana and Mysore, under native administration. The Age of Consent Bill, just referred to, passed by the Government in 1891, establishing the age at which a legal marriage could be consummated at twelve years for the girl, created considerable excitement among conservative Hindus, but has been accepted with quiet satisfaction by the

Christian communities repudiate the custom.

---

[1] *The Indian Social Reformer*, August 22, 1897, p. 402. The author is indebted to Dr. James Sommerville (U. P. C. S. M.), of Jodhpore, Rajputana, for an account of the valuable services of Colonel Walter.

[2] *The Double Cross and Medical Missionary Record*, November, 1895, p. 232.

[3] See Vol. I., pp. 120, 121.

majority.[1] " Child marriage," writes the Rev. Dr. Downie (A. B. M. U.), of Nellore, "is losing its hold on the people. This is due directly to missions." Societies for the express purpose of discouraging infant marriages are now springing up in different sections of India. The Christian leaven is working mightily.[2]

Other results somewhat less direct, but still plainly in the line of sequence, may be recorded. We note among these the formation of societies for social reform where this subject, among others, is brought forward for discussion and ad- Reform agitation ex-
tending throughout
Indian society. vocacy as a matter of pressing and vital impor- tance. Resolutions are introduced dealing with the practice in a spirit of deprecation, and in some instances of severe reprobation. Thorough reform measures are urged in papers and ad- dresses by educated natives, well calculated to exert a wide influence in changing public opinion. Every meeting of the National Social Con- ference affords an opportunity for renewed assault upon the custom of infant marriage, and thus through the press reports strong and able protests from representative men are scattered broadcast throughout India.[3] Local conferences, although less noted as representative gather-

---

[1] A full discussion of the question of infant marriage in India may be found in the standard work of Mr. B. M. Malabari, on " Infant Marriage and Enforced Widow- hood," published at Bombay.

[2] The Rev. L. L. Uhl, Ph.D., a Lutheran missionary of Guntur, India, writes that there is, as the effect of mission influence, "a wide prevention of early marriages and of the consequent evil results. Many thousand intelligent young men and women who become Christians and are instructed in mission schools for a number of years learn the folly of forced marriage and wish to exercise the right of choice."

[3] At the Conference held at Calcutta in December, 1896, the Hon. Justice Ranade, in a searching arraignment of the social evils of India, referred hopefully to this problem as follows : " About the question of infant and unequal marriages there is unanimity of public sentiment, which is being slowly but surely educated to perceive the necessity of adopting a higher standard of age both for boys and girls than the one which satisfied the generation that is past. Thanks to the marriage laws passed in Mysore, the sentiment in favour of legislation on the subject is ripening gradually to action. Meantime private efforts to raise the marriageable age to four- teen for girls and to twenty for boys are being actively encouraged among some of the very highest families by the more advanced reformers in all parts of the country, without meeting with much opposition from the orthodox classes."— *The Indian Magazine and Review*, March, 1897, p. 119.

At the Conference of 1897, held at Amraoti, the same able advocate delivered an inaugural address upon " Revival and Reform," in which, among other subjects, that of infant marriage was discussed, with special emphasis upon the present hopeful outlook. *The Indian Social Reformer*, January 16, 1898, pp. 157, 158.

At the Conference of 1895, Dr. Bhandarkar condemned energetically the unequal marriages of old men to young girls, and presented an indictment of the whole prac-

ings, are held in various places, and stimulate zeal for reform in the same direction. In the second Provincial Social Conference of Madras, held April 18, 1897, nine resolutions bearing upon the evils of Indian society were introduced, and, after full discussion, passed. *The Indian Social Reformer* of April 25th presents a full report. The reference to the subject in hand was as follows: " In view of the economical and physical evils inseparable from the system of early marriages, this conference urges upon the community the importance of adopting energetic measures for discouraging such marriages, and of asking for the introduction of legislation on the lines of the Mysore marriage regulations." It is customary also to have lectures delivered at stated intervals before various reform associations; in some instances the lecturer is a woman, and the audience is composed exclusively of Hindu ladies. All this is in the line of promoting changes which can only come as the result of persistent and untiring agitation. Something really new, and very remarkable when we consider the parties involved, was a public indignation meeting held at Madras, and attended by about five hundred people. The meeting was called for the purpose of protesting against the marriage of a native judge, a gray-haired man of fifty-four, with a child ten years of age. A prominent native lawyer presided upon the occasion, and the proposed union was made the subject of vigorous denunciation, a formal resolution being adopted as follows: " That this meeting regrets that Rai Bahadur C. Venkoba Chariar should at his age, and in spite of his education, have resolved to marry a girl of ten years, and takes this opportunity to protest against a system which allows such ill-assorted marriages to take place without disapproval." [1]

An important step in the progress of marriage reform in India still remains to be noted. It is the action of the late Maharajah of Mysore, who, in 1893, instituted marriage regulations in that large State which represent the high-water mark of Indian legislation under purely native auspices. According to the provisions of the Act, a girl in Mysore below eight years of age is regarded as an infant, and a boy under fourteen in the same light, and any person who causes, aids, or abets the marriage of either of these, and any man above eighteen who himself marries an infant girl, shall be punished with imprisonment for a term which may extend to six months, or with

Advanced legislation in Mysore.

tice of early marriages, based not only on physical objections, but also upon those of a social and historical character.

[1] *The Indian Social Reformer*, December 6, 1896, p. 104.

a fine, or with both. A further stipulation is that any man over fifty who marries a girl under fourteen is liable to be punished with imprisonment for two years, or with a fine, or with both. Mysore ranks second in importance among the Native States of India, and has a population of about five millions.[1] Legislation of this character may seem to us of little significance, but no one who is familiar with public sentiment, immemorial custom, and the violent social and religious prejudices of society in India, can fail to see the import of the step, especially as the act of a native Hindu ruler who was not a Christian, although kindly and generously disposed towards missionary work. The action made a powerful, almost startling, impression throughout India, and has formed a rallying-cry for similar legislation elsewhere.[2]

The most recent, and in some respects the most noticeable, example of the spread of this spirit of reform is the effort on the part of two members of the present Legislative Council of Madras to secure the passage of a Bill for the prevention of infant marriage throughout the Presidency. In one of these proposed Bills the age of ten years is named as the limit in the case of the girl, which, it will be noted, is

---

[1] *The Chronicle*, January, 1894, pp. 22, 23; *Work and Workers in the Mission Field*, February, 1895, pp. 72–75, October, 1898, p. 401. The regulations will be found in full in *Work and Workers in the Mission Field*, December, 1893, pp. 519, 520, and in *The Indian Social Reformer*, February 6, 1898, p. 182.

[2] These regulations are not by any means a dead letter, and although the Maharajah himself died December 28, 1894, and the government of the province during the minority of his successor is in the hands of an administrator, the Dewan Sir K. Sheshadri Iyer, K. C. S. I., still they are enforced with impartiality and considerable vigor, as the following editorial note in *The Indian Social Reformer*, May 31, 1896, indicates: "We are glad to learn that the Dewan Sir K. Sheshadri Iyer is determined to put down with a strong hand infant marriages in Mysore, as is proved by the fact that not a week passes but some venerable bridegrooms or the guardians of infant victims are brought to book for their share in a hymeneal atrocity. The punishments are, as a rule, not very severe, which is but right, seeing that these poor fellows are, after all, the creatures of society. It is society as a whole that should be whipped into common sense."

Another note from the same journal, February 8, 1896, is worth quoting as an additional illustration of the free and firm tone with which Indian reformers, while still Hindus in religion, are accustomed to refer to this reprehensible feature of Indian social life: " We have long thought Government should pass a marriage law for the Hindus who glory in the most absurd custom of child and infant marriages. If *sati* can be prevented, we do not see why infants who are married when they know absolutely nothing of the world cannot be given an option as to their continuing in matrimonial bonds when they become of age. Those who talk big on the sanctity of marriage will feel horrified at this idea. But we think, and we deliberately commit our thought to writing in these columns, that marriage can be satisfied only by true love, mutual trust and respect, perfect equality, and unity of convictions and aspirations."

higher by two years than the age fixed in the Mysore regulations. The other Bill names eight years as the limit, following in this respect the legislation in Mysore. The two Hindu gentlemen who are the leaders in the agitation are prominent in both political and social circles. They seem to have conceived independently of each other the purpose to introduce these Bills to the Legislative Council of the Madras Government, neither of them being connected with social re- form organizations, but basing their opposition to the custom of infant marriage on the claim that it is an innovation and corruption not au- thorized by the Shastras. The Hon. R. Pillai, who advocates in his proposed Bill the limit of ten years for the girl, names "liability to criminal prosecution" as the penalty of non-compliance. The Hon. J. Mudaliar, who places the limit at eight years, proposes "imprisonment or fine" as possible punishments to parents, guardians, or other per- sons who transgress. These incidents are noteworthy, because of the clear indication they give of a movement from within the higher official ranks of Hindu legislators, and are for this reason a salient indication of advancing public opinion.[1]

Although child marriage as found in India is a far more serious evil than elsewhere, yet in all Asiatic and African countries it prevails to an extent which justifies earnest efforts to introduce more humane and sensible customs. Female edu- cation is immensely helpful to this end, and the general elevation of the social status of woman is working steadily in the same direction. Woman herself ceases to be a mere chattel, and marriage becomes less and less a matter of bargain and sale, in proportion to the degree of education, refinement, and self-respect which she attains. In China, Japan, and Korea, a truer estimate of the Christian dignity of marriage already pervades mission communities, and is beginning to be accepted more widely. A higher consideration is now shown for the preferences and feelings of those immediately concerned in a marriage contract. In ordinary Chinese society gross deception often characterizes a betrothal, and this, of course, generates discontent and unhappiness.[2] Christian customs do away with these objectionable features.

Missions are every- where rebuking the bar- barity of child marriage.

---

[1] Cf. *The Christian Patriot* (Madras), February 5, 1898, which contains the text of both Bills; also *The Indian Social Reformer*, January 30, 1898, February 13, 20, and 27, 1898, and March 13 and 27, 1898, for articles, discussions, and vari- ous memoranda bearing upon the subject.

[2] "Marriages are arranged by parents through go-betweens, usually without reference to the wishes of the young people or their suitability to each other, but

In Moslem lands the old barbarism will yield slowly, but when Christianity breaks the iron bondage of Mohammedan custom, as it is bound to do, a happier day will dawn for the victims of the harem system, who are now practically without protection. From the South Seas, amid the grossest traditions of savagery, a missionary writes concerning changes in the Island of Tongoa: "Marriages were arranged by parents while the parties were infants. . . . Since the influence of Christianity has been felt on the islands, this hateful custom has fallen into disrepute. Marriages are now arranged by the young men and maidens themselves."[1] In the Island of Java, where the Dutch missionaries have been so busy, many improvements in social customs may be noted. Marriages among the Mohammedan populace take place when the girls are only seven, but among the Christian converts they are deferred until they are fourteen or fifteen years of age, and "then permitted only on the request of the youth and the consent of the girl."[2] From the Island of Trinidad comes the decisive statement, through the Rev. J. Morton, D.D., of the Canadian Presbyterian Mission, that "child marriage is abolished, and children are not forced to wed against their wishes." When we reflect upon the social value of true and happy marriages, the import of changes like these is manifest.

always with regard to the social standing, wealth, and prestige of the families, and the advantages the alliance may bring. In the present state of society the only provision to be made for a woman's support is marriage. Women have no claims upon their own relatives, but only on those of their husband, and the reliance of both men and women for care and support in sickness or old age, and for decent burial, is on their sons and daughters-in-law; therefore everybody ought to marry early, and the more helpless and dependent boys and girls may be—blind, deaf, crippled, imbecile, epileptic—the more important that they be married; boys, so that they will have somebody to wait upon them; girls, so that they will have somebody to support them. There are no charitable institutions of any class in China for the relief of such unfortunates. Their only hope is marriage. Go-betweens, like everybody else here, will lie, and sometimes they are deceived, and etiquette requires that neither of the young people shall be seen before the wedding-day by any member of the other's family, so it often happens that a desirable match is made for these unfortunates. If such a thing is not possible, they are mated with each other as best may be. I know two young men, each of whom on bringing home his bride on his wedding-day found her an idiot, and one young girl in a high family was married to a badly deformed imbecile, covered with loathsome sores; and I am acquainted with other similar but less grievous cases. Christianity has already established in China many families whose lives are governed by Christian principles, and whose members live together in the enjoyment of great happiness."—The late Mrs. C. W. Mateer (P. B. F. M. N.), Tungchow, China.

[1] Michelsen, "Cannibals Won for Christ," pp. 135, 136.

[2] *The Gospel in all Lands*, May, 1895, p. 505.

238 CHRISTIAN MISSIONS AND SOCIAL PROGRESS

5. ALLEVIATING THE SOCIAL MISERIES OF WIDOWHOOD.—In many heathen lands a widow is "a widow indeed" in the sorrow, isolation, and bondage of her lot. The fact that death has deprived her of a husband places her under a ban, and robs her of even that limited meed of consideration which is shown to ordinary womanhood. The climax of this cruel status was in that saturnalia of heathenism, the *sati*, or burning alive of widows, once so prevalent in India. The first protest ever made against it with any aggressive purpose was in 1799, by a missionary, William Carey, and this was the beginning of the agitation for its overthrow.[1] The final abolishment came only after fully thirty years of persevering effort, when the British Government, with Lord William Bentinck as its honored instrument, issued in 1829 its memorable order for the legal prohibition of *sati*. The action of the Government referred, of course, only to British India. *Sati* was still practised for some time in the Native

The origin of the agitation for the abolishment of sati.

---

[1] Dr. Carey wrote in 1801: " I consider that the burning of women, the burying of them alive with their husbands, the exposure of infants, and the sacrifice of children at Saugor, ought not to be permitted, whatever religious motives are pretended, because they are crimes against the State."

In a letter of Carey's, inserted in his Biography by Dr. George Smith (p. 94), one of these horrid rites which Carey himself witnessed in 1799 is described. He and his colleagues continued the agitation against *sati*, and struggled to induce the British Government to forbid the custom. They proceeded to fortify their appeal by collecting evidence of the extensive prevalence of the crime. Careful investigation in 1804 revealed the fact that within a circle of thirty miles around Calcutta more than three hundred widows had been immolated on the funeral pyre during a period of six months. Lord Wellesley was then Governor-General, but just as Carey had almost succeeded in securing the intervention of the Government, Lord Wellesley retired from office, and it was in 1829, fully a quarter of a century later, before the Act was finally passed, while, as Carey waited and prayed, " every day saw the devilish smoke ascending along the banks of the Ganges and the rivers and pools considered sacred by the Hindus." Thus years of enforced delay witnessed the destruction of 70,000 victims of this atrocious iniquity. The proclamation of Lord William Bentinck abolishing the *sati*, and declaring it to be punishable as homicide, reached Dr. Carey one Sunday morning when he was engaged in preparation for his preaching service. He immediately called for some one else to take his place, and seizing his pen, he translated the order into Bengali, and had it issued in the *Bengali Gazette*. " If I delay an hour," he exclaimed, " to translate and publish this, many a widow's life may be sacrificed." Thus, on the 4th of December, 1829,—" memorable date," as Dr. Smith calls it, " to be classed with that on which, soon after, 800,000 slaves were set free,—' the Ganges flowed unblooded to the sea ' for the first time." Consult Smith, " Life of William Carey," pp. 65, 94, 247, 252; Horne, " The Story of the London Missionary Society," p. 99; Bliss, " The Encyclopedia of Missions," vol. i., p. 235.

States, but it grew more and more into disrepute. An incident is given by a lady missionary in a paper in commemoration of the sixtieth year of the Queen's reign, entitled " Progress among the Women of Bengal during the Reign of Queen Victoria," published in *The Indian Evangelical Review* for October, 1897, which shows that the burning of widows and slaves was still possible in some of the Feudatory States in 1839. The account is as follows: " Four of the wives of Ranjit Singh (of the Punjab), veiled and clothed in white silk, held the hands of the corpse as he was about to be cremated. Seven of his fair and beauteous slave girls sat at the body's feet while the flames from the sandalwood and aloes consumed all that was mortal of their master, after the son, Dhulep Singh, had fired the pyre. The blaze of that funeral pyre cast a lurid light on the Native States of India in 1839, of which we know nothing in 1897." The Abbé Dubois, in " Hindu Manners, Customs, and Ceremonies," describes similar scenes where he himself was present.[1]

The cessation of this ghastly crime, which, it may be noted, had no support in early Vedic literature,[2] although a most important gain in the direction of reform, was not all that was to be desired for the alleviation of the widow's lot. Further ameliorations of the condition of Indian widows. Christian missions have been working steadily and with strenuous purpose for nearly a century to lift still further the burdens and mitigate the woes which rest upon widowhood. The British Government, so far as it felt justified, has given its powerful coöperation in overcoming the barriers existing in Hindu society, chiefly by reason of caste rules, superstitious prejudices, and social customs, which make the marriage of widows so difficult. Indian public sentiment, however, fortified by flinty obstinacy, has been stubborn and sullen about accepting any change in the traditional status. The Widow Marriage Act, passed by Lord Canning in 1856, simply removed legal obstacles to such marriages, but it has met with little support from Hindu concurrence, and its provisions have been to an amazing extent a dead letter for over forty years. *The Indian Social Reformer* for June 20, 1897, in an editorial on " Sixty Years of Social Progress," estimates the entire number of widow marriages during that period to be not more than two hundred. As we shall see, they have gradually become more frequent of late years. The Rev. David Downie, D.D., of Nellore, says : " Widow marriage is increasing. This is due directly to missions." Another

1 See vol. ii., new ed., 1897, chap. xix., pp. 359–370.
2 Wilkins, " Modern Hinduism," p. 377.

missionary—the Rev. W. A. Wilson (C. P. M.), of Rutlam—writes that "there is good evidence that through the spread of Christian teaching widows are now better treated. The belief that a husband dies because of his wife's sins is being slowly displaced by other views of the divine providence, and the anger of her husband's relatives is not vented upon her as when she was looked upon as cursed of the gods and the direct cause of the calamity. Her sufferings are still great enough, but there is reason to believe that, where the truths of Christianity are at all well known, her miseries are greatly mitigated. Public opinion is changing, and is making itself felt."

The lamentable features of Indian widowhood have been briefly stated in Vol. I. (pp. 123, 124),[1] where it is shown that nearly every fifth woman in India is a widow, and that the total number of these unfortunates is at present not less than twenty-five millions. The evils which follow in the train of this strange and cruel ostracism, affecting as it does in so many instances the tender years of innocent girlhood, only accentuate the call for a complete revolution in Indian thinking upon this subject. The prejudice against widow marriage is still almost prohibitive throughout India, especially among all the higher castes, with the exception of certain sections of the North-West Provinces, where considerable freedom in the matter is tolerated.[2] A perusal of the writings of Indian reformers, whether Hindu or Christian, reveals at once to those who read between the lines the terrible helplessness of a widow's lot, and the perilous temptations which crowd around her. She is looked upon by the great majority of Hindus as an easy victim, a species of social outcast, and the destined prey of wanton passion. She herself, being doomed to a loveless and lonely isolation, is without the natural safeguards of self-respect and protection which she needs. The chaotic state of Hindu sentiment on this subject is apparent when we contrast its inflexible attitude towards young widows, whom it consigns for life to an unnatural deprivation, with the sanction it gives to the immediate remarriage of a widower any number of times, and, as often happens, it may be the union of old men with young girls hardly in their teens. Mr. B. M. Malabari has described in his courageous way many of the dark features of this burden of Indian widowhood—the almost inevitable fall of the widow, infanticide with hot ashes choking the breath

The gradual passing of a strange and cruel ostracism.

---

[1] Cf. also Dubois, "Hindu Manners, Customs, and Ceremonies," new ed., 1897, vol. ii., p. 356.

[2] Crooke, "The North-Western Provinces of India," pp. 228, 229.

of her new-born babe, or possibly a hasty recourse, before the child is born, to a ceremony which is suggestively called "a cold suttee."[1]

A careful distinction is made by educated Indian reformers, in the discussion of this question, between the status of widowhood when it is voluntarily maintained, and the law of Hindu society enforcing perpetual widowhood under the ban of contumely. In an address at the Social Conference held at Poona, 1895, Mr. K. Natarajan, in moving a resolution on the disfigurement of child widows, spoke as follows: "With regard to widows, I personally feel, and there are a large number of us who feel, that the sentiment which impels a man or woman, out of regard to the memory of the dear departed, to lead a life of pure, unworldly celibacy is one which appeals to all that is holiest in human nature. With widowhood as such we have no quarrel. But we ought to make a distinction between that which is enforced and that which is voluntary. Voluntary widowhood is holy; enforced widowhood is an iniquity. It is the enforced character of our system which makes it so great an evil. The disfigurement alluded to in the resolution makes this custom a hideous iniquity."[2]

If we turn now to inquire what has been actually accomplished by missions in India in the direction of reforming these evils, we note the existence of societies especially for the aid of widows, having in view the alleviation of their lot and the elevation of their lives. The Indian Widows' Union, auxiliary to the Church of England Zenana Missionary Society, is doing a kindly and efficient service in this sphere of ministry. At the Chicago Columbian Exhibition a medal was awarded for needlework done in an Industrial Institute for Widows connected with the above-named society. There are also in India reform societies established under missionary and

The mission crusade supported by the coöperation of native reformers.

---

[1] "And woe be to her [the widow] if she belongs to a respectable family. Then they get up a ceremony in her honour, which they call a *cold suttee.* They serve her with the best of viands, they ply her with sweet intoxicants, and they cap her last supper on earth with something that will settle their business. The widow is soon cold in death, and is forthwith carried off to the burning-ground (the pious Hindu can't keep a corpse in his house for ten minutes). This *cold suttee* means a double murder. Let us hope it is a very rare practice."—Gidumal, "Behramji M. Malabari: A Biographical Sketch," p. 198.

[2] *The Indian Social Reformer,* January 11, 1896. Cf. article in *The Church Missionary Intelligencer,* November, 1893, on "Missions or Science the Maker of India's Homes?" by the Rev. G. Ensor, especially pp. 809, 810; also article on "Social Progress in India," by the Rev. T. H. Whitamore, in *Work and Workers in the Mission Field,* June, 1894, pp. 250–252.

native auspices, usually under the title of "Widow Remarriage Associations," the object of which is to encourage and facilitate the marriage of widows by moral and social support. The memorable crusade of Mr. B. M. Malabari[1] has now become only one of many heroic efforts on the part of enlightened Hindus to create a change of sentiment in Indian society upon this vexing problem. He has had as contemporaries and followers such accomplished Indian reformers as Rao Sahib Mahipatram Rupram Nilkanth, C.I.E., Iswar Chandra Vidyasagar, C.I.E., Rao Bahadur Veeresalingam Pantulu, and Madhavdas Raghunathdas,[2] the latter of whom was called "a champion of Hindu widow remarriage," and whose home at Girgaum, near Bombay, was known as the "Widow Marriage Hall," owing to his readiness in allowing it to be used for the celebration of such marriages, and the refuge from persecution which it afforded to Hindu widows. Since 1871 more than twenty-five widow marriages have taken place within its doors, and others have followed since his death in 1896, as his son, Mr. Bhagwandas Madhavdas, seems to cherish views similar to those held by his father.

Thus the colossal and Hindu-heartrending revolution involved in the marriage of innocent young girls who have become widows goes bravely on. It is still such a paralyzing innovation that every widow marriage which occurs in India is regarded among reformers as a proper opportunity for congratulations, and for somewhat sensational references in the Hindu public press.[3] The fact is slowly gaining credence, on the strength of the judicial opinion of learned pundits, that widow marriage is not contrary to the Vedas and Shastras.[4]

---

[1] Gidumal, "Behramji M. Malabari: A Biographical Sketch," pp. 195–201; Karkaria, "India: Forty Years of Progress and Reform; being a Sketch of the Life and Times of Behramji M. Malabari," pp. 119–130.

[2] *Progress*, May, 1896, p. 126.

[3] In the Ninth Indian National Social Conference of 1895 the resolution upon widow marriage began as follows: "The Conference expresses its satisfaction that this year, as in the two or three years past, some ten marriages of widows have taken place, five in the Presidency of Bombay, one in Madras, and four in the Punjab, and it congratulates Dewan Santrama, of Lahore, on the moral courage shown by him in this connection."— *The Indian Social Reformer*, January 18, 1896, p. 151.

[4] "A high-caste Hindu at Lahore, Dewan Sam Ram Chopra, has given his widowed daughter in marriage, and has publicly stated that the pundits of Benares, Allahabad, Jammu, and other places, have pronounced that remarriage was allowed by the Vedas and Shastras. He also said that a committee of gentlemen had been formed with the object of arranging for the marriage of child widows, with due regard to caste and family."— *The Indian Magazine and Review*, February, 1896, p. 111.

Special service in the elucidation of this fact has been rendered by Pundit Iswar Chandra Vidyasagar, late Principal of the Sanscrit College, Calcutta.[1] Every meeting in the interest of social reform gives more definite expression and imparts an added impulse to the agitation. As an illustration we may quote the resolution which was moved at the Second Provincial Social Conference of Madras, held April 18, 1897, which is as follows: "While readily acknowledging that a life of voluntary abnegation is worthy of respect in man and woman alike, this Conference considers it unjust and inhuman to force upon women, especially young girls, a life of celibacy, accompanied, as it is, with circumstances of painful humiliation. It therefore urges on the communities in which widow marriage is prohibited the justice and desirability of abolishing the existing restrictions on the remarriage of widows."[2] Addresses which are often weighty and powerful pleas for the deliverance of Indian widowhood from its crushing stigmas are generally a feature of these gatherings.[3]

The Maharani-Regent of Mysore, herself now a widow, is taking a kindly and sympathetic interest in the welfare of the women of that State who have suffered the same affliction that she has recently experienced. She has opened in her school two special classes for training adult Hindu widows for the profession of teaching, and there is a prospect that her powerful influence will be still further exerted on behalf of widows.[4] The spirit of protest on the part of native Hindu reformers is especially directed just now against the customary disfigurement of widows. The shaven head is a bitter and cruel affront to Hindu women. *The Indian Spectator* says truly that "this is and ought to be a crime. Hardly lives a widow who agrees to it of her free will and accord." It is the contention of this able journal that the "law should step in to protect all minors. Many a parent, even orthodox

---

[1] *The Indian Magazine and Review*, March, 1896, p. 163; April, 1896, pp. 205, 206.

[2] *The Indian Social Reformer*, April 25, 1897, p. 267.

[3] Examples may be found in the address of Mr. K. Srinivasa Rao, B.A., at Poona (see *The Indian Social Reformer*, February 1, 1896, p. 164), and in a lecture by Mr. G. Parameswaran Pillai, B.A., Editor of *The Madras Standard*, at a meeting of the Saidapet Hindu Social Reform Association, March 28, 1896 (*ibid.*, April 4, 1896, p. 237). In response to a prize offered by *The Indian Social Reformer* for the best contribution on the subject of widow remarriage, an article of some length, dealing with the crucial, salient points of the theme, by Mr. A. Sethuraman, B.A., of Mahboob College, Secunderabad, is published in full, *ibid.*, May 23 and 30, 1897.

[4] *The Indian Magazine and Review*, December, 1895, p. 643; *The Christian Patriot*, Madras, July 4, 1895.

ones, will inwardly bless Government if it makes the disfigurement of widows below sixteen, with or without consent, a crime punishable under the Indian Penal Code."[1] This indignity, it may be noted, is not called for in the ancient sacred books of the Hindus.[2]

No statement of the hopeful aspects of this reform movement would be complete without mention of the homes for widows which are now established in many places throughout India, and will no doubt grow in numbers as time goes on. Chief among them may be mentioned that of the Pundita Ramabai, in Poona, whose romantic history is referred to so often in current missionary literature.[3] She was born of Hindu parentage in April, 1858, her father being a learned Brahman pundit, and was married at the age of sixteen to a Bengali gentleman, a graduate of the Calcutta University. She became a widow after nineteen months of happy married life. A little daughter was born to her a few months before her husband's death, whom she named Manorama, or "Heart's Joy." She afterwards engaged as a lecturer in the advocacy of a higher life and larger opportunity for Hindu women, and founded in Poona a society of ladies, known as the Arya Mahala Somaj, for the promotion of education among native women and the discouragement of child marriage. Later she visited England, and enjoyed there educational opportunities which fitted her for future responsibilities. Her contact with Englishwomen at St. Mary's Home, Wantage, and at the Ladies' College at Cheltenham, was a blessing to her. In 1886 she visited America, where she studied thoroughly the kindergarten system. Work for Indian widows was the chosen field of service towards which she looked, and with this in view a society called the Ramabai Association was formed in Boston in December, 1887, which pledged her a stipulated support for ten years. She returned to Bombay, and founded the Sharada Sadan, or "Widows'

The notable services of Pundita Ramabai on behalf of Indian widows.

---

[1] Quoted in *The Indian Social Reformer*, August 30, 1896, p. 408.

[2] "The leading lawgivers of old times, and the great epics Ramayana and Mahabharata, make no mention of it [shaving the head in mourning] in the many detailed accounts they give of funeral obsequies and subsequent mournings. On the contrary, they describe widows with 'dishevelled hair.' Down to the times of Buddhism we find no trace of the practice. The earlier lawgivers allow widows a remarriage."—Article from *The Indian Spectator*, quoted in *The Indian Social Reformer*, May 16, 1897, p. 295.

[3] For a sketch of her life, consult Chapman, "Sketches of Some Distinguished Indian Women," pp. 26–47; Murdoch, "Sketches of Indian Christians," pp. 220–227; *The Missionary Review of the World*, September, 1897, pp. 669–674; *The Outlook*, May 29, 1897, pp. 243, 274.

Indian Widows from famine districts received
at Pundita Ramabai's Home.

A Group of Child Widows in the
Ramabai Home, Poona.

Indian Widows in Pundita Ramabai's Home
a few months after admission

A CHRISTIAN REFUGE FOR WIDOWS IN INDIA.

Home," which was afterwards removed to Poona, where it is still conducted.

Ramabai's views on some of the essentials of evangelical truth had up to this date not attained the status of clear conviction which was subsequently reached. Her school was established without a distinctively religious purpose, and without the intention of proselyting in the interests of Christianity, although full liberty of conscience was accorded to every inmate.[1] Subsequently her faith in evangelical Christianity became more pronounced, and gave a decided tone and direction to her religious life. The result of this was that several of the widows under her care were brought, as it was thought, too directly under Christian influence. This awakened much opposition on the part of the Hindu supporters of her Home, which culminated in the withdrawal of several from her advisory committee, and caused in 1893 a violent outbreak of criticism and false accusations. She bore this with courage and fortitude, and an unshaken loyalty to her convictions. A reconstruction of the committee of the institution followed, and since then it has been conducted as a Christian Home, with a manifest power to mould the religious views and practices of its inmates, so much so that twelve of them, about two years later, sought Christian baptism, which aroused another storm of protest.[2] The number had increased to twenty-

---

[1] " Ramabai has promised not to proselytise, and that engagement she has faithfully kept. Some have confused this promise with a pledge not to influence. To *that* she did not commit herself, for it would have been promising an impossibility. No one with a strong personality can help making an impression upon others. The most powerful influence is often the most unconscious. Ramabai's pupils can no more help being moulded by her than they can help breathing the same atmosphere, and if some of them are drawn towards Christianity by the noble exemplification of it they see daily before their eyes, neither she nor they are to be blamed. Were Ramabai incapable of thus silently and involuntarily moving those with whom she is brought into daily contact, she would not have possessed the individuality necessary to originate and carry out the difficult task she has undertaken."— *The Indian Magazine and Review,* April, 1894, pp. 201, 202.

[2] " A Bombay Christian paper pertinently remarks: ' Did the city of sacred bulls and secular bears expect other results from the working of a Christian Home for Hindu widows and orphans? Pundita Ramabai first offered to start her work in the interests of Brahmanism, and lavish promises were made her; sore at heart and disappointed in her countrymen, this daughter of Maharastra went over to another land and another faith. She returned from the United States bringing with her the funds for founding a Home for high-caste Hindu widows. Those who sent their wards to her institution did it with their eyes open; we fail to see any breach of faith so far on Ramabai's part. She has not tried to force Christianity on its inmates. If her example has been too catching for the girls, and too striking a contrast to that afforded by their parents and guardians, what is more

three at the end of 1896, and to forty-eight in 1897.[1] This was without any compulsory attendance upon Christian teaching, and was entirely the outcome of their voluntary search for truth, and intelligent insight into what Christianity really means.

Pundita Ramabai's reply to those who were so offended at the conversion of some of her protégées is at once vigorous and opportune. She says: "They are mourning for these girls, for they think they are lost to society, and that the nation has been made weak by this loss of strength. These good people never think of the thousands of young widows who are yearly led astray, and whose lives are wantonly destroyed by men like themselves. They never think of mourning for them, and for the hundreds of innocent lives that are sacrificed upon the unholy altar of caste. . . . Men who live in open sin, daily violating the rules of morality, and who are plagues of society, are received and honored everywhere in their caste; while a man following his conscience, either by marrying a widow or by embracing Christianity, is made an outcast, and persecuted."[2] She continues with a stinging exposé of the inconsistencies of Hindu religion and practice.

Her Home has steadily grown in usefulness, and the number of inmates has increased from year to year.[3] She began in March, 1889,

natural than that the girls should become Christians? The conclusion to which we are driven is that the present outcry is a revival of the old policy of the Brahmans, to do nothing themselves, and abuse all who attempt to do something for the little widows of India.'"—Quoted in the *Woman's Missionary Friend*, March, 1896, p. 246.

[1] " Report of Annual Meeting of the Ramabai Association, held March 16, 1898," pp. 17, 18.

[2] Quoted from *The Indian Christian Herald* in *The Missionary Review of the World*, December, 1896, p. 932. Cf. also *The Sentinel*, February, 1896, p. 17, and " Report of the Ramabai Association for 1895."

[3] The Orthodox Brahmans of Poona and vicinity have undertaken to establish a rival " Home for Widows," under strictly Hindu control. The project was intrusted to the care of Professor Karve, a gentleman who is, no doubt, fully competent; yet, according to the *Indian Spectator*, its success is still far from assured. The *Spectator* thus sums up the result: " He [Professor Karve] has been quietly working for it for the last two years, travelling from place to place, giving lectures, distributing pamphlets, and appealing for private help. For all his pains, he has been able to collect less than five thousand rupees, and this from scarcely more than a hundred and fifty gentlemen. What is the secret of his failure? The *Dnyanodaya* has the following pertinent reply: ' In all deference to Professor Karve's sincerity and patient endeavors, we dare to say that the difference is that between an imitation and the genuine thing. Men have fought and spent enormous sums for the Kohinoor, but we do not hear of life and wealth sacrificed for a paste dia-

with only two inmates; in 1892 there were forty-three, including thirty widows; in 1896 there were fifty-seven, which number in 1897 had increased to seventy-five.[1] When the fearful fam- ine of 1897 arose, Ramabai extended her efforts to reach the famine-stricken widows and girls of Cen- tral India. During a tour in the Central Provinces, she found many young widows and deserted wives not only starving, but in great moral danger, owing to their distress and helplessness. From these waifs of famine and ostracism, she gathered, during repeated visits, nearly five hundred, including many young girls who were neither widows nor deserted wives. Some two hundred of these were dis- tributed among different missions, while about three hundred high-caste girls were placed at Kedgaum (also written Khedgaon), a few of them going to her Widows' Home in Poona. She is erecting buildings at Kedgaum (a place thirty-four miles from Poona, where she had previously purchased some land), which will accommodate nearly three hundred girls, in place of the temporary bungalow which had been hired. A large wing has been added to the school building

A stirring and romantic story of God's provi- dential leadings.

mond. The Pundita is genuine. Her whole heart and soul, all that she has, has gone to the saving and bettering of widows. A widow herself, she believes there is something from which widows can be saved, and some one to whom they can be led to their temporal and spiritual bettering. She believes and she acts. Professor Karve sees and admires, and says: " Let us do likewise, leaving out the Christianity of it." But Professor Karve is not a widow! He does not see in the light of the Divine Love how forlorn, loveless, and sad is the state of the Hindu widow, nor does he know by experience what the Divine Saviour can do to elevate, purify, and ennoble the human soul in whatever state it may be found.' "—Quoted in *The Christian Patriot*, August 14, 1897.

1 " The Sharada Sadan, to-day, is worth $50,000, without one rupee of debt upon it. Through it have passed three hundred and fifty child widows and girls, the average number in the home being fifty. The past year [1897] closed with seventy-five. Fourteen pupils have been trained as teachers, nine of whom are teaching in different schools, and two have opened schools of their own. Of eight trained as nurses, five are employed. Of seven trained as assistants to missionaries, five are employed. Seven are matrons, two are housekeepers; while ten have happy homes of their own, and were not married before they were twenty-one. Of the three hundred and fifty who have been in the Sadan for a longer or shorter time, forty-eight have become Christians, twenty-three of whom are voluntary Christian workers; all of these retaining the Hindu customs and costumes. The greater part of this large work has been accomplished in less than nine years, for in the storm of 1893 thirty-one pupils were removed from the Sadan, through the influence of the Poona Advisory Board after its resignation, so that fifty of the present number have been under instruction less than five years. In two years thirty of the attend- ing pupils will be ready to go out as wage-earners."—" Report of the Annual Meeting of the Ramabai Association, held March 16, 1898."

in Poona. A report dated October, 1897, states that "about ninety of these new girls have accepted the Lord Jesus as their Saviour." An account of events still more recent, published in *The Indian Witness* of November 26, 1897, announces the baptism by the Rev. W. W. Bruere of one hundred and sixteen women and child widows at Poona, and on November 15th one hundred and eight women and girls at Kedgaum.[1] The semiannual report (July, 1898) of the "Mukti Home," as it has been named, at Kedgaum, announces the baptism of thirty more of its inmates, and gives the total on its roll at that date as two hundred and thirty. The girls thus gathered are portrayed as at first "nothing but skeletons, and wild like the beasts of the jungle."[2] The physical, intellectual, and spiritual blessings which will come to them through this rescue at the hands of Pundita Ramabai, who can estimate?

Could there be a more stirring and romantic story of God's providential leadings than appears in the history of this brave widow? Is there a more significant illustration of what He has in prospect for those Indian Christians who are prepared to serve Him among their fellow-countrymen? Krupabai Satthianadhan, who once visited Pundita Ramabai, has given an interesting account of her work. In describing the inmates of the Home, she says: "They seemed to have shaken off all prejudices, and in the new atmosphere of freedom and intellectual development to have acquired some force of character and a determination to improve themselves. Everything they attempt, whether singing or reading or talking, they do naturally, without any of that false modesty and affectation which characterise Hindu girls of their age. How much fuller, brighter, and healthier the life of our girls would be if they could only throw off the trammels of supersti-

---

[1] Quoted in *The Baptist Missionary Review* (Madras), January, 1898, pp. 28, 29, and *The Missionary Review of the World*, April, 1898, p. 281.

[2] Their appearance is thus described by one who was present and witnessed their arrival at Kedgaum: "They are a sad, pitiful sight when first they come! How shall I describe them? Some are almost too weak to move, some through want of cleanliness and proper food are so covered with sores that it is painful to look at them, others through sheer poverty have been reduced to wearing the same article of clothing for such a long time that it is impossible to stand near them without feeling faint through the unhealthy odour proceeding therefrom. Praise the Lord for what a few months in the Home have done for such! They are not only clean, and the majority of them strong and healthy, but they have been wonderfully toned down through the Christ-influence that has been exerted over them, and now instead of quarrelling and fighting, they gladly do anything for one another, or for those who are in charge of them."—*White Already to Harvest*, October, 1897, p. 8.

A group of famine refugees gathered by
Mrs. Bruere, (M. E. M. S.), Poona.
(See page 395.)

The Pundita Ramabai, and a group of
widows, in the Shárada Sadan.
(The Pundita in white.)

A little widow and her adopted
orphan child.
(See note, page 249.)

THE PUNDITA RAMABAI AND HER WIDOWS' HOME.

tion and prejudice, and breathe the healthy atmosphere of innocent enjoyment and culture! Pundita Ramabai's work is national in its effects, for the widows that she is training will no doubt take the lead in the emancipation of the women of India. They have no demands on their time, and no ties. If they can make life more useful, more intellectually, innocently happy, the married women will be sure to follow and make life in their homes worth living." [1] The pledges of the Ramabai Association expired in 1898, and further provision has been made for conducting her institution through the efforts of an organized committee which has undertaken to secure the financial support required.

Special work on behalf of widows has been assumed by various other agencies in India. The London Missionary Society has an Industrial Home in Calcutta for the assistance of Christian widows. The Church of England Zenana Missionary Society has an Industrial Institute for Widows at Amritsar, in the Punjab.

From the funeral pyre of heathenism to the loving care of Christianity.

Her Majesty Queen Victoria was pleased to accept in her Jubilee year a curtain embroidered by one hundred widows connected with this institute. It is to be noted "that the incident is of special interest, because until sixty-eight years ago [1829] these women would have been burned alive on the funeral pyre of their husbands." [2] The American Presbyterian Mission at Jalandhar, in the Punjab, has a class for Hindu widows, with sixteen pupils. A Widows' Industrial Home has been opened at Beawar by the United Presbyterian Mission of Scotland. A Widows' Fund, from which assistance is rendered to those who need aid, has been established at Nazareth, in Tinnevelly, by the Society for the Propagation of the Gospel. Mention should be

[1] Satthianadhan, " Miscellaneous Writings," p. 95.
The Outlook for May 29, 1897, publishes a letter from Helen S. Dyer, of Bombay, in which the following incident is given in connection with the sudden expansion of the Pundita Ramabai's work occasioned by the distress of the famine ▸ " The attitude of the older inmates of the Sharada Sadan in this emergency has been most helpful. They agreed to eat cheaper food, and live in a poorer way, to make it easier to take in these poor waifs. They have joined in caring for and making them feel at home. Among the new-comers were some little girl widows, and one or two babies who were connected with them and could not be separated. The older girls volunteered to adopt these as foster-children, and have devoted themselves lovingly to their care. One little scrawny mite was adopted by a lassie of fourteen who had herself in infancy been cast out to die. When the other girls twitted her on the ' monkey face ' of her protégée, she calmly replied: ' To adopt a nice and pretty child is good, but to take an ugly one is love.' "
[2] India's Women, October, 1897, p. 218.

made also of a Brahman Home at Baranagar, near Calcutta, conducted by Mr. and Mrs. Sasipada Banerjee. Mr. Banerjee's work has now expanded to include not only a Home for Widows, but a female boarding-school, and a normal class for the training of teachers. He and his wife long ago gave up their faith in idolatry, and became disciples of the Brahmo-Somaj; but the school is not known as distinctively Christian, as it is his theory that caste should not be interfered with, and that Hindu widows should feel free to come there without apprehension that it might involve revolutionary changes in their religious life. Mr. Banerjee has fought a brave fight with the prejudices of Indian society, and his enlightened views of what should be done for the education of the women of India, and the mitigation of the miseries of Hindu widowhood, deserve all praise.[1]

In other lands it is apparent that Christianity, wherever missions have introduced it, is exerting a powerful influence in modifying the cruel exactions and doing away with the old legal disabilities which affect the status of widows. A new law has recently been passed in Korea, abrogating the rule which limited the right of widows to marry only those of inferior rank, and allowing full liberty in this respect without regard to caste.[2]   In Old Calabar, as a result of missionary intervention, the custom of compelling widows to remain in their houses in filth and wretchedness after the death of their husbands, until " devil-making " was over, which sometimes imposed seclusion for a period of seven years, has been abolished. The requirement is now that there shall be but one month of mourning on the part of widows, and after that no further restraint shall be put upon them.[3] At another place on the West Coast, where the Mission of the American Presbyterian Church is established, a converted African king has issued some strange decrees, which may be called the Magna Charta of widowhood among those wild races.[4]   In Aneityum, in the New Hebrides, the evils of female infanticide and the strangulation of widows have long

Mitigation of the widow's lot in other lands.

---

1 " Some Noted Indians of Modern Times," p. 98; *The Indian Magazine and Review*, June, 1895, p. 298; August, 1895, pp. 428–434.

2 *Woman's Missionary Friend*, August, 1897, p. 52.

3 Dickie, " Story of the Mission in Old Calabar," p. 79.

4 Mrs. Reutlinger, of the mission, writes from Benito in 1896: " Our Kombe King and his chiefs have just been in council, and have decreed some new laws, among which is the following: Widows are to be allowed liberty to settle as they please, and to marry whom they will, and in a case where the woman has been long in the husband's family, only half the dowry paid is required to be returned, if she chooses to leave the family of her deceased husband and make her home elsewhere."

ceased. "During the first seven years of his residence, Dr. Inglis counted sixty widows who, but for the new religion, would have been strangled according to native law." Thus writes the Rev. J. H. Lawrie, formerly a missionary in the New Hebrides.[1]

6. MITIGATING THE ENFORCED SECLUSION OF WOMAN.—The isolation of woman, accompanied by the strict espionage to which she is subjected in most Eastern lands, is the result of the brooding suspicion which rests upon social intercourse. Men distrust other men, and all men distrust more or less all women. In some religious and social environments this state of suspicion is more intense than in others. We find its extreme form in Mohammedan society and among aristocratic circles in nearly all Oriental countries. It has become to such an extent a part of the social economy of life that it will not be safe to disturb it until nobler views of the relation of the sexes, more civilized conceptions of the status of woman, and a larger increment of chivalry and chastity have been introduced into the moral tone of society. Wherever Islam has established itself severe restraints have been put upon woman, and the veil has been dropped over her person. Christian or Hindu communities surrounded by Moslems, in order to protect their own women from public insult and annoyance, have had to conform some of their customs, to a greater or less extent, to those current among their Moslem neighbors. In India, with all high-caste Hindus as well as Mohammedans, an extreme measure of seclusion and espionage has become characteristic of the zenana system, although it is acknowledged by Hindus themselves that a wonderful change has taken place within the last thirty years.[2] Before the advent of the Moslem women had far more liberty than is at present granted them.[3] It should be noted that even now the zenana system is not enforced in

The social problems of the zenana system.

---

[1] *The Free Church of Scotland Monthly*, May, 1897, p. 108.

[2] "In Bengal, Hindu women had for centuries been kept in a state of seclusion; this may have been partly due to Mohammedan influence, but, whatever was the cause, thirty years ago the position of the Hindu women in Bengal was most deplorable. The state of things is altogether different now. As regards the seclusion of Hindu women, the change has been of a marvellous character."—From an address by Mr. Manomohun Ghose before the National Indian Association, printed in *The Indian Magazine and Review*, February, 1896, pp. 63, 64.

[3] "The Origin of Hindu Zenanas," by the Rev. Thomas Evans, Mussoorie, *The Missionary Herald of the Baptist Missionary Society* (London), February, 1897, p. 94.

all parts of India, nor is it customary with the agricultural population, or to any great extent with the lower classes of Hindu society.

The attitude of missions towards this seclusion of woman in the East should be one of prudence and reserve. These formal barriers of custom and external restraint may not safely be thrown

The proper attitude of down with undue haste, or at least until efficient missions to the zenana. moral safeguards can be substituted in their place.[1]

Nothing is more distressing to an Oriental woman of natural refinement than a breach of custom, involving on her part what is counted to be a moral shame. Public sentiment, however, is so focussed upon artificial standards, and so occupied in exacting external conformity to social habit, that the inner spirit of modesty counts for little in comparison with the outer form, nor is it always accorded the respect to which it is entitled, or granted its rightful privileges. These changes will come with "sweeter manners, purer laws," and nobler insight into social morals. The difficulty of dealing in any arbitrary way with the terrible rigor of Mohammedan and Hindu custom regarding the treatment of woman has been revealed in connection with the effort of the British Government to enforce sanitary requirements during the recent prevalence of the plague. The most pressing demands of a hygienic code are of no weight whatever to the Moslem, if they involve the slightest violation of established traditions governing the sanctities of his harem. Hindus and Mohammedans, therefore, conceal the presence of disease, and bar out from their homes all medical supervision. Any amount of suffering, and even death itself, seems to be preferable to making the least concession to unwelcome or too intrusive sanitary regulations.[2]

---

[1] " It would be a calamity if the zenana doors were all opened wide to-morrow, because male society is not in a fit state to allow of this with safety. The influence of our Lord in promoting genuine morality is spreading rapidly, and the doors everywhere are ajar. In thousands of cases they are at least half open, as it were. If the stable and righteous government of the English, and the influence of Christ through His missionary servants, male and female, continue, the evils of the zenana system will pass away in time."—Rev. J. P. Ashton (L. M. S.), Bhowanipore, Calcutta, India.

[2] In *The Spectator* of April 3, 1897, is an article on " Indian Doctors and the Plague," in which the following startling incident is given, illustrating in a dramatic form the intensity of Mohammedan and Hindu fanaticism regarding matters of this kind: " A Mussulman lady was attacked by the plague, and, as she might be a centre of infection, was ordered by the doctors to be removed to a hospital. Her husband protested violently, and finding the doctors resolute, first shot his wife dead, and then himself. Observe that he did not shoot the doctors. That would have been a mere act of revenge, having no effect on the protection of his home,

In view of this state of feeling it is apparent how impossible it would be for men to engage in any kind of zenana work. It is a department of service appointed by Providence to Christian women, and while it is true that Moham- A providential call to medan and Hindu women in the zenanas are not Christian womanhood. usually so unhappy as one would imagine, and are not generally begging for deliverance, yet the significance of a change in the zenana code, and the benefits which may be expected to accrue thereby to Eastern society, can hardly be overestimated. The whole system is not only a stronghold of ignorance and degradation; it is also an impenetrable screen for almost every possible kind of iniquity and cruelty. *The Times of India*, a leading journal of Bombay, although not in sympathy apparently with zenana missions, has no hesitation in condemning the zenana. " From a sociological point of view," it remarks, " it is plain that a system which perpetuates limitations already far too heavy in the East, imposed upon the normal development of half the race, and a corresponding class of sentiments which make rather for the lowering than the raising of the type in the other half, stands as condemned." [1]

The part which Christian missions have to play in the effort to mitigate this enforced seclusion of woman is to cultivate the spirit of manly and womanly virtue, to establish relations of purity, honor, and mutual confidence between the sexes, and to introduce wholesome simplicity, moral chivalry, and refined freedom into the home life of the East. This they have accomplished already in thousands of Christian communities, where a large measure of brightness and cheer has come into the social life of woman, without any undue demission of those formal restraints which, in view of the moral tone of Oriental society, are required for safety and self-respect. The very presence of Christian women, native as well as foreign, is a ministry to the higher nature of a hitherto inhibited womanhood, and suggests brighter and fairer possibilities of life outside the petty slavery of its present lot, without in any sense lessening the sacred halo of domestic virtue. In the zenanas, where life is so shrouded, dwarfed, and to a certain extent

whereas his object was to prevent what he deemed dishonour falling upon him and on his house. This may be called an extreme case, and the Mussulman may have been a man of violent temper; but so far as we know his coreligionists, they would all agree that he had done his duty, and would wish under the same circumstances, and supposing an armed revolt to be hopeless, to have grace enough to follow his example."

[1] Quoted in *The Christian Patriot* (Madras), February 14, 1895.

paralyzed both morally and intellectually, the sweet, womanly visitor with her message of Christian love and hope, and the suggestion of a better and freer life, becomes a symbol of another world of thought and custom, not only teaching lessons of religious truth, but illustrating by her own personality a nobler type of womanhood, exemplifying liberty without the loss of self-respect, and revealing a modesty which is in no sense bounded by lattice bars. Her refined womanliness and social dignity are recognized as entirely independent of the *purdah* and all that it signifies—a parable which it is not easy, as Indian society is constituted, for the inmates of a zenana to comprehend.[1]

It is difficult to name with confidence the person to whom belongs the credit of initiating zenana work as a missionary method, or to designate with certainty and precision the time **Who began Christian** and place of its inauguration. In "The Indian **effort in the zenanas?** Missionary Manual," by Dr. Murdoch (fourth edition, p. 471), we find the following statement: "The Rev. T. Smith, a colleague of Dr. Duff, first proposed, in 1840, a scheme for the home education of women of the upper classes; but at the time it met with no practical response. A beginning was first made by the Rev. J. and Mrs. Fordyce in 1855, through Miss Toogood, with the cordial coöperation of Mr. Smith. Soon afterwards the work was taken up by missionary ladies, Mrs. Sale and Mrs. Mullens.[2] It has

---

[1] " In Oriental lands, even more than in Western countries, fashion is omnipotent, and the power of social respectability is so potent that almost any unveiled woman in the East would gladly surrender her liberty if she could gain the social promotion which is implied in belonging to the zenana. True enough, the women who are subject to this system are always very glad to get a glimpse of the outdoor world, but only one in a hundred would accept the life of unveiled women if they had the opportunity. They would shrink with fear from such a proposal, as if it implied a surrender of moral character."—Thoburn, " The Christless Nations," p. 86.

[2] The late Mrs. John Sale died at Helensburgh, Scotland, February 8, 1898, at the advanced age of eighty. She went to India with her husband in 1849, under appointment as a missionary of the Baptist Missionary Society (English). In *The Zenana Missionary Herald*, the monthly publication of the Baptist Ladies' Association, we find the following information concerning her entrance upon zenana visitation: " It was in 1852, about three years after leaving England, that Mrs. Sale began to try to reach her Indian sisters in the villages about Barisal. In 1854 she obtained access to a native gentleman's house in Jessore, and from that time slowly but surely gained access to other houses. In 1858 she was a welcome visitor in many zenanas in Calcutta; but in 1861 came the summons to accompany her husband to England. To whom should her work be given? Few sympathised with her in it. It seemed so dangerous and questionable to many that they strongly opposed the idea of any good coming from it, and urged Mr. Sale not to allow his wife to engage in it. But the Lord was leading her, and provided some one to take up

Lady missionaries in the court of the Zenana Mission House, Peshawar, India.

Station Class at Sa-yong, Fuhkien, China.
(Miss Codrington in the second row.)

WOMAN'S MINISTRY TO WOMAN IN INDIA AND CHINA.
(C. E. Z. M. S.)

since extended to all parts of India." In "The Women of India," one of the "Papers on Indian Social Reform," also prepared by Dr. Murdoch, and published at Madras, we find the additional statement that "until 1861 nothing was done in the North-West Provinces, but the late Mrs. Winter, who had labored for four years as a zenana visitor in Bengal, soon afterwards commenced the work in Delhi" (p. 47). It is reported elsewhere that the Society for Promoting Female Education in the East was organized in 1834, in response to the appeals of Dr. David Abeel, who visited England at that time to plead the cause of female education in the East. This society was formed for the purpose of giving instruction to women in the zenanas of India and in their homes in China, and it is stated that one of its missionaries succeeded, in 1835, in gaining access to a zenana in Calcutta, thus becoming the first zenana missionary.[1] The Indian Female Normal School and Instruction Society was organized in 1852, largely through the influence of the late Dowager Lady Kinnaird, who may be regarded as its founder, and to the end of her life its patron and mainstay. Out of this effort sprang the Church of England Zenana Missionary Society and the Zenana Bible and Medical Mission. As the inspiring purpose in the founding of the Indian Female Normal School and Instruction Society was work in the zenanas, to it also, and to Lady Kinnaird, its founder, belongs a share of the honor of initiating the zenana campaign. In still another connection it is recorded that "to Mrs. Sale, the wife of the Rev. John Sale, for many years a missionary in the Backergunge District, and then in Calcutta, is due the honor of having turned the

the service she must lay down. Mrs. Mullens, of the London Missionary Society, gladly accepted the responsibility, and followed up the effort with vigour and wonderful success. Mrs. Sale came home and pleaded with great earnestness for ladies to take up this hitherto neglected work. One and another caught the glow of her enthusiasm. She was herself convinced that the Lord had opened a great and effectual door which none but women could enter, and where a stupendous work was waiting for Christian women to do."—Quoted in *The Zenana Missionary Herald* of the Baptist Ladies' Association (London), March, 1898, p. 117. See *ibid.*, April, 1898, pp. 135-138.

1 Article on "Progress among the Women of Bengal during the Reign of Queen Victoria," in *The Indian Evangelical Review*, October, 1897, p. 189. Cf. also "A Handbook of Foreign Missions," p. 209 (American ed., p. 179). Of the Society for Promoting Female Education it is stated: "Not long after its commencement [1834] four Hindu gentlemen actually consented to allow a lady to visit the secluded women of their houses, and teach not only needlework but reading from Christian school-books. This was the inauguration of zenana work. In 1842 they sent out the first agent for direct zenana work on a larger scale: Miss Burton was appointed to commence the work at Bombay."—"Woman in Missions," pp. 76, 77.

first sod and entered the first Hindu zenana with the message of salvation. Very soon after this Mrs. C. B. Lewis conceived the idea of
organizing a zenana mission."[1] This resulted in the formation of the
Baptist Zenana Missionary Society in 1867. In the Centenary Volume
of the Baptist Missionary Society of London we read that "Mrs. Sale's
first entrance into the zenanas in 1856 [1854?] was a great emancipation act" (p. 87). In *The Missionary Review of the World* (May, 1895,
p. 371) it is declared that the first zenana teaching ever attempted in
the East was by missionary women, in 1851, among the thirty wives and
royal sisters of the King of Siam. Still another statement indicates
that to the womanly insight of a native lady of the Christian community of Madras belongs the credit of first introducing in Southern India
the method now known as zenana work. Mrs. Anna Satthianadhan
as early as 1863 began her life of Christian service in Madras, and soon
after commenced to visit the homes of her Hindu pupils.[2]

Although we may not be able to determine with absolute assurance
what may be properly regarded as the original movement towards
zenana work, yet this much is certain, that it was
under the pressure of Christian missionary zeal
that the idea came into being and in various
directions was practically put in operation. That
credit is due to the Rev. Dr. Thomas Smith and the Rev. and Mrs.
John Fordyce, Free Church of Scotland missionaries in Calcutta, for
very early proposals in advocacy of such a work, and among the very
earliest practical efforts to establish it in Indian zenanas, is sufficiently
clear. The Rev. E. Storrow, who went to Calcutta as an agent of the
London Missionary Society in 1848, has just published what may be
regarded as authoritative information bearing upon the subject in his
volume entitled "Our Indian Sisters." He states that in 1840 the
young missionary Thomas Smith advocated publicly the plan of Chris-

Zenana missions the outcome of a Christian missionary impulse.

---

[1] Paper by Mrs. Robinson upon the history of the Baptist Zenana Mission in
Bengal, printed in *The Zenana Missionary Herald* of the Baptist Ladies' Association,
September, 1897, pp. 487-491.

[2] " In 1863 she accompanied her husband to Madras, and soon found her voca-
tion in life. The honour of inaugurating that important branch of Christian effort
known as zenana teaching belongs to Mrs. Satthianadhan. The work grew out of
a little school she had for Hindu girls in her own house. It was indeed very trying
at first; but her patience, enthusiasm, and deep longing to make known to her
Hindu sisters the Gospel message gave her success, and after six years' hard labour
the Church Missionary Society and the Church of England Zenana Missionary
Society took up the work she had commenced, but placed her in sole charge of
it."—Satthianadhan, " Sketches of Indian Christians," p. 41.

tian ladies forming classes for instruction in the zenanas, and that this proposal was acted upon for the first time through the efforts of the Rev. and Mrs. John Fordyce, in 1855, Miss Toogood being the first British teacher. It is acknowledged, however, that four English ladies, Mrs. Tracey, Miss Bird, Mrs. Sale, and Mrs. Mullens, had given instruction previous to this date in some of the zenanas. Mr. Storrow's conclusion is stated as follows: "But the honor of erecting zenana teaching into a system, and of popularizing it by public advocacy and efficient practical organization, belongs to Mr. Fordyce and Dr. Thomas Smith."[1]

The Rev. C. Silvester Horne, in "The Story of the London Missionary Society," probably experienced the same difficulty as has the author in determining to whom should be assigned the precedence in the matter of zenana missions. He remarks: "Where many noble workers were contemporaneous, it would be invidious to select any single one as the absolute first to occupy the field, but certainly Mrs. Mullens (L. M. S.) was among the very earliest in drawing attention to the opportunity of visiting Hindu ladies in zenanas." The date which he assigns for her formal entrance upon the work was after her return to India (in 1860) from a visit to England. This missionary method has now been adopted by even Hindus and Mohammedans, and education in the zenanas has been gradually put into practice by enlightened natives. The result of all this will appear more and more, and its magnificent power in the making of a new India cannot be overestimated.[2]

It is recognized that education conducted in the zenanas is a very expensive system, and is serviceable rather as a temporary makeshift until the cause of female instruction shall command more fully the support of public opinion. The British Government has assisted by some "grants in aid" to missionary and other agencies engaged in this work of home training. Mr. H. B. Grigg, who was for many years Direc-

---

[1] Storrow, "Our Indian Sisters" (American ed., "Our Sisters in India"), p. 215. Cf. also *The Free Church of Scotland Monthly*, October, 1898, p. 244.

[2] "The marvellous opening up of Hindu and Mohammedan homes to our zenana missionaries and their native assistants, the hundreds who are daily hanging upon their lips for instruction, and the close and tender ties of friendship that are being formed, assuredly herald the coming of Christ. Of all the lines of preparation we have been considering, none more certainly speaks of divine foreknowledge and love than this. None is more pregnant with hope. None more certainly foretells the speedy conquest of India for Christ."—Article by the Rev. Francis Ashcroft, in *The Missionary Record*, July, 1894, p. 191. Interesting articles on the progress of zenana missions may be found in *The Gospel in all Lands*, September, 1895, pp. 436–438, and in *The Baptist Missionary Review* (Madras), April, 1896, pp. 132–139.

tor of Public Instruction in the Madras Presidency, states in one of his reports: " This method of extending education among women is no doubt at present proportionately very expensive. . . . The system is, to my mind, in itself admirably suited to the conditions and circumstances of the country, and calculated to be of immense help to the progress of Indian women."[1]   Education pure and simple is, however, but a small part of the benefit which has come to Indian women through zenana visitation.   The touch of sympathy has quickened the higher life.   New subjects of thought and fresh themes of conversation have been introduced.   Nobler ideals have been stimulated, and, above all, a knowledge of Christ and His power to bless the soul has been imparted to multitudes of Indian women.   A promising movement has been started even among Hindus, having in view the home education of women, and so far as missionary work in the zenanas is concerned, we have gathered as yet but the first-fruits.   The influence of this movement is yet to be felt among the 140,000,000 women of British India and the Native States, and future homes of India are to be brighter and purer through this ministry of Christian womanhood behind otherwise sealed and guarded doors.

In Mohammedan lands still under the sway of strict Islamic traditions only the woman missionary can gain access to the harem.   It will be a long and somewhat discouraging process to produce any change of sentiment in Moslem society and bring about a relaxation of its rigorous customs.   Here and there we read of quiet work in Mohammedan communities on the part of missionary women seeking to teach the truth to ignorant minds, but the day of wide opportunity is not yet.   In Egypt the United Presbyterian and Church of England Missions are availing themselves of the special privileges which the present political status affords.

The relaxation of the zenana system must come gradually.

In China and Korea seclusion is customary, but it is not so universal, or carried to such a fanatical extreme, as is the case in Hindu zenanas or Moslem harems.   There is, however, the same impracticability of access, except through women visitors, native and foreign.   The Bible-women in China render valuable service.   Such schools for their training as the one formerly conducted by Miss Adele Fielde at Swatow, and many others, have a distinct sphere of usefulness, the importance of which can hardly be overstated.   Among the higher classes of China the seclusion to which women are subjected is sometimes little better than imprisonment.   A missionary worker of the Church of Eng-

---

[1] Satthianadhan, " History of Education in the Madras Presidency," p. 226.

land Zenana Missionary Society, late at Foochow, reports a visit to the home of a mandarin where the ladies had not been outside the door for six months.[1] Miss F. M. Williams, in her recent volume, writes of visiting houses where there are " girls over twelve years of age who may not go out of their homes until they are married." [2] Missions are doing much to mitigate the severity of these restrictions among the middle classes, and to some extent in higher circles. Not the least valuable service they render is in preparing the way for a gradual change of custom, without at the same time imperilling the moral safeguards of social intercourse.

7. IMPROVING THE CONDITION OF DOMESTIC LIFE AND FAMILY TRAINING.—That Christian missions are moulding the home life of heathen lands after the pattern of a finer ideal and a nobler culture is beyond dispute. Wherever Christian homes are established parental duty and responsibility become sacred in a new and hallowed sense; purer desires are kindled for the moral welfare of children; larger hopes are cherished in the family horoscope; special watchfulness characterizes domestic training; parental pride and effort centre about a sweeter and finer type of character, and a higher mission in life is sought for the children of the household. The domestic intercourse of all members of the family circle has a kinder and lovelier tone; there is a refined reticence about matters which were once paraded with shameless vulgarity; there are new standards of modesty; much that was unseemly and coarse has vanished as if it knew that it was no longer welcome. Christianity in its own marvelous way everywhere differentiates the Christian from the heathen home. In a statement of the nature, work, and aims of Protestant missions in China, laid before the Tsung-li Yamen in 1895 by American missionaries, to be presented to the Emperor as a summary of missionary principles,[3] a very clear and explicit paragraph deals with filial piety in the Christian sense. Emphasis is given to the Fifth Commandment, and the teachings of Christ and the Apostles on the duty of children to parents and of parents to children are commented upon with discernment and precision. The statement is typical of the attitude of missions to home life throughout the world, and there is no lack of evidence that Christian-

The differentiation of the Christian from the heathen home.

[1] *India's Women*, June, 1894, p. 257.
[2] Williams, " A New Thing," p. 55.
[3] *The Chinese Recorder*, February, 1896, pp. 67, 68.

ized homes in mission fields are the wonder and delight even of otherwise unresponsive heathen.[1]

Beautiful and impressive signs of the coming of Christ into heathen environments are often observable, but there is none more striking than this new creation of the Christian family. Some of these sanctified homes which missions have established amid surroundings of moral and physical degradation are among the very brightest and most unique trophies of the light and healing of the Gospel to be found upon the face of the earth. It is a long step towards social regeneration when the family becomes a religious institution—sacred in its privileges and opportunities—and is made instrumental in the upbuilding of Christ's kingdom among men. Heathenism has always claimed the right to exercise its unlovely absolutism in the hallowed realm of family experience.[2] Christianity has ever placed strict limits to the power of authority in the family, and has declared with the emphasis of a mighty imperative that the law of love rules and that a high standard of parental as well as filial obligation must prevail. On the other hand, it has not failed to teach the sacred duty of wise and loving government, a much-needed lesson, within as well as without the bounds of Christendom.

Christian missions have introduced, in the first instance, the concrete example of home life as exhibited in the missionary family. "The first thing the Protestant missionary does among the heathen,"

---

1 " Christianity has given this city some beautiful homes. First of all, it has created a charming domestic life, affection between husband and wife, the Christian training of children, a family circle mutually loving and trusting each other. Neatness and order are maintained in the house, while the clothing and the person are kept clean. Such homes are an object-lesson in this great city, and are not without considerable influence. The heathen do not have such homes."—Rev. Chauncey Goodrich, D.D. (A. B. C. F. M.), Tungcho, China.

" The difference between Christians and non-Christians in conjugal and family faithfulness is well known all over the country."—Rev. J. B. Porter (P. B. F. M. N.), Kyoto, Japan.

" In many a village the Protestant houses might be pointed out by a stranger, because of the flower in the window, the tidily kept children, or the decent approach; and not unfrequently the first outward and visible sign of a man or woman's interest in evangelical truth is the cleanlier person, the more careful attire, or the improved style of living in the home."—Rev. Robert Thomson (A. B. C. F. M.), Constantinople, Turkey.

2 Storrs, " The Divine Origin of Christianity," Lecture V.; Schmidt, " The Social Results of Early Christianity," pp. 188–208; Weir, " Christianity in Civilization," pp. 47–62; *The Biblical World*, December, 1896, p. 479.

CHRISTIAN FAMILIES IN CHINA AND SYRIA

wrote the late Dr. E. A. Lawrence, "is to establish a home. He approaches them not as a priest, not simply as a man, but as the head of a family, presenting Christianity quite as much in its social as in its individual character- The missionary's home istics. This Christian home is to be the transform- an object-lesson. ing centre of a new community. Into the midst of pagan masses, where society is coagulated rather than organized, where homes are degraded by parental tyranny, marital multiplicity, and female bondage, he brings the leaven of a redeemed family, which is to be the nucleus of a redeemed society. . . . This new institution, with its monogamy, its equality of man and woman, its sympathy between child and parent, its coöperative spirit of industry, its intelligence, its recreation, its worship, is at once a new revelation and a striking object-lesson of the meaning and possibility of family life."[1] In the second place, missions have established in the minds of natives a new conception of home, as illustrated in the more refined life and habits of native Christian families.[2]

[1] Lawrence, "Modern Missions in the East," pp. 196, 197.

"The missionary and his family have a wonderful influence for the elevation of domestic life among the natives. They see how he respects his wife and treats his children. They are also taught that woman is not inferior to man as an intellectual and responsible being, and learn to exercise patience and protect her as the weaker vessel. This change is seen first in Christian families who are more intimately associated with the missionaries and come under the influence of Bible teaching. But it is fast extending to those heathen families who are more directly in contact with missionaries and native Christians. I know many Hindu families in which the wives are treated very differently since the men have become acquainted with the missionaries. A feather will show whence the wind blows."—Rev. Robert Evans (W. C. M. M. S.), Mawphlang, Shillong, Assam.

[2] "We have now in our Christian communities many comfortable homes, where children are cared for and educated, all of whom would have suffered beyond description if their fathers had not been rescued from the opium habit."—Rev. Frederick Galpin (U. M. F. M. S.), Ningpo, China.

"Native Christians are strongly impressed with the desirability of marrying only ' in the Lord.' ;The happy homes of Christians affect the heathen very favorably. Last week a man came to a friend of mine, bringing his idol, the ' God of Riches,' which he presented to him, saying: ' We never have any peace in our house. I am told if I give up idols and believe on Jesus my home will become a little heaven on earth. Here is my idol.' The cleanliness, sanitary improvements, and decent arrangements for sleeping (instead of the usual indecencies) impress the heathen favorably."—Rev. Joseph S. Adams (A. B. C. F. M.), Hankow, China.

Cf. article in *The Church Missionary Intelligencer*, November, 1893, on "Missions or Science, the Maker of India's Homes?" by the Rev. G. Ensor.

It requires only a glance at the old-time features of domestic life in different lands to realize how great this change is.   The Rev. Dr.

The old *versus* the new domesticity in Turkey.

Charles C. Tracy, in a suggestive volume on the influence of missions in Asia Minor, has a chapter entitled " The Gospel in the Family," in which a brief description is given of family life as it existed before the advent of the missionary in the Turkish Empire.   " We have been told," he writes, " with the utmost frankness by men of the older type that they began to beat their wives as soon as they were married, supposing it necessary to do so in order to bring them into proper subjection; that they did it at the outset from principle, as something which must be done, or unhappy results would follow." [1]   Another missionary in Asia Minor, in a letter to the author, dwells at some length upon the blighting results of the earlier family life in that mission field. He regards the true home as unknown until the advent of Christian missions.   In its place was the one room, often filthy and unwholesome, in which the whole family herded, the absolute and irresponsible sovereignty of the head of the family, with its unreasonable caprice and self-assertion, marriage at an unseemly age of immaturity, and artificial standards of family intercourse almost incredible in their stupidity and unnaturalness.   " For a mother," he writes, " to show any special fondness for her babe in the presence of others would be sure to expose the child to the terrors of the evil eye; for a husband and wife on meeting after a long absence to show any sign of recognition or to exchange even a word while in the presence of others would be the height of immodesty; for them to correspond while absent from one another even for a year would be improper, or at least would be smiled at as a sort of sentimentality; if any letters are exchanged upon important business they should be written by a child or a neighbor.   While these and similar notions still hold sway over the great majority, yet there is a very considerable class of people who have been sufficiently influenced by enlightened and evangelical views to perceive their folly and in many cases completely to emancipate themselves from such thraldom." [2]

[1] Tracy, " Talks on the Veranda in a Far-Away Land," p. 131.

[2] Similar statements from those entirely familiar with home life in Asiatic Turkey may be quoted:

" There was no real family life—no home life—in any part of Asia Minor before the Gospel came.   That has brought with it the home,—the true Christian home,— and the enlightenment which has come from Christian schools and the customs which Christianity always carries with it."—Rev. J. L. Barton, D.D. (A. B. C. F. M.), formerly missionary in Asiatic Turkey.

" Great progress has been made in improving the general condition of women

Internal sweetening of domestic life has been attended also by external reconstruction of the houses of the people. " Formerly these homes," writes the Rev. C. Frank Gates, D.D., of Harpoot, Turkey, "were of a very low type. In the village of Midyat fifteen years ago there was scarcely a house of more than one story, and they were all without windows and chimneys. The hole in the roof by which the smoke was supposed to find exit was never directly over the fire, lest some enemy should come upon the roof and throw down gunpowder; the door never opened directly into the room in which the family lived, but was guarded by grain-bins and the like, lest some foe should shoot them down before their own fire. The whole region was in a state of constant warfare, one family or tribe against another. One of the first effects of missions in that region was to oppose and check this spirit of barbarism and strife. The village of Midyat has been largely renovated. There are now many houses of stone, two stories high, furnished with stoves, chairs, clocks, and other furniture, and having windows of glass. As the houses have improved, family life has been elevated to a higher plane."

Some of the strange amenities of heathen family life in India are indicated by the following quotation from a native journal forwarded to the author by the Rev. R. McCheyne Paterson, B.D., Gujrat, Punjab : " At home the boy is a great pet of his parents, who allow him unlimited indulgence, irrespective of good or evil, and to expect any moral training here is simply an incongruity. If the father happens to abuse the boy, the latter is at liberty to retaliate in the vilest language imaginable; and this, instead of being discouraged, is regarded as a source of pleasure by his parents. The mother delights to hear her boy use abusive language, because it sounds sweet and charming; while the father thanks his particular god for his mercy in having brought the little hero safe to the age when he is able to talk obscenely. The grandmother cracks her fingers as a token of Oriental affection, and the boy is happy. A child from the age of two is taught to abuse

among all classes of the people; they have become better educated, and with this have been better treated by their husbands and male friends, being released to a very marked extent from abuse in the matter of heavy outdoor work and corporal punishment. I remember a wealthy Armenian in Kessab who once told me that he was very anxious to join the Protestant community, but he felt that his wife needed physical punishment pretty frequently, and he said he knew that the sentiment in the Protestant Church was so strong against any such treatment that he would be turned out of the Church very promptly at the first offense."—Harris Graham, M.D., of Beirut, Syria. Dr. Graham was formerly a missionary in the Central Turkey Mission of the A. B. C. F. M.

every member of the family, for it brings good luck into the house, and by the time he aspires to the age of ten he has at his command the whole standard volume of family vituperation."

In Japan the typical domestic life of the older régime, while it is far removed from barbarism, has nevertheless some deplorable signs of

Deplorable features of native homes in many mission fields.

degradation. Chief among them may be named the parental absolutism, which is abused in so many instances by the forcing of daughters or sisters to enter upon a life of shame. While filial fidelity is much emphasized and sometimes beautifully illustrated, the equally binding obligations of parents are grievously misunderstood and misused.[1] In China the family government of heathen homes is almost totally lacking in wise and conscientious discipline and training of the young. "It is contrary to their theories to restrain or govern little children, and they are permitted to follow their own sweet will unless they chance to do something which rouses the anger of the parents, in which case they revile them, strike them on the head, or beat them unmercifully. The penalty is never proportioned to the real gravity of the offense, but a mistake, an accident, a sin of ignorance, is quite likely to be visited with severe chastisement, while lying, reviling, and bursts of angry passion will often only call forth a smile which will encourage their repetition. To the Chinese mind the punishment of a child, except as one is impelled to it by anger, seems an impossibility."[2]

A missionary in Africa writes, in a letter to the *Journal des Missions Évangéliques*, concerning the family life of the Pahouins, "whose children are old and corrupt before they are grown up, whose hopeless, joyless lives are gloomier and darker than the huts of bark in which they live, but at the breath of Christian love these little ones, whom Jesus cares for, grow young again, become playful, and begin to laugh with the good, clear, healthy laughter of our children."[3]

---

1 *The Japan Evangelist*, February, 1896, p. 135.
2 Miss J. E. Chapin (A. B. C. F. M.), Peking, in *Woman's Work in the Far East*, May, 1895, p. 9.
3 *The Chronicle*, October, 1895, p. 271.
Statements from other mission fields are of a similar tenor: "Nothing that I see in the social life about us here is more painful to me than the way in which children are brought up. They drink in falsehood and all forms of deception with their mother's milk. Cruel and undeserved punishment is attended with a fondling love so tender that it cannot bear to hear the child cry, until all perception of the deserts of right and wrong conduct is obliterated from the child's mind, and the daily life is a contest between children and parents, as to which shall outwit the other. Obedience is an unknown virtue, and the worst elements in the child's na-

It is safe to say that as the result of Christian missions great and blessed changes are apparent in thousands of homes. In every community where they have been planted we can enter native Christian families where the sweet cadence of domestic intercourse is full of gentleness and mellow kindliness. Dr. Tracy, in his volume before mentioned, has given a pleasing sketch of one of these new homes which has sprung into being under mission influence in Asia Minor. "Knocking at the gate," he writes, "we are admitted into a neat court by a bright little boy, and are met at the door of the house by a smiling young woman. We are ushered into a pretty little parlor and seated. This young woman is a wife at the head of the house, and the chosen companion of her husband by her own free consent. She comes and gives us a hearty greeting, with a warm grasp of the hand. There is no veil on her face, no abject position or expression. Her tongue is free, her face is shining, her heart is glad. Here are two or three bright children already longing for school. The mother is a lady. She speaks intelligently upon various subjects. She is training her little ones in the fear and love of God, and teaching them to think and understand. She tells them stories from the Bible, interests them in the best things, watches the words of their mouths, keeps them away from the bad company always met with in the street. She teaches them truthfulness; she never frightens them with hobgoblin stories to secure obedience, as the custom is; she is careful to tell them no lies of any kind. She asks to be excused a moment or two, that she may call her husband from the garden; he will be so glad to see us. While she is absent, notice the contents of the room. See a neat

A new type of domestic life in the Turkish Empire.

ture have almost unrestrained freedom."—Rev. P. H. Moore (A. B. M. U.), Nowgong, Assam.

"In Chile there is wanting the Christian home. Parents love their children; children love each other, but they do as they please, and early form habits of drinking, gambling, and immorality."—Rev. J. M. Allis (P. B. F. M. N.), Santiago, Chile.

"There is no family life in these heathen communities. The children in early life live with their mothers, and, like them, belong to no caste. When the males grow older they mix with the men, and children of both sexes hear the filthy conversation of the grown-up people, nothing being too immoral to be concealed from them. No love is lost between parents and children, and the latter disobey their parents when young and neglect them when grown up. Brought up amid immorality in their purely heathen state, they become prepared for immoral acts. Before they came under Christian influence, when the youth of both sexes met, the first and perhaps only subject of conversation was immorality. This was almost, if not altogether, universal."—Rev. William Gunn, M.D. (F. C. S.), Futuna, New Hebrides.

center-table with a pretty cover of crochet-work, made by her own hand. On it a nice lamp is placed, a Bible, and a weekly news-paper. On the wall is a little bookcase. We get a most hearty greeting from the husband; the little child three years old goes all around and kisses our hands. The lady prepares delicious coffee, which she serves, smiling and chatting gayly. Husband and wife are happy in their own home, managing their house and their children with no interference. Love and good-will and wisdom blossom out here. What has made the difference? The Gospel, and nothing else. This lady was educated in the seminary for girls. There she learned to love the Lord; there she acquired both discipline and useful knowledge. She was taught what life is for, and how to use it. She was trained in the knowledge of the best things. She and her husband have been instructed in sound principles. Here you observe the result."

Another missionary from the far interior of Turkey writes: "It is a very conspicuous fact that where the Gospel has gained an entrance into a house or village, 'home' means much more than it did. There is a more intelligent outlook upon the world at large. The whole appearance of the house and family shows more cleanliness and neatness. During a recent visitation of the cholera some five hundred died in this city, but among them there was not a single Protestant, an exemption which was noted also in Mardin. This was very plainly due to the greater cleanliness in their homes and in their mode of living."[1] The following attractive picture is from the letter of another correspondent in the Turkish Empire: "If there is one sweet spot on earth on which the angels love to gaze, it is a truly Christian home. Here and there among the multitudes of the inhabitants of this land, such a spot is now found. Gentle manners and tender love, morning and evening family worship, kindly counsel, warning and instruction, tidiness and thrift, intelligence and education, and over all and through all the spirit of humble, joyful Christian sincerity. Next to the actual salvation of individual souls, these are the results that most rejoice the heart of the true missionary, and testify to the value of his work."[2]

Bishop Caldwell, of India, once remarked, after a tour in Tinnevelly: "In passing from village to village you can tell without asking a question which village is Christian and which is heathen." Of the

---

[1] Rev. John A. Ainslie (P. B. F. M. N.), Mosul, Turkey.

[2] Rev. Edward Riggs (A. B. C. F. M.), Marsovan, Turkey. Cf. also the account of exercises at the dedication of the Memorial Column in Beirut, in commemoration of the opening of the first school for girls in Syria. *The Church at Home and Abroad*, October, 1894, pp. 301, 303.

Group of pupils in the Beirut Female Seminary.

THE MAKING OF BETTER HOMES IN SYRIA.

(P. B. F. M. N.)

late Rev. David Mohun, one of the native pastors in the employ of the Church Missionary Society, an associate writes that among his prominent characteristics was " the fatherly way in which he brought up his children and gave them the best education possible for a poor pastor, thus exemplifying a true type of Christian family life." At the Centenary of the London Missionary Society, in 1895, the Rev. E. Lewis, of Bellary, gave a very forcible description of the influence of the Gospel in one of the native families in India, telling of the confession of a mother who contrasted the home of her Christian son with that of another who was a fakir, and whom she had formerly adored, while almost hating her converted son. She remarked: " My Christian son's home is heaven, and I would never wish to see a better heaven; my fakir son's home is a dunghill, yea, hell itself." [1]

The making of better homes in India, Japan, and China.

A missionary remarks: " Christianity has given to Japan an ideal for domestic life such as never had been known in this land before—a Christian home." " Many who take no other interest in Christianity," states the Rev. T. T. Alexander, D.D., of Tokyo, "are deeply impressed with the higher and happier tone of family life among our converts, so much so that the words ' Christian home' have come to be understood and used by many who do not know English, as expressing the ideal household." " There is not a child in Japan," declares the Rev. D. C. Greene, D.D., " who does not live a markedly different life from that of the children of thirty years ago. The whole atmosphere which he breathes is permeated by the new thought of the value of the individual." [2] The Rev. J. G. Fagg, of Amoy, China, writes that " infanticide is not practised by Christians; the husband treats his wife kindly, and brothers their sisters, while the conduct of one towards another in a Chinese Christian home is something that amazes the heathen."

In the dismal social wastes of Africa, amid the abominations of native degradation, a Christian home was unknown until Christianity entered the native huts and kraals. Now we may read even of royal homes where love reigns. It is said of Khama that " he has abolished *bogadi*, or the purchase of wives by cattle, and introduced the law of marriage by free choice, at an age when young men and young women are capable of forming such an attachment intelligently." In his capital " there are scores of native homes where the

Transformed huts and kraals among savage races.

---

[1] *The Chronicle*, June, 1895, p. 166.
[2] Pettee, " A Chapter of Mission History in Modern Japan," p. 188.

children are brought up to honor Christ." [1]   In Tembuland there are Young Women's Christian Associations, in which the rule is that "when a girl belonging to the Association is married she carries a Bible in her hand into the church." [2]   Let us hope that this is typical of the influence of Scriptural principles in after life.   "The change of moral atmosphere in the Christian as compared with the heathen home will be of incalculable benefit to the children of the next generation." [3] The Rev. Charles D. Helm, of Matabeleland, writes, in the same strain, that "Christian home life is a vast improvement."   Mr. Andrew Smith, formerly a Free Church of Scotland missionary in Cape Colony, in a series of papers on native social questions, has devoted one to the advocacy of the upright and sufficiently ventilated house for native homes, in place of the ordinary hut.   "The Kaffir community," he writes, "should be impressed with the idea that their elevation as a race is impossible until they build proper houses, and that there is a deep and impassable gulf between themselves and Europeans as long as they live in huts." [4]

In the South Pacific Islands it is the plan of the Malua Training Institution, at Upolu, Samoa, to receive married students and teach them how to make homes after the Christian pattern.   The Rev. J. E. Newell reports the results as revealed in the lives of its graduates: "Those who have settled as missionaries in the Samoan out-stations or in New Guinea have in all cases exemplified these ideals in their own

---

[1] Hepburn, "Twenty Years in Khama's Country," pp. 122, 284.
[2] *The Christian Express*, March, 1897, p. 41.
[3] Rev. Robert Laws, M.D., D.D. (F. C. S.), Kondowi, Livingstonia, British Central Africa.
[4] "Short Papers Chiefly on South African Subjects," p. 39.
A South African missionary also writes: "We not infrequently see even the heathen native building a ' square, upright house ' instead of the ' oval beehive hut.' These square houses are not generally of brick, it is true, but of hard wood, upright poles, or posts, set two feet into the ground, running up from eight to nine feet above-ground, then filled in with a kind of ' basketwork,' and plastered with ' ant-heap and sand, mixed.'   This is durable and forms a good smooth surface, and when the house, with its windows and doors and two or three rooms, is whitewashed, it makes, with its ant-heap floor, hard-polished by rubbing down, a very comfortable dwelling, better than the peasantry of Ireland and Europe often have.   This is the general style of house in this station, but here and there we see brick houses, well furnished; all have tables and chairs, and usually bedsteads of some sort.   Fifty years ago the family lay on the floor, with the fireplace in the middle of the hut, and the feet of the sleepers pointing to this fireplace, while, often occupying a part of the circle, tied up next the wall, were a number of cattle."—The late Rev. H. M. Bridgman (A. B. C. F. M.), Natal, South Africa.

homes, and have thus introduced a beneficial change in the islands where they have gone." The contrast between the Christian and heathen homes, as, for example, in Arorae, one of the Gilbert Islands, is as great as that between light and darkness. In the West Indies, especially Jamaica, the testimony of missionaries as to the improvement in home life and the training of children is similar. The Rev. Egerton R. Young, writing of "Life among the Red Men of America," tells of an incident which illustrates how Christianity makes tender the hearts of Indian sons.[1] At Lesser Slave Lake, Athabasca, Canada, the Church Missionary Society has a "Children's Home" conducted by the Rev. and Mrs. G. Holmes. "A Beaver Indian woman walked a hundred miles with a baby in her arms, in order to commit her two children to Mr. and Mrs. Holmes, having heard that they 'loved children and taught them to live good lives,' and though she 'knew her heart would be sore when she left them,' she 'determined to come at any cost.' Mr. Holmes says of the importance of this and similar institutions : ' The more I see into the home life of the Indians, the more I am convinced that our homes are the only means of saving the children. The whole atmosphere of the camp is polluted with immorality, and, humanly speaking, it is impossible for any child to grow up pure in heart or mind under such influences.' " [2]

The Oriental conception of family life, although sadly marred in practice, has still much of the simplicity and clinging affection of the patriarchal system. If the havoc and ruin which the gross sins of heathenism have wrought can be repaired, and the power of Christian love, with refined instincts and customs, be introduced, the home life of the East will become most beautiful. No people in the world can make better and happier homes than the representatives of these

The possibilities of a beautiful home life in the Orient.

---

[1] " But look, the chapel doors are thrown open. Ah! there's a sight that brings a lump to my throat and tears to my eyes. Two great Indians, men twenty-eight or thirty years of age, with their hands have made a chair, and over their hands and shoulders there was a blanket thrown, and seated on that chair, with her arms around their stalwart necks, the poor old invalid mother is being carried to the house of God by her own sons. Another brother goes ahead down the aisle. We have no backs to our plain seats, so he folds up a blanket very nicely and puts it down as a soft cushion, and mother is seated upon it, and one of the big fellows sits down beside her and puts his strong arm around her, and she lays her head against his manly breast. Ah! there comes a dimness in my eyes as I see that, and I thank God for the transformation. The mother burned to death is paganism ; the mother carried by her sons to the house of God is Christianity."

[2] "Annual Report of the Church Missionary Society, 1896," p. 397.

old civilizations of the Orient, provided Christianity has its rightful influence. If the results achieved seem as yet meagre and fragmentary, it should be remembered that Christianity in its attempt to reconstruct the family in non-Christian lands is dealing with a thoroughly disorganized institution, in most instances a pulverized moral ruin which cannot be put into form again except by patient preparation and infinite effort. Then, again, let us remind ourselves that only of late, even in Christendom, under the stimulus of sociological study, has there been any proper appreciation, from a scientific point of view, of the fundamental value and immense capabilities of the family as a social factor and dynamic force. Yet how clearly an intelligent Christian woman of India discovers the value of proper family nurture may be seen in the writings of Krupabai Satthianadhan, who published a little essay on the "Home Training of Children," so full of practical wisdom and Christian tenderness that it would be profitable reading even in the best of homes.[1]   Much of a similar tone can be found in the writings of Japanese and Chinese converts.   The Orient under the culture of Christianity will some day be a paradise of homes.

8. RENDERING AID AND PROTECTION TO CHILDREN.—Closely allied with the moral training of children is the problem of their aid and protection.   In a brutish environment they are surrounded by many perils arising from the ignorance and cruelty of parents or the heartlessness of others who may have authority over them, and they are liable to be without adequate relief in the sufferings incidental to sickness, accident, neglect, and the distress which comes with public calamities like famine and plague.   In some countries they are exposed to the awful sufferings occasioned by the slave-trade.   If regulative legislation concerning employment, and even societies [2] established for

The perils of childhood in the realms of barbarism.

---

[1] "Miscellaneous Writings," pp. 9–15.

[2] It should be noted that the system of protective legislation which has been called the " Children's Charter " is a comparatively recent aspect of civilization.   It has been said that " every statute upon the Statute-Book for the protection of the helpless subjects of the Crown has been passed during the reign of Queen Victoria." The same writer remarks : " When the Queen ascended the throne, the great Juggernaut Car of unscrupulous commercialism, private greed, and domestic inhumanity rolled upon its way, with none to hinder." The Victorian era has placed the State in an entirely new attitude towards children.   Mr. W. Clarke Hall has summarized this remedial legislation under three heads : " (1) The Employer and the Child, which treats of the various acts for ameliorating the lot of children engaged in fac-

the aid, protection, and oversight of children, are needed in civilized lands,[1] how much more are remedial measures necessary in the irresponsible realms of barbarism! The whole subject of childhood, its mysteries, its possibilities, its perils, its opportunities, and the duties it imposes, seems to have stimulated a distinct phase of scientific investigation and philanthropic effort. A " Congress of Child-Study " has taken its place among the numerous conventions of our times.

The scandals of ancient heathenism as revealed in its attitude towards child life are well known. The unlimited authority of parents, the exposure, abandonment, and sale of children, the atrocious cruelties and mutilations incident to the slave-trade, need not be dwelt upon. The same heartless crimes prevail to a notorious extent throughout heathendom even at the present day. The dread advent of famine almost everywhere in Asia and Africa dooms thousands of children to neglect and suffering, while in some instances it leads to their sale to shameless panderers to lust. Slave raids and slavery itself inevitably bring heartrending sorrows and sufferings to the young. At the convention of the Indian National Woman's Christian Temperance Union held at Poona in 1896, it was declared that India was greatly in need of a " Society for the Prevention of Cruelty to Children," and it was eventually decided to make this a department of the work of the W. C. T. U. in India.[2] In Calcutta an independent organization for this purpose was formed in 1898, under the title of " The Society for the Protection of Children in India" (S. P. C. I.). Mr. Justice Pratt was elected President, and the formation of branch societies and committees was encouraged.[3] Hindu mothers, in their ignorance and

The crimes of ancient heathenism in its treatment of children still perpetrated in some parts of Asia and Africa.

---

tories, mines, brick-fields, agricultural gangs, on canals, and as chimney-sweepers, etc.; (2) the State and the Child, which embraces the humanised corrective systems of reformatories, industrial schools, and courts of summary jurisdiction; and (3) the Parent and the Child, which shows the efforts which have been made to lessen parental misrule and neglect." Cf. Hall, "The Queen's Reign for Children."

[1] " The New York Society for the Prevention of Cruelty to Children has during twenty-two years received and investigated 102,501 complaints, involving more than 307,503 children; obtained 36,981 convictions, and rescued 56,160 children from vice, from suffering, and from destitution. Its reception-rooms during the past fifteen years of their establishment have sheltered, clothed, and fed 24,932 children, and furnished 233,370 substantial meals. Day and night, in summer and in winter, its doors are never closed. No child has ever been turned away without temporary shelter. Two hundred and fifteen similar societies with a like object have been organized throughout the United States, and eighty-one others in foreign lands."

[2] *The Sentinel,* February, 1897, p. 23.   [3] *Ibid.,* October, 1898, p. 134.

thoughtlessness, are in the habit of terrifying childish hearts by alarming falsehoods concerning demons, hobgoblins, and malignant monsters. Upon this subject an Indian woman writes: " How many devils are summoned up, what forms are given them, and what grisly monsters are made to lie in the dark all night, ready to swallow or harm the poor innocent little one! All this a Hindu child alone knows and can tell. Fear, a kind of dread of the unknown and unseen, takes possession of the child." [1] The tales of cruelty to childhood in heathen lands are harrowing, and sometimes almost incredible. It is a cause for gratitude that natural affection and instinctive love of children are, as a rule, so prevalent among many Oriental races, and exercise such a mighty restraint in the case of thousands of dependent infants.

What Christianity has done in general for children is one of the brightest chapters in its social history. " If no other change," writes Dr. Storrs, " had followed the coming of the religion of Jesus, this change in the attitude of civilized society, with its multiplied instruments, its vaster enterprises, its prouder hopes, and its bolder ambitions, towards the weakness of childhood, is surely one to impress and delight us. It seems to me to repeat the example of the Master Himself, and to bring the Christendom which now honors, blesses, and consecrates that childhood nearer to Him than all cathedrals ever builded!" [2] The asylums, homes, reformatories, industrial schools, and hospitals for children, which are now a feature of Christian civilization, are sufficient to show that the example of Christ in His tender ministry to the little ones, and in His " coronation of childhood," has not been lost upon His followers.

Christianity's ministry to childhood one of the brightest chapters in its history.

Christian missions have not been able to do much as yet in the direction of organized effort, but a steady, and in many instances successful, moral influence has been exerted. Instruction, precept, example, and the introduction of more intelligent and sensible methods have done much to lessen the evils which afflict the young. The Christian impulse in the parental heart is distinctively humane in its tendencies. Natural affection and the ties of kinship are, of course, everywhere influential in safeguarding the interests of children; but ignorance, superstition, barbaric customs, and the brutal lapses to which human nature is so strangely addicted, are all in array against the weak and helpless childhood of the world. Christianity not only softens the heart and stirs the sympathies, thus giving a new sacredness to infant life, and creating

---

1 Krupabai Satthianadhan, " Miscellaneous Writings," p. 13.

2 Storrs, " The Divine Origin of Christianity," p. 146. Cf. also *ibid.*, Note XIV, p. 464, for quotations from the early Christian fathers.

A Kindergarten Group at Smyrna.

(A. B. C. F. M.)

a social conscience regarding its treatment, but it addresses itself with a vigorous imperative to the quickening of philanthropic and reverent views of duty to children as an important part of human society.

Fresh illustrations of this kindly ministry to childhood present themselves in the noble work of the American missionaries in Asia Minor who have received and still care for many desolate orphans who lost parents and guardians in The rescue of orphans the recent dreadful massacres. Many a helpless and famine waifs. child has also been rescued in the famine districts of India and saved from lingering suffering and death by the hand of missionary philanthropy. "We have two orphans in our home," writes the Rev. C. E. Petrick, of Sibsagor, Assam, "who are Eurasians, their father being an Englishman. They are fine little girls, and when they were offered to us it was said that if we did not take them they would be sold for an evil purpose in Calcutta. They have been delivered from a life of shame, to which, no doubt, many orphan girls in Assam are consigned."

In Japan work for children has already assumed some importance. Miss Alice Haworth, of the Presbyterian Mission, observes: "It is one of the surest signs of hopeful Christian progress when Japanese men of character, as well as women, begin to recognize the value of personal attention to neglected children."[1] The Rev. K. Tomeoka is at present seeking to establish a Christian Reform School to be located probably at Tokyo. The object in view is to save Japanese children who are in danger of becoming criminals. In Kobe there is a Children's Home, similar to what is known here as a day-nursery, where the children of the poor are cared for while their parents are engaged in earning their livelihood. The splendid work of Mr. Ishii in his Okayama Orphanage is one of the direct fruits of missions. Full particulars concerning it will be found in the section on orphanages. Mention should be made also of Judge Miyoshi's projected institution for criminal children, which no doubt will be evangelical in its spirit and aims. The kindergarten has become popular among the Japanese, who are specially fond of children. A sad and dark feature of home life in Japan, the sale of daughters for an evil purpose, has been much restricted, and is fast becoming repugnant to the moral sentiments of the people. This change may be traced to the influence of Christianity.[2]

---

[1] *Woman's Work for Woman*, September, 1896, p. 240. Cf. also an article by Miss A. Buzzell on the subject of work for children in Japan, in *The Japan Evangelist*, December, 1896, p. 73.

[2] " What has thus changed the moral sentiments of the people? The answer is, Christianity. With the spread of the Gospel comes naturally and of necessity the

We find here and there, in letters and reports from Africa, statements concerning what are called "Nursery Missions," chiefly in the stations hitherto conducted by Bishop Taylor, of the "Nursery Missions" Methodist Episcopal Church. Of this unique and homes for slave children. method the Bishop writes: "The children are redeemed from heathenism, and are being trained for missionary work. The Divine Founder of missions adopted but a dozen disciples for special missionary purposes. We prize the careful nursery training of about a dozen little children for each station much more highly than we do public-school teaching, however needful in its own line of service."[1] In regions where the slave-trade is carried on it sometimes happens that a whole group of children will be rescued, with hardly any possibility of restoring them to their homes. In fact, they are sometimes so young as to be unable to give the slightest intimation as to whence they came. The English and Scotch missionaries of Central and Eastern Africa are accustomed to receive these waifs and train them in homes set apart for the purpose. Thus in a variety of ways missions are seeking to save the children. With slender means and limited facilities little can be done in comparison with the vast needs, but an example may be set, a standard established, and the saving efforts of Christian nurture and philanthropy be put in operation. Thus as Christianity becomes more powerful a blessed and holy ministry in the name of Christ will be inaugurated.

9. DIMINISHING INFANTICIDE.—All that has been said, in the previous section, with reference to the aid and protection which missions are instrumental in securing for children, Parental thuggism in applies to their deliverance from the criminal India. brutality of infanticide. If they are aided and protected in life, they are saved thereby from the inhuman clutches of the child murderer. This parental thuggism has shadowed for unknown generations the birth-hour of infant daughters

elevation of woman, and it is to Christianity that the world must again look for hope. Under Buddhist teaching these sales have gone on for centuries. Shintoism has done nothing to improve the situation and give to woman the rights which belong to her as an individual. Not until the coming of Christian enlightenment do we find any relief or hope. But with the present rate of social progress in Japan, the sale of girls will soon be a custom wholly of the past."—Rev. David S. Spencer (M. E. M. S.), Nagoya, Japan.

1 *The Christian*, November 8, 1894.

in India and China, and among the savage races of all heathen countries. Tribal or family pride in regard to marriage stimulates the fear that no suitable alliance will be found for a daughter, and thus she may become an occasion of humiliation to the parental honor. The temptation to avoid this risk, and at the same time to escape from the expense and trouble involved in arranging a marriage, is strong enough in thousands of instances to stifle natural feeling and consign the helpless infant as a living victim to this Moloch of selfish vanity. Mr. W. Crooke, in his recent volume on "The North-Western Provinces of India," states some shocking facts concerning the former prevalence of this crime among certain tribes of North India.[1] At the beginning of the present century infanticide by drowning, and especially by throwing infants to the crocodiles and sharks at Saugor Island and other places, was a common occurrence. This statement has been sometimes challenged by zealous and possibly ignorant defenders of Hindu character, but the Parliamentary documents and correspondence, and the regulations proclaimed by the British Government to abolish it, are all on record and give irrefragable proof that this despicable and unnatural custom prevailed.[2] The Government went so far as to place a guard at Saugor Island, near the mouth of the Hugli River, below Calcutta, to prevent these atrocious acts, which were usually performed in fulfillment of vows made under the influence of superstition.

Concerning infanticide in China and elsewhere enough has been reported in Vol. I., pp. 128–135. The author desires here to correct an impression which may have been given by what was written (Vol. I., p. 134) on the doom of twins in Africa. The facts as there stated are strictly true so far as they apply to the section referred to on the West Coast. In the interior, however, and in regions not far from the head waters of the Congo River, there are certain tribes among

---

[1] He refers to the well-known fact that it is a point of honor with the Rajputs, Jats, Gujars, and other tribes, to find for their daughters husbands of superior rank, and that among a certain clan, known as the Chauhans, there was not in 1843 a single female child (p. 136). Cf. also Dubois, " Hindu Manners, Customs, and Ceremonies," new edition, 1897, pp. 506, 612.

[2] Cf. *The Indian Evangelical Review*, January, 1897, article entitled " Papers Relative to Infanticide by Drowning, Practised by the Hindus at Saugor and Other Places, 1794–1820," pp. 297–302, in which the Government regulations are given in full.

" In 1802 the Marquis of Wellesley published an order declaring infanticide to be murder, and punishable with death, and yet so late as the year 1836 it was estimated by a Rajput chief that as many as 20,000 infant girls were destroyed annually in the Provinces of Malwa and Rajputana alone."—*The Indian Evangelical Review*, April, 1898, p. 386.

whom quite the opposite feeling seems to be found, since they extend a welcome to twins and treat them with special honor.[1]

If we inquire what saving power has been exerted on behalf of these innocents, we should not fail to note the measures, most creditable to Christian rule, which are taken by the British Gov-
The efforts of the British Government in India. ernment in India for the suppression of infanticide. The iniquity is a difficult one to eradicate. It was not considered murder until so declared by British authority, since parents were regarded as having the power of life and death over their children. As before stated, it has been prohibited by the Government since 1802, and was made a crime according to the Penal Code Act of 1860, while still another Act requiring the registration of all births was passed in 1870, with a view to restricting infanticide. In addition, a strict watch was established over the relative proportion of boys and girls reported as born. In this way the crime has come more and more under an official ban, although there is still no assurance that it is not perpetrated secretly either by neglect, or other methods which defy the detection of the Government. *The Indian Social Reformer* of March 21, 1897, in an editorial on " Female Infanticide in the Punjab," intimates as much as this. An article in *The Calcutta Review* for January, 1897, deals with the subject historically, and shows that it is a practice of very ancient origin, which is not by any means at an end. The Pundita Ramabai is quoted as asserting "the prevalence of infanticide in some parts of India in spite of laws for its repression." [2] Dr. Carey and others of the early missionaries were earnest advocates of aggressive legislation on the part of the Government long before the present regulations were adopted. " The first reform he helped to effect," says a biographer of Dr. Carey, " was the prohibition of the sacrifice of children at the great annual festival at Gunga Saugor." [3] All honor, too, is due to humane British officials

---

[1] The late Bishop Crowther wrote as follows : " Many thousand twin infants have been barbarously destroyed by some tribes, while others spare these infants, and worship the supposed goddess as generous."

Mr. F. S. Arnot, in writing of pioneer mission work in Garenganze, states : "Twins, strange to say, are not only allowed to live, but the people delight in them."—Arnot, " Garenganze," p. 241.

[2] *The Sentinel,* February, 1897, p. 23; *World-Wide Missions,* September, 1898, p. 13. In one of the Thakur villages of the North-West Provinces, a census taken in 1897 revealed the fact that eighty-five per cent. of the children were boys and only fifteen per cent. were girls. See *The Indian Evangelical Review,* April, 1898, p. 510.

[3] Creegan, " Great Missionaries of the Church," p. 55. Cf. also Thoburn, " India and Malaysia," p. 186.

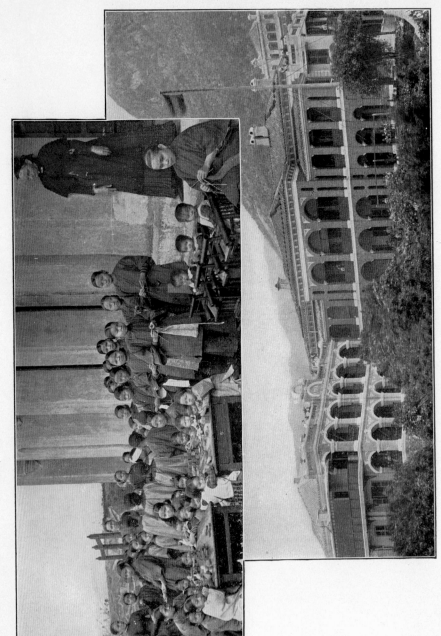

A Group of Inmates.

THE BERLIN FOUNDLING HOME, HONG KONG.

(Supported by the Berlin Ladies' Missionary Association.)

who have used their influence and exerted their authority to repress this secret enormity of Hindu society.

In China, where no Christian Government is on the alert, missionaries have found a more immediate responsibility resting upon them to save infant life. In a recent volume by Irene H. Barnes, entitled "Behind the Great Wall," is a chapter on "The Cry of the Chinese Children." Special efforts of missionaries in China. The statements of several of those devoted women who were murdered at Kucheng, 1895, are given as to the prevalence of infanticide in that section of China (the Province of Fuhkien), and the efforts of Miss Elsie Marshall and Miss Hessie Newcombe to rescue these little waifs are described.[1] A glance at letters from the field will reveal how often these abandoned infants are rescued by missionaries and in some way cared for.[2] At Hong Kong is a missionary institution known as the Berlin Foundling Home, which is maintained by the Berlin Ladies' Association. An organization is reported in connection with the work of the London Missionary Society in China, "for saving baby girls from destruction." In the same paragraph is found the following statement: "In all our churches we have a stock of old clothes so as to provide for the children whom the mothers cast away. Then we have pamphlets issued pointing out the wickedness of the custom of infanticide."[3] Under the restraints of Christianity the crime has diminished to a considerable extent.[4] It is true that the Chinese Government has issued decrees forbidding infanticide and has established foundling hospitals for the reception of baby girls, but the care given in these institutions, and the provision made for the children, are, as Miss Gordon-Cumming states, "without any pretense to cleanliness or comfort." She writes: "It is needless to say that the miserable children are horribly neglected, and the sound of their ceaseless, pitiful wailing is heard even before we enter this abode of infant misery."[5] The Rev. M. Mackenzie, of the English Presbyterian Mission, states that the evil has decreased in South China, and this result he traces in part to "the example of Christian parents sparing the lives

---

[1] Barnes, " Behind the Great Wall," pp. 91–98. Cf. also Johnston, " China and Formosa," p. 30.

[2] *Life and Light for Woman*, March, 1894, p. 142; *Heathen Woman's Friend*, September, 1894, p. 68.

[3] " Report of the Religious Tract Society, 1894," p. 167.

[4] Johnston, " China and Formosa," p. 31. See *Regions Beyond*, June, 1897, p. 279.

[5] Barnes, " Behind the Great Wall," p. 94.

of all their children."[1]   "How is it that you keep your girls?" inquired Mr. Bonsey, of the London Mission, Hankow, as he visited some Chinese homes where there were several of them.   "We see that the Christians are keeping their girls, and we think, perhaps, we might be able to do the same," was the reply.[2]   The Rev. J. Macgowan (L. M. S.), of Amoy, writes that through the influence of Christianity "foundling institutions were established which are still carried on, and now have fully two thousand children in connection with them.   These children are kept for a certain time, and then given to people who are childless, or who wish to rear them to become future daughters-in-law.   Thousands of women are alive to-day who but for Christianity would have been put to death."[3]

One of the older missionaries of the American Board at Foochow remarks that in that region forty years ago, according to native statements, about sixty or seventy per cent. of the female infants were drowned at birth, or destroyed in some other way.   Missionaries, however, made such an impression by their appeals and protests that the ruling class sought to put a check upon the prevailing tendency, and about twenty years ago a proclamation engraved upon stone was set up by the roadside in prominent places, announcing that "the drowning of female infants is forever forbidden."   It was supplemented by official notices threatening severe punishment to parents guilty of the crime, and a lighter punishment to neighbors who failed to report it. The result has been so effective that infanticide in that vicinity occurs now only infrequently.   Still another cause coöperated, no doubt, to check the evil.   The price of marriageable girls rose so high that the preservation of infant daughters became a profitable speculation.   The same missionary, the Rev. Charles Hartwell, states that missions in that section "have had a great influence in heightening the regard paid to the female sex."   The Rev. Gilbert Reid writes to the author that "missions have tended to make more sacred the life of girls, and to lessen the evil of infanticide."

Another part of the world which has long been notorious for this

[1] *The Monthly Messenger*, June, 1897, p. 160.
[2] *Ibid.*, August, 1893, p. 175.
[3] "I recall one happy household, father and mother both earnest, consistent Christians; they had six daughters and no sons.   It is almost certain that, if it had not been for the influence of Christianity in and around their family, some of these bright, merry children would have been suppressed at birth, and that there would have been no peace and good-will in the family.   It is also possible that a second wife might have been brought into the home."—Rev. John Murray (P. B. F. M. N.), Chinanfu, Shantung, China.

iniquity is the South Seas, where missionary success has in many instances entirely abolished the custom. Even in some of the islands where Christianity has only as yet a partial hold, "the practice of infanticide, once so common, has been very much reduced." It is stated in a review of mission results in the Pacific that "in the Christian communities infanticide, formerly so prevalent, is now thought of only with abhorrence."[1] The Bishop of Tasmania, in an account of his visit to the Solomon Islands in 1892, quotes Bishop Patteson as lamenting in his day (1866) the scarcity of children and the terrible frequency of infanticide. While it is true that the crime of child murder may not have been wholly abolished, yet it has been greatly reduced.[2] At the present time the wives of the native teachers in San Cristoval are often instrumental in saving infant lives, as they have received instructions to offer their services and extend protection to babes newly born.[3] In the missionary occupation of New Guinea much good has been done by the South Sea Island teachers in checking this evil. It is reported that "on Darnley Island, Gucheng, the teacher, had done well. In a few months this brave fellow practically stamped out the custom of strangling infants at birth."[4]

Checking infant murder in the South Seas.

In Africa, also, missions are in conflict with this strange aspect of human savagery. Among the West Coast tribes, where the murder of twins is so common, we find the communities of native Christians altogether purged of the unnatural custom. The records of Gospel progress have everywhere this significant commentary: "The people have given up twin murder and human sacrifices." A letter from Ikorofiong, one of the United Presbyterian mission stations in Old Calabar, contains the following auspicious item of information: "A month or so ago twin children were born to one of our church-members, and they have not only been kept and well cared for, but both the parents are delighted with them, and told us that they were sure that God would bless the children. When we go to see them the mother is so happy and bright that it is a real joy to meet her. To many of the women here the greatest calamity that can befall them is to give birth to twin children."[5] It is recorded of the late Rev.

A happier day for twins on the West Coast.

---

[1] *The Chronicle*, September, 1894, p. 212. Cf. also Alexander, "The Islands of the Pacific," pp. 94, 476.

[2] Montgomery, "The Light of Melanesia," pp. 166, 167. [3] *Ibid.*, p. 168.

[4] Horne, "The Story of the London Missionary Society," p. 400.

[5] *The Missionary Record*, November, 1894, p. 317.

Hugh Goldie, of Old Calabar, that, in the early days of the mission, he and Mr. Waddell, with Mr. Anderson, "determined to take their stand against the prevalent custom of twin murder. They found that this reform was even harder to accomplish than the abolition of human sacrifices." The efforts towards this end were stoutly opposed by the native chiefs, and especially by the women themselves. At last King Eyo, of Creek Town, decreed that the murder of twins or their mother was henceforth to be a capital crime, but, since the mother and her infants *could not be permitted to live in the town*, a place outside should be found for them. This was in 1851. Since then the battle has been fought and won, and in the agreement of 1878, drawn up between the British Consul at Old Calabar and the leading men of the country (a document which Consul Hopkins declared to be possible only because of missionary influence), the first article condemns the crime under consideration.[1] The influence of the Scotch Presbyterian missionaries in Old Calabar at the present time is commented upon by a recent traveller, with special mention of their success in suppressing infant murder.[2] The Rev. George Grenfell, an English Baptist missionary of the Upper Congo, writes that "the constant enunciation of the teaching that human life is sacred has established a sentiment which is preventive of much infanticide, and has saved the lives of many who would otherwise have been sacrificed, in accordance with the cruel customs and superstitions of the country."

The Reports of the Universities' Mission refer to the decrease of child murder in East Africa, which in one place, at least, was so "horribly general that in 1895 our missionaries knew of at least forty children killed in Kologwe Town alone, at or shortly after birth."[3] The Scotch missionaries of British Central Africa announce a similar diminution wherever their work has extended. The venerable M. François

---

[1] The text of the article is as follows: "Whoever wilfully takes the life of a twin child or children shall be adjudged liable to the penalty of death. Any persons wilfully concealing any fact that may come to their knowledge of the murder of twins shall be considered accessories of the fact, and shall be liable to such punishment as the consul shall direct. Mothers of twin children in future shall have full liberty to visit the town, and buy and sell in the markets, the same as any other women, and they shall not be molested in any way."—Dickie, "Story of the Mission in Old Calabar," p. 78.

[2] Captain Boisragon, in his volume on "The Benin Massacre," refers to Miss Mary M. Slessor, one of the missionaries, as follows: "She has got such a hold over the people that all killing of twins and such like evil customs have been absolutely stopped." His reference is to the district of Okoyong, where Miss Slessor resides. See *The Missionary Record*, March, 1898, p. 96.

[3] "Report of the Universities' Mission to Central Africa, 1896," p. 8.

Coillard, of the Société des Missions Évangéliques de Paris, in his recent fascinating volume, speaks of infanticide as "fearfully common" among the Barotsi of the Upper Zambesi Valley, in the very heart of Central Africa south of the equator, and states that there is virtually no recog- nized sentiment against it. "Public opinion," he writes, "does not in the least deter from these revolting atrocities."[1] M. Coillard and his devoted wife have done much to check this and similar brutal practices in the Zambesi Valley. What such a fight with the tyranny of custom means cannot be realized except by those who have had some personal experience among primitive races. The murder of infants in Galla communities seems to have been a prevalent evil which missionary influence has succeeded in lessening.[2] In Madagascar a conspicuous effect of Christianity wherever it has penetrated is that infanticide is a thing of the past.[3]

The infant death-roll of an East African village.

The degraded Indians of North and South America have often been guilty of the murder of children, but the restraining power of missions has become manifest. "We have been very much grieved of late," writes a missionary among the Chacos of Paraguay, "at the number of young children who have been murdered, and have been forced to take severe measures with those who carry on this horrible practice." A man who had been guilty of the crime was severely reproved, and a promise obtained from him that he would not kill another child. He has kept this promise. Other instances are given in which children have been thus saved.[4] According to a law of the

Degraded Indians in North and South America learn lessons of compassion from their missionary teachers.

---

[1] Coillard, "On the Threshold of Central Africa," p. 399.

[2] "Infanticide is common among the Gallas. The first-born child, especially if a female, must be thrown into the woods to starve or be eaten by wild animals. *As the result largely of palavers with missionaries,* many of the Gallas have come to see the folly of obeying such a cruel custom, and a few months ago Boru Dolu (the king elect) and seven other leading men in this station publicly announced their determination to give up the abominable practice. The Gallas of other towns will no doubt follow suit."—Rev. R. M. Ormerod (U. M. F. C. S.), Golbanti, East Africa.

[3] "Infanticide used to prevail to such an extent that hundreds of infants born in Madagascar were murdered every year. That is a thing of the past. No month is now considered unlucky for the 'little stranger' to make its appearance in, and the spark of life is never unnaturally extinguished in any infant in those parts of Madagascar where Christianity has been planted, and where it has successfully taken root."—Rev. J. Pearse (L. M. S.), Fianarantsoa, Madagascar.

[4] *The South American Missionary Magazine,* September, 1897, p. 139; October, 1897, p. 156.

Chacos, if a mother dies leaving a little babe, the child must be buried alive with her. When this emergency arises it is the habit of missionaries to plead for the life of the child, and they are oftentimes successful.[1] The same custom of infanticide and burying the child alive with its dead mother prevailed in Greenland before the introduction of Christianity. "Among the Eskimos baby girls are sometimes smothered, and in hard times old people are left to perish, or are put to death by their relatives."[2] The Indians of North America, especially the far Northwest, are known to be guilty of infant murder. Dr. Sheldon Jackson writes of the Eskimos of Alaska, that "they sometimes destroy their offspring, particularly if the child is a girl."[3] The Rev. E. H. Edson, a missionary of the Protestant Episcopal Church in Alaska, states that "infanticide is very common."[4] From the wild north land, towards Great Bear Lake, the missionaries of the Church Missionary Society also report that the killing of infant girls is not uncommon. Christian converts confess that in their heathen days they have been guilty of killing infants.[5]

Thus the evidence seems conclusive that Christian missions are pleading and contending for the sacredness of infant life, wherever they have an opportunity to grapple with the despicable crime of child murder.

III.—RESULTS OF A HUMANE AND PHILAN-THROPIC TENDENCY

"The God that answereth by orphanages, let Him be God," is a challenge which Christianity does not fear to give. The sentence simply puts in graphic form the unanswerable argument of Christian philanthropy in support of the divine origin of the Gospel. We have presented evidence that missions have created a new basis of personal character and a better environment for individual development. It has been shown that they have implanted a nobler spirit in the family, bringing to it blessings and hopes hitherto unknown. We shall now advance the claim that they have also stimulated impulses and started

The humanitarian value of missions.

---

1 "South America: the Neglected Continent," p. 152.
2 *The Gospel in all Lands*, December, 1894, p. 539.
3 *The Church at Home and Abroad*, January, 1894, p. 7.
4 *The Spirit of Missions*, November, 1895, p. 471.
5 Headland, "Brief Sketches of C. M. S. Missions," Part III., p. 180.

movements which have wrought for the more general welfare and happiness of mankind by promoting humane policies, banishing cruel customs, securing the relief of suffering, and providing for the comfort of the dependent and helpless classes of society. Many and impressive specifications present themselves in this connection, which call for careful investigation, and, as we shall see, yield a generous reward to the patient student.

1. HASTENING THE SUPPRESSION OF THE SLAVE-TRADE AND LABOR-TRAFFIC.—The very mention of this subject calls to mind the name of a great missionary, one whose memory is garlanded with a tribute of world-wide admiration and whose life fitly symbolizes the historic attitude of missions towards this colossal wrong. It was *Livingstone a pioneer in the modern crusade against the slave-trade.* in 1852 that Livingstone began his heroic journey from Cape Colony northward into Central Africa, and during a period beginning not long after that date, and lasting until his death on the shore of Lake Bangweolo, in 1873, his voice rang through Christendom in denunciation of this detestable crime. It was not far from the noble mission church at Blantyre that Livingstone, in 1861, accompanied by an exploring party of the Universities' Mission, first wrenched the slave-sticks from the necks of a captive gang of slaves.[1] Sir Harry H. Johnston, in an historical sketch of the suppression of the slave-trade in British Central Africa, writes : " Dr. Livingstone, however, appeared on the scene, and his appeals to the British public gradually drew our attention to the slave-trade in Eastern Central Africa, until, as the direct result of Livingstone's work, slavery and the slave-trade are now at an end within the British Central Africa Protectorate, and are fast disappearing in the regions beyond under the South Africa Company ; and the abolition of slavery in Zanzibar will shortly be decreed as a final triumph to Livingstone's appeal." [2] It is now almost half a century since this intrepid

---

[1] An illustration of the Blantyre Church is given in Vol. I., p. 459.

[2] Johnston, " British Central Africa," p. 157.

Dr. Blaikie, in his " Life of David Livingstone," refers in the following terms to his influence both before and after his death, as a pioneer in the extermination of African slavery: " The heart of David Livingstone was laid under the mvula-tree in Ilala, and his bones in Westminster Abbey; but his spirit marched on. The history of his life is not completed with the record of his death. . . . From the worn-out figure kneeling at the bedside in the hut in Ilala an electric spark seemed to fly, quickening hearts on every side. The statesman felt it; it put new vigor into the

explorer entered the dark realms of African cruelty. Marvelous progress has been made in the destruction of this cursed traffic, and one may even hope that the jubilee anniversary of Livingstone's first blow at the slave-trade will witness its virtual overthrow in Africa, except as it may still lurk in hidden recesses of the Continent. Events which have transpired within a brief period, such as its suppression in British Central Africa, its prohibition by official decree in the Niger Protectorate, including the immense *Hinterland* of the Royal Niger Company, and the abolishment not only of the slave-trade but of the status of slavery in the Zanzibar Sultanate, all show the rapid march of stupendous changes throughout Africa.

The story of the attitude of Christian nations towards the slave-trade, from about the beginning of the sixteenth to the first decade of the nineteenth century, is a dark and dismal chapter in the annals of mankind, but happily it is now past history. It is a dreadful record of what has been called the "Christian slave-trade" to distinguish it from the Mohammedan traffic.[1] While it is true that nations Christian in name were sadly compromised by their unworthy representatives in promoting this vile traffic, yet we should not fail to note that under the pressure of an aggressive Christian protest, on the part of conscientious citizens, these same nations were also active in its suppression, the eyes of their people having been opened to its enormities and abominable wickedness. The influences which brought about the abolition of the traffic in slaves throughout the British Empire, in 1807, are described by Dr. Ingram as largely Christian. "It is unquestionable," he writes, "that the principal motive power which originated and sustained their efforts was Christian principle and feeling." The statement is made with reference to the members of the Committee appointed in 1787 for the Abolition of the Slave-Trade throughout the British Empire, who, after a struggle lasting twenty years, accomplished their

The Christian origin of the first efforts to suppress the traffic in slaves.

---

despatches he wrote and the measures he devised with regard to the slave-trade. The merchant felt it, and began to plan in earnest how to traverse the continent with roads and railways, and open it to commerce from shore to centre. The explorer felt it, and started with high purpose on new scenes of unknown danger. The missionary felt it,—felt it a reproof of past languor and unbelief,—and found himself lifted to a higher level of faith and devotion. No parliament of philanthropy was held; but the verdict was as unanimous and as hearty as if the Christian world had met and passed the resolution: 'Livingstone's work shall not die: AFRICA SHALL LIVE'" (pp. 480, 481).

[1] Ingram, "A History of Slavery and Serfdom," pp. 140–154; Froude, "English Seamen in the Sixteenth Century."

purpose.[1]   Other civilized nations followed in quick succession, the United States acting simultaneously with Great Britain.

The treaty agreements between the Christian Powers did not, however, put a stop to an illicit traffic carried on for over half a century in defiance of international agreements.   The struggle to secure coöperation among the nations in establishing really effective barriers to the prosecution of the trade resulted in extended, difficult, and discouragingly futile negotiations.   The refusal of the United States Government to assent to the Right of Search prolonged the existence of the slave-traffic in spite of all efforts to suppress it.   The year 1838 is declared to be the worst on record since the formal abolishment of the African slave-trade, in respect to the mortality and misery inflicted by it.[2]   It was at this juncture that Sir T. Fowell Buxton began his crusade against the evil, and was instrumental in securing a government expedition for the discovery and capture of slavers on the African coast.[3]   Efforts looking to its overthrow have increased up to the present hour under the auspices of civilized governments, Great Britain playing the leading rôle, and offering the services of her navy and the coöperation of her officials at critical points.   To the latter belongs a meed of special praise in this noble humanitarian crusade.[4]   The Brussels Conference of 1889–90

1 " A History of Slavery and Serfdom," pp. 160, 163.

2 *The Church Missionary Intelligencer*, June, 1897, p. 425.

3 It is stated that in 1837 " the American importation was estimated as high as 200,000 negroes annually.   The total abolition of the African trade by American countries then brought the traffic down to perhaps 30,000 in 1842.   A large and rapid increase of illicit traffic followed, so that by 1847 the importation amounted to nearly 100,000 annually.   One province of Brazil is said to have received 173,000 in the years 1846–49.   In the decade 1850–60 this activity in slave-trading continued, and reached very large proportions.   The traffic thus carried on floated under the flags of France, Spain, and Portugal, until about 1830; from 1830 to 1840 it began gradually to assume the United States flag; by 1845 a large part of the trade was under the stars and stripes; by 1850 fully one half the trade, and in the decade 1850–60 nearly all the traffic, found this flag its best protection. . . .

" On the outbreak of the Civil War, the Lincoln administration, through Secretary Seward, immediately expressed a willingness to do all in its power to suppress the slave-trade.   Accordingly, June 7, 1862, a treaty was signed with Great Britain granting a mutual limited Right of Search, and establishing mixed courts for the trial of offenders at the Cape of Good Hope, Sierra Leone, and New York.   The efforts of a half-century of diplomacy were finally crowned; Seward wrote to Adams : ' Had such a treaty been made in 1808, there would now have been no sedition here.' "— Du Bois, " The Suppression of the African Slave-Trade," pp. 143, 150.

4 For a valuable summary of well-authenticated historical data, cf. Du Bois, " The Suppression of the African Slave-Trade," chap. ix., on " The International Status of the Slave-Trade, 1783–1862."

agreed upon tentative provisions for the suppression of the slave-trade, which should now, however, be revised and made more effective. This subject, with that of the supply of alcoholic liquors and firearms to natives, will, it is hoped, be considered and dealt with at an early day in a way to promote the higher welfare of native races.

Let us begin our survey of the direct service which Christian missions have rendered with a glance at the situation on the East Coast of Africa. A brief summary of historical facts Missions and the East concerning the East African slave-trade will be Coast slave-trade. found in Vol. I., p. 141. As there stated, the treaty between England and the Sultan of Zanzibar, in 1873, consummated through the special efforts of Sir Bartle Frere and Dr. (afterwards Sir) John Kirk, prohibited the traffic in the sultanate, including the Island of Pemba. When an English protectorate was established over the Sultanate of Zanzibar, in 1890, the stipulations of this treaty were accepted and confirmed by the Sultan. So far as it affected the trade itself, however, its inefficiency became notorious. In Great Britain the pressure of the opponents of slavery was steadily brought to bear upon the Government to abolish altogether its status in Zanzibar, as the only effective measure for bringing the traffic in slaves to an end, since the legal existence of slavery was a constant stimulus to the illicit trade. The British Government finally abolished the status of slavery in Zanzibar and Pemba on April 6, 1897. During all these years missionaries have had an influential part to play in furthering this consummation. They have given prompt information of any infraction of the treaty of 1873 which fell under their notice, and have coöperated with cordial sympathy, so far as their circumstances would allow, in all efforts of the Government and of the British East Africa Company. Of late years they have spoken and written with much urgency concerning the duty of the Government to put an effectual stop to the cruelties and scandals which marked the continuance of slavery under the British flag. They have been specially active and useful in opening homes and refuges for rescued slaves, in establishing schools for their instruction, and in some instances training them to be teachers and preachers of the Gospel in connection with mission work.[1] On January 1, 1889, the number of runaway slaves

---

[1] Bishop Maples relates the following incident in one of his letters from Zanzibar, in 1877, concerning a rescued slave who had been trained by the mission: "One of our boys, John Briton, was taken (as a slave) in the following manner: He was being hurried off to Arabia in a dhow, when a man-of-war appeared. The Arabs popped John in a bag and hauled him up into the rigging. 'What's that?' said the officer of Her Majesty's ship as he boarded the dhow. 'A bag of grain,' answered

harbored at mission stations within the territory of the British East
Africa Company on the mainland was found to be 1422.[1]

The services of the Swedish missionaries on the mainland to the
north of Mombasa are highly spoken of by Mr. Donald Mackenzie in
his report upon the slave-trade on the East Coast.[2] The Church
Missionary Society's Home for Rescued Slaves at Frere Town, Mombasa Harbor, is doing an effective and admirable service. It is practically a continuation of the African Slave Asylum formerly (1860–74)
located at Nasik, India, where those faithful attendants of Livingstone,
who bore his body to the sea-coast, were trained.[3] The United Methodist Free Church stations, north of Mombasa, are centres of humane
activity. German missionaries are also conducting work in German
East Africa, with Dar-es-Salaam as a basis. At Kisserawe, an inland
station, provision is made for the reception of liberated slaves.

The Universities' Mission to Central Africa is throughout its ter-
ritorial extent one of the most effective agencies in East Africa for
the suppression of the slave-trade. It has nobly
carried out the desires of its founder, Dr. Living-   The redemption of the
stone, by receiving all freed slaves committed to   old slave-market at
                                                        Zanzibar.
its care, some of whom have been trained for the
native ministry. Its station Magila, in Usambara, on the mainland, is
a modern city of refuge for the victims of the traffic. Christian villages
are springing up on the main routes into the interior as far as Lake

the Arab. But the officer progged it with his sword. This went very much *against
the grain*, for John squealed out, and thus was rescued."—" Chauncy Maples, Bishop
of Likoma," pp. 87, 88.

In a letter of the previous year, before he himself became a bishop, he speaks of
the arrival at Zanzibar of fifty slaves captured by a British ship off Pemba, and states
that " the Bishop means to take them all in, and has just gone off to Dr. Kirk to
negotiate matters. The greater number are adults; they will go, of course, to the
shamba at Mbweni [a station of the Universities' Mission south of Zanzibar]. The
rest, if possible, we shall take in here [Kiungani]."—*Ibid.*, p. 60.

[1] Letter of George S. Mackenzie on "Slavery in East Africa," in *The Mail*
(London *Times*), April 13, 1896.

[2] *The Anti-Slavery Reporter*, December, 1895, p. 213.

[3] It was chiefly through the efforts of the Church Missionary Society that the
Parliamentary Committee of 1871 was appointed, which in the following year resulted in Sir Bartle Frere's mission to Zanzibar. "In 1874 the Rev. W. S. Price,
formerly in charge of the Asylum for Rescued Slaves at Nasik, Western India, was
sent out; some two hundred African Christians from the freed slaves entrusted to his
care were collected as the nucleus of an industrial colony; land was purchased for a
settlement, which was named Frere Town, in honour of Sir Bartle Frere; and some
five hundred rescued slaves were, in 1875, received from Her Majesty's cruisers, and
housed, fed, instructed, and led to work for their living."—" Report of the Church
Missionary Society, 1894," p. 35.

Nyassa, and are homes of freedom for the hunted African. A succession of noble bishops—Mackenzie, Tozer, Steere, Smythies, Hornby, Maples, Richardson, and Hine—have all been men of energy, power, and humane enthusiasm. Bishop Tozer gave special attention to the training of rescued slave children, and it was in Bishop Steere's day that the dramatic master-stroke of purchasing the property adjacent to the old slave-market at Zanzibar, and devoting it, with the market itself, to mission uses, was carried out. In the fine and stately Christ Church Cathedral, erected near the site of the old slave-market, three native Africans were ordained to the ministry on September 22, 1895. Within the sound of their voices as they took the vows of consecration were a hospital, a school, a home for released slaves, and the Universities' Mission houses at Zanzibar. What a redemption is this of the place where slaves by the hundreds were once publicly offered for sale in one of the most notorious slave-shambles of the world! In these latter days it has been a stirring sight, now and then, to witness the arrival at the headquarters of the Universities' Mission of a newly rescued cargo of slaves brought in by a British man-of-war, and to see them kindly and sympathetically cared for as free human beings upon the very spot where hundreds of thousands in the past have been bought and sold. That old slave-market at Zanzibar has become one of the brightest spots on the East Coast of Africa. The illustration of Christ Church Cathedral will give the reader a glimpse of the noble uses to which Christianity has now consecrated this former scene of heathen suffering and shame.[1] An Industrial Mission, supported by the Society of Friends in England, has been lately established on the Island of Pemba, with the special object of providing employment for slaves who have been able to secure their freedom under the recent decree of partial abolition.[2] The abrogation, in 1897, of the status of slavery was a welcome move, but not soon enough to prevent long and weary years of misery, which mark the slave annals of Zanzibar and the East Coast. In spite of some defects in the workings of the decree, it never-

1 " Look at the two pictures—rows of men, women, and children, sitting and standing, and salesmen and purchasers passing in and out among them, examining them, handling them, chaffering over them, bandying their filthy jokes about them, and worse scenes still going on in all the huts around; and then, in the same spot, see instead the priest and preacher, the teacher, the physician, the nurse, the children crowding to be taught, the grown men coming to hear of God and Christ, the sick and suffering finding help and health. Look at these two pictures and is it not a blessed and a glorious change, and is it not worth a life to have made it possible? " —Rowley, " Twenty Years in Central Africa," p. 227.

2 *The Anti-Slavery Reporter*, November–December, 1897, p. 248.

Hospital at Mombasa, East Africa
(C. M. S.)

The late Bishop Maples   Bishop Richardson
(Portraits by Elliott & Fry)

Christ Church Cathedral, Zanzibar
(U. M. C. A.)

The Christian Redemption of an African Slave-Market.

theless exists, and so forms the basis for persevering efforts on the part of missionaries and philanthropists to secure in the near future such an effectual execution of it as shall make the abolishment of slavery throughout the sultanate a reality, and, moreover, insure its benefits to those who are as yet virtually helpless even to take advantage of their freedom.

Before turning from Zanzibar to the southward we may note the establishment, by the Arabian Mission of the Reformed Church of America, of a school at Muscat for liberated slaves who have been rescued in transit from the East Coast to the Arabian and Persian markets. The Rev. P. J. Zwemer, since deceased, reported, late in 1896, the capture of some slave-dhows in the vicinity of Muscat, containing in all forty-four slaves. On application by Mr. Zwemer to the British Consul at Muscat, eighteen of these, all under twelve years of age, were handed over to him to train. The enterprise has been generously sustained by friends in America, and it is gratifying to reflect that on the distant and somewhat inaccessible coast of southeastern Arabia American missionaries are on the watch for rescued slaves whom they may redeem unto God and His salvation.[1] The Rev. James Cantine, of the Reformed Church Mission, sends word quite recently (July, 1898) that the limit of eighteen should by no means be insisted upon, as is apparently the case by direction of the Board in America. He announces the arrival, just previous to the date of his letter, of a captured slave-dhow, and continues as follows: "By express direction of the Board I was prevented from making further application for any boys of suitable age who might be on board. Our lads were quite excited at the news, and wished me to go at once to the English Consulate to see about getting others. On my telling them that I had no

The school for rescued slave boys at Muscat.

---

[1] In a recent report by Mr. Zwemer we find the following paragraph: "Although the experiment is not yet completed, the results so far are most gratifying, and the boys are making excellent progress in morals and education. Immediately after they came they were put into manual training, making baskets, sewing, and housework. Ignorant of any language but Swahili, it was thought best that they be taught English first. After primary instruction by means of charts, they showed enough mental capacity to warrant the expense of a teacher; and S. M. David, an Indian Christian, formerly a teacher in the Church Missionary Society Freed-Slave School at Nasik, India, came to Muscat on September 15, 1896. All the boys have since made such rapid progress in the ' three R's ' that they are almost prepared for the first Indian standard. The health of the lads has been good, with one exception, and they are apparently perfectly at home in the Muscat climate. Instruction is given them from the Bible and by means of a simple catechism; their moral sense is growing, and many of them begin to realize the opportunity of the new life open before them. —" The Arabian Mission: Statement Number Nine, 1897," p. 8.

extra food, they said that each would share his plate of rice with a new boy. The question of the extension of the Freed-Slave School is something for its friends and supporters in America to decide for themselves. The opportunity is before us!"[1]

In Uganda, where the mission of the Church Missionary Society, founded in 1877, is now (1898) just reaching its majority, there is a record of almost exclusively missionary influence Mackay and his associates teach the rights of humanity in Uganda. working with swift and marvelous precision for the abolishment not only of the slave-trade, but, as we shall see in the next section, of domestic slavery as well. Dr. Blaikie, in his "Life of David Livingstone," recognizes the services of a countryman of Livingstone, Mr. A. M. Mackay, of the Church Missionary Society, in securing the abolition of the slave-trade by King Mtesa, as having "contributed mainly to this remarkable result." It was Mackay who appealed to the rulers of Uganda to respect the rights of humanity and honor human beings as too precious to be bought and sold like cattle, and so successfully did he plead that a strong sentiment was created against the traffic in slaves. How different is this from the old way, of which the late Mr. Pilkington wrote: "No protest was heard when women and children were sold into the hopeless misery of Arab slavery." What this check to the slave-trade in that section of Africa means for the relief of suffering and the deliverance from appalling cruelties may be discovered by reading the chapter entitled "On the Banks of Lake Tanganyika," in Johnston's "Missionary Landscapes in the Dark Continent." The accounts there given of the horrors of slave-raiding in that region for the supply of slaves to the Waganda people, among whom Mackay labored, are deeply harrowing to humane sensibilities. The country around the northern end of the lake, according to the reports of Emin Pasha, was the hunting-ground of the slave-raiders, who disposed of their victims among the Waganda.[2] In the abolition of domestic slavery in Uganda,

1 "The Arabian Mission: Field Report Number Twenty-six," pp. 5, 6. Cf. also for confirmation of the existence of the slave-trade at the present time on the Arabian coast, *The Anti-Slavery Reporter*, July–August, 1898, pp. 190–192.

2 The following extract is from the pen of Emin Pasha: "I have heard and seen terrible things on my way to the Albert Lake. I followed the traces of one of these robbers, Omar Ben Chalid, for six days, and counted fifty-one fresh corpses emaciated to the bone. Thirty-nine of the victims had their skulls shattered. Twelve hundred persons are said to have been dragged to Mengo, there being twenty to thirty negroes of either sex bound to each chain. Twenty-seven, including four women, who had succeeded in escaping, met us, half dead with hunger."—Quoted by Mr. Johnston, p. 258.

The whole chapter by Mr. Johnston should be read, as a revelation of the atrocities of the slave-trade around Lake Tanganyika as late as 1890.

a fact which we shall mention more particularly in the next section, it was the Protestant chiefs, inspired by missionary instruction, who made for themselves in this respect a record which shall "be told for a memorial" of them, wherever the history of missions is written.

Let us now pass southward, noting *en route* the pioneer services of the missionaries of the London Missionary Society at the southern end of Lake Tanganyika, and recognizing with gratitude and admiration the efforts of the Moravian and German missionaries who are located north of Lake Nyassa, almost in touch with their English brethren of the London Society. In *Periodical Accounts*, the magazine of the Moravians, is related an incident, giving the details of the rescue, in 1894, by Baron von Eltz, an official of the German Protectorate, of two hundred and eleven slaves who were being transported to the coast. A large number of these were delivered to the Moravian missionaries at Rungwe, and the remainder consigned to the more southerly stations of the Moravian and Berlin Societies, at the northern end of Lake Nyassa.[1] Still farther to the southeast we find at Newala, an interior station of the Universities' Mission, that some of the powerful chiefs in that vicinity refrain altogether from the slave-trade. "Perhaps the greatest testimony to our influence," wrote the Rev. R. F. Acland-Hood, in a communication concerning work at Newala, "is the fact that the most important chiefs are not slave-traders." [2]

Stories of rescue from the mission stations south of Lake Tanganyika.

Our entrance into the British Central Africa Protectorate brings us to the scene of recent important transactions, which, it is to be hoped, have permanently arrested the slave-traffic within the borders of Nyassaland. In these stirring events gallant British officials have directed the military operations, and Scotch and English missionaries have coöperated by rendering humane services to hundreds of slaves who were rescued in circumstances of extreme misery and suffering. This martial campaign, under the direction of Sir H. H. Johnston, Her Majesty's Commissioner in British Central Africa, has extended over a number of years, and one after another of the ruthless slave-raiders has been brought low, and his nefarious business ruined.[3] Makanjira, Kawinga, Zarafi, Mwazungu, Mwasi, Mponda, Tambala, Mpemba, and especially the cruel Mlozi, have all been crushed. In this valiant and repeated appeal to arms Commissioner Johnston has

The gallant crusade in British Central Africa.

[1] *Periodical Accounts Relating to Moravian Missions,* June, 1894, p. 308.

[2] *African Tidings,* December, 1896, p. 139.

[3] *The Missionary Review of the World,* October, 1895, pp. 754–756, and June, 1896, pp. 440, 441.

been the leading spirit, and in some instances has borne a personal part. Associated with him at different times were his fellow-officers, Deputy Commissioner Sharpe, Lieutenant Alston, Captain Stewart, Captain Cavendish, Lieutenants Coape-Smith and de Herries Smith, Dr. Poole, Major Edwards, Sergeant-Major Devoy, and Mr. Swann. In the campaign against Mlozi, in 1895, a prominent part was borne voluntarily by some English officers who were enjoying a holiday excursion in Central Africa, when the duty of subjugating Mlozi suddenly arose. The expedition resulted in his capture and execution.[1] That autumn campaign of 1895 is memorable in this respect, that it secured the release from the clutches of the slave-raiders of 1184 slaves. Of this number 596 were set free by the overthrow of Mlozi. A further result is the apparent death-blow to the slave-traffic around Lake Nyassa. We say apparent, for it is likely that secret efforts may be made to renew it, which, it is to be hoped, will be unimportant and futile.[2]

In conjunction with these interesting events just mentioned, we should note carefully the valuable help and coöperation of missionaries in supplementing and rounding out the benefits which flow from the energetic action of the British authorities.[3] The Universities'

---

[1] White Book, "Africa, No. 4, 1896." See also *The Anti-Slavery Reporter,* March–April, 1896, pp. 73–75 ; and Johnston, " British Central Africa," pp. 130–144.

[2] The Rev. Alexander Dewar, a Free Church of Scotland missionary, located on the Stevenson Road, northwest of Lake Nyassa, in a recent report gives the particulars of one of these unsuccessful attempts. His words are interesting also as giving a glimpse of the part taken by missionaries in supplementing and completing the results of this war upon the slave-trade. He writes as follows : " In our last report mention was made of Mlozi's fall and our satisfaction. Contrary, however, to general belief, slaving has since then been going on all around us, several caravans having been attacked. Last week, while the resident official of the British South Africa Company was superintending work near Fife, an Arab caravan was reported. He at once set out, capturing one of the Arab leaders—the other committing suicide to escape capture—and securing a large lot of ivory. Fifty-seven slaves were also rescued, and these, so far as their homes can be ascertained, are being returned. Some were so small that they could give no account of themselves. Six of these poor little things have been handed over to our care, while others are to go to the London Missionary Society's station at Fwambo. We are trusting some friends will be so interested in these little ones as to support them."— *The Free Church of Scotland Monthly,* March, 1897, p. 63.

[3] " The great agents in stopping the slave-trade must be the European Governments who have taken the country under their protection, but the work of Christian missions necessarily tends in the same direction, though by different methods, namely, by converting the raiding tribes to Christianity. Hence the great importance of our mission to the Yaos."—Rev. J. S. Wimbush (U. M. C. A.), Kota Kota, British Central Africa.

Mission House and Garden, Rungwe,
North Nyassaland.

Group of Freed Slave Children.

Sewing School, Rungwe.

Mother and Child.   Freed Slaves.

HAPPY SCENES ALONG THE OLD SLAVE-ROUTES.

(M. M. S.)

Mission to Central Africa has in its Constitution a clause indicating as one of its chief objects "the *ultimate extinction of the slave-trade.*" [1] In the furtherance of this object its first Bishop, Charles Frederick Mackenzie, during his journey up the Zambesi Valley, entered into agreements with the various chiefs, securing from them pledges that they would refrain from the traffic in slaves.[2] These initial efforts are typical of the spirit with which Scotch and English missionaries have assumed their part in this humane crusade. The lamented Dr. William Affleck Scott, of the Church of Scotland Mission at Blantyre, contracted his fatal illness during the expedition against the slave-raiding chief Kawinga, which he accompanied in the capacity of a medical man to look after the wounded.[3] The Rev. Robert Laws, M.D., of the United Presbyterian Church, who is now in the service of the Free Church of Scotland Mission in Livingstonia, in summing up the results of twenty-one years' work in that region, among other things refers to the wonderful progress towards the overthrow of the slave-trade.[4] Enough has been said to show that, while it is not the function of missionaries to draw the sword upon the slave-trader, it is their high privilege to participate in the extirpation of this cruel business by personal labors in the sphere of benevolent and humanitarian ministry. A permanent efficacy and a higher usefulness are thus given to military victories, since the additional moral and social benefit of a hopeful future is secured to the freedmen through a religious and industrial training.

The value of missionary coöperation in supplementing military victories.

In the Upper Zambesi Valley, among the wild Barotsi, is the scene of the memorable labors of the Rev. François Coillard and his noble

---

1 Anderson-Morshead, "The History of the Universities' Mission to Central Africa," p. 434.

2 The Bishop's treaty with the Manganja at Magomero, south of Lake Shirwa, in August, 1861, is as follows: "(1) That all the chiefs then present should solemnly promise, on behalf of themselves and people, that they would not buy or sell men, women, and children again. (2) That all captives found with the Ajawa should be perfectly free; that no chief or person should claim any one of them, but that they should have the liberty to go to whom they liked and where they liked. (3) That all the chiefs present promise that they will unite to punish any chief who sells his own people or the people of any other chief, and that each chief will punish any of his own people found guilty of buying or selling men, women, and children for slaves. (4) That if any Portuguese or other foreign slave-dealers came into the land, they would drive them away, or at once let us know of their presence."— Rowley, "Twenty Years in Central Africa," p. 57.

3 *The Church of Scotland Mission Record*, June, 1895, p. 189.

4 "Report on Foreign Missions of the United Presbyterian Church of Scotland, 1897," pp. 20, 21.

wife, the latter now buried at Sefula, in the heart of South Central Africa. In that deep isolation, amid the depressing savagery and cruelty of those untamed tribes, M. Coillard, as often appears in his recently published volume, was continually struggling to place some restrictions upon the barbarities of the slave-traffic. His success with Lewanika was a triumph of personal influence and patient effort. " There is progress," he writes, " with regard to slavery. Recently a man led an ox to his chief. ' I want a man,' he said. ' Will you get me one? Here is the price.' ' Why, where do you come from,' answered the chief, ' that you think you can still buy slaves under Lewanika?'"[1] In his concluding chapter he writes concerning the Barotsi kingdom : " Unquestionably, a great change is already operating in the country, which will become more marked as time goes on : the interdiction of spirituous drinks, of the slave-trade, and of the barbarous practice of ' smelling out sorcerers'; increasing security of property; and respect for human life,—tokens of civilisation, of a real need felt by the Barotsi themselves for developing their industrial tastes and talents: these, in various domains, are victories which the Gospel has won over paganism. ' And it is not only the good we may have done,' as a friend wrote to me; ' it is the evil—and who could fathom it?— that the presence of the Gospel has hindered.'"[2] The venerable author's description of an incident he once witnessed, when a large number of prisoners, mostly women and children taken in war, were to be distributed among the Barotsi victors, is of graphic and painful interest as illustrating that process of social vivisection which is so often a commonplace feature of African warfare.[3]

The triumph of missionary influence in the Upper Zambesi Valley.

To the southward of these scenes we reach the moral oasis of Khama's country. This Christian ruler has forbidden by law all purchase of slaves in his territory.[4] A native African convert, it may safely be said, uniformly ceases to be a friend to the slave-trade. It was a Christian queen in the neighboring Island of Madagascar, who, in 1877, " decreed that all slaves imported into the island should be set free." This was the final blow to the slave-trade in her realm. A treaty made with Great Britain for its suppression had existed for half a century, but it had never been sufficiently effective to abolish the illicit traffic.

[1] Coillard, " On the Threshold of Central Africa," p. 401.
[2] *Ibid.*, p. 639.   [3] *Ibid.*, pp. 471–473.
[4] Hepburn, " Twenty Years in Khama's Country," p. 122.

In the early history of the extreme southern section of the Continent, now under British rule, we find mention of the slave-trade as tolerated by the Dutch and French colonists.[1] The extension of British authority resulted in its practical extinction, although it has continued until quite recently among the native tribes.

The struggle in South Africa.

South African traditions, however, are not wholly in sympathy with the views which prevail upon this subject in Great Britain, and there seems to exist at the present time a certain laxity in the social customs of Cape Colony concerning the treatment of native prisoners of war. The establishment of a system of "indenture," which is fully acknowledged by the public press of South Africa, and pronounced by dignified British journals to bear a perilous resemblance to the proceedings of a slave-market, has elicited a loud murmur of dissatisfaction in Great Britain.[2] The missionaries of all societies in South Africa have not failed for nearly a century to do what they could to prevent the slave-trade wherever it has been found, and to lessen its brutalities among the native tribes.

If we now advance up the West Coast of the Continent, we meet with the Rhenish and Finnish missions in German Southwest Africa, and that of the American Board, which has its principal station at Kamundongo (formerly Bihé), in Angola. The missionaries of all these societies do what they can to mitigate the barbarities of inter-tribal slave-raids. Upon the high table-lands of Portuguese territory inland from Benguella, we find Mr. Heli Chatelain and his colleagues,

The Philafrican Liberators' League and its work.

---

[1] Wilmot, "The Expansion of South Africa," pp. 34, 92.

[2] *The Spectator* of October 30, 1897, p. 583, contains the following paragraph: " *The Cape Times* of September 29th gives an account of a visit to the slave-market opened by the Cape Government in Cape Town, at which the Bechuana prisoners are disposed of to farmers who desire indentured labourers. Probably the account is a little written up, but the ugly fact remains that a specially odious form of slavery— the sale of prisoners of war—has come into existence. But though we feel bound to make a protest in regard to the reaction against the English view of slavery which is taking place in South Africa, we do not say that the home Government is to blame. We gave responsible government to the Colony, and we cannot take back that gift. What we can do is to insist that the Imperial forces shall never be used to put down native risings without a strict agreement that the Colonial Office is to participate in the final settlement. Under ordinary circumstances we must look to the growth of a healthier sentiment in the Colony itself. We are glad to see signs of this in the meeting of the South African Political League, presided over by Mr. Rose-Innes, an account of which is given in a telegram in Thursday's *Times*. It is evident that

representing the newly organized Philafrican Liberators' League, having its headquarters in New York City. They are just inaugurating at Caconda a work specially designed to offset the evils of the internal slave-traffic, by establishing colonies where freed and rescued slaves may be educated and trained for future usefulness. The object of the organization, as stated in its published documents, is: "(1) To gather and diffuse authentic information regarding slavery and the slave-trade in Africa. (2) To found, in Africa, refuges and settlements of liberated slaves, in accordance with the Brussels Act." Mr. Chatelain, with a party of helpers, sailed from New York in July, 1897, to open his first station. His own leadership is regarded by all who know him as a guarantee of wisdom, prudence, and untiring effort towards the consummation of these humane plans.

Still northward, in the Congo Free State, we come upon regions which have long been smitten and decimated by Arab slave-traders, who have entered the country of the Upper Congo

Military expeditions and missionary toils in the Congo Valley. from Zanzibar and the East Coast.[1] The expedition under Commandant Dhanis, of which Dr. S. L. Hinde was a prominent member, was organized by the authorities of the Congo Free State in 1892, and resulted in the fall of the Congo Arabs in 1894. It has been instrumental in dealing a death-blow to that brutal system of plunder and rapine which has so long desolated the eastern portions of the Congo Free State. The operations of the campaign culminated in the fall of Nyangwe and Kasongo, important cities of the Manyema country, lying directly west of the northern end of Lake Tanganyika.[2] The credit of this achievement belongs to the Congo Government, and to the energetic leader of the expedition, although the methods of the Congo authorities may not in all cases be worthy of commendation. Missionaries are now located at many points in the Congo Valley. Some of them are occupying isolated stations, where they are in constant contact with the awful and disgusting features of mid-African savagery. Their reports, and the simple narrations of their heroic and patient work, often reveal the steady influence they are exerting for the overthrow of the hidden abominations of intertribal warfare, human sacrifice, cannibalism, and

---

Mr. Rose-Innes and his friends are bestirring themselves in the matter of the treatment of the natives. That is a hopeful sign. One meeting of protest at Cape Town is worth a hundred at Exeter Hall."

Cf. also *The Christian*, October 7, 1897, and *The Aborigines' Friend*, March, 1898, p. 309.

[1] Hinde, "The Fall of the Congo Arabs," pp. 1-3.   [2] *Ibid.*, pp. 169-193.

slave-raiding. Many prisoners of war who would be destined for the slave-shambles have thus been rescued (sometimes by ransom), and as free men and women have been trained and educated. It is stated in a recent report of the Southern Presbyterian Church of the United States that in one of its stations there were some seventy or eighty natives who had been ransomed.[1] Of the wisdom of thus ransoming slaves we are not prepared to pronounce an opinion. There seems, however, to be the possibility of thereby giving some covert encouragement to the slave-trade, which is liable to be misinterpreted by the natives themselves. We note that M. Coillard, of the French Mission on the Upper Zambesi, was strenuously opposed to this plan.[2] Dr. Snyder, of the Presbyterian Mission, writes, under date of June 15, 1894, that the Congo officials were often ready to hand over to the missionaries freed slaves, and thus relieve the question of all complications. He and his good wife, who has since died, reported that they had just received from the State a present of " ten boys, two women, and eight girls," making, with others under their charge, forty-four liberated slave children in their care at that time.[3]

As we move northward and follow the coast-line of the African Continent as it curves towards the west, we come to the scenes of the colonial slave-trade which terrorized and decimated the West Coast for two centuries and a half. There **A brighter day on the** is perhaps no other part of the world which in **West Coast.** modern times has been the scene of such inhuman cruelties as those which were perpetrated by unworthy representatives of Christian nations engaged, under the impulse of greed and selfishness,

[1] " Foreign Mission Report of the Southern Presbyterian Church, 1894," p. xxxvii.

[2] Coillard, " On the Threshold of Central Africa," pp. 152, 153.

Dr. Cust, in his " Notes on Missionary Subjects," has commented upon the subject of purchasing slaves, even with the best of motives, in the following terms : " There is another practice which missionary societies should not tolerate. I have seen notices of its existence in missions on both sides of the Atlantic. I allude to the purchase of Negro boys and girls by missionaries in Africa, for the best and holiest purposes, and yet the practice has in it the germs of much evil. As long as there is a demand for children, the kidnappers and slave-dealers will find it worth their while to continue the trade. It matters not to them whether the little girl is to find her way into the harem or into the mission school ; it is a question of so many dollars as purchase-money. It is not likely that parents would sell their own children, or tribesmen children of their own tribe ; the children must be stolen, and then sold. The Roman Catholics make this part of their system, and glory in it."—Part I., p. 12.

[3] *The Missionary*, November, 1894, pp. 483, 484.

in this scandalous traffic.[1]   Thanks to Christianity, this disgrace has ceased to rest upon civilization, and a day of liberty is surely dawning for the whole West Coast.

The Royal Niger Company, representing British authority, has now the command of the vast *Hinterland* lying inland from the Niger Coast Protectorate, east of the Niger River and north of the Binue, and bounded on the north by an irregular line extending westward from Lake Chad to a point about midway between Sokoto and Say.   To this extensive region the name of Nigeria has been given.   According to the Anglo-French Agreement of 1898, a large section of Borgu, west of the Niger, bounded on the west by a line extending from a point ten miles north of Ilo (a town on the Middle Niger just above Gomba) to the eastern boundary of Dahomey, is also secured to British control. The successful expeditions of the Royal Niger Company, in 1897, for the deliverance of Nupé from Fulah oppression, and the capture of Ilorin and Bida, have established the Company's supremacy in all that region.   Nupé and Eastern Borgu may now be regarded as British territory.   A steady struggle on the part of the Government with the slave-trade, so awfully prevalent in Sokoto and the populous Hausa States, has marked the extension of British administration.

The brilliant outcome of the expeditions of 1897 against the slave-raiding Fulah tribes was the proclamation by Sir George T. Goldie, Governor of the Royal Niger Company, of the abolition of the legal status of slavery throughout its territories, the decree to take effect June 19, 1897, upon the occasion of Her Majesty's Diamond Jubilee.[2]   The object of this campaign was chiefly for the extirpation of the slave-traffic in the protected Native States, and the

A veritable Jubilee in the Niger *Hinterland*.

---

[1]   Du Bose, " Memoirs of Rev. John Leighton Wilson, D.D.," pp. 212–215.

[2]   Sir George T. Goldie's proclamation is an historic document, as admirable in its terseness and force as it is striking in its far-reaching significance.   It is as follows:

" WHEREAS, a Resolution of the Council of the Royal Niger Company, Chartered and Limited, dated the Twenty-seventh day of October, One Thousand Eight Hundred and Ninety-six, authorises me to act in all respects on their behalf during my visit to the Niger Territories, and that all acts done by me in respect of the Government of the Niger Territories and the affairs of the Company during that visit shall be taken to be done by the Council;

" I HEREBY DECREE on behalf of the Council as follows:

" 1. On and after the Nineteenth day of June, One Thousand Eight Hundred and Ninety-seven, the legal status of Slavery shall stand abolished throughout the portion of the possession of HER GRACIOUS MAJESTY THE QUEEN OF GREAT

result is characterized in an editorial of *The Times* (London), February 11, 1897, in the following terms: "It seems not unreasonable to hope that in the downfall of Nupé the slave-trade has suffered the severest check it has undergone since the abolition of the traffic between this same West Coast and America." Dr. Harford-Battersby, in a letter to *The Mail* of February 12, 1897, expresses his opinion that "a great blow has been struck at the internal African slave-trade," and further on in his communication makes the following statement: "It must not be forgotten that the earliest approaches which were made to Nupé by our countrymen were largely through the aid of missionaries. To Bishop Crowther's tact in gaining the confidence of the native rulers is due much of the success that has followed English trade with the Upper Niger, and the present offers an almost unrivalled opportunity for missionary work in this part of Africa." What these victories and this blow at the slave-trade, in fact at slavery itself, mean for the future of those vast regions is incalculable.[1] It is not only a powerful guarantee looking to peace and prosperity, but by one quick stroke it is a release from untold suffering and sorrow, which would inevitably attend the continuance of slavery and the slave-trade in those populous regions at the hands of fiendish native despots.

The coast colonies for a generation or more have been in large measure freed from the traffic, and in the achievement of this result missionary coöperation is entitled to a conspicuous share of the honor which justly belongs to the efforts of the British Government. With the advent of the first agents of the Church Missionary Society in Sierra Leone, as early as 1804, the campaign against the slave-trade was commenced. The missionaries landed in Sierra Leone, but soon after settled at the mouth of the Pongo River, about

The redemption of the coast colonies.

BRITAIN AND IRELAND and EMPRESS OF INDIA, which is known as the Niger Territories.

"2. The Supreme Court of the Niger Territories is charged with the interpretation of this Decree by decisions given from time to time.

"Given under my hand, this Sixth day of March,
"One Thousand Eight Hundred and Ninety-seven,
"GEORGE TAUBMAN GOLDIE,
"Governor.
"ASABA, NIGER TERRITORIES, March 6, 1897."

Quoted in *The Anti-Slavery Reporter*, April–June, 1897, pp. 138, 139.

[1] "Report of the Church Missionary Society, 1897," p. 64. Cf. also Vandeleur, "Campaigning on the Upper Nile and Niger," especially the Introduction by Sir George T. Goldie.

one hundred and twenty miles to the northwest, in what is at present French territory. " It is impossible," writes Bishop Ingham, "not to admire the splendid courage with which those first missionaries entered upon, and persevered in, a death-grapple not only with the climate, but with European and African slave-dealers." [1] Little is known among Christian people as to what has been actually going on during the larger part of the nineteenth century, in the continuance of the slave-trade, on the African West Coast, in spite of all efforts to break it up. We have upon record, however, the testimony of missionaries who have been there on the ground fighting these awful atrocities, and who describe scenes of which they themselves were eye-witnesses. Extracts from the writings of two of them will suffice. [2]

It was the Rev. John Leighton Wilson, D.D., an American Presbyterian missionary to the West Coast, who, in 1850, when the British **How an appeal to the** Government was preparing to withdraw its African **British Government by** squadron from service, on the ground that it was **an American missionary** **kept its squadron on** doing little for the extirpation of the slave-trade, **the West Coast.** prepared a strong and able appeal urging that this should not be done, and giving good reasons for the request. The document was put into the hands of Lord Palmerston, who directed that an edition of ten thousand copies should be printed and distributed

---

[1] Ingham, " Sierra Leone After a Hundred Years," p. 195.

[2] The Rev. C. F. Frey, of the Church Missionary Society, wrote from Sierra Leone, in 1845, as follows : " In going from Kissy to Free Town, I met with a scene of misery which made such an impression on my mind that I shall scarcely ever forget it. About four hundred rescued Africans, old and young, of both sexes, were proceeding towards Kissy hospital. They had just come from a slave-vessel, and were in a most heartrending condition. Some, not being able to walk, were carried, while others supported themselves by sticks, looking, from the starvation they had endured on board, more like human skeletons than living beings. I have since been informed that, within a short time, about a hundred of them died. What crime had these poor creatures committed that they should be thus treated? It was ' the love of money,' truly designated ' the root of all evil,' in those who are called civilised people, which had brought them into this condition. . . . If Christians in Europe could have but one peep into such misery, they would more frequently pray for the propagation of the Gospel of Peace in Africa."—Ingham, " Sierra Leone After a Hundred Years," p. 245.

The Rev. John Leighton Wilson, D.D., an American Presbyterian missionary to the West Coast, wrote from Gaboon, in 1842, as follows : " I have visited all the settlements on the river in this immediate vicinity. There was one scene in these excursions which particularly affected my heart. I refer to the interior of a slave-factory on the opposite side of the river. I cannot enter into details, but, suffice it to say, my curiosity will never prompt me again to visit a similar scene of human degradation. Think of four hundred and thirty naked savages of both sexes, of all

in influential quarters. It was this monograph which quieted all opposition in England to the retention of the squadron at its post of duty. Lengthy extracts from the memorandum are given in the Life of Dr. Wilson.[1]

The recent successes of the Royal Niger Company in subduing Nupé by the capture of Bida, its capital, Ladi, one of its strongholds, and Ilorin, should remind us that the earliest British explorations of the Niger Valley were participated in by missionary agents, among them Mr. Schön and Mr. (afterwards Bishop) Crowther, *The bearing of early missionary efforts upon the slave-trade in the valley of the Niger.* who in the year 1841 were thus engaged, and that the destruction of the slave-trade was one of the prominent objects then in view. Again, in 1854, in another of these exploring journeys Mr. Crowther selected the sites of mission stations at Onitsha, Gbebe (Igbegbe), and Rabba. In 1857 he once more participated in a more formal expedition under the auspices of the British Admiralty, for the further exploration of the Niger and its tributaries. The steamer "Dayspring," which carried the expedition, was wrecked by striking a rock not far from Rabba. Mr. Crowther on this account spent a considerable time in that region, making a careful study of the whole situation. Subsequently he was appointed Bishop, representing the Church Missionary Society in its Niger Coast Mission, and had an influential part in the great conflict with the slave-raiders who were desolating those regions.[2]

Let us glance for a moment at the early history of this Mr. Crowther, afterwards Bishop of the Niger. He was a young Yoruban lad, who, in 1821, was seized by a Mohammedan slave-raider, but afterwards rescued, and, in 1825, was baptized by missionaries, under the

ages, sizes, and conditions, brought together in one enclosure, chained together in gangs of twenty, thirty, or forty, and all compelled to sleep on the same platform, eat out of the same tub, and in almost every respect live like so many swine. More than this, on the middle passage they must have quarters still more circumscribed, and live on much scantier fare. God reigns, and this vile traffic in human beings must come to an end."—Du Bose, " Memoirs of Rev. John Leighton Wilson, D.D.," pp. 217, 218.

[1] At the conclusion of these extracts, the biographer comments as follows: "Thus ends this great State paper. His voice was heard by the English nation, and her people accepted the three conclusions : First, That the squadron had done much for Africa; Second, That it must be continued till its work was accomplished; and, Third, That the fastest ships be placed in this service till the slave-trade come to an end."—*Ibid.*, pp. 218-226. See also Wilson's " Western Africa," pp. 430-451.

[2] Cf. article on " Nupé—Past Endeavors and Present Opportunities," by C. F. Harford-Battersby, M.D., in *The Church Missionary Intelligencer*, March, 1897, pp. 169-173.

name of Samuel Crowther.   He was educated in the Fourah Bay College of the Church Missionary Society, and was ordained to the ministry in 1843.   After a time he unexpectedly met his mother and also a brother and two sisters near the scene of his early seizure, and was the means of their conversion.   In 1857 he founded a mission in the Niger country, and in 1864 he was appointed Bishop of the Niger. During most of his life, amid many perils and hardships, he opposed most earnestly the slave-trade, and every other cruel heathen custom of the Niger region.   His wife, like himself, was rescued from a slave-ship, and was blessed with a Christian training by the missionaries. Their six children, all Christians, are living useful lives, three of them actively engaged in mission work.   To one of them, Archdeacon Crowther, the author is indebted for valuable documents from his father's papers, and for information kindly furnished concerning missions in the Niger Coast Protectorate.[1]   A memorial church at Cline Town commemorates Bishop Crowther's life.   The Rev. H. W. Tucker, of the Society for the Propagation of the Gospel, speaks of the mission which Bishop Crowther founded, as follows: " By this mission the horrible slave-trade has received a great check; the practice of human sacrifice is at an end within the Niger country, and the neighboring chiefs find themselves unable to procure slaves to be immolated by their priests.   Instead of the indolence which accompanies the easy gains of the slave-dealer, commerce, with its attendant activity, has been introduced far up the rivers." [2]

Bishop Crowther—the story of his rescue and subsequent services to the cause of freedom.

Mr. William A. B. Johnson, with others, was sent out to Sierra Leone by the Church Missionary Society in 1816, and was busy during the seven years of his life there in receiving the rescued slaves as they were landed by cruisers, and bringing them under Christian instruction, by which they were trained for usefulness.[3]   In 1822 there were two thousand freed slaves in the mission schools, and thousands more were reached by Christian teaching.   The Governor of the colony, in commenting upon the fact, remarked: " The hand of Heaven is on this." Dr. Cust, in one of his papers, entitled " A Word to those who do not Recognize the Divinely Imposed Duty of Evangelization," refers to missionary intervention in arresting slave-dealing, and in the course of his remarks says: " What but strong Christian influence would have

[1] Cf. Creegan, " Great Missionaries of the Church," pp. 125–140; Pierson, " The Miracles of Missions," Second Series, pp. 107–126.

[2] Tucker, " Under His Banner," p. 188.

[3] Pierson, " Seven Years in Sierra Leone " (Life of W. A. B. Johnson).

Mission Workshop, Christiansborg, Gold Coast, Africa.

Home for Freed Slaves, Kumassi.

A HOME FOR SLAVES ON THE GOLD COAST.

(Ba. M. S.)

done it, and who but missionaries would have supplied the facts about slave-dealing and been foremost in the conflict? The Christian mission is the complement of the Slavery-Abolition Society: the two make one power. Sierra Leone and Frere Town are proofs of this."[1]

It was Sir T. Fowell Buxton's appeal in his book on "The Slave-Trade and its Remedy" which incited the United Presbyterian missionaries in Jamaica, soon after the abolition of slavery in the West Indies, to establish a mission in Old Calabar, in the eastern section of what is now the Niger Coast Protectorate. The Rev. H. M. Waddell, their first missionary, went out in response to an appeal from King Eyamba and several of his chiefs, who offered protection and a gift of ground at Duke Town. In 1844 the Presbytery of Jamaica responded to this call of opportunity, and since then the Old Calabar Mission, which was adopted in 1847 by the United Presbyterian Church of Scotland, has borne its full part in the struggle with the slave-traffic, especially in that section where it has been located.[2] The missionaries of the Wesleyan Methodist Church of England, early in the second decade of the century, began their work at Sierra Leone, and have also taken an active part in this prolonged conflict. One of their finest mission churches in West Africa, the Buxton Chapel at Freetown, is named after Sir T. Fowell Buxton. The captured slave-vessels were many of them stranded in what is known as "Destruction Bay," not far from that city, where they either went to pieces or were broken up. Much of the timber of these doomed ships has been appropriated to missionary uses. The mission house of the Wesleyans at Freetown, and also the neighboring Zion Chapel, were erected of material obtained from this source. Missionaries of the Wesleyan, Basel, and North German (Bremen) Societies, in the Gold Coast Colony, Togoland, and Kamerun, have contributed by sympathy and active coöperation, wherever the opportunity has presented, towards hastening the doom of the West Coast slave-trade. In some of their churches many of the converts were formerly brought as slaves from the interior, and escaped to the shelter of British protection, where they found Christian instruction through the good missionaries of the Basel Society.[3]

Missionaries of all societies hastening the hour of full deliverance in West Africa.

1 Cust, "The Gospel Message," p. 166.
2 Dickie, "The Story of the Mission in Old Calabar," pp. 9–13.
3 "The Basel Evangelical Mission on the Gold Coast, from 1828 to 1893," p. 19.

Far off the West Coast is the Island of St. Helena, which in 1847 became a part of the Diocese of Cape Town, and since 1859 has been made the seat of its own bishopric.   It has often

A good work for rescued slaves in St. Helena. happened that slaves from captured slavers have been landed on this island, where they were cared for by the bishop and his colleagues with great kindness.   So numerous were the slaves thus discharged at St. Helena that the British Government provided an institution especially for their reception.   Upon one occasion, when the Bishop of Cape Town was making a visit to the island, a slave-ship containing five hundred and sixty souls arrived there.   At the same time there were already three hundred in the hospital on the shore.   Bishop Claughton, the first bishop of the See of St. Helena, was accustomed to labor with loving assiduity in these seasons of emergency.   His successors, and others of the English clergy, have worthily followed in his footsteps.   The slaves are not only freed, but employment guarded by proper restrictions is found for them in the West Indies.   During some years as many as three thousand Negroes were landed at St. Helena, and after a period of a few months, spent under Christian instruction, a settlement was arranged for them in some way which secured to them their freedom. For those who were permanently invalided, or suffered from blindness, as many of them did, provision was made upon the island, where they were the recipients of patient and careful Christian ministrations.[1]

Along the northern coast of the Continent the slave-trade has existed for centuries.   A grim feature of the cruel piracy of the Bar-bary corsairs was the seizure of human beings,

Efforts old and new on behalf of freedom in North Africa. many of them Christian natives of Europe, who were captured upon piratical expeditions of pillage to the Mediterranean islands of Sicily, Sardinia, and Corsica, and even to the coasts of Italy and Spain, and thence trans-ported into captivity in the Barbary States.   During the latter part of the sixteenth century, and through the two succeeding centuries, even to the nineteenth, these deeds of rapine continued.   Among those who were thus captured, in 1575, was Cervantes, the well-known author of "Don Quixote," who spent some years in slavery in Algiers.[2]   Much attention was devoted by several ecclesiastics of the Roman Catholic Church in the Middle Ages to the rescuing and extending of compas-sionate ministrations to these bondmen, and to others enslaved by

[1] Tucker, "Under His Banner," pp. 152–157.
[2] Ingram, "History of Slavery," pp. 274–278. Cf. also "The Barbary Cor-sairs," by S. Lane-Poole, in The Story of the Nations Series.

Moors and Saracens. For this purpose also two permanent religious orders were founded, namely, the order of Trinitarians, and that of Notre Dame de la Merci.[1] Although the influence of Christian Powers has been directed, through diplomatic pressure and by the aid of various treaties, to the suppression of the slave-trade in the North African countries, the efforts have not proved wholly efficacious, except in the cases of Egypt and Algiers. In Morocco, Tunis, and Tripoli there are still slave-markets (Vol. I., pp. 139, 140). Even at the present time the traffic in Morocco is open and scandalous. Under date of November, 1897, details of slave-sales at Safi, on the west coast of the sultanate, were published in the newspapers of Tangier.[2] It is interesting to note that a committee of European ladies residing in Tangier has addressed appeals upon the subject to the philanthropic societies in Europe organized and conducted by women. *The Anti-Slavery Reporter* (November–December, 1897, p. 262), in commenting upon this fact, remarks: "This is as it should be, for the public indignities offered to women in the slave-markets of Morocco are a scandal of which all Europe ought to be ashamed."

The British Government, in 1895, established a convention with Egypt for the suppression of slavery and the slave-trade, signed on behalf of Great Britain by Lord Cromer.[3] The execution of this definitive agreement will no doubt prove a permanent check to the Egyptian slave-trade, and the advance of British rule into the Soudan will result, let us hope, in an effective blow at the inner sources of slave-trading conspiracy. The Home at Cairo for the protection and care of liberated female slaves has secured an annual grant of three hundred pounds from the Egyptian Government. The missionaries in Egypt have been in full sympathy with the efforts of the British Government to put a stop to the slave-traffic of the Nile Valley, and have coöperated with the authorities as they have had opportunity. In the Turkish Empire they have not failed to give information to European officials, especially British consuls, whenever they were aware of the secret transactions of traders who were bringing slaves to Mohammedan cities with a view to selling them.

There are two regions which still remain to be mentioned, where missionary influence has been helpful in opposition to this evil. One

Missionary coöperation with British officials in Egypt and Turkey.

[1] Ingram, "History of Slavery," pp. 278–281.

[2] *The Anti-Slavery Reporter*, November–December, 1897, pp. 261, 263.

[3] The text of the Convention is given in full in *The Anti-Slavery Reporter* for December, 1895, pp. 269–272.

is the Pacific Islands, and the other the East Indies. What has been known as the Kanaka traffic (the significance of which is a trade in human beings, since the word "Kanaka" in Hawaiian means "man") was for nearly thirty years, or from its inauguration in 1863 to its supposed "regulation" in 1886, and its suppression in 1890, a most atrocious species of the kidnapping slave-trade. By it natives were torn from home and kindred, and transported to virtual slavery in Queensland and elsewhere throughout Australasia.[1] It was in retaliation for this kidnapping of natives that Bishop Patteson was killed at Nukapu, one of the Santa Cruz Islands; but the martyrdom of this noble missionary bishop served to call the attention of the people of England to the horrors of the Kanaka traffic, and through the trenchant exposure of its shameful features by Melanesian missionaries the subsequent efforts of the British Government to regulate and control it were prompted.[2] The provision which the authorities had made to place proper restrictions upon the traffic proved to be ineffective in many important respects, and a proposed revival of it, in 1891, for the supply of the Queensland labor-market, called out the strenuous efforts of missionaries to check it. Its evils seem indisputable, although, in the opinion of some who are entitled to speak concerning the matter, the condition of the natives, when once located on the Queensland plantations, is not without beneficent features. A strong statement, based upon nearly a lifelong observation, by the Rev. George Brown, D.D., of Sydney, Secretary of the Methodist Missionary Society, clearly points out, however, that to the native islanders the traffic is a burdensome and cruel evil, which should not be tolerated.[3]

The situation in 1892 was such as to impel the venerable Dr. Paton, whose life has been given to missionary service in the New Hebrides, to enter upon a campaign of public protest and personal effort to secure the effectual suppression by the British Government of this shocking evil, which, on the authority of a Royal Commission, had been already condemned in severe terms, as "one long record of deceit, cruel treachery, deliberate kidnapping, and cold-blooded murder." For this purpose he visited England, where he was able to convince people of influence that there was an urgent call for action, and, at the request of Lord Ripon, Secretary of State for the

The battle with the Kanaka traffic.

The appeal of Dr. Paton to the British and American Governments.

---

[1] Michelsen, "Cannibals Won for Christ," pp. 153–156.

[2] Montgomery, "The Light of Melanesia," pp. 157–159, 249.

[3] *Work and Workers in the Mission Field,* November, 1892, pp. 323–325.

Colonies, in December, 1893, he drew up a memorandum presenting a valuable and powerful summary statement of the whole question, in which the objectionable aspects of the case were presented with great force and unsparing plainness.[1] Dr. Paton had previously to this visited America in the autumn of 1892, as a delegate to the Presbyterian Council at Toronto, and while in the United States he sought to influence the Government to coöperate with other nations in the suppression of the traffic in slaves and rum in the New Hebrides. So effective have been the steps taken by the British Government, largely, no doubt, as the result of Dr. Paton's energetic appeals, that at the present time the system may be regarded as freed from its most objectionable features, and likely to cease altogether, as under present regulations neither safe nor profitable. Coolies from India have in most instances been substituted for the Kanakas, and, owing to the supervision of the British Government in India, this plan is

[1] Copious extracts from this memorandum are printed in *The Anti-Slavery Reporter*, January, 1894, pp. 24–31, and *The Christian*, January 18, 1894. The concluding paragraphs are as follows : " I do solemnly assure your Lordship, without bias or prejudice against planters, agents, or crews, that the *system* of securing Polynesian labour for the Queensland plantations is a relic of the bygone and barbarous past, a veiled system of slavery, robbed to some extent of its bloodshed and murder, but carried on by deceit and allurement, by bribes and plausibility, through the agency of trained native decoys, under cover of armed boats, crews, captains, and Government agents, in regions far from the vigilant eye of the law (save for the occasional visit, hailed with joy by missionaries and natives, of one of Her Majesty's ships with its noble officers, men of honour, of kindly heart and noble bearing, who so impartially seek to administer justice and uphold the dignity of the Queen and Nation). I repeat that, while humanity is at a very low ebb among the South Sea labour-collectors, while such deeds can be perpetrated on *speechless natives* whose dark bodies alone are desired for the energy that can be forced out of them to fill the coffers of white men, while the planters own labour-ships and hire captains and crews, and while a handsome premium is given all round for Kanaka recruits, the traffic is bound to be a curse and a degradation to all engaged in it, a disgrace to the colony that legalises it, and a blot on the fair name of Britain.

" I entreat your Lordship to hear the heartfelt plea of an old man, burdened with the evils that are heaped upon his defenceless people, just as they are emerging from the long, black midnight of gross heathenism and cannibalism. Oh, that my beloved country would rise and stamp out this foul system ; that the land of Wilberforce and Clarkson, that the Britain whose blood and treasure have been freely sacrificed to enable her to assume the proud position of a nation that never owns a slave, a nation that prefers death to bondage—that my own loved home-land would add to its roll of glorious triumphs this : that her children must not and shall not disgrace her name by playing with a deadly system that has led in the past, and must in the future lead, to abuse, bloodshed, and God-dishonouring cruelty, little short of that accursed thing called slavery ! "

subject to proper restrictions and regulations. Where European protectorates have been established in the South Seas, especially by Great Britain, the "blackbird traffic," as the slave-trade is called, has been put under a rigorous ban, as in the Fiji and Gilbert Islands.[1] In the Eastern Archipelago, especially under Spanish and Portuguese rule, the slave-trade has existed for centuries. Wherever the Dutch have ruled it has been extirpated, and here and there even slavery itself has been abolished, but the liberation has come very slowly, and in certain localities only within a few years. The influence of the Dutch missionaries may be said to have contributed to this result.[2]

Thus, wherever Christian missions in their onward movement have crossed the blood-stained trail of the slave-trade, they have sought to mitigate its horrors, and have always gladly and often most efficiently assisted in its suppression.

2. AIDING IN THE OVERTHROW OF SLAVERY.—Although slavery and the slave-trade are closely connected, yet they are not identical, and should, therefore, be distinguished. The slave-

The inevitable revolt of Christianity against slavery. traffic is far more of an offense to the moral sense of mankind than slavery, and the revolt against it has generally been in advance of the condemnation of slavery. The latter may exist long after the former has been abolished. In fact, even in modern times, the movement for the extinction of slavery has been historically from one to two generations later than the suppression of the traffic. The verdict of Christianity has been consistently in opposition to both these great historic scandals, except in cases where individual self-interest, or the moral paralysis which is often produced by an environment of slavery, has distorted the judgment of misguided interpreters of biblical teachings on the subject. Christian missions have faced both evils on many fields, and have waged against them a sturdy warfare of moral antagonism, which in some instances has been a powerful factor in producing practical results of momentous value, as was true also in the early history of Christianity.[3]

---

[1] Alexander, "The Islands of the Pacific," p. 339.

[2] Guillemard, "Australasia," vol. ii. (Stanford's "Compendium of Geography and Travel"), pp. 92, 315, 322, 338.

[3] Brace, "Gesta Christi," p. 53; Schmidt, "The Social Results of Early Christianity," p. 215; Storrs, "The Divine Origin of Christianity," pp. 161–167, 488–493.

The most striking instance in modern mission history of a successful moral crusade against slavery is the memorable campaign of the missionaries in the West Indies, which culminated in British legislation for the total abolition of slavery in 1834. This decree, however, did not become effective until 1838. Jamaica, which was chiefly the scene of these stirring events, was discovered by the Spaniards in 1494, on the second voyage of Columbus to the Western world. For over a century and a half Spanish rule, characterized by much heartless and brutal treatment of the native populations, wrought only sorrow and moral evil to the island. A victory by the British, in 1655, gave them the military supremacy, which was followed, in 1661, by the establishment of a civil government. As previously under Spanish, so, unhappily, under British rule, the slave-trade, conducted by both Spanish and English traders, grew to frightful proportions. The island became a perfect inferno of slavery, and the lowest depths of moral degradation and of civil injustice and absolutism were reached.[1]

The missionary campaign in Jamaica can hardly be said to have begun until the entrance of the Moravians in 1754, although the Church of England had been established there since 1662, not, however, devoting itself to missionary efforts at that early date. The Methodists followed in 1789, the Baptists in 1814, and the United Presbyterian Church of Scotland in 1824, although the Scottish Missionary Society had previously made an unsuccessful effort to open a mission on the island by sending out the Rev. Joseph Bethune in 1800. In 1835 the London Missionary Society and the Society for

The memorable campaign of missions for freedom in the West Indies.

---

[1] The burning words of William Knibb, the heroic missionary who was so influential in securing the final abolition of slavery, may serve to characterize the abominable social conditions which were incidental to West Indian slavery early in the nineteenth century. He writes: " The cursed blast of slavery has, like a pestilence, withered almost every moral bloom. I know not how any person can feel a union with such a monster, such a child of hell. For myself, I have a burning hatred against it, and look upon it as one of the most odious monsters that ever disgraced the earth. The slaves have temporal comforts in profusion; but their morals are sunk below the brute, and the iron hand of oppression daily endeavours to keep them in that ignorance to which it has reduced them. When contemplating the withering scene my heart sickens, and I feel ashamed that I belong to a race that can indulge in such atrocities. It is in the immorality of slavery that the evil chiefly consists. I can easily account for persons becoming familiarised with slavery, and having a dislike to the slaves, as they are very trying; but it ought ever to be remembered that this proceeds from the system, and that the owner has a large portion of the blame attaching to himself."—Smith, " William Knibb: Missionary in Jamaica," pp. 8, 9.

the Propagation of the Gospel also began work in Jamaica. The latter society had rendered aid to the local clergy by grants of books, and by contributions of money towards the partial payment of their passage, since 1703, but its foreign missionary work proper began in 1835, with an apportionment of an allowance from its Negro Instruction Fund to aid in educating the Negroes of Jamaica. Its first missionaries reached the island the next year.[1] It is worthy of note that the original purpose of these early missionary efforts was *the religious instruction of the slaves*. In fact, the Scottish Missionary Society, which introduced the Presbyterian Church into Jamaica, was led to undertake its work at the solicitation of some Scotch owners of property in Jamaica, who urged the Society to "send out missionaries to the slaves on their estates," the owners themselves offering to bear half the expense.[2]

It was the policy of the missionaries in those early times not to attack slavery publicly or seek its overthrow, a method which, in view of the overwhelming power of the slave interest, would then have been hopeless. The very fact, however, that they were friendly to the slaves and devoted to their spiritual welfare excited the suspicion and animosity, and in the end the persecuting violence, of the great majority of slave-owners. Laws were passed forbidding any spiritual teaching on the part of the missionaries among slaves, and it soon became manifest that, while slavery lasted, the Gospel would be under a ban, and mission work would be bitterly antagonized. A formidable insurrection of the slaves was quietly fomented by non-missionary agencies during Christmas week in 1831. When it finally broke out the missionaries were charged with inciting it. Against this false accusation a complete vindication has since been established, but at the time the pro-slavery party vindictively used its power to persecute them, and to put down the insurrection with horrid cruelty. The leader of the rebellion, a slave named Samuel Sharp, was executed, "attesting with his last breath the innocence of the missionaries, and declaring that if he had listened to their instructions he should never have come to that awful end."[3] A purpose to expel the missionaries from the island was fully formed, and an effort made to accomplish it.

The hostility of the slave-owners to the missionaries.

---

[1] Pascoe, "Classified Digest of the Records of the Society for the Propagation of the Gospel in Foreign Parts," pp. 195, 229, 885.

[2] Robson, "The Story of Our Jamaica Mission," p. 26.

[3] Smith, "William Knibb: Missionary in Jamaica," p. 23.

Rev. J. M. Phillippo.   Rev. W. Knibb.

        Rev. T. Burchell.   Rev. John Wray.

Rescued slaves brought to Zanzibar, captured from slave-dhows by Her Majesty's ship London.

MISSIONARY HEROES IN THE ANNALS OF FREEDOM.

In the meantime, William Knibb, at the instance of his colleagues, sailed for England, to unite with Messrs. Burchell and Phillippo in an appeal to British Christians. He sailed from Kingston, April 26, 1832, and on his arrival at London, in June, the three champions of liberty, all of whom were Baptist missionaries to Jamaica, began their campaign.[1] The preparatory work of four noble philanthropists, Sharp, Clarkson, Wilberforce, and Buxton, whose names will ever be associated with the downfall of slavery in the British Empire, had already influenced public sentiment in Great Britain. The addresses of these missionaries from Jamaica, especially those of the eloquent Knibb, produced a powerful and instantaneous impression, as they went from one large assembly to another throughout England and Scotland. The Imperial Parliament passed, August 7, 1833, the Act of Emancipation, which by royal assent became law August 28th, abolishing slavery in Jamaica and all British colonies after August 1, 1834. This legislation, involving, as it did, the payment of twenty million pounds as compensation to the slaveholders for the forcible manumission of the bondmen, was a splendid triumph for freedom, not only in the annals of missions, but in the history of humanity. Knibb, Burchell, and Phillippo returned to their missionary labors in Jamaica, where serious duties awaited them. The final consummation of the Emancipation Act did not take place, however, until August 1, 1838, the first year of Queen Victoria's reign.[2]

> Knibb, Burchell, and Phillippo — a brave triumvirate.

As passed by the British Parliament the Act was marred and fettered by a stipulation that the slaves should remain in a state of apprenticeship during four years from August 1, 1834, before receiving absolute freedom. The planters, in their rage, took advantage of this opportunity to wreak their vengeance upon the Negroes, and committed violent excesses in the infliction of punishment and torture. The Island of Antigua alone was an exception, for reasons which we shall state presently. On the 1st of August, 1838, the great triumph of justice in Jamaica came, and eight hundred thousand human beings were freed forever from bondage, amid the wildest rejoicings and the most heartfelt thanksgivings. The Negroes fully understood that this freedom had come to them through the intervention of Christian missionaries, and their services of praise and gratitude were marked by a holy and chastened joy, and were deeply religious

> A rejoicing multitude of freedmen in Jamaica give thanks to God and His missionaries.

[1] Smith, " William Knibb: Missionary in Jamaica," pp. 35–48.
[2] " The Centenary Volume of the Baptist Missionary Society," pp. 190–193.

in spirit.[1] The whole history of the service rendered by missions to the Negro population of the West Indies is a sociological study which illustrates in a convincing manner their social benefits to a degraded and downtrodden race. Jamaica, in contrast with the neighboring Island of Haiti, affords also a luminous example of the blessings which Christianity in its purity brings to a people who receive it.

The chronicles of missions in South America, especially in British Guiana, are also not without illustrations, although on a less imposing scale, of the services of missionaries to the cause of human freedom. In the early history of the London Missionary Society, the Rev. John Wray was sent to Demerara (now part of British Guiana). He arrived at his destination in 1808, where he came in contact with the miseries of slavery, which in that region was attended with gross barbarities. The same animosity which had been manifested in Jamaica characterized the attitude of the slave-owners towards the missionaries, and the London Missionary Society's agents became an offense to these vengeful masters. "To attempt to make the Negroes Christians was in the eyes of the planters of those days criminal." It was clearly seen by them that "to introduce Christianity was to intro-

The heroic struggle of the early missionaries in Demerara.

---

1 Smith, "William Knibb: Missionary in Jamaica," chap. vi. ; Robson, "The Story of Our Jamaica Mission," chap. iv. ; Pitman, "The West Indies" (Outline Missionary Series), pp. 27–31.

"Mr. Knibb gives a thrilling account of the joy of his people on the occasion of full freedom. His chapel was crowded with slaves, who spent the hours in praise and prayer, until the clock pointed nearly to twelve on the night of the 31st of July. As it pealed out the stroke of twelve, the people rose, and broke out into a loud cheer, which was only interrupted by sobs and thanksgivings. The next morning a coffin was buried, containing a chain, handcuffs, iron collar, and other insignia of slavery, while the people uplifted their voices in the following words :

"'Now, Slavery, we lay thy vile form in the dust,
    And, buried forever, there let it remain ;
    And rotted and covered with infamy's rust
    Be every man-whip and fetter and chain.'

"At Montego Bay, at Brown's Town, at Spanish Town, and at other places throughout the island, rejoicings were loud and long-continued. Yet we have the testimony of historians that nothing unseemly occurred. It was said by one : ' There was joy without riot, triumph without reproach, multitudes without confusion, while religion assumed the undisputed precedency over the soul-exhilarating scenes.' Sir Lionel Smith, the Governor of Jamaica, uttered the following memorable words : ' Out of the eight hundred thousand oppressed slaves set free in one day to equal rights and liberty, not a human being of the mass has committed himself in any of the dreaded offences.' "—Pitman, "The West Indies," pp. 30, 31.

duce the spirit of freedom, and to hasten the day of emancipation." The Society's work in British Guiana may be designated as *a mission to slaves* for the purpose of humane ministrations and Gospel instruction to a crushed, forsaken, and despised people. A stirring account of this heroic struggle is given in a beautiful and impressive chapter of "The Story of the London Missionary Society," by the Rev. C. Silvester Horne (pp. 146–170). The obstructive attitude of the colonial authorities towards every attempt to teach and elevate the slaves, the bitter hostility of the planters, the intrepid and self-sacrificing efforts of Wray, Davies, and Smith, the disheartening hindrances, the cheerful toils, the courageous devotion, and the memorable successes of twenty-five years of conflict, are all told by Mr. Horne with a fullness of detail which is impossible in these pages.

The Emancipation Act of 1834 brought relief, and gave a brighter outlook to what may be regarded as one of the forlorn hopes of mission history. We do not wonder that this quarter of a century of heroism has been embalmed with grati- A missionary's exposé tude and pride in the records of the London Mis- of colonial slavery in British Guiana. sionary Society. The account of John Wray's visit to England in 1811, to seek the repeal of iniquitous legislation, and his triumphant return, cannot be read unmoved.[1] The unsparing

---

[1] " In the midst of many encouragements, and at a time when Mr. Wray was able to report that there was a better feeling towards his work among several of the neighbouring planters, the dreaded blow fell. This was nothing less than a Government proclamation forbidding the slaves to assemble, for any purpose whatsoever, before sunrise or after sunset. Any Englishman taking part in such illegal meeting was liable to a fine of fifty pounds; the slaves were to be subject to very severe punishments. The proclamation was issued in 1811. It was, of course, an absolute barrier to any instruction during the week-days, as the slaves worked from sunrise to sundown. Mr. Wray was regarded as a very quiet, patient, and peaceable man. Possibly the authorities imagined he would tamely submit; if so, they were mistaken. He first of all demanded an interview with Governor Bentinck, to whom he stated his case. The Governor assured him that if he were caught breaking the law he should be banished from the colony. Wray's reply to this was that he would not break the law, but would go direct to England and make his appeal at headquarters. With his usual determination, he walked straight to the docks, and found a ship that was to sail for England in a few days, with a cargo of cotton. The captain assured him that all the berths were choked with cotton-bales, and that he could not take passengers. Wray replied that he did not want a berth, but would sleep on the bales. He must go to England *at once*. The terms were arranged. . . . On June 16, 1811, John Wray sailed for England. If Governor Bentinck imagined that he could intimidate this young missionary, he had evidently reckoned with the wrong man.

" Six weeks among the cotton-bales was probably not the most congenial position

exposé of the conditions of colonial slavery in those days, sent home in 1822 by the Rev. John Smith, is perhaps the most powerful and scathing presentation of the subject that can be found, and bears upon its face the marks of absolute authenticity and truthfulness. The principal points of the indictment are summarized in Mr. Horne's volume as follows: " In the colony there are about four hundred slaves to five whites able to bear arms. The slaves live in huts, that only deserve the name of kennels, and are turned out at six in the morning by the drivers cracking their whips as they might at a number of horses or cattle. Work goes on till six in the evening, and often half through the night as well. The Sunday rest is not properly observed, as they are then 'employed in other ways. The slaves work in gangs under a black ' driver.' Punishment consists in a man or woman being stretched out on the ground —hands and feet tied to stakes—and then beaten with the whip, sometimes to the extent of a hundred lashes. If the work is not finished, the slave who is behindhand is put into the stocks, in prison, and kept there all night. Cases are frequent in which slaves, after cruel beatings, have been detained many days, and even weeks, in the stocks, that the marks on their backs might not be seen. The only furniture allowed the slave is one iron pot for the family, and a blanket for each individual. Children from twelve years old upwards must work just the same as grown men and women. The slaves have no time to clean their huts, and they keep their fowls in them, so that the state of filth is inconceivable. Their food consists of vegetables and salt fish. Their moral life is naturally very low and degraded; but even here, Mr. Smith asserts, they compare favourably with the whites, whose licentiousness and profanity are abominable. No wonder that he concluded his letter with the words: ' To nurture this system of slavery is a foul blot

in the world; but the voyage had to be made somehow, and ' the King's business requireth haste.' After a brief stay at Liverpool, Wray pushed on to London, and easily enlisted Wilberforce and Stephens on his side. His case was duly presented and enforced; and he soon had the gratification of knowing that missionary work in Demerara, and other colonies where slavery existed, was saved. By Government decree, on all plantations where the planters offered no objection, the slaves might meet at any hour between 5 A.M. and 9 P.M. on Sundays, and between 7 A.M. and 9 P. M. on week-days. In six months from the time of his sailing from Demerara, Wray was back again, having secured his charter. Governor Bentinck naturally was not cordial. He had been clearly beaten, and he did not accept defeat manfully. For some time he made no formal announcement that the former proclamation was withdrawn. But his term of authority was at an end. In April, 1812, he was superseded, and the new Governor was entirely favourable to the missionaries."—Horne, " The Story of the London Missionary Society," pp. 152, 153.

on the British character, which every lover of his country should dedicate his whole life to efface.' " [1]

Let it be noted that in 1823 what was regarded as an important victory in the interest of the slaves in Demerara was gained through British legislation. And what was this new law for which at that time thanks were given in the name of humanity? It was "that slaves should not be worked more than nine hours a day, and that women should not be flogged." We read that when the news reached Demerara it "was received with great indignation by the planters," and that the Governor refused to proclaim it. Distorted rumors of the withholding of some good tidings so excited the Negroes that an insurrection followed, which was put down with frightful cruelties. The Rev. John Smith was falsely accused of aiding and abetting in rebellion, was tried by court martial, and publicly sentenced to be hanged. This sentence was not executed, but Mr. Smith was confined in a loathsome, malarious prison-cell, where he fell a victim to a swift and fatal illness. He lies in an unknown grave in Demerara, but in life and in death he was a hero, and his name deserves to be written high on the roll of honor in the annals of human freedom.[2] In 1836 the Rev. S. R. Murkland and his wife sailed for Demerara under appointment of the London Missionary Society. It is reported of Mrs. Murkland that through her instrumentality more than a thousand Negro slaves learned to read the Word of God.[3]

An honored name in the annals of freedom.

The Moravian Missionary Society has also an honorable record in connection with the emancipation of slaves in the West Indies and in Central and South America. As early as 1732 its missionaries entered the Danish West Indies, and in 1756 the mission on the Island of Antigua was established. It was by the advice of the Anglican, Wesleyan, and Moravian missionaries that Governor Macgregor, in 1834, promptly gave effect to the Emancipation Act, and saved

The romantic story of Moravian achievements in the West Indies and Dutch Guiana.

---

[1] Horne, "The Story of the London Missionary Society," pp. 160, 161.

[2] "One cannot help thinking with even deeper reverence and tenderness of another and a nameless grave [not Wray's] in Demerara, the precise situation of which no man knows, where he sleeps who, for his consistent and chivalrous devotion to ' the poor and him that hath no helper,' was sentenced to a felon's death, and died in a felon's cell. Doubtless he has his reward, not only in that rest which remaineth for the people of God, but in that day of liberty which he saw not, but which he greeted afar, and in the honour and reverence which all true children of freedom will ever feel for John Smith of Demerara."—*Ibid.*, p. 170.

[3] *The Missionary*, April, 1896, p. 183.

thirty thousand slaves from four years of apprenticeship.   The religious instruction of the missionaries is declared, in the preamble to the official document, to be the secret of the fitness of the Antigua slaves to receive immediate manumission.   It was announced that the decree of freedom would take effect August 1, 1834.   Upon the evening of July 31st, the slaves gathered in the historic Spring Gardens Church, at St. Johns, Antigua, and Bennet Harvey, a Moravian missionary, preached to them as a congregation of slaves for the last time, from the text, "Sanctify yourselves; for to-morrow the Lord will do wonders among you."   Shortly after eleven o'clock the roll of thunder was heard, increasing in loudness as midnight approached.   "It is Massa breakin' de chains, Hallelujah!" exclaimed the wondering throng. The stroke of midnight brought the day of freedom amid deep, ecstatic joy.[1]   The mission of the Moravians in Dutch Guiana was chiefly devoted, at an early date, to the welfare of the slaves, including Negroes, bushmen, and coolies.   The black population of Surinam, which has been won to Christianity, is indebted almost exclusively to the missionaries of this Society for its knowledge of the Gospel.   Even as early as the opening of the present century, 1645 of the Indian and slave population of English and Dutch Guiana were enrolled as Christians in connection with their missions.[2]   The Moravians were especially commissioned by the Government of Dutch Guiana as far back as the beginning of this century to take pastoral charge of the slaves and prisoners at the government posts.[3]   A baptized membership of over twenty-eight thousand is now found in their missions in Dutch Guiana. Of this number 8584 are adult communicants.[4]

The African Continent is just at present in a special sense the arena of missionary activity on behalf of slaves.   These efforts, however, are not put forth directly or forcibly for the suppres-
The rôle of missions in   sion of slavery, but rather with a view to the culti-
the overthrow of
slavery.   vation of an anti-slavery sentiment in native minds,
the encouragement and hastening of a policy of abolition in European administration, the mitigation of existing barbarities, and the provision of settlements, homes, and schools for the care and training of liberated slaves.   The missionary agencies which have been referred to in the previous section, as participating by moral sympathy and humane coöperation in the effort to suppress the slave-

[1] Thompson, "Moravian Missions," p. 111.   See also article by the Rev. F. Clemens, in *The Illustrated Missionary News*, April, 1895, pp. 65, 66.
[2] Thompson, "Moravian Missions," p. 149.   [3] *Ibid.*, p. 150.
[4] *Periodical Accounts of the Moravian Missions*, September, 1898, p. 578.

trade, might with equal propriety be mentioned here as exerting a steady pressure against slavery,[1] and extending a helping hand, wherever opportunity offers, for the alleviation of the misery it brings. It often happens that political and military authorities, in the exercise of their legal right to rescue the victims of the slave-trade, or to liberate those who are held in illegal bondage, find themselves embarrassed by the demand for the personal care and training of these unfortunate natives, who are suddenly ushered into freedom, with no provision for them in their friendlessness and helplessness. It is just then that the missionary agency steps in with a beneficent ministry and the offer of a temporary refuge, an industrial settlement, or an educational institution, including the assurance of friendly help and useful training.

The importance of this feature of missionary service at the present stage of progress in world-emancipation is manifest when we take note of the marvelous providential impulse which has been given within a very few years to the cause of universal abolition. Proclamations of freedom are echoing throughout the African Continent from Nyassa to Cairo, and from Zanzibar to Nigeria. Human avalanches of freedmen have been let loose, and lie in ignorance and moral disorder around the centres of missionary activity. In one single year the status of slavery has been abolished in the Niger Territories on the west, and in the Zanzibar Protectorate on the east.[2] The year

A marvelous era of emancipation and missionary opportunity.

[1] " There is no need to show how Christianity tends to counteract this social evil. The two things are incompatible, and where Christianity exists, and in proportion as it spreads, so will slavery die a natural death, and it is, very gradually, giving way. For hundreds of years it has gone on, with no single voice raised against it. Now for the first time the natives are hearing that it is wrong, and the voice of protest will year by year gather force and volume, as the number of native Christians, pledged by the baptismal vow to have nothing to do with slavery, increases."—Rev. J. S. Wimbush (U. M. C. A.), Kota Kota, British Central Africa.

[2] The decree of abolition, so far as the Zanzibar Protectorate is concerned, has not been as satisfactory in its workings as the friends of emancipation in England have desired. In the first place, it was stipulated that compensation should be made to the owners of slaves set free. Again, while the precise intent of the phrase " abolition of the legal *status* of slavery" may not be historically open to question, as Mr. Alexander contends (*The Anti-Slavery Reporter*, March–June, 1898, pp. 91–94), it is evident that the government interpretation put upon it in the Zanzibar decree assigns to it the meaning that a slave, though legally free, is not practically so until he proves himself entitled to and actually secures his papers of emancipation from the proper authorities. Intimidation, ignorance, or some other hindrance may keep him from doing this, although there is no legal restraint upon his formal application, and in this way the practical results of the decree may develop very slowly. Strange to say, also, its privileges are denied in the case of slaves who are concu-

1897 will be memorable in the history of the world as witnessing the legal manumission of probably not less than twelve million slaves. In the Nyassaland Protectorate the leaders in the traffic have fallen, and the powerful Yao nation is rapidly coming into touch with civilizing influences. The Commissioner of the single district of Blantyre reports, in 1895, that there is a population under his care which he estimates at 22,206 souls, and that this number consists largely of "the slaves released during the expeditions of the last twelve months."[1]   The victory not long since of the British over Lobengula, the Matabele king, has subdued the strongest native supporter of slavery and heathenism south of the equator.   The Arab slave-traders in the region of the Upper Congo have also been defeated.   Tippu Tib is no longer able to decimate whole sections of Central Africa, while the notorious ravagers of Nyassaland are brought low.   In the Island of Madagascar, as if in sympathy with the upheavals of the neighboring continent, there was a shout of triumph and joy one September morning in 1896, when a million slaves awoke to find themselves suddenly and forever free.   So unexpectedly was the announcement made by the French authorities that some of the slaveholders knew nothing of it until their own slaves made a morning call to announce their freedom.

bines. The decree was issued in the name of the Sultan, and its execution was unfortunately left largely in the hands of native administration, which has been exceedingly reluctant to give it due effect.   There is reason to hope that all this will in time be remedied.   In the meantime, the interpretation which is put upon the fact that the decree touches only the legal *status*, and the way in which this is distinguished from instant and effective manumission, are points worthy of note.   The distinction is well stated in the following paragraph from the London *Times:* " It is important to notice this difference between the abolition of the legal *status* of slavery and the abolition of slavery pure and simple.   By the abolition of slavery pure and simple, as it was carried out in the British possessions under the Act of 1834, every slave is actually freed.   By the abolition of the legal *status* of slavery the support of the law is withdrawn from the maintenance of the condition of slavery, and the slave is put in a position to claim his freedom if he chooses.   Until he so chooses he remains a slave, but the continued acceptance of his slavery is a purely voluntary agreement on his part, of which the law refuses to take cognizance.   He cannot be sued in any Court on the ground of his alleged servile *status*.   Any act which would be a penal offence if committed against the person or property of a free man becomes equally an offence against him, and he has in every respect the rights of a citizen. The law as promulgated under the late decree gives, not freedom, but a permissive right to freedom, to every inhabitant of Zanzibar and Pemba who chooses to claim it."   For further and recent information concerning the results of the decree, see Blue Book, " Africa, No. 6, 1898 "; *The Anti-Slavery Reporter*, July–August, 1898; and *The Church Missionary Intelligencer*, October, 1898, pp. 721–735.

[1] *The Christian Express*, September, 1896, p. 141.

The result of this swift onward movement of emancipation is seen in the frequent mention by missionary correspondents from Africa of the sudden call at various points to minister to slaves rescued from the caravan or the dhow, or to those who have stepped from a state of slavery into that of freedom.   "A Stolen Boy Rescued," "An Unlooked-for Arrival," "Another Catch of Slaves," "An Intercepted Caravan," are now familiar headings in African missionary communications.   The capacity of places provided by the various missions for the reception and care of slaves is liable to be taxed to the utmost by the unexpected arrival of parties, varying in size, which have been snatched out of the clutches of the trader.[1]   How thoroughly and cordially this coöperation of missionary service is appreciated by English and other officials is well illustrated by the statement of Sir John Kirk, former Consul-General in Zanzibar, who writes: "Without the Mission I do not know how otherwise I could have provided for the welfare of the many poor slaves who, when freed, fell into my hands. They had to be taught what freedom was, and how as free men they could live.   All this has been done under the Mission, and now a large class has grown up in Zanzibar, looking to the British Agency and the Universities' Mission for protection and advice.   Apart from this much good has been done on the mainland."[2]   The whole case has been put

Missionary care of liberated slaves.

[1] *African Tidings*, March, 1894, p. 24.

[2] Another and very recent testimony is from Mr. Basil Cave, C.B., Her Majesty's Consul at Zanzibar, who in an address at the anniversary of the Universities' Mission, in June, 1897, spoke as follows: "You are doubtless aware that, in spite of all the efforts that have been made to check and put a stop to the traffic in slaves, and in spite of the fact that those cruel raids of former times have, at any rate so far as the English and German spheres of interest are concerned, been effectually checked, yet cases do arise more or less frequently when little boys and girls— sometimes older, but generally younger—kidnapped on the coast, or on the island, and brought to Zanzibar for sale, and perhaps subsequently transhipped to Arabia, fall into the hands of the English or Zanzibar Government representatives, and receive their freedom in the Consular Court.   I remember on one occasion when as many as seventy were rescued in this way—mostly children.   I think you will agree with me that it would be utterly unsatisfactory, I might say inhuman, if we were merely to hand them a certificate of freedom, and dismiss them to take care of themselves; for most of them would have nowhere to go, and they are utterly incapable of looking after themselves and their own interest and welfare.   So we find it very difficult often to know how to arrange for their future disposal.   But, fortunately for them and for us, the doors of this Mission's houses in Zanzibar are open to all of them, from little wee mites trying to toddle along by Miss Mills' side at Kilimani, to the old men and women, who, whenever it is possible, are allowed to find a place on the shamba at Mbweni; and, I assure you, I have more than once been very severely

in a few words, by a writer, who, in referring to the slave population of Zanzibar and Pemba, calls attention to two striking facts of the situation: first, that it "lies prostrate at the feet of the greatest empire in the world, uneducated, unevangelized"; and, second, that "it awaits the succor of the Christian Church." The Government has now in a measure discharged its duty by the decree of legal emancipation. It remains for the Church, through the instrumentality of missions, to rescue the spiritual nature of this unenlightened multitude, and bring it into the freedom and hope of the Gospel.

It may, we think, be historically demonstrated that Christianity, if not indeed the only moral agency, is at least the most effective one which has waged an aggressive warfare upon sla-

The Christian Church and its historic attitude towards slavery. very. Its cardinal truth of the brotherhood of man, based upon the divine Fatherhood, and involving spiritual equality in the sight of God, as well as the essential value of all human souls, is irreconcilable with the condition of servitude. At the communion-table of Christ the relationship of master and slave becomes the merest fiction, while before the face of the Creator, in whose likeness all men are made, the insistence upon such a relationship involves an intolerable assumption and injustice. It was a custom in the early Church for Christian masters to free their slaves, as an act of piety. While this is all true, still great caution, patience, and wise moderation are necessary on the part of the Church in refraining from violent attacks upon slavery where it is firmly established as a social institution. The influence of Christianity will inevitably work out a fruitage of freedom. The prevalence of the Christian spirit will ultimately change, enlighten, and humanize public sentiment, and culminate, albeit slowly, in permanent reforms. Where this spirit, however, has been lacking, little, if anything, has been done. The struggle was a severe one in early Church history, despite earnest protests and vigorous action in opposition to slavery on the part of many of the spiritual leaders. The conflict lasted through the religious formalism of the Middle Ages, although the consistent attitude of the true Christian heart was revealed in that beautiful ritual of manumission: "I, in the name of God, thinking of the love of God, do free this

handled by Miss Thackeray and Miss Berkeley, not, as you would suppose, because I have sent too many, but because I have not kept up a sufficiently constant supply to engage all their attention in training miserable, half-starved, naked savages into well-fed, well-clothed, and happy Christian children. I think you will agree with me, ladies and gentlemen, that if the Mission did nothing else, that is a work for which we ought to be deeply grateful."—*Central Africa*, July, 1897, pp. 106, 107.

slave from the bonds of servitude." Even towards the middle of our present century, slavery still remained one of the unsolved problems of civilization, until England led the van in the march of emancipation, and by the decree of abolition achieved, to her honor, what Mr. Lecky has described as "one of the three or four perfectly virtuous acts recorded in the history of nations." [1]

Modern missions, from their earliest contact with African slavery, have been true to their high trust. The movement towards freedom has been slow, but its initial stages have an honored place in the annals of all our great missionary organizations. The Church Missionary Society's Report for 1810 states that the school at Rio Pongas, on the West Coast of Africa, contained some slave boys redeemed by the missionaries. Again, in 1811, it is recorded that Governor Maxwell, of Sierra Leone, consigned six Negro children to the missionaries for education, and that these six children represented "the first instance of African slaves, liberated by British cruisers, committed to the missionaries of the Church Missionary Society." [2] A previous effort to instruct the slaves is recorded as early as 1798, concerning a Christian man at Stellenbosch, South Africa. In the memoirs of Mr. Borcherds it is asserted that a certain Mr. Johan Nicholas Desch held a meeting at Stellenbosch every Sunday for the instruction of slaves. Nothing of the kind seems to be on record again until 1824, when, at the same place, "a school-room and church were built by subscription,

Modern missions have been true to their trust.

---

[1] Bishop Barry, in his Hulsean Lectures, in referring to the history of the colonial churches, touches upon the relation of the Christian Church to slavery, especially in the West Indies. The following paragraph, although written with particular reference to colonial church life, expresses the true attitude of missions towards this world-problem : " It was obvious that only by the progress of the true ' humanity ' of self-sacrifice of the strong for the weak, which has to fight against the lower spirit of selfishness, and of the faith in right principle, which steadily refuses to ' do evil that good may come,' could an institution so deep-rooted and engrained in social life be gradually cast out. It was the task of Christianity to create and foster that higher humanity, under the sense of a common Fatherhood of God and a common salvation in Christ—to enunciate the great principle, ' No longer a slave, but a brother beloved in the Lord,' and leave it to work on the minds and hearts of the people. So had the slavery of serfship been gradually destroyed in Europe ; so now the question, ' Am not I a man and a brother ? ' which is to us somewhat obsolete, was to be asked in relation to a wider brotherhood of all humanity. The real battle had, of course, to be fought at home ; the Church in the West Indies had simply to act as an auxiliary, and meanwhile prepare both masters and slaves for the coming change."—" The Ecclesiastical Expansion of England," p. 240.

[2] *The Church Missionary Intelligencer*, December, 1893, pp. 894, 896.

and solemnly opened on the 5th of February, the then Governor, Lord Charles Somerset, and the authorities of the village being present." [1]

The past half-century has witnessed the establishment of vastly increased facilities for caring for the spiritual, intellectual, and industrial welfare of African slaves. Without repeating in too much detail references to agencies in different parts of Africa, enumerated in the previous section, it is still worth while to note that these facilities are available for freedmen delivered from slavery, as well as for those who are rescued from the slave-raider's caravan or the Arab dhow. The Universities' Mission has its educational institutions, its shambas (industrial plantations), and its settlements at Zanzibar and on the mainland. At Kiungani, near the city of Zanzibar, is a training-college, in which many of the pupils received were "raw slaves from the dhows." [2] Mbweni, a flourishing shamba, and the scene of Miss Thackeray's devoted labors, shelters over a hundred released slave girls. At Kilimani, in a refuge for little boys who have been snatched from slavery, Miss Mills and Miss Clutterbuck have one hundred and sixteen lads under their care. [3] Upon the mainland, at Kichelwe, not far from Dar-es-Salaam, is an interesting and independent colony of some three hundred released slaves, who have constituted themselves an orderly community, and, at their own request, are under the spiritual ministrations of a native deacon, provided for them by the Universities' Mission. They are diligent, industrious, and happy, and have.built for themselves a place of worship. [4]

The rapid growth of missionary facilities for ministering to freedmen.

The Church Missionary Society has founded at Frere Town, opposite Mombasa, a freed-slave settlement, with a home where rescued slaves are cared for by the agents of the Society. This asylum was established in 1874, at the recommendation of Sir Bartle Frere, after his visit to Zanzibar, in 1872, for the purpose of negotiating a treaty prohibiting the slave-trade. The Annual Report of the Church Missionary Society for 1897 records the interesting fact that Bishop Tucker had ordained at Frere Town the first liberated slave

Settlements and homes for freed slaves in Africa.

---

[1] *The Christian*, July 23, 1897, " Letters from South Africa," No. 26.

[2] " The released slaves under our charge owe everything to the mission—religion, education, instruction in a trade or profession. There are growing up many young men who are skilled handicraftsmen, who have been taught their trade by Indian masters whilst they lived with us in the Mission."—Rev. G. M. Lawson (U. M. C. A.), Zanzibar.   [3] See illustration, Vol. I., p. 134.

[4] *Central Africa*, February, 1896, p. 28.

Native Deacons of the Universities' Mission, Zanzibar

Mbweni School Girls, Zanzibar.   All rescued from Slave-dhows.
(Miss Berkeley in doorway, Miss Garrett on the right.)

FROM THE SLAVE-DHOW TO FREEDOM IN CHRIST.
(U. M. C. A.)

to enter the ministry from the ranks of those educated at this settlement.[1] The English Friends have just founded in Pemba a Mission for Liberated Slaves, and the English Methodist Free Churches, the German, and the Swedish missionaries have similar agencies on the mainland.

At Kisserawe, near Dar-es-Salaam, the German East African Missionary Society has a home for freed slaves, who are gathered from surrounding German territory. The Evangelical African League of Germany has also selected a salubrious site in Usambara, East Africa, where it intends to locate a colony of freedmen. If we pass on to British Central Africa, we find the missions of the Established and Free Churches of Scotland, and also the Universities' Mission, that "illuminating triumvirate," all grappling with the question of slave education, which has been thrust upon them by the swift developments of providence. The last report of the newly established Livingstonia Institution, on the northwest coast of Lake Nyassa, as given by Dr. Laws, its founder and organizer, announces one hundred and seventy-seven pupils, many of whom had marched in the ranks of slave-caravans, and had been led out of that dreary pathway into the light of a Christian home. Dr. Laws writes that it is impossible to know whence some of them came, as "they were carried away from their native places in slave-gangs when very young."[2] In the schools of the Scotch missions "may frequently be seen rescued slave children side by side with the children of their captors, a singular consummation of union among friends and foes."[3] At the Free Church Institution in Lovedale are classes of liberated slaves. At Freetown, on the West Coast, is Fourah Bay College, under the Church Missionary Society, and in the Old Calabar Mission of the Scotch United Presbyterians similar institutions are conducted. Christian work in Lagos may be described as largely a mission to slaves. Wesleyan missions in Gambia, Sierra Leone, and on the Gold Coast, and German efforts in Togoland and the Kamerun, are face to face with slavery as a vanishing social factor, leaving in its wake a mighty task for Christian hearts and hands. A Swiss society for the relief of African slaves has been formed, which will make Ashanti the scene of its operations, where the Basel missionaries are already engaged in the same benevolent service. In the Congo Valley, and, in fact, wherever missionary stations are located, sooner or later will the touch of Christianity reach the slave.

[1] "General Review of the Year," Church Missionary Society, 1896–97, p. 5.
[2] "Report of the Free Church of Scotland Missions, 1897," p. 89. See also "Report of the Livingstonia Mission, 1897–98," p. 4.
[3] *The Church at Home and Abroad*, September, 1897, p. 171.

Another feature, however, of the missionary crusade against slavery demands our notice ; namely, the moral pressure which missionaries themselves have personally exerted in moulding public opinion in Christendom, and in quickening the native conscience concerning the moral aspects of the institution. It is to a notable extent through missionary teaching and example that the idea of brotherhood based upon humanity has been exemplified and enforced. They have always insisted that "justice should be color-blind, and ignorant of class distinctions." Their hands have often been lifted to stay the blow of the lash, or to unloose and destroy instruments of torture. If government authorities have been slow to recognize the rights of humanity, missionaries have brought to bear upon them whatever influence they could command. If, as happily has been the case in many instances, the civil Government has instituted a humane policy, missionaries have joyfully coöperated. One of the earliest and most important illustrations of missionary exertions on behalf of freedom in Africa was the passing of the Emancipation Act of 1834. As we have seen in previous pages, that memorable event was to a noticeable degree due to the advocacy of earnest and eloquent missionaries from Jamaica. South Africa's share in its results consisted in the liberation of nearly thirty-six thousand slaves in Cape Colony, and an allotment of about three million pounds from the indemnity of twenty million pounds voted by Parliament as compensation to colonial slaveholders. A few years later we find Krapf and Rebmann representing the Church Missionary Society on the East Coast, and laying the foundation of the steady anti-slavery policy of its East African missions. Both of these heroic missionaries were anti-slavery pioneers in Eastern Africa.[1]

In 1852 Livingstone entered upon his Central African explorations. Subsequently, in 1861, with the late Bishop Mackenzie and the late Rev. Horace Waller, of the Universities' Mission, Dr. John Kirk, and others, he conducted an exploring expedition up the Zambesi to the

The service of missions in moulding public opinion in Christendom and in native communities.

---

[1] " Krapf and Rebmann, like Livingstone, were pioneers. Like him, they saw little direct fruit of their labours, though Rebmann remained in East Africa for twenty-nine years (1846–75) without once going home. The latter was found by Sir Bartle Frere, in 1873, at Kisulutini, quite blind, but immersed in his dictionaries and translations, and surrounded by a few faithful Wanika. The indirect results, however, of their work have been immense, for they have led, as we have seen, to all Central African exploration. Both retired to live at Kornthal, in Germany; Rebmann living long enough to hear of Stanley's ' Appeal to Christendom,' written from Uganda, Krapf even witnessing the occupation of Uganda and the Congo Valley by missionaries."—Thornton, " Africa Waiting," p. 85.

southern end of Lake Nyassa. The moral pressure exerted by Livingstone in his memorable appeals on behalf of the African slave is beyond all estimate. From the time that he first seized and cast off the slave-sticks from the necks of African captives, at Mbame's, on the borders of the Shiré Highlands,[1] until the day of his death, in 1873, and even to the present hour, the telling impact upon Christendom of his burning words and heroic life has been immense and incalculable.

As early as 1854, in the history of the Old Calabar Mission, the question of the attitude of the native Church towards converted slaveholders, slaves, and freedmen, reached a crisis. There were many complications. "Once a slave, always a slave," was an unwritten law of society. Owners had the power of life and death. Society was composed of two classes, slaveholders and their slaves. The law took no cognizance of free servants. Masters were not accustomed to sell their slaves except for some serious crime. If it was necessary to get rid of them, they killed them. The moral alertness of missionary influence and changed public sentiment was equal to the emergency, and a declaration was agreed upon, which every converted slaveholder signed when admitted to the Church. Christian civilization has reached no higher and finer coign of vantage for the discernment of humane duties than is revealed in that remarkable declaration.[2]

In the recent struggle for the abolition of slavery in Zanzibar the missionaries of the Church Missionary Society, the Universities' Mission, and also those connected with the new enterprise on behalf of slaves in Pemba, under the auspices of the English Friends, have almost all brought vigorous and continuous advocacy to bear in behalf of decisive action, although they have differed somewhat as to the expediency of immediate and total emancipation. The public

The attitude of missionaries towards the problem of slavery in Zanzibar.

---

[1] Anderson-Morshead, "The History of the Universities' Mission to Central Africa," p. 24.

[2] The document referred to reads as follows: "Believing that all men are equal in the sight of God, and that, under the Gospel, there is in Christ Jesus neither bond nor free, I hereby, as a servant of Christ, bound to obey the commands of God's Word, promise, in the sight of the great God, my divine Master, that I shall regard those persons placed under my care, and formerly held by me as slaves, as *servants*, and not as *property;* that I shall give them what is just and equal for their work; that I shall encourage them to obtain education for themselves and their children, and to attend on such means of religious instruction as the Church may be able to afford them; that I shall dispose of none of them for the mere purposes of gain; that I shall do so only in the case of those who, being chargeable with criminal offences, would be liable to be put to death were they to remain in Calabar, and

utterances and published letters of Bishop Tucker, which have appeared repeatedly in *The Times*, *The Record*, *The Church Missionary Intelligencer*, and *The Anti-Slavery Reporter*,[1] have been especially forcible and influential. The Bishop, in 1896, forwarded to the Consul-General at Zanzibar a memorial signed by himself and thirteen of his associate missionaries in Uganda, expressing "the very earnest hope that the legal status of slavery in Mombasa, Zanzibar, and Pemba may be abolished without delay"; basing this appeal upon the undoubted fact that "the existence of a legalised condition of slavery in these places is more or less intimately connected with slave-raiding and trading in the interior of the Continent." This memorial was forwarded by the Consul-General to the Foreign Office in London, and appears in one of the Government Blue Books.[2] The Bishop also recently made a test case in the Provincial Court at Mombasa in behalf of a slave girl cruelly treated, and secured judgment giving her freedom.   This case is important in several respects.[3] The estimate which is put upon Bishop Tucker's advocacy of the policy of abolition may be inferred from the following quotation from an editorial in *The Record*, July 2, 1897: "The question of slavery on the Zanzibar coast has now, *mainly owing to the persistence of Bishop Tucker*, been placed upon a better footing." The Church Missionary Society itself also participated in this campaign of moral pressure, by passing a resolution in December, 1896, expressing the opinion of its Committee "that the time had fully arrived to give effect to the long and definite promise of the Government to abolish the status of slavery in the dominion of the Sultan of Zanzibar, including Mombasa and all the country within the ten-mile limit, and

---

who can be legally banished in no other way; that I shall endeavour as far as I can to secure the making of laws to promote personal freedom; that, as soon as it can be done, I shall legally set free all those under my care; and that, in the meantime, I shall treat them with kindness and equity, it being my constant aim to act upon the command of the Lord Jesus Christ, to do unto others as I would wish them to do unto me."—Dickie, "Story of the Mission in Old Calabar," pp. 51, 52.

[1] *The Times*, June 23, 1896, April 15, 1897, January 26 and April 19, 1898; *The Record*, May 8, 1896; *The Church Missionary Intelligencer*, August, 1898, p. 625; *The Anti-Slavery Reporter*, March–June, 1898, pp. 67–82.

[2] "Africa, No. 7, 1896"; *The Church Missionary Intelligencer*, August, 1896, p. 616. See also *ibid.*, February, 1897, pp. 93, 94, and *The Anti-Slavery Reporter*, May–July, 1896, p. 126. In *The Anti-Slavery Reporter* for July, 1897, and July–August, 1898, there is an extensive résumé of public opinion in England, as revealed in the journalistic press, upon the question of slavery in Zanzibar and its abolition.

[3] *The Anti-Slavery Reporter*, March–June, 1898, pp. 73–82. See also *The Church Missionary Intelligencer*, September, 1898, pp. 678–690, and October, 1898, pp. 721–735.

earnestly and respectfully pressing upon Her Majesty's Government the urgent necessity for prompt and resolute action in the matter." [1]

In British Central Africa the influence of missionaries has been steadily coöperating with the government forces in the magnificent campaign against the slave-trade. The agents of the Universities' Mission, and of the Scotch Established and Free Church Missions, have counted the contest with the slave power as one of the most militant and pressing of their responsibilities, and the value of their moral training over the native mind has been freely acknowledged by British authorities. The London Missionary Society, through the efforts of the Rev. J. D. Hepburn and others of its agents, has accomplished a work of permanent value in educating native public sentiment among the Bamangwato and the Batauana, in South Matabeleland. Mr. Hepburn repeatedly refers to his desires and struggles to overcome the cruelties of slavery, and no one can read his accounts without being impressed with his success in reaching the native conscience and creating a reversal of immemorial custom and a revolution in public opinion, wherever his strong personal influence was felt. In speaking of his pleadings with the Bamangwato on the subject of slavery, he says: "Well does the day stand out when in my Bible class I remonstrated with a prominent member of my church, who maintained that Masarwa were not people, but were only dogs without souls. Has that day passed forever? Shall it nevermore return? Has eternity fallen on it to draw over it the screen of its own eternal silence? Then what estimate shall that trifle be valued at, and what angel of God is equal to the calculation? Let it go down as one of the trifles of Christian missions; yet, as I have said, it made my glad heart sing." [2] Khama, the Chief of the Bamangwato, a Christian convert and friend of Mr. Hepburn, was of one mind with him on the subject of slavery. Mr. Hepburn's appeals to the Directors of the London Missionary Society were not without avail. He spent his life in an atmosphere which was fairly stifling with the moral disorders and sickening atrocities of African slavery, but he left his impress in changed lives and new impulses pervading the native society where he had lived. [3]

The part they have taken in Central and South Africa.

[1] " Report of the Church Missionary Society, 1897," pp. 66, 67.

[2] Hepburn, " Twenty Years in Khama's Country," p. 266.

[3] The following extract will give a glimpse of the spirit in which he toiled: " The next morning, Sunday, May 1st, I discoursed on the great mercy of God in Christ Jesus, dwelling upon it at length, until I felt that the hearts of the people had warmed to it, and then I contrasted it with cruelty in whatever form, and especially

To the northwest of Mr. Hepburn's sphere of service, in the valley of the Upper Zambesi, among the degraded Barotsi tribes, is the scene of the life-labors of the Rev. F. Coillard, of the **Champions of freedom in the Upper Zambesi and Congo Valleys.** French Evangelical Society, who describes slavery as "at the very foundation of the social edifice" of African communities in that section. The truth of this statement is illustrated by the singular fact that even the Barotsi children would bring their slaves with them to the mission school. The complications resulting from this curious situation were both amusing and startling. The tact and ingenuity of the good French missionary and his wife were abundantly exercised in trying to do good to the slaves as well as the masters, without at the same time breaking the strict code of etiquette, and thereby incurring some real danger.[1]

In the valley of the Congo the missionaries of different societies have striven to make some headway in overcoming native customs and changing public opinions upon the subject of slavery. The natives have come to look upon these good men as champions of humanity and freedom. The following extract from a letter from Mr. Gilchrist, of the Congo-Balolo Mission at Lulanga, gives us an insight into what is

---

denounced cruelty to their wives, who were their equals, to their children, who were their own flesh and blood, and to their slaves, who bore God's image, and for whom Christ died equally with themselves; and I pointed out the injustice of taking the bones and flesh, the marrow and sinews which God had given to another man, and using them as if they were their own, without any payment in return. I did not speak mincingly, and I did not spare the Batauana slaveholders; but I did not forget that there was another side of the question to be considered, and as I knew that I had a large number of Bakoba slaves hearing me, I told them I should return to the subject in the afternoon, and that I had a word specially for them."—Hepburn, "Twenty Years in Khama's Country," pp. 190, 191.

[1] In his volume, "On the Threshold of Central Africa," M. Coillard writes (p. 286): "Each of our little people has come with a number of slaves, more or less; some of these attend school, and place themselves behind their masters. But we have not yet arrived at making them understand that the teaching is for them too."

An incident related in another connection gives rather a startling emphasis to the possible results of clashing with the terrific etiquette of African society. The author states: "We could have returned to Sefula with a number of young girls, if we had wished, and had been able to do so. But how could we resist the entreaties of the king, who besought us at least to receive his own daughter, Mpololoa, a nice child of ten or eleven? We ended by consenting, on condition that she should come quite alone, without slaves, and should be entirely left to our discretion. Instead of one,

meant by this humane championship of the missionary on behalf of slaves: "The news came to me just in the nick of time that the chief had sent a slave across the river to a cannibal town, to be killed and eaten, on account of his ailments. I at once set out for the place; most of the people made for the bush, but to the few who remained I gave directions to have the man brought at once before me at our station. Next day they presented him. His story made me shudder, as also the sight of his hands and arms, which were in a fearful state, preparatory to his being killed and eaten. He said they had put him into the execution chair the previous day, but, finding they had no salt to eat with him, delayed killing him for two days. Before execution the arm, wrist, and thumb are compressed between two pieces of wood, firmly tied, and left until the pain becomes excruciating; the victim is then ready for decapitation. Needless to say, I assured the poor fellow that he could sit down with perfect safety on our place, and that his master had henceforth no claim on him. 'Ah, if it were not for you,' often exclaim the men and boys of the station, and the slaves in the town—'if it were not for you, *Mundele Inglese*, some of us would have our necks cut! We don't want you to go away.'"[1] The Rev. James Johnston, in a chapter on "Missionary Advance up the Congo Water-way," refers to this aspect of missionary service as follows: "In speeding the daybreak of emancipation on the Congo and its tribu-taries, glorious deeds have been wrought by the American Baptist Mis-sionary Union, the Swedish Society, the Congo-Balolo Mission, the English Baptists, and the co-workers with the apostolic William Tay-lor, whose respective ensigns and missionaries have alleviated sorrow,

---

three came, and with a suite of slaves suitable to their rank. 'What!' the princess Katoka had exclaimed, 'let our children go to Sefula without slaves? Never!' In vain we sent them back; some persistently remained, 'lying low' at Litia's and ap-pearing now and then. We had to make an exception in favour of two little slaves of the same age as the king's children, who share their amusements and come to school; and one other exception for Sanana's nurse, who has never left her."

In a foot-note to the above we find the following tragic illustration recorded:

"The training of these young people was no easy matter, since the sanctity of their persons was such that it was not permitted *literally* to lay a finger on them. One day, while some building was going on at the station, a serf, running round the corner with a bundle of thatch in his arms, met the king's little daughter, who was running in the contrary direction, and by accident the tip of a reed brushed her eye. In an hour's time, before M. Coillard had even heard of the occurrence, the man was dead, executed by the child's attendants."—*Ibid.*, pp. 334, 335.

[1] *Regions Beyond*, February, 1894, p. 83.

lessened cruelty, dispelled ignorance, broken slave-chains, conquered paganism, and triumphantly uplifted the Cross of Christ."[1]

The recent notable action of Sir George T. Goldie, on behalf of the Royal Niger Company, in abolishing slavery in the Company's terri-

The moral coöperation of missionary agents in Nigeria and Madagascar.

tories, is a bold stroke for which full credit is due to this noble British official. The author is not able to throw any light upon the matter, but he ventures to suggest that it would be an interesting study to ascertain what part the moral influence of mission work in the Niger Protectorate has had in coöperating to bring about this consummation. In connection with the cessation of slavery in Madagascar, the Rev. W. E. Cousins writes: "The acceptance of Christianity has done much in later years to prepare the way for abolition. The Church recognized no distinction between slaves and others, free children and slave children being taught in the same schools. A slave might even become a pastor, or preacher, or deacon, in the church of which his owner was a member."[2] While this is true, Madagascar has been somewhat slow in accepting the Christian view of slavery. Progress, however, has been made in the right direction under the steady pressure of Gospel principles, as is manifest in an incident related by one of the agents of the London Missionary Society. In the year 1876 a missionary ventured to speak on the subject of emancipation, but his remarks were not received with favor. In 1893, however, the Rev. R. Baron took occasion, in his address as Chairman of the Congregational Union in that island, to advocate earnestly the policy of emancipation. Another spirit was apparent in the reception given to this appeal. He put the matter before them in the following effective way: "All Christian nations," he said, "have now abolished slavery—except—except—" and after a pause he added, in a kind of stage-whisper, and with both hands to his mouth—"except you in Madagascar." His discourse was wisely conceived, and he insisted that slavery must in the end disappear before the progress of Christ's kingdom.[3] It is not surprising that the reluctance of the Christian churches in Madagascar to discharge their full duty in this matter should have been sharply criticized by Dr. Cust[4] and others, but it is sufficiently obvious that this reluctance has been exceptional, and is out of sympathy with the true and universal spirit of missions.

[1] Johnston, " Missionary Landscapes in the Dark Continent," pp. 195, 196.
[2] *The Missionary Review of the World*, April, 1897, p. 285.
[3] *The Chronicle*, January, 1894, p. 19.
[4] Cust, " Notes on Missionary Subjects," Part II., pp. 25, 47; *The Anti-Slavery Reporter*, August–October, 1897, p. 229.

Still another phase of the results which have followed the moral crusade of missions against this evil remains to be noted. It is the responsive action of the native conscience in deference to the instruction of missionaries concerning the true attitude of Christians to slavery. An illustration of this is presented in that remarkable declaration signed by forty native chiefs in Uganda, in 1893, who voluntarily, after they had become Protestant converts, determined wholly to abolish domestic slavery. Their brief statement is a unique document in the history of missions and in the annals of human freedom. It reads as follows: "All we Protestant chiefs wish to adopt these good customs of freedom. We agree to untie and free completely all our slaves. Here are our names as chiefs." How simple, how suggestive, how dramatic, is this noble act! It would seem as if nothing further was necessary to vindicate the weighty protest which the Gospel, when honestly, sincerely, and conscientiously received, brings to bear in opposition to slavery.[1] A similar and hardly less remarkable incident is reported by the Rev. A. G. MacAlpine, of the Free Church of Scotland Mission at Bandawè, on the western shore of Lake Nyassa. An account of it will be found in the foot-note on p. 215 of this volume.

In Mr. Hepburn's narrative of his work are several accounts of native Christians having liberated their slaves, as a matter of con-

The response of the native conscience to the anti-slavery influence of missions.

---

[1] *The Church Missionary Intelligencer,* August, 1893, p. 606.

The full significance of this action is explained by Bishop Tucker in one of his letters concerning it: "It may be asked, How will the slaves themselves be affected by this measure? First of all, there will be no more bartering of men, women, and children, like so many cattle. The buying and selling of human beings will forever come to an end (I wonder what the opponents of the retention of Uganda will say to this!). Again, one of the great incentives to war will be removed. At present one of the chief inducements for one Central African tribe to wage war with another is the hope of capturing slaves. This will no longer operate in Uganda, should this measure be adopted. People need not fear that a large number of destitute freed slaves will be wandering about the country without means of subsistence. On being freed by their masters they will naturally take the place of the *bakopi,* i.e., free men who hold their land on a service tenure. Happily there is plenty of land unoccupied, and it only needs to be taken up and cultivated, and at once there will be employment for the slaves and an increase in the prosperity of the country. Whichever way the matter is looked at, there seems to be nothing but good that is likely to be the outcome, whether it be for the slaves themselves or their masters. Then the effect on the nations and tribes around will be great. It will soon be noised abroad that the Waganda have declared for freedom, and a yearning for the same blessing will take possession of many a downtrodden soul. The movement has begun, and none, thank God, can stay it. The Gospel has not lost its ancient power."— *The Church Missionary Intelligencer,* October, 1893, p. 757.

science.[1]   Other instances are on record of converts, in defiance of all tradition, undertaking, in a spirit of Christian love, evangelistic work among slaves, or, as owners, granting them their freedom.   An incident reported by Dr. A. Watson, of Egypt, finely illustrates this statement.[2]   The liberated slaves of Jamaica originated a project of missions among African slaves, which resulted in the formation of the Cameroons Mission of the Baptist Missionary Society of England, afterwards transferred to the Congo.   When these Jamaica freedmen, who had been kidnapped from the West African coast, were desirous of carrying the Gospel to the heathen lands whence they had been taken, it was suggested to them that it was a perilous undertaking and might result in

Christian converts become liberators and evangelists to those in slavery.

---

[1] Hepburn, " Twenty Years in Khama's Country," pp. 95, 166, 167.

Dr. Laws, of the Free Church of Scotland Mission, on the shores of Lake Nyassa, reports an incident which may be quoted in further illustration. " Slavery and the slave-trade," he writes, " are, or were, prominent features of heathen life in this country.   Political changes are striking at the latter by suppression, but domestic slavery can be abolished only by the effect of the Gospel.   As an example of what I have seen, I may mention the case of a poor half-paralyzed slave I saw in Angoniland, lying on a dunghill in want and nakedness, spurned by all, and considered useless by his master.   The grace of God changed the heart of that master and his brothers, and the poor slave was no longer treated as an ousted cur whose days of usefulness were done, but taken in and fed, and cared for as one of the family."

[2] " When our mission began, in 1854, the number of slaves in Egypt must have been great.   Almost every family, Moslem, Christian, or Jewish, able to purchase a slave, had either one or more.   The influence of Christian missions in Egypt has been opposed to this institution, and while other agencies have helped to restrict trade in human chattels, still the chief factor in creating a public opinion, on the basis of intelligence instead of force, has been Christian missions.   Not a few slaves have been freed by our own members, as it was one of the principles of our church not to receive slaveholders to membership.   In one case, perhaps twenty years ago, I was appointed by our native presbytery to examine an elder elect for ordination, and in doing so it appeared that he owned a slave.   I told him that this was a serious objection.   He had never thought on the subject before.   I talked over the matter with him in a brotherly manner, and he heard all I had to say, and then replied that he would think about it, and give me a reply the next morning.   On meeting with him next day, he said it appeared now to him that it was contrary to the spirit of the Gospel to hold slaves, and that he would in the evening announce before the assembled congregation that his faithful servant was no longer his slave.   This he did, saying that the man was free to go or stay.   Having been well treated by his master, he remained with him as a son, and when the elder died, a few years after, the former slave took his master's place as leader in the congregation, and is now one of our local preachers."—Rev. Andrew Watson, D.D. (U. P. C. N. A.), Cairo, Egypt.

their being enslaved again. They answered: "We have been made slaves for men; we can be made slaves for Christ."[1]

The Roman Catholic Church has participated heartily in this effort to alleviate African slavery. The campaign of Cardinal Lavigerie among the European churches of that communion was producing hopeful results when interrupted by his lamented death. The "Armed Brothers of the Sahara," and the "White Teachers," represent organized attempts on the part of the Roman Catholic Church to break up the slave-trade and extend a helping hand to Africans freed from slavery. This humanitarian service on the part of Roman Catholic missionaries is not only worthy of admiration, but serves as a modern offset to the unhappy historical notoriety of Bishop Bartolomé de las Casas, who first suggested, in 1517, to the Spanish King Charles, the importation of Negro slaves from Africa to Hispaniola (Haiti), thereby encouraging, if he did not inaugurate, the awful slave-traffic of succeeding centuries, which makes such a dismal chapter in the history of the human race. It should be noted, however, that Las Casas subsequently recognized with extreme regret the grave nature of his mistake, and did what he could to atone for his lamentable error.[2] No candid reader of these facts will be likely to question the prominent part which Christian missions have taken in the emancipation of Africa.

The honorable efforts of the Roman Catholic Church.

Slavery was a well-known fact in British India until 1843, when its legal status was abolished by the British authorities.[3] The direct appeals of missions may have had little to do with this event, but we can discover the undoubted sympathy of missionaries with the purpose of the Act from the fact of the inauguration at that early date, in South India, by the Rev. J. M. Lechler and his wife, of the

The abolition of slavery in India.

---

[1] "The Centenary Volume of the Baptist Missionary Society," p. 156.

[2] Ingram, "History of Slavery," pp. 143–145.

[3] The legality of slaveholding came to an end when the Council of India passed, with the assent of the Governor-General, what is known as "Act No. V. of 1843," on April 7th of that year. The text is as follows:

"An Act for declaring and amending the Law regarding the condition of Slavery within the territories of the East India Company.

"I. It is hereby enacted and declared that no public officer shall, in execution of any decree or order of Court, or for the enforcement of any demand of rent or revenue, sell or cause to be sold any person, or the right to the compulsory labour or services of any person, on the ground that such person is in a state of Slavery.

"II. And it is hereby declared and enacted that no rights arising out of an alleged property in the person and services of another as a Slave shall be enforced

London Missionary Society, of "a philanthropic society for purchasing the freedom of slaves."[1]   In that caste-ridden country the false views of society, illustrated by slavery, were deeply lodged in social theory and practice, and have been slow to yield to higher principles.   Missions have been a great and aggressive power in educating public sentiment, and in gradually undermining and weakening the artificial barriers which caste and slavery have erected.   The prostrate classes are beginning to rise ; the spirit of human lordship is not so assertive as it was ; a consciousness of self-respect is springing up in downcast hearts ; education is spreading among all sections of society, while equality before the law has become an unquestioned fact.   A philanthropic conception of not only the possibility, but also the justice and duty, of relief to humanity as such, in its hours of need, has forced its way into the higher life of India.

Slavery for debt, and what is known as labor slavery, having in them a voluntary element, are not reached by government regulations in any effective way.   The relationship which is

How missionaries are helping those in slavery for debt.

established by debt amounts to a state of serfdom, sometimes involving whole families ; for while there is no actual purchase or sale, yet the authority over the person is not virtually different from that involved in domestic slavery.   The influence of missions in mitigating this state of things is not so manifest, but nevertheless it is real.   Dr. L. L. Uhl, a Lutheran missionary at Guntur, India, writes that Christianity, by the development of manhood, the spread of education, and the practical help which missionaries can secure, "is bringing relief to the serfs, and gradually removing labor slavery."   The same may be said with reference to missionary influence in Assam.   An illustration of this is given by the Rev. Robert Evans, of the Welsh Calvinistic Methodist Mission,

by any Civil or Criminal Court or magistrate within the territories of the East India Company.

" III. And it is hereby declared and enacted that no person who may have acquired property by his own industry, or by the exercise of any art, calling, or profession, or by inheritance, assignment, gift, or bequest, shall be dispossessed of such property or prevented from taking possession thereof on the ground that such person, or that the person from whom the property may have been derived, was a Slave.

" IV. And it is hereby enacted that any act which would be a penal offence if done to a free man shall be equally an offence if done to any person on the pretext of his being in a condition of Slavery."—*The Indian Evangelical Review*, January, 1897, p. 302.

1 *The Chronicle*, June, 1896, p. 124.

who has interested himself in seeking to put an end to the indefinite prolongation of the term of service in the case of debt slavery. He writes: "After I began to be known, some of the slaves who were very cruelly treated by their masters came to tell me their trouble. When I was sure of a genuine case of ill-treatment, I would urge the slave to sue his master before the British Government, and would promise to back him. We brought some cases from different neighborhoods before the court, and urged the magistrate to fix upon a certain number of years for service, at the end of which the slave would be free. It soon became known throughout the country, and in this way many have been set free who would otherwise have been slaves all their lives long. The system is still far from being done away with, but the masters know that if they are cruel to their slaves they cannot retain them under those conditions. They must be kind to them. In this way Christianity has made a wonderful difference in the treatment of such people throughout the country." The value of this change in the possible fortunes of one in the clutches of debt slavery is evident from the fact that in some instances a man has been kept in practical bondage for years by an arrears of not more than twenty or thirty dollars, without in the meantime reducing in the least the amount of his indebtedness. The British Government has, of course, abolished the status of slavery in Assam and Burma.

"In Siam," writes the Rev. W. C. Dodd, of the Presbyterian Mission in Laos, "human slavery has been much mitigated by the coming of Christianity. In the portion of the Lao country in which we have our mission work established, the people are tributary to Siam. The King of Siam has become so influenced by contact with the missionaries and with Christian people and Christian nations that he is making an effort towards the gradual abolition of slavery for debt. This, in addition to what the missionaries have been able to do towards creating a public sentiment, both by precept and example, in favor of freeing those who are in servitude, has largely mitigated the condition of slaves for debt in very many places, and it has almost entirely abolished slavery among those who profess Christianity."

Again, in China, where domestic slavery usually takes the form of concubinage, "Christianity," writes the Rev. J. Macgowan (L. M. S.), of Amoy, "is the only power that speaks out definitely and decisively on this subject. It says slavery is wrong, and must not be tolerated. It will listen to no excuses. The voice of tradition and the pleadings of custom are unheard, and it says sternly that it will have no tampering with the liberty of the person, and that it will never consent to the extinguishing of the natural affection which God has implanted in the human heart, both for the comfort of the children, and for the elevation of the nature of the parents. Many of these enslaved women have been delivered by Christianity."

Mr. Macgowan relates the following incident to illustrate the above statement: " Many years ago a man became a Christian. All the rest of his family were opposed to this step. Besides his wife and several sons he had a slave who acted as a concubine. Both husband and wife were fond of her. She was a clever, executive woman, who managed the business of the household with great ability. When the man asked for baptism, he was told that before his request could be complied with he must give his slave woman freedom, and be content to live alone with his wife. He was ready for any sacrifice, but the two women were not. The wife would not part with her servant, neither would the latter part with her master. At length the slave, seeing the determination of the man to live according to Scripture teaching, gave her consent. A young man of unblemished character was obtained, who was willing to marry her; one of the sons was handed over to her, and a present of money, and one fine day she was transformed from being a slave into a respectable woman and a wife. After a time she became an earnest Christian, and for many years she has been a deaconess in the church to which she belongs."[1]

---

[1] In shocking contrast to the above is the following statement illustrating the awful possibilities of slave life in China. The Rev. J. Walter Lowrie writes, from Paotingfu, in March, 1897, in a private letter to the author, of an event which had occurred at that place during the week previous to his writing. He states that " while the bearers of a coffin were proceeding through the streets to the potter's field, accompanied by the family servant of an official, from whose house the coffined remains were brought, they distinctly perceived a movement within the coffin, and insisted upon stopping for an examination, saying that they had been hired to bury a dead person, and objected to burying a living one. The official's servant strenuously objected, and only deepened the suspicions of the bearers by the nervous anxiety which he exhibited. The party were soon surrounded by a crowd, hungering for some new thing. The box was opened, and the form of a slave girl about seventeen years of age was disclosed. She was still living, but was rendered speechless by the fact that her tongue had been literally pulled out by the roots. It seems that she had attempted suicide by hanging, in order to escape her owner's cruelty, but had been cut down, and out of revenge had been thus horribly mutilated, and was about to be buried alive. She survived but a few days. As she was *only a slave girl*, the opinion here is that nothing will be done by the magistrates towards the punishment of the criminals. The whole city is familiar with the names of all the parties concerned."

In Korea, where missions have not been long established, little has been done directly by Christian agencies to uproot slavery. In connection with the recent political reconstruction it was nominally abolished, although the decree is said to be entirely ineffective. Bondage in the form of serfdom rather than slavery has existed for centuries, but it has of late been less prevalent than formerly. The great majority of the slaves are women.[1] The subject of the abolition of slavery, brought into view as a humane ideal of Christianity, has enlisted the sympathy of men of prominence and wealth, some of whom have voluntarily freed their slaves. The Independence Club, an organization of high social standing in Seoul, recently declared unanimously against servitude, and voted to exert its influence in securing freedom to those in bondage. The Vice-President, the Hon. Yi Wan Yong, manifested his sincerity in advocating the emancipation of slaves in Korea by his own example in manumitting thirty-one bondmen whom he had previously owned.[2]

The growth of public sentiment in Korea against slavery.

Thus, wherever we have traced the influence of Christian missions in discrediting slavery, we have found that they have taught and wrought in the interests of freedom, and that they are an honored and useful coadjutor to the enlightened policy of Great Britain and other European Powers, in the universal extinction of this ancient curse of human society. In their sphere of moral incitement and tutelage they take the front rank, and represent a beneficent and aggressive agency which is practically without a rival in regions of the earth where the traditions and usages of bondage still linger.

3. ABOLISHING CANNIBALISM AND INHUMAN SPORTS.—The entrance of Christian missions among savage races has invariably branded with shame the loathsome habit of feasting upon human flesh, and in the case of converts has extinguished the desire for this brutal gratification where it has previously existed. Christianity insists upon the sacredness of human life, and implants those refined instincts which are sure to turn with disgust from the orgies of a cannibal feast.

The story of Christian progress in the Pacific Islands is full of testimony confirmatory of this general statement. The people of the Hawaiian Group, over which the American flag now waves, were redeemed from the degradation of this bestial gluttony by the labors of

[1] *The Korean Repository*, October, 1895, pp. 366–372.
[2] *Ibid.*, November, 1897, p. 438.

missionaries. That the Hawaiians were formerly addicted both to cannibalism and to infanticide is a fact which seems to be based upon authoritative testimony.[1]   The Christian converts of Hawaii, in their turn, became missionaries to the Marquesas Islands, and were instrumental in delivering the inhabitants from the same odious customs.

Pacific Islands redeemed from cannibalism through missions.

The incident of President Lincoln's letter to the Hawaiian missionary Kekela, thanking him for the rescue of Mr. Whalon, the mate of an American ship, just as the latter was about to be killed as the victim of cannibals, has been mentioned elsewhere (p. 19).[2]   In the Hervey, Society, Samoan, Loyalty, Fiji, and New Hebrides groups, except in some localities where missions have not yet penetrated, this fact of the extinction of cannibalism is one of the most striking features of their modern history.

The change came in some instances almost immediately after the entrance of Christianity. The Island of Rarotonga, in the Hervey Group, was first visited in 1823 by Mr. Williams, who in 1827 took up his residence there. As early as 1834, he wrote concerning the inhabitants: "When I found them in 1823, they were ignorant of the nature of Christian worship, and when I left them in 1834, I was not aware that there was a house in the island where family prayer was not observed every morning and evening." The report of the same mission in 1841 contains this significant statement: "One of the most consistent members of the Church, and an active evangelist, was in the days of his youth a cannibal."[3]   On the little Island of Mbau, among the Fijis is a great stone with a history. It was once used as a place of slaughter for the victims of cannibalism, but was removed by the native converts to a Christian church, and, having been hollowed out, was consecrated as a baptismal font. The murderous baptism of blood has given place to the gracious baptism of cleansing. This incident is typical of the amazing transformations which are manifest in the social condition of many of these islands.[4]

Not very long ago the ship "Scottish Dale" was wrecked on Vatoa, known also as Turtle Island, in the Fiji Group. The crew were alarmed when they saw a native boat bearing down upon them,

---

[1] Jarves, "History of the Hawaiian Islands" (fourth edition, with Appendix), pp. 43, 44.

[2] Laurie, "Missions and Science" (The Ely Volume), p. 421.

[3] Alexander, "The Islands of the Pacific," pp. 267-272.

[4] *Ibid.*, pp. 405, 407. See also *Work and Workers in the Mission Field*, June, 1898, pp. 241, 242.

and put forth every effort to flee from the clutches of those whom they supposed to be cannibal savages. When they reached the harbor of Suva, on the southern coast of Viti Levu, a distance of nearly two hundred and fifty miles, and found that they were under the protection of the British flag, they congratulated themselves upon their narrow escape from death. Their alarm was needless, as missions had already transformed the Vatoans from cannibals into kindly and humane Christians, and the speed with which they were hastening towards the "Scottish Dale" was simply indicative of their desire to help the unfortunate mariners. The sailors were told at Suva that "they would have been safer in Vatoa than in any civilized European State, as the Vatoans were Christians, and had saved many shipwrecked crews, giving them food and lodging free, and preserving stranded goods, which they restored faithfully to the owners."[1] The striking contrast between the new times and the old is apparent if we compare statements taken from the journals of John Hunt, the great Wesleyan missionary to Fiji, describing the horrid atrocities of the Fijians before Christianity entered, with the changes which were manifest even as early as 1839. "The cannibals of Viwa," he reports, under date of February 28, 1839, "having embraced Christianity, have lost their love of human flesh."[2] Under date of January 7, 1839, he writes in one of his letters of the former barbarities at Rewa, but adds: "There is no cannibalism at Rewa now, and many of the people have embraced Christianity."[3] A still more vivid insight into the social transformation which marks the present happier era in Fiji is given in an incident recorded in our current literature, that the grandchildren of these former savages have contributed thirteen thousand rupees to the famine sufferers in India. Can cannibals be rescued from their brutal customs by the power of the Gospel? Yes, and they can be made to sympathize to the extent of generous liberality towards a strange and distant people who are famishing for bread. We are prepared to believe a remark recently made concerning these once outcast Fijians, that they are "the most law-abiding community in the world."

The Loyalty Islands yield us evidence not less striking. The story of Pao, the Rarotongan evangelist, and his memorable and perilous struggle to introduce the Gospel into Lifu, is familiar to readers of

The story of the Vatoans and the "Scottish Dale."

---

[1] *The Chronicle*, July, 1897, p. 167, quoted from the *Allgemeine Missions-Zeitschrift.*

[2] *Work and Workers in the Mission Field*, February, 1896, p. 61.

[3] *Ibid.*, June, 1894, p. 234.

South Sea mission literature.[1]   When he first went there, in 1842, he not only literally preached the Gospel to cannibals, but was himself a marked victim, his murderers at one time having been selected and assigned to their task, but at the signal for despatching him not an arm was raised.

Pao and his victories at Lifu.

Amid many perils he still continued his brave campaign, although sometimes the very hour appointed for religious worship would be chosen also by his savage neighbors for one of their inhuman feasts.   In 1852 a deputation from the London Missionary Society visited the island, and reported that "cannibalism had been stamped out."[2]   Pastor Lengereau, a French missionary who formerly resided on the Island of Maré, one of the Loyalty Group, speaks of the great things that have been accomplished there.   "Thirty-five years ago," he states, "seven sailors cast upon Maré were eaten by natives, who, in common with all the inhabitants of the island, were cannibals. Now the whole population is civilised, and cannibalism has ceased."[3] More significant still is the statement of Dr. Gill to the effect that on the occasion of a recent visit to the Loyalty Islands, he found "a band of twelve ex-cannibals, educated and mighty in the Scriptures," ready to go with him and the Rev. A. W. Murray to instruct the heathen of New Guinea.[4]

Due north of the Loyalty Islands are the New Hebrides— Erromanga, with its bloody memories; Tongoa, the scene of the Rev. Oscar Michelsen's story of "Cannibals Won for Christ"; Vate, where faithful Samoan teachers have toiled, and where some of them have been martyred; Tanna, the missionary home of the venerable Dr. Paton; Aneityum, forever consecrated by the labors of the Rev. John Geddie; and also Aniwa and Futuna.   All of these islands a generation or so ago were the scenes of unspeakable barbarities. The changes are marvelous.   In place of cannibal feasts on Ambrym, there is now established a missionary hospital under the care of Dr. Robert Lamb.[5]   The Erromangans, once ferocious in their love of human flesh, and with an evil fame as the murderers of missionaries, are now "reckoned among the most gentle, kind-hearted, and willing

"Cannibals won for Christ" in the New Hebrides.

---

[1] Cousins, "The Story of the South Seas," pp. 148–154; Horne, "The Story of the London Missionary Society," pp. 213–215.

[2] Horne, "The Story of the London Missionary Society," p. 215.

[3] *The Missionary Record*, June, 1894, p. 180.

[4] Gill, "From Darkness to Light in Polynesia," p. 383.

[5] "Annual Report of the New Hebrides Mission, 1896," p. 19.

Bishop of Waiapu, New Zealand, and Melanesian Boys.

Maori Girls' School of the Misses Williams,
Napier, New Zealand.

of Christian people." [1]   At Erakor, on the Island of Vate, there is a centre of Christian light and civilization.[2]   Mr. Michelsen relates some striking incidents of Tongoa: "Cannibalism is now a thing of the past.   The Prince of Peace reigns over two thousand natives."   He tells the story of a party rescued from Epi, a neighboring island, where cannibal customs were still known.   The liberation was by Tongoans, who brought these native friends to their island as a place of refuge.   Among those thus delivered was an aged chief, who, upon arriving at Selembanga, a mission station in Tongoa, recalled the fact that thirty years before he had been there as an invited guest at a heathen feast, and "was one of those who helped to eat forty Purau men, whom the people of Selembanga had slaughtered.   Now, having been saved from the same fate, he was welcomed in a spirit of compassion by those who had learned a better way of life."   The refugees remained several years on Tongoa, were converted to Christianity, and afterwards went back to Epi to live in peace with their former enemies, who had promised faithfully that, if they returned, no harm should come to them.[3]   Mr. Michelsen writes, at the conclusion of one of his chapters (p. 117), concerning the death of a certain native preacher: "This was the last martyr on Tongoa for the faith of Christ, and it was the last cannibal feast on the island."

The Maoris were once addicted to these horrid practices,[4] but a cannibal Maori is not now to be found within range of Christian influences, if indeed a single one exists.   The latest and freshest triumphs are in New Guinea, the home of the "man-catcher."   The missionaries of the London Society, such men as Lawes, Chalmers, Pearse, Hunt, Walker, Dauncey, Abel, and others, with the efficient aid of native preachers and teachers from distant islands in the South

Fresh triumphs in New Guinea.

---

[1] *The Missionary Record*, December, 1894, p. 338.

[2] Horne, "The Story of the London Missionary Society," p. 211; Hodder, "The Conquests of the Cross," vol. iii., pp. 424, 425.

[3] Michelsen, "Cannibals Won for Christ," pp. 79-84.

[4] "The stories of their [the Maoris'] cannibalism are revolting.   They differed from the other Polynesians in that, besides feasting on enemies who were killed in battle, they specially fattened slaves for their feasts.   A poor slave girl would sometimes be commanded by her master to fetch fuel, light a fire, and heat an oven, and then would be knocked on the head, and cast into the oven.   One cannibal testified that, when he first heard the missionaries speak of the sinfulness of eating human flesh, he thought their words were very foolish, and questioned whether it was any more wicked to eat a man than a dog, or pig, or any other animal; but remembering the words, he did not relish his next cannibal feast, and finally loathed the sight of

Seas, once noted for cannibalism,[1] are transforming the wild natures
and ferocious customs of that savage people, until, as Mr. Chalmers
wrote of East Cape in 1882: "All these things are changed, or in
process of change. For several years there have been no cannibal
ovens, no desire for skulls. Tribes that formerly could not meet but
to fight now assemble as friends, and sit side by side in the same house
worshipping the true God."[2] At an isolated station on Milne Bay,
directly opposite the house of the teacher, stand some cocoanut-trees,
which are "simply tattooed with the records of the men who have been
killed and eaten in that village." It seems that it was customary to
cut a notch in the tree upon the celebration of each cannibal feast.
All this has now ceased, let us hope forever, in that little village, where
a messenger of the Gospel—a converted native from distant Samoa—
is teaching of Christ.[3] From the outposts of Australia, the Moravian
Mission at Mapoon, on Cullen Point, reports similar changes.[4] The
missionary societies of the Netherlands in the Dutch East Indies have
done much, wherever their work has extended, to eradicate the custom.
The late Dr. J. L. Phillips, who visited those islands in 1895, was told
that there were at present no cannibals in Sumatra.[5]

The cannibalism of Africa is confined largely to the regions of the
Congo and its tributaries, and to the *Hinterland* of the West Coast.
Wherever mission work has been established, it
A moral tonic for   is noticeable that within the area of its influence
African appetites.   this evil is under a ban. The English and
American missionaries in the Congo State are
many of them face to face with this brutal custom, which, according
to Captain Hinde's recent book, "The Fall of the Congo Arabs," prevails under conditions of exceptional atrocity.[6] The little groups of
converts, it need hardly be said, are the pioneers of a better sentiment,
although as yet their example is but an insignificant force amid the
wild millions of those vast regions. The Presbyterian Mission in the
vicinity of the Gaboon is working among the Fan (written also "Fang")
tribes, who are notorious for their love of human flesh. The English

such food, and became a Christian."—Alexander, "The Islands of the Pacific,"
pp. 359, 360.
 [1] Horne, "The Story of the London Missionary Society," p. 407.
 [2] Chalmers and Gill, "Work and Adventure in New Guinea," p. 251.
 [3] *The Chronicle*, August, 1892, p. 193.
 [4] *Periodical Accounts Relating to the Moravian Missions*, December, 1894,
p. 393; *The Missionary Record*, May, 1893, p. 157.
 [5] *The Missionary Review of the World*, September, 1895, p. 685.
 [6] Hinde, "The Fall of the Congo Arabs," pp. 62–69, 89, 131, 175, 282–285.

and Scotch missions in Lagos and Old Calabar have to contend with the same vicious tendencies. The late Bishop Crowther, in one of his papers on African missions, relates a typical incident. It happened that in a tribal war about one hundred and fifty prisoners were taken, who were divided among the conquerors. Eleven of these captives were assigned to chiefs who were Christian converts, and the remaining one hundred and thirty-nine fell to the lot of heathen rulers. The latter were killed and eaten, but the eleven were spared by the Christian chiefs.

Some of the Indian tribes of South America are known to have been long addicted to cannibalism. It is supposed that the word itself is derived from the Caribs, or Caribales, aboriginal inhabitants of islands off the northeast coast of South America, notorious for their man-eating propensities.[1] The Indians of Tierra del Fuego were shameless cannibals, until the South American Missionary Society established its work among them. Their tendencies in this respect have been completely changed. The Rev. S. J. Christen, of the Presbyterian Mission, Santiago, Chile, writes of them as follows : " Formerly the poor shipwrecked sailors who had the misfortune to be thrown on those inhospitable shores were almost invariably butchered and eaten ; to-day, influenced by the Gospel of Christ, they give assistance and shelter to the unfortunate. The Chile Government some years ago made public recognition of this fact, complimenting the Rev. Thomas Bridges, who was working among them, and sending to the poor Indians a number of cows and oxen as a premium for their humanitarian spirit."

The passing of cannibalism in Tierra del Fuego.

The same brutal passions that are gratified in cannibalism find indulgence also in cruel sports. As Christianity has had its part to play in the overthrow of gladiatorial contests,[2] so at the present day, wherever inhuman pastimes are known, every possible effort is made by missionaries to check and abolish them.

4. ARRESTING HUMAN SACRIFICES.—The humanizing influence of missions, wherever they have entered, has been an unfailing remedy for this ghastly rite. The Gospel doctrine of forgiveness, based upon the

---

[1] Josa, " The Apostle of the Indians of Guiana: Memoir of the Rev. W. H. Brett," pp. 104–106.

[2] " There is scarcely any other single reform so important in the moral history of mankind as the suppression of the gladiatorial shows, and this feat must be almost exclusively ascribed to the Christian Church."—Lecky, " History of European Morals " (American ed.), vol. ii., p. 34.

sacrifice of Christ, has also taught both its folly and its worthlessness. That which Christianity has made only a grim tradition of the early paganism of our ancestors is still to be found in the present-day haunts of darkness. Not to go back to the old Syrian and Phœnician times, we may find among the Teutons, the Druids, and the Aztecs much nearer traces of these atrocious crimes, and it is hard to realize that even to-day the same sun which shines upon us often looks down in some other lands upon a dismal ritual of murder in the name of religion, though in reality chiefly for the gratification of barbaric pride.

What Christianity has done to abolish human sacrifices.

On the West Coast of Africa, that hotbed of abominations, we soon come into contact with the horrors of human sacrifices. They are far less numerous, to be sure, than they were a generation or so ago, but the quivering flesh and streaming blood of scores of victims in that dreary *Hinterland* behind the thin line of West Coast civilization cannot even now be concealed. "Benin, the City of Blood," is the title of a recent volume, describing with lurid realism the scenes of a West Coast inferno in 1897.[1] A British expedition to Kumassi, in 1895, put an end to a similar carnival of crime, and destroyed the power of Prempeh, that king of beastliness and cruelty. The royal mausoleum at Bantama, with his official shambles, has been destroyed. His "Festival of the Yams," with its six hundred victims, is no longer celebrated with ghastly immolations. The fetich-trees are not now soaked to the roots with the life-blood of his victims. His horrid mandate of the sacrifice of one of his slaves, for his entertainment each night before he slept, has ceased. He can no longer offer four hundred virgins, that their blood may be mixed with the mortar to form a richer red in the painted stucco of his palace.[2] Truly, the city of Kumassi was rightly named "Death Place," where the executioners were such conspicuous members of the king's personnel that a whole quarter of the city was assigned to them. This guilty wretch is now a prisoner in Sierra Leone, under official guardianship, and the government of Ashanti is in British hands. The executioners' knives were all handed over,

The breaking up of a West Coast inferno.

---

1 Bacon, "Benin, the City of Blood."
2 Sanderson, "Africa in the Nineteenth Century," pp. 77, 294, 307; Macdonald, "The Gold Coast, Past and Present," p. 286; Kemp, "Nine Years at the Gold Coast," pp. 251, 256; *The Free Church of Scotland Monthly*, March, 1897, pp. 64, 65; *Work and Workers in the Mission Field*, August, 1898, p. 324; *The Mail* (London), April 15, 1896, containing extracts from an article published in *The Sierra Leone Messenger*, by the Rev. Canon Taylor Smith, acting chaplain to the Ashanti Expedition.

with much official ceremony, to the late Sir William E. Maxwell, who was then the Governor.

This, however, is a story of British arms; there is another record of missionary suffering and heroism, which complements it. The Rev. Friedrich Ramseyer and his wife, of the Basel Society, had previously penetrated into these haunts of cruelty. They were there made captives in 1869, and for four years were at the mercy of their bloody persecutors. Their deliverance came when Sir Garnet Wolseley's victorious expedition arrived in 1874. Mr. Ramseyer now writes with joy that he is again in Kumassi, and that it is once more a station of the Basel Society. He speaks of his return in 1896 as if it were a dream, and refers gratefully to the kindness of the British Governor and his friendliness towards the mission. The people are glad to be delivered from Prempeh's tyranny, and hail the good missionary as one of their old friends.[1] The Wesleyan Missionary Society is also now reinstated in its work at Kumassi. An incident illustrates the joy with which the new régime has been welcomed. It is stated that "while on a tour through the country, the British Governor caused the military band which accompanied him to play one evening in the street of a certain town. Among the crowd which gathered to listen was a woman who could not resist the influence of the music, and who began to dance and sing. Pains were taken to discover what she sang, and it was found that every improvised verse ended with the words, '*No more the knife! No more the knife!*'"[2]

"No more the knife" in Kumassi.

The records of the Old Calabar Mission of the United Presbyterian Church of Scotland yield clear and emphatic data upon the subject we are now considering. Human sacrifices, both as acts of worship and as tributes of honor to the dead, were commonplace events when the missionaries first entered the country. Slaves by scores and hundreds were sacrificed through pure wantonness, and with absolute unconcern for human life. The pioneers, Waddell, Goldie, and Anderson, took a strong, unflinching stand in opposition to these customs. Finally, in 1850, occurred the death of two chiefs, and the occasion was a time for action. Several wives and slaves had already been made victims, when Mr. Anderson appealed to the king, and, through tact, firmness, and the power of his personal influence,

A Society for the Suppression of Human Sacrifices in Old Calabar.

[1] *The Mission World*, August, 1896, p. 376, quoted from the *Allgemeine Missions-Zeitschrift*.

[2] *The Free Church of Scotland Monthly*, September, 1896, p. 219.

he succeeded in putting a check upon the proceedings. The king and the chiefs met with the missionaries in the church palaver-house, and "agreed to pass a law that human sacrifices should be abolished, and that life should not be taken unless for crime." The following day the missionaries rallied the people, and, supported by public sentiment, a "Society for the Suppression of Human Sacrifices in Old Calabar" was formed. So firm and decisive were the efforts made that on the 15th of February, 1850, the law was passed, and although it was difficult at once to enforce it fully, there was steady progress, until human sacrifices became a thing of the past.[1] Victories like this have since been won in other sections of the country, and when King Eyo died, December 3, 1858, "there was not a drop of blood shed. Many of the slaves took to flight, but his Christian retainers remained, and without fear performed the last offices for the dead. Only twelve years before this the death of a king would have implied the slaughter of hundreds." [2] Other kings have since died within the field occupied by the mission, but without the bloody scenes enacted in former days.[3] A similar story is told by the Rev. J. J. Fuller, who landed on the West Coast of Africa in 1845, and lived to see "the old custom of burying the living with the dead wiped out and gone." [4]

The Yoruba Mission of the Church Missionary Society has a record not of uninterrupted success, but of steady effort and final victory. If a chief now dies, it is more than likely that no sacrifices will be offered, but if the old temptation should conquer, there will be not more than one or two victims, and they will be slain in secret, whereas previously they would have been killed by scores.[5] Bishop Phillips, a native of Lagos, writes: "The influence of Christianity upon the horrible customs connected with human sacrifices in this country is gradual, but marked. The public parading of the victims before the immolation was first discontinued. Next the opinion as to the usefulness or beneficial results of a human sacrifice was changed, so that it came to be generally acknowledged as wanton cruelty. Then it was practised clandestinely, and now it has been abandoned (we trust) altogether." In "A Life for Africa" is a significant incident

The triumph of a solitary burial at African funerals.

---

[1] Dickie, "Story of the Mission in Old Calabar," p. 38.

[2] *Ibid.*, p. 63.

[3] *The Missionary Record*, October, 1893, p. 286; November, 1895, p. 311; March, 1896, p. 75; *Woman's Work for Woman*, June, 1896, p. 158.

[4] *Illustrated Africa*, June, 1894, p. 10; Pierson, "The New Acts of the Apostles," pp. 267-269.

[5] "Report of the Church Missionary Society, 1894," p. 26.

relating how Dr. Good succeeded in "having the dead safely buried alone," and thus dealt an effective blow at witchcraft and its attendant custom of burying a woman alive in the grave of her husband. "Within two years after," writes his biographer, "three witch-doctors in the district abandoned their calling." [1] We read of missionaries facing the same dread emergencies in the valley of the Congo, and remonstrating with excited crowds, at the time of funeral ceremonies, on the wickedness and folly of these needless sacrifices. One of the missionaries of the Baptist Congo Mission writes: "I cannot help contrasting the spirit exhibited during this affair [an attempt to prevent a human sacrifice] with that shown about two years ago." Then all remonstrance was in vain, but in this case it was successful.[2] In Uganda, as far back as 1893, the missionaries persuaded the king to give up the custom of murdering all his brothers when he came to the throne.[3] In Zambesia the Rev. F. Coillard so influenced King Lewanika that "for four years he has not offered a human sacrifice, or allowed his subjects to practise this rite." [4]

The readers of Mr. Michelsen's book on missions in the South Seas, and of Dr. Gill's "Life in the Southern Isles," will find examples of the power of Christianity to stay these inhuman rites. In a narrative given in the latter volume, entitled "Saved from Sacrifice," the story of Makimou, an old native, is related, to the effect that *A new order of peace-offerings in the South Seas.* again and again, before the Gospel entered his island home of Mangaia, he was marked as a victim for sacrifice, but was saved through the intervention of powerful friends. In his own words he gives this testimony: "Still I believed that I must die, and in my turn be offered. But, blessed be Jehovah, not long after the offering of Reonatia, the Gospel was brought to Mangaia. I then learned with wonder that the true peace-offering is Jesus, who died on Calvary, in order that all the wretched slaves of Satan might be freed. This was indeed good news to me." After some years the king, chiefs, and the body of the people embraced Christianity and burned their idols, and Makimou was saved.[5] The wondrous story of other Christianized islands certifies to the same transforming power of the missionary evangel.[6]

[1] Parsons, "A Life for Africa," pp. 272, 273.
[2] *The Monthly Messenger*, March, 1893, p. 68.
[3] *The Church Missionary Intelligencer*, March, 1893, p. 202.
[4] Johnston, "Missionary Landscapes in the Dark Continent," p. 141.
[5] Gill, "Life in the Southern Isles," p. 327. See also Michelsen, "Cannibals Won for Christ," pp. 120–122, 131.
[6] *The Chronicle*, July, 1893, p. 194; August, 1894, p. 181.

The existence of the custom of human sacrifices in India, until the advent of British rule, cannot be denied. The Abbé Dubois gives explicit testimony to this fact.[1] The Khonds, in

The suppression of human sacrifices in India.

Orissa, one of the aboriginal hill tribes, seem to have attained a revolting preëminence in the practice. Mission work among them has been largely instrumental in changing all this, and under the British Government such immolations are suppressed by law.[2] It becomes a simple truism that where Christianity enters, and the Gospel illumines the mind and softens the heart, human sacrifices are regarded as an abomination, and are no longer offered.[3]

5. BANISHING CRUEL ORDEALS.—The barbarous ordeals of heathendom must be regarded as one of the most vulnerable points of non-civilized society.   If there is such a thing as

The foolishness of heathen wisdom.

native common sense, it is hard to understand why it has not long ago wrought out a deliverance of its own ; yet the same stupid and atrocious performances have gone on for centuries, and seem to be beyond remedy except through guidance, help, and courage supplied from some outside source.   The Christian teaching concerning a gracious, good, and almighty God, at once the protector of the innocent and the judge of the guilty, satisfies the demand for justice and affords a refuge from the terrors of demonology.   Education gives enlightened views of the natural world and our relations to it, while it delivers the mind from the dismal spell of superstition.   Those who are taught the truths of science can no longer be made to submit to the arbitrament of poison or to the

1 " Hindu Manners, Customs, and Ceremonies," pp. 652–654.   On the general subject of sacrifice as a feature of Hinduism, see an instructive article by Dr. F. F. Ellinwood, in *The Missionary Review of the World*, November, 1898, pp. 827–833.

2 *Regions Beyond*, January, 1897, p. 24.

3 *The Christian Patriot* of Madras for December 24, 1896, in an editorial on the Indian famine, calls attention to a suggestive remark from *The Times*, as follows: " Before we conclude, we briefly allude to an interesting observation made by *The Times* on this subject.   This journal shows how famine serves as a criterion of the changes that are taking place in native opinion.   It points out that years ago natives regarded famine as a sign of divine wrath, and betook themselves to propitiatory rites.   But things have altered now.   Instead of looking to miracles wrung from heaven by sacrificial rites, and even by human offerings, the Indian now scans the weather forecast, and if divine interposition is looked for, it is expected in the wind currents.   Though the orthodox Hindus still regard famine as a visitation, the average among them no longer thinks of resorting to sacrifices."

torture of fire as tests of moral guilt. We who are born into the freedom of knowledge can little comprehend the limitations of those in the grim thraldom of total ignorance. We who enjoy the privilege of appealing to divine and human justice can but feebly realize the agony and demoralization of those who regard themselves as the victims of evil omens and unseen foes, or as already condemned by the verdict of fate. Strange as it may seem, the dislodging of these satanic devices is not easy. The struggle in African mission fields to discredit the insignificant esere-bean as the arbiter of guilt or innocence has been a desperate conflict; yet where Christian missions have gained a vantage-ground the battle has been fought and won, and the poisonous bean, which was so long both judge and jury on the West Coast of Africa, has been relegated to its proper place as an ordinary product of nature.

In the history of the Old Calabar Mission, under date of 1852, we read of the death of a native king, and of the immediate recourse to the ordeal of drinking the powdered esere-bean by the suspected parties, in order to discover who caused his illness, on the supposition that if guilty, "they would retain it and die; if innocent, put it up and live." It is stated that all who drank it at that time died. There were resolute and courageous missionaries in Calabar in the early fifties. "Waddell, with his zeal and spirituality, Goldie, with his scholarly tastes and calm perseverance, Anderson, with his courage and dash, made a strong triumvirate." With them were associated others of like qualities. Among the signs of progress which were reported a little later were the following: "When Eyo's house was burned down, and property to the value of some thousands of pounds destroyed, it was a distinct victory to the cause of Christ that no one was accused, and no esere-bean employed to discover the culprit, as would inevitably have been the case but for the influence of the Gospel upon the king."[1] In 1855 some suspected natives who were doomed to undergo the poison ordeal fled to Mr. Anderson's house for protection. He harbored them, not without serious peril to himself, and by the intervention of a British consul from Fernando Po the repudiation of the ordeal was secured. Again and again Anderson fought this dread iniquity, until, in 1878, a document was drawn up by Her Majesty's Consul, Mr. Hopkins, and the leading men of the country. It is Mr. Hopkins's own statement that this agreement was made possible by missionary influence and teaching. Articles III. and IV. are as

The banishment of the poison ordeal.

[1] Dickie, "Story of the Mission in Old Calabar," pp. 44, 45.

follows: "(3) Any person administering the esere-bean, whether the person taking it dies or not, shall be considered guilty of murder, and shall suffer death. (4) Any persons taking the esere-bean wilfully, either for the purpose of committing suicide, or for the purpose of attempting to prove their innocence of any crime of which they may have been accused, shall be considered guilty of attempted murder, and shall be fined as heavily as their circumstances will permit, and shall be banished from the country."[1] What more decisive trophy of their victory could Christian missions present?

Bishop Ferguson, of Liberia, writes of the conversion of the Grebos to Christianity, and the consequent abolishment of the ordeal by poison.[2] In fact, on the Gold Coast persons have been known to declare themselves Christians for the sake of escaping the perils of witchcraft and the deadly poison ordeal, since it has become an accepted dictum that Christianity will not tolerate these cruelties.[3] Dr. Franklin P. Lynch, an American Baptist missionary in the Congo Valley, writes of his conflicts with the native tribes in the endeavor to break up the *nkasa* (poisonwood) palavers, and of his success, after a flagrant and fatal case, in securing a formal agreement signed by all the neighboring chiefs, in which they pledged themselves "to prevent any further administration of *nkasa* in the territory." They moreover stipulated that no *nganga* (medicine-man) should be allowed to make a charge of witchcraft within their dominions, and that no one should be taken elsewhere in order to receive the poison.[4]

Corroborative testimony from the Rev. Robert Laws, M.D., writing from the borders of Lake Nyassa, indicates that the poison ordeal has been "almost abolished within a great part of the sphere of his mission."[5] In a private letter to the author he remarks: "In the neighborhood of Bandawè, where the effects of the Gospel have been most marked, the use of the ordeal has almost disappeared, and when resorted to, the fact is concealed as much as possible." The Rev. J. S. Wimbush, of the Universities' Mission, writes from the southern shores of the lake, that while poison-drinking and other witchcraft used to be quite common on the Island of Likoma, these things "seem now to have come to an end, and public opinion is setting against them."

[1] Dickie, " Story of the Mission in Old Calabar," p. 79.
[2] *The Church Missionary Intelligencer*, May, 1894, p. 364.
[3] *The Christian Express*, February, 1895, p. 28.
[4] *The Baptist Missionary Magazine*, October, 1896, p. 508.
[5] " Foreign Mission Report of the United Presbyterian Church of Scotland, 1897," p. 21. See Dr. Laws's statement as to its former prevalence, in Vol. I., p. 164.

Among the wild parishioners of Pastor Coillard was Lewanika, the King of the Barotsi. He was much given to terrorizing his people by ordeals, and one day he found himself in unlucky circumstances which forced upon him the tempta-   A court preacher's tion to resort to desperate measures. Pastor Coil-   straight talk to African royalty. lard on hearing of this made a strenuous endeavor to check the impending disaster. " Directly this news reached us," he writes, " I took a canoe and went to the capital. The king seemed pleased to see me—his heart was full; he passed a great part of the night in my hut, talking. I spent the whole of the next day in private interviews with his principal councillors, and in the evening they were all assembled at my place with their master. But that did not suffice. The next day, Sunday, at the two meetings, I preached on the Sixth Commandment: 'Thou shalt not kill.' I leave you to imagine how they opened their eyes when they heard me enunciate and develop this truth, here so new and strange, that man is the creature, the *exclusive* property of God, that kings and governors are only the shepherds of the people, and servants who will have to render an account of their stewardship. However much I shrank from the task, I had to denounce the atrocity of a superstition which so lightly sacrificed so many human lives, and the intrigues which had produced these last events. I felt the full importance of the occasion, and the grandeur of the ministry committed to me. Oh, how tremblingly I had gone to Lealuyi! —how I besought my Master for fidelity, for strength, and the power of a burning love! They understood my address quite as well as the purpose of my visit. The people, astonished, said, ' Ah, yes, indeed!' The king hung his head, and said to the Gambella, ' The words of the *Moruti* have sunk into my heart.' The councillors came to me in private, to beg me to repeat them to him; and he himself in his turn asked me to say them all again to his ministers. They made me all sorts of fine promises: no more ordeals by boiling water, no more poison, no more burning at the stake." [1]

Pastor Coillard no doubt saved lives at that time, and the spirit with which he then discharged his high duty indicates clearly enough the tact and energy with which he has conducted this long struggle. He writes a little further on as if he realized that a temporary success of this kind did not necessarily mean the final break-up of a long-established custom. " But let us not deceive ourselves," he remarks; " it is not at the first blast of the ram's horn that one can overthrow or even shake the walls of superstition. It is one of Satan's chief strong-

1 Coillard, " On the Threshold of Central Africa," p. 288.

holds.   But we shall redouble the blows, we shall dig mines, and happy shall we be if we can succeed in making a breach!"   If the venerable pastor does not live to see the day of final and confirmed triumph, yet his name and courageous services will be forever associated with the deliverance of his flock from the terrors of the poison ordeal.

In Madagascar a decisive result is reported by a resident missionary, of the London Society.   "Trial by ordeal," writes the Rev. J. Pearse, Fianarantsoa, "used to be the popular way of decid-

No more deadly ordeals in Madagascar and in India. ing between the supposedly innocent and the guilty, and hundreds of guiltless men and women were thus cruelly murdered every year.   Now the fatal draught is never mixed, and the deadly cup is never put to the lips of any accused persons."   In India this species of savagery is forbidden by authority of the British Government.   Devotees are still found who subject themselves to much suffering by self-imposed ordeals, but such exhibitions as hook-swinging and murderous self-mutilation are now prohibited, though not as yet entirely suppressed.

6. Initiating the Crusade against Foot-Binding.—A peculiar interest attaches to this struggle to dislodge an ancient and barbaric

The missionary verdict concerning the wanton torture of childhood in China. custom, since the purpose of the endeavor is to release innocent childhood from wanton torture. Just as the sunny and frolicsome days of Chinese girlhood are beginning, during the fateful fifth or sixth year, this grim decree of mutilation lays its hand upon the little victim, holds her in its relentless grasp for months and years of pain, and then turns her loose to a maimed and fettered life.   Until recently hardly a word of protest has been raised by the ethics, the philosophy, the common sense, or the humanitarian instincts of China, while this piercing and needless suffering has been inflicted from generation to generation.   If pressed by argument, or confronted with the question of *Cui bono?* in many instances intelligent Chinese will frankly acknowledge that foot-binding is senseless and cruel.   There is a well-known saying among them, that "for every pair of small feet there is a *kong* full of tears"—a *kong* being the Chinese equivalent for "pail."   The offset to this, however, and by far the more powerful sentiment, is that "a woman's feet and hair proclaim what kind of a woman she is." The desire for feet after the type of the "Golden Lilies" seems to control parental feelings and capture the imagination even of suffering childhood.   The custom is entrenched in the social system of China, though it is acknowledged to have no support from Confucianism. The present Manchu dynasty even repudiates it in the royal palace and the higher circles of Manchu society do not conform to it. Nevertheless the effort of Kang He, a former emperor, to abolish it by royal proclamation utterly failed, and he was advised by his councillors that any endeavor to compel its suppression would occasion a widespread and dangerous rebellion.

Christian missionaries, while deeply sensible of the magnitude of this evil, and of the desirability of reform, have also realized the overwhelming difficulties and threatening perils which would be involved in an unwise attempt to deal prematurely and in a spirit of compulsion with this most delicate question. They have, therefore, exercised great prudence and self-restraint, at the same time that they have been expectant and alert, availing themselves of every opportunity to prepare the way for a great change. There was, naturally, some difference of opinion among them as to whether it was wise to meddle with the custom. Many who deeply deprecated its existence were yet inclined to let it alone, in the hope that in the course of time it would die out or remedy itself. Within the present generation, however, and especially during the last decade, a more militant and aggressive attitude has been assumed. Missionary women throughout China are now thoroughly aroused, and, with mingled tenderness, tact, energy, and courage, have resolutely inaugurated an ardent crusade. A new public sentiment upon the subject is springing up on every side, and the iron rule of fashion is weakening. The glory of the " Golden Lilies " is fading, and the Creator's ideal is beginning to be honored and recognized. The Rev. John Macgowan, of Amoy, remarks in one of his recent volumes: "It is amazing with what heroic fortitude the women of this country have endured a custom that entails a lifelong misery. It has such a hold, however, upon all classes of them that no imperial legislation has ever been able to affect it in the slightest degree. The only force that will be able to banish it from the country is Christianity. Much has been effected by that already, and to-day hundreds of girls and women within the Church, now pioneers in the movement for freedom, are rejoicing in the liberty that never would have come to them but for the Gospel of Christ." [1]

Foot-binding has sometimes been lightly spoken of as not a matter of serious moment, and an issue which should be left to the Chinese to settle for themselves. No student of the well-being of society can

> *The difficulties of dealing with foot-binding.*

[1] Macgowan, " Pictures of Southern China," p. 308.

thus regard it when he realizes that it almost necessitates domestic slovenliness and dirt, is a stimulus to false and utterly artificial pride, leads
to enforced idleness, produces much ill-health, oc-
casions excruciating suffering, cripples the person,
diminishes the capacity for useful service in every
sphere of a woman's life, and is an incitement
to the crime of infanticide.[1]   It is hard to understand the almost
impregnable fixedness of a custom wholly evil, and based upon purely
artificial and imaginative standards; yet the magnitude of these difficulties no one appreciates more vividly than the missionaries themselves.   "The most noteworthy struggle of the year," writes Mrs.
Goodrich, of the American Board, in 1895, "has been at Kalgan,
where Miss Etta Williams has fought Satan in his stronghold of pride
(for the Kalgan feet are 'so dainty and pretty'), and convinced some

A social indictment
of bound feet.

---

[1] A description of the method of foot-binding has been given in Vol. I., p. 212;
but we insert here another, from an authoritative source, giving in graphic English
the result of personal observation during many years of residence in China: "Long
bandages of calico, about two inches in width, are prepared, and the process is
begun by turning all the toes, except the large one, under the soles of the feet.   In
the early stages the children suffer agonies.   Every day the bandages are tightened,
and the toes driven still further from the place where Nature has appointed them,
until the instep, amidst pains that only those who have endured them can comprehend, is thrust forward in this unnatural manner.   Still the bandages do their cruel
work, fastened by the hand of a mother from whose heart custom has expunged all
the more generous and tender feeling for her offspring, and a chasm is made between
the heel and the fore part of the foot, whilst the instep becomes convex in shape,
instead of concave.   The morrow comes, and the cruel torture is resumed, and no
tears can stay the hand that inflicts it.   The toes, in spite of the fiercest protest
from Nature, are pressed by brute force still further under the soles, and the instep
bones, unable to bear the strain, crack and break, and yet the mother, untouched by
the wreck she has made of her girl's feet, draws the bandages tighter and still more
tight, till at length, through the infinite suffering of her daughter, she has reached
the very ultimate limit to which her art can go, and the feet are so reduced in size
that they can be put within the narrow confines of the shoe.   But it must not be
supposed that the torture ends when the process of binding has been completed, and
when flesh and blood have been cramped within the very narrowest possible bounds.
When the beau-ideal has been reached, in order to get the feet into the small, doll-
like shoes, the unfortunate victim of this hideous custom is compelled from this time
forward, whenever she walks out, to stand with her feet, not in the ordinary natural
way, but in an inclined position, with the heels considerably elevated above the toes.
She thus really throws the whole burden of her body upon the latter; and, in order
to ease the strain upon them, a ball of cloth is fixed in the after part of the shoe upon
which the heel may rest, thus relieving the pressure upon the big toe, which cannot
be cramped, for fear of fatal consequences."—Macgowan, "Pictures of Southern
China," pp. 307, 308.

Pupils in the Girls' High School of the Woman's Foreign Missionary Society.

Asbury Methodist Episcopal Church.

(The Asbury Church is new, and was erected by native workmen, under the superintendence of Prof. Gamewell, of Peking University. It is one of the finest church buildings in China. Its Sabbath-school, attended by both adults and children, numbers one thousand.)

of the Christian mothers of the sin of foot-binding. It was a battle such as you in America cannot comprehend." [1] In some sections of the country there is hardly any test of the moral courage, fortitude, and patience of a Chinese woman which can compare with that of allowing herself to be the possessor of natural feet, and appearing in public as God made her.

The origin of the practice cannot be settled by any authoritative historical record. Some Chinese writers have asserted that it began in the time of the Tsi dynasty (A.D. 501). Others, and the latter is more probably the correct view, trace it only to the days of the Tang dynasty (A.D. 975). All agree that it was a device of some favorite of the imperial harem, but the purpose which it was intended to serve is not so clear. It has been said that the object was to disguise a natural deformity. Another version states that it was the wile of a royal concubine, a celebrated beauty who won the heart of the king by her graceful dancing, and that the origin of the term "Golden Lilies" as applied to small feet is the king's exclamation of admiration: "Every step she takes she causes a lily to grow." Dr. Faber and Dr. Edkins both advocate the later origin; the former argues that, strictly speaking, it is not a legal custom, since it is against the usage of Chinese antiquity, and made its appearance fourteen hundred years after the time of Confucius. It is not, therefore, supported by the teachings of the Chinese sages, and is, moreover, contrary to the expressed will of some of the members of the present dynasty. [2]

The origin of the custom.

The earliest aggressive efforts on the part of missionaries of which the writer can find any trace occurred in 1870, when a school, the name of which is not given, is mentioned in which the custom was not allowed. Another reference, as early as 1872, is found concerning the girls' school of the Methodist Episcopal Mission, Peking, where the contention for unbound feet as a matter of Christian principle has been steadily and successfully maintained. Mrs. Grace Stott (C. I. M.) also opened a school at Wenchow, in 1874, in which no foot-binding was permitted. The pioneer anti-foot-binding society

The initial movement for its suppression.

---

[1] *Life and Light for Woman*, November, 1895, p. 503. The sad tidings have recently been received of the death of Miss Williams, which occurred, after a brief illness, at Kalgan, May 30, 1898.

[2] *Woman's Work in the Far East*, May, 1894, p. 120; August, 1894, p. 33. Cf. also article by Dr. Faber, in *The Chinese Recorder*, April, 1893.

was established in Amoy in 1874,[1] chiefly through the efforts of the Rev. John Macgowan, of the London Missionary Society, with the hearty coöperation of other Amoy missionaries. A pledge was drawn up and signed at the first meeting of the society by over forty women who were prepared to unite in the movement. The organization has flourished, and now, according to recent information, it numbers over a thousand members.[2] In the "Records of the Shanghai Conference of 1877" (p. 132), an essay on this subject is found, contributed by Miss S. H. Woolston, then of the American Methodist Episcopal Mission at Foochow, in which the following statements are made: "It is well understood in the Foochow missions—in two of them, at least— that preachers and church-members are not to bind the feet of their daughters." It is also stated that the preachers themselves in the Methodist Mission "made a rule prohibiting the practice among church-members." The distinction between the higher classes, with bound feet, and the lower classes, consisting of slaves and hard-working women, with unbound feet, is noted, while the appearance of a third class, respectable and at the same time neither slaves nor work-people, and yet having unbound feet, is commented upon as having already sprung up. It was asserted that this latter class was destined to increase and become identified with Christianity. The prophecy of that essay has already been fulfilled. It is apparent from the discussion which followed its reading that the missionaries had strong convictions upon the subject, but were acting in the matter with wisdom and self-restraint. In the "Records of the Shanghai Conference of 1890" there are indications of progress, although the subject is not so prom-

---

[1] *The Chinese Recorder*, October, 1895, p. 497.

The following extract from a letter of Mrs. L. W. Kip, dated Amoy, July 7, 1874, and furnished to the author by Dr. H. N. Cobb, Secretary of the Reformed Church Board of Missions, refers to the organization of this society: "Last winter, at one of our missionary conferences, the subject of small feet was brought up, and it was thought we might institute a society the members of which would pledge themselves not to bind their girls' feet. After a great deal of talk, a pledge-book was printed, and a meeting for women only was appointed for Friday, July 3d, in one of our churches. There were about seventy present in the body of the church; in the pulpit were three missionary gentlemen and two Chinese pastors. After prayer and addresses, all who were willing to take the pledge were invited to sign their names, or rather make their marks. Then we ladies had a chance to do our part, and we each went round to those of our own classes who, we knew, were willing to join, but who, perhaps, would not have courage to come forward alone, and brought them up to sign, and in that way we secured over forty names at once."

[2] "Christianity is the only force that would dare to attack such a widespread system as foot-binding, backed as it is by the gentry, the scholars, the wealthy

inent, as no doubt it will be in the coming conference which will probably be held in 1901.

The awakening of a more general interest among the Chinese in
favor of the suppression of foot-binding, and we may also say the
quickening of a more aggressive spirit among missionaries themselves, became manifest in 1893   The organization of a
more aggressive
and 1894. The action of the Shanghai Mission-   crusade.
ary Association, taken December 5, 1893, appoint-
ing a committee to "deal with the whole question, with full power to
act," seems to have stimulated a progressive and widely extended campaign against the custom. The committee entered into correspondence
with missionaries throughout China, and brought to light the fact that
there was much latent interest in the subject, and that excellent work
was being accomplished here and there in cultivating a spirit of revolt
against such grievous exactions. Under the auspices of this committee
mass-meetings were held in Shanghai, and an anti-foot-binding society
organized, known as the "Tien Tsu Hui." Other mass-meetings have
been held and other societies formed in rapid succession in various
communities, until the statement made in a missionary communication
in 1894, that "all China seems to be aroused on the question of foot-
binding," is quite true within the limits of mission influence. Since
1894 missionary correspondence from China has been full of references
to this subject. The Tien Tsu Hui, or "Natural-Foot Society,"
under the direction not alone of missionaries, but of the wives of consuls and other prominent foreigners in Shanghai, is fully equipped for
its work, and is engaged in issuing a supply of literature in which the
custom of foot-binding is condemned. Prizes have been offered for
the best essays upon the theme by Chinese authors. The Tientsin
Committee of the Tien Tsu Hui, in response to its recent offer of

middle class, and by the instincts of the women, who feel that they would be degraded were they to leave their feet unbound. Seventeen years ago an anti-foot-
binding society was formed in Amoy, and all were invited to join it. The object
was to do away with this cruel and unsightly custom. Some of the better spirits
joined at once, but great opposition was manifested by others. Public meetings
were held, where essays both for and against it were read, and which were afterwards discussed both by friend and foe. The result is that to-day over a thousand
persons are connected with the society, and now public opinion in the churches is
opposed to foot-binding. The idea which originated in Amoy has spread to other
places in China, and to-day in different parts of this great empire a vigorous crusade
is being carried on against the inhuman practice. Only Christianity could have
accomplished this, for so strong was the hold it had on all classes of society that
imperial legislation against it was unable to control it in the slightest degree."—
Rev. John Macgowan (L. M. S.), Amoy, China.

such a prize, received one hundred and seven essays, coming from four provinces.[1]   Meetings have been and will continue to be held for discussion, and local committees are being formed in many towns.   The efficient organizing Secretary, Mrs. Archibald Little, the wife of an English merchant residing at Chungking, is indefatigable in her efforts to extend the usefulness of the society.   One of the most recent steps has been the preparation of a memorial to the Emperor, praying for his intervention to put a stop to the custom throughout the empire. The International Women's Union also united in the presentation of this memorial, which was forwarded to the Tsung-li Yamen by Minister Denby.   This official body, however, respectfully declined to assume the responsibility of placing it before the Emperor.

A survey of the progress already made in this good cause may be taken from Shanghai as a centre, where the new crusade seems to have had its origin.   In that city "foot-binding is not The progress in Central allowed " in St. Mary's Hall, a school of the Epis- and Southern China. copal Mission, and in the Presbyterian boarding- school the custom is opposed by both teachers and pupils.   In a society of Christian women under the direction of Miss Posey forty members have pledged themselves against it.[2]   If we turn southward, we find at Hangchow the girls' boarding-school of the American Mission (Southern Presbyterian), reporting through Miss Davidson that "from the first it has taken a firm stand against this evil, and no girl has been allowed to enter whose feet were not unbound." The school has more applicants every year than can be accommodated.[3] At Ningpo is a society which, in 1894, had not yet celebrated its first anniversary, but already a number of Christian women there had unbound their feet.   At Funghwa a little group of women, under the influence of Miss Britton, of the China Inland Mission, have had the courage to break with the custom.   One of the earliest efforts was made at Wenchow, when, twenty-five years ago, Mrs. Grace Stott, of the same mission, founded a boarding-school in which no bound feet were to be admitted.   The school grew in numbers, and is now full, with a waiting list of those who are ready to comply with the condition.[4] At Kweiki, in Kiangsi, is a school of twenty-five girls, under the charge of Miss McCulloch (C. I. M.), "all with unbound feet."   At Foochow a decided sentiment against foot-binding exists, and special efforts are

---

[1] *The Chinese Recorder*, July, 1898, p. 358.
[2] " Station Reports of the Central China Mission, 1893–94," pp. 12, 15.
[3] *The Missionary*, February, 1895, p. 80.
[4] Stott, " Twenty-six Years of Missionary Work in China," p. 55.

reported, not only on the part of missionaries, but of prominent Chinese, to secure its cessation. It is stated that on the Island of Haitang, where the American Methodist Mission is established, "nearly all the Christian women either have natural feet, or have unbound them," and that the daughters of the Christians are quite free from the infliction. At Amoy, as we have seen, there is a large and flourishing pioneer society of over a thousand members. From Formosa the Rev. W. Gauld (C. P. M.), of Tamsui, writes: "Among Christians there is a growing opinion against it, and many have given it up." At Swatow a beginning has been made. At Canton "none of the Christians bind the feet of their daughters, and to allow them to remain the natural size is becoming more and more consistent with respectability and a good position in society." In the Canton Female Seminary of the American Presbyterian Mission, in the year 1890, there were ninety-two girls, and of this number only five had bound feet.[1]

Starting out again from Shanghai, in a northerly direction, we reach Nanking, where there is a school of the Methodist Episcopal Mission, in which the rule is to unbind the feet. In the boarding-school of the Foreign Christian Missionary Society, with an enrollment of fifty-two, "all the girls who had bound feet have unbound them." **Bulletins from North China.** At Chinkiang "increased interest" is reported, and excellent work is being done towards "setting the prisoners free." Mrs. Killie states that at Ichowfu a movement has been commenced for releasing the feet of the children in the girls' school. The Rev. Dr. Corbett, of Chefoo, writes that "within a year not a few of our women—some of them well advanced in life—have unbound their own feet, and pledged themselves to do all they can to prevent their friends and neighbors from following this cruel custom." In September, 1894, an anti-footbinding league was formed in Chefoo, and there is a group of Chinese Christian mothers in the city, most of whom were educated at mission schools, who can be relied upon not to bind their daughters' feet.[2] The late Mrs. C. W. Mateer reported from Tengchow that of the thirty-two pupils in the Girls' High School "all but four had unbound feet, and this was one of the strongholds of the practice." From Pang-Chuang, Miss Wyckoff, of the American Board, announces the formation of a society with a membership of fifty-eight, and states that no girl with bound feet is admitted to the boarding-school.[3] From Tientsin Miss

---

[1] " Records of the Missionary Conference, 1890," p. 221.
[2] *Woman's Work for Woman*, February, 1895, p. 36.
[3] *Woman's Work in the Far East*, August, 1894, pp. 63, 64.

Stanley, of the same Board, writes with satisfaction that she "has four girls all ready to go to Peking, who have unbound feet." In the girls' school of the London Missionary Society at Peking there has been a rising tide of aversion to this injurious practice, and one girl after another has unbound her feet, until out of thirty-seven there was, in January, 1894, "only one little cripple left."[1] The Bridgman School of the American Board at Peking has taken the stand "that it will receive no more girls with bound feet." In 1893 an anti-foot-binding society was formed in the capital, with an enthusiastic membership.[2] The Rev. Dr. Goodrich, of Tungcho, near Peking, states that a sentiment is springing up against this detestable custom. He writes: "This is wholly due to missions, and especially to our missionary ladies. I predict that in a score or two of years foot-binding will be rapidly passing away, at least in North China. In this city there are about forty women and girls with natural feet." The struggle to subdue this almost invincible evil in Kalgan, one of its strongholds, goes bravely on. Mrs. Moir Duncan writes in 1895, from Hsianfu (Singanfu), Shensi Province, in the far interior: "Three years and a half ago, one young woman faced the inevitable ridicule of her fellows, and unbound her little feet. Since then over seventy have followed her example. Of these two are more than seventy years of age, some over sixty, many over fifty, and all agree in testifying to the increased comfort they enjoy from their unbound feet. Add to these the scholars and ex-scholars of our boarding-school, and you have over one hundred and twenty witnesses silently reproving the cruel and crippling fashion we long to see utterly abolished."[3] A later report in 1898 gives the number as one hundred and fifty.

Entering now the great valley of the Yang-tse Kiang, we find at Kiukiang, where all classes of women bind their feet, a hearty antagonism to the miseries of foot-binding in the school of the Methodist Mission, under the charge of Miss Stanton. It is stated that Kiukiang was the home of the first girl in Central China who was allowed to grow up with unbound feet. An interesting incident is related in connection with a mass-meeting held at the time of the Annual Meeting of the Central China Mission, October 29, 1894. Mrs. Shie, the mother of this same girl, better known, perhaps, by her translated name of Mrs. Stone, was invited to make an address upon the occasion.

The story of reform in the Yang-tse Valley.

---

[1] *Quarterly News of Woman's Work*, July, 1894, p. 70.
[2] *The Missionary Herald*, September, 1893, p. 349; November, 1896, p. 471.
[3] "Report of the English Baptist Missionary Society, 1896," p. 66; 1898, p. 72.

She related an incident from her own personal experience, saying that "when their first daughter was born the father knelt beside her bed, and together they consecrated the little one to the Lord, and registered their vow that her feet should never be bound." Years after we find this daughter, bearing the new name of Mary Stone, standing upon the platform at the commencement of Michigan University, receiving her medical diploma in anticipation of her return to her native city to open a hospital there for Chinese women.[1] Her picture appears opposite page 193. Soon after the meeting referred to an anti-foot-binding association was formed at Kiukiang, with a membership of sixty-two. In an article published in 1897, Mrs. Archibald Little reports that at Kiukiang she "had the pleasure of seeing in the American Methodist Episcopal School forty bright, healthy-looking girls with unbound feet." There are also fully as many Chinese women in that city who have released themselves from the bonds.[2] At Hankow, still further up the Yang-tse, we read of meetings in the interests of this reform.[3] The Rev. William Deans, of the Church of Scotland Mission at Ichang, writes that " Christian missions help in the suppression of foot-binding, as church-members generally do not bind the feet of their girls." At Chungking, the residence of Mrs. Archibald Little, a vigorous society has been formed, called the " Natural-Foot League," a union organization supported by the four Protestant missions in that place. At a meeting held in 1896, sixty Chinese men were present, and all but six indicated that they were opposed to foot-binding. A still later report states that there were five successful anti-foot-binding meetings among the Chinese in Chungking during the winter of 1896–97. A society composed of Chinese men is one of the latest developments. One of the gatherings was marked by a unique feature in the form of a prize shoe competition. " Competitors had been invited to send in shoes of original design for unbound feet, not less than five Chinese inches in length. Thirty pairs were sent. Prizes were given for the three pairs which secured most votes from the visitors." [4] A presentable and attractive shoe seems to be one of the essentials of a successful reform movement. If the Chinese women could see something pretty to step into with their unbound feet, many of the imaginary

1 *The Chinese Recorder*, May, 1895, pp. 244, 245; *The Messenger* (Shanghai), February, 1896, p. 27.

2 *The Chinese Recorder*, July, 1897, p. 321.

3 *Ibid.*, July, 1895, p. 347.

4 *Woman's Work in the Far East*, November, 1897, p. 142; *The Chronicle*, March, 1898, p. 63.

hardships of the change would vanish. We pass over another long stretch of the Yang-tse, and come to Suichaufu (Suifu), where the good cause seems to have excited unusual interest. At Chentu, a point still further into the interior of far western Szechuan, we reach apparently the outposts of the anti-foot-binding movement. A society has been formed, and the question of reform taken up under promising auspices by the missionaries of all three societies working in that city.[1]

These scattered fragments of information which the author has been able to cull from current missionary literature, although no doubt they present in an inadequate way the real vitality and growing momentum of the movement, yet serve clearly to indicate that there is a determined, though quiet, crusade now organized, which is destined to achieve the overthrow of an ancient and monstrous wrong. A correspondent of *The Spectator*, writing from Shanghai, under date of December 20, 1897, gives a striking account of the unexpected favor with which the anti-foot-binding movement has been received in the higher circles of Chinese society, and records a manifest inclination among the women of superior rank to take an active part in urging the reform. They have even gone so far as to project a school intended for girls of the upper classes of society, which contains in its prospectus the following astonishing and revolutionary sentiment: " Foot-binding is a wicked custom; so, after having been admitted into the school, the girls shall advise each other to unbind their feet. For the present both those with feet bound and unbound shall be similarly admitted, but after the lapse of a few years girls with bound feet shall not be admitted." The writer of the communication states that special invitations were extended, by the Chinese committee having this plan in charge, to all the officers and patronesses of the Tien Tsu Hui, or " Natural-Foot Society," which had been organized in Shanghai. Moreover, a union meeting had been held between Chinese and foreign communities for the suppression of foot-binding. A Chinese society had just been established, composed of men of high standing and great influence, and it was " their intention to ask the Superintendents of Northern and Southern Trade to petition the Emperor that children born after the twenty-third year of Kuang Hsü [i.e., 1897] should not be recognized as of standing unless they had natural feet." Petitions, it is stated, have been presented to the viceroys of several provinces, praying for

The coming fate of the " Golden Lilies."

1 *Woman's Work in the Far East,* November, 1895, p. 118; May, 1898, pp. 17-20.

Mrs. C. A. Killie, and some of her pupils, Ichowfu, China.
(P. B. F. M. N.)

CHINESE GIRLHOOD WITH SMILING FACES AND UNBOUND FEET.

the enforcement of the ancient law against foot-binding.[1] A petition from the *literati* to the officials at Foochow is reported, urging that the practice be prohibited.[2] Several of these accomplished scholars have exercised their literary gifts by translating anti-foot-binding proclamations into rhythmical measures, and have adopted the novel expedient of employing the blind and the poor to commit them to memory and recite them throughout the city of Foochow.[3] All this clearly indicates that the hour of China's deliverance from this wretched custom is surely coming.

In initiating this valuable reform all attempts at compulsion have been avoided. Quiet appeals to conscience and common sense, a vigorous effort to dissipate prejudice and mould public opinion, and a resolute stand on the part of many missionary schools not to have Christian education identified with this unchristian usage,

A quiet appeal to the piety and common sense of Chinese Christians.

are the main elements of urgency in the campaign. In seeking to influence Chinese converts much stress is laid upon the Scriptural doctrine of the sacredness of the body, and the obligation to honor the will of God, while practical and humane considerations are not ignored. In a few instances a pledge not to participate in foot-binding has been made a condition of church-membership, but this is far from general, and is not in accordance with the views of probably the majority of missionaries in China, however earnestly they may be disposed to advise in the matter. The appeal for reform is addressed not to women and to mothers of girls only, but to mothers of boys, and to young men themselves, urging them to relax their insistence upon bound feet as a condition of marriage. Hymns have been composed, full of anti-foot-binding sentiment, which are sung with fervor in schools and Christian assemblies. Poems of a more classic poetic flavor are addressed to the *literati*. Prize essays treating of the subject are printed and distributed; notices and memorials are posted in public places; more formal petitions to those in authority are presented; resolutions are passed by mission meetings and conferences; [4]

---

[1] *The Spectator*, March 19, 1898, p. 406; *The Missionary Review of the World*, January, 1898, pp. 52–55; *The Outlook*, April 23, 1898, p. 1021; *The Independent*, March 17, 1898, p. 16.

[2] *The Missionary Herald*, December, 1897, p. 514.

[3] *The Church Missionary Intelligencer*, April, 1898, p. 300.

[4] The Southern Presbyterian Mission of the United States, at its annual meeting held in Shanghai, September, 1895, after full discussion, reaffirmed its former attitude of opposition to foot-binding. *The Messenger* (Shanghai), October, 1895, p. 158.

The Annual Meeting of the Central China Mission of the American Methodist

and direct appeals to God in prayer are made by hundreds of devoted missionaries and Chinese Christians, imploring Him to hasten the overthrow of this evil. Then, again, there is the quiet but no doubt effective influence of a well-shaped shoe constantly worn in the presence of Chinese women, as an object-lesson of comeliness and good taste. "I think we should dress our feet neatly," writes a missionary lady, "lest the natives should say that they are untidy as well as large." In the same line of appeal to motives the power of which cannot be questioned is the effort to provide a type of Chinese shoe which will secure a minimum of offense to the sensibilities with a maximum of room to the extremities. The prize competition for a pleasing model shoe, before referred to, is thus explained.[1]

Special use is made of the powerful agency of literature, and the coöperation of the native press in some instances has been secured. Illustrated booklets and tracts also have been issued.[2] A poem has been written by Mrs. Chen, of Hangchow, and translated by Dr. Edkins.[3] A still more remarkable contribution is an appeal against foot-binding, written in Wenli, the classic language of Chinese students, by Mr. Chow, of Suichaufu (Suifu), who is himself a member of the *literati*, and whose strenuous indictment of the custom is regarded, considering its author, and the fact that it is based upon Confucian and Chinese ethics, as a very remarkable and influential document.[4]

Some help from unexpected sources.

Episcopal Church, held at Kiukiang, October, 1894, convened in mass-meeting for the discussion of the question. The outcome was an anti-foot-binding movement inaugurated in a hopeful and enthusiastic spirit. *The Chinese Recorder*, May, 1895, p. 244.

The Hinghua Conference of the same Church gave expression to no uncertain sentiment concerning what it called "an accursed custom." *The Chinese Recorder*, July, 1897, p. 343.

At the Woman's Conference of the Methodist Episcopal Mission, held at Peking, papers were read deprecating the evils resulting from this practice. *Woman's Work in the Far East*, May, 1897, p. 82.

The Annual Methodist Episcopal Conference in North China, which assembled September 15, 1897, at Peking, took action that "all preachers should keep their families free from the practice, and that they should exhort all church-members to abandon it in their households."—An article on "Our Work in North China," by the Rev. S. L. Baldwin, D.D., in *The Christian Advocate* (New York), December 2, 1897.

[1] *The Chinese Recorder*, July, 1897, pp. 321, 322.

[2] One by Pastor Kranz, and another by Mr. Sez, the native pastor of a church at Shanghai, are well known.

[3] It is published in *Woman's Work in the Far East*, August, 1894, p. 30.

[4] *The Chinese Recorder*, December, 1896, p. 584; July, 1897, p. 323.

It is being distributed by tens of thousands in Western China. Other prominent men have added supplementary and confirmatory statements, so that in its present form it is somewhat of a consensus, with the imprimatur of the *literati*.[1]

An interesting compilation might be made of the views of Chinese advocates of the reform. At a conference of native preachers connected with the Wesleyan Mission, held at Wusueh, Hupeh Province, the practice was strongly condemned. One of the preachers "deeply regretted that the light of the Gospel had come to him too late to save his daughters from the pain they had suffered."[2] The address of Mrs. Shie, at Kiukiang, has been already mentioned (p. 360). A Chinese woman was a successful competitor for the prize essay at Shanghai, in 1896. Her treatment of the theme was thorough and spirited.[3] Among the papers presented at the Woman's Conference of the Methodist Episcopal Mission at Peking was one by Mrs. Wang, who apparently discussed the subject with a spice of Chinese humor.[4] Dr. Kin, a medical officer of the Military College of Tientsin, has delivered a lecture on the folly and wickedness of footbinding, which he characterizes as "horrid and most barbarous." An abstract of his lecture may be found in the *Woman's Missionary Friend*,

> Native Christians awakening to their duty.

---

1 The correspondent of *The Spectator*, previously mentioned, has the following paragraph in his letter: "Chinese *literati* are writing tracts against foot-binding; Chang Chih Tung, the one incorruptible viceroy of China, and the most respected, is circulating a tract with a preface by himself; whilst Kung Hui Chung, one of the lineal descendants of Confucius, writes: 'I have always had my unquiet thoughts about foot-binding, and felt pity for the many sufferers. Yet I could not venture to say it publicly. Now there are happily certain benevolent gentlemen and virtuous daughters of ability, wise daughters from foreign lands, who have initiated a truly noble enterprise. They have addressed our women in animated exhortations, and founded a society for the prohibition of foot-binding.' And this descendant of the great sage, hereditary guardian of the ancient ways, does not denounce the foreign ladies, but is collecting their tracts and himself circulating what he thinks the best bits put together out of them."—*The Spectator*, March 19, 1898, pp. 406, 407.

2 The following resolution was unanimously adopted by the Conference: "The preachers desire to say that they hold the practice of foot-binding to be a very hardhearted and hurtful one, an offense against the handiwork of God, and therefore a sin, an injury to a parent's love, a worldly custom, and opposed to reason. They request the members to pray for the guidance of the Holy Spirit in this matter, and to act in accordance with that guidance: so that if He make it clear to them that binding is lawful, to continue binding; but if He show them that it is wrong, to abolish it."—*The Illustrated Missionary News*, October, 1894, p. 153.

3 *The Chronicle*, September, 1896, p. 211.

4 "Mrs. Wang, who, three years ago, decided to consecrate her feet to the

October, 1897, p. 113. He there announces his purpose to found a school for Chinese non-Christians where no children with bound feet will be received.[1]

Surely the power of missions to work a social revolution by their unique and persuasive methods, and to discredit an evil custom, however strongly entrenched, has here a brilliant illustra-

The approaching downfall of an evil custom.

tion. It cannot be said that foot-binding is to any noticeable extent abolished in that vast empire, yet it is manifestly true that nothing has ever so disturbed its sway over Chinese society as this quiet missionary crusade. In time, perhaps much sooner than we expect, it will be entirely banished and despised as a relic of ignorance and barbarism. When that day comes there can be no uncertainty as to who began the assault, and to whom the chief honor of the victory belongs.

7. PROMOTING PRISON REFORMS, AND MITIGATING BRUTAL PUNISHMENTS.—A humane code of penal administration, and the punishment of criminals by methods which will encourage reformation, are now among the recognized insignia of civilization. Christian humanitarianism deserves the credit of having introduced these amendments into the modern code of penology.[2] We are especially indebted to the efforts of John Howard[3] and Elizabeth Fry[4] for early and memorable services in behalf of prisoners. The reform has come at a comparatively late period in the world's history, and has progressed slowly. The Bastille, and other overcrowded prisons, were found in France as late as the eighteenth century, while *lettres de cachet* were still in use, and even at the close of that century the dungeon, the torture chamber, and the *oubliette* were not wholly abolished.[5]

While Christianity devotes most of its energies to the creation and nourishment of a social morality in harmony with Scripture standards

Lord, and who, at our last Conference, said regretfully that her little toes still belonged to the devil, as she could not straighten them out, spoke of the suffering endured by little girls during the first stages of foot-binding."— *Woman's Work in the Far East*, May, 1897, p. 82.

1 *Woman's Missionary Friend*, August, 1897, p. 42. Cf. also for another expression of native opinion, *ibid.*, October, 1896, p. 99, and *Woman's Work in the Far East*, August, 1894, pp. 35-37.

2 Brace, "Gesta Christi," p. 400.

3 Born near London, 1726; died of the plague at Kherson, Russia, 1790.

4 Born near Norwich, England, 1780; died in 1845.

5 Wines, "Punishment and Reformation." Cf. chaps. iv. and v. for a succinct account of the cruel devices of barbaric penology which were formerly in vogue.

as the best safeguard of human welfare, yet it does not neglect the task of rescuing degenerates. It is of its very essence that it cannot give up any section of society as hopelessly lost, or be complacently content with even a certain percentage of social waste. On the contrary, it is "not *willing* that any should perish." It must therefore have its ministry of instruction and hope even to prisoners. Prison Reform Associations, however, all date from the present century. European Prison Congresses were held on the Continent as early as 1846, but the present organization, with its broader international basis, assembled for the first time in London, as late as 1872. The American National Prison Association was organized in 1870, but local State associations were of earlier date.[1] Great reforms have been instituted, yet in certain aspects there is still in many places a call for better things.[2] The true spirit of a prison system, and the prime essential to its highest success, were clearly announced by General Brinkerhoff, the President of the National Prison Association of the United States, in his Annual Address for 1897.[3] In striking contrast with this noble sentiment is the fact that at present all religious influence or instruction seems to be ruled out in French reformatory methods, if a recent incident truly represents the status.[4]

The reformed penology Christian in its origin.

[1] Cf. articles by the Rev. George S. Mott, on "Christo-Penology," in *The New York Observer*, October 15 and 22, 1896.

[2] *The Outlook*, March 13, 1897, p. 726; December 18, 1897, p. 937.

[3] After emphasizing the importance of moral and religious education in our public schools as a preventive of crime, he continued as follows: "In this last message I want to put it on record, with all the emphasis I can command, that if we are to make any large progress in the reformation of prisons, or in the prevention of crime, or in the betterment of mankind, we must utilize more fully than we have heretofore the religious element which is inherent in the universal heart of man. . . . If this be true, then it follows, as the night the day, that every prison officer, every teacher in our schools, and especially every editor of a newspaper, ought to be profoundly religious; for it is only by the education of our people in the eternal verities of God and the future that society at its best can be developed and saved, and the divine right of all men to ' life, liberty, and the pursuit of happiness ' can be fully secured."—*The Outlook*, December 4, 1897, p. 792.

[4] At the meeting of the Prison Congress in Paris, in 1895, many of the delegates were invited by the French Government to visit a newly erected reformatory school at Montesson, capable of accommodating some four hundred boys. Mr. Wraskoy, chief of the Russian prison administration, after surveying the buildings, asked, " And where is your church or chapel? " The reply was: " We do not need one." Further inquiries revealed the fact that French reformatory institutions were inclined to ignore religious instruction in the training they imparted. *The Missions of the World*, August, 1895, p. 302.

Punitive methods among barbarous and semi-civilized nations are still marked by many shocking features.[1] In some sections of the world Christian missionaries have been able to do A remarkable response to humanitarian principles in Japan. little to change immemorial usages, but here and there they have succeeded in greatly modifying or abolishing existing evils. Our survey may well begin with Japan, where there has been a remarkable response to humanitarian principles in the matter of prison reformation. Recent statistics report 120 prisons in the empire, with 80,000 inmates, a proportion of 2 in every 1000 of the population. All attempts at improvement in prison administration date within thirty years. In 1869 an office was created in Japan for the supervision and direction of the prison system,[2] and in the following year a reform code was instituted, which was, however, quite too general and indefinite in its provisions to be of any great practical service, although its spirit and purpose were excellent. Shortly after this date, in 1873, John C. Berry, M.D., a missionary of the American Board, had his attention called to the sanitary condition of the Hyogo Prison, situated in the suburbs of Kobe. Its state was at that time found to be so unsatisfactory that Dr. Berry obtained permission from the authorities to inaugurate some reforms. He subsequently secured a permit from the Japanese Minister for Home Affairs to inspect other prisons in various places. This compliance on the part of the Minister was accompanied by a request that a report should be made directly to him. Dr. Berry's response was published and widely circulated, and resulted in the preparation of a circular on the subject of an improved penal system. This document, largely a rescript of Dr. Berry's elaborate statement, may be regarded as the initial step in the inauguration by the Japanese Government of its

---

1 Cf. Henderson, " An Introduction to the Study of the Dependent, Defective, and Delinquent Classes," chap. xxv., for an historical review of the social treatment of criminals.

2 The author is indebted for this information, and other data of value, to an article by the Rev. Kosuke Tomeoka, on " The Prison System of Japan, Past and Present," published in *The Far East*, August, 1897. Mr. Tomeoka is a graduate of the Doshisha College, and has become greatly interested in prison reform. The perusal of the volume by Dr. Wines on " Punishment and Reformation," now translated into Japanese, had an influence in quickening his desire to devote himself specially to this philanthropic service. He visited America in 1895, and spent a year in the study of penology and practical prison administration. The author had the pleasure of meeting him during this visit, and was much impressed with his sincerity and singleness of purpose. Since his return to Japan he has given his attention to the subject with renewed enthusiasm, and is now, in spite of the opposition of the Buddhists, serving as government chaplain for Sugamo Prison, Tokyo.

present enlightened policy in prison administration.[1] Further efforts were characterized by important and definite advances, and repeated revisions of prison regulations, with the appointment of responsible officials to carry them out. A Government Training-School for Jailers was founded in 1890.

In 1891 a movement was begun in the Hokkaido, the most northerly of the principal islands of Japan, which, with five large prisons, had become a sort of Botany Bay. The chief administrator of these prisons, appointed in that year, was Mr. Oinue, whose conception of his duty seems to have been characterized by intelligent discernment and much practical wisdom. His view of the moral, intellectual, and physical needs of his wards led him to institute a system of instruction and religious ministry which produced the happiest results. The care of the prisoners was handed over to Christian chaplains ; Sabbath-schools and Bible classes were established, at which the attendance was entirely voluntary ; lectures and other profitable entertainments were provided ; good literature was put into circulation ; magazines dealing especially with the subject of prison reform and helpful ministry to the criminal classes were started ; and the whole movement was along the advanced lines of humanitarian penology. An exceedingly interesting account of this effort, under the title of "Applied Christianity in the Hokkaido," has been given by the Rev. William W. Curtis, a missionary of the American Board, then located at Sendai, but now at Sapporo.[2] In his missionary tours Mr. Curtis has visited all the prisons of the Hokkaido, and inspected them thoroughly, receiving special courtesies from Superintendent Oinue. His estimate of the whole system is high, and the results of the ministry of Christian chaplains have commanded the respect of the Japanese officials. While Gospel instruction is not made in any sense compulsory, and in fact goes on side by side with moral lectures based upon Confucian and Buddhist classics, yet its influence has been great, and the

Prison reforms in the Hokkaido.

[1] The reforms suggested in this circular cover the following points: " 1. The sanitary condition of the prisons. 2. The training of prison officers. 3. The classification of criminals according to their age and the nature of their crime. 4. Prisoners shall be duly paid, provided the wages be laid aside for their benefit on their release from confinement. 5. Criminals shall be taught better, rather than subjected to cruel punishment. 6. Religious instruction shall be given to prisoners. 7. Prison architecture shall be improved."— *The Far East*, August, 1897, p. 335.

[2] *The Missionary Herald*, January and February, 1894. The article has also been published as a leaflet by the American Board, and in *The Japan Evangelist* for April and June, 1894. Cf. also *The Missionary Herald*, November, 1894, p. 486.

fact of its acceptability is encouraging. In one of the prisons Mr. Curtis found 510 prisoners studying the Bible, and 148 of them were following a course of daily Bible readings published in a Japanese Christian periodical. A magazine called *The Sympathy* was issued by these faithful instructors, and had a large circulation among the inmates of the prisons. A *Journal of Prison Reform* was also established for the advocacy of an enlightened policy in the management of prisons.

A Japanese Christian has the honor of being a pioneer in this philanthropic ministration to prisoners. Mr. T. Hara, one of the earliest converts, was baptized in 1874, and, after a remarkable experience of providential prepara-

A Japanese friend of prisoners.

tion for this service, has become a devoted and energetic worker on behalf of this hitherto neglected class. His first position as moral instructor was in the " Receiving Prison," located at Hyogo, a suburb of Kobe, for the temporary detention of prisoners before they are sent to their permanent place of incarceration. Subsequently he went to the newly established prison in Kushiro Province, Hokkaido, where all the inmates are sent for a period of not less than twelve years. There he was appointed a prison chaplain by Mr. Oinue, and was joined later by Mr. Tomeoka, who afterwards served in the same capacity in the Sorachi Prison. Others were assigned to similar positions—Mr. Otsuka to Kushiro, Mr. Makino to Tokachi, and Mr. Yamamoto to Abashiri. All of these young men are graduates of the Doshisha. Thus five large prisons of the Hokkaido became places of Christian instruction in charge of Japanese chaplains.[1] These devoted officials were accustomed to take an interest in

---

1 Mr. Curtis calls attention to some interesting statistics, which we quote from " A Chapter of Mission History in Modern Japan," by the Rev. James H. Pettee. They are found in an article by Chaplain Hara in *The Journal of Prison Reform*, and were compiled from data gathered by a canvass of the convicts at Kabato. They yield the following results: " The 1449 inmates are classified from an educational standpoint as follows: number of educated, 66; of somewhat educated, 319; of illiterate, 1064, showing that the criminal classes are very largely illiterate. These three classes are considered from a religious standpoint with the following result (the term 'religious' of course includes the various beliefs of the land): Of the 66 educated men, 34 are religious, 25 somewhat so, and but 7 wholly irreligious. Of the 319 somewhat educated, 80 are religious, 142 somewhat so, and 97 wholly irreligious. Of the 1064 illiterate ones, only 33 can be included in the religious column, 233 are somewhat inclined to religion, while 798 are wholly irreligious. The illiterates are further separated into those who can and those who cannot read the alphabet (*kana*). Of those who cannot read it, only 1 can be called religious, 58 are somewhat religious, while 422 are wholly irreligious. The table thus brings into vivid light the value of education as preventive of crime, and the far greater value of reli-

the welfare of their prisoners after they were discharged, and to follow them with their sympathy, counsels, and prayers. Mr. Hara sent out upon a recent New Year's day 156 postal cards to discharged prisoners, with a view to maintaining a Christian watchfulness over them. The replies numbered 142, and their purport clearly indicated that the spiritual ministrations of the prison were not lost.

The good work above referred to has received, let us hope, only a temporary check through the resignation of Mr. Oinue, owing to dissatisfaction in high quarters with his methods, and the crowding out of the Christian chaplains by Buddhist interference. The present superintendent in the Hokkaido, Mr. Hata, is, however, kindly disposed towards Christianity, and extended every courtesy to the Rev. G. M. Rowland, of Sapporo, upon a recent evangelistic visit to one of the prisons. It may safely be said that the striking results of introducing evangelical instruction in the Hokkaido prisons vindicated its value in the eyes of all unprejudiced observers in Japan. The watchword of prison reform under Christian auspices has been sounded. Mr. Hara and his associates are alert and active in their efforts to carry on their work elsewhere, and they have not lost sight of the prisoners who were formerly under their personal influence. A periodical has been established by Mr. Hara, which is freely distributed among them. His tabulated statistics in regard to these discharged prisoners state that, of the first one hundred names entered, ninety-six are in regular employment, and most of them are giving promise of becoming good citizens.[1] We find in the *Asylum Record* of February, 1897, published at the Okayama Orphanage, an account of the way in which Mr. Hara met two hundred and fifty Hokkaido convicts who were brought to Sugamo Prison to be liberated. He stood at the prison door with more than a hundred jinrikishas, into which he placed these released men, and conveyed them to his Home for Discharged Prisoners, where they passed their first night of freedom. The next morning he preached to them an earnest sermon, full of love and good advice, and the result was that fifty-six of them decided to remain in Tokyo and earn their livelihood under his instruction and protection. The remainder departed to their homes with hearts full of kindly feeling towards their Christian benefactor.[2]

An enlightened prison system an established fact in Japan.

gious education. It may perchance have a significance as bearing on the question whether missionary work should include educational as well as evangelistic methods."

[1] *The Missionary Herald*, June, 1896, pp. 235–237; May, 1898, p. 191.

[2] *Asylum Record* (Okayama), February, 1897, p. 7.

Mr. Hara's efforts are attracting the attention of benevolent Japanese and foreign residents, and we trust that all the aid he requires may be provided. The statement issued by him in 1897 reports sixty-two discharged prisoners as inmates of his Home in Tokyo. In addition he has charge of 109 others, who find employment elsewhere, while friends are looking after 136 more.[1] It is not too optimistic to say that a kindly ministry to prisoners is now an established feature in Japanese Christian circles. Devoted men will be raised up to engage in the service, and Japanese Christianity may be trusted to appreciate its opportunity and discharge its obligation. Mr. Curtis remarks that Mr. Hara, as truly as Neesima, or Sawayama, or Ishii, has found his special mission.

Other efforts on behalf of prisoners may be chronicled in connection with the Okayama Orphanage of Mr. Ishii, where an annex for ex-convicts has been established. A group of these men in his Home for Discharged Prisoners is presented in the illustration facing this page.

The Home for Discharged Prisoners at Okayama.

The unique methods adopted in the Hokkaido have not extended throughout Japan, but here and there are indications that Christian ministry in the prisons is not going to be placed under a ban. At Sumoto Prison opportunity has been given for Christian instruction to the inmates.[2] At Morioka the Rev. E. Rothesay Miller has at times conducted religious services in the prison. The Salvation Army has established a Prison-Gate Home at Tokyo, where industrial education serves as an aid in the reformation of ex-convicts. The Rev. T. Ito has opened a Home for Discharged Prisoners at Yokohama, where spiritual instruction is combined with industrial training. Before its inmates start out for their work in the morning a Christian service is held. Mr. Miyoshi, formerly President of the Supreme Court of Japan, has interested himself in the founding of a Christian reformatory for children in Tokyo.[3]

Two things are apparent from this survey: first, Christian missions have been influential in hastening the introduction of an improved prison system; second, Christian Japanese have been alert in seeking the welfare of prisoners, and befriending them when they are discharged. Japanese prisons are as yet in many respects seriously defective, so much so that British residents are protesting vigorously against

[1] *The Japan Evangelist*, June, 1897, p. 291. For a biographical sketch of Mr. Hara, see *The Christian*, June 16, 1898.

[2] *The Japan Evangelist*, February, 1896, p. 195.

[3] *Ibid.*, December, 1896, p. 95; January, 1897, p. 102.

Inmates of the Okayama Home for Discharged Prisoners, in connection with the Okayama Orphan Asylum.

WORK AMONG DISCHARGED PRISONERS IN JAPAN.

the possibility of their being liable to incarceration therein after the new international treaty goes into effect in 1899.[1] No Oriental nation, however, can compare with Japan in the excellence of its penal administration.[2]

Judicial and punitive methods in Korea were until very recently scandalous and cruel to an extent hardly credible. A change seems to have been brought about, partly through the influence of the Japanese, who have had much to do with Less cruelty to prisoners in Korea. shaping the course of events during the transitional period which has followed the war between Japan and China. Mrs. Bishop sufficiently intimates from her own personal knowledge the summary methods formerly in use in the name of justice and for purposes of punishment.[3] The new clemency lately shown in the trial and treatment of criminals, without the torture, intimidation, and coercion hitherto practised, is referred to in recent numbers of *The Korean Repository* as a subject of congratulation.[4] There is perhaps little in this change which can be credited directly to missionary influence, yet it is indirectly traceable to the enlightenment which missions have introduced. In a report of the Pyeng Yang station presented in 1897 by the Rev. Graham Lee, of the Presbyterian Mission, he states that at Christmas the Christians of that place took up a contribution for the benefit of prisoners sufficient to purchase a Christmas dinner and a book for each inmate of the two jails. He speaks of the incident as exciting a feeling of wonder throughout the town, resulting in the general verdict that "the Christians had done a very commendable thing."[5]

The judicial cruelties and horrible punishments prevalent in China are well known. A Chinese lawyer in Hong Kong, who had been educated in England, is stated by Dr. Graves to have expressed the opinion that "China's first and China's great need of reform in her methods of punishment. greatest need is reform in her legal procedure and prison discipline."[6] So unalterable are Chinese ways that little has been accomplished in discrediting or mitigating these atrocities. Christianity is not as yet sufficiently influential in the empire to transform national customs, nor have missionary agents the

[1] *The Mail* (London), July 11, 1898.

[2] Cf. an article on "Japanese Criminal Law," by the Rev. J. H. De Forest, D.D., in *The Congregationalist*, August 18, 1898.

[3] Bishop, "Korea and Her Neighbors," pp. 264, 265, 441, 450.

[4] *The Korean Repository*, April, 1896, p. 170; November, 1896, p. 452.

[5] *Ibid.*, October, 1897, p. 366.

[6] Graves, "Forty Years in China," p. 96.

prestige to enable them to mould official opinion. Here and there efforts have been made by individual missionaries to reach prisoners with the Gospel message or through Christian literature, but that China has actually modified to any perceptible degree her barbarous penal system cannot be claimed.

In India the prevalence of English judicial processes, and the establishment of a humane prison system, are in pleasing contrast with former

An enlightened treatment of criminals in India.

punitive cruelties.[1] "The influence of Christian law," writes the Rev. S. H. Kellogg, D.D., of the Presbyterian Mission, "has modified the treatment of criminals immensely. Even in the Independent States barbarous executions, as by trampling with elephants, etc., have ended, though I am told that in the Native State of Rewa, a few years ago at least, a hand was still cut off for theft." The prison administration of the British Government renders it unnecessary for Indian missionaries to attempt other than evangelistic work among prisoners. Here and there efforts of this kind are reported, such as the Prison-Gate Home in Ceylon established by the Salvation Army.[2] In Burma special services are held in some of the jails.

If we cross to the African Continent, we find a dominant spirit of cruelty, culminating in inhuman methods of punishment as its most

The checking of punitive atrocities in Africa.

dramatic exemplification. The Rev. T. R. Buckley, of the Church Missionary Society in Uganda, in a recent report gives a few suggestive intimations of the change which has come in that country since the introduction of Christianity. He writes of having met in his tours men and women whose eyes had been plucked out and their ears cut off by order of those in authority, often in punishment for trifling offenses.[3] Who can restrain expressions of thankfulness, while reading of these mutilations, that the authority of British law and the guidance of Christian truth are now firmly established in Uganda? Unhappily, it cannot be claimed that European administration in all sections of Africa has been free from injustice. In some instances there is reason to fear that there has been inhumanity, as recent events in the Congo State indicate. The action of the King of Belgium, in 1896, in establishing a Commission for the protection of Congo natives from the cruelties of traders and irresponsible State officials, shows plainly that some intervention of the kind was demanded. This Commission,

---

1 Dubois, " Hindu Manners, Customs, and Ceremonies," p. 673.
2 The Army reports in all eleven such institutions in foreign lands.
3 " Report of Church Missionary Society, 1897," p. 127.

so far as nominated by King Leopold, was composed exclusively of missionaries, and it is to be hoped that the authority vested in its members will enable them to exercise an effective guardianship over the Congo people.[1] A communication from Dr. Sims, of Leopoldville, a member of the Commission, reports: "The State is doing better towards us and the natives, and officers and traders are being constantly punished. This is cheering intelligence to those who have been acquainted with the unbridled license formerly shown by the lower officials of the Congo State towards the natives and the missionaries who sought to befriend them. A new era of safety and freedom from oppression seems to have begun for the native Congo people." [2] The Rev. George Grenfell, of the English Baptist Mission, who is Secretary of the Commission, gives an account, in a recent letter, of his successful efforts to rescue from a cruel death three victims who had been condemned on the charge of witchcraft.[3]

The horrors of the West Coast, and the shambles of Kumassi, are happily under the ban of civilized authority. It is an undeniable fact that missionaries have had much to do with the banishment of penal cruelties in Africa. In Mada- **Work among prisoners in Madagascar.** gascar work among prisoners is a recognized branch of missionary service. At Fianarantsoa the agents of the London Missionary Society have a Gospel service in the prison every Sunday morning, besides visitations during the week.[4] The Rev. James Sibree (L. M. S.), of Antananarivo, writes to the author: "Formerly soldiers were burned alive for desertion, and theft in markets was punished by immediate stoning to death; but both have long been forbidden by law. The old custom of inflicting the death penalty for numerous offences, accompanied by the reducing of wife and children to slavery, is now obsolete and replaced by mild and merciful punishments." In Morocco, under Mohammedan rule, fiendish outrages upon prisoners are reported from time to time.[5] Little can be accomplished where the authority of Islam is supreme, to alle--

---

[1] The text of the decree issued by King Leopold constituting a Commission for the protection of natives in the Congo State is printed in *The Baptist Missionary Magazine*, June, 1897, p. 200. Cf. *The Independent*, October 8, 1896.

[2] *The Baptist Missionary Magazine*, October, 1897, p. 543.

[3] *The Missionary Herald of the Baptist Missionary Society* (London), February, 1897, p. 74.

[4] *The Chronicle*, May, 1894, p. 122.

[5] *The Anti-Slavery Reporter*, January–February, 1898, pp. 58–60. See also a letter from the Howard Association to the British Foreign Office on the treatment of prisoners in Morocco, published in *The Mail* (London), August 5, 1898.

viate these horrors.   The stories which Turkish prisons could tell of what has happened within their doors, even during the past decade, would make the world shudder.

The thoughtful reader will understand why prison reform must necessarily occupy a secondary place among the activities of missions. It is, for several reasons, a side issue, but enough has been said to show that the spirit of compassion is inherent in Christianity, and that the tendency of missionary influence is to plant in society a public sentiment which will be strongly opposed to the inhuman treatment of criminals.   Cruelty is inevitably ostracized from a Christian community, and humanitarian principles are sure finally to gain the ascendancy.

8. SECURING HUMANE MINISTRATIONS TO THE POOR AND DEPENDENT.—In his "Christian Charity in the Ancient Church," Dr. Uhlhorn

Christianity quickens a compassionate spirit towards the poor and dependent.

has an interesting sketch of the growth of a benevolent spirit towards the poor and dependent in early Christian history.[1]   The same story of softened hearts and compassionate ministrations can be traced to-day wherever Christianity has been planted throughout the modern heathen world.   "The Christian religion," writes Mr. Lecky, "was designed to be a religion of philanthropy, and love was represented as the distinctive test or characteristic of its true members.   As a matter of fact, it has probably done more to quicken the affections of mankind, to promote piety, to create a pure and merciful ideal, than any other influence that has ever acted upon the world."[2]

Let us begin with a nation whose reputation for callousness in the presence of suffering is notorious.   The Chinese, of all the peoples to

Teaching lessons of sympathy to Chinese hearts.

be found in the world who profess an ethical consciousness and claim to be civilized, seem to have the least natural compassion for helplessness and misery.   This statement is not intended to convey the idea that there are no instincts of kindness and compassion in any individual Chinese heart, but that a non-sympathetic attitude of stolid indifference is almost universal, so much so as to be regarded as a national characteristic.   There are here and there native asylums for lepers, for the blind, and for foundlings, but in many instances these

---

[1] Pp. 141–159.   Cf. also Schmidt, "The Social Results of Early Christianity," pp. 237–275; Storrs, "The Divine Origin of Christianity," pp. 273, 322, 495, 496.

[2] Lecky, "History of the Rise and Influence of the Spirit of Rationalism in Europe" (American ed., 1888), vol. i., pp. 329, 330.

can be traced either in their origin or their present activities to the stimulus of missions.[1] As regards the efforts on behalf of foundlings and blind girls, there is frequently grave cause for suspecting motives far from benevolent in character.[2] We have good evidence that Christian missions have inaugurated a significant change in the traditional insensibility of the Chinese towards helpless dependents. They have certainly established a new standard of consideration for the unfortunate classes. Facilities for ministering to the blind, the deaf and dumb, foundlings, the aged and feeble, the distressed poor, lunatics, and the victims of sudden calamity, are illustrations in point.

The miseries of the blind in China, where they are found in large numbers as compared with European countries, are truly pitiful, as all diseases of the eye are beyond the skill of Chinese practitioners. Uncleanly habits, total neglect, exposure to the fierce glare of the sun, and the ravages of disease are responsible for either the total blindness or defective vision of a vast throng in that empire. An estimate by Miss C. F. Gordon-Cumming, who has interested herself on behalf of this neglected class, is that there are about five hundred thousand blind persons in China, or one in every six hundred of the population, and even this proportion is thought by some to be too small.[3]

A notable work for the blind in China.

[1] " I think I am right in stating that Chinese foundling asylums unconnected with Christian missions, and the charitable distribution of medicines, clothing, etc., to the poor, owe their origin, or, at any rate, their present life and energy, to the high example and influence of Christian charity, especially in connection with our medical missions."—The Ven. Arthur E. Moule, B.D. (C. M. S.), Archdeacon of Shanghai, China.

" In the famine of 1889 it was not until the missionaries had been distributing funds, contributed by foreigners, for several months, that the Chinese Government began to extend relief in a systematic way. Benevolent institutions and the philanthropic spirit have always existed among the Chinese, but a new impetus has been given to kindly deeds by the notable charities of the missionary organizations."—Rev. Gilbert Reid, Peking, China.

" The Chinese have some benevolent instincts, but their development is limited and fitful. Christianity at once expands their narrow view of charity. It encourages the attempt to do something for particular cases. Thus far the wider problem of dealing with masses, and with tendencies by way of prevention, is quite too large for the infant church to grapple with, but the force is there."—Rev. Arthur H. Smith (A. B. C. F. M.), Pang-Chuang, China.

[2] " As a whole, the Chinese seem to think that, besides begging, the only occupation open to blind men is fortune-telling, and to blind women prostitution, and from this sad alternative they are not even protected by the native asylums."—" Records of the Shanghai Conference, 1890," p. 298.

[3] *Work and Workers in the Mission Field*, November, 1893, p. 471.

The calamity of blindness among the Chinese seems to be attended
with the most lamentable incidental results to morality.   " The morals
of the adult blind are appalling," writes a missionary, so that effort on
their behalf is not only humanitarian, but, if successful, it is crowned
with their rescue from moral ruin.

The Mission to the Blind, organized by the Rev. W. H. Murray,
of Peking, is entitled to special notice and commendation in this connection.   Mr. Murray's original purpose in China, where he went in
1871, was to enter the service of the National Bible Society of Scotland,
as a colporteur.   He took up his residence in Peking in 1873, and,
while engaged in the discharge of his duties, visited many places and
often spent days in the streets of the large cities.   He became much
interested in the blind, whom he met everywhere, and who seemed to
be not often reached by ordinary mission agencies.   In response to
a personal impulse to devote himself to their welfare, he began to
think and plan how he could benefit them, and a few years later
commenced his special mission on their behalf.   His efforts to
produce some available method for their instruction resulted in what
is practically a most useful adaptation of the existing systems to
Chinese uses.   He first reduced the number of syllabic sounds in
that language to 408, and having assigned raised symbols to these
sounds, he has been able to facilitate reading by the blind through the
sense of touch.   His system is admirably suited to the Mandarin, and
in time may possibly be adapted to other Chinese dialects, although the
use of romanized letters for this purpose is at present more current in
South China.   Some difference of opinion exists as to the comparative
availability of the two systems, but for the Mandarin dialect of North
China Mr. Murray's method seems to fulfill the conditions of success,
and his work among the blind has enlisted the hearty admiration and
support of all who are familiar with it.[1]   Mr. Murray's visits to Great
Britain have enabled him, through the assistance of friends, greatly to
increase the mechanical facilities of his plant, and to extend its philanthropic activities.   His School for the Blind in Peking has become one
of the missionary features of the place, and the generous coöperation of
a Scotch committee, largely through the instrumentality of Miss C. F.
Gordon-Cumming, gives encouragement to hope for still more extensive
effort.   He is now able to provide native teachers of his system, who
can instruct the blind in other places.[2]

[1] " Records of the Shanghai Conference, 1890," pp. 302-306; *The Chinese
Recorder*, April, 1897, pp. 185-189.

[2] Articles upon Mr. Murray's work will be found in *The Missionary Review*

There are other schools for the blind in various sections of China. That at Hankow, in the valley of the Yang-tse, which was founded in 1888 by Mr. Crossette, an American missionary, and has since been conducted by the Central China Wesleyan Methodist Lay Mission, is a most beautiful charity, combining industrial work with religious instruction.[1]   Another institution at Chinchew, known as "Light-for-the-Blind Hall," is under the charge of Miss Graham, of the English Presbyterian Mission, and also has its industrial department.   The Protestant Episcopal Mission supports an asylum for this class at Shanghai, with sixty inmates.   Miss Codrington, of the Church of England Zenana Missionary Society, has just commenced a work for the blind at Kucheng, where the new house set apart for the purpose was quickly filled with twenty-eight inmates.   At Canton Dr. Mary Niles has a school for blind girls, with twenty-seven pupils, a charity which in China is specially beneficent in its results.   At Taiwanfu (changed by the Japanese to Tainanfu), on the neighboring Island of Formosa, the English Presbyterians have a school for the blind, which, under the faithful supervision of the Rev. William Campbell, is truly a fountain of blessing to that afflicted class.   Various industries are taught to the pupils, and they are trained to be self-supporting, self-respecting Christians.   Their usefulness in life is thus assured, while some of them go forth to become organizers and teachers of similar institutions elsewhere.[2]

No reference to the benevolent work of missions for the blind would be complete without mention of the medical and surgical services of

Schools and asylums for the sightless.

---

of the World, May, 1897, pp. 349–353; *The Review of Missions,* February, 1897, pp. 465–471; *The Missionary Record of the United Presbyterian Church of Scotland,* July, 1896, pp. 215, 216.

The discussion as to the relative merits of Mr. Murray's method as compared with the romanized-letter system seems to have arisen partly as the result of some overstatements in advocating the superiority of the former system.   There are no doubt excellencies in both, and while the Murray system may be suited to the Mandarin dialect, it is still an open question as to whether it is as well adapted to the southern dialects of China, where the romanized system is in general use. Those who desire to look into the merits of the subject will find articles bearing upon the matter in *The Chinese Recorder,* July, 1895, pp. 336–338, and June, 1896, pp. 270–284.   Cf. also "The Blind in China: A Criticism of Miss Gordon-Cumming's Advocacy of the Murray Method" (London, Sampson Low, Marston & Co.).

[1] *Work and Workers in the Mission Field,* November, 1893, pp. 471–475; March, 1896, pp. 100–105.

[2] Johnston, "China and Formosa," p. 319; *The Monthly Messenger,* November, 1895, p. 255; March, 1896, p. 61.

missionary physicians.   The first operation for cataract in Manchuria
was successfully performed by Dr. Dugald Christie, of the Scotch United
Presbyterian Mission, at its hospital in Mouk-
The work of missionary   den.[1]   In all parts of China missionary surgeons
surgeons in China.   are giving sight to darkened eyes.   It is impossible to enter into detailed references to such every-
day facts of their experience.   Dr. Douthwaite, of the China Inland
Mission at Chefoo, in telling of one of these cases of restored vision,
relates that the grateful patient, upon his return home, gathered together
all the blind people he could find, and shipped about twenty of them
in a boat to Chefoo, commending them to the physician's care.[2]   Another pathetic story illustrates the profound impression made by the
surgical skill of our missionaries.   A patient was successfully treated
for cataract in the London Mission Hospital at Hankow.   On his
return home he was besieged by a group of blind men, who besought
him to lead them to the foreign doctor where they could obtain the
same healing ministry.   A strange procession of forty-eight blind men
was then formed, each one holding on to a rope in the hand of the one
before him, and marched a distance of two hundred and fifty miles to
Hankow, where nearly all were cured, and in some instances let us
hope the higher blessing of spiritual healing was given.[3]

Another excellent work is that for deaf-mutes.   The pioneer effort
in China for these unfortunates was the school of Mrs. Mills, of the
American Presbyterian Mission at Chefoo.   Mrs.
The school for deaf-   Mills was attracted by this department of philan-
mutes at Chefoo.   thropy before she went to China, and found
there a happy sphere of usefulness by establishing
a school for the deaf and dumb in connection with her missionary
service.   As yet her work is confined to boys, but she hopes in time
to open also a school for girls.   The difficulty of adjusting scientific
methods to such a language as the Chinese is truly formidable.
Mrs. Mills has put into use a phonetic alphabet, which seems to serve
admirably with her Chinese pupils.   An interesting feature of the work
is that it is supported by deaf-mutes in Christian countries.[4]   It is
impossible to estimate the percentage of this class in a land like
China.   There are a large number, and there are also many more who

---

[1] Christie, " Ten Years in Manchuria," p. 21.

[2] *Mercy and Truth*, September, 1897, p. 197.

[3] *The Messenger* (Shanghai), December, 1894, p. 182.

[4] *Woman's Work for Woman*, February, 1893, pp. 37-39; *Regions Beyond*,
May, 1895, p. 242.

are simply deaf. The late Dr. Mills "found over thirty deaf-mute boys from five to fifteen years of age" during one of his missionary tours.

The fame of Dorcas has been spread abroad through China, not only in the Scripture story, but by societies imitating her good deeds. The Chinese name of one of these benevolent circles is "Help-the-Needy Society," and it is under the charge of Mrs. Bridie, of the Wesleyan Mission, Canton. It has introduced the inevitable bazaar, and is distributing its garments quite like one of its sister organizations in Christendom.[1] Still another, known by the standard title of "Dorcas Society," is conducted at Swatow by Miss Mary K. Scott, of the American Baptist Mission. Then there are poor funds, and widows' funds, and refuges for homeless beggars, and the quiet charities of the churches, all representative of the spirit of love inspired by the Master. We are not able to find many traces of organized Christian work for the insane in China. Dr. John G. Kerr, of Canton, has for many years been desirous of establishing an asylum for this unfortunate class, and has recently been able to accomplish his wish.[2] Kindly care of the aged and dependent is often sadly lacking, but the influence of Christianity is stimulating humane interest. Dr. MacKay, of Formosa, writes that formerly the old and feeble there were neglected and despised, but that now they are cared for, at least in Christian communities.

Charitable movements in Japan, apart from Christianity, are not lacking, but their resultant until recently has been slight, and even during the modern régime the advance has been, in comparison with other progressive changes, not what one would naturally expect. There are, however, some interesting official and private charities which it is a pleasure to note. In the reconstruction of the laws incidental to the Restoration there has been introduced into the Poor Law of Japan a provision for government relief by means of a reserve fund, amounting to about two million pounds, the interest of which is to be devoted to the aid of the poor and indigent who may be the victims of famine, earthquake, fire, and other calamities. Mention should be made also of an institute for the blind and dumb at Tokyo, founded about 1875, by a philanthropic society called the *Rakuzenkwai*, organized by some prominent Japanese citizens. The Emperor became a contributor, and through his help a building was erected, which was opened for the admission of a few blind pupils in 1880. Subsequently,

Doreas societies among the Chinese.

Charitable movements among the Japanese.

---

[1] *Work and Workers in the Mission Field*, November, 1897, pp. 454-456.
[2] *The Church at Home and Abroad*, November, 1898, p. 390.

in 1885, the direct control of the school was assumed by the Department of Education, and, according to a late report, there were forty-six blind and eighty-five mute pupils in the institution. Another small school at Tokyo and also one at Kyoto have been recently opened.[1] It is perhaps too early to pass judgment on a matter of this kind, yet the apparent failure of the Japanese as a people to grasp benevolent ideals, and to organize schemes of relief and charity with the same earnestness with which they have adopted other Western ideas, is somewhat disappointing.[2] On the other hand, the rapid growth of Christian philanthropy is creditable and full of encouragement, and, what is still more remarkable, these evangelical institutions for charitable purposes command, in many instances, the support of non-Christian Japanese of the official and wealthy classes.[3]   In the terrible earthquake of 1891, and in the destruction caused by the devastating seismic wave of June 15, 1896, the native Christians, under the leadership, especially in the latter instance, of the pastors of Morioka, discovered a practical call to duty to which they responded in a spirit of generous sacrifice.[4]

In a statistical census of the Christian institutions of Japan, recently prepared by the Rev. J. H. Pettee, of Okayama, a section, containing sixty entries, is devoted to schools for the poor, one to orphan asylums, reporting nineteen entries, another to homes for various classes,

---

[1] *The Japan Evangelist,* June, 1897, pp. 266, 267; *The Baptist Missionary Magazine,* June, 1898, p. 217.

[2] The Rev. William Elliot Griffis, D.D., an acknowledged authority on Japan, has commented upon this status as follows : " Though the nation is to-day ground down under the awful load of taxes that keeps the mass of the people poor and ignorant, though, no doubt, many are made rich, one in Tokyo, Osaka, òr Kyoto looks almost in vain for great schemes of benevolence, hospitals, asylums for the insane, for the blind, and for diseased and suffering humanity.   One does indeed find a few hospitals maintained by the Government, but even these are ridiculously few compared with the number in Christian countries ; while for the special classes, for orphans, the blind, the dumb, the insane, the lying-in mothers, one is appalled to find that, outside of those under Christian or foreign auspices, and one blind and dumb school of the Government, such things hardly exist.   The finest buildings in Japan are the Government offices, the houses of the high officials, and the military barracks, but a Girard College or Cooper Institute, or those institutions which even in colonial America were hopefully common, are practically unknown in boasting Japan.   Large-minded philanthropists are as rare as white crows."—*The Missionary Review of the World,* September, 1897, p. 656.

[3] *The Missionary,* September, 1897, p. 415.   The fact is stated on the authority of the *Kirisutokyo Shimbun,* a Japanese paper.

[4] "Nineteenth Report (1896) of the Council of Missions Coöperating with the Church of Christ in Japan," pp. 52-60.

mostly dependents, giving fourteen entries, and still another to hospitals and dispensaries, represented by sixteen entries—all of these being under Protestant Christian auspices, and not including a nearly equal number under Roman Catholic supervision. This is surely a most commendable and cheering exhibition of the charitable fruitage of Christianity in Japan. A representative institution for the blind is the Draper Christian Blind School, at Yokohama, with thirty pupils. This school was founded by Mrs. Draper, widow of the Rev. G. Draper, D.D., of the Methodist Episcopal Church, who died in 1889, while on a visit to his son, a missionary in Japan.[1] Others are the blind school at Gifu (C. M. S.), with fifteen inmates, and the school for blind men at Takata, with ten students.[2] Industrial work is a feature of these institutions. The Scripture Union for Japan has now forty-five blind persons in its membership, an interesting fact when noted in connection with the recent publication of the Gospel of Luke in Japanese by the American Bible Society, and the projected issue of other books of the Bible for the use of the Japanese blind. Various aspects of benevolence are represented by relief societies, such as that of Mr. Takahashi, in Tokyo, and the work of Mr. Osuga for feeble-minded children, in conjunction with his orphanage at Oji. There is also a home for the aged and destitute at Nagoya, reporting twenty-seven inmates. These results show clearly that Christianity has not failed to quicken the grace of charity in the Japanese heart, a statement which is fully sustained by the judgment of resident missionaries.[3]

A census of Christian charities in Japan.

---

[1] *The Japan Evangelist*, August, 1896, pp. 328–330.

[2] " Annual Report of the Methodist Missionary Society of Canada, 1896–97," p. xxvii.

[3] " Orphanages, homes for ex-convicts, prison reform movements, efforts to give poor children education, and benevolence in cases of great disaster, are taking forward strides under the fostering of Christianity."—Rev. S. W. Hamblen (A. B. M. U.), Sendai, Japan.

" A society has been established in this city for relief in case of distress by earthquake, fire, or flood. The little Christian community furnishes an executive officer and about one-third of the membership."—Rev. Henry Stout, D.D. (Ref. C. A.), Nagasaki, Japan.

" A year ago last summer, and also the previous summer, this province suffered terribly from floods. The Christians organized relief work, following up their gifts of rice and money with educational and evangelistic work. This charity, together with the orphan asylum, gave them a recognized standing, and has led to a great change of feeling toward Christianity."—Rev. James H. Pettee (A. B. C. F. M.), Okayama, Japan.

" Organized charities are making wonderful progress, and the best of it all is that

In India there is much suffering among the poor and dependent.   It is pleasant to record that there are instances of large-hearted benevolence among the wealthy natives of the country, especially the Parsis.[1]   At Bombay a *dharamsala*, or charitable institution, costing eighty thousand rupees, was built many years ago by the late Sir J. Jejeebhoy, a philanthropic Parsi, who subsequently placed it under the direction of the District Benevolent Society.   One hundred and fifty of its inmates are lepers, and live in separate quarters.   There are other well-known Parsi philanthropists, among whom is Sir D. M. Petit, Bart., who for some time has been identified with benevolent work in Bombay.   Among Hindus, there are Sir M. Nathoobhoy, C.S.I., of Bombay, who has constructed a *dharamsala* at Walkeshwar; Rao Bahadur Mudaliar, of the Deccan, whose princely contributions to famine relief and to the support of famine orphans deserve grateful recognition; Iswar Chandra Vidyasagar, C.I.E., who has spent large sums for the maintenance of widows and orphans; and King Nasir-ud-Din Hyder, who established the King's Poorhouse at Lucknow.   These public benefactors are examples of many who might be mentioned with honor in this connection.

Examples of benevolence among natives of India.

The entrance of Christianity into India has stimulated and broadened the spirit of benevolence, and introduced some beautiful charities. The welfare of the blind, of whom there are possibly half a million in British India, including Burma and Ceylon, has not been neglected.[2]   In connection with the Sarah Tucker College (C. M. S.) at Palamcotta, there are classes, organized by Miss Askwith,—the first of the kind in the Madras Presidency,—for both blind boys and girls, and also for deaf-mutes.   Industrial training is part of the educational course.   The report of 1896 states, regarding the graduates of the class for the blind, that seven are already employed as teachers, having

Mission efforts for the blind in India.

in almost every case they have their source in Christianity.   This is victory."— Rev. David S. Spencer (M. E. M. S.), Nagoya, Japan.

[1] Cf. "Some Noted Indians of Modern Times," pp. 60, 68, 87, 95, 109; Bailey, "Glimpses at the Indian Mission Field," p. 104.

[2] "According to the census of 1891, out of a population of some 274,000,000 there were 458,868 blind.   Including Burma and Ceylon, there would probably be about half a million who, according to the census, are reported blind.   But this estimate, large as it is, must be far below the real number of the sightless who need to be provided for.   The census takes no note whatever of the people whose sight is so seriously defective as to render them for educational purposes practically blind, and these form a very large proportion."— *The Christian*, October 11, 1894.

A trio of rescued famine waifs.
Two of them blind.

Miss Hewlett.   Miss Sharp.

St. Catherine's Hospital, Amritsar.

A group of famine boys, St. Catherine's, Amritsar, saved through hospital treatment.
Many still delicate, some blind.

GOOD ANGELS OF CHILD LIFE IN INDIA

passed the government examinations successfully. One of them has established a school in Pannevellei, his own village, where he gives instruction to ten pupils. An "Association for Work among the Blind" has been formed, under the auspices of the Madras Missionary Conference, and chiefly through the instrumentality of the Rev. T. P. Dudley. Much painstaking work had previously been done by Mr. L. Garthwaite, formerly Government Inspector of Schools, and also by the Rev. Joshua Knowles, of Travancore.[1] Mr. Garthwaite has arranged an alphabet which can be adapted to any language of India, and has published primers of instruction. An institution for the education of the blind is about to be established at Bangalore. There is a school at Amritsar, under Miss Hewlett, in which twenty-seven blind pupils—all Christians—are under instruction. The work of a Bible-woman at the Amritsar dispensary is suggestive of the service which can be rendered to Christianity by its blind converts.[2] At Poona the Church of Scotland Mission has a special department in its orphanage for sightless girls. At Calcutta a medical mission home and orphanage for blind, crippled, and destitute children has just been established, under the direction of Mr. and Mrs. J. Norman. At Lucknow the American Methodists have a school for the blind, and the Canadian Presbyterians have a class at Ujjain. Medical missionaries are busy everywhere with their skilful ministrations to those whose vision can be restored by surgical service. In some sections of India ophthalmia is prevalent and as many as three hundred operations on the eyes within a month are reported by physicians of the Church Missionary Society in Kashmir.[3]

[1] *The Christian*, October 11, 1894; *The Harvest Field*, December, 1896, p. 471.

[2] "A peculiarly bright, happy-looking girl of about eighteen, sitting down at the beginning of the morning in one of our Amritsar dispensaries, with her large Gospel of St. Matthew, in Dr. Moon's system of raised characters for the blind, open on her knees; she can see nothing, but her fingers move swiftly across the page, and she begins to read better than some persons who have the use of their eyes! As the morning goes on, all the sick who come for medicine will listen with astonishment and pleasure, and she will have opportunities of witnessing for Jesus to those who ask her a reason for the hope that is in her. She was once herself in the darkness of Mohammedanism, and in the Blind School found Christ. She is now a rejoicing and consistent Christian. Do you think that, as we stood and watched her delight in reading the comfortable words of our Saviour Christ, we asked ourselves if to bring such to the Lord were work worth doing? Rather, is it not a service which angels might envy?"—Barnes, "Behind the Pardah," p. 126. Cf. also Hewlett, "They Shall See His Face."

[3] "Report of the Church Missionary Society, 1895," p. 183; *The Church Missionary Intelligencer*, August, 1898, pp. 611, 612.

Schools for the deaf and dumb are also to be found. A prominent one at Calcutta, founded in 1893, is under the charge of Mr. J. N. Banerji, an educated Hindu. This zealous philan-

Schools for the deaf and dumb at Calcutta and Bombay.

thropist has taken a deep interest in what is apparently his life-work. He visited England and America, spending some time at the Gallaudet College in Washington in studying the best systems of deaf-mute instruction, and has recently returned to Calcutta, prepared to conduct his work according to the most improved methods.[1] This school is not under the auspices of any missionary society, although the majority of the trustees are Christians, and some of them missionaries. It is to be hoped that Mr. Banerji's efforts may receive some financial recognition from the Indian Government. The need for institutions of this kind in India is indicated by his statement that if provision were made in that country for the deaf and dumb in proportion to the efforts put forth in America, it would imply the existence there of four hundred and fifty schools for that class, instead of the two now existing,[2] the number of deaf-mutes to be cared for being estimated at fully two hundred thousand. An institution similar to that in Calcutta exists at Bombay. That missionaries will not fail, even amid their multiplied responsibilities, to give attention to the welfare of this neglected class, is indicated by the fact that a committee has been appointed by the Calcutta Missionary Conference to take up the subject of instruction for deaf-mutes.[3] An interesting paper on this theme was presented to the Conference, in February, 1897, by the Rev. K. S. Macdonald, D.D., and tentative plans were made for inaugurating special work for these unfortunates.[4] As before mentioned, there is a class for deaf-mutes at the Sarah Tucker College in Palamcotta.

At different places in India a unique ministry has been established among the poor. A picturesque and at the same time impressive exam-

[1] *The Indian Magazine and Review*, August, 1895, pp. 436–438; February, 1896, pp. 107–109; March, 1897, p. 165; *The Independent and Nonconformist*, May 20, 1897; "Report of the Calcutta Deaf-and-Dumb School, 1894–95."

[2] *The Congregationalist*, May 14, 1896.

Mr. W. S. Monroe, of the State Normal School, Westfield, Massachusetts, in an article on "The Education of Defective Children," published in *The Congregationalist* of August 12, 1897, states that "for every 100,000 children in the public schools of America, there are 559 children in schools for the deaf, 215 in schools for the blind, 416 in institutions for mentally deficient children, and 1123 in juvenile reformatories."

[3] *The Harvest Field*, December, 1896, p. 466.

[4] *The Indian Evangelical Review*, July, 1897, pp. 56–65.

ple of this is called the "Beggars' Church," and was instituted by Dr. Colin S. Valentine at Agra. He arranged for a gathering on Sabbath mornings of the poorest of the poor within his compound for a religious service attended by a distri- The "Beggars' Church" bution of alms. This has resulted in the formation at Agra. of a church with an attendance sometimes as large as eight hundred, of whom nearly three hundred are blind. The appearance of this congregation is so pathetic that visitors have been known to shed tears on beholding it. There is reason to believe that many of those who thus assemble have become Christian disciples.[1] A similar charity, entitled the "Garden Service," is conducted by Miss Harvey, of the Zenana Bible and Medical Mission, at Nasik. Her sympathies have gone out also towards suffering animals. She has interested herself in rescuing many of them from the cruelties of the people, and has succeeded in establishing a hospital for them, under the direction of a local committee. It is supported by the united gifts of the municipality, the Government, and voluntary contributors. Through the liberality of Sir D. M. Petit, Bart., a Parsi gentleman, a permanent hospital building for this purpose is to be provided, which is to bear his name. Only those who have lived in the East can realize the need and value of an object-lesson like this of kindness to dumb animals. Among the various projects of the Salvation Army in India is a plan for the establishment of peasant settlements on waste lands, where the extremely poor may be located, with the hope that they will thus become able to support themselves. The subject of systematic provision on the part of the various missions, for the poverty-stricken, is attracting attention, and the establishment of well-ordered poorhouses has been advocated by a recent writer.[2]

In Siam, Burma, and Assam, the idea of some practical ministry to those overtaken by infirmity or calamity is beginning to be a recognized part of the Christian social code. At Rangoon the "Diamond Jubilee Friend-in-Need Society" has just been organized, and, with the Rangoon Branch of the Madras Native Christian Association, is devoted to the welfare and assistance of Indian Christians. "The Siamese," writes Miss Mary L. Cort, "are learning to help unfortunate sufferers from fire or flood, instead of calmly looking on and saying that 'they did not have merit enough to deserve a better fate.'"[3]

---

[1] *The Christian*, November 19, 1896; and March 17, 1898.

[2] The Rev. J. R. Hill, in *The Indian Church Quarterly Review*, October, 1898. Cf. *The Christian Patriot*, October 1, 1898, p. 4.

[3] "Christianity and missions have brought light and life to many poor persons

In Persia our missionary physicians have their skill taxed in dealing with the terrible diseases of the eye. Many a blind person passes from the mission hospitals into the light of

Sight for blind eyes in Persia. restored vision. Dr. Cochran, of Urumiah, relates some of his experiences in this line: " One day there came, from Van, in Turkey, a company of men, Turks, Armenians, and Nestorians, nine in all, five of them with sore eyes—ten of the worst eyes I ever saw in a single group. They had experienced all sorts of difficulties by the way, from cold at night and heat by day, from robbers, and from passport and customs officers on the frontier, and had at last reached us after ten days' journey. For two of them we could do nothing; the rest were helped more or less. One, who was wholly blind, went home with his vision partially restored by the aid of an artificial pupil, and was as happy a man as one could wish to meet. We have had several interesting cases of cataract, interesting because the patients, being blind, were so rejoiced to regain their sight. One, a little Moslem girl, perhaps fourteen years old, had been blind for a year. I removed a cataract from one eye, and by the time she had the bandages taken off and found her eyesight renewed, it was the date of their great feast. Her father, who had often visited her and reported her favorable progress to his family, asked leave to take her home, so that her mother and friends, who did not believe that her sight was recovered, could have a ' feast of thanksgiving together.' "[1]

In the Protestant churches of Asiatic Turkey careful provision is made for the poor. Benevolent societies have been formed, and, in some instances, hospitals and temporary work for sufferers from earthquakes and other disasters have been organized in evangelical communities. In times of war, famine, and distress, and especially amid the sufferings which were occasioned by the Turkish atrocities, missionaries have distinguished themselves by benevolent ministrations. Thousands

in Assam who would otherwise, in all probability, have starved. They have also brought into the country a new idea altogether, namely, that no distinction should be made on account of nationality. The help which can be given should be extended to all alike. This principle is taught to the Christians, who receive it very well on the whole, and from them it will be imparted to others. As the influence of Christianity extends, this idea will undoubtedly be adopted by boards and municipalities, so that the very poor will not be left to starve. It is an undeniable fact that almost every movement for the good of the community is started in some way by the missionaries, and the native Christians who are under their instruction."—Rev. Robert Evans (W. C. M. M. S.), Mawphlang, Shillong, Assam.

[1] Wilson, " Persia: Western Mission," pp. 267, 268.

of lives have been saved, and many hearts cheered, by the faithful and kindly relief administered by those who were made the almoners of the bounty of Christendom. Recent instances recorded are but the last of a long series of such ser- Benevolent ministry to vices, especially those rendered during and after the and Egypt. war of 1877–78. A venerable patriarch among the American missionaries, Dr. Elias Riggs, now eighty-eight years of age, has long interested himself in work for the blind. He has prepared portions of the Scriptures by the use of a few simple characters arranged to supply the needed symbols, and has published the Gospel of St. John in this form.[1] Missionary physicians at such centres as Beirut are rendering a priceless ministry to many afflicted with the grievous maladies so dangerous to the sight in Syria. In Egypt, where diseases of the eye prevail, a special benefit attaches to skilful medical and surgical services. The British Syrian Mission conducts at Beirut some schools for blind men and women, and has also another at Tyre. At Jerusalem a class of blind girls was formed in 1896, by Miss Ford, and in 1897 a home and school for this dependent class was founded, now under the charge of Miss M. J. Lovell. A British Ophthalmic Hospital, maintained by the Order of St. John of Jerusalem in England, is also ministering to the relief of multitudes who flock to it from the city and the surrounding country.

The treatment of the insane in Western Asia has long been a dreadful feature of social demoralization. To be sure, they are generally regarded as holy, and for that reason allowed to wander about at will, although they are sometimes The first asylum for the tormented by the jeers and persecutions of the insane in Syria. baser element of the population. Under Christian missions the first really organized attempt to do anything for the insane in Syria has been undertaken through the instrumentality of Mr. Theophilus Waldmeier, formerly of the Friends' Mission on Mount Lebanon. A committee, composed largely of Christian missionaries, with representatives also of the foreign and native communities of Syria, has been formed, and through the exertions of Mr. Waldmeier a substantial fund is now secured for the establishment of a home for the insane on Mount Lebanon, and a purchase of property has been consummated. The accounts given in the prospectus of this undertaking, of the shocking treatment to which the violently insane in the Levant are usually subjected, emphasize the great need of this kindly charity.[2] Thus

---

[1] *The Missionary Herald*, August, 1898, p. 297.

[2] *The Missionary Review of the World*, August, 1897, pp. 613–615; *The Outlook*,

Christian missions, even in such a comparatively civilized part of the world, are saying the first word for this neglected class.   Let us hope that this enterprise may be instrumental in quickening throughout Western Asia a new conception of the duty of society to those bereft of reason.

We cannot longer follow these attractive clues.   A single instance from the African Continent must suffice.   The good Khama has revolutionized the whole attitude of his people towards the miserable pariah tribes in their vicinity.   It is usual for the powerful native communities to look upon their pariah neighbors as wild beasts, who may either be left to perish, or hunted for sport and spoils.   Khama has taught his people a better way, and has persuaded them to help these former outcasts to a higher life and to win them by kindly treatment.[1]   A resident missionary of South Africa, the Rev. John W. Stirling, of Kaffraria, makes an interesting statement bearing upon our present theme.   He says: " Perhaps in nothing is the benefit accompanying the Gospel more noticeable than in the attention now given to the infirm and the aged.   In former days, when any one had reached the stage of not being able to help himself or others, he was

Lessons of kindness in Africa and the South Seas.

June 19, 1897, p. 467; *Medical Missions at Home and Abroad,* April, 1897, pp. 279–281; *The Literary Digest,* November 21, 1896; *The Christian,* November 5, 1896.

[1] Mr. Selous may here be quoted: " A generation ago all the Bakalahari lived the life described by Dr. Livingstone and others.   They wandered continually, under a burning sun, over the heated sands of the Kalahari, without any fixed habitation, and ever and always engaged in a terrible struggle for existence, living on berries and bulbs and roots, on snakes and toads and lizards, with an occasional glorious feast on a fat eland, giraffe, or zebra, caught in a pitfall; sucking up water through reeds, and spitting it into the ostrich-egg shells in which they were wont to carry it, and altogether leading a life of bitter, grinding hardship from the cradle to the grave.   In fact, they were utter savages, joyless, soulless animals, believing nothing, hoping nothing, but, unlike Sir Walter Scott's Bothwell, fearing much, for they were sore oppressed by their Bechuana masters, and often became the prey of the lions and hyenas that roamed the deserts as well as they.   Now many of the wild people have been induced by Khama to give up their nomadic life.   He supplied them with seed-corn, and, as may be seen at Klabala and other places, the Bakalaharis of the present day hoe up large expanses of ground, and grow so much corn that, except in seasons of drought, they know not the famine from which their forefathers were continually suffering.   In addition to this, Khama and his head men have given them cattle, sheep, and goats to tend for them, from which they obtain a constant supply of milk.   In fact, it may be said that Khama has successfully commenced the work of converting a tribe of miserable nomadic savages into a happy pastoral people."—Selous, " Travel and Adventure in South-East Africa," pp. 112, 113.

taken out of doors and left to the tender mercies of the wolves. The thought of the sacredness of human life is gradually, if slowly, percolating into the heathen mind, and has already done much towards ameliorating the lot of decrepit parents and friends."

The old ways in the South Seas may be learned from the journals of John Hunt, an early missionary to Fiji. "We have had some new instances," he writes in 1839, "of the deep depravity of the people. They are literally 'without natural affection.' It is their common practice to bury their old people alive in order to put them out of the way. The custom of burning widows in India is as nothing to this. That is done from superstition, but this from insensibility, and disregard both of God and man. The other day we heard of a woman who had been suffering from a cold and was unable to work. This was considered a sufficient reason for killing her, though she was young, and, excepting this indisposition, of a vigorous constitution. The queen, to whom she belonged, thought it was better to strangle her and throw her into the river. A Tonga man who has embraced Christianity, succeeded with the aid of a woman of the queen's household who is also a Christian, in rescuing her from this fate, and she was taken to the man's own house, where she now is. We hope she will soon recover and praise the Lord for His goodness. Another woman, of some rank, has just been strangled and buried. This seems to be the distinction between the rich and the poor: the poor are generally buried alive, and the rich are strangled. A woman who was put into the grave some time since desired to sit upright, but the wretch who was burying her did not find it convenient to himself that she should be in that position, and he therefore put his foot on the poor creature's breast, and thrust her down." [1]

The above incidents serve the double purpose of illustrating the cruelties of heathen practices, and also the new resolves of mercy and rescue which Christianity at even that early date had put into the native heart. Expand this symbolic object-lesson a thousand times, and it would not prove an exaggeration of the growth of charitable instincts and practices now observable in the native Christian communities of the Pacific.

9. ORGANIZING FAMINE RELIEF.—The entire world is rarely, if ever, free from the scourge of famine. A portion of the earth's population is always liable to be in the grasp of this giant woe. Now it

[1] *Work and Workers in the Mission Field*, February, 1896, p. 62.

is an African tribe, anon it is an Asiatic people, or the natives of some island of the sea.   The recent harrowing scenes in India have reminded us of this.   The service which Christian missions

A delightful chapter in the annals of philanthropy.

in many lands have been able to render in such times of misery and despair is a delightful chapter in the annals of philanthropy.   It has attracted comparatively little attention in the busy world, but we may believe it has been written on high in the unfading record of those things which have been done unto Christ.   Among His own memorable words is a distinct reference to compassionate ministry of this kind, when He says: "I was an hungered, and ye gave Me meat."

The section in Vol. I. (pp. 229–238) dealing with poverty and famine gives some account of the prevalence of this grievous calamity in the world.   The most helpless regions of the

The sorrows of India in 1896-97.

earth in times of great distress are those where no civilized authority exists, and where all systematic modern facilities for coping with national disaster are lacking.   The truth of this statement becomes more manifest when we reflect that the vast resources of such an experienced and highly organized government as that of British India are taxed to the utmost, and are barely able to cope efficiently with the enormous burdens of widespread famine among a dense population, which even in ordinary times is wretchedly poor.   The years 1896 and 1897 will be memorable in India for the combined miseries of famine and plague, and still more memorable for the energetic and largely successful efforts of the Government and of missionary agencies to mitigate the sufferings of the people.   The region of famine was in the central and northern provinces of the country, and a population of fully seventy-two millions was more or less affected by it.   Of this number about thirty-seven millions were in the section of veritable "famine," and the remainder in the region of "scarcity."[1]

---

[1] A valuable and authoritative survey of the progress of the British Government in its efforts to cope with Indian famine, and the immense advances in the effectiveness of its provisions, within the past quarter of a century, is found in an article by Sir Roper Lethbridge, K. C. I. E., entitled "India in the Sixtieth Victorian Year," published in *The Imperial and Asiatic Quarterly Review*, July, 1897.   He calls special attention to the services, at the time of the Bengal famine in 1873–74, of Dr. George Smith, then editor of *The Friend of India*, and now Secretary of the Free Church of Scotland Missions.   Dr. Smith was at that time the Calcutta correspondent of *The Times*, and his ardent advocacy of the duty of a more vigorous policy in dealing with conditions of famine had a marked influence in quickening the British conscience and in stimulating official action.   The energies of Sir Richard Temple,

A Group of Famine Victims, Jabalpur.

An Emaciated Trio.   Mother and Child.

A Famine-stricken Group at Panajar.

SNAP SHOTS AT THE FAMINE OF 1897, IN INDIA.
(W. M. S.)

A vivid conception of the beneficent work accomplished by missionaries during the recent famine may be obtained from their own descriptions in personal communications and published accounts. An article by the Rev. J. P. Haythornthwaite, of Agra, in *The Church Missionary Intelligencer*, March, 1898, is of special value. *The humane ministry of missionaries.* In many instances this service has included the rescue of the helpless and dying—those who, either through desertion or weakness, were unable to save themselves. Thousands of children were in this condition, many of whom, having lost their parents by death, would have been an easy prey to the scourge. In some places the missionaries have organized relief work resembling that instituted by the Government, in which employment of a useful kind, and frequently for the public benefit, has been given to the needy multitudes.

An example or two from hundreds which might be quoted must suffice. The Rev. J. O. Denning, of the Methodist Episcopal Mission, Narsinghpur, wrote to the author, under date of October 25, 1897: "We have been in the midst of the famine for two years. Thanks to the good Lord, it is now abating. The scenes that we have witnessed have been awful. I have seen no picture that equals the original. I have looked upon men, women, and children lying under trees and by the roadsides, dying of hunger. We have helped to save life and relieve pain. My wife and I have rescued nearly seven hundred children and put them into mission schools. Almost all of them were orphans, having been made so by the famine. We shall have four hundred orphan boys on our hands when this emergency is over. We shall do our best to educate them, some more, some less, according to their ability, and shall teach each one a trade, so that he can do something for himself. We shall endeavor to lead all to a personal knowledge of Christ. We teach carpentry and shoemaking, and have started orange and banana orchards, also a poultry-yard and a farm, and

Lord Northbrook, Lord Lytton, and others, established an effective scheme of government relief which has been of the highest service and proved efficiency during the tremendous strain of the recent visitation. The article is based upon personal observations of the admirable workings of the whole system, made during a recent visit to India. The author gives it as his opinion that no one need die of starvation in India who will seek government aid in time of distress and will abide by the regulations controlling its distribution.

Articles upon the recent famine will also be found in *The Indian Magazine and Review* for April and May, 1897. British government publications upon India may also be consulted. See also *Evangelical Christendom*, May, 1897, p. 146, and *The Church Missionary Intelligencer*, March, 1898, pp. 180–189.

shall soon have a vegetable garden. We hope, too, in the near future to teach printing and telegraphy. Our aim will be to make the boys useful. We now have a splendid plant for the orphanage and school, but we need money for their support until they are able to do for themselves. A boy can be fed and clothed during the whole year for fifteen dollars. I have about three hundred famine sufferers on relief work. All told, about seven hundred persons get their daily bread from funds sent me for famine relief. On the 26th of September I baptized ten of the relief workers and sixty-eight of the boys."

The Rev. Rockwell Clancy, of the same mission, writes under date of February 17, 1897, from Allahabad: "We have received in all two hundred and fifty children, and finding it impossible to keep all who came to us, we decided to establish in our compound a depot for the distribution of famine children. From this depot we have sent ten girls to a Presbyterian mission, seventeen to our orphanage at Bareilly, twenty to our school at Cawnpore, fifty-nine to the mission of the Society for the Propagation of the Gospel at Cawnpore, and thirty-five to Ajmere. Our workers in the famine-stricken villages are busy collecting orphan children. Yesterday two native workers brought in fifty-eight of them, and have returned to their villages for more. I received a letter from a friend this morning offering us a lot of boys. A few days ago more than fifty girls from Jabalpur passed through this station to our school at Aligarh; and on Tuesday thirty-eight girls were sent on to our school at Bareilly, in addition to the seventeen above named. If we had the accommodation we could take in hundreds of children." [1]

The Rev. A. Campbell, of the Santal Mission of the Free Church of Scotland, has conducted for months a system of relief employment involving several kinds of work, for both men and women, and gratuitous distribution of food to the aged and helpless and to famished infants and children, which has been a means of deliverance to a total of over five thousand souls. Aside from that, some three thousand others have received relief more or less regularly. Mr. Campbell writes: "We have been privileged during the last seven and a half months to minister, at the lowest computation, to the wants of eight thousand people, and this has been accomplished by the mission staff, slightly strengthened, along with their regular duties." [2]

1 *The Gospel in all Lands*, May, 1897, p. 244.

2 *The Free Church of Scotland Monthly*, August, 1897, p. 186, and November, 1897, p. 269.

Examples like these might be culled from the records of almost every missionary society having work in the regions affected.[1] The Pundita Ramabai's noble services in the rescue of girls and widows from the famine districts are well known.[2] Dr. Jessica Carleton, of the American Presbyterian Mission, Ambala, is reported as having two hundred needy women on her roll, mostly aged widows. The Rev. E. D. Price writes of "eleven Church Missionary Society relief centres, and, including orphans and other children, twenty-five hundred human beings on daily relief." [3] The Rev. J. E. Clough, D.D., aided by the pastors and evangelists of the American Baptist Mission among the Telugus, has had the oversight of from two to five thousand natives employed at the quarries on the Ongole hills in labor for the support of themselves and their families.[4] A special feature of these efforts has been the gathering of hundreds of orphans into mission schools and orphanages. This rescue work for children is illustrated by a photograph facing p. 249, representing a group of famine waifs under the care of Mrs. Bruere, of the American Methodist Mission at Poona. "The famine," she writes, "is too terrible to describe. It is enough for us to know that parents sell their children to secure the price of food, or push them into wells, putting them to death in order that they may not see them suffer." In January, 1897, Mrs. Bruere had one hundred and three children, both boys and girls, under her charge. The testimony of one who has studied the subject, not from the standpoint of a missionary, but rather as a student of social conditions in India, may be found in an article by Mr. Julian Hawthorne, entitled "The Real India," in *The Cosmopolitan* of September, 1897.

Spiritual harvests in times of physical famine.

Another aspect of this matter which deserves special notice is the readiness with which native Christians in parts of India not affected by the famine, and also in other mission fields, have contributed to the relief of the sufferers. "A little native Presbyterian church in Korea, of about one hundred members, forwarded sixty dollars towards the Indian famine fund." Still another Korean congregation collected fifty-six dollars, and the Presbyterian churches in Seoul gave

Liberal contributions from native Christians of other lands.

---

[1] The "Report of the Kurku and Central India Hill Mission, 1897," devoted specially to an account of famine relief, is an excellent example.

[2] *The Sentinel*, February, 1897, p. 26; March, 1897, p. 35; April, 1897, p. 45; and July, 1897, p. 87.

[3] *The Church Missionary Intelligencer*, December, 1897, p. 914.

[4] *The Baptist Missionary Magazine*, September, 1898, p. 541.

over sixty dollars to the same fund. It is a significant comment upon this fact that "not a cent was contributed to the famine fund by non-Christian Koreans." The gift of £844 from the Fiji Islands to the Mansion House Indian Famine Fund has already been mentioned (p. 42). A contribution amounting to more than one thousand rupees was sent by the native members of the English Baptist congregations of China for their suffering fellow-Christians in India. Another gift for the same purpose, amounting to forty dollars, was sent by the Christians of Kusaie, one of the Caroline Islands, and still another was forwarded, for transmission, to the British Consul at Kobe, by a little group of believers on Okinawa, one of the Loochoo Islands.[1]

We have confined our attention almost entirely to the events of 1896–97, but the services of missionaries in previous famines have been equally beneficent, energetic, and fruitful of good. The accounts of the work of Dr. Clough and many others in the famine of 1877,[2] and in those of 1873–74 and 1866, yields the same testimony of faithful and heroic labors. In the year 1837, when the present Queen of Great Britain came to the throne, a terrible famine raged in Hindustan. It was said that "British residents at Agra and Cawnpore could not take their evening drive because the corpses —too numerous for burial—lay by the roadside." In 1897, after a period of sixty years, a marked change in the method and efficiency of famine relief was observable, when between three and four millions were successfully aided by government and missionary agencies. The funds for this immense undertaking were supplied mostly by the British Government, but the gifts of missionary societies, charitable organizations, special philanthropic committees, and donations secured through the personal efforts of missionaries, have amounted to a goodly and most effective contribution.

These benevolent ministrations have effected very much more than the mitigation of physical suffering and the saving of life. The spiritual results attained in past visitations, and no doubt to be duly recorded in connection with more recent experiences, have been a vast gain to Christianity in India. After the great famine of 1876–78 Dr. Clough baptized 9606 converts within six months. It was the beginning of

(margin note: What missionaries have done in previous Indian famines.)

---

[1] *The Indian Witness*, November 5, 1897; *The Missionary Herald of the English Baptist Missionary Society*, January, 1898, p. 21; *The Missionary Herald* of the American Board, August, 1898, p. 293; *From Month to Month*, one of the serial letters of the Church Missionary Society, dated July 18, 1898, p. 3.

[2] *The Missionary Record*, April, 1895, pp. 106–109.

The group on the left represents six little orphan girls, victims of the famine, as they appeared when rescued. The group on the right represents the same girls, in the same relative position, three months after their reception by Miss Hewlett and Miss Sharp, at Amritsar, India.

The Pathos and Joy of a Rescue from Famine.

(C. E. Z. M. S.)

an advance which is now represented by 111 churches, 51,878 communicants, 647 schools, and 11,930 pupils.[1]   Out of these ministrations have sprung flourishing orphanages, asylums, homes for widows and the aged, dispensaries, hospitals, churches, and even thriving missions. Hundreds of the present preachers, evangelists, and teachers in India, when children, were the inmates of orphanages, where they were nourished, trained, and saved from destruction.[2]

Years of spiritual plenty following years of physical dearth.

In passing on to China we cannot linger to speak in any detail of the philanthropic services rendered, in 1893, by the Presbyterian missionaries in Laos.   Through the bounty of American benevolence, nearly ten thousand dollars were disbursed by them in faithful and compassionate ministries to that suffering people.   In China the work of missionaries in periods of famine is a noble and memorable record.   That vast country has been the scene of some of the most frightful calamities in modern history.   The visitation of 1877–79, which centred in and around the Province of Shansi, has been perhaps rightly designated as the greatest famine known in history.   The victims are estimated by the Rev. Timothy Richard, who himself participated in the relief distribution, as amounting to at least ten millions. Many missionaries of various denominations shared in this work.[3] Two of them who labored devotedly have recently died, the Rev. John L. Nevius, D.D., of the Presbyterian, and the Rev. David Hill, of the Wesleyan Mission.   The lives of many thousands were saved at that time.   A tablet has been erected by the natives in North China to commemorate the services of Christian missionaries in those awful days. Upon it is inscribed that in the crisis of the greatest need there occurred "a truly heavenly phenomenon, an awe-inspiring event, for certain English preachers of doctrine,—namely, David Hill, Timothy Richard, and others,—moved by the calamities of the Chinese populace, came with expression of the wealth and fine feeling of their country, and began by distributing several thousands of dollars, visiting the famine-stricken villages, making minute and personal inquiries, and presenting either one or two or three thousand cash to each person.   This they continued to do until, at the beginning of 1879, the sum total of their charity

"A truly heavenly phenomenon" commemorated in China.

[1] "Annual Report of the American Baptist Missionary Union, 1898" (see statistical tables opposite p. 212).

[2] Cf. article by the Rev. J. E. Robinson, Calcutta, entitled "How will the Famine bear on Missions?" in *Regions Beyond*, June, 1897, pp. 247–250.

[3] "Centenary Volume of the Baptist Missionary Society," pp. 121–123.

must have amounted to more than fifty thousand ounces of silver."
The inscription, it is declared, was set up to "everlastingly hand down
their names to a thousand ages." In recognition of their services, these
missionaries were subsequently offered the rank of mandarins by the
Emperor, an honor which they did not think it wise to accept.[1] The
overshadowing woe of such a sore famine seems to dwarf all other seasons of privation, but a condition of dearth is almost chronic in China,
and in some sections of the country missionaries are engaged almost
every year in efforts to relieve want. The famine of 1888–89 was also a
time of widely extended suffering, affecting five provinces.[2] The services of the late Mrs. C. W. Mateer, who at that time supervised the
distribution of aid to an enrollment of over fifty thousand persons,
were especially noteworthy.[3]

The story of relief work among the Armenians during the recent
massacres is fresh in our minds. The service was shared by various
agencies, not least among them the American missionaries scattered throughout the country, at almost
every prominent centre of population. Numerous accounts of the emergencies which arose, and
the duties they were called upon to discharge, have been published
in the secular and missionary periodicals of 1896 and 1897.[4] In previous visitations in Asia Minor and in Syria, especially during 1860, at
the time of the massacres on Mount Lebanon, when so many thousands

The record of missionary benefactions in Armenia, Persia, and Arabia.

---

[1] *The Review of Missions*, July, 1897, pp. 2, 3.

[2] " During the last thirty years, over and over again, missionaries have acted as
the distributers of money or grain contributed by foreigners, and also, to some extent, by wealthy natives, for relief purposes. Indeed, there is hardly a year in
which some work of this kind is not demanded. The most fearful famine which
even China has ever known, perhaps unparalleled in any other country or age, was
that of 1877–79, whose centre was the Province of Shansi. It is supposed that in
Chihli a quarter of the people perished, and in Shansi even a larger number. The
efforts to relieve the sufferers cost the lives of four or five missionaries, one of them
a beloved colleague of my own. Again, in 1888–89, five provinces were affected,
and very large sums raised and distributed. It is only just to add that on every
such occasion it has been found that the native merchants and gentry have been ready
to come nobly to the help of their suffering countrymen."—Rev. Jonathan Lees
(L. M. S.), Tientsin, North China.

[3] *The Chinese Recorder*, May, 1898, p. 220.

[4] *The Review of Reviews* (American edition), April, 1896, pp. 444–449; *The
Christian*, September 24, 1896; Harris, " Letters from Armenia," pp. 193–198;
Life and Light for Woman, November, 1895, p. 506, March, 1896, pp. 105–109,
October, 1897, p. 443, and December, 1897, pp. 542–544; *The Missionary Herald*,
November, 1895, p. 466, March, 1896, p. 106, April, 1896, p. 155, and March,
1897, pp. 99–102.

Indian orphans who were rescued in the famine of 1877.
(W. M. S.)

Armenian orphans rescued from famine and massacre. Now in Talas boarding-school.
(A. B. C. F. M.)

THE AFTER REWARDS OF A FAMINE RESCUE.

were homeless and hungry, memorable service was rendered by resident missionaries.[1]   In Persia their names are forever associated with benefactions in times of distress.   Dr. Cochran and the late Dr. Shedd, among others, have rendered invaluable aid.   The drought and famine of 1879–80 enlisted the ministrations of nearly all the missionary circle. Refugees sent over the Persian border from Turkey by the recent atrocities have been cared for as far as practicable by members of the mission in Western Persia.   The Keith-Falconer Medical Mission in Southern Arabia has done good service in relieving those enfeebled by famine.[2]

In the primitive environment of savagery, famine is not met by organized assistance.   The people migrate, or wander, from place to place, hopeless and helpless, in the vain search for supplies.   Under these circumstances, as often   Services to starving happens in Africa, missionaries render about the   Africans. only ¦aid which can be expected.   The Rev. F. Coillard makes some interesting statements which reveal his influence in persuading native chiefs to pay attention to the needs of their people at such times.   The Rev. J. D. Hepburn, in an account of his missionary life in Khama's country, tells of the bewilderment of the native church when he first undertook to induce them to attempt systematic efforts to prevent starvation.[3]   In the famine of 1895 in Usagara, ter-

[1] " The missionaries of the American Board in Asia Minor have been the means of relieving distress and saving hundreds, nay thousands, of lives in numerous famines which have afflicted Asiatic and European Turkey.   For example, in 1873–74 I was myself a member of a committee which raised and distributed some thirty thousand pounds sterling in the form of food and clothing, and seed for sowing, to sufferers from a famine in the great Province of Cesarea.   Rev. W. A. Farnesworth, D.D., and his associates and native fellow-laborers were the chief agents for the distribution of relief, and they devoted themselves to the work without any remuneration, performing the service with much sacrifice and most commendable fidelity, regardless of differences of race or religion.   Indeed, if I mistake not, the larger number of recipients of aid were Mohammedan Turks.   Again, in 1876–77, our missionaries in Bulgaria were invited by another Constantinople committee to convey assistance to the distressed Bulgarians.   Also, in recent years, signal service to humanity has been rendered by the mission staff in raising funds and bringing relief to famine sufferers in the Provinces of Adana, Mardin, and Erzroom."— Rev. J. K. Greene, D.D., Constantinople.

[2] Dr. Young, of Sheikh-Othman, writes: " Last month there were 2029 attendances at the dispensary, and I do not think I am exaggerating in saying that forty per cent. of these cases were caused by the famine, and that the best medicine one could give them was vegetable food or milk dietary."— *The Free Church of Scotland Monthly*, November, 1898, p. 269.

[3] " Twenty Years in Khama's Country," p. 127.

rible scenes were witnessed by resident missionaries while they devoted themselves with unsparing zeal to the relief of the sufferers.[1]

Surely further details are not needed to make manifest the fact that a humane and faithful service has been done by Christian workers in many fields to stay the ravages of famine, and to rescue, in Christ's name, those who were "ready to perish."

10. INTRODUCING MODERN MEDICAL SCIENCE.—If we search for the crowning benefaction which missions have brought to the nations, we will find none, other than the Gospel itself, which surpasses in value the establishment of modern medical and surgical practice among ignorant, deluded, and suffering peoples. The truth of this statement derives emphasis from the fact that medical ministry is not only a physical benefit, but also an evangelistic agency of great power. Pain has a message to the soul as well as an admonition to the body, and the medical missionary seeks to impress its spiritual lesson at the same time that he mitigates its physical pangs. The patient is in a receptive and expectant mood, and medical science serving in love, and instructing in the name of the Master, arrests the attention and carries conviction, as if it were in truth what it has been called, "the modern substitute for miracles."

The immense scope and suggestiveness of the theme are almost bewildering. As we reflect upon it, the mind wanders over dreary centuries of misery, during which mankind has been tortured by superstitious ignorance and cruel quackery. It pictures the prejudices which it was necessary to overcome, the suspicions which had to be allayed, the responsibilities which could not be avoided, and the risks which had to be taken by courageous missionary pioneers.[2] It thinks of the professional nerve and fortitude still required, the careful instructions to be given, the many inconveniences to be faced, the grave dangers to be guarded against, the repulsive persons to be handled, the frightful cases to be treated,—often alone, with no skilled assistants,— and the heavy disappointments which sometimes have to be borne. It contemplates the struggle, in many cases prolonged, which medical

The heroic significance of medical service in foreign fields.

---

[1] *The Church Missionary Intelligencer*, April, 1895, pp. 275–277; *Central Africa*, July, 1895, pp. 107–110; August, 1895, pp. 124–129.

[2] *The Missionary*, January, 1898, p. 19; *Woman's Work for Woman*, November, 1897, pp. 301–303.

Dr. Philip B. Cousland, and his Hospital Assistants.

Burns Memorial Hospital.

HOSPITAL AND MEDICAL STAFF, CHAOCHOWFU, CHINA.
(E. P. C. M.)

missionaries have passed through in securing suitable facilities for their growing work [1] and the patient fidelity which has been needed in order to establish, in the face of jealous opposition and malicious detraction, the superior merits of their scientific methods as compared with the old style of practice. It notes with admiration the quiet vindication of professional honor and rectitude which has been achieved in spite of violent and unjust accusations, the composure with which ingratitude, based often upon ignorance, has been overlooked, and the forbearance which has been exercised in dealing with unreasonable and childish exactions. Then comes the vision of achievements, vast and benefi- cent, which it is impossible to record in human language, although they have been written upon the hearts of grateful peoples in many lands. In missionary literature much space is now devoted to medical service, and some references to recent sources of information upon this broad theme are here inserted.[2]

---

[1] The experience of Dr. Cousland (E. P. C. M.) in establishing the Burns' Memorial Hospital at Chaochowfu, China, well illustrates this aspect of medical missionary service. See *The Monthly Messenger*, March, 1897, pp. 68, 69.

[2] Cf. Lowe, " Medical Missions : Their Place and Power "; also " Primer of Medical Missions "; Laurie, " Missions and Science " (Ely Volume), pp. 406–416; " Report of the London Missionary Conference, 1888," vol. ii., pp. 101–139; Wherry, " Missions at Home and Abroad," pp. 335–348; " The Medical Arm of the Missionary Service," a pamphlet published by the A. B. C. F. M. ; " The Stu- dent Missionary Enterprise " (Report of the Student Volunteer Convention, Detroit, 1894), pp. 204–219; " The Student Missionary Appeal " (Report of the Student Volunteer Convention, Cleveland, 1898), pp. 483–508; Mackenzie, " Christianity and the Progress of Man," pp. 102–104; Graves, " Forty Years in China," pp. 220–253; Foster, " Christian Progress in China," pp. 162–195; Tracy, " Talks on the Veranda," pp. 222–237; Houghton, " Women of the Orient," pp. 461–492; Bryson, " John Kenneth Mackenzie, Medical Missionary to China "; Maxwell, " W. Burns Thomson : Reminiscences of Medical Missionary Work "; Christie, " Ten Years in Manchuria "; files of *The Double Cross and Medical Missionary Record; Medical Missions at Home and Abroad; Mercy and Truth;* and *Quarterly Papers of the Edinburgh Medical Missionary Society;* Annual Reports of the Edin- burgh Medical Missionary Society, the Medical Missionary Association, the Inter- national Medical Missionary Society, and the International Medical Missionary and Benevolent Association ; *Regions Beyond*, October, 1895, pp. 403–406; November, 1895, pp. 459–463; *The Missionary Review of the World*, September, 1895, pp. 678–682; September, 1897, pp. 695–697; *The Missionary Herald*, July, 1897, pp. 266–268; *Mercy and Truth*, June, 1897, pp. 132–139; *Medical Missions at Home and Abroad*, March, 1897, pp. 260–263; *The Indian Evangelical Review*, October, 1897, pp. 207–214; *The Missionary*, December, 1898, pp. 549–552; *The Review of Missions*, January, 1899, pp. 436–439 (reprint of preceding article). Cf. also p. 40 of this volume.

The subject cannot be thoroughly studied without noting the fact that far more attention has been given to the appointment of fully trained medical agents by American and British societies than by their sister missionary organizations on the Continent of Europe. This no doubt has been the result of deliberate choice on both sides. As the case now stands, there are at present 338 American, 288 British, and 27 Canadian medical missionaries in the various fields, as compared with 20, the total number for all the societies of Continental Europe, and 7 for Australasia. It should be said, however, that it has been customary in several of the Continental societies to have many of their outgoing missionaries receive a practical training in medicine, which, without securing to them the regular diploma, enables them to prescribe the simpler remedies, and to give useful directions in cases of ordinary illness. In some individual instances this foundation of medical knowledge has proved the basis of growing skill and efficiency, so that valuable services have been rendered by non-professional practitioners.

Medical agencies popular with American and British societies.

A similar disparity also exists in the employment of women as missionary physicians. Included in these totals, there are 127 American, 73 British, and 9 Canadian women holding medical diplomas, who are at present serving in the field, as compared with one representative from the Continental societies.[1] The author is informed, however, that several young women are now taking a medical course, with the expectation of receiving appointment from societies on the European Continent. The admirable services, moreover, rendered by the skilled nurses sent out from some of the European societies, especially by the Kaiserswerth Deaconesses, should be carefully noted here as contributing much to the efficiency of medical and surgical practice in the hospitals. British and American societies as well have furnished their quota to the nursing staff. There are many Florence Nightingales and Sister Doras in foreign mission hospitals, whose services are rendered in a spirit of cheerful devotion to a round of duty which nothing but love for the Master could transfigure with the joy and charm of privilege. "Ye did it unto Me" can be truly said of all such loving ministry. For our present purpose, however, we count as medical missionaries only those who have received the regular diploma, and at the present time (1899) we find that the total number in the foreign field is 680, of whom 470 are men and 210 are women.

---

[1] Mrs. Morten Andersen, M.D., Thabor, Shevaroy Hills, South India, who is connected with the Danish Missionary Society.

As this summation is intended to represent only professedly missionary agencies, the physicians in connection with the Countess of Dufferin's Fund in India and Burma (often designated the Lady Dufferin Association) are not included. The philanthropic service of that useful organization is worthy of all honor, but as it confessedly does not seek to evangelize, the author has not considered himself at liberty to introduce it under the caption of missionary statistics. He has not thought it justifiable, either, to include native medical employees in the mission fields, unless they have received foreign diplomas, and have been regularly sent out by a missionary society, and enrolled among its foreign missionaries. In a few instances this is the case, and these have been reckoned in the list. He has thought it best also not to count nurses who have not received a full medical training, and they are not here classed as medical missionaries, although their services are of great value in hospitals and in connection with surgical cases.

It has come to light in the examination of reports that the Board of Foreign Missions of the Presbyterian Church in the United States of America (North), including its Women's Auxiliaries, has a total of 83 medical missionaries on its roll, of whom 50 are men and 33 women—the largest number of any single society or board in the world. The Church Missionary Society, with a total of 55 (49 men and 6 women), has the most numerous medical force of any British agency. If, moreover, we add the ten women physicians of the Church of England Zenana Missionary Society, the total becomes 65, with 16 instead of 6 women. The American Presbyterians, above mentioned, also lead all others in the number (33) of medical women now in the foreign service, and the Methodist Episcopal Church (U. S. A.) follows with 29 on its roll. The foreign missionary field having the greatest number of medical missionaries is China, with 243, of whom 166 are men and 77 are women. The next in rank is India, with 168, of whom 83 are men and 85 are women. If those in Burma (13) and in Ceylon (3) were added the total would be 184.

The rapid progress of medical missions has been astonishing. The statistics just given for India indicate this when compared with a statement made by Dr. C. S. Valentine, at the Annual Meeting of the Edinburgh Medical Missionary Society, in 1897. He remarked that "thirty-nine years ago there were only about seven medical missionaries in all India." The Church Missionary Society reported, in 1897, that more than one tenth of the whole number of missionaries sent out that year for the first time were qualified doctors. The

Rapid growth of medical missions.

total of physicians entered on its roll, March 1, 1899, is stated to be fifty-five.[1] The Report of the Zenana Bible and Medical Mission for the year ending December 31, 1895, gives a statistical statement of its medical work, with the following striking results: In 1885 the number of individual patients treated by its missionaries was 2222; in 1895 it was 21,092. In 1885, also, the total of treatments in dispensaries was 6000; in 1895 it was 66,582.[2] At the Student Volunteer Convention held in Cleveland in 1898, Mr. Douglas M. Thornton, a delegate from Great Britain, stated that among British students those preparing for medical service had increased greatly in number, so that, in fact, the majority of the Student Volunteer body were now studying medicine.[3] The Church Missionary Society, with its characteristic alertness, has instituted a special Prayer Union in connection with its Medical Missionary Auxiliary, to be called "The Order of the Red Cross." Its object is to quicken prayer, enlist service, and arouse interest in this expanding department of mission enterprise.[4]

Traces of a desire to consecrate medical science to missionary purposes are evident in the early movements of modern missions. An

Early movements on behalf of medical missions.

English official, General Christopher Codrington, Governor of the Leeward Islands, in his will, dated February 22, 1703, bequeathed valuable plantations in the Island of Barbados to the Society for the Propagation of the Gospel in Foreign Parts, with the stipulation that the property be kept intact, and that an institution be maintained there in which the students "shall be obliged to study and practise Phisick and Chirurgery as well as Divinity, that by the apparent usefulness of the former to all mankind they may both endear themselves to the people, and have the better opportunities of doing good to men's souls whilst they are taking care of their bodies."[5] Owing to difficulties occasioned by litigation, it was not until 1745 that a building was opened for use. The Codrington College, Barbados, stands to-day as a monument of the broad views and generous liberality of a distinguished layman who saw clearly the usefulness of

1 *Mercy and Truth*, January, 1899, p. 23.

2 Annual Report, issued in 1896, p. 18.

3 "The Student Missionary Appeal," p. 61.

4 *The Church Missionary Intelligencer*, January, 1899, pp. 69, 70; *Mercy and Truth*, January, 1899, p. 5.

5 Pascoe, "Classified Digest of the Records of the Society for the Propagation of the Gospel in Foreign Parts, 1701–1892," p. 197.

Elizabeth Sleeper Davis Memorial Hospital for Women, Peking.
(M. E. M. S.)

Victoria Hospital, Damascus.
(E. M. M. S.)

NEW HOSPITALS IN CHINA AND SYRIA.

physical healing as a missionary agency. The early Danish missions to India also sent out some medical men in 1730 and 1732.[1] The Moravians, as well, were represented by two physicians sent to Persia in 1747.

Since, however, these early efforts of the Danes and Moravians in the eighteenth century did not result in the permanent establishment of a medical service, it may be truly said that it is hardly more than an ordinary lifetime since the majority of medical missionary pioneers entered the fields. Dr. Asa Dodge went to Palestine; Drs. Van Dyck and De Forest to Syria; Drs. Azariah Smith, Lobdell, Pratt, Jewett, Nutting, and West to Asia Minor; Dr. Grant to Persia; Dr. Parker (1834), and soon after Drs. Lockhart, Hobson, Macgowan, Mc-Cartee, Happer, and Kerr, to China; Drs. Thomas and Scudder to India; Dr. Hepburn to Japan; and Drs. Vanderkemp and Livingstone to Africa. The pioneers among women physicians were Dr. Clara A. Swain, who went to India in 1869, and Dr. Lucinda L. Combs, who entered China in 1873, both of the American Methodist Episcopal Church. The first with a regular diploma to go from England (in 1880 to India), was Dr. Fanny J. Butler (C. E. Z. M. S.). The present medical staff in the foreign field is almost entirely a growth of the last half-century, and especially of the last two decades. Dr. Davidson (L. M. S.), on January 14, 1864, wrote: "To-day I began building the hospital, the first in the Island of Madagascar. It shall stand at Analakely as a testimony to our humanity, our science, and our Christianity."[2] Again, on May 9, 1865, Dr. Elmslie (C. M. S.) wrote: "To-day is memorable in the history of the Kashmir Medical Mission, from the fact that I opened my dispensary this morning." He writes again on the last day of the same month: "Opened my small hospital to-day. It accommodates from four to five patients."[3] At the present time that little extemporized hospital started on Dr. Elmslie's veranda is a well-equipped and extensive plant, where, according to a recent annual report, there were 38,573 treatments and over 500 major operations during the year. From still another distant field, Ambrym, in the New Hebrides, come similar tidings. Dr. Lamb, of the New Hebrides Mission, writes in the autumn of 1897: "Much interest centres in the experiment— the first made in this part of the world—of founding a hospital on a

A roll-call of pioneers in many fields.

---

[1] Sherring, " The History of Protestant Missions in India," p. 14.

[2] Maxwell, " W. Burns Thomson: Reminiscences of Medical Missionary Work," p. 159.

[3] *Mercy and Truth,* August, 1897, p. 175.

cannibal island, and utilizing it as an engine for breaking down savagery by the power of Christian love." [1]   It requires a vivid imagination to realize what these philanthropic efforts mean to the people among whom such institutions are established.

The usefulness of the medical arm of the missionary service is indisputable.   It breaks down opposition, dissipates prejudice, and wins

The value of medical missionary work.

its way to the hearts and homes of the high and the low, the rich and the poor.   It receives the highest official recognition, and thus facilitates the employment of all other agencies. [2]   The foreign doctor is a *persona grata* even in palaces and halls of state.   Missionary physicians render help by their advice, and often by their personal services, in the establishment of sanitary measures in hitherto neglected communities.   Extensive excerpts might be given, from sources worthy of confidence, vindicating the exceptional value of this department of missions, but it must suffice to indicate a few in a foot-note. [3]

Another feature of great interest in connection with this subject is the provision which has been made in many fields to train medical

The importance of schools of medicine in mission fields.

students from the native races, who will represent among their own people the scientific skill and approved methods which have been introduced through missionary agencies.   In some instances schools of medicine, with a competent faculty and fine equipment, have been established.   The one connected with the Syrian Protestant Col-

---

[1] *Edinburgh Medical Missionary Society Quarterly Paper*, May, 1898, p. 276.

[2] " I do not claim that Western medicine established Christianity in Japan, but that Christianity, in introducing medicine, brought into the country a power which, under God's blessing, has been one of the most softening influences upon the Japanese mind, and has, so to speak, been everywhere a forerunner of the divine message."—W. N. Whitney, M.D., formerly of the United States Legation, but now of Akasaka Hospital, Tokyo.

" Owing to the medical skill of Dr. Mackenzie and Dr. Leonora Howard (now Mrs. King), the celebrated Premier, Li Hung Chang, and his wife, Lady Li, have for years been strong supporters of Western medicine, and now, in addition to the hospitals erected by them, both for men and for women, a special training-school for medical students has been established, at the expense of the Government, for training physicians and surgeons for the army and navy."—Rev. Gilbert Reid, Peking, China.

[3] *Mercy and Truth*, June, 1897, p. 138; September, 1897, p. 197; November, 1897, p. 249; *The Missionary Review of the World*, September, 1897, pp. 695-697, 708; *The Church Missionary Intelligencer*, November, 1895, p. 862; *The Chronicle*, November, 1895, p. 303; *Work and Workers in the Mission Field*, February, 1897, p. 79; Macgowan, " Pictures of Southern China," p. 203.

Students of Medical Department, Syrian Protestant College

The Medical Faculty.

FACULTY AND STUDENTS OF THE MEDICAL SCHOOL, BEIRUT.

lege at Beirut, and similar facilities, such as those found at Agra, Neyoor, Lodiana, Bareilly, and Kalimpong, in India, the medical instruction at Moukden, Foochow, Soochow, Canton, Fatshan, Hong Kong, and Chungking, in China, and also the training-classes of from half a dozen to a dozen pupils at a number of the hospitals in various fields, are examples sufficiently illustrative of this important phase of medical effort.[1] The Tientsin Medical College, founded by the London Missionary Society, has passed under Chinese control, but continues to give the modern training required by Western science, some of the instructors having been pupils of Dr. Mackenzie.[2] In certain of the institutions mentioned women are taught, and special classes for them are conducted in many of the hospitals. Chang Chih-tung, a prominent viceroy in China, was reported, in 1897, as seeking the services of Drs. Meigii Shie and Ida Kahn, with a view to their acceptance of positions in the medical department of a school for women which it is the desire of the authorities to found in Shanghai, and which is said to be the forerunner of a university for women to be established in the future.[3] The medical education of Indian women has assumed new importance under the auspices of the Lady Dufferin Association, which, in 1898, reported two hundred and forty female students under its charge in medical schools and colleges in India. The Campbell Medical School in Calcutta has a class for native girls, in whose behalf the Lady Elliott Hostel has been built by the same Association. A similar provision has been added at the Calcutta Medical College, and in a few other places in India. The North India School of Medicine for Christian Women, at Lodiana, has been recently organized, and the medical departments of some of the universities are open to women students. These facts are indicative of revolutionary changes in the social status and prospects of woman in India, which are due largely to the introduction of medical science among missionary agencies.[4]

[1] See article on " Medical Schools in China," by the Rev. George A. Stuart, M.D., in *The Chinese Recorder*, October, 1896, pp. 494–501.

[2] " Report of the London Missionary Society, 1894," p. 63.

[3] *Woman's Missionary Friend*, December, 1897, p. 170.

[4] The Rev. T. E. Slater (L. M. S.), of Bangalore, South India, calls the author's attention to the following statement of a distinguished official:

"Sir Charles U. Aitchison, one of the Lieutenant-Governors of the Punjab, wrote in *The Baptist Missionary Herald*, May, 1887: ' It was at the suggestion of the missionaries that I have this year introduced a system of government grants-in-aid to hospitals and dispensaries. It is to the example set by missionary ladies in mission hospitals, and in house-to-house visitation, that the present widespread

The formal establishment of medical training, notable as it is, does not represent the educational impetus to be traced to medical missions.

A revolution in native practice.

Independently of organized facilities for instruction, missionary physicians have in their private capacity as practitioners exerted a manifest influence over native students and physicians, who have derived from them valuable knowledge and new methods of practice, to their own advantage and the benefit of their patients. Of Dr. J. C. Berry, of Japan, it is said that he gave much attention to instructing native doctors how to proceed in the treatment of disease in accordance with the best medical knowledge. At one time he was teaching a band of one hundred and twenty native physicians. The superiority of Western methods was immediately appreciated by the Japanese, and the Government soon decided to send a number of medical students to Europe to qualify themselves, and then return to practise in their native land. Several of those who enjoyed these advantages are now well-known professors in medical institutions in Japan.[1] The stimulus of these new ideas reaches also the old practi-

demand for medical aid and medical training for the women of India is mainly due. Apart from the strictly Christian aspect of the question, I should, *from a purely administrative point of view*, deplore the drying up of Christian liberality to missions as a most lamentable check to social and moral progress, and a grievous injury to the best interests of the people.'"

Bishop Thoburn writes on this subject as follows: " What this means to the young women and girls of India I can hardly make you understand. I have myself seen twenty young ladies, all daughters of village converts, in attendance at a medical college. These girls had spent their childhood in extreme poverty. Their fathers had been accustomed to earn about two dollars a month, and to occupy a very low social position in the village community. But one of the girls on graduation stepped at once into a position worth twenty-five dollars a month, an income which in the eyes of the simple villagers, no doubt, seemed princely. A new career has thus been opened to the womanhood of India, while relief from pain and sickness in a hundred forms has been secured for all coming generations to uncounted millions of Indian women. All this is to-day, under God, owing to missionary ladies, and I am glad to be able to testify that more young women are offering their services for medical work abroad than ever before. The door is still wide open to Christian workers of this class, and the great movement has probably only begun." —Thoburn, " The Christless Nations," pp. 107, 108.

[1] Page, " Japan: Its People and Missions," p. 107.

" In the principal cities of Asia Minor the very best and most reliable physicians are generally the pupils of the missionary physician and celebrated surgeon Henry S. West, M.D., who labored for many years seeking to heal the bodies and souls of men in Sivas, the capital of this province, and with whom it was my privilege to be associated during the last seven years of his life."—Rev. Edward Riggs (A. B. C. F. M.), Marsovan, Turkey.

tioners, who often adopt the better methods, and discard many of the irrational expedients which characterized their former practice. Thus an entire transformation is gradually being wrought in medical science throughout the country.[1] "Medical work," writes the Rev. W. P. Chalfant, of Ichowfu, China, "aside from its benevolent and evangelistic aspects, is disseminating among the intelligent classes more correct ideas of anatomy and physiology, which must sooner or later revolutionize native practice."

Dr. George W. Holmes, a Presbyterian missionary at Hamadan, Persia, writes of this aspect of the case: "Medical mission work is making its influence felt very decidedly, not alone in the case of the eight young men taught, or under instruction, but also in the higher professional and ethical standards already apparent in the ranks of the native physicians with whom we come in contact. Much is hoped for in this direction." The author is indebted to Dr. James Sommerville, a missionary of the Scotch United Presbyterian Church, residing in Jodhpore, India, for the following significant statement: "I was gratified lately by receiving a request from one of the nobles of this State for the services of a Christian native doctor to give medical aid to his people. The physician was to have the fullest permission (a stipulation made by myself) to preach Christianity, as he should have opportunity. This preference for the services of a Christian, to be selected by and employed under the supervision of a Christian missionary, and at the charge of a man still professing Hinduism, and of the proud, conservative Rajput race, constrained by his very position to main-

---

[1] "Many of the early missionaries to Japan were physicians, and in this capacity contributed much to the introduction of modern medical science. Dr. Hepburn's services as a scholar, a lexicographer, and a translator can never be overrated; but for many years his principal duty was the practice of his medical profession, and a goodly number of the Japanese natives, both high and low, obtained their first conception of foreign, rational medicine from the benefits which Dr. Hepburn's skill brought to their suffering bodies. Dr. D. B. Simmons went out to Japan as a medical missionary, but afterwards devoted himself entirely to the practice of his profession. He served the local government at Yokohama as the superintendent of a hospital, and in many ways benefited the country by promoting the use of foreign medicine. Dr. Berry, of the American Board, has in like manner contributed materially to the replacing of the old, absurd system of medical ideas (it cannot be called a science) by the more reasonable methods of Western science."—David Murray, Ph.D., LL.D., Late Adviser to the Japanese Minister of Education.

"What grand names," writes Dr. Griffis, "are Simmons, Hepburn, Berry, Whitney, Harwell, Taylor, Cutter, McCartee, in the medical annals of Japan!" —Article on "America in the Far East," in *The Outlook*, December 31, 1898, p. 1053.

tain both racial and religious traditions, is very unusual. Taken in connection with the facts that such a choice was made deliberately, according to the wishes of the late bearer of the title as expressed in his will, and that he had designated a sum of money to endow the appointment, it is an incident which bears testimony in a most signal manner to the impression which our Christian morality and life have made upon the Hindu mind."

In some instances, as, for example in India, and to a less degree in China, the Government has recognized the duty of introducing facilities for medical training, but it is not an assumption to say that the first inspiration to this movement was attributable in large measure to missionary example and counsel. Training-schools for nurses have been founded in some fields as supplemental to a higher medical course. A fine example of this is the Doshisha Nurses' Training-school, at Kyoto, Japan.

Mention should also be made of the preparation of medical literature, including a few scientific periodicals, such as *The China Medical Missionary Journal*, the organ of the Medical Missionary Association of that country, and the *Chinese Medical Journal*, edited by Wan Tun-mo, resident surgeon of the Alice Memorial Hospital, Hong Kong, and *Medical Missions in India*, edited by Dr. Husband of Ajmere. The services of Dr. Hobson, Dr. Mackenzie, and Dr. Kerr in China, of Dr. Van Dyck and Dr. Post in Syria, and of many others, have been notable in this respect. Tracts dealing with the subject of sanitation, the treatment of epidemic diseases, and the preservation of health, have been published, especially during periods of danger. The first medical congresses convened in Eastern lands have been held under missionary auspices, as the one at Calcutta in December, 1894. The Medical Missionary Society in China, with headquarters at Canton, held its sixtieth annual meeting in January, 1899, and the Medical Missionary Association of China dates from 1886. The former coöperates with the American Presbyterian missionaries in supporting a large hospital plant. The spirited example of professional fidelity and *esprit de corps* manifested by missionary physicians in times of public peril, or in private practice, has been of value in introducing a higher code among native practitioners. In addition, the liberality of wealthy natives, especially in India and China, has been enlisted in promoting the establishment and support of hospitals, and in providing benevolent ministries for the suffering. Quite recently, at Madura, in India, large gifts were received from native princes and merchants for

Modern medical literature introduced by missionaries.

Dr. and Mrs. Browne.   Dr. and Mrs. Clark.

The natives in the above group are all Christians, and mostly converts of the Amritsar Medical Mission.

THE MEDICAL STAFF, AMRITSAR, INDIA.

(C. M. S.)

the building of a hospital, which is now completed and under the care of Dr. Van Allen, a missionary of the American Board. Late news from Uganda informs us that the King of Toro, to whom reference is made on page 16 of this volume, is building a hospital—surely a sign that his heart is responding to the promptings of Christian benevolence.[1]

The use of anæsthetics, the introduction of vaccination, and the intelligent treatment of the epidemic diseases which make such awful havoc in the teeming centres of Oriental life, are due, as a rule, to missionary physicians, although a notable exception should be recorded in the case of China. Dr. Alexander Pearson and Dr. T. R. Colledge, who were not officially connected with any missionary society, were the pioneers of modern medical practice in China. The former introduced vaccination in 1805, seven years after Jenner announced his discovery in Great Britain, and Dr. Colledge established the first benevolent institution for the help of natives in need. He was also the principal founder, and during forty years the President, of the Medical Missionary Society in China. Both these distinguished physicians were in the employ of the East India Company, but rendered much philanthropic service in their time. While this is true, Dr. Parker's position of honor remains, as the first medical missionary to China, and the founder (1835) of the first missionary hospital in that great empire.[2] In Northern Siam, Dr. McKean, a resident Presbyterian missionary, has been appointed official vaccinator by the Government, and through his persevering efforts the present generation of Laos children will soon all be inoculated. More than three thousand persons were thus treated by him in a single year. It is within the memory of Dr. McGilvary that only by argument, appeal, and even payment for the privilege, could the opportunity to vaccinate be secured. Dr. Bradley, who introduced the practice into Lower Siam, was obliged to hire a man to submit to the operation, and as he declined at the last moment, another one had to be found. In 1894 the Siamese Government made vaccination, at its own expense, compulsory.

The medical treatment of opium victims in China is now a striking feature of missionary effort. Although permanent cures are not often effected, unless the awakened conscience of the patient, and the spiritual energies of Christian faith coöperate with medical skill, yet every poor degenerate is a potential victor, and

> **Missionary doctors bearers of the best gifts of modern science.**

1 *Mercy and Truth*, February, 1898, p. 32.
2 Foster, "Christian Progress in China," p. 162.

notable instances of entire recovery are rewarding those who engage in this service.[1]

Turning our attention to various fields, what has been said in general will be found illustrated by concrete examples in many lands.

In no part of the world, however, has medical

What medical science has done for China and India.

science been more urgently needed, or accomplished more important results, than in China and India, where vast populations have dwelt for centuries in total ignorance of the laws of hygiene and sanitation, or of the first principles of an intelligent practice of medicine and surgery. Hundreds of shocking incidents pertaining to these as well as other countries could be brought forward to prove the truth of this statement, but the reader surely does not require to be tortured into conviction concerning such indubitable facts.[2]

In India the saving benefits of medical science are apparent. Before the English occupation there were no hospitals or dispensaries in all the land.[3] Even at the present time it is estimated that only five per cent. of the population is practically reached by existing facilities. The usual expedient when a fatal termination of disease seems to be imminent is to remove the patient from the house, and, if possible, place him on the banks of the Ganges. This ominous procedure

[1] Mr. F. E. Shindler, of the China Inland Mission, at Kihchau, writes under date of April 20, 1898, as follows : " For nearly ten years it has been our custom at this station to open an opium refuge annually during the winter months, with the result that about thirty men and women (mostly men) have broken off the habit each year." He mentions the cases of several individuals who have been lifted from the depths of bondage and misery to a happy Christian experience. " We have twenty-six members on the church roll, fourteen of whom were formerly opium-smokers."

[2] " The amount of disease and suffering in China is very great, and the methods of native medical practice tend rather to increase than to lessen it. The rich and poor alike suffer. Ignorance, superstition, and filth are as apparent and potent among the wealthy as among the poverty-stricken. Diseases are left to the unaided powers of nature, or, what is far worse, are treated by crude and inappropriate methods. Scientific diagnosis and rational treatment are an impossibility even to the most wealthy, for the reason that a requisite knowledge of medicine cannot be said to exist in China at the present time."—Article by the Rev. George A. Stuart, M.D., in *The Chinese Recorder*, October, 1896, pp. 494, 495.

Cf. article by the Rev. W. R. Lambuth, M.D., D.D., on " Medical Missions in China," in *The Missionary*, February, 1894, pp. 51–54; March, 1894, pp. 93–96; republished in *The Medical Missionary Record*, May, 1894, pp. 99–101. Cf. also *Work and Workers in the Mission Field*, July, 1896, pp. 305–307; *The Missionary*, December, 1898, pp. 549–552; and *The Review of Missions*, January, 1899, pp. 436–439.

[3] " Papers on Indian Religious Reform :" see paper entitled " India Hindu and India Christian," p. 7.

becomes the signal for an indescribable scene of lamentation on the part of friends.[1]   One of the hopeful and notable features of the progress of missions in India is the rapid development of medical study and practice by native women.   This has been already referred to, especially in connection with the Countess of Dufferin's Fund, which reported, in 1898, twenty-eight lady doctors of the first grade, seventy assistant surgeons, second grade, and seventy hospital assistants, third grade. The twenty-eight medical women of the first grade have all qualified by a thorough course, and are on the British Medical Register; the others are Indian-born and Indian-educated, and of many nationalities, castes, and creeds.   During the year 1897 about 1,327,000 women were treated by those identified with this organization.   The total of foreign and native medical women of all grades, inclusive of trained nurses, connected with all British societies in India, not excepting the Lady Dufferin Association, may be safely estimated as at least three hundred, and of this number seventy-four are fully qualified medical women.   If we deduct, for reasons already stated (p. 403), the twenty-eight physicians of the Lady Dufferin Association, the total number of officially qualified medical women sent to India by British missionary societies is forty-six.   The Lodiana Medical School for native Christian women, and the opportunities offered by the admission of women to the medical colleges of Calcutta, Madras, Bombay, Lahore, and Agra, promise large accessions in the near future.[2]   When the students now in training are added, the number will be more than doubled. In Burma, where the medical work of the American Baptists is growing in volume, and in Siam, especially in Laos, where the American Presbyterians have an able staff of physicians, the benefits may be said to be as marked as in India.

In Japan and Korea striking progress is also to be noted.   The practice of missionary physicians in Japan has been instrumental in stimulating the desire on all sides for a better knowledge of Western methods.   Medical schools and a number of hospitals are now established under Japanese auspices.   The training for nursing and the study of medicine have become especially popular with Japanese women.   There are a large number of such medical students gathered

A warm welcome to the missionary physician in Japan and Korea.

---

[1] *The Missionary Herald of the Baptist Missionary Society* (English), February, 1898, p. 57.

[2] Cf. article by Mary Scharlieb, M.D., on "Medical Women in India," in *The Indian Magazine and Review*, September, 1897, pp. 441–447.   See also *The Imperial and Asiatic Quarterly Review*, October, 1896, pp. 298–305, 406–415;

in Tokyo.[1]   An interesting article by John C. Berry, M.D., on "The Medical Missionary Work of the American Board in Japan," gives salient facts concerning the part taken by that society in the introduction of this branch of modern science into the empire.[2]   In Korea the people have received the missionary physician with special favor.[3]   In 1895, during the terrible epidemic of cholera, which was especially severe in Seoul, the missionaries of various denominations living in that city, assisted by devoted Korean Christians, rendered during the long summer months services marked by great personal risk and sacrifice, which were gratefully recognized by the Government, and will never be forgotten by multitudes of the population.[4]

In Mohammedan lands, over which the spirit of fatalism has long brooded, the promotion of the scientific practice of medicine is changing the attitude of the people towards public calamities, and is placing in an entirely new light all epidemic as well as ordinary diseases.   In Arabia, a centre of medical work has been established in connection with the Keith-Falconer Mission of the Free Church of Scotland, near Aden, where Dr. J. C. Young is stationed, and with whom Dr. J. R. Morris has now become associated.   The

The victory of medical skill over fatalism in Moslem lands.

The Indian Social Reformer, August 2, 1896, p. 370; Barnes, " Behind the Pardah," pp. 193–210; *India's Women*, April, 1895, pp. 149–155, September, 1897, pp. 199–201; *The Church at Home and Abroad*, April, 1895, pp. 312–315; *The Missionary Review of the World*, April, 1897, pp. 280–282; *The Edinburgh Medical Missionary Society Quarterly Paper*, August, 1897, pp. 178–180.

[1] *Regions Beyond*, January, 1897, p. 36.

[2] *The Missionary Herald*, July, 1894, pp. 278–281.

[3] *The Korean Repository*, January, 1898, p. 32.

" ' That doctor did not come from America, but from heaven,' exclaimed the wondering Korean courtiers as the missionary Allen left the palace.   Their prince had been wounded, and was dying from loss of blood, thirteen native surgeons having tried in vain to stop the bleeding by pouring molten wax into the wound.   The American missionary's treatment saved his life, and won an entrance for the Gospel into the court of hermit Korea."—*Regions Beyond*, February, 1894, p. 76.

[4] *The Korean Repository*, September, 1895, pp. 339–344.

" During the epidemic of 1895, at Seoul, Korea, whether as inspectors, or as physicians and nurses in the two cholera hospitals, nearly all the members of the two Presbyterian Missions, the Baptist Mission, and the medical staff of the Methodist Mission, were engaged in fighting cholera.   It was work hard and trying, both to the health and sympathies of the workers.   It was done in the heat of summer, after a year of mission toil, just when tired bodies needed rest; done night and day, in the midst of suffering and grief, among the dying and the dead.   But, again, it was undertaken for Christ's sake and for humanity, and that made all the difference in the world.   A number of Korean Christians cheerfully joined in the perilous task,

Dispensary—Rear View.   Robert Clark Wards.

Dr. Henry Martyn Clark.   Students' Quarters.

Dispensary and Operating Rooms—Front View.

SCENES AT THE AMRITSAR HOSPITAL, INDIA.

(C. M. S.)

fame of Dr. Young's skill has so penetrated the interior that his patients journey sometimes from ten to fifteen days to visit him. Another effort is under the auspices of the Reformed Church of America, at Busrah and Bahrein, on the eastern coast of the Arabian peninsula. Three medical missionaries, Dr. H. R. L. Worrall, Dr. Sharon J. Thoms, and Mrs. Thoms, who is also a medical graduate, are now at these outposts. In the Turkish Empire, a large and important medical school is conducted at Beirut, where scientific training of high grade is given, and the tone and standard of practice have been thereby greatly raised in Syria and Palestine. The American Board has its missionary physicians stationed throughout Asia Minor, as the names of Drs. Parmelee, at Trebizond, Dodd, at Cesarea (where a hospital has just been opened), Carrington, at Marsovan, Raynolds, at Van, Thom, at Mardin, and Ussher, at Harpoot, indicate.

In Persia, Dr. Joseph P. Cochran, at Urumiah,[1] and Dr. G. W. Holmes, at Hamadan, both of the American Presbyterian Mission, have charge of two busy centres of medical effort, where instruction is also given to classes of native students. Dr. Carr, of the Church Missionary Society, and his associates, conduct a hospital at Julfa. Other stations, such as Tabriz, under Dr. W. S. Vanneman, and Teheran, under Dr. J. G. Wishard (successor to Dr. W. W. Torrence), where a hospital is now established, should be mentioned. Dr. Wishard has just graduated his first class of medical students. In connection with the Persia missions are some accomplished women physicians—Dr. Mary E. Bradford, at Tabriz, Dr. Emma T. Miller, at Urumiah, Dr. Mary J. Smith, at Teheran, and Dr. Jessie C. Wilson, at Hamadan. Dr. Emmeline M. Stuart, and Dr. Urania Latham, of the Church Missionary Society, are at Julfa. Mr. M. G. Daniel, a native of Persia, who has written a volume on the modern development of the country, speaks with enthusiasm of the influence of Dr. Cochran, and of the commanding position which medical missions have assumed among all ranks, from the Shah to the peasant. He states that "the name 'hospital' was unknown there

The high standing of medical missions in Persia.

and it is a cause for gratitude to God that, while death was all about us, like the destroying angel in the households of Egypt, none of the foreign community, and but two or three of the Korean Christians in the city, were taken away by the dreadful disease."—Rev. D. L. Gifford, in *Woman's Work for Woman*, August, 1896, p. 213.

[1] A sketch of Dr. Cochran appears in *The Double Cross and Medical Missionary Record*, January, 1898, p. 5.

until the missionaries came," and that hundreds died of smallpox before the introduction of vaccination by medical missionaries.[1] The establishment of modern medical science through mission agencies clearly marks a humanitarian epoch in Western Asia.

The African Continent for unknown generations has been under the dreadful delusions of fetichism and witchcraft, while supposed masters in these occult mysteries have posed as healers of disease. Many of the pioneer missionary physicians of the Dark Continent have found themselves face to face with these cruel charlatans, and have succeeded in overthrowing their devices. The revolutionary effects which must follow the destruction of witchcraft and quackery are far-reaching. The immemorial sway of ignorance and deception is already waning.[2] Wherever missions have entered the Continent they are slowly supplanting the ancient terrors of the native quack by the introduction of medical knowledge. In the interior, where the Church Missionary Society, the Universities' Mission, the Scottish missionaries,[3] the American and English Baptists, the London Missionary

Supplanting the terrors of the native quack in Africa.

---

[1] Daniel, " Modern Persia," pp. 196–203. Cf. also Wilson, " Persia: Western Mission," pp. 7, 258–290.

[2] " Do you suppose that when the missionary societies began to send medical missionaries to Africa they had any very clear idea as to what the greatest potency of physicians and surgeons would prove to be? It is already found in some places that these specialists are striking at the very root of an evil which, perhaps more than any other one influence, keeps the native African degraded. That is the superstition which has invested the fetich-doctor with mysterious power over human life and happiness. No man can grow intellectually while he believes the fetich-doctor can exorcise the evil spirits that make him ill, or sell him charms that will bring victory in battle. No man can progress so long as a greedy chief, eager to seize the little property his subject has gathered, may call in the fetich-man to declare him a witch and condemn him to death. The glimmer of an idea is dawning upon many of these people, that the real healers are these men who have come among them, and that there is nothing supernatural about their skill. They are beginning to see the imposition that has kept them prostrate."—Paper by Cyrus C. Adams, on " Some Results of the African Movement," in " Africa and the African Negro: Addresses and Proceedings of the Congress on Africa, Atlanta, 1895," p. 38.

[3] Captain Lugard, in ' The Rise of Our East African Empire," has expressed his view of the value of medical missions in Africa, and, incidentally, of the work of the Free Church of Scotland missionaries on Lake Nyassa, as follows: " Beyond doubt, I think, in the initial stages of savage development, the most useful missions are the medical and industrial. A combination of the two is, in my opinion, an ideal mission. Such is the plan of the Scotch Free Church on Lake Nyassa. The medical missionary begins work with every advantage. Throughout Africa the ideas

Society, and the French Evangelical Society, have penetrated, the gentle heart and the healing touch of the Christian physician have entered upon their sacred mission. The Rev. F. Coillard, with that enthusiasm which so often characterizes his writings, has expressed his desire for medical skill as a missionary agency among the Barotsi. He writes: " Oh, if I could but grow young again, how ardently I would apply myself to the study of medicine! And, thus furnished with the fullest possible equipment, medical and theological, with what joy I would go forth to relieve the physical and moral miseries of these poor heathen! They do not understand how it is that the messengers of Jesus, ' who healed all manner of disease,' cannot cure those of the body as well as those of the soul. A cure is in their eyes a proof of our apostleship. And can we blame them? "[1]

In almost every instance in the experience of medical missionaries in Africa, it was at first a fight with smallpox, but wherever the physician has gone he has carried with him treatment by vaccination. Again, it is a protest against the excruciating and perhaps even fatal torture of a helpless patient. Some exhibition of medical and surgical skill has finally conquered prejudice, the tidings have been carried in all directions, and from far and near the patients have come in throngs to seek the benefit of such mysterious healing. The medical missionary has thus become the representative of the new religion, with power to work wonders which to native eyes seem little less than miracles. As time goes on, the dispensary and hospital are introduced, and constitute a Mecca of healing towards which thousands make their pilgrimage.

In the neighboring Island of Madagascar much attention has been

of the cure of the body and of the soul are closely allied. The ' medicine-man' is credited not only with a knowledge of the simples and drugs which may avert or cure disease, but, owing to the superstitions of the people, he is also supposed to have a knowledge of the charms and *dawa* which will invoke the aid of the Deity or appease his wrath, and of the witchcraft and magic (*ulu*) by which success in war, immunity from danger, or a supply of rain may be obtained. As the skill of the European in medicine asserts its superiority over the crude methods of the medicine-man, so does he in proportion gain an influence in his teaching of the great truths of Christianity. . . . The medical missionary, moreover, gains an admission to the houses and homes of the natives, by virtue of his art, which would not be so readily accorded to another. He becomes their adviser and referee, and his counsels are substituted for the magic and witchcraft which retard development."—Quoted in *The Free Church of Scotland Monthly*, January, 1894, p. 16.

[1] Coillard, " On the Threshold of Central Africa," p. 583.

given to medical work, and also to the instruction of native physicians, by the London Missionary Society, the English Friends, and the Norwegian Missionary Society, as has been shown by the Medical Missionary Academy at Antananarivo, and the extensive hospitals at Antananarivo, Fianarantsoa, Antsirabe, and in the Sihanaka district. Some of these buildings have been requisitioned by the French, and it seems unlikely that they will be restored to their former owners and devoted again to their original purpose.

Other lands share in the benefits.

In the West Indies, Mexico, and the South American Continent, medical missions have been introduced to some extent. The degraded Indians of North and South America, whose methods of treating disease are shocking in their cruelty, have not been neglected. A journey of 1200 miles in canoes must be taken into the heart of Brazil, to reach one of these Indian outposts up the Tocantins River, where Dr. and Mrs. James A. Graham, both of whom are medical missionaries, have been sent by the Missionary Pence Association of Great Britain. Here and there in the Pacific Islands the same beneficent service has been rendered by the Wesleyan and London Missionary Societies and the American Board, which have been heralds of the Gospel in the South Seas.

The introduction of scientific medical knowledge, with its modern facilities, is an incident of surpassing interest in missionary achievement, and an event of benign import in the spiritual, social, and physical history of mankind. It is not sufficient to consider it abstractly and dwell upon its general significance; we must inspect it more closely in its practical outcome and its present varied activities. To this purpose the following section is devoted.

11. CONDUCTING DISPENSARIES, INFIRMARIES, AND HOSPITALS. —These institutions are important and necessary adjuncts to modern medical science. Its introduction calls for them, as art calls for its tools, or industry for its mechanical facilities and its "open door." It is not desirable to repeat in this section much that has been sufficiently dwelt upon in the preceding pages. Our object will be attained if we can give even glimpses of the real magnitude and splendid efficiency of these institutional plants, located at many points in mission fields, with here and there a reference to the men and women who serve them. To do justice to this theme would require an entire volume.

Dr. Elizabeth Reifsnyder (on the left), Miss McKechnie (now Mrs. Thomson), and their Assistants.

THE MARGARET WILLIAMSON HOSPITAL, SHANGHAI.

(W. U. M. S.)

An attempt to visit in person the widely scattered stations throughout the world, where the six hundred and eighty medical missionaries
at present in the field are located, would occupy
no small portion of a lifetime. We should have to
penetrate four hundred miles within the Arctic
Circle, in order to reach Point Barrow, on the
What it would involve
to shake hands
with the missionary
doctors of the world.
northern shores of Alaska, where only a yearly mail is delivered to Dr.
and Mrs. Marsh, home missionaries of the Northern Presbyterian
Church of America.[1]   Upon the journey thither, we must call at Sitka,
Ketchikan, Circle City, and Point Hope, where Presbyterian and, in
the last three stations, Protestant Episcopal medical missions are
planted.   We should have to traverse the wilds of the Canadian northland, and sail along the coast of Labrador, where, on behalf of the
Mission to Deep Sea Fishermen, Dr. Wilfred T. Grenfell and his
associates have established hospitals, and cruise from station to
station in their hospital ships, and where the Moravians also render
medical services to the people.[2]   Still due north of Labrador, off the
bleak shores of Cumberland Sound, is Blacklead Island, where Mr. C. G.
Sampson, associated with the Rev. E. J. Peck, of the Church Missionary Society, is " doctoring and visiting the people at all hours of the
day and night." [3]   Thence we must cross to Greenland, and touch at
some of the Moravian and Danish outposts, where missionaries minister
to the sick in the most northerly mission stations in the world.[4]   In
our long journey we should have to skirt the coasts of Africa and Asia,
and penetrate great waterways like the Nile, the Zambesi, the Congo,
the Niger, and the Yang-tse. We should be obliged to climb the
Himalayas, and even scale their heights to Srinagar and Leh, at
which latter outpost Dr. Ernest Shawe, of the Moravians, has lately
settled.   It would be necessary to land upon distant shores in the
deep calm of the tropics, and upon rocky islets in isolated groups of
the vast Pacific.[5] We should be compelled to round Cape Horn, and
journey among the Araucanians and the Chacos of the Argentine plains.
We should have to visit the Indies, West and East, not omitting the
Moravian stations on the coasts of Central and South America, and

---

[1] *The Church at Home and Abroad,* December, 1897, p. 451.

[2] Grenfell, " Vikings of To-day," pp. 44, 100, 207, 213, 214; *The Congregationalist,* March 4, 1897; *Periodical Accounts Relating to Moravian Missions,*
December, 1897, pp. 375–377.

[3] *The Church Missionary Gleaner,* January, 1899, p. 2.

[4] Upernivik, on the western coast, is in latitude 72° 48′ N.

[5] *Edinburgh Medical Missionary Society Quarterly Paper,* May, 1898, p. 276.

lonely outposts in the depths of the Continent.   Thus we should have to wander around the world in perpetual zigzags, often availing ourselves of the facilities of modern travel by railways and steamships, but sometimes in sailing vessels, small boats, or canoes, again on horseback, or riding on elephants, camels, mules, bullocks, or donkeys, in sledges, carts, jinrikishas, palanquins, hammocks, or wheelbarrows, and now and then on the shoulders of carriers, or, where all else failed us, plodding our own way over mountains and plains, across desert wastes, through pathless forests and tangled jungles, in endless variety.   He must be a good traveller and live many years who would compass this immense achievement.

An excursion through China alone for the inspection of medical missionary institutions would be no easy task.   They dot the coast provinces from Pakhoi to Moukden and Kalgan,

*An excursion through
China alone would
be no easy task.* on the north, extending still southward to Hoihow and Nodoa, in Hainan, and northward to Kirin and Kwanchengtzu, in Manchuria.   They are in the far interior, westward of Hankow and Wuchang, beyond Chungking and Suifu, at Tungchuan, Chautung, Kiating, Chentu, and Lanchau. Within this circle of outposts we may visit one hundred and fifty cities, towns, or villages where the good ministry goes on with its unceasing activities.   It would be interesting to speak of this work in detail, but quite impossible with our present limitations.   We can call only here and there for a glimpse at some typical plants which may be considered as representative of all.

Moukden, in Manchuria, is a station of the United Presbyterian Church of Scotland, with a hospital and dispensary for men, and the same provision for women, where the sum total of

*A call at Moukden and
Canton.* treatments given annually to patients, according to a recent report, was 31,703.[1]   At Canton we find the American Presbyterians (North), the American Board, and the United Brethren in Christ conducting medical work, in connection with which 70,500 annual treatments are

---

[1] In the record of hospital statistics the distinction between individual patients and the number of treatments should not be ignored.   In most instances the returns of medical work, as recorded in the published reports, give the number of separate treatments rather than the number of individual patients, some of whom may be treated several times during the course of the year, and each visit counted as a treatment.   In some cases, on the other hand, only the number of actual patients is given, without counting their return visits for repeated treatment.   In certain instances it is not clear whether patients or treatments are intended in the returns. A careful comparison of data where both the patients and the treatments are given

recorded in the latest available reports. Dr. Hager's itinerating dispensary and Dr. A. A. Fulton's medical boat are included in the above summary, as also the work on the Island of Honam, in charge of the Woman's Missionary Association of the United Brethren in Christ. Dr. John G. Kerr, a veteran in the medical missionary ranks of China, has served in the Canton Hospital for forty-five years. His record of operations in lithotomy is said to exceed that of any other living surgeon.[1] The total of cases treated in that hospital and its dispensaries during this period is 1,156,965. The rapid increase in number is apparent from the fact that fully one half of the above have been received within the last ten years. The Canton Hospital is owned and supported by the Medical Mission Society in China, and in its medical and surgical requirements is served by missionaries of the American Presbyterian Church. Its number of treatments during the year 1897 (41,354) is the largest of any missionary hospital in China.

At Shanghai, an important centre, there are four hospitals and several dispensaries, representing the Woman's Union Missionary Society, the American Protestant Episcopal Church, and the Seventh-day Baptists, with a total, according to late reports, of 61,662 yearly treatments. A large hospital located on the grounds of the London Missionary Society, and served spiritually by L. M. S. missionaries, is not controlled by that society, so its returns

A visit to Shanghai, Swatow, Foochow, Amoy, and a thousand miles westward to Chungking.

indicates that the number of patients multiplied by three will fairly represent the average number of treatments, and, *vice versa*, that the number of treatments divided by three will give the number of individual patients. In the statistics given in this section concerning the work of different hospitals and dispensaries, the returns recorded, unless expressly stated to signify patients, indicate the number of separate treatments annually, which may be considered as averaging in a few instances two, but usually three, times the number of individual patients. Some accepted system of recording medical statistics, used in common by all societies, is greatly needed, in order to save confusion and insure accuracy. Nothing in the published returns has fallen under the author's eye more complete and admirable than the tables given in the " Report on Foreign Missions of the United Presbyterian Church of Scotland, 1898," p. 67, a copy of which is here appended.

STATIONS.	DISPENSARIES.					SURGICAL OPERATIONS.					IN-PATIENTS.			VISITS.
	Male.		Female.		Total.	On Males.		On Females.		Total.	Male.	Female.	Total.	Number.
	New Cases.	Old Cases.	New Cases.	Old Cases.		Major.	Minor.	Major.	Minor.					

[1] *The Church at Home and Abroad,* November, 1898, p. 390.

are not included in this aggregate of yearly treatments. A word of explanation seems to be required concerning the peculiar status of this fine institution. It is supported by the foreign community of Shanghai, and served by foreign resident practitioners not identified with any missionary agency, although its spiritual interests, as stated before, are in the care of missionaries of the London Society. It cannot, therefore, be wholly classed as a missionary institution, but it is a pleasure to emphasize its usefulness and call attention to its immense activities. According to a recent report it registered 92,513 annual treatments of out-patients, and also a list of 1127 in-patients. At the Margaret Williamson Hospital, of the Woman's Union Missionary Society, also at Shanghai, we shall find Dr. Elizabeth Reifsnyder and her associate, Dr. Emma Garner. The former has been in charge of the hospital since its establishment in 1884, and during these years has received over 200,000 individual patients, many of whom have returned for repeated treatments. The daily average of those to whom she and Dr. Garner minister in hospital and dispensary is over one hundred, coming from many cities and villages. Dr. Reifsnyder's skill in surgical cases has been a great boon to her patients. Some tumors have been removed by her which are thought to be larger than those of any other successful operations recorded in the practice of surgery.[1] Special care is taken to supplement these medical services by religious teaching. The hospital is visited regularly by Miss Mary J. Irvine, and two native evangelists also aid, chiefly in the dispensary. It is interesting to learn that about half the support of the hospital is received from the Chinese themselves.

More than a thousand miles in the interior, almost due west of Shanghai, is Chungking, where the American Methodists, the English Friends, and the London Missionary Society have a record in their hospitals and dispensaries, according to recent reports, of 50,118 annual treatments. It may be noted that this is about one hundred and fifty a day throughout the year. There are many other places which seem to demand a word of description and comment. The English Presbyterians receive in their hospital at Swatow, under the care of Drs. Alexander Lyall and John M. Dalziel, over 2500 *in-patients* annually, the largest number of this class of patients cared for at any single missionary institution in foreign mission fields. The Women's Missionary Association of the same Church is about to increase the plant by opening a Woman's Hospital. At Foochow the American Methodists, through their Woman's Society, conduct two

[1] " The China Mission Hand-Book " (first issue, 1896), p. 266.

Exterior and Interior Views.

The S. Wells Williams Pavilion of Margaret Williamson Hospital, Shanghai.
(W. U. M. S.)

hospitals and three dispensaries exclusively for women, where 18,794 treatments were given last year. At Amoy the new building of " Hope Hospital," of the Reformed Church in America, was opened April 27, 1898. During the first seven months since his recent return to Amoy, Dr. J. A. Otte, who is in charge of the hospital, has seen 6000 patients and performed 319 operations, none of the latter having been attended with fatal results. A joyous record is this, and so we could continue to follow a luminous pathway of healing ministry from city to city throughout the empire. The total of mission hospitals in China is 122, and the number of dispensaries is 242.[1]

1 The number is so large that only a partial record can be inserted here. The following list of important centres of medical work in China is restricted to stations reporting more than 15,000 annual treatments. More complete returns may be found in the "Centennial Survey of Foreign Missions."

STATION.	SOCIETY.		TREATMENTS.
Taiku	A. B. C. F. M.		15,249
Tungcho	A. B. C. F. M.		16,400
Chinanfu	P. B. F. M. N.		16,467
Chingchowfu	E. B. M. S.		16,692
Chinchow	P. C. I. M. S.		16,749
Chuwang	C. P. M.		16,759
Amoy	L. M. S.	6,553	16,837
	Ref. C. A.	10,284	
Chiningchow	P. B. F. M. N.		17,646
Chinchew	E. P. C. M.		17,802
Pakhoi	C. M. S.		18,146
Tungkun	R. M. S.		18,347
Ichowfu	P. B. F. M. N.		19,050
Hong Kong	L. M. S.		21,171
Hankow	W. M. S.	10,822	21,822
	L. M. S.	11,000	
Tsunhua	M. E. M. S.		22,487
Ningpo	C. M. S.	6,236	23,448
	A. B. M. U.	6,936	
	U. M. F. M. S.	10,276	
Kieng Ning	C. M. S.		23,818
Chefoo	C. I. M.		24,096
Paotingfu	A. B. C. F. M.	11,782	25,541
	P. B. F. M. N.	13,759	
Pang Chuang	A. B. C. F. M.		26,125
Chentu	C. M. M. S.	15,000	26,329
	M. E. M. S.	11,329	
	C. I. M.	(no returns)	
Swatow	A. B. M. U.	13,381	28,122
	E. P. C. M.	14,741	

The most prominent medical service in Japan has been under the auspices of the American Board, but it has now passed in large part into the care of the Japanese. The native Chris-

Medical results in Japan, Formosa, and Korea.

tians of the Kumiai churches have shown themselves ready to assume responsibility in this department. The hospital and dispensaries at Osaka and Kobe have been retained by the Board in charge of Dr. Wallace M. Taylor. At Akita, on the northwest coast of the main island, the Foreign Christian Missionary Society has medical work conducted by Dr. Nina A. Stevens. Mrs. Stevens seems to be the only woman physician, among the foreign missionaries, at present in charge of a dispensary in Japan. She reports 1750 patients treated annually, and two Japanese women pupils taking a course in practical medicine. The Protestant Episcopal Missionary Society is actively engaged at Tokyo and Osaka,

(Continued from p. 423.)

STATION.	SOCIETY.		TREATMENTS.
Soochow	P. B. F. M. S. P. B. F. M. N. M. E. S.	9,260 (new) 20,424	29,684
Moukden	U. P. C. S. M.		31,703
Chouping	E. B. M. S.		33,116
Wuchang	P. E. M. S. W. M. S. L. M. S.	20,370 7,510 6,000	33,880
Foochow	A. B. C. F. M. M. E. M. S.	21,695 18,794	40,489
Tientsin	M. E. M. S. L. M. S.	23,213 17,932	41,145
Nanking	M. E. M. S. F. C. M. S. A. F. B. F. M.	21,357 17,555 4,000	42,912
Hangchow	C. M. S.		43,097
Chungking	M. E. M. S. L. M. S. F. F. M. A.	38,259 6,859 5,000	50,118
Shanghai	W. U. M. S. P. E. M. S. S. D. B.	30,610 26,475 4,577	61,662
Canton	P. B. F. M. N. U. B. C. A. B. C. F. M.	49,354 19,896 1,250	70,500
Peking	L. M. S. P. B. F. M. N. M. E. M. S. A. B. C. F. M. S. P. G.	30,717 30,000 28,590 7,080 3,313	99,700

Operating Room of Hope Hospital.
Dr. J. A. Otte, and Assistants.

Buildings of Hope Hospital, and Woman's Annex.
(The funds for the Woman's Hospital were given in the Netherlands.)

THE HOPE HOSPITAL, AMOY, CHINA.

(Ref. C. A.)

with a sum total of 18,307 annual treatments. In some centres medical work which was originally established through foreign missionary effort has been placed under Japanese control, as, for example, the Doshisha Hospital, Dispensary, and Nurses' Training-school. In Formosa the Presbyterian Churches of England and Canada have planted medical facilities—the former at Tainanfu, the capital (formerly called Taiwanfu), where 11,113 patients are reported, and also at Chianghoa, where it is proposed to open a hospital. A hospital for women is also soon to be established at Tainanfu by the Women's Missionary Association of the English Presbyterians. The Canadian Presbyterian Church conducts the MacKay Hospital and Dispensary at Tamsui, reporting 6411 treatments, and at many places in the island dispensaries are opened at intervals by the missionaries of that Church and their native assistants.

In Korea the principal societies engaged in medical operations are the American Presbyterians (North and South), the American Methodists (North and South), and the Society for the Propagation of the Gospel. Hospitals or dispensaries are maintained at Seoul, Chemulpo, Fusan, Kunsan, Wonsan, Tagoo, Pyeng Yang, Chunju, Songdo, and Makpo. The total number of annual treatments reported from these stations is about fifty thousand.

In India medical agencies are found upon a scale of great magnitude, and yet if we attempt to estimate the necessities of that immense country, we soon realize how scattered and fragmentary, after all, is the service rendered, in proportion to the incalculable needs of that teeming population. It is not practicable to attempt to locate and describe in detail the 103 hospitals and 254 dispensaries which missions have planted in prominent centres of India. From Srinagar and Leh, in Kashmir, among the Himalayas, to the Island of Ceylon, at its southern extremity, the entire peninsula is dotted with medical stations. In the statistical tables in "Centennial Survey" detailed returns of these various hospitals and dispensaries will be given, so far as the author succeeds in obtaining them. The work of the Church Missionary Society at Amritsar, in the Punjab, in charge of Dr. Henry Martyn Clark and Dr. A. H. Browne, and that of the Church of England Zenana Missionary Society, in the same city, under the direction of Miss Hewlett and her associates, some of whom have received a medical training, represents the largest number in annual treatments reported from any single mission station of the world. The united returns of these two societies at Amritsar rose in 1897 to 157,893, but later reports give 116,997. The patients treated annually in all these hospitals and dispensaries reach a total of many hundred thousands, as may be inferred from the facts given below.[1]

The American Board has work in Ceylon, conducted on Jaffna Island, with a yearly list of 6286 treatments. The Woman's Auxiliary of the Wesleyan Mission has also four dispensaries in Ceylon, the chief one being at Batticaloa. Under the same direction is the Wiseman Hospital and Dispensary at Wellimada in Uva Province. The returns from these sources indicate 8347 annual treatments.

In Burma the American Baptists have six hospitals and eight dispensaries, but it has been difficult to obtain exact returns concerning them. The number of individual patients, so far as ascertained, is 24,042. It is not altogether clear, however, that some of these returns do not represent treatments rather than patients, and, if this is so, it would seem to be a fair estimate to reckon the total of treatments as about 50,000. In Northern Siam, among the Laos people, the American Presbyterian Board of Foreign Missions (North) supports four hospitals and six dispensaries, giving

Hospitals and dispensaries in Burma, Siam, Malaysia, and the Pacific Islands.

---

[1] In mentioning centres of medical work in India, owing to limitations of space, those only are given which report 15,000 or more annual treatments. They are as follows:

STATION.	SOCIETY.	TREATMENTS.
Sabathu	P. B. F. M. N.	15,000
Codacal	Ba. M. S.	15,020
Ahmednagar	A. B. C. F. M.	15,563
Allahabad	P. B. F. M. N.	15,887
Jammulamadugu	L. M. S.	16,212
Cherapoongee	W. C. M. M. S.	16,225
Krishnagar	C. E. Z. M. S.	16,905
Dindigul	A. B. C. F. M.	17,709
Lodiana	S. F. E. E.	18,371
Jhelum	U. P. C. N. A.	18,613
Bilaspur	C. W. B. M.	20,075
Bareilly	M. E. M. S.	20,325
Ferozepur	P. B. F. M. N.	20,494
Indore	C. P. M.	21,841
Quetta	{ C. M. S. 12,107 / C. E. Z. M. S. 10,675 }	22,782
Batala	C. E. Z. M. S.	24,003
Lahore	P. B. F. M. N.	24,960
Calicut	Ba. M. S.	25,750
Kalimpong	C. S. M.	26,077
Agra	E. M. M. S.	26,117
Nasirabad	U. P. C. S. M.	26,561

Nursing Staff of Kaiserswerth Deaconesses.

The Hospital Building.

(Medical faculty of Syrian Protestant College in attendance as physicians and surgeons.)

THE JOHANNITER HOSPITAL, BEIRUT, SYRIA.

nearly 22,000 annual treatments. In Lower Siam, under the same Board, are a hospital and three dispensaries, with a total of yearly treatments reaching 4500. In Malaysia the American Methodist Episcopal Mission has medical agencies in Singapore and Penang, and the Netherlands Missionary Society has a large hospital and dispensary at Modjo-Warno, in Java, where 26,624 yearly treatments are reported. Among the Pacific Islands there is a new medical service at Ambrym, in the New Hebrides, where a hospital and dispensary, under the care of Dr. Lamb, have been recently opened by the New Hebrides Mission. Among the Samoan Islands the London Missionary Society conducted an important dispensary on Savaii for many years, until, in 1895, Dr. Davies retired. Since that date the author can find no record of its continuance. The International Medical Missionary and Benevolent Association has its medical agents, and maintains a sanitarium at Apia. This society has also established similar work at Rarotonga, and has another sanitarium at Honolulu.

In the Moslem countries of Western Asia—Arabia, Persia, Turkey, Syria, and Palestine—medical missions are conducted with vigor, and occupy a very important and strategic position in missionary operations. In Arabia the Reformed Church of America has dispensaries at

(Continued from p. 426.)

STATION.	SOCIETY.		TREATMENTS.
Neemuch	C. P. M.		27,671
Nagpur	F. C. S.		28,694
Delhi	E. B. M. S.	16,794	29,205
	C. M. D.	12,411	
Thana	F. C. S.		30,178
Ranipettai	Ref. C. A.		30,667
Sialkot	C. S. M.	20,641	33,209
	U. P. C. N. A.	12,568	
Ranaghat	R. M. M.		35,589
Tank	C. M. S.		38,527
Lucknow	Z. B. M. M.		38,607
Srinagar	C. M. S.		40,079
Jodhpore	U. P. C. S. M.		41,511
Nazareth	S. P. G.		45,260
Madura	A. B. C. F. M.		48,670
Bannu	C. M. S.		52,167
Udaipur	U. P. C. S. M.		55,331
Neyoor and Branch Dispensaries	L. M. S.		61,763
Dera Ghazi Khan	C. M. S.		62,963
Ajmere	U. P. C. S. M.		83,622
Amritsar	C. M. S.	74,682	116,997
	C. E. Z. M. S.	42,315	

Busrah and Bahrein.   The Free Church of Scotland has a hospital and dispensary at Sheikh Othman, near Aden, where, according to a late annual report, 14,308 treatments were recorded. In Persia the American Presbyterians (North) and the Church Missionary Society have effective medical agencies.   The Archbishop's Mission fails to specify any medical work since the retirement of its missionary physician in 1897.   At Julfa the Church Missionary Society hospital and dispensary report 21,893 treatments, with also a separate dispensary for women and children, giving 11,569 additional treatments.   The Westminster Hospital, and the Howard Annex for Women, at Urumiah, in charge of the Presbyterian missionaries, are important institutions, the treatments numbering 11,230.   The Ferry Hospital, and two dispensaries, at Teheran, report 16,936, and the Whipple Hospital and Dispensary for women, and the dispensary for men, at Tabriz, 11,556 as their annual quota, while at Hamadan, under the same society, the missionary physicians give 12,356 as the number representing their yearly visits.

The fame of the missionary doctor in Arabia, Persia, and Asia Minor.

In Asiatic Turkey the medical service of the American Board, conducted at Cesarea, Marsovan, Mardin, Harpoot, and Van, amounts to an annual total of 17,499 treatments.   The Azariah Smith Hospital at Aintab, under the care of the Central Turkey College, with Dr. Shepard in charge, reported last year over 4000 patients, with 20,964 separate visits for treatment.   Dr. Caroline F. Hamilton and Miss Trowbridge devote themselves to the women's department.   The Church Missionary Society has work at Baghdad, and the Jewish Mission Committee of the Church of Scotland conducts the Beaconsfield Memorial Hospital and Dispensary at Smyrna, now (1899) about to be considerably enlarged by a new building, and by the addition of a training-class for nurses.   The Friends' Medical Mission among the Armenians, the Free Church of Scotland, and the Kaiserswerth Deaconesses are represented in Constantinople by hospitals and dispensaries.

In Syria medical work is scattered over a large area, and is under the direction of various missions.   The Johanniter Hospital and Dispensary at Beirut are supported by the Knights of the Order of St. John of Berlin.   They are in charge of the excellent Kaiserswerth Deaconesses, and served by the able Medical Faculty of the Syrian Protestant College.   Dr. George E. Post, the senior member of the medical staff, has labored here for many years, with professional skill and great usefulness.   His colleagues, Drs. Graham, Adams, Webster, and Moore, are men of high qualifications both as instructors and as prac-

A fine medical service in Syria and Palestine.

A Corner of the Children's Ward.

Students and Patients at the Clinic.

The Operating Room. Dr. Post seated by Patient.

SCENES AT THE JOHANNITER HOSPITAL, BEIRUT, SYRIA.

titioners. Returns for 1898 give the number of patients during the year as 12,360. An itinerating dispensary is maintained by Dr. Mary Pierson Eddy, of the Presbyterian Mission, who in her latest annual report stated that 51 places had been visited, where a total of 7070 treatments were given. The patients came from 216 different villages in Mount Lebanon and Syria. At Tripoli Dr. Harris reports 7082 patients, with a list of 524 surgical cases. The Reformed Presbyterian Church of the United States conducts a hospital and dispensary at Latakia, in which over 8000 treatments were given in 1898. They have medical work also in Larnaca, Cyprus. The Reformed Presbyterians of Scotland are occupying Antioch, and the English Presbyterians are at Aleppo. The British Syrian Mission has medical work at Tyre and Baalbec. The Free Church of Scotland, through its efficient physician, Dr. William Carslaw, administers a dispensary at Shweir. The Edinburgh Medical Missionary Society has stationed Drs. F. I. Mackinnon and Brigstocke at Damascus, where 10,000 treatments are reported in connection with the new building for the Victoria Hospital and Dispensary. In the same city Dr. Masterman, of the London Society for the Jews, according to late returns, attended to 7092 cases. The Friends' Foreign Missionary Association has a well-appointed hospital and dispensary at Brummana, under the care of Drs. B. J. and A. J. Manasseh, with 6309 patients, according to a recent report. The Palestine and Lebanon Nurses' Mission has a cottage hospital and dispensary at Baakleen. Medical work as a matter of private benevolence is also conducted at several places.

In Palestine quite a field of operations for medical missions is found. The London Society for the Jews has a large hospital and dispensary at Jerusalem, which in 1896 recorded 33,722 treatments, and has also stations at Hebron and Safed, where more than 20,000 prescriptions are furnished yearly. The Kaiserswerth Deaconesses have a hospital and dispensary in Jerusalem, with 5500 treatments. The Order of St. John of Jerusalem, an English organization, maintains the British Ophthalmic Hospital, under the direction of Dr. Cant, where skilful ministrations are given to many patients suffering from painful diseases of the eye. The Church Missionary Society is at Acre, Nablus, Gaza, Kerak, and Salt, and the sum total of visits reported at these stations is 55,063. The Free Church of Scotland is at Safed and Tiberias, where its physicians during the year 1897 attended to 31,310 calls. The Mildmay Mission reports from Hebron 9064 treatments. The list of visits at the Jaffa Medical Mission, according to recent returns, is 10,256. The Edinburgh Medical Missionary Society has work at Nazareth, with a record of 8000 treatments annually, and the American Friends at Ramallah have some 5000 callers at their dispensary.

Turning now to Africa, we find along the Mediterranean coast the North African Mission, with medical stations at Fez, Casablanca, Tangier, Tetuan, Tripoli, and Sousse, representing The medical invasion of a total of 28,665 annual treatments. The Mildmay Africa. Mission is at Tangier, and reports 2008 visits. The Southern and also the Central Morocco Missions have gone still further into the interior of this fanatical kingdom with their medical forces. The Church Missionary Society conducts a good service at Cairo. It is ready to enter Khartum, but as yet has not received the Sirdar's permission to establish a medical mission except at Fashoda and vicinity. On the West Coast its stations are at Abeokuta, Ibadan, Obusi, and Onitsha, and a recent entrance has been made into Hausaland. On the East Coast it has either its hospitals or dispensaries at Mombasa, Mpwapwa, Rabai, Jilore, Kisokwe, Luba's, and Mengo. At the latter place the *first hospital* in Uganda was opened nineteen centuries after Christ, with a service of dedication, on May 31, 1897. Without undertaking to give more specialized data, it is sufficient to say that the efforts of the Church Missionary Society in these various stations represent a sum total of 100,000 treatments annually.

The medical services of the numerous societies engaged in missionary operations in Africa are far too extensive to mention in further detail. Almost every section of the Continent where there is foreign occupation shares in the advantages of these benevolent efforts. The mere enumeration of the principal societies having medical agencies, in addition to those already mentioned, gives an impressive idea of the magnitude of this enterprise.[1] In Egypt are the United Presbyterians of America and the Kaiserswerth Deaconesses; in Sierra Leone the United Brethren in Christ; in Liberia the American Protestant Episcopal Mission, and the Lutheran General Synod (American). On the Gold Coast are the Basel missionaries, on the Slave Coast their North German brethren, and in Old Calabar the United Presbyterians of Scotland. The Qua Iboe Mission is on the river of the same name, just west of Old Calabar. Within the French possessions north of the Congo is the Gaboon and Corisco Mission of the American Presbyterians. The Congo Free State is occupied by the American and English Baptists, the Southern Presbyterians of the United States, the Congo Balolo, and the Swedish Missions, and in Angola is the American

---

[1] Cf. Noble, "The Redemption of Africa," pp. 551–561, for an interesting résumé of medical missions in Africa.

Medical Staff and Students, Tungkun Hospital.

Village of Tungkun (near Canton).

Hospital Buildings, Tungkun.

MEDICAL WORK OF THE RHENISH MISSION IN SOUTH CHINA.

Board.   All these missions give more or less attention to medical agencies.   In the eastern section of the Continent, there are Swedish missionaries in Abyssinia, and in German territory is the Evangelical Missionary Society of German East Africa.   On the borders of Lake Tanganyika are stations of the London Mission.   In Zanzibar and Pemba, and from thence in a southwesterly direction to British Central Africa, is the Universities' Mission, which, around Lake Nyassa and Lake Shiré, unites with the Free Church of Scotland and the Church of Scotland in the occupation of British Central Africa.   In this vicinity is the Zambesi Industrial Mission, to which Sir Brampton Gurdon has presented two fully equipped hospitals, as an expression of his appreciation of the value of the service it is rendering to that part of Africa. The American Methodist Episcopal Mission has opened a station at Inhambane, in Portuguese East Africa.   The Evangelical Missionary Society of Paris has just sent a medical man with Pastor F. Coillard on his return to labor among the Barotsi.   We find also the United Presbyterians of Scotland, the Free Church of Scotland, the American Board, the Society for the Propagation of the Gospel, the South African General Mission, and the Swiss Romande Mission in the Transvaal, all engaged at the southern extremity of the Continent. Medical agencies are found in each of these different and widely separated missions.

An event of importance in the medical missionary expansion of South Africa was the opening, July 15, 1898, of the Victoria Hospital at Lovedale.   This beautiful building, costing £4000, is virtually a gift to the Foreign Missions *The new Victoria Hos-* Committee of the Free Church of Scotland by *pital at Lovedale.* British donors, aided by local subscribers and the Government of Cape Colony.   Mr. David A. Hunter, an honorary missionary, has been active in securing the large share given by British contributors.   The hospital is also to provide the facilities for training native women as nurses, and young men in ambulance service.   The institution has been put in charge of Dr. M'Cash, of Glasgow, and Miss Wallace, a nurse from Guy's Hospital, London, both self-supporting missionaries, and highly qualified for service in their respective departments.   Sir Gordon Sprigg, Prime Minister of the Colony, officiated at the opening ceremonies, in a spirit of hearty and sympathetic appreciation of the missionary work at Lovedale.[1]

In the Island of Madagascar the London and Norwegian Societies and the English Friends have established superior medical facilities at

[1] *The Christian Express*, August, 1898, pp. 113, 117; *The Free Church of Scotland Monthly*, October, 1898, p. 246.

considerable expense. Before the recent military campaign by the French, seven hospitals and ten dispensaries were in service, in which, according to a conservative estimate, some 40,000 annual treatments were given. Unhappily, the fine hospital at Antananarivo was requisitioned by the French authorities in 1895, also the one at Isoavinandriano was taken, and that at Antsirabe was destroyed by fire in 1896. Eight new dispensaries have, however, been recently opened, concerning which only very imperfect statistics have as yet been received. On the South American Continent and in Mexico this department of effort has received the attention which the societies endeavoring to meet the needs of these vast fields have been able to give. The South American Missionary Society among the Araucanian and Chaco Indians, the South American Evangelical Mission in Uruguay, the Moravians in Surinam, the Methodist Episcopal Mission in Mexico, and that of the Seventh-day Adventists, are the chief factors in the fields of the Western Hemisphere. In the hospital and dispensary of the Methodist Society at Guanajuato, and in the two dispensaries at Romita and Silao, an aggregate of 7221 treatments is reported in its last annual statement.

A word about Madagascar and the Western Hemisphere.

The reader who has pondered these impressive statistics cannot fail to discover that they represent services of incalculable value to the world. All attempt to emphasize or enlarge upon this point will be in vain in the case of one who, learning these facts, has not already recognized their significance. The world would be bereft indeed of an immeasurable consolation if medical missions should cease to minister to its sufferings.

These efforts for the relief of distress have wonderfully quickened the spirit of compassion in mission lands among all classes of people, and have inclined them to treat the sick and infirm with more kindly consideration. In place of the neglect and harshness so often exhibited towards the helpless in heathen communities, a disposition to minister to them in tenderness has been awakened. Restoration to health has been sought for those who heretofore would have been left to be the victims of disease. The beneficent results of thus developing the spirit of kindliness in callous hearts are revealed in the brighter outlook for thousands of sufferers who are now helped in their misery rather than doomed by their misfortunes. From the West Coast of Africa, Dr. R. H. Nassau writes: " Neglect of the sick is very much modified. Formerly even the relatives of the insane or

Some beneficent results in native society.

of those afflicted with chronic illness would fling them into the river or sea. I hear no more of such actions, and I am sure the change is not caused by fear of the Government." From Rangoon, Burma, the Rev. Dr. J. N. Cushing speaks especially of the more sympathetic treatment of the poor and sick brought about by the influence of missions. "It is nowhere more conspicuous," he writes, "than in the case of epidemics or contagious diseases, like the smallpox, among the mountain peoples. In the olden times, when maladies of that kind broke out, those attacked were conveyed to solitary places in the jungle, and abandoned. This is much rarer now than formerly, and seems to me to be due greatly to the better ideas that Christianity has planted in the communities on the mountains." The Rev. Robert Evans writes from the neighboring country of Assam of the blessings that missions have brought to those smitten with disease, in teaching the people how to care for them and save them from the results of neglect. Native churches in different fields have arranged to care for the sick and needy, and have organized special funds for that purpose. The training of nurses, especially in Japan and India, has provided an intelligent ministry at the bedside of the suffering, where hitherto hopeless incompetency and perilous ignorance held sway. The example of missionaries in ignoring all distinctions of caste or sect or rank in the hour of helplessness and distress has taught a lesson of humanity where it has been greatly needed. Could we stand by the sufferers in many lands, and ask them to tell us of the blessings which missions have brought to them in the hour of illness, we should hear a mighty volume of testimony, the sincerity and truthfulness of which it would be impossible to doubt.

12. FOUNDING LEPER ASYLUMS AND COLONIES.—"The lepers are cleansed," was a sign in Christ's day (Matt. xi. 5), and the spiritual healing and kindly care of these smitten ones are characteristic of the ministry of Christianity in modern missions.[1] The estimate of their total number in the world, given by Miss Kate Marsden, as reaching 1,300,000, is probably below the true figure. Leprosy is made a type of sin in the Old Testament, representing both its un-

The Leprosy Conference of 1897, at Berlin, and its conclusions.

---

[1] The following sources of information are available: Bailey, "A Glimpse at the Indian Mission Field and Leper Asylums in 1886–87," and "The Lepers of Our Indian Empire: A Visit to Them in 1890–91"; Carson, "The Story of the Mission to Lepers in India"; Annual Reports of the Mission to Lepers in India and the East; *Without the Camp*, the attractive quarterly organ of the same Mission;

cleanness and its destructive power.   In recent times some new light has been thrown upon its mysterious genesis and the processes of its resistless development when once established in the system.   The Leprosy Conference held at Berlin in October, 1897, states as its conclusions that the disease is communicated by a bacillus which enters the organism probably through the mouth or the mucous membrane, and that it attacks only mankind.   It is pronounced contagious but not hereditary, and as hitherto not yielding to remedies.   The above statement as to its contagiousness should not, however, be understood as implying that it is infectious in the common sense of that word, nor even that it is contagious simply through touch or ordinary contact, but rather as pointing to the fact that the reception of the bacilli by means of some kind of inoculation, as through a wound or otherwise, or their entrance into the system by the mucous membrane, is the usual way of contracting it.   This limitation is required if we are to be guided by the experience of multitudes of workers and attendants who come into constant touch with lepers in homes and asylums for long periods of time, often dressing the wounds day after day, and yet escape all contagion.   The fact that leprosy is not hereditary seems to be well supported, as the children of lepers, if smitten, receive the contagion, to all appearances, through intimate contact with their parents, and not through the channel of physical heredity.   If segregated or reared apart from their parents they give no sign of the disease.   The effort to establish homes for the untainted children of lepers is therefore a charity which is in the highest degree useful and encouraging.[1]

An elect work, in every way admirable, for those afflicted with leprosy, has been established under the auspices of the Mission to Lepers in India and the East, having its office in Edinburgh, and in whose behalf Mr. Wellesley C. Bailey, the founder and efficient Secretary and Superintendent, has long labored with assiduous devotion.[2]   Mr. Bailey, who was originally connected with the Mission

Founding of the Mission to Lepers in India and the East.

Marsden, " On Sledge and Horseback to the Outcast Siberian Lepers "; " Report of the Leprosy Commission in India, 1890–91 "; " Report of the Third Decennial Missionary Conference Held at Bombay, 1892–93," vol. i., pp. 96–119; *Church of Scotland Home and Foreign Mission Record,* October, 1895, June, 1896, September, 1897; *The Missionary Review of the World,* May, 1897, pp. 345–349, and May, 1898, pp. 330–337; Hodder, " Conquests of the Cross," vol. iii., pp. 499–510.

[1] *Without the Camp,* January, 1898, pp. 34, 35.

[2] Mission to Lepers in India and the East (founded 1874), Wellesley C. Bailey, Esq., Secretary and Superintendent, 17 Greenhill Place, Edinburgh. While the Mission aims to minister to the physical needs, it gives special atten-

A Group of Patients at the Sabathu Asylum.
(P. B. F. M. N.)

TYPICAL CASES OF LEPROSY IN INDIA.

of the American Presbyterian Church in the Punjab, as early as 1869 had his attention especially drawn to the condition of lepers at the Ambala asylum of that mission. A hearty interest in the victims of the dreadful malady was at once aroused in his mind, and he soon found himself conscious of a clear call of Providence to a direct service on their behalf, a duty which he has discharged with enthusiasm and success. He labored in Ambala for a time, and in 1874 visited Great Britain, where he awakened the desire among Christian friends to organize a special work for this neglected class. A society was formed, which has been generously supported from the outset. It has grown and flourished and wrought, until it occupies at the present time a unique position of usefulness among the beneficent forces of missions.

Its plan of operations is independent, and at the same time coöperative. It has its own institutions, and also aids other missions in their work for lepers. Prominent missionary societies, to the number of eighteen, in various Eastern fields, are in alliance with it in its chosen sphere of effort. Its field was originally confined to India, but has now been extended to include Burma, Ceylon, China, and Japan. Its stations in India, Burma, and Ceylon number forty-two, in China six, and in Japan two, making a total of fifty. In these countries twenty asylums or hospitals are owned by the Mission itself, although other societies share in the expense and labor of conducting them. In addition, there are eleven institutions for lepers owned by various societies, towards the support of which the Mission to Lepers contributes. Under its auspices in some instances, and in others under the direction of missionary societies, fourteen homes for the untainted children of lepers have been established. There are also places where provision for the care of lepers has been made either by the Government or through private benevolence, in which opportunity has been given to agents of this and other missionary societies to impart Christian instruction, an aim which is specially prominent not only in the conduct of this Mission, but in the work of all societies, as is apparent from the large proportion of Christians in leper institutions. The total number of inmates in the institutions of the Mission to Lepers, including adults and children, as reported in *Without the Camp*, January, 1899, is about 1500, and those in institutions aided by it equal about 1800, making a total of 3300 who share in the benefits of its ministry. Of this number 1466 are Christians, of whom 492 were baptized in 1897.

Its extensive and admirable work.

tion to "the maintenance of Christian instruction and worship" wherever its operations extend.

The Mission to Lepers in India and the East, although occupying at present the place of honor, does not by any means represent the first or the only efforts for these afflicted ones.

Earlier efforts on behalf of lepers.

Dr. Carey in 1812 witnessed the burning of a leper, and was so impressed by the need of some interposition on behalf of this class of sufferers that he established probably the first leper hospital in India. It was located at Calcutta.[1] The Moravians as early as 1822 were at work among the lepers in South Africa, especially in connection with a government asylum founded in 1818, which was afterwards enlarged, and in 1846 was removed to Robben Island, not far from Capetown. This service of the Moravians ceased upon the appointment of a chaplain of the Church of England in 1867. In Dutch Guiana they are also laboring among the lepers segregated in a government colony at Groot Chatillon. They have, moreover, a beautiful Home for Lepers in Jerusalem.[2] Many prominent agencies, such as the Church Missionary Society, the London Missionary Society, the Church of Scotland, the Free Church of Scotland, the United Presbyterian Church of Scotland, the Friends' Foreign Missionary Society, the Wesleyan Missionary Society, the Basel and the Gossner Missions, the American Presbyterian, Baptist, Methodist, and Congregational Churches, and others, also share in this good work.

A visit to these various homes, asylums, colonies, and hospitals, we venture to say, would be one of the most quickening and cheering missionary lessons which could be given to Christian people. On the other hand, an inspection of the dreadful condition of those helpless and neglected outcasts who are still unreached in their isolation, herded together in hovels, where no charitable hand is extended to aid them, and left to perish by a living death, would powerfully impress the humane feelings of every visitor. The benign nature of the work done on their behalf by missions would be all the more strikingly revealed in contrast with their desperate misery when left to rot away in their filthy huts.

India, including the Native States and dependencies, contains, according to the census of 1891, 119,044 lepers.[3] This number, however, is considered by those well informed on the subject as much lower than the facts would justify. The officials of the Mission to Lepers regard 500,000 as not too high an estimate. They state as the

---

[1] Smith, " The Life of William Carey," p. 256.
[2] La Trobe, " Work among Lepers by the Moravian Church."
[3] " Report of the Leprosy Commission in India, 1890-91," p. 182.

Patients at Meal-time.

Calisthenics by Women Patients.

The Children's Room.
(These little ones, it is hoped, are untainted.)

The Home—Exterior View.

The Moravian Home for Lepers, Jerusalem.
"Jesus Hilfe."

result of their investigations that there are 600,000 more in China and 200,000 in Japan, and if we add those found elsewhere in the world, an estimate of 2,000,000 of these unfortunates would not seem excessive. We may visit in India many scenes of acute misery among the lepers, but at the same time we should find there the most extensive efforts for the mitigation of their miseries. When Lord Lawrence was Viceroy he found occasion to insist upon these three precepts in his government of the Punjab: "Thou shalt not burn thy widow; thou shalt not kill thy daughters; thou shalt not bury thy lepers."[1] The British Government has provided large asylums in some of the prominent centres, as Bombay, Calcutta, Madras, Saharanpur, Srinagar, Trivandrum, Rawal Pindi, Colombo, and elsewhere. In these institutions full opportunity is given to various missionary societies to labor for the spiritual welfare and comfort of the inmates. Asylums controlled and supported by Christian agencies are scattered throughout India, "from the Himalayas to Cape Comorin."

An important service in India.

The Gossner Mission at Purulia conducts the largest work for lepers in British India, the buildings being owned by the Mission to Lepers, which also contributes liberally towards its support. The asylum and colony combined, under the supervision of the Rev. H. Uffmann, contain 545 inmates, nearly all of whom are Christians. Mr. T. A. Bailey, of Poona, a brother of the Secretary of the Mission to Lepers, who, in 1897, paid a visit to Purulia in the interests of the society, reports a never-to-be-forgotten scene which he witnessed, when 61 of the lepers were baptized one Sabbath morning.[2] The Gossner Mission has also opened another asylum at Chandkuri, with 65 inmates, and the Mission to Lepers is about to erect for them a new building. At Tarn Taran, in the Punjab, the Church Missionary Society, through its devoted agent, the Rev. E. Guilford, has ministered spiritually since 1882 in the municipal asylum, containing 186 inmates, of whom 51 are Christians. The little congregation of lepers increased, until a church building became a necessity, and one was erected for their special use. At Dehra the MacLaren Asylum, a government institution aided by the Mission to Lepers, is in charge of a superintendent who is interested in the religious welfare of its inmates. The Rev. J. F. Ullman, a Presbyterian missionary, had the spiritual super-

The largest leper asylum in British India.

---

[1] Smith, "The Life of William Carey," p. 257.
[2] *Without the Camp*, April, 1898, p. 46.

vision of the asylum until his death in 1896.   Out of 135 lepers within its doors, 55 are Christians.

One of the oldest asylums in India is that at Almora, conducted since 1849 by the London Missionary Society, and the scene for forty years of the loving labors of the Rev. J. H. Budden.   It has 122 inmates, of whom 109 are Christians.   Provision for lepers at Almora had been made as early as 1840, through the efforts of Sir Henry Ramsay, of the Indian Civil Service, but in 1849 the undertaking was committed to the care of the London Missionary Society.   It is estimated that more than 400 inmates have become Christians during their stay in this asylum.   At Chandag an interesting work is conducted by the American Methodist Episcopal Mission.   The buildings are provided by the Mission to Lepers, and many of the eighty-one inmates are Christians.   Within ten miles of its location there are 500 lepers, who, as far as possible, are ministered to by Miss Mary Reed, the missionary in charge.   At Sabathu the American Presbyterians have another institution, with 81 inmates, 39 of whom are Christians.   A ward for Europeans was added to this asylum in 1896.   At Ambala the same society has conducted a work since 1855, in the establishment and financial support of which General Sir Hope Grant took an influential part, when, as a colonel, he was stationed there in that year.   At present there are 23 inmates, every one of whom is a Christian.   Lady physicians have had charge of the asylum for some years, and it is now directed by Dr. Jessica Carleton. The American Methodists maintain work of much interest at Asansol, with 72 under their care, 30 of whom are Christians.   At Patpara, Mandla, the Missionary Pence Association of England, under the auspices of the Church Missionary Society, purposes to erect the Victoria Leper Asylum at an early date, through the proceeds of its million-farthing fund.   The list of institutions is too long to enumerate in full.[1]   It is difficult to distinguish always with precision the share in

---

[1] The following are in addition to those mentioned above, and give the statistics of some other stations where there is work for lepers.   In almost every instance financial aid is provided by the Mission to Lepers.   Still other stations might be mentioned, but full details concerning them will be found in the " Centennial Survey."

STATIONS.	SOCIETY.	INMATES.	CHRISTIANS.
Raniganj	W. M. S.	74	43
Bhagalpur	C. M. S.	67	13
Poladpore	M. L.	65	34
Allahabad	P. B. F. M. N.	48	7
Ellichpore	K. C. I. H. M.	48	5

these benevolent efforts assumed by the Mission to Lepers, but it is safe to say that in almost every case there is financial coöperation, and in many places the buildings are provided and owned by that society.

A beautiful feature of this ministry to leprous parents is the provision of homes for their untainted children, now made at many stations, in almost every instance wholly or in part supported by the Mission to Lepers. There is no doubt a predisposition in the offspring of lepers to contract the disease, yet, as before stated, it has been decided that it is not hereditary, and therefore if these children can be segregated and kept apart from their parents, there is reason to hope that they will wholly escape the dreaded peril. These homes, as the number of converted inmates indicates, are places of Christian nurture. At Purulia the Gossner Mission Home has 70 untainted children, all of whom are Christians, and in the following instances also every inmate is a Christian: Almora, 20; Trivandrum, 22; Tarn Taran, 16; Neyoor, 6; Raniganj, 5; and Asansol, 4. There are other asylums at Chandkuri, Poladpore, and Lohardugga, concerning which the returns in this particular are not so definite. The number of children thus sheltered in the homes of the Mission to Lepers is 205, and in institutions aided by it 81, making a total of 286.

A beautiful charity for untainted children of leprous parents.

Missionary work among lepers involves resolute sacrifice and genuine heroism. A brave heart, unshrinking hands, tireless patience, and readiness to risk all in this unselfish ministry, are essential in one who would undertake the service. A brief chapter from the life of a devoted worker is sufficient to make this clear. In North India, on the southern spurs of the Himalayas, is Chandag, the home of Miss Mary Reed, of the American Methodist Episcopal Mission. She is

Service on the heights, or the story of Mary Reed.

(Continued from p. 438.)

STATIONS.	SOCIETY.	INMATES.	CHRISTIANS.
Neyoor	L. M. S.	46	33
Baba Lakhan	U. P. C. N. A.	43	43
Roorkee	M. E. M. S.	36	28
Roha	M. L.	32	32
Patpara (Mandla)	C. M. S.	32	3
Calicut	Ba. M. S.	25	8
Allepie	C. M. S.	24	9
Hurda	F. C. M. S.	22	22
Lohardugga	G. M. S.	20	14
Dharmsala	C. M. S.	20	16
Wardha	F. C. S.	16	16
Chamba	C. M. S.	16	12

a missionary to lepers, and lives there among them on the slopes of those eternal hills, in pathetic yet cheerful isolation, happy in the joy of her Master's service. Her only companion in her modest home on Chandag Heights is a leper girl sharing her cottage. Within is every sign of taste and refinement, and an atmosphere of Christian love and consecration. Without are fragrant flowers scenting the mountain air, and scenes of lofty grandeur as the eye rests upon the snow-clad peaks. A few friends venture to visit her now and then, but the reality of her isolation appears in the guest-tent pitched without her home, and the separate table at which she eats her meals, so that there may be the least possible danger from contagion, for Miss Reed herself is a leper.[1] Close by we shall find the sphere of her labors in a large leper colony, of which she has the sole charge. The quarters for the women are near her home; those for the men are about a mile away down the mountain. The land which has been set apart for these purposes includes about one hundred acres, "the whole side of the mountain," and here she has the oversight of an asylum consisting of separate homes for special aspects and stages of the disease, a dispensary, a hospital, and a chapel, with the necessary quarters for caretakers and attendants. In all, 81 lepers are under her supervision, men, women, and

---

[1] Dr. Martha A. Sheldon, of the Methodist Mission in Bhot, spent the Christmas of 1896 with Miss Reed, and wrote an interesting account of her visit, which was published in the *Woman's Missionary Friend*, March, 1897, and also in *Without the Camp*, July, 1897. The following extract gives a glimpse of home life and heart experience on Chandag Heights: " In the evening we had dinner together; Miss Reed sitting at her little table with separate dishes, and I at another, eating chicken, curry and rice, and peaches from far-away America. We talked with many a ripple of laughter as we enjoyed our meal in the cozy little dining-room, where the wood fire burned cheerily. Then what an evening we had together! There were heart experiences to tell, difficulties of the work to recount, and travails of soul over wayward ones to relate. In the course of the conversation, I asked Mary, ' Do you think the disease is making any progress with you?' She said: ' I feel that it will never be any worse for others to bear than it is now, yet I am conscious of its presence within, especially during the last few months; but I feel the power of God upon me in holding me quiet. There are days, too, when the external symptoms are aggravated and more noticeable. Then again they recede. What I pass through in my experiences no one knows. The furnace is only heated a little hotter. What dross there must have been in my nature!' she added. 'No, Mary,' said I; ' it is all for the glory of God, and He has honored you in choosing you to suffer for Him and to show His keeping power. Not you only, but many, many are blessed with you.' But I feel deeply that so far as human help is concerned she is walking in the furnace *alone*, and that there is only One who can enter in and comfort her. Later, at the sweet-toned organ, the gift of kind friends in America, we sang several hymns, including the one beginning, ' Father, whate'er of earthly bliss Thy sovereign will denies,' and the Christmas one, ' Hark! the herald angels sing.' "

MARY REED.

Miss MARY REED, Missionary to Lepers.
(M. E. M. S.)
The Home of Miss Reed, Chandag Heights.

SERVICE ON THE HEIGHTS, CHANDAG, INDIA.

children. Of this number 64 are Christians. It is now her eighth year of happy toil in this scene of earthly suffering, where, with a prayerful heart and an unfaltering step, she is leading a company of Christ's chosen ones through great tribulation towards the heavenly gates. How it all came about is a strange and touching story.

Miss Reed was born in Ohio, in 1857, and in 1884 went to India as a missionary of the Woman's Foreign Missionary Society of the Methodist Episcopal Church, and entered upon zenana work at Cawnpore. In 1890 she be- *A touching narrative of her consecration and victory.* came conscious of a strange physical disability, and thinking that her health was failing, returned to America on a furlough. While at home came the dread suspicion and subsequent discovery that the mysterious malady was leprosy. At first the agony of her situation was overpowering, but she wrestled in prayer, and triumphed. She quickly decided to give her life to work among the lepers in India, and her thoughts turned to Pithoragarh, among the foot-hills of the Himalayas, at the base of Chandag Heights, where a group of these outcasts lived, in whom she had already become interested. Her convictions as to the nature of her disease were confirmed by every specialist she consulted. She kept it a secret, however, from father, mother, brothers, and sisters, with the exception of one sister, and returned to India in 1891. She proceeded to Pithoragarh, informing her friends by letter of her purpose, and her reason for choosing this service. Since then she has conducted her wonderful work at Chandag, and has built up an institution which in many respects is a model of order and well-arranged facilities.

Now, after seven years, comes the glad announcement that there is ground for hope that the progress of the disease has been checked, and that eventually she may fully recover her health. Physicians who are specialists examined her in *Glad tidings of Miss Reed's returning health.* the spring of 1898, and although they could not declare her entirely free from the virus, yet they pronounced her practically cured to the extent that the disease was regarded in her case as incommunicable. Later tidings seem to confirm the hope that absolute and permanent healing has been given by the Great Physician. She wrote late in 1898 as follows: "I have divinely given health, and there is no cause for anxiety. I could go home without jeopardizing any one, and I look so well that none need fear."[1]

We have dwelt in detail upon Miss Reed's experience, as an illustration of the supreme consecration involved in work for lepers. There are special aspects of this case which give peculiar beauty and pathos

[1] *Woman's Missionary Friend*, January, 1899, p. 236.

to her story, but there are many others among Christian missionaries in India and elsewhere who offer themselves with the same courage and devotion for this heroic service of love.

In Burma the Home for Lepers at Mandalay, founded by the Rev. A. H. Bestall in 1891, and soon after its establishment placed under the charge of the Rev. W. R. Winston, of the Wesleyan Methodist Mission, is the first institution of its kind in that country.[1] Mr. Winston's ill health has compelled him to retire, and it is now under the superintendence of the Rev. A. Woodward, to whom the author is indebted for the photographs illustrating the Home. There are 114 inmates, and "all but the latest comers are Christians." At Singapore Mrs. F. H. Morgan, an American Methodist missionary, visits a company of lepers who have been segregated by the Government. Her compassionate ministry is greatly welcomed by these sufferers.[2] At Lakawn, among the Laos people, the native Christians, aided by their children who sold the contents of a Christmas box to secure some benevolent funds, have been supporting twenty leper families. Dr. W. A. Briggs, a medical missionary of the Presbyterian Board at that station, has informed the author of a beautiful custom which has been adopted by the native members of that church. The communion is held monthly, and at every preparatory service a collection, not always of money, but more frequently of provisions, is taken for the aid of destitute lepers who live in their own village, not far away. The church also appoints two deaconesses who attend to the distribution and seek to do some spiritual ministry among them. There is something so genuine, so true to the instincts of Christian feeling, so suggestive of the "all things in common" spirit, in this plan, that it seems like a reproduction among simple native believers of an incident from the early history of the Church.

At Pakhoi, in Southern China, the Church Missionary Society has one of the finest institutions of the kind in the foreign field. It is a department of the more general hospital, but, while in the same compound, is quite isolated. It was founded in 1891, and is the largest hospital for lepers in China. The latest report, forwarded to the author by Dr. E. G. Horder, the physician in charge, gives the number of inmates as 140, of whom 110 are men, and 30 women

Efforts for lepers in Burma.

Fine institutions in China.

---

[1] *Work and Workers in the Mission Field*, July, 1895, p. 270, and April, 1896, p. 166. Cf. Also Winston, "Four Years in Upper Burma," pp. 251–266.

[2] *The Gospel in all Lands*, September, 1898, pp. 414, 415.

Rev. W. R. Winston, and a Group of Leper Children.

Women Patients.   Rev. A. Woodward, Superintendent, on the left.

Dispensary, Operating Room, Hospital Wards, and Church.

THE HOME FOR LEPERS, MANDALAY, BURMA.
(W. M. S.)

and children. The constant attention to their wounds, involving as it does about 18,000 separate dressings annually, requires a routine of daily labor, in the accomplishment of which competent lepers have been taught to assist, as will be seen in some of the accompanying illustrations. There are other asylums and hospitals, notably one at Hiau Kan, not far from Hankow, under the London Missionary Society, which was opened in 1895, and was the first of its kind in Central China. It has 24 inmates, all of whom are Christians. A large institution is conducted at Hangchow by the Church Missionary Society, consisting of a leper asylum for men, a hospital for women, and a home for untainted children, with also a convalescent home. The Mission for Lepers shares in the work at Hangchow, as also at Hiau Kan. Drs. Main and Kember are in charge at Hangchow, and Mrs. Main gives special attention to the women. In all, 25 inmates are reported, of whom 15 are Christians. The Church Missionary Society is engaged in efforts of a similar character at Foochow, Kien Ning, Lo-Ngwong, and Kucheng. At the latter place a church is about to be erected, and it is proposed to establish as soon as possible a home for untainted children. The American Methodist Episcopal Mission ministers to a leper village at Hinghua, where 20 out of a group of 50 have become Christians. These institutions represent but the beginning of this charitable work in the great Empire of China, where there are multitudes stricken with leprosy. It is of interest to note that Mr. and Mrs. Felix R. Brunot, of Pittsburg, Pa., have placed in the hands of the missionary society of the Protestant Episcopal Church (U. S. A.) the money to build and endow a leper home at Nganking, on the Yang-tse River.

Mission efforts on behalf of lepers in Japan are of recent origin. The only institutions as yet founded date from 1894 and 1895. The home called "Ihaien," situated at Meguro, a southern suburb of Tokyo, was established in **New enterprises in** 1894, by Miss Kate M. Youngman, of the Ameri- **Japan and Korea.** can Presbyterian Mission, aided by the Rev. J. C. Ballagh, Mr. S. Ito, and Dr. Otsuka, who is the present manager, under the general supervision of Miss Youngman. The object of this home, while distinctly evangelistic, is the shelter and care of helpless outcasts. The Mission to Lepers furnishes a grant for its support, and it reports 18 inmates, 6 of whom are Christians. A new hospital at Kumamoto, under the care of Miss H. Riddell and Miss G. Nott, of the Church Missionary Society, has been recently opened, with the promise of great usefulness. According to the latest returns, there are 24 patients, of whom 10 are Christians.[1]   In Korea no organized work has been attempted as yet, but Dr. Vinton, of Seoul, writes: "It is expected that before long an institution for the reception and treatment of these outcasts will be established in Korea, through the coöperation of the Mission to Lepers in India and the East."[2]

Little is known as to how extensively leprosy prevails in Africa, but judging from the data obtainable from those sections under European supervision, it is found to a moderate extent throughout the greater part of the Continent. In South Africa a considerable increase in the number of lepers is apparent.[3]   Segregation laws were enacted by the Cape Government, and put into operation in 1891. The result has been a large accession of inmates to the government colony on Robben Island, near Capetown.   The public hospital, although founded much earlier, was transferred thither in 1846, and since 1867 a chaplain of the Church of England has been maintained there by the Cape Government.   The present incumbent, the Rev. W. U. Watkins, is eminently fitted in every way for the position. The colony is a large one, numbering in 1893 more than 500 men, women, and children.[4]   This service, previous to the appointment of a Church of England chaplain, was performed, as before stated, by the Moravian missionaries, who entered upon it in 1822, when the asylum was at Hemel-en-Aarde.[5]   The servants of the same society are also providing for these outcasts within the bounds of their mission north of Lake Nyassa, where the disease has been found to be somewhat prevalent.[6]   Leper work is reported by the Hermannsburg Mission at Mosetla, in the Transvaal.   The government asylum at Emjanyana, Kaffraria, is visited by the Rev. S. J. Wallis, a missionary of the Scottish Episcopal Church, who gives some encouraging accounts of his efforts to instruct the inmates.   In the Island of Zanzibar there is a leper colony near Zanzibar City, where Dr. A. H. Spurrier, a resident

The lepers of Africa.

---

[1] "Annual Report of the Church Missionary Society, 1898," p. 394; *The Church Missionary Intelligencer*, August, 1898, p. 583.

[2] *The Missionary Review of the World*, September, 1898, p. 671.

[3] *The Christian Express*, May, 1895, p. 66; *The Church Missionary Intelligencer*, September, 1895, p. 698.

[4] *The Mission Field* (S. P. G.), October, 1897, pp. 375–379.

[5] Bliss, "Encyclopedia of Missions," vol. i., pp. 544, 545; La Trobe, "Work among Lepers by the Moravian Church," p. 11; Noble, "The Redemption of Africa," pp. 449–451.

[6] *Periodical Accounts Relating to the Moravian Missions*, December, 1897, p. 390.

Interior of Stewart Ward.   View of Mission Compound, including the General and Leper Hospitals.

Lepers Waiting for Admission.   Dressing the Wounds of Leper Patients.

SCENES AT THE LEPER ASYLUM, PAKHOI, CHINA.

(Conducted by the Pakhoi Medical and Leper Mission, in connection with the C. M. S.)

English layman, renders voluntary service as a superintendent and adviser. The following statement indicates the peril to which these poor creatures are subjected if left without some guardianship on the part of missionaries or civil authorities. "Only think," writes a missionary lady from Zanzibar, "Dr. O'Sullivan was taking care of a leper at Pemba, but had to come to Zanzibar, and when he returned, to his great regret he found that the people had buried the poor man alive, because he was of no use. It is time the lepers had some friends." [1]

In Madagascar the London Missionary Society, through two of its missionaries, the Rev. A. S. Huckett and his wife, secured in 1892 funds for the establishment of a leper settlement. It is located upon a hill named Ilena, about four miles from Fianarantsoa, and was opened in February, 1895. It is called by a name signifying "Village of Hope." Mrs. Huckett has devoted herself to this kindly charity. Thirty-seven inmates are reported, and a church of ten members.[2] Still another institution of the London Missionary Society is at Isoavina, sheltering 25 inmates. The funds for its establishment were raised by the Rev. P. G. Peake, who erected the buildings in 1895. It is his purpose not to charge the London Missionary Society with its support, but to interest the native church in assuming the obligation. The Norwegian Missionary Society has provided excellent accommodations for lepers at Antsirabe, consisting of a leper colony, with forty houses, a church, and a hospital. Three hundred inmates are reported, of whom two hundred are Christians. A special building is about to be erected for the children of leprous parents. Norwegian deaconesses aid in this work of mercy. Still another asylum, under the care of the same society, is located in the vicinity of Fianarantsoa, and enrolls 30 inmates. The United Norwegian Lutheran Church of America has also a leper home and an orphan asylum on the Island.

"Villages of Hope" in Madagascar.

The French Roman Catholic missionaries have rendered a service for lepers in Madagascar which deserves grateful recognition. At least two hospitals are spoken of in connection with their mission. They have also a leper home at Port of Spain, Trinidad, where Dominican nuns are the nurses, and again at Mandalay, where Father Johann Wehinger, who has been named the Father Damien of Burma, has charge of St. John's Leper Asylum.

[1] *African Tidings*, February, 1898, p. 19.
[2] "Report of the London Missionary Society, 1897," p. 167; *The Chronicle*, July, 1895, p. 182, and August, 1898, p. 202.

In Palestine the beautiful leper home in charge of the Moravians at Jerusalem, founded in 1867, and called "Jesus Hilfe," is not only one of the ornaments of the city, but also a monument of Christian charity in the land where our Saviour once healed the sick. The late Bishop La Trobe, of the Moravian Church, who died in 1897, in his ninety-fifth year, labored for the establishment and prosperity of this institution, which was the pride and joy of his old age. Since 1891 it has been under the charge of Mr. and Mrs. Schubert. At the close of 1897, 29 inmates were reported.[1]

The Moravian Asylum at Jerusalem.

In acquiring the Hawaiian Islands the United States Government added over a thousand lepers to its dependent classes. They are segregated on the Island of Molokai, the scene of Father Damien's sacrificing efforts for the relief of their miseries. The Hawaiian Government has been accustomed to appropriate over a hundred thousand dollars annually for their support. Our American administration will surely care for these helpless wards, and the Christian Church will not fail to provide for them the spiritual privileges and consolations of the Gospel. After the death of Father Joseph Damien, who labored among them for some twenty years, and was himself finally smitten with the disease, dying, in 1889, a victim to its ravages, his brother Pamphile, accompanied by a band of priests and nuns, took up the work, aiding Father Damien's surviving comrade, Joseph Dutton. Protestant missionary work among them has also been conducted, under the auspices of the Hawaiian Evangelical Association, which has established a church, with a stated pastor, a Young Men's Christian Association, a Sunday-school, a gymnasium, and a reading-room.[2] Still another leper colony which is maintained by the Melanesian Mission, is situated in the Banks Islands, but further particulars concerning it are wanting.

The lepers of Molokai.

An encouraging and from a social point of view important aspect of the efforts on behalf of lepers, is the prospect that native philanthropy will be stimulated and directed into this channel, so that a disposition to treat them kindly and provide for their needs will take the place of previous neglect. In India the corner-stone of a leper hospital has recently been laid by the Maharaja of Kolhapur, and the Maharaja of Kashmir has just placed the leper asylum at Srinagar under the care

[1] *Periodical Accounts Relating to Moravian Missions*, June, 1898, p. 503.

[2] See article by Bishop E. R. Hendrix, D.D., on "The Leper Island of Molokai," in *The Independent*, August 26, 1897.

of Dr. Neve, of the Church Missionary Society. Incidents like these would seem to indicate that there is hope that more active sympathy in regard to lepers will be quickened among native residents in foreign lands.

13. ESTABLISHING ORPHAN ASYLUMS.—In times of special calamity and suffering in mission fields there are multitudes of children who are bereft or deserted or thrust into some sudden peril of body or soul. The care of these defense- The appeal of imperilled less little ones, who in most instances are orphans, childhood. represents a department of mission activity which is most attractive and hopeful. The impulse which prompts to these efforts is both evangelical and humanitarian, and the result is notable for its spiritual fruitage and also for its ultimate advantage to society. Unprotected children are peculiarly exposed in an atmosphere of heathen vice, and easily become the victims of sinister designs, or are entrapped for evil purposes. It is wholly congenial to the spirit of missions, and in accord with its highest aims, to rescue the young from moral peril and physical distress, and gather them into homes of Christian training. Their circumstances are often so pitiful, and their situation so agonizing in its helplessness and misery, that missionaries are compelled by every instinct of humanity and every impulse of Christian sympathy to assume responsibilities which more than tax their resources. Many an orphanage in mission lands has been created by the mandate of necessity, and is conducted in response to an imperative call of Providence.

In the Turkish Empire such an emergency recently arose in connection with the Armenian massacres of 1894–95, which desolated hundreds of families, and left many helpless orphans. Missionaries have gathered such into The recent emergency homes and asylums, where they are trained under in Asia Minor. Christian instruction to be of service to their generation. Throngs of children, homeless and friendless because deprived of their natural protectors, have thus been thrown upon the kindly ministries of those who, with brave hearts and willing hands, shared with their native friends the perils of that cyclone of horrors which lately swept over Asia Minor. It is not an exaggerated estimate to state the number of children who were cast, in a condition of almost total dependence, upon the charity and care of mission agencies, as fully 50,000, and of this number some 10,000 had been suddenly orphaned.   Everything possible has been done by the missionaries, supported by the beneficent gifts of Christendom, to meet this emergency, yet so extensive was the need that much was of necessity left undone, or accomplished only in part.   Through the aid, however, of American, British, Swiss, and German Christians, the goodly number of 4000 little orphans are now under permanent watch and guardianship in the various asylums which have been planted in almost every centre of American mission work in Asia Minor.[1]

At Van, under the care of Dr. G. C. Raynolds, there are some 300 orphans, while an additional 400 are provided for in stations not far away.   At Sivas, in charge of Mrs. Hubbard, are five places of refuge, with two in neighboring villages, accommodating in all 280 little waifs.   The Swiss Committee, presided over by Professor Godet, of Neuchâtel, renders special aid at this station.   Five times as many orphans might have been taken had circumstances permitted. At Marash, where Mrs. Lee was in charge, over 200 were gathered, and four other homes were opened under different auspices.   At Harpoot, under the motherly care of Mrs. Barnum, aided by Miss Hattie Seymour, there is another flock of 220 little ones, and a similar band has been gathered at Choonkoosh, up in the neighboring mountains of Kurdistan.   Other new homes have been opened in Harpoot, until seven orphanages are now reported in the city, and four more not far away, while an aggregate of nearly 600 little ones are cared for at out-stations in the Harpoot field.

Missionary protection and shelter for bereft children.

At Urfa Miss Corinna Shattuck, with Miss E. M. Chambers as her associate, gathered around her a group which numbered 256.   A German orphanage, supported by a fund raised and dispensed under the direction of Dr. Lepsius, has also been established in this place, with 250 inmates.   At Bitlis the Misses Ely have been caring for 100 children.   At Hadjin Mrs. Coffing has had charge of 100 more.   At Brousa an orphanage has been conducted since 1875, and a branch has recently been opened at West Brousa for the Armenian orphans, both of which are under the supervision of a native pastor, the Rev. Gregory Baghdasarian.   In addition the United Swiss Committee has an institution at West Brousa.   At Aintab the asylum of the American Board has 75 inmates, and since 1876 the Rev. H. Hovhanessian has conducted a native orphanage, enrolling at present 256

1 *The Missionary Herald*, December, 1897, pp. 501–503, May, 1898, pp. 204–208; *Life and Light*, March, 1897, pp. 107–109; *Evangelical Christendom*, July, 1898, p. 209; *The Mission World*, January, 1897, p. 23.

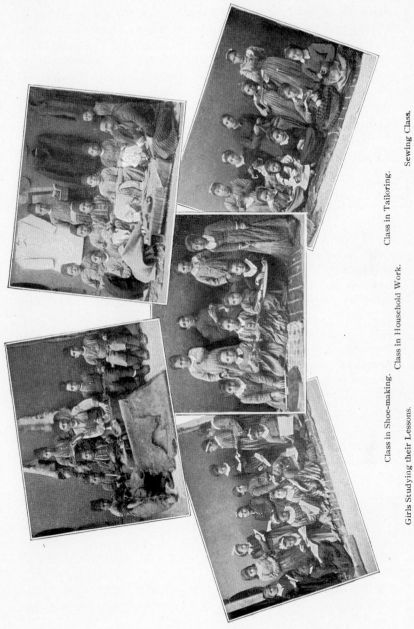

Class in Shoe-making. Class in Tailoring.

Girls Studying their Lessons. Class in Household Work.

Sewing Class.

ORPHAN GROUPS AT HARPOOT, TURKEY.

(A. B. C. F. M.)

inmates. The " Friends of Armenia," in England, *The Congregation-alist* of Boston, *The Christian Herald* of New York City, the Red Cross Society, and other philanthropic agencies have aided gener-ously, by means of special subscriptions secured through their solicita-tions, in caring for hundreds of the Armenian orphans. Other stations where this good work goes on under direct missionary supervision are Mardin, Diarbekir, Erzerum, Zeitun, Bardezag, Malatia, Marsovan, Cesarea, and Smyrna. At the latter place the Kaiserswerth Deacon-esses have a large orphan home, with 120 inmates, and the American German Baptist Brethren another, with 25 in their care. At Constanti-nople also the Relief Committee of Frankfort-on-the-Rhine supports an asylum with 50 inmates.

South of Asia Minor, in Syria and Palestine, we find at Beirut such noble institutions as the Zoar Orphanage of the Kaiserswerth Dea-conesses, and the St. George's Orphanage, the latter in charge of Miss Taylor. These are for girls, the former with 130 inmates, and the latter with 67. There is an industrial school for orphan boys at Sidon, under the supervision of Dr. George A. Ford, of the Presbyterian Mission. At Nazareth the Society for Promoting Female Education in the East has a fine institution, founded in 1870, in which are 75 inmates, and in Jerusalem the Kaiserswerth Deaconesses are rendering faithful service in the Talitha Kumi Orphanage, with a roll at present numbering 115 beneficiaries. The Bishop Gobat Memorial School, as it is now called, was originally opened by the good Bishop as an orphanage upon Mount Zion. Its scope, however, under the Church Missionary Society, has been enlarged into an educational institution. In Persia a large orphan asylum has been established since 1880 at Geogtapa, near Urumiah, in charge of a native Protes-tant known as Deacon Abraham, and is supported by Christian friends in England. It has now 60 inmates, and since it was founded over 300 orphans have gone out from its shelter trained for usefulness.

In India efforts on behalf of this special class have assumed un-wonted proportions. The roll-call of mission institutions in 1898 ex-tended to 124 orphanages or homes, with an ag-gregate of about 8000 children gathered within their doors. Of all foreign fields India surely stands in the front rank in respect to the extent and excellence of work in this department.[1] This is no doubt due in large measure to the calamities which periodically sweep over the

Orphan homes in Syria and Palestine.

Noble institutions in India.

[1] *Woman's Missionary Friend*, October, 1897, p. 91.

country.   Famines, plagues, pestilences, and the ever-present woes of
poverty have brought multitudes of children into a condition of helpless want.   In the early days of missions to India not a few little ones
among the cruel and superstitious Khonds were snatched from the peril
of lingering death as living sacrifices.[1]   Every great famine has left a
heritage of perishing orphans to the care of the missionaries, who have
received them literally by the hundreds, and out of such experiences
have grown many benevolent institutions.

The famine visitation of 1896–97 filled to overflowing every existing orphanage, and necessitated the opening of many new ones.   The

Rev. and Mrs. J. O. Denning, of Narsinghpur, res-
Indian orphans rescued during the famine of 1896-97. cued 700 children, nearly all of whom were
orphans, distributing many of them in various mis-
sion schools.[2]   The Friends' Foreign Missionary
Association (British), in its report for 1898 (p. 33), states that it has
gathered 500 children into orphanages at Seoni and Sohagpur, which
with its two asylums at Hoshangabad, having 317 inmates, makes a
sum total of 817 at present under its care.   The recent famine harvest
of the American Methodist Episcopal missionaries is over 2000 orphan

---

[1] " Year by year thousands of children were ruthlessly stolen from their native
villages, and sold to the wild Khonds.   Fattened by them for slaughter, they were
brought out on the day of sacrifice, and the livid flesh was cut piece by piece from
the suffering victim, and presented as a propitiatory offering to the earth-spirit.   Men
abandoned to paroxysms of emotion accompanied the bloody rite with music and
song, saying to the victim : ' We have bought you with a price, and it is therefore
no sin to offer you to the goddess '; and addressing the Khond deity with the
invocation :

> ' Hail, mother, hail! hail, Goddess Bhobanee!
> Lo! we present a sacrifice to thee;
> Partake thereof, and let it pleasure give,
> And in return let us thy grace receive.'

"Jesus Christ still ' seeks and saves that which is lost,' and in the spirit of His
Palestine mission *seeks first that which is most lost.*   He is the Deliverer of the oppressed.   He sets at liberty them that are appointed unto death.   Swayed by His
indwelling, and guided by His Spirit, the Orphan Asylum [at Cuttack, Orissa] was
established as early as 1836, and six boys and three girls who had been ' decreed for
sacrifice,' but were rescued from their deluded murderers, found a new home and
new parents within its walls.   And before the efforts of Government to suppress
these cruel practices were crowned with success, not less than seventeen hundred
victims were rescued, and at least two hundred and fifty of them had the advantages
of our schools."—" The Centenary Volume of the Baptist Missionary Society, 1792–
1892," pp. 258, 259.   Cf. also Lyall, " Natural Religion in India," p. 46; Sutton,
" Orissa," p. 229; *The Indian Evangelical Review*, October, 1897, pp. 190, 191.

[2] *The Missionary Review of the World*, April, 1898, p. 295.

children.[1] Their work in this department is exceptional in its extent. Their orphanage at Aligarh has 475 inmates, of whom 200 are girls; at Bareilly they report 350 girls; at Allahabad, in their two orphanages, are 275; at Poona, 262; at Narsinghpur, 250; at Jabalpur, 215; at Shahjahanpur, 175. The Church Missionary Society reports in its institution at Patpara, 200; at Gorakhpur, 140; at Clarkabad, 133; at Sharanpur, 112; at Benares, 113. The Society for the Propagation of the Gospel has two orphanages at Cawnpore, with 240 inmates, and the London Missionary Society one at Mirzapur, with 130. The Basel Missionary Society has 179 in its asylum at Udipi, and 173 at Chombale. The American Reformed Episcopal Mission, in its institution at Lalitpur, shelters 140 children. At Jabalpur the Wesleyan Missionary Society has two orphanages, with 132 inmates. The efforts of the Christian Woman's Board of Missions resulted in the rescue of 750 children, many of whom were retained in its asylum at Mahoba. The list is too long to enumerate further. Several additional institutions appear in a foot-note.[2]

[1] *The Harvest Field*, November, 1897, p. 433.

[2] The following list includes only institutions reporting more than fifty inmates. In the statistical tables of "Centennial Survey" fuller details will be found.

LOCATION.	SOCIETY.	INMATES.
Pakur	M. E. M. S.	110
Saugor	S. E. N. S.	110
Almora	L. M. S.	107
Mahoba	C. W. B. M.	106
Borsad	P. C. I. M. S.	105
Agarpara	C. M. S.	103
Fatehgarh	P. B. F. M. N.	102
Calcutta	W. U. M. S.	100
Saharanpur	P. B. F. M. N.	92
Anand	P. C. I. M. S.	89
Codacal (Paraperi)	Ba. M. S.	88
Cuttack	E. B. M. S.	84
Nagpur	F. C. S.	81
Pithoragarh	M. E. M. S.	79
Surat	P. C. I. M. S.	77
Damoh	F. C. M. S.	76
Chikalda	K. C. I. H. M.	71
Mungeli	F. C. M. S.	70
Dharwar	Ba. M. S.	70
Roorkee	S. P. G.	70
Bilaspur	C. W. B. M.	69
Raniganj	W. M. S.	68
Madras	M. E. M. S.	66
Kotageri	Ba. M. S.	66

In many instances industrial training in various trades is given. The children are educated to be skilled workmen, and are enabled to support themselves when older, thus becoming in-

Successful training in various industries.

dustrious members of society. From Lalitpur Mrs. E. M. Bacon writes that the weaving of cotton cloth is one of the specialties of the orphanage. At Hassan, under the Wesleyan Mission, the making of caps is a feature, and in this the girls do such excellent work that "the Hassan caps are known throughout a considerable part of India, so that orders come from all parts of the country, not only to the orphanage, but to the several stations where the girls are now found, and thus the mission is helped, and the chronic poverty of the Christian families is to some extent relieved." [1] At Clarkabad they are busy with their spinning-wheels. At Shahjahanpur the boys are manufacturers of tools, shovels, and wire-spring mattresses. Rope-making is taught to blind lads, and a dairy-farm has also been started, with forty cows, so that the business of supplying the British troops near by with milk and butter has been undertaken, to the extent of about eight hundred pounds of butter per month. In her Widows' Home and Orphanage at Chunar, Miss Margaret Patteson seeks to train faithful ayahs and cooks, and to prepare candidates for the higher instruction needed to become Bible-women and skilled nurses. The social benefits of this combination of Christian and industrial training must be apparent to all. Thousands of children have thus been saved, to reflect honor upon the Christian profession, and to serve their generation in honest and productive occupations.

Peculiar interest attaches to work for orphans in Japan, for the reason that it is so largely conducted by native Christians. The earliest effort of the kind was the Okayama Asylum,

The story of the Okayama Asylum.

founded in 1887 by Mr. and Mrs. J. Ishii. It is a cheering illustration of the power of Christianity to bring forth its fruits in the Japanese character, and to inspire in them as in others a spirit of service. It is a sign of God's purpose both to call the Christians of Japan to works of benefi-

(Continued from p. 451.)

LOCATION.	SOCIETY.	INMATES.
Bhaisdehi	K. C. I. H. M.	60
Mulki	Ba. M. S.	59
Allahabad	Z. B. M. M.	57
Cawnpore	W. U. M. S.	57
Bhagalpur	C. M. S.	55
Hassan	W. M. S.	55

[1] *Work and Workers in the Mission Field*, February, 1897, p. 55.

ZOAR ORPHANAGE AND ITS PUPILS, BEIRUT, SYRIA.

"The God that answereth by orphanages, let Him be God."

The Zoar Orphanage is conducted by the Kaiserswerth Deaconesses of Germany, and has 130 inmates. Sister Sophie, the Directress, is seated in the centre of the second row.

cence, and to sustain them in Christian labors involving personal devotion and sacrifice. More than that, it is an evidence of the readiness of Japanese converts to respond in faith and love to such demands upon their consecration.

Mr. Ishii was of samurai parentage, and was born at Takanabe, in the Province of Hyuga, in 1865, and converted to the Protestant faith in 1884. Early in his Christian career he was deeply impressed by reading such books as "Self-Help," by Smiles, and accounts of the efforts of Dr. Guthrie and John Pounds on behalf of poor children. In 1886, not long after receiving these impressions, Mr. George Müller visited Japan, and the story of his great work for orphans at Bristol fascinated and inspired this young Japanese, who himself has now come to be known as "the George Müller of the Orient." In 1887, as he was about to enter upon the practice of medicine, after a successful preparatory course of study, he began his mission by taking to his home a poor lad, the son of a widow. This boy has remained with him, and is designated as the original orphan of the institution. Mr. Ishii soon gathered others around him, befriending and aiding them, while depending upon prayer for special help and guidance in his undertaking. Thus his orphanage was begun in the village of Kamiyasuji, where he was then residing. He soon removed it to Okayama, and hired an old temple for his purpose. Around this temple his extensive plant has grown, until it is one of the most prominent of the Christian charities of Japan. It has been a work of toil and sacrifice, and often of much anxiety, conducted in a spirit of intense and constant prayer. Gradually it became known among those who were glad to minister to its support. Friends increased in number, and their gifts grew more bountiful. Mr. Ishii was greatly blessed from the outset by the friendship and support of the Rev. James H. Pettee and family, missionaries of the American Board at Okayama. Mr. Pettee has published abroad the unique features of the undertaking, and given information concerning its needs.[1] It has friends at present on every continent, and there are many in Great Britain and America who

> "The George Müller of the Orient."

[1] Cf. a pamphlet by Mr. Pettee, entitled "J. Ishii and His Institution, Japan's Chief Apostle of Faith: The George Müller of the Orient, and His Unique Orphanage," printed at Yokohama in 1892. Cf. also "Mr. Ishii and His Orphanage," an illustrated pamphlet by the same author, printed at the Asylum Press, Okayama, 1894.

Mr. Pettee introduces the first pamphlet with the following tribute to the man and his work: "Mr. J. Ishii, of Okayama, is perhaps the most widely known living Japanese Christian. Not only from end to end of this Eastern land is his

contribute regularly to its support.   Just as its financial year in 1897
was closing, a debt of over nine hundred dollars seemed to be impending, but a letter was even then on the way from America with a gift of
a thousand dollars from Miss Elizabeth Billings, of New York, which
reached the treasury just in time to cancel the debt and close the
year's accounts with a small balance on the right side.

The Okayama Asylum passed its tenth anniversary on September 22,
1897.[1] The plant has grown until it includes several buildings, the facilities for conducting various industries, an annex

The record of a
bright decade.

with a farm and a mill for preparing rice, in the
Province of Hyuga, situated on the Island of Kiu-
shiu, and a boat as a means of transport.   The
printing department is located in a building purchased with funds
contributed by Christian Endeavor Societies, Dr. F. E. Clark having
opened the subscription list with a generous gift.   Its periodical, *The
Asylum Record*, is published in English, and there is a Japanese edition,
the *Kojiin Shimpo*, or "Asylum News."   Twelve other periodicals are
printed by workmen at the Asylum Press.   The following industries are
also taught in connection with the Orphanage: the cultivation and
cleaning of rice, farming, carpentry, weaving, the raising of silkworms,
navigation, and the manufacture of some useful commodities, such as
matches, and straw braid for hats.   It is the desire of the founder to
make the institution self-supporting as far as possible, and to secure a
sufficient endowment to guarantee its financial needs.   There could
hardly be found in all Japan a more instructive illustration of the

worth respected, but his name has gone out into all Christendom as a synonym for
fearless faith and practical piety.   His simple trust in God is as refreshing as it is rare."

[1] Mr. Pettee at the end of the first decade records his judgment of the work
done.   He writes: "We would sum up the results accomplished as follows: over
five hundred needy people, mostly children, befriended and led into a larger and better
life; a spirit of self-help and large-hearted benevolence planted in many young hearts;
an inspiring example set to scores of similar institutions, Christian, Buddhist, and
secular; a world-wide interest aroused in this one work and the principles on which
it was founded.   These principles may be defined as faith voicing itself in intense
prayer, biblical teaching as the only true basis of a correct and useful life, an earnest
spirit of self-help developed in the face of stern trial, and a love for others that is
the highest socialism.   The Asylum has done all this, and is still true to the faith
of its earlier years, still believes in prayer and realized answers to prayer, the simple Gospel of a crucified Redeemer, a high spiritual life, and tireless activity in
labors of love.

"For all that it has done through suffering and success, it gives to God the glory,
and in a spirit of joyous praise, of humble devotion, and of renewed courage, it
starts out for the next great goal a half-score years ahead."— *The Asylum Record*,
October, 1897, p. 5.

Mr. Ishii,
Founder and Superintendent Okayama Orphanage.

The original orphan,
ten years after admission.

Mrs. Ishii,
Mother of the Orphanage.

The Press Building of the Okayama Orphanage.
(A contribution from Christian Endeavor Societies.)

A NOTABLE PHILANTHROPIC ENTERPRISE IN JAPAN.

(See pages 452–455.)

possibilities of Christianity among that impressible people than the Okayama Orphanage of Mr. and Mrs. Ishii, with its 278 inmates.

Since its establishment, other institutions, under native auspices, have sprung up in different parts of the empire. Prominent among them is the "Morning Star Orphanage," at Nasunohara, under the direction of Mr. S. Hongo, with 41 in- *Other fine institutions under Japanese direction.* mates. There is still another at Mombetsu, in the Hokkaido, under the direction of the Rev. Taketaro Hayashi. The Rev. E. Rothesay Miller, of the Reformed Church Mission at Morioka, writes to the author commending in high terms the service rendered by Mr. Hayashi. The plan of administration was conceived by the latter while he was a pastor in the Hokkaido. The financial support is derived from government lands, reclaimed and cultivated with a view to making the orphanage entirely a self-supporting institution. For the "sterling qualities" of the enterprising young pastor Mr. Miller has "a high admiration." At Oji, near Tokyo, there is a fine asylum with 55 inmates, under Protestant Episcopal auspices, and conducted by Mr. A. Osuga. It has recently been named the "Holy Trinity Orphanage," and is intended especially for girls. Mr. Osuga, who is greatly respected by missionaries in Japan, has turned his attention also to the education of feeble-minded children, and intends to make this a distinctive feature of his benevolent work. The native congregation of St. John's Protestant Episcopal Church at Osaka is supporting St. John's Orphanage. At Maebashi Mr. H. Kaneko superintends the Jomo Orphanage. Another, at Kobe, is in charge of Mr. K. Yoshikawa. There is also an institution at Tokyo, established by a Christian teacher, who devotes to it all his property, and at Yokohama a Japanese church-member of the Methodist Episcopal Mission has opened his own home for the reception of orphans. At Gifu the Nobi Orphanage is under the direction of Mr. Y. Igarashi, and at Hiramatsu Dr. T. Nishi conducts the Kyusai Kojiin. Let it be noted that all these institutions have been founded since Mr. Ishii's initial effort in 1887.

There are others under foreign mission auspices, as the two at Kanazawa, one maintained by the Canadian Methodists, and the other founded and independently supported by the efforts of the Rev. and Mrs. T. C. Winn, of the *The efforts of missionary societies on behalf of orphans in Japan.* Presbyterian Mission. At Kumamoto there was an American Methodist Episcopal institution, but it has been very recently removed to Koga. In Nagoya the Canadian Church Missionary Association supports the Yoro-in Asylum. Near Osaka is an American Protestant Episcopal institution known as the "Widely Loving Society," under the superintendence of Mr. J. Kobashi, where a fine training in farming is given to the pupils, who now number 23. At Tokyo Miss Kate M. Youngman, of the Presbyterian Mission, has for several years counted a little group of orphans as members of her own household, and has cared for them with loving oversight. The Anglicans have also the John Bishop and St. Andrew's Orphanages at Tokyo, while still another is conducted there, under the care of the Canadian Methodists. At Chofu the American Baptists have an asylum. This rapid development of humane charity so largely under native direction gives cheering assurance that Japanese Christianity will do its duty towards orphans. Industrial training is a feature in many of these orphanages, and the work done by the pupils often renders the institutions partially self-supporting. At Kanazawa brushes of various kinds are made and sold to provide for the expenses of the asylum. It may be noted also that the Buddhists have founded some similar institutions, the most important of which is the Fukuta-Kwai, in Tokyo.

In Korea an orphanage at Chemulpo was opened by the late Dr. Landis, of the Anglican Mission. At Seoul a Home for Destitute Children has lately been established, under the charge of Miss Ellen Pash and Miss Jean Perry, the responsible oversight being in the hands of a local council, with Dr. Underwood as Chairman. Some native Christians in Japan are purposing to carry their orphanage work into Korea. The Okayama Orphanage has already sent a part of its benevolent fund, raised in honor of the completion of its first decade, to aid in the founding of an asylum for Korean orphans at Seoul. The Roman Catholic Church has for some time conducted an institution in that city, under the charge of the Sisters of St. Paul de Chartres. All this shows clearly that though evangelistic work is still so new in that land, even the more indirect results of missions are beginning to appear.

In China one of the oldest and most interesting orphan asylums is the Berlin Foundling Home at Hong Kong, opened in 1850. The late Mrs. B. C. Henry was so touched, some years ago, by the perils of orphan girls at Canton that she founded a modest orphanage, which she conducted for several years, and in which many little waifs were saved from the dismal fate which threatens destitute and deserted daughters in China.[1] At Amoy is a home for infant girls,

A beginning in Korea.

An interesting work for foundlings and orphans in China.

[1] Henry, "The Cross and the Dragon," p. 311.

under the charge of the English Presbyterian and Reformed Church Missions. The ladies of these missions established it because they felt keenly the need of a place of refuge for baby girls whose sad fate they desired to avert.[1] At Foochow is the Mary E. Crook Memorial Orphanage, in charge of Methodist missionaries, with 34 inmates, and near by, at Kucheng, the Church of England Zenana Missionary Society has 30 little protégées in the " Bird's Nest Foundling Asylum." It was here that Miss Hessie Newcombe and Miss Elsie Marshall suffered martyrdom, while engaged in their service of love. At Shanghai, St. Mary's Orphanage, of the Protestant Episcopal Mission, reports 40 girls. Other institutions are at Nanking, Hinghua, and Chinkiang. Roman Catholic missionaries have devoted themselves especially to these benevolent efforts for orphans and foundlings in China. In Manchuria alone about 1500 boys and girls are in their asylums.[2] Unusual interest attaches to orphanage work in this empire, in view of the prevalence of infanticide, as well as for reasons already indicated. At Singapore there are 49 inmates in the Mary C. Nind Home, under the charge of Miss S. Blackmore, of the American Methodist Mission.

Orphanages are conducted here and there in the South Sea Islands, among them one which was founded in the New Hebrides, by Dr. Paton. In Australia there is work of this kind carried on by the Moravians. In Madagascar the London Missionary Society and the English Friends have each an orphanage at Antananarivo, in which are 39 children. Other asylums are maintained under the care of the Norwegian Society at Antananarivo and Antsirabe, and under the direction of the United Norwegian Lutheran Church of America at Fort Dauphin. The London Society also has one at Ambohimanga. In the neighboring Island of Mauritius is the Rose

Rescue work for children in various fields.

[1] " The lady missionaries had its establishment laid on their hearts by what they saw round about them of the fate of many of the girls born into Chinese homes. There is scarcely a Christian woman in the Church who has not, in her heathen days, killed one or more of her girls. In one case Miss Johnston mentioned, nine out of ten girls had been killed by their own mother. Miss Johnston was one day visiting the Mission Hospital at Amoy, when a woman came in crying, with a baby in her arms. The little thing was going to be blind, and the doctor could not help her. The woman said, ' I must throw her away; I cannot keep her.' The child had been given to her by its mother. She was sorry to have the little baby die, but she could not possibly be encumbered with a blind girl! The ladies of the Mission took the little thing from the woman, and then, thus led into it, they raised money in Amoy, rented a house, and set up their Babies' Home."— *The Monthly Messenger*, May, 1894, p. 112.

[2] *The Independent*, July 25, 1895, article on " Mission Work in Manchuria."

Belle Orphanage of the Church Missionary Society, with 51 girls on its roll.

On the Continent of Africa some institutions especially for orphans are reported. Their number would be larger were they not more properly classed as training-schools or homes for rescued slave children. In connection with the Delta Pastorate there is provided at Bonny a shelter for orphans, under the care of Mrs. Crowther, and at Harper, Cape Palmas, the American Protestant Episcopal missionaries have gathered 56 girls into St. Mark's Orphan Asylum. At Capetown, St. George's Orphanage, with 40 girls, is under Anglican supervision. Canon Booth has established an orphanage at Durban, Natal, among the Indian coolies. The Swedish Church has also opened institutions in various portions of Zululand, and the South African General Mission has an asylum at Capetown. The Presbyterians have a children's home at Luebo, in the Congo State, and the only orphanage in Morocco is conducted at Casablanca by missionaries of the North Africa Mission. Homes for rescued slave children maintained by the Universities' Mission, such as that under the care of Miss Mills and Miss Clutterbuck at Kilimani, are mentioned elsewhere in this volume (p. 322).

The South American Missionary Society has institutions in South America, at Tekenika and at Ushuaia, in the "Land of Fire," and another at Alberdi, in Uruguay. At San Bernardo, in Chile, is the Powell Orphanage, begun under the auspices of the Methodist Episcopal Mission, but now independently supported. The first Protestant orphanage established in Argentina was founded at Buenos Ayres by Mr. W. C. K. Torre, in 1894, and is still conducted by him. The Orphan Home of the Anglican Church in Trinidad has 190 inmates. The Rev. W. D. Powell has opened an institution at Toluca, Mexico, and the Moravians one for Indian children at New Fairfield, Canada.

14. PROMOTING CLEANLINESS AND SANITATION.—Cleanliness is a social virtue, and Christian missions foster it in many lands where dirt is domesticated in the homes of the people, and where disgusting slovenliness—in many instances intolerable filth—is more or less characteristic of the individual. A Christian convert in almost any mission field is sure to become more prepossessing and more tidy in person and environment, to an extent which is differential. The Rev. Dr. J. L. Barton, formerly a missionary in Asia Minor, writes on this point: "We find that those who have accepted the Gospel immediately

Missions an incentive to personal cleanliness.

The itinerating dispensary of Dr. Mary Pierson Eddy. The photograph of the encampment was taken near the village of Furzul, on the eastern slope of Mt. Lebanon. Patients have assembled from neighboring villages, and are awaiting treatment. Dr. Eddy stands on the right, in the door of the tent. Her last annual report stated that she had visited 51 places, and administered 7,070 medical treatments during the year. Her patients came from 216 different villages.

WOMAN'S MEDICAL WORK IN SYRIA

(P. B. F. M. N.)

evince a desire to change the sanitary conditions of their homes as well as their villages. Many families who before were content to occupy the same winter quarters as their cattle, in dark, unventilated stables, now build additional rooms either upon the top or at the side, and live separately. A mind aroused by the Gospel at once appreciates the fact that man is higher than the animal, and so worthy of a better place in which to live." Dr. G. C. Raynolds, of Van, Turkey, states: "A much greater regard to the laws of health, in the arrangement of homes, in attention to cleanliness of the person and of the household, is apparent." Dr. George E. Post, of Beirut, corroborates these testimonies as follows: "Missions have done much to teach personal cleanliness and household hygiene. The homes of all girls educated in mission schools are conspicuous for their betterment in this regard. Protestant families are models to all in the matter of neatness and freedom from slovenly habits."[1] This is partly the result of example and the recognition of the simple charms of refinement, and partly the instinct of higher self-respect in the convert. It is an encouraging response to the practical influence of school life and training, and often illumines and beautifies the new homes of pupils who are beginning domestic life for themselves after a course of education. It casts by contrast a shadow

---

[1] Missionaries in other lands express the same judgment: " One striking fact following the acceptance of Christianity has been the improvement in the clothing, housing, and food of the people. The outcome of these bettered conditions is apparent in a generally improved state of health, and by a marked decrease in infant mortality. This last point—the high death-rate among infants—is one of the most striking features of heathen life to a medical man, and its diminution is the more noticeable."—Rev. Robert Laws, M.D., D.D. (F. C. S.), Kondowi, Livingstonia, British Central Africa.

" A few among the natives have learned that ' cleanliness is next to godliness,' and their persons, their homes, and the surroundings of those homes, are models of neatness."—Rev. J. Pearse (L. M. S.), Fianarantsoa, Madagascar.

" It is refreshing to see the clean houses and villages of Christians, instead of the filthy heathen hovels of previous years."—Rev. G. L. MacKay (C. P. M.), Tamsui, Formosa.

" The Christians, as a matter of fact, improve their homes and home surroundings, are more alive to the importance of pure air and water, of good food, rest, and sufficient exercise. Indirectly, at least, Christianity has brought them the knowledge of sanitation, and directly it has taught them the sacredness of all life, and the duty we owe to ourselves and others in the matter of health."—Rev. J. Morton, D.D. (C. P. M.), Trinidad.

" Insanitary conditions, arising from burying the dead in the dwellings of the living, filthy clothing, and unwashed bodies, are very much altered. No government authority in this; simply the influence of our example and our schools, even upon those who are yet heathen."—Rev. Robert H. Nassau, M.D. (P. B. F. M. N.), Baraka, Gaboon, West Africa.

of reproach and discomfort over the old customs, and insures a measure of discontent with conditions that are foul and objectionable. It is a charming spectacle to behold this new cleanliness of the person and the home, and to see the whole life becoming more orderly and wholesome.

Although these changes, in almost every instance where they occur, are distinctively Christian, yet it is not true that there is universal filthiness, individual and social, in the Oriental world.

An awakened desire for sanitary reform. Among the higher classes of the older civilizations there is often little to offend a casual observer, although an exception must be made to this statement in reference to the insanitary disposition of garbage. In the streets and homes where even the best people reside, sometimes in the wealthiest quarters of the largest cities, filthy conditions are apt to prevail, while among the rank and file in the lower walks of life the public highways and the dwellings are usually in a state which is loathsome. This is a stumbling-block in the path of civilization and social betterment. It ruins the water-supply, breeds the germs of frightful diseases, and is the chief source of those plagues and pestilences which cut a swath through whole sections of society. The heathen world has been long at the mercy of these insanitary conditions, and thousands, even millions, of victims have paid the penalty. The indirect benefits of missions in securing improved surroundings and introducing remedial measures are not at once apparent to a casual observer, and can be discovered only by considerable searching and inquiry. Reports from every direction indicate that there is much to be said on this subject. The Rev. L. L. Uhl, Ph.D., a Lutheran missionary at Guntur, India, writes: "The poorer people have learned through us the power of acting unitedly to accomplish some good end, especially the securing of a better water-supply. Through Christian efforts whole communities have already been led to give up the eating of non-slaughtered beasts. In many places the habit of devouring the flesh of diseased animals and of carrion has entirely ceased, and the people are more intelligent and brighter-looking for this reform. It is the Christians who call attention to the decaying, unburied carcasses, and to the washing of clothes in drinking-tanks." [1]

_____

[1] "The supply of good drinking-water which the natives enjoy in many places is due almost altogether to the missionaries. They have also done much in getting the people, chiefly the Christians, to remove their villages to healthier localities. The houses being made of timber and bamboo, it is not difficult to carry them from one place to another. In some communities the mortality is very great; but by the

India has always been noted for its neglect not only of every hygienic precaution, but in certain respects of the simple decencies of living. Missions, of course, have had little to do officially with the establishment and enforcement of modern sanitary regulations. The British Government is discharging this gigantic task as far and as fast as the serious difficulties allow.[1]   Missions, however, have much to do in preparing the people to welcome and respond to the efforts of the Government in this direction.   It is the ignorant and bigoted children of superstition, the thronging pilgrims, the fanatical devotees, the slaves of custom, the men and women whose lives are stagnant, and whose outlook has no gleam of better things, who are intractable and immovable.   Hearts and minds into which the light of mission instruction and culture has entered are ready for a sweeter and more wholesome existence.[2]

Helpful coöperation with the Government in India.

advice of the missionaries they move to healthier places, and the change in some cases has been marvellous.   For instance, there was a village in my district, consisting of about one hundred persons.   Within twelve years, about sixty of them, chiefly children, had died there.   In a few years more they would probably have died out altogether; but where they are now, the atmosphere is healthful, and the water-supply good, so they flourish and multiply.   The older people have renewed their strength, and the children are strong and vigorous."—Rev. Robert Evans (W. C. M. M. S.), Mawphlang, Shillong, Assam.   Cf. also an article on "Training in Hygiene," by Mrs. H. Morrow, M.D., of Tavoy, Burma, in *The Baptist Missionary Magazine*, May, 1898, pp. 181, 182.

" The poor sanitation is another evil that has greatly diminished in Brazil since the introduction of the Gospel.   The city of Campinas, which for so many years was scourged by the ravages of yellow fever, is now in excellent condition, with well-drained streets and an abundant supply of pure water.   Many of the improvements made in this city, and many of the sanitary measures adopted, were due, I think, either directly or indirectly, to suggestions made by our missionaries."—Miss Charlotte Kemper (P. B. F. M. S.), Lavras, Brazil.

[1] Cf. articles on " The Indian Doctors and the Plague," in *The Spectator*, April 3, 1897, and on " Segregation Camps in India," in *The Missionary Herald*, October, 1898, pp. 385–387.

Statements concerning the unsavory and abominable habits of the people may be found in articles on " Indian Village Life—Its Present Urgent Want," by M. B. Colah, M.D., in *The Indian Magazine and Review*, August, 1894, and on " Indian Sanitation," by A. Rogers, *ibid.*, June, 1897.   See also an article by Dr. Mackichan, in *The Free Church of Scotland Monthly*, March, 1897, p. 61, and a statement concerning " The Disinfection of Wells in India," in *The Independent*, March 25, 1897, p. 16.

[2] " The moment a strange visitation, like the plague, appears in the midst of the people, they fly with offerings to their gods, while a matter-of-fact administrator endeavours to indoctrinate them with the laws of hygiene, and offers them disinfectants and other preventives.   Practical and calculating though our countrymen are in

Mission schools are giving instruction in the laws of health and the dangers of neglected sanitation.   Dr. John Murdoch, Secretary in Southern India for the Christian Literature Society, has appealed to the universities, petitioning that the subject of hygiene shall be made a requirement for matriculation examinations.[1]   The same zealous worker for the good of that land has published an admirable pamphlet of fifty-two pages on "Sanitary Reform in India."   It is issued at Madras, under the auspices of the Christian Literature Society for India, as one of the series of "Papers on Indian Social Reform."   Its chapters on "Pure Water," "Good Food," "Village Sanitation," and many other timely themes, would, if heeded, save thousands of lives and untold suffering throughout the country.   Among the "Simla Tracts," compiled at the request of W. Coldstream, Esq., C.S., Deputy Commissioner of Simla, for the use of the village people, is one written by the late Rev. M. M. Carleton, of the Presbyterian Mission, on "Good Health and Good Crops," and another, on "Cleanliness," by Edith M. Brown, M.D., the Principal of the North India School of Medicine for Christian Women, at Lodiana.

Dr. Murdoch and his campaign of sanitary reform in India.

Miss Florence Nightingale, long known to the world as a devoted philanthropist, has interested herself for some years in the effort to secure what might be called a Health Mission to Rural India, by commissioning those suited for the service to visit Indian villages and give lectures on hygiene, making practical suggestions as to sanitation.[2]   In this plan she has been warmly assisted by native reformers, such as Mr. B. M. Malabari, of Bombay.   In fact, the advocates of sanitary reform among the natives of India are in most instances either Christians, or disciples of the somajes, sects which have usually arisen from the imperfect assimilation of Christian teaching. Among the latter may be named Rao Bahadur S. Mudaliar, who is de-

Miss Florence Nightingale and her Health Mission to Rural India.

most things, in this particular direction they believe this characteristic saying: ' It is the will of our gods; let it work without let or hindrance.'   To face and fight appears impious; all that they care to do is to petition their gods to stay the pest destroying them.   Sentiments like these stand against sanitation, the people rejecting the saving hand, and, worse still, turning at times fiercely on their rescuers. Therefore it is necessary to exercise great forbearance, and wean them from the folly of believing that the divine will is an isolated force quite uninfluenced by human endeavours.   We should then teach them the truth contained in the simple words, ' God helps those who help themselves.' "— *The Christian Patriot*, Madras, November 12, 1898.

[1] *The Independent*, April 29, 1897, article on "The Bubonic Plague."

[2] *The Indian Magazine and Review*, September, 1898, pp. 239–241; *The Indian Social Reformer*, December 20, 1896, p. 122, February 7, 1897, p. 176.

scribed as a man of liberal education, a member of a somaj in Bellary, the object of which is "the moral, spiritual, and social elevation of all classes and castes." He is said to have secured to his native town of Bellary "entire immunity from cholera and other epidemic diseases," and has been noted for humanitarian service to the poor, and especially for his interest in the cause of temperance.[1]

The Government of India is almost powerless to enforce sanitary laws behind the closed doors of the homes, even when the perils of the plague threaten whole communities. Mission influence through education and zenana visitation is far more penetrating, and at the same time can develop a public opinion in support of cleanliness. No trace of fatalism in Christian communities.

At Ahmednagar, strange to say, native plague inspection committees were organized when the dreaded visitation threatened in 1897. Let it be noted, however, that these committees were formed in the Christian community at their own instigation.[2] The late Rev. J. F. Burditt, of the American Baptist Mission in India, in a paper upon "Work among the Depressed Classes," calls attention to the subject of sanitation as worthy of the efforts of missionaries, and emphasizes the "tendency of regenerate souls to keep the body and its surroundings pure."[3]

One or two aspects of this subject are worthy of special note. In some instances the services of missionaries during the prevalence of the plague have been acknowledged by the British Government in terms of marked appreciation. Among those who have thus received cordial recognition for their beneficent efforts is the Rev. James Smith, a missionary of the American Board at Ahmednagar, of whom it was said in the government report that "his assistance to the Plague Administration of Nagar City has been invaluable."[4] The Government recognition of the services of missionaries during the prevalence of the plague.

[1] "Some Noted Indians of Modern Times," pp. 94–97.

[2] Dr. Julia Bissell, of the American Board, reports as follows concerning this undertaking: "Energy and enthusiasm were shown in this movement, and two committees, one of four and one of three members, were appointed to visit near and distant Christian homes, respectively. The objects of these committees were: (1) to give suggestions on cleanliness of the individual and of the home and surroundings to any who needed them; (2) to impress on them the connection of dirt with contagious diseases; (3) to quiet fears; and (4) to explain to them the meaning of anti-plague measures adopted in the city, their importance to the public health, and the reasons for complying cheerfully and promptly with them. The committees assembled twice a week to report on work done and obstacles met, and did excellent service."—*Life and Light for Woman*, September, 1898, p. 401.

[3] "Report of the Third Decennial Missionary Conference, Held at Bombay, 1892–93," p. 13.

[4] *The Missionary Herald*, August, 1898, p. 294.

Government Plague Committee specially mentioned Mrs. Ball, of the Church Missionary Society at Karachi, and recorded its high appreciation of the "unwearying care, kindness, and sympathy" shown by her in her ministrations at the Convalescent Hospital.[1]

Another striking fact which arrests the attention is the exceptional immunity of native Christians during the prevalence of deadly visitations of disease. The testimonies from various

The remarkable immunity of native Christians.

directions upon this point are too explicit and uniform to pass unnoticed. The missionary magazines of 1898 speak repeatedly upon this point. The following sentences may be quoted: "In general, throughout the Presidency there have been very few cases of plague among Protestant Christians, and still fewer have proved fatal. Faith in God's protecting power, readiness to further all rules of the municipalities, and personal cleanliness have conduced, we believe, to their marked exemption."[2] A missionary of the Free Church of Scotland comments as follows: "A remarkable feature of this later as well as of the earlier epidemic is the comparative immunity of our native Christians from the plague. It is probable that careful, regular, cleanly, and right living has had much to do with it."[3] Concerning a recent visitation of cholera at Khammamett, Miss Wells, of the Church of England Zenana Missionary Society, reports: "Not one of the mission party or workers was attacked, and among the Christians in Khammamett there were only five cases, all mild, and all yielding to treatment."[4] The Rev. A. R. Cavalier, of the Zenana, Bible, and Medical Mission, writes from India, where he was visiting the various stations of that society: "There are over fifteen hundred native Christians in Bombay. During the outbreak only six of them were attacked, although many exposed themselves to constant risk in their efforts to minister to the sick."[5] A recent official Health Report of Bombay strikingly confirms the exceptional healthfulness of the Christian community of that city.[6]

[1] *The Church Missionary Intelligencer*, October, 1898, p. 779.

[2] *Work and Workers in the Mission Field*, August, 1898, p. 343.

[3] Extract of letter from Poona, by the Rev. John Small, in *The Free Church of Scotland Monthly*, March, 1898, p. 66.

[4] *India's Women*, October, 1898, p. 240.

[5] *Mercy and Truth*, May, 1898, p. 99.

[6] The comparative mortality among the various races and castes for a week early in June, 1898, is given as follows:

Low-caste Hindus ....52.95 per 1000
Mohammedans..................................45.93 "   "
Jains..... ....45.35 "   "

The author has been impressed with similar statements in private letters from missionaries, forwarded to him from different fields. The Rev. Dr. C. F. Gates, of Harpoot, Turkey, writes: " In time of cholera it has been noticed that the evangelical communities were to a marked degree free from the plague, so that in the region of Cilicia a Turkish official said: ' How is it, O ye Protestants; has God spread His tent over you that you are so spared?' I attribute this largely to the greater cleanliness and less fear of death prevailing among evangelical Christians." Other testimonies as to this remarkable exemption might be given, but the few mentioned are sufficient to indicate that the more cleanly habits are a boon to native Christian communities in foreign lands.[1]

The paragraph in Volume I. (p. 222) describing the sanitary condition of China emphasizes sufficiently the need of a purifying crusade among its people. In the foreign concessions of some of the large cities, notably Shanghai and Hong Kong, scrupulous care is taken by the English and other European authorities to maintain proper sanitation; but the native quarters, as is the case in the towns and villages throughout China, are steeped in filth.[2] The Chinese themselves seem to be incorrigible, and live on in dogged cheerfulness amid suffocating odors and sickening foulness, such as would madden Occidental sensibilities. The plague comes as a matter of course, and yet if sanitary measures are enforced, the populace

Cleanliness a Christian virtue in China.

(Continued from p. 464.)

Europeans	27.63 per 1000	
Caste Hindus	26.37 "	"
Parsis	24.10 "	"
Eurasians	24.01 "	"
Jews	20.71 "	"
Bhattias	13.17 "	"
Brahmans	9.58 "	"
Native Christians	8.75 "	"

Quoted from *The Times of India*, and *The Church of Scotland Home and Foreign Mission Record*, January, 1899, p. 11.

[1] " It may be truthfully said that the general health of the Protestants as a body has been greatly improved by their superior intelligence in regard to the laws of health, and by the attention which they have given to the sanitary condition of their homes. The four weekly religious newspapers published for many years—one of them for forty-eight years—by the American Mission at Constantinople have from the beginning contained special articles, and given valuable information, in almost every issue, touching disease and the laws of health and sanitation."—Rev. J. K. Greene, D.D. (A. B. C. F. M.), Constantinople, Turkey.

[2] Macgowan, " Pictures of Southern China," pp. 86, 163.

grow furious, as if their dearest idols and their most sacred rights were being desecrated. It would seem that a Chinese must become a Christian before he will either appreciate or practise cleanliness, and even then he is painfully deliberate about it.[1] " At the time of the plague," writes Dr. Mary H. Fulton, of Canton, "the Christians were careful to whitewash their walls, if owners would permit them—many of whom would not, however, fearing it would bring 'bad luck.' They were also particular about disinfectants."

The same remarkable phenomenon, of the exceptional safety of Christians, is reported even in the recent visitation at Hong Kong. The

Plague-proof Christians.

Rev. C. Bennett, of the Church Missionary Society, writes that the question was asked by heathen Chinese in Hong Kong: "How is it that you Christians do not take the plague? We have had processions and fire-crackers, and made presents to our gods, but all in vain; we are dying by hundreds." In commenting upon this fact he remarks: "Certainly the Christians have been preserved in a most marvellous way, although living in some of the worst parts of the city. We have lost, out of two hundred, only three adults and one child. One of the former was an old woman eighty years of age, and the other two can be specially explained." [2]

The Rev. Willard L. Beard, of the American Board, at Foochow, reports that for the first time in its history a street-cleaning corps has

Missionary sanitation.

been set to work in the city. It is the result of a petition presented by the missionary named, in co-operation with some native friends, for permission to form a street-cleaning corporation.[3] Under the head of "Practical Questions," the Rev. F. Ohlinger discusses the possibility of sanitary changes in the architecture of Chinese dwellings, and proposes that special missionary literature shall be put forth with a view to securing some beneficial reforms.[4] During the recent visitation of the plague at Amoy, the native Christians of the city cleansed their own homes, and seized the opportunity to do missionary work in behalf of more wholesome living. They prepared leaflets for distribution, in which Christian truth and timely information suited to the emergency were mingled, and put them into the hands of the populace. Many of the panic-stricken people were led to turn from superstitious

---

[1] *The Monthly Messenger*, October, 1894, p. 233.
[2] *The Church Missionary Intelligencer*, August, 1894, p. 754.
[3] *The Missionary Herald*, December, 1897, p. 514.
[4] *The Chinese Recorder*, August, 1898, p. 398.

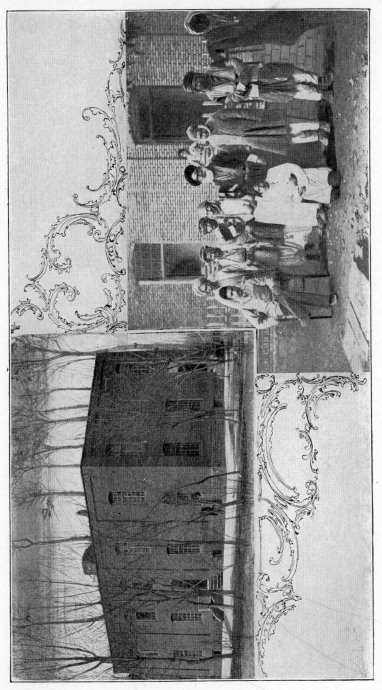

WESTMINSTER HOSPITAL, AND A GROUP OF PATIENTS, URUMIAH, PERSIA.
(P. B. F. M. N.)

and idolatrous devices to needed precautions, and some, let us hope, to an intelligent trust in God.[1]

In Korea, at least in the capital, a great change has been noted within a year or two. Mr. M'Leavy Brown, the English Commissioner of Customs, seconded by the Governor of the City, Ye Cha Yun, who once studied the municipal administration of Washington, has effected a radical metamorphosis in the sanitation of Seoul.[2] "A new thing in the capital—a garbage company. Now for solid work! " says *The Korean Repository* of August, 1896. If not missionary work in its official form, this must be considered as an independent lay effort for the public good. The Rev. David S. Spencer, of Nagoya, Japan, writes concerning that country: " The improvements in public sanitation are cause for great rejoicing. All this is modern, and may be covered by a period reaching back only seventeen years. The changes are along the line of water-supply for cities, improved sewerage, better construction of houses, careful supervision of shops selling meats and vegetables, and systematic arrangements for quarantine and the fighting of contagious diseases. The date within which all this has occurred shows plainly to what the reforms must be attributed. The average of life is increasing rapidly here, and great emphasis is placed upon the importance of proper sanitation."

A fact of interest appears in some sections of the world where civilization, or rather the material and seamy aspect of it, has apparently exacted the gradual extinction of native races as the price of its introduction. It is noticeable that where Christianity has entered it has retarded and in some instances is actually preventing this extinction. There are illustrations of this in some of the Pacific Islands. " In consequence of the conformity of the natives to the laws of health and morality, and of wise medical care provided for them by mission agencies and by new and intelligent governments, their bodily health is promoted, while their spiritual natures are improved. As the missionaries have sometimes rescued native infants from being buried alive by their savage parents, so they are rescuing native races from extinction; and although greatly diminished in numbers, those races will continue as monuments of the power for good in the foreign mission enterprise." [3] In India, especially, the increase of the popu-

The benefits of sanitary reform among native races.

---

[1] Article by the Rev. John A. Davis, on " The Plague in China," in *The Christian Intelligencer*, February 3, 1897.

[2] Bishop, " Korea and Her Neighbors," p. 435.

[3] Alexander, " Islands of the Pacific," p. 476.

lation as the result of good government, and better social and sanitary conditions, is so marked as to suggest problems not free from anxiety to its rulers.

In tropical Africa a service which promises to be of great value not only to missionaries and merchants residing there, but to the vast native population as well, is the recent appointment by the British Government of an expert commission to investigate the mysterious black-water fever, so fatal to Europeans in Africa. Missionary representation had a share, at least, in securing this action on the part of the authorities, the British Medical Association joining in the appeal by passing a resolution urging upon the Government the desirability of such an investigation. These commissioners are to meet at Blantyre, a mission station in British Central Africa, and let us hope that their labors will result in the discovery of such remedies as will prove a blessing to coming generations in Africa.[1] The proposed School for the Study of Tropical Diseases, about to be established in Liverpool by the British Colonial Office, may prove of value to missionaries, as well as to physicians who are preparing to practise in the tropical colonies of Great Britain.[2]

An expert study of mysterious African fevers.

15. MITIGATING THE BRUTALITIES OF WAR.—Fierce and cruel passions are excited by war, so that even the minimum of suffering which the powerful restraints of civilization and the better instincts of humanity have been able to secure is still appalling in its extent and severity.

The still, small voice of Christian compassion.

In the bloody conflicts of barbarous nations or savage tribes, where these modifying influences have not been exerted, ghastly brutality has characterized strife. Even in modern times we find little, if any, improvement in the spirit and methods of heathen warfare. The stories of Asiatic and African struggles between native races within the present century would not differ essentially from those of the great pagan nations of antiquity. To a certain extent the customs of Western civilization may have been introduced in connection with colonization, but at the same time deadlier weapons have been put into the hands of natives, or used against them, without their recognition of the obligation of mercy towards non-combatants and those who are sick and wounded. Turkey and Persia, in Western Asia, and

[1] *The Missionary Record*, October, 1898, p. 289.
[2] *The Times* (London), November 12, 1898, and March 11, 1899.

China, in the Far East, fairly represent the methods of warfare which prevail throughout that Continent, except where Western rule has insisted upon the modern code. The ordinary accompaniments of conflict in Africa are appallingly represented by the barbarities of the Mohammedan nations (except Egypt) along its northern shores, and by the bloodthirsty fierceness of its interior tribes. Missions as yet have been able to modify but slightly, and only indirectly, these sad and dreadful aspects of uncivilized strife; but where the Christian spirit has entered it has shown, as in all international history, its readiness to challenge and condemn all needless cruelty, and its power to create a nobler sentiment in favor of humane regulations and saving ministry.[1]

It is perhaps not desirable merely for the sake of the argument to put forward too exclusive a claim for Christianity as the source of the new spirit manifested by Japan in conducting her recent war with China. It is, however, a contention which is well within the bounds of probability, and supported by evidence worthy of confidence, *The new humanitarianism in Japan.* that Christian principles, with their mysterious power to mould public opinion, have influenced in a forcible and decisive way the leaders of the New Japan. The desire of the Japanese Government and people to enter the ranks of civilization and command the respect of Western nations is no doubt also a factor in the case. Its participation since 1886 in that great international agreement represented by the Red Cross, made all the more impressive by the fact that, in 1889, the Emperor himself accepted the presidency of the national society formed by the Japanese, also represents a commanding influence in favor of humanitarianism. An independent national association, identical in its purpose, had been formed in 1877, by some of the leading spirits of Japan, even earlier than the acceptance of the Red Cross Convention. This organization was known by its Japanese title, " Hakuaisha " (" Society of Benevolence "), and during a civil insurrection then raging it ministered in a spirit of compassion to the sick and wounded on both sides. It was afterwards (1886) united with the Red Cross Society of Japan.[2] The International Society of the Red Cross, while not in any insistent or exclusive sense Christian, is nevertheless based upon essentially

---

[1] Cf. Storrs, " The Divine Origin of Christianity," Lecture VI., on " The New Conception of the Duties of Nations towards Each Other," for a luminous exposition of the modifying power of Christianity upon warfare. Cf. also Schmidt, " The Social Results of Early Christianity," pp. 276–289.

[2] *The Japan Evangelist,* April, 1895, p. 207; *The Missionary Herald,* July, 1895, p. 290.

Christian principles and inspired by Christ-like motives. It is true that in joining it no nation makes a profession of Christianity, but simply agrees to adopt the creed and practice of a broad humanitarianism in dealing with the sick and wounded of either party; yet this policy of compassion to enemies is distinctively Christian in its spirit and aims. The systematic and organized effort to provide relief for suffering not only in war, but, as the broader code of Red Cross service stipulates, to arrange also for ministry and help to victims of pestilence and public calamities in general, is historically an outcome of the Christian religion. It is to be noted that Japan accepted what is known as the American amendment, giving this more general scope to the Red Cross service, and that at the present time there are in the empire one hundred and seventy thousand Japanese members of the society, and several fine hospitals devoted to Red Cross purposes.

While considerations like those just noted should not be ignored or minimized, yet it would be an unwarranted assumption to claim that they represent all the factors in the case. Whence has come this new respect of the Japanese for civilization, and this desire to be counted worthy of a place among those nations of the earth included under the collective name of Christendom? Whence this awakening of humane aspirations, and this zealous effort to adopt and practise nobler methods of warfare? Is it possible to eliminate altogether the influence of Christianity in accounting for these things? Missionary instruction for over a generation has been working like leaven in Japanese thought. The leading minds of the country have acknowledged the power of Christian teaching, and some of them have openly accepted Christianity, while others have rendered their homage to it in secret. All have felt, consciously or unconsciously, its pervasive and weighty influence over the better nature, and its incitement to nobler ways of living. Whatever measure of reserve it may be proper to maintain in publicly claiming for Christian missions the credit of developing Japanese humanitarianism, there is good reason for the friends of that enterprise to cherish a sober and happy assurance that God has used the introduction of Christianity to mould public opinion and give to the Japanese a new vision of those things which truly exalt a nation.[1]

How far is Japanese humanitarianism traceable to missions?

[1] The following order, issued September 22, 1894, by Count Oyama, Minister of State for War, is worthy of a place of high honor in the modern history of Eastern nations. It contains instructions to the Japanese army upon the conduct of the war with China, and is as follows:

" Belligerent operations being properly confined to the military and naval forces

Bringing in the Patients.

Patients Waiting for Treatment.
(Dr. Donald W. Carr standing on the right, in front of the stairs.)

HOSPITAL SCENES AT JULFA, PERSIA.
(C. M. S.)

The Rev. David S. Spencer, of Nagoya, a missionary of the Methodist Episcopal Church, writes to the author: "Brutality in war is a thing of the past with the Japanese. No one point in the recent sad conflict with China gave more pleasure to the real friends of Japan than did the spirit she exhibited towards the conquered. **Let the Japanese themselves decide the question.** In the hospitals the Chinese sick and wounded lay side by side with the Japanese, receiving treatment from the same physicians and nurses, who all wore the Red Cross uniform, showing the organization they represented. The treatment of prisoners was kind and generous. The men had the same food as the Japanese soldiers in the barracks, and a real interest in their personal and moral welfare was manifested by the Japanese officers in charge. When the time came for them to be sent home, many begged to be allowed to stay. This chapter in the

actually engaged, and there being no reason whatever for enmity between individuals because their countries are at war, the common principles of humanity dictate that succour and rescue should be extended even to those of the enemy's forces who are disabled either by wounds or disease. In obedience to these principles, civilized nations in time of peace enter into conventions to mutually assist disabled persons in time of war, without distinction of friend or foe. This humane union is called the Geneva Convention, or more commonly the Red Cross Association. Japan became a party to it in June, 1886, and her soldiers have already been instructed that they are bound to treat with kindness and helpfulness such of their enemies as may be disabled by wounds or disease. China not having joined any such Convention, it is possible that her soldiers, ignorant of these enlightened principles, may subject diseased or wounded Japanese to merciless treatment. Against such contingencies the Japanese troops must be on their guard. But at the same time they must never forget that, however cruel and vindictive the foe may show himself, he must nevertheless be treated in accordance with the acknowledged rules of civilization; his disabled succoured, his captured kindly and considerately protected.

" It is not alone to those disabled by wounds or sickness that merciful and gentle treatment should be extended. Similar treatment is also due to those who offer no resistance to our arms. Even the body of a dead enemy should be treated with respect. We cannot too much admire the course pursued by a certain Western country which in handing over an enemy's general complied with all the rites and ceremonies suitable to the rank of the captive. Japanese soldiers should always bear in mind the gracious benevolence of their august Sovereign, and should not be more anxious to display courage than charity. They have now an opportunity to afford practical proof of the value they attach to these principles."—Quoted from *The Japan Daily Mail*, in *The Japan Evangelist*, October, 1894, pp. 59, 60.

Cf. also the following sources for admirable articles showing the fidelity of the Japanese, as a rule, in observing these principles: " Japan's War Record," by the Rev. J. H. De Forest, D.D., in *The Golden Rule*, February 7, 1895; "Japan and the United States: A Contrast," by the Rev. J. D. Davis, D.D., in *The Independent*, February 14, 1895; " Japanese Women and the War," by Miss Umé Tsuda, in *The Independent*, May 9, 1895.

history of modern Japan is highly encouraging, and in it the Christian worker glories, whether he be native or foreign.   The sense of joy is heightened when we hear many Japanese, from officers to coolies, attribute this grand moral victory to the influence of Christianity among them.   With what pride do our Christians point to the Red Cross work as a result of our blessed religion!"

The testimony of another eye-witness comes from the Rev. Henry Loomis, the agent of the American Bible Society in Yokohama.   His statement is as follows: "Within the past two

The best "open-door policy" for the Far East.

months I have visited the principal military hospitals, and found the sick and wounded Chinese prisoners receiving the same treatment as the Japanese."   The Rev. Thomas T. Alexander, of the American Presbyterian Mission, Tokyo, thus expresses his judgment: "No discussion of this subject can be closed without reference to the enlightened and humane policy of Japan in the conduct of the war with China. This policy is not only a pleasant surprise to everybody, but it is a revelation to the majority of the Japanese people themselves.   Such treatment of one's enemies is unheard of in the annals of war in these Eastern lands.   The question naturally comes to their minds, 'Why this change?'   That it is not wholly due to material and secular causes is plain to every intelligent observer.   The consequence is that the thoughts of the people are being turned to Christianity, and that the military authorities gladly encourage and assist in the distribution of the Scriptures among the soldiers.   Many thousand copies of the Bible, or portions of it, have thus been circulated within the last month among a class of men who hitherto have for the most part been guarded carefully against Christian influences." [1]

[1] The following additional statements have been received by the author directly from missionaries in Japan:

" The working of the Red Cross Society and its beneficent labors in connection with the recent war between China and Japan are one of the most interesting and hopeful signs of the times.   The barbarities of war have been much lessened, and the amenities of life have been greatly increased, by the incoming of the Christian religion.   All thoughtful and sensible people admit this."—Rev. Julius Soper (M. E. M. S.), Hakodate.

" Much might be said about the conduct of the recent war, which was upon the most approved, modern, civilized, and, if you please, Christian principles.   It would not be possible to prove that missions have had no influence in bringing about this condition of affairs.   There are certainly not a few men in both branches of the service who are Christians.   There are churches at each of the three naval stations.   And who can know what influences are exerted by the Christian work done in the barracks and hospitals at Hiroshima, the temporary capital and point of

The sympathies of Japanese Christians have been especially enlisted on behalf of the sick and wounded, and in helping the needy families of absent soldiers. In Hiroshima, an army and navy centre, the Christian community organized itself into what was called an "Army Comfort Society," which worked heartily for both the physical and spiritual benefit of the soldiers. This society received support also from Christians elsewhere, and was regarded with favor by government officials.[1] The striking contrast of all this with former methods of warfare practised by the Japanese is illustrated by an incident which at the time so stirred the feelings of the nation as to secure a commemorative tomb of stone at Kyoto, known as "Mimizuka," or the Ear Monument. This memorial was erected on a mound over the buried ears which the Japanese had cut from thousands of vanquished Koreans and brought home as trophies of their victories in Korea some three centuries ago.[2] The policy of mutilation has been supplanted by that of humane consideration for vanquished enemies.

An "Army Comfort Society" in the land of the "Mimizuka."

In China also, through the initiative and practical aid of missionaries, some Red Cross work was inaugurated during the recent war with Japan. The characteristic verdict of the Chinese authorities was that nothing of the kind was needed, certainly not for their enemies, nor indeed for their own suffering soldiers, who when wounded or sick were condemned as useless.[3] Dr. Dugald Christie reports the establishment of a Red Cross hospital at Newchwang, in December, 1894.[4]

Pioneers of the Red Cross in China.

contact with the seat of war? Also, who can tell how much the brilliant career of Field-Marshal Yamagata reflects what he has seen and admired in his earnest Christian wife?"—Rev. Henry Stout, D.D. (Ref. C. A.), Nagasaki.

[1] *The Missionary*, April, 1895, p. 164.

[2] Griffis, "The Mikado's Empire," p. 245; Chamberlain, "A Handbook for Travellers in Japan," third edition, p. 301.

[3] Cf. Volume I., p. 171.

[4] Dr. Christie writes concerning this Red Cross effort as follows: "The need of such work became more and more apparent. One of the most deplorable features of this war is that practically no provision is made for the wounded by the Chinese military authorities. There are neither ambulance corps nor medical officers in the army, and when a man is wounded, he is usually left to die on the field, or escape as best he can. Many hundreds must have succumbed to exposure and neglect whose lives could have been saved had they been properly cared for. The news of the opening of our hospital spread rapidly through the army, and the patients whom we discharged cured did much to establish the confidence of the soldiers in foreign treatment."—*The Missionary Record*, July, 1895, p. 207.

The older mission records of work in various fields yield facts which are of significance as revealing the practical influence of missionaries in checking the cruelties which were customary features of warfare. In Persia the wild Kurdish chiefs held the early missionaries in such esteem that through their interposition the wholesale massacre of entire communities was averted.[1]   In Syria, during the civil wars of Mount Lebanon, especially in 1860, the homes of missionaries were places of refuge and safety, and their intervention saved multitudes from being put to the sword.[2]   Further illustrations might be quoted concerning Dr. Moffat's "exertion to prevent the Bechuanas from taking fearful vengeance on the wounded,"[3] and the exceptional behavior of the Malagasy, under their Christian Queen Ranavalona II., in the war of 1874.[4]   The good Queen established during her reign a branch Society of the Red Cross, and favored its activities even in the case of the native allies of the French.[5]   In the recent war with France the Christian women of Madagascar were most active in ministering to the soldiers.

The services of early missionaries in restraining massacre.

Previous statements made in other sections concerning the influence of missions in hastening the suppression of the slave-trade, in abolishing cannibalism and human sacrifices,—all of which have been incidental features of tribal conflicts,—might also be put in evidence here as showing the manifest tendency of Christian teaching to mitigate in many important respects the deplorable features of savage warfare.

[1] Laurie, "Missions and Science" (The Ely Volume), revised edition, p. 477.

[2] "In the following spring, when the Druses attacked the Maronites of Abeih, Dr. W. M. Thomson, at no little personal risk, effected a cessation of hostilities between the Maronites, in the strong castle of one of their leaders, and the Druses, who would soon have starved them out or stormed their stronghold.   Nor did he cease his good offices till he saw them safe on their way to Beirut under the protection of the British consul-general.

"It was a curious illustration of the power of missionaries for good that, in a later war between the same parties in the same locality, the house of the Rev. S. H. Calhoun was filled for six months with the silver ornaments and .other precious things of the Maronites, left there without either receipt or written pledge of any sort, to save them from the Druses; and no sooner did the appearance of French ships of war in the harbor of Beirut embolden their owners to take them away, than the Druse women hastened to deposit their valuables in the same place of safety, fearing the retribution which might follow.   They who thus equally command the confidence of opposite parties in a civil war cannot but greatly alleviate its horrors, and be sources of great temporal blessings to all around them."—*Ibid.*, p. 477.

[3] Horne, "The Story of the London Missionary Society," p. 83.

[4] Townsend, "Madagascar: Its Missionaries and Martyrs," p. 151.

[5] Noble, "The Redemption of Africa," p. 282.

The Moukden Hospital, its Medical Staff, and Students.
(Dr. Dugald Christie in the centre, on the right; Dr. D. D. Muir on the left.)

MEDICAL MISSIONS IN MANCHURIA.

(U. P. C. S. M.)

16. INSTILLING A PEACEABLE AND LAW-ABIDING SPIRIT.—Wherever Christian converts have been won and gathered into churches, they form peaceable and law-abiding communities; this is their reputation both as individuals and as a class. It is not meant, of course, that they are perfect, and free from all tendencies to alienation and strife, but that, as a rule, they seek to live in harmony, are not revengeful, respect mutual rights, obey the laws, favor peace rather than war, and the pursuit of honest industries rather than plunder and rapine, while in their social environment they constitute a leaven of good citizenship.

Peaceable communities the outcome of missions.

This is noticeable even among savage races, where turbulence and lawlessness have been the rule. The very idea of responsible citizenship has come with Christian teaching. Testimonies to this effect are not wanting from those who have had opportunities of personal observation in Africa or elsewhere.[1] Major J. R. L. Macdonald, R.E., in referring to the development of peaceful civilization in Uganda, remarks that "a large share in its accomplishment is undoubtedly due to the patient toil of the Christian missionaries."[2] Sir Harry Smith, a former Governor of Kaffraria, declared that "the frontier would be better guarded by nine mission stations than by nine military posts."[3] Mr. Joseph Thomson, the well-known African explorer, in a lecture before the Royal Geographical Society of London, speaks in terms of admiration of the moral influence of the Scotch missionaries in Nyassa-

The political value of missions as an aid to tranquillity.

[1] See Liggins, " The Great Value and Success of Foreign Missions," pp. 32, 33.

[2] Macdonald, " Soldiering and Surveying in British East Africa, 1891-94," p. 143.

Major Macdonald was the Chief Engineer of the preliminary survey for the Uganda Railway, and was Acting Commissioner before the establishment of the British Protectorate. He had, therefore, the best of opportunities to speak advisedly upon the subject of missions. His words leave no one in doubt as to his favorable opinion. He writes: " The effect that education and the influence of the missionaries have had on this intelligent and powerful people is almost incredible. . . . Instead of a savage heathen kingdom, where a man's life was rated at the price of an ox, and a woman was an article of barter, and where justice went to the highest bidder, the Uganda of to-day is a well-ordered State, steadily improving in the arts of civilisation and culture, where no man can lose his property or his life at the arbitrary will of the great, or without a fair and open trial. This alone is no small thing to have achieved, and a large share in its accomplishment is undoubtedly due to the patient toil of the Christian missionaries, who have adhered steadfastly to their self-imposed task through the stormy times of war and through the dark days of persecution."—*Ibid.*, pp. 143, 144.

[3] Thompson, " Moravian Missions," p. 401.

land, especially in leading turbulent tribes into the paths of peaceful industry.[1] The services of the Rev. P. Hargreaves, a missionary of the Wesleyan Methodist Church of South Africa in Pondoland, as a peacemaker and counsellor of the natives when tempted to war, are acknowledged with appreciation in the public journals of Cape Colony, and upon two distinct occasions he received the thanks of the Cape Government for his mediation.[2]   The influence of Khama, the Christian chief of the Bamangwatos, has been recognized by the British Government.   "Out of the ruins of anarchy, lawlessness, and general disorder," wrote the late Rev. J. D. Hepburn, "he has been building up law, order, and stability."[3]

Within the sphere of the Mission of the United Presbyterian Church of Scotland in Kaffraria, the "orderly and peaceful behavior and the Christian fidelity of the converts" in times of political upheaval and warfare have been noticeable in repeated instances.   In connection with the uprising of 1851–53, it is stated that, "with the exception of the Christian converts, almost the whole of the Kaffirs took part in the war."[4]   A recent visitor at a Moravian mission station about eighty miles from Capetown, where there is a native community of three thousand, comments upon the fact that "there is but one policeman at Genadendal, and he is also the postmaster, which will show the characteristic quiet of the settlement."[5]

Another striking illustration is presented in the story of the transformation of the Angoni, those inveterate warriors and marauders of British Central Africa, into a peaceful, law-abiding people.   They found their way some seventy years ago from Matabeleland to Lake Nyassa, bent upon rapine and plunder, and have since been the terror of the whole country west of Lakes Tanganyika and Nyassa, until the Scotch missionaries won them over to peaceful pursuits, and

Warriors and marauders won over to peaceful pursuits.

---

[1] *The Missionary Record*, January, 1893, p. 24.

[2] *Work and Workers in the Mission Field*, September, 1894, p. 368; October, 1894, p. 406.

[3] Hepburn, "Twenty Years in Khama's Country," p. 122.

The Rev. Brownlee J. Ross (F. C. S.), of Cunningham, Transkei, South Africa, writes to the author as follows: "I think it is quite the fact, among the South African tribes, that Christianity is the first and strongest agent in enabling them to rise above the clan and tribe feeling. It gives them their first idea of the value of man as man. It alone seems able to make them feel what philanthropy is, and so leads on to the giving up of intertribal hatred and jealousy. They argue that Christianity must be supernatural, for it alone can bring men of different clans and tribes together in peace and friendship."

[4] Slowan, "The Story of Our Kaffrarian Mission," pp. 35, 40, 109.

[5] *Service for the King*, April, 1896, p. 79.

reaped among them a Christian harvest of astonishing fruitfulness.[1] Similar reports are at hand concerning the work of the Church of Scotland missionaries among the tribes of Lomweland, and the efforts of the Universities' Mission among the Yaos.

In the region of the Upper Zambesi, to the west of British Central Africa, for the first time in the history of the warlike Barotsi, a war which was about to be commenced with a neighboring tribe has been prevented, through the intervention of M. Jalla, a missionary of the French Evangelical Society.[2] Of the late Mr. George L. Pilkington, of the Church Missionary Society, Captain Charles H. Villiers, of the Royal Horse Guards, who served under Sir Gerald Portal in Uganda, writes: "He accompanied the Waganda, at their special request, as their chaplain on the Onyoro expedition, living with them throughout the entire campaign, and was the cause of their abandoning all their former ideas of warfare, and behaving as well as civilized troops."[3] The Christian King of Toro, on the western borders of Uganda, who has been mentioned on page 16 of this volume, makes a significant statement in a letter dated September 14, 1898, and addressed to the Secretaries of the Church Missionary Society. In the true spirit of Christianity, he seems to rejoice in the tranquillity throughout his realm, when he writes: "And also, my friends, I thank you for praying to God to keep us in these great wars, because war had surrounded the whole country, but at our place we remain at peace, right up to the present time we are at peace."[4] In the Life of Bishop Smythies, late of the Universities' Mission to Central Africa, there are many instances recorded of successful peacemaking on the part of the Bishop between hostile African chiefs. His influence, and also the respect which his goodness of character and dignified presence called forth, were so great that he was able upon frequent occasions to prevent war and reconcile bloodthirsty enemies.[5]

In West Africa the missionaries in Old Calabar have been messengers of concord, where there was formerly perpetual strife between native tribes. "Were we ever before so long without killing people as since you came?" remarked the Bulè to the late Dr. A. C. Good, who had opened a pioneer station among that interior

[1] *The Free Church of Scotland Monthly*, September, 1897, p. 212, September, 1898, p. 222; *Medical Missions at Home and Abroad*, February, 1896, pp. 76, 77; " Foreign Mission Report of the Free Church of Scotland, 1896," p. 87; Noble, " The Redemption of Africa," pp. 340, 341.

[2] *The Missionary Record*, April, 1898, p. 131.

[3] *The Mail* (London), January 12, 1898.

[4] *The Church Missionary Intelligencer*, January, 1899, p. 149.

[5] *Central Africa*, February, 1899, p. 19.

tribe.[1]   An incident mentioned in the " Report of the Methodist Episcopal Missionary Society for 1895 " (p. 25), referring to its missions
on the West Coast, is worthy of record as showing
Native Christians strive   true courage and a desire for peace on the part of
to promote peace.   native Christians. The account is as follows : "The
Barraka nation has been engaged in war with a con-
tiguous nation for more than a hundred years.   It is not their custom to
march in a solid body and fight it out, but they waylay small parties on
their farms, and the women when gathering wood and carrying water are
butchered in cold blood. To cross the boundary lines between the hostile
parties is death. But Jasper, one of our native local preachers at Barraka,
received a commission from God, about a year ago, to cross the death-
line alone, and go straight to the king of the belligerent nation.   He
immediately obeyed orders, and told the king that God had sent him to
see him, and to ask him to assign a house in which he and half a dozen
of his fellow-Christians from Barraka might pray to the God that made
the heavens for him and his people. The king received him kindly
and granted his request ; and at the time appointed Jasper and his band
of praying men assembled in the house assigned, and commenced their
work—the reconciliation of two heathen nations that had been at war
for more than a hundred years. After they had prayed a few nights,
Jasper submitted another proposition to the king, requesting him to
order a peace palaver to be held each day in conjunction with the
prayers of each night. The king consented, and issued an order for the
assembling of his councilors. Jasper's band prayed twenty-eight nights
(on two or three occasions they prayed all night), until a permanent
peace was effected between the two belligerent nations, and now they
are hand and glove in mutual attachment."

The South Sea Islands were once scenes of ferocious tribal wars,[2]
with hardly a year of continuous quiet, but many of them are now the
homes of peaceful communities. Professor David,
The delights of peaceable   of Sydney, in a recent address at a missionary meet-
intercourse *versus* the   ing in New South Wales, Australia, has given his im-
policy of mutual de-   pressions of the value of mission efforts in the South
struction.
Seas, having just returned from a tour among the islands, during which he
came in contact with the work of the London Missionary Society. His
remarks are full of pointed testimonies to the civilizing power of missions. A concluding sentence summarizes his judgment as follows : "The

---

[1] *Woman's Work for Woman*, June, 1894, p. 148.
[2] Stair, " Old Samoa," pp. 242-258.

result of the work of the London Society has been that it has brought peace where before there was war, civilization where before there was savagery, and morality where before there was immorality." [1] In many instances missionaries have been the mediators between warlike nations bent upon mutual destruction. [2] Native chiefs have often been persuaded to abandon their wars of conquest or revenge, and to favor a policy of peace. [3] Christianity, in fact, has now a political as well as a social value, in the estimation of the inhabitants of these islands, as a restraint upon the passion for blood, and a guarantee of peaceful inclinations. [4] The Rev. William Gunn, M.D., a missionary of the Free Church of Scotland in the New Hebrides, comments upon this fact as follows: " Christianity brings the natives together in friendly and peaceable contact. In Christian Aneityum the people can travel without danger. When the Gospel began to extend, this result was a wonderful sign to those who had formerly lived under the influence of heathenism. Visitors can go to other islands without fear of being captured as slaves or seized by cannibals. To a certain extent this is true of the whole group, but especially so in the Christian and partially Christianized islands."

Sir William Macgregor, M.D., K.C.M.G., upon the occasion of his recent retirement from the position of Governor of British New Guinea, which he had held for ten years, addressed a letter to the resident missionaries of the London Society, in reply to a resolution passed by them appreciative of the wisdom and value of his administration. His words are weighty and of special note as the testimony of a government official of high standing. In the course of this letter, which was dated August, 1898, he remarks: "It can never be overlooked that the pioneers in civilising this place were the members of the London Missionary Society. The work of the Society in this country I probably value higher than does any other person, but that is only because I know it better. Although not the first mission in this colony, it was the first that could obtain a permanent footing and make its influence felt. What your Mission has already effected here in the work of humanity can never be forgotten or ignored in the history of the col-

Official testimony from the Governor of New Guinea.

---

[1] Quoted in *The Chronicle*, November, 1898, pp. 256–258.

[2] Michelsen, "Cannibals Won for Christ," pp. 59, 62.

[3] Cousins, " The Story of the South Seas," p. 60; Paton, "Autobiography," vol. ii., p. 171; *The Missionary Herald*, December, 1897, p. 497.

[4] Horne, " The Story of the London Missionary Society," p. 207; Michelsen, "Cannibals Won for Christ," p. 84.

ony; and the great names of Chalmers and Lawes will long continue to be incentives to younger men to keep the Mission up to its former and present high standard of usefulness, while steadily enlarging its field. Will you kindly convey to the ministers and teachers of the Mission my sincere and cordial thanks for their loyal coöperation, and assure them of my lasting sympathy with them in their unselfish and generous task in British New Guinea?"[1]

Among the Indian tribes of North and South America, Christian missionaries assume the rôle of peacemakers. The warlike instincts of these wild aborigines, so far as they have come under the influence of missions, have been tamed, and they have been taught to love the avocations of peace. The United States Census Report for 1894 says concerning the Indians of Alaska that "religion is doing more to keep the natives within peaceful pursuits than all the combined forces of military and civil government."[2]   Dr. Sheldon Jackson, in an interesting account of the venturesome overland expedition sent by the United States Government, in the depths of an arctic winter (1897–98), for the relief of whalers imprisoned in the ice near Point Barrow, on the north coast of Alaska, calls attention to the influence of mission work in making travel safe among the wild Eskimos of those frozen realms.[3]   The Right Rev. Bishop Reeve, of the Diocese of Mackenzie River, in the far Northwest of Canada, speaks of the frequent wars which formerly occurred in that section between the Eskimos and the Indians, and asserts that since the Indians have become Christianized they are no longer hostile, but fraternize with their Eskimo

The taming of Indian warriors.

---

[1] Quoted in _The Chronicle_, January, 1899, p. 22.

[2] _The Review of Missions_, September, 1898, p. 149.

[3] " In this connection," writes Dr. Jackson, " it is appropriate to call public attention to the influence of the mission schools in making arctic Alaska safe for the transit of white men.   In 1890, when the Congregational Mission was established at Cape Prince of Wales, no whaler had dared drop anchor in the neighborhood of that village for ten years; and the stationing of missionaries there was considered by the captains of the whalers as a foolhardy undertaking.   They were placed there, however, and now ships can anchor and their crews go on shore with safety.   When, in 1881–83, Lieutenant Ray, United States Army, was placed in charge of the international polar expedition at Point Barrow, a turret was built at one corner of his house and armed with cannon to protect his party from the natives.   Now the Presbyterian Mission has so civilized the people that no fortified habitation is necessary.   The natives not only provided the shipwrecked sailors with food from their own scanty supply, but also with necessary fur clothing.   The influence of the missions made possible Lieutenant Jarvis's heroic trip unarmed."
—_The Evangelist_, January 26, 1899.

neighbors.[1] In another article by Bishop Reeve, in *The Church Missionary Gleaner* for November, 1896 (p. 167), he speaks of his diocese as "a country of undisturbed peace."

Off the Pacific coast of Canada are the Queen Charlotte Islands, inhabited by lonely groups of Haida Indians, among whom the Church Missionary Society labors. This tribe was once known as one of the fiercest of the Northwest. In their little settlement of Massett at present there is not a single heathen remaining. Its inhabitants are engaged in peaceable occupations, and live an orderly and quiet life.[2] The results of American missions among the Indians of the United States confirms the statement concerning the uniformly pacific disposition of Indian converts to Christianity. It was noted in connection with the recent Exposition at Omaha, in which a thousand Indians participated, that only thirty-five years ago the town, then small and unimportant in comparison with its present dimensions, was threatened by an invasion of Sioux warriors. It is perfectly safe to assert that if the Indian tribes could be converted *en masse* to Christianity, and receive just and fair treatment from the nation, the era of Indian wars would be over.

A striking confirmation of this assertion is found in the notable results of missionary work among the Indians of Dakota, under the direction of Bishop William Hobart Hare, who has been called the "Apostle to the Sioux." For twenty-five years he has labored among them, and during that time he has won over to Christianity more than five thousand. Many of them were famous warriors, but they have long since forsaken the trail of blood, and given themselves to peaceful pursuits. The annual assemblage of Christian Indians from the various tribes within the bounds of Bishop Hare's diocese is said to represent "the largest number of communicants of the Protestant Episcopal Church which gathers at any diocesan convention or convocation in all America." Out of twenty-five thousand Indians within the limits of the mission, over nine thousand have been baptized, and nearly three thousand confirmed, while about fifty churches and chapels have been built, and also four boarding-schools. It would be hard to find a peace-loving Indian who had not in some way been touched by the influence of Christianity, and, on the other hand, one is not likely to meet a Christian Indian on the war-path.[3]

[1] *The Gospel in all Lands*, December, 1894, p. 539 (quoted from *The Canadian Church Magazine*).

[2] *Awake*, September, 1898, p. 103.

[3] See article entitled "An Apostle to the Sioux," in *The New York Tribune*, October 16, 1898.

The story of Missionary Duncan and his Metlakahtla settlement on the Pacific coast of Canada is well known. He established there a model community, whose watchword was "Peace,"

A peaceful Indian paradise.

and where orderly living was secured in place of the turbulent savagery of the Indians. In 1887 a colony from the original settlement removed to Annette Island, which is part of the United States Territory of Alaska. The order, morality, and peace maintained among the people of this New Metlakahtla are not surpassed in any centre of civilization. In 1888 the Commissioners of the Canadian Government, in their report on the condition of disturbed districts in British Columbia, stated that the Metlakahtla Indians "were in happy contrast to all others, and were a credit to their instructors."[1] Similar testimony might be quoted regarding the peaceful developments among the Chaco Indians of South America.[2]

Among the older civilizations of the Orient, where a measure of respect for government and the authority of law exists, mission converts are in good repute for their conscientious-

Quiet and orderly living characteristic of Oriental Christians.

ness and obedience. It is the testimony of a prominent Japanese that "the Christian subjects of Japan are conspicuous for orderly conduct and faithful discharge of obligation." In the official "Statement of the Nature, Work, and Aims of Protestant Missions in China," recently (1895) presented to the Emperor, emphasis is laid upon the fact that the Christian religion inculcates obedience to civil rulers.[3] Chinese

---

[1] "Report of the Church Missionary Society, 1898," p. 430.

[2] *The South American Missionary Magazine*, February, 1898, p. 29, May, 1898, p. 88; *The Missionary Review of the World*, October, 1895, p. 787.

The following practical evidence of the civilizing influence of missions among the Chacos is at hand: "A. Busk, Esq., an extensive landowner in Paraguay, has offered to the South American Mission the free grant of nearly two square miles of territory for the purpose of forming a missionary settlement. He declares himself moved to this by their ' extremely rational and humane mode of managing and civilising the Paraguayan Chaco Indians, which will, without question, be of great advantage to the Chaco landowners, even leaving aside all philanthropic motives.' He concludes his munificent offer in these terms : 'If I can at any time be of service to the Society I shall be most happy, and I wish it all prosperity in its workings in the Paraguayan Chaco, which, if continued in the way they have been commenced, will be of inestimable advantage to the Indian population, to those who have pecuniary interests in the country, and to the Government of Paraguay, by transforming semi-barbarians into peaceable, law-abiding citizens.' "—*The Missionary Record*, November, 1892, p. 389.

[3] *The Chinese Recorder*, February, 1896, p. 66.

officials acknowledge that Christians are peaceable, and distinguished by quiet and sober living. In the recent riots native converts not only did not participate, but exhibited much courage and loyalty in seeking to restrain the violent passions of their countrymen and to protect foreigners from the rage of the mobs.[1] Missionaries from China write of the disposition on the part of Christians to seek redress for their wrongs through legal channels rather than by violence. Their patience under injury and their avoidance of lawsuits are also commended.

In India, where thuggism and other outrages once prevailed, the strong hand of British authority has worked a mighty change; yet it took the Government thirty years to abolish these crimes by a vigorous campaign of punishment.[2] It is not a rash statement to say that the genuine conversion of a community or a tribe to Christianity effectually banishes these dark deeds. Concerning the Garos it is stated that, as the result of mission work among them (there were nine hundred baptisms in 1897), " they are now a law-abiding and peace-loving people "; yet in 1867 the Commissioner described them as "bloodthirsty, desperate, and incorrigible." [3]

Missionaries from the Turkish Empire speak unhesitatingly of the influence of the Gospel in creating a respect for law and promoting the vocations of peace. The Rev. Robert Thomson, of Constantinople, writes to the author in reference to Bulgaria, that "the late Prime Minister, Mr. Stambuloff, officially endorsed on a certain document his judgment that no more loyal or law-abiding citizens could be found than the Protestants." [4]

[1] " It is only a few days since that an intelligent Chinaman made the following remark: ' If the Gospel you preach were generally accepted, we should need no prisons, and could do without magistrates.' Native Christians are gradually earning a good name as law-abiding citizens, as men and women who can be trusted, and who will not wantonly injure their neighbors."—S. P. Barchet, M.D. (A. B. M. U.), Kinhwa, China. Cf. also an article entitled " The State of Affairs in China: An Inside View," in *The Independent*, February 9, 1899.

[2] Crooke, " The North-Western Provinces of India," p. 135.

[3] *The Baptist Missionary Review* (Madras), July, 1898, p. 271.

[4] Dr. H. O. Dwight (A. B. C. F. M.), of Constantinople, reports the following incident: " A missionary upon one of his tours met a Turkish official, and ascertaining that his destination was the village of Sardoghan, inquired of him whether the people of that place were troublesome. ' That village,' said the officer, ' is a most curious case. The inhabitants until about ten years ago were drunk every week, were quarrelsome, and given to all kinds of rascality, so that we had several of them in prison almost all the time. They have since become quiet, law-abiding, and respectable, and give us no trouble.' " Dr. Dwight's further statement of the fact that within ten years past a large number of the inhabitants of the village re-

The spirit of forgiveness and forbearance which Christianity inculcates is one secret of its peaceable trend. This directly reverses the immemorial heathen code of vengeance and re-

The passing of blood-feuds in native Christian communities.

taliation, which has been the incentive to the wild, dark passions of blood-feuds, to which may be traced so many cruel deeds. The biography of the Rev. W. H. Brett, for forty years a missionary in British Guiana, contains several narratives of his remarkable success in leading into peaceful relations "tribes who formerly punished each other with rancorous hatred, . . . but are now united in peace and love."[1] Dr. Gill, in writing of Polynesia, remarks: "Heathenism separates and sets at enmity individuals, families, and tribes. Christianity unites, and heals ancient feuds. The *lex talionis*, or law of blood-revenge, was one of the chief reasons why the South Sea Islanders were rapidly degenerating when Christianity arrested their downward progress."[2] In place of the lust of vengeance and the avenger's mission, often handed down from generation to generation, the Gospel doctrine of forgiveness has given life and security to entire communities.

Blood-feuds were numerous and deadly in Japan until recent times. The code of retaliation was so obligatory that "a weak spirit in this respect was completely ostracized." A missionary now writes: "The very samurai, who gloried most in this purpose of revenge before they were brought under the power of Christian enlightenment, represent the class which furnishes our best preachers of the Gospel; and those same preachers are the men who plead for the manifestation of the spirit of forgiveness and love taught by the Sermon on the Mount. Blood-feuds have ceased, and men in this land are increasingly inclined to find their impulse to revenge controlled by the sacrifice on the cross."[3] In

ferred to have been converted to evangelical Christianity and are seeking to live as their Bible teaches is a sufficient explanation of the curious phenomenon which puzzled the Turkish official.

[1] Josa, "The Apostle of the Indians of Guiana: A Memoir of the Life and Labours of the Rev. W. H. Brett," pp. 96, 126, 143.

[2] Gill, "From Darkness to Light in Polynesia," p. 382.

"The life of the clan among the ancient Samoans entailed blood-revenge. With the introduction of Christianity, blood-feuds were practically abolished. Recently, and whenever an outbreak of war revived heathen associations and aroused old passions, there has been a renewal of the practice. But the genius and spirit of Christianity have been repeatedly shown in the spirit of forgiveness which one and another have with their latest breath manifested. As the last words of the dead are considered to be binding on the living, this has put an end to the feud."—Rev. J. E. Newell (L. M. S.), Malua Institution, Samoa.

[3] Rev. David S. Spencer (M. E. M. S.), Nagoya, Japan.

China, Burma, and India, missionaries have often acted as peacemakers. " Sectional feuds have almost entirely disappeared, and the brotherhood of the Karen race is recognized," are the words of the Rev. **W. I.** Price, of Henzada.[1] Dr. Robert Laws, of British Central Africa, pronounces it " one of the most evident blessings following the preaching of the Gospel that peace has been established between tribes who formerly were constantly at enmity."

It is not necessary to multiply illustrations, for it seems to be clearly demonstrated by experience that Christian missions become the harbinger of peace and security wherever they enter turbulent and lawless communities. Were they triumphant everywhere, surely no moral force could be more hopefully relied upon to hasten throughout the earth that day of regnant peace and happy brotherhood when,

" Every tiger madness muzzled, every serpent passion kill'd,
Every grim ravine a garden, every blazing desert till'd,
Robed in universal harvest, up to either pole she smiles,
Universal ocean softly washing all her warless Isles."

In concluding this prolonged review of the humane results of missions, we feel confident that no thoughtful reader will fail to note the significance of these cumulative facts as illustrating this aspect of our theme. It should be borne A solid basis for mission-
in mind, moreover, that this particular phase of ary optimism.
the argument is only one of several briefs of evidence brought forward under the general title of " Contributions of Christian Missions to Social Progress," yet is it not clear that, were this line of proof our only dependence, it would be no mean demonstration of the benignity, value, and power of the Christian religion as a social force for the betterment of mankind? We need not ignore, however, as we close this volume, other themes that have occupied our attention —the moulding power of missions upon the character and habits of the individual, and their ennobling, purifying, and hallowing influence in family relationships. We may still add to these their heroic assaults upon every species of brutality and outrage, their courageous defense of the helpless, their relief to the distressed, their ministrations to the suffering, their wholesome lessons in the arts of clean and peaceful liv-

[1] " Blood-feuds have been very prevalent and deadly in the mountain communities. Villages that have become Christian have refused to keep up such feuds, and heathen villages with which they were at enmity have felt the influence, and allowed the feuds to lapse."—Rev. J. N. Cushing, D.D. (A. B. M. U.), Rangoon, Burma.

ing, as recounted in this final review of their humanitarian victories, and we have an expanding record of social progress for which Christians may well thank God and take courage. There are also other considerations of solid worth to be presented in a subsequent volume.

Is it not evident that, of all " Good Workmen " whom the Master owns, the Christian missionary is the one who could least be spared by the sinful, ignorant, and suffering millions of mankind? Though he toils in comparative obscurity, amid many difficulties and discouragements, yet he, of all human seers, has the vision of assurance in response to the poet's question:

> " After all the stormy changes, shall we find a changeless May? "

He knows that he is sowing the seeds of a nobler life for the race. He is confident that the God of spiritual harvests will make fruitful his desert planting, and that the moral springtide of the world will surely come, when "the Sun of Righteousness shall arise with healing in His wings." In that high service of man which reaches the lowest depths of his need, and searches for him in the dark and distant haunts of his degradation, a place of rare honor may surely be assigned to the messengers of Christ among unenlightened races. Into their hands have been entrusted the priceless treasures of the Gospel, the hopes, delights, and incentives of moral culture, and all the nobler possibilities of a true civilization. They are the bearers of the choicest gifts of God into the sterile and impoverished life of the old social systems.

> " Poor world! if thou cravest a better day,
> Remember that Christ must have His own way;
> I mourn thou art not as thou mightest be,
> But the love of God would do all for thee."